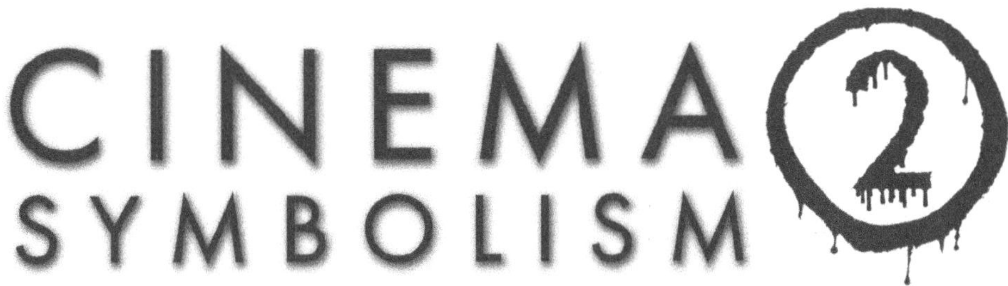

CINEMA SYMBOLISM ②2

MORE ESOTERIC IMAGERY IN POPULAR MOVIES

CINEMA SYMBOLISM 2:
MORE ESOTERIC IMAGERY IN POPULAR MOVIES

by
Robert W. Sullivan IV, Esq.

Front Cover: (top left) Ralph Fiennes as Lord Voldemort in
Harry Potter and the Deathly Hallows – Part 2;
(top right) Natalie Portman as Nina Sayers in *Black Swan*;
(bottom left) Maleficent in *Sleeping Beauty*;
(bottom right) Jack Nicholson as Jack Torrance in *The Shining*;
and (center) Hugo Weaving as V in *V for Vendetta*.

Book layout by Rebekkah Dreskin
Editor: Wendy Tucker
Revised and reedited by Deadwood Publishing LLC., 2019 ©

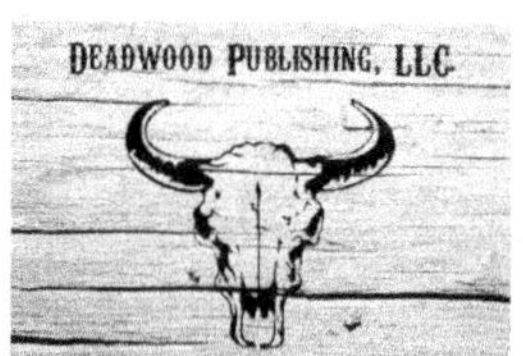

Published by **DEADWOOD PUBLISHING, LLC.**, Baltimore, Maryland, 2017.

CONTENTS

- Season 1, Chanel Oberlin promotional poster, *Scream Queens*
- Chanel Oberlin as Smurfette, *Scream Queens*, Season 2
- Original *Dracula's Daughter* half-sheet movie poster
- Madeleine Elster's spiraling hair, *Vertigo*
- *Portrait of Carlotta Valdes*, *Vertigo*
- Alfred Hitchcock's silhouette, *Alfred Hitchcock Presents*
- Mary Samuels and Norman Bates enter mother's bedroom, *Psycho II*
- Elizabeth blindfolded, *9 ½ Weeks*
- Anastasia Steele blindfolded, *Fifty Shades of Grey*
- Cancer's astrological symbol

Chapter I

- Antique golden medallion of the sun god *Sol Invictus*
- Diagram of the sun placed upon the equinoxes and solstices
- *The Adoration of the Golden Calf* by Nicolas Poussin
- *Moses* by Michelangelo
- The Hebrew Kabbalistic Tree of Life

Chapter II

- Saturn's astrological symbol
- *The Reward of Cruelty* (Plate IV) engraving by William Hogarth
- Guy Fawkes' dark lantern, Ashmolean Museum, Oxford, England
- The Cross of Lorraine
- The Minutemen, 1940, *Watchmen*
- Cremation of Care ritual, Bohemian Grove
- Bohemian Grove insignia

Chapter III

- The Mystery Man, *Lost Highway*
- Diane Selwyn, *Mulholland Drive*

Chapter IV

- Spaceship Earth at Epcot, Walt Disney World, Orlando Florida
- The Roman god Janus

PREFACE

"No reason. I just like doing things like that."
– Luther, *The Warriors*, 1979.

"How about I dance the Black Swan for you?"
– Lily, *Black Swan*, 2010.

"I know, I know, but it does make a fine jest,
the kind of jest that would amuse Satan."
– Prince Prospero, *The Masque of the Red Death*, 1964.

"We played the Cobb Energy Performing Arts Centre you bitch."
– Aubrey Posen, *Pitch Perfect*, 2012.

"Enough! Enough! You better start talking asshole!
Because we got shit we need to talk about. We're already freaked out.
We need you acting freaky like we need a fucking bag on our hip."
– Mr. White, *Reservoir Dogs*, 1992.

"Good and evil, there never is one without the other."
– Merlin the Magician, *Excalibur*, 1981.

"You never had a rope around your neck,
well I'm going to tell you something. When that rope starts to pull tight,
you can feel the Devil bite your ass."
– Tuco Benedicto Pacífico Juan María Ramirez (a/k/a the Ugly),
The Good, the Bad and the Ugly, 1966.

"Of course I intended on changing my jacket
this evening before the fish and goose soirée."
– Jack Torrance, *The Shining*, 1980.

"He used to say, 'sometimes you need to do something bad
to stop you from doing something worse.'"
– India Stoker, *Stoker*, 2013.

re esoteric and occult symbols, icons, themes and undercurrents intentionally placed in films or do they appear by happenstance? To this author the answer is yes; like mysterious Masonic rituals, arcane symbols and themes are deployed in movies to both conceal and reveal; they are a cinematic Sphinx whose ageless riddles require deciphering. Otherwise, it would all be a coincidence, and there is no such thing as a coincidence. Hollywood eccentric, psychic, and showman the Amazing Criswell (1907-1982) adroitly echoed this sentiment when he wrote, "No one, but no one is superstitious; for coincidence is the language of fools."[1] However, there is no uniform agreement so opinions can vary. As nebulous as it may sound, the answer to this question is sometimes *yes,* while occasionally the answer is *no*. The context in which these esoteric themes and symbols materialize is critical to decoding movies. In some films, these symbols hide arcane meanings, while the same symbol in another movie can have a different, but legitimate, interpretation; in some films an omnipotent eye in a triangle is just that: an attention-grabbing emblem employed for theatrical purposes.[2]

The nexus between movies and the occult was first analyzed by this author in *Cinema Symbolism: A Guide to Esoteric Imagery in Popular Movies* (2017, Second Edition). It is beyond dispute that Joseph Campbell's (1904-1987) mythological monomyth, discussed in his book *The Hero with a Thousand Faces* (1949), heavily influenced writer, producer, and director George Lucas. Numerous elements of the monomyth, or the hero's journey, appear in Lucas' *Star Wars* saga; his grandiose Space Western is a study in comparative religion and mythology. To this author, it's obvious that the characters in the *Back to the Future* trilogy personify deities from the Egyptian Osirian Cycle while Zemeckis' time-traveling films hide numerological motifs as well. There is no doubt that the sublime philosophies presented in the Wachowski Siblings' *Matrix* films, much like Ridley Scott's *Blade Runner* (1982), are Gnostic, metaphysical, and occult.

Gnosticism, in general, is a belief system that holds that the spirit was positive, and matter or materialism was an illusion. According to

---

1 Criswell, *Criswell's Forbidden Predictions based on Nostradamus and the Tarot*, p. 1.
2 This author stresses that esoteric symbolism in cinema is, most often, intentionally placed there by the filmmakers. However, like everything in life, there is an exception to every rule.

the Gnostics, the material world is governed by a lesser god: a botched Jehovah known as the demiurge; while spiritual salvation *qua* gnosis is obtained by learning to know thyself via sagacious practices, such as meditation, yoga, or the study of arcane wisdom. Esoteric knowledge is identified with the sacred feminine, Sophia. Sophia (Σοφία, Greek for wisdom) is critical to Hellenistic philosophy and religion, Platonism, Gnosticism, and both orthodox and mystical Christianity. The Gnostics venerate Sophia, a wisdom goddess, as do some Neopagan, New Age, and feminist-inspired goddess spirituality groups. In the Gnostic tradition, Sophia is analogous to the human soul but also simultaneously one of the feminine aspects of God. "Sophia, Wisdom itself, beautiful as the moon, great as the sun, terrible as marshaled rank of armies, pure because nothing of defilement can touch her, honorable because the image of goodness itself, powerful because being one she can do all things, kind because she visits the nations that are sacred to her and makes men friends to God and prophets."[3] "For Philo, as for the Gnostics, Sophia is the 'Mother of the Logos.' The central role given to the Divine Feminine by the Pagan philosopher, the Hellenized Jews of the intertestamental period and later by the Gnostics is strong evidence for a direct line of evolution linking these three traditions together."[4]

To the Gnostics, the pursuit of divine gnosis led to the pleroma: the abode of God and of the totality of the divine powers and emanations. This god is known as the Monad: the unfathomable godhead of the spiritual realm. Gnostic films work on two levels: they awaken viewers to the possibility that they have been dwelling in a dream; they offer paths out of this dream into a realm where no one sleeps.[5] In both instances, the Gnostic film crashes the old system and envisions a new dispensation.[6] For example, the insomniac Gnostic philosopher Tyler Durden (Brad Pitt), an alchemical trickster and explosive wizard (cf. the magical sage Hermes Trismegistus), of 1999's *Fight Club* speaks of the demiurge, "You have to consider the possibility that God does not like you. He never wanted you. In all probability, he hates you. This is not the worst thing that can happen," because "…We don't need

---

3 Frances Yates, *Giordano Bruno and the Hermetic Tradition*, p. 311.
4 Timothy Freke and Peter Gandy, *The Jesus Mysteries*, p. 182.
5 Eric Wilson, *Secret Cinema*, p. 35.
6 *ibid.*

him."[7] Durden, a fictitious creation[8] of his alter ego the Narrator, or Jack (Edward Norton), leads a full-blown Gnostic rebellion against the demiurge by initiating Project Mayhem: the destruction of modern society and its obsession with materialism, status, and wealth. By annihilating the hylic world, Durden is ravaging the false illusion–its banal trappings–which the demiurge sustains and perpetuates. Materialism is torn down epitomized by imploding buildings during *Fight Club's* final moments making way for a new mystic vision to stand in their place.

Fight Club's Gnosticism thrives in *They Live* (1988) wherein demiurge-like extraterrestrials secretly rule planet Earth by using all forms of media and advertising to create an illusion. The aliens employ subliminal and hypnotic OBEY, CONFORM, MARRY AND REPRODUCE, SLEEP, CONSUME, and to have NO INDEPENDENT THOUGHT mind-control advertisements to keep humankind in perpetual stasis–drowning man and woman's divine spark–while hiding in plain sight. Much like Tyler Durden, an unemployed drifter, Nada (Spanish for *nothing*), played by "Rowdy" Roddy Piper (1954-2015) initiates a rebellion against the aliens, many of whom are power brokers, exposing them and their materialistic subterfuge to the world. Being *nothing*, Nada is anti-wealth and anti-materialism thus anti-demiurge; by revealing the humanoid extraterrestrials, Nada will supply gnosis by awakening humanity to the illusion placed before it, anticipating Neo (Keanu Reeves) in *The Matrix* (1999), thereby outmaneuvering the mind-controlling skull-faced creatures. The demiurge's shadow is cast upon Joh Fredersen (Alfred Abel, 1879-1938) in 1927's *Metropolis*. Fredersen is a wealthy, ruthless tyrant who oversees a vast urban dystopia, Metropolis, in which there is a significant separation between the spiritual, philosophical lower class and the decadent, wealthy upper class; Fredersen sees workers as machine-like slaves who labor endlessly to maintain the luxury and technology (cf. materialism) of his city.

However, if one wishes to view the Gnostic demiurge in film, one of the best examples is Bela Lugosi's (1882-1956) armchair sub-deity from Ed Wood's (1924-1978) sixty-five-minute transvestite apologia *Glen or*

---

7 Hermes Trismegistus associates with the trickster, Mercury, because the former is an agent of change. He (or she) removes the hero from the constricts of everyday life, placing him (or her) on an adventure of gnosis and salvation.

8 Durden could also be interpreted as the Narrator's daemon which, in ancient Greek and Hellenistic mythology, was a spirit guide or fate.

Glenda (1953). Billed in the credits as "Scientist," Lugosi's eccentric demiurge pulls the strings of humanity to fix, or at least reconcile, cross-dressing men. While rationalizing transvestism, he admits that mistakes are made, admonishing humankind to, "Dance to that which one is created for," suffocating all notions of individuality. He has no problem tinkering with humanity to satisfy the needs of his narrow ego. Implying Manichean duality (e.g. good versus evil, spirit and matter, light against dark, i.e., Zoroastrian dualism), Lugosi's demiurge describes the film's two protagonists: "One is wrong because he does right, and one is right because he does wrong. Pull the string!" Lugosi's demiurge sees the sexes as illusionary: they can be (and should be, depending on the circumstances) distorted, altered, and rearranged regardless of consequence. The difference between Wood's films and those of Lucas, Ridley Scott, and the Wachowskis is that Wood knew next to nothing about Gnosticism, the esoteric, and its impact on popular culture. Wood's knowledge of the occult was limited to Universal horror films most notably *Dracula* (1931), *Frankenstein* (1931), *The Mummy* (1932), and *The Wolfman* (1941), and lurid pulp magazines. But there is Bela Lugosi portraying the Gnostic demiurge, manipulating the material realm, erroneously guiding humankind into pansexual oblivion. So how can this contradiction be reconciled?

In *Cinema Symbolism*, I put forth the theory that esoteric iconography appearing in film unintentionally is the result of what Swiss psychiatrist and psychotherapist Carl G. Jung (1875-1961) called the *collective unconscious*. This psychological paradigm holds that particular imagery and symbols related to mythology, religion, legends, and the occult are so hardwired to the human psyche–embedded in humankind's anthropological makeup–that the forms and images materialize, in artistic expressions, regardless of the director or producer's intentions. Jung's theorem is a practical answer (or explanation) when a movie's director, writer, or producer denies the intentional placement of arcane symbols and themes in film. Jung's achievement–broadly–was to demonstrate that this unconscious was not separate, uniquely exclusive to the individual, but was collective as well, and that beneath that level, perhaps endlessly, are other reservoirs of consciousness or, in terms of the human condition, unconsciousness. These fundamental discoveries form the basis of all the more recent investigations of supernatural belief by Depth Psychology.[9] According to Jung, the collective unconscious is part of the *unus mundus* (one world) which is the concept of an underlying unified reality from which everything emerges and to which everything returns. Jung borrowed the term *unus mundus* from Belgian philosopher, translator, alchemist, physician, and bibliophile Gerhard Dorn (ca. 1530-1584), a student of the famous alchemist, occultist, and astrologer Paracelsus (1493-1541). Jung's collective unconscious echoes Plato's (427-347 BCE) Theory of Forms which asserts that non-material abstract (but substantial) forms or ideas, not the material world of change, possess the highest and most fundamental type of reality. Thus, this concept explains Lugosi's portrayal of the demiurge in spite of Wood's apparent ignorance of the subject matter. Components of the collective unconscious include, but are not limited to, magic, astrology and the zodiac, sorcery, lunar and solar folklore, the anthropomorphizing of the stars, constellations, planets, and numinous folklore. These provide the raw material of what Jung termed *archetypes*. Since this arcane imagery is subconscious, the individual may have limited understanding of it as a whole but not cognizant of its discrete power and influence. Cinema often draws from the secret treasure trove of symbols and ideas dwelling in the collective unconscious; they hide in the celluloid not seen by the casual moviegoer. This hidden, beneath-the-surface archetypal imagery often enhances plotlines, informs us of a director or producer's instincts, influencing character development thus revealing the movie to be more than just a film. Instead, cinema itself becomes an epic narrative, living artwork, designed to explore the human experience both negatively and positively. In other words, movies are a reflection of the human condition on psychological, metaphysical, conscious and subconscious levels; cinema is our current mythology.

For example, 1978's *Halloween* transformed the holiday and, in doing so, the fabric of society. Before John Carpenter's film, Halloween was a holiday for children when adolescents costumed themselves and went out trick-or-treating for confectioneries. Carpenter's grim movie returned the holiday to its pagan roots, when darkness not only covered the land, but was celebrated as well. After the film, Halloween was perceived as a day and

---

9 See Douglas Hill and Pat Williams' *The Supernatural*, pp. 25-26.

night when evil and death–a boogieman[10] personified by Michael Myers–were given license to roam the land to terrorize the living. Its customs were no longer mere child's play; rather, the celebration of the autumnal harvest, such as carving jack o' lanterns from pumpkins and dressing as demons, witches, and hobgoblins, became protective talismans against the unseen malevolence that forever stalks October 31st. Cinema can also be prophetic: Thomas "Neo" Anderson's passport expires (or dies) on September 11th, 2001, anticipating the terrorist attacks on the World Trade Center and Pentagon. *The Matrix* reference is particularly disturbing considering the film is about beginning and end, death and rebirth. During the opening credits of 2000's *The Patriot*, Benjamin Martin's (Mel Gibson) handmade wooden rocking chair weighs exactly 9 pounds, 11 ounces. When he sits in the chair it collapses, causing Martin to come crashing down. The horrors of September 11th, 2001 can also be found in 1981's *Escape from New York* wherein an Al-Qaeda-like terrorist organization called the National Liberation Front seeks to strike a blow against American imperialism by crashing an airliner–Air Force One–into lower Manhattan. September 11th, 2001, appear in the pilot episode of *The Lone Gunmen* (original airdate 4 March 2001) which involved a government conspiracy to hijack a commercial airliner, fly it into the World Trade Center, blaming the act on terrorists to gain support for a new profit-making war.

The Net (1995) anticipated the coming internet revolution when, via the advent of social media in the 2000s, privacy is scarce because everyone's life is online. The Pentagon and the United States Navy, employing the 2009 movie *Transformers: Revenge of the Fallen*, subtly announced to the world that an electromagnetic railgun was no longer the domain of science fiction and video games, having constructed one

---

10 cf. the Haitian Tonton Macoute (Uncle Gunnysack), a mythological monster kidnaping and punishing unruly children by snaring them in a gunnysack, carrying them off to be consumed for breakfast. Echoing this mythology is Krampus, a horned, anthropomorphic figure in German-speaking Alpine folklore. According to traditional narratives around the figure, Krampus punishes children during the Christmas season having misbehaved, in contrast with Saint Nicholas rewarding well-behaved ones with gifts. Krampus' spirit finds a home in Sam (Quinn Lord) from 2007's *Trick 'r Treat*. The childlike Sam is an impish pumpkin-headed creature that punishes and, in some instances, kills those who do not respect the traditions and folklore of Halloween. Etymologically, the name "Sam" comes from Samhain, which was the Gaelic festival marking the end of the harvest season (October 31st-November 1st), and the beginning of winter or the darker half of the year. Today, we celebrate Samhain as Halloween, welcoming the seasonal darkness, anticipating the birth of the sun at the winter solstice.

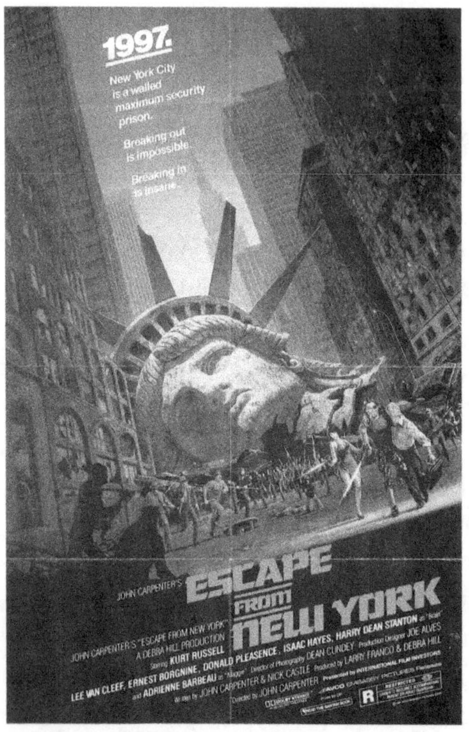

Escape from New York one-sheet movie poster. Directed by John Carpenter, the film exhibits stark 9/11/01 imagery thirty years before the terrorist attacks on Lower Manhattan suggesting that Jung's collective unconscious is not only inherited, but in some instances, anticipates future events. Carpenter's film also employs Gematria: the assignment of number values to letters to forge an occult relationship, conveying an occult meaning or agenda within the words or phrases. Gematria originated as a Babylonian-Greek system of alphanumeric code-cipher, merging later with Jewish culture. In the dystopian movie, the President's airplane, Airforce One, is designated David 14; David refers to the Bible's King David, the second king of the United Monarchy of Israel and Judah, reigning from ca. 1010–970 BCE. King David is regarded as a righteous and effective king. He was feared in combat, but was tempered by his ability to effectively dispense civil and criminal justice. According to the New Testament he was an ancestor of Jesus (Matthew 1:1-17, Mark 10:46-48, Luke 3:23-38, Romans 1:1-4, 2 Timothy 2:8, and Revelation 22:1). In Hebrew, David equals 14 (D=4, V=6, D=4; 4+6+4=14) thus David 14 transforms the President (Donald Pleasence, 1919-1995) via his aircraft's code number into a quasi-divine figure, a Biblical patriarch. The President, along with the contents of his briefcase, avert a nuclear apocalypse, ensuring the survival of western civilization.

not only in the film, but in reality, as well. The 2009 film *Knowing* predicts the Gulf of Mexico oil disaster of April 2010, and the 1982 comedy, *Hanky Panky*, features a Gene Wilder (1933-2016) character named Michael Jordon. Jordon, from Chicago, anticipates the rise to stardom of basketball superstar Michael Jordan, drafted by the Chicago Bulls in 1984, a mere two years later. Could it be that Jung's collective unconscious is not only inherited, but predictive as well, foretelling the future? Or could there be a dark conspiracy at work; put another way, is this imagery evidence of predictive programming[11] or, alternatively, is this art imitating life imitating art? Is there an Illuminati-like order that runs Hollywood and if so, are hidden symbols and themes in movies part of their sinister agenda? What about the government's involvement with Hollywood? It is evident that the 1942 James Cagney (1899-1986) film *Yankee Doodle Dandy* was government propaganda; the movie is an anti-fascist rallying call to whip-up support for the Allied cause, quelling dissension to America's entry into World War II.

---

11 The author will address the issue of Predictive Programming in the Conclusion.

* * * *

Hidden codes, the occult, and the ancient mysteries are a source of endless fascination, challenging the movie-going audience to both decipher and understand these arcane treasures, when concealed by filmmakers. The intertwining of the occult with entertainment predates Hollywood: Shakespeare's preoccupation with the ghosts, witches, Neoplatonism, Rosicrucianism, astrology, and fairies is understood as deriving as less from popular tradition than from deep-rooted affinity with the learned occult philosophy and its religious implications;[12] so it is today with the entertainment industry. Attempting to locate hidden clues and symbols within film–unravel their mysteries–provides even another level of entertainment when one watches a movie; it challenges the viewer to play a game of chess with the filmmakers: to decode their celluloid masterpieces. Seeing is not enough, rather one must observe to comprehend cinema's esoteric imagery. Films provide the raw material–almost a passion play–enabling the viewer to take a magica Throughout the inhabited world, in all times and under every circumstance, l journey, revisiting ancient myths and numinous legends, some hidden, some more visible. The audience is watching visual sorcery in a theater–itself a church-like atmosphere complete with aisles and pew-like seating–which can cause one to laugh or cry, feel happy or sad, terrified or exhilarated; one can leave a movie theater transformed by the manufactured light they have just experienced. In *The Book of Black Magic*, Masonic author A.E. Waite (1857-1941) provides insight into this arcane psychological philosophy:

> The ordinary fields of psychological inquiry, largely in possession of the pathologist, are fringed by a borderland of transcendental experiment into which pathologists may occasionally venture, but it is left for the most part to uncharted explorers. Beyond these fields and this borderland there lies the legendary wonder-world of Mysticism, Magic,

---

12 See Frances Yates' *The Occult Philosophy in the Elizabethan Age*, pp. 89-90 and Yates' *The Rosicrucian Enlightenment*, pp. 182, 189. It has been suggested that William Shakespeare (1564-1616) was Sir Francis Bacon and the Rosicrucian Knights of the Helmet; see Manly P. Hall's *The Secret Teachings of All Ages*, Chapter XXXVIII, "Bacon, Shakspere [*sic*], and the Rosicrucians," pp. 539-551. See also Manly Hall's *The Lost Keys of Freemasonry*, p. 277, where he cites Bro. Hugh James commenting on a paper, *Some Notes of the Legends of Masonry*, by William Harry Ryland, "Look into the mystic symbolism of the Shakspere [*sic*] trilogy–'The Tempest,' 'The Midsummer Night's Dream,' and 'The Winter's Tale.'"

and Sorcery, a world of fascination or terror, as the mind which regards it is tempered, but in either case the antithesis of admitted possibility. There all paradoxes seem to obtain actually, contradictions logically coexist, the effect is greater than the cause, and the shadow more than the substance. Therein the visible melts into the unseen, the invisible is manifested openly, motion from place to place is accomplished without traversing the intervening distance, matter passes through matter.[13]

One thing is for sure: movies are part of this wonderworld of mysticism and sorcery; they provide the viewer a universe of fascination, terror, or both. Veiled themes, hidden symbols, arcane emblems and esoteric archetypes concealed in film augment this visual magic adding substantially to the film's mystery. The movie maker's wizardry is not limited to the celluloid itself; the one-sheet movie poster for 1982's *E.T. The Extra-Terrestrial* is an allusion to Michelangelo's (1475-1564) famous mural within the Sistine Chapel, only an alien–not the Abrahamic God–is the progenitor of humanity. Film–esoteric pieces of animated art–present logical paradoxes where darkness exists in light and characters contradict themselves while seemingly making total sense in the context of the story. For better understanding we must lift the veil to peer into the world of cinema symbolism, both exoteric and esoteric. Occult symbolism elevates the film to a neo-dimension of myth and legend, transcending popular culture. Whether these hidden undercurrents and icons are intentional or unintentional is a question which adds to the film's mystique.

When not intentional, or manipulated by a hidden hand, Jung's collective unconscious theorem provides a legitimate explanation how these arcane symbols and themes arise in movies. However, one must bear in mind that many in Hollywood's filmmaking industry are aware of the occult imagery and esoteric doctrines. When these hidden symbols turn up in movies it is of little surprise to this author; in most cases, these obscure yet powerful emblems and themes are deliberately placed, of this there is little doubt. Often a movie explores a myth or its component parts; on universal mythology and the life experience Campbell writes:

Whether we listen with aloof amusement to the dreamlike mumbo jumbo of some red eyed witch doctor of the Congo, or read with cultivated

---

13 Arthur. E. Waite, *The Book of Black Magic*, p. 17.

rapture thin translations from the sonnets of the mystic Lao-tse, or now and again crack the hard nutshell of an argument of Aquinas, or catch suddenly the shining meaning of a bizarre Eskimo fairy tale, it will always be the one, shape-shifting yet marvelously constant story that we find, together with a challengingly persistent suggestion of more remaining to be experienced than will ever be known or told.

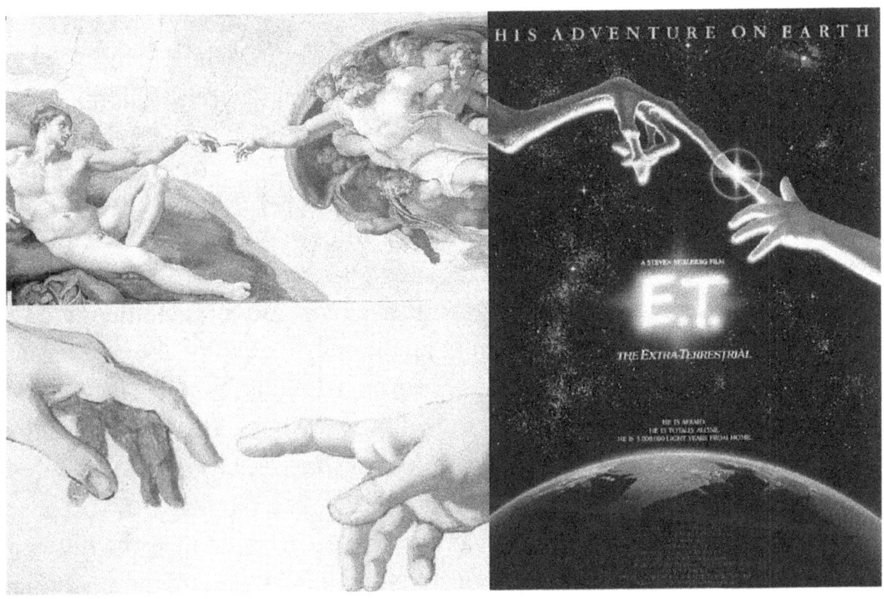

(Left Top and Left Bottom) God creates Adam in Michelangelo's fresco on the ceiling of the Sistine Chapel, Rome. (Right) Michelangelo's art becomes the one-sheet movie poster for *E.T. The Extra-Terrestrial*. The poster changes the hands of Adam and God into the hands of Elliott (Henry Thomas) and E.T. suggesting the possibility that extraterrestrials–not the God of Abraham–are responsible for humankind's creation.

Throughout the inhabited world, in all times and under every circumstance, the myths of man have flourished; and they have been the living inspiration of whatever else may have appeared out of the activities of the human body and mind. It would not be too much to say that myth is the secret opening through which the inexhaustible energies of the cosmos pour into human cultural manifestation. Religions, philosophies, arts, the social forms of primitive and historic man, prime discoveries in science and technology, the very dreams that blister sleep, boil up from the basic, magic ring of myth.

The wonder is that the characteristic efficacy to touch and inspire deep creative centers dwells in the smallest nursery fairy tale–as the flavor of the ocean is contained in a droplet or the whole mystery of life within the egg of a flea. For the symbols of mythology are not manufactured; they cannot be ordered, invented, or permanently suppressed. They are spontaneous productions of the psyche, and each bears within it, undamaged, the germ power of its source.

What is the secret of the timeless vision? From what profundity of the mind does it derive? Why is mythology everywhere the same, beneath its varieties of costume? And what does it teach?[14]

If it teaches one thing, it is this: the story of the human condition, what it holds sacred, and its belief system and values. Cinema pervades this time-less vision because film presents legends under a variety of guises thereby, alchemically, making the celluloid active, almost alive. The cinematic flight from empirical reality might open to an alternative reality above conscious-ness.[15] The reveries of the popular screen could bloom into dreams of eterni-ties beyond reason; the images overwhelming the individual mind could well usher one to a collective unconsciousness, a shared panorama of symbols.[16] Cinema's attenuation of realism need not be limitation but a virtue because, in the hands of a wily filmmaker, esoteric symbolism transforms the movie into a spiritual medium: a realization of invisible worlds, ungraspable thoughts, and immanent potencies.[17] Jung's collective unconscious and synchronicity theorems transcend cinema, as does mythology and legend, Gnosticism, the occult, Neoplatonism, theology, mysticism, religion, Freemasonry, magic, and astrology. This tome's Introduction provides an outline of this material so do not pass it over. Welcome to *Cinema Symbolism 2: More Esoteric Imagery from Popular Movies*.

Robert W. Sullivan IV, Esq.
13 November 2013
Baltimore, Maryland, United States.

---

14 Joseph Campbell, *The Hero with a Thousand Faces*, pp. 1-2.
15 Wilson, *Secret Cinema*, p. 147.
16 *ibid.*
17 *ibid.*

INTRODUCTION

"The Devil take me?
Not for some considerable time, I trust."
– Dr. Anton Phibes, *Dr. Phibes Rises Again*, 1972.

"The battle with the guards was magnificent.
Your skill is extraordinary.
And I was going to ask you to join us."
– Mr. Han, *Enter the Dragon*, 1973.

"You see none of it was real. It was illusion.
Your art, your science, it was all a nightmare.
And now it's done. Finished."
– Matthias, *The Omega Man*, 1971.

"The saucers are up there, and the cemetery's out there,
but I'll be locked up in there."
– Paula Trent, *Plan 9 from Outer Space*, 1959.

"So do I, in you and in what you believe.
I've been an eager student but
I've held back from the final ceremonies,
and now I'm ready to join you at the invocation."
– Juliana, *The Masque of the Red Death*, 1964.

"I'll do things to you that are beyond all known philosophies!
Wait until I get my devices!"
– Durand-Durand, *Barbarella*, 1968.

"Hold on, fuck off."
– Clarence Beeks, *Trading Places*, 1983.

There are more to movies than what meets the naked eye. In the post-modern age, cinema has the unique ability to place formal cleverness, arcane imagery, and symbolism onto celluloid to create occult realism. Esoteric symbols and themes are right before our eyes, but we have not been trained to see them; when it comes to this sublime visual sorcery, most seem to suffer intellectual vertigo. This symbolism is hiding in plain sight, and once educated the disorientation will fade away.

In *Star Wars: The Force Awakens* (2015), the conscientious Stormtrooper FN-2187 (John Boyega) frees Poe Dameron (Oscar Isaac) from the clutches of the First Order. His numeric designation, 2187, is a reference to Princess Leia's (Carrie Fisher, 1956-2016) Death Star jail cell number, 2187, in *Star Wars: A New Hope* (1977). The esoteric nexus is this: Leia is held captive in cell 2187 eventually freed–rescued–while Dameron is likewise liberated–rescued–by FN-2187. Most people are not aware that in 1981's *Evilspeak*, the medieval satanic Father Esteban (Richard Moll) is a hardcore rendition of Dominican friar, Renaissance occultist, and Neoplatonic philosopher Giordano Bruno (1548-1600).[18] Esteban is sent into exile by the Inquisition while his real-life counterpart Bruno was burned at the stake as a heretic after being found guilty by the Inquisition.[19] Did you know that actor Charles Gray (1928-2000) portrays an Aleister Crowley (1875-1947) analogue named Mocata in *The Devil Rides Out* (1968)? During a sabbath, Mocata summons the Goat of Mendes, Baphomet, mirroring Crowley's practice of the *Sacred Magic of Abramelin the Mage* is designed to conjure demons. One may not know that Crowley's spirit resides in black magicians Adrian and his son Steven Marcato[20] (cf. Mocata) in 1968's *Rosemary's Baby*; Marcato the elder conjures the living Devil at the Bramford. In 1999's *The Sixth Sense*, the surname of the boy who can see ghosts, Cole Sear (Haley Joel Osment), implies a seer: a person through spiritual insight sees what the future holds. Sear's ghostly visions give him insights into the past which can affect the present and alter the future.[21]

---

18 In the First Edition of *Cinema Symbolism* (2014), I identified Dominican Friar Tommaso Campanella (1568-1639) as an analogue to Esteban; see Chapter VII. After consideration, I believe that Bruno is a better comparison. This change was made in the second edition of *Cinema Symbolism*, but naturally remains in all first edition copies.

19 See Robert Sullivan's *Cinema Symbolism*, Chapter VII.

20 Portrayed by Sidney Blackmer, 1895-1973.

21 Sullivan, *Cinema Symbolism*, Chapter XI.

Or that in *Magic* (1978), the Fats dummy was created specifically to look like Anthony Hopkins to symbolize the shadow, evil side of Hopkins' character Charles "Corky" Withers. Did you know that the characters of Johnny Charles Bartlett (Jake Busey) and his female accomplice Patricia Ann Bradley (Dee Wallace) from Peter Jackson's *The Frighteners* (1996) are based on real-life American killers Charles Starkweather (1938-1959) and his female lackey Caril Ann Fugate? Starkweather was executed in the electric chair for killing eleven people, just like his cinematic counterpart Bartlett, sentenced to the electric chair for massacring hospital workers; Johnny thus identifies Starkweather as his role model. Caril Ann Fugate, whose precise role in the Starkweather murders is still not known, is paralleled by Patricia Ann Bradley. Bradley feigns innocence yet secretly assists Bartlett echoing Fugate whose innocent persona was likewise thought to be a ruse. Her first name, Patricia, evokes Patricia "Patty" Hearst, taken hostage by the Symbionese Liberation Army (SLA), then brainwashed into sympathizing with her kidnappers helping them rob banks in the 1970s. Johnny Bartlett is named after Velda and Marion Bartlett, who were the second and third victims of Charles Starkweather. In a strange twist of fate, Starkweather and the Bartletts are buried in Wyuka Cemetary in Lincoln, Nebraska; murderer and victims are not one hundred yards away. Lastly, art imitating life can be found in *Back to the Future III's* (1990) Clara Clayton (Mary Steenburgen) who personifies female astronomer Marie Mitchell (1818-1889). Clayton, being interested in the stars, is naturally attracted to Doc Brown (Christopher Lloyd), the scientist. The two polymaths fall in love while stargazing.

Were you also aware that Susie Salmon (Saoirse Ronan) from Peter Jackson's *The Lovely Bones* (2009, based on the novel by Alice Sebold) is a girl representing the dying solar age of Pisces? Although Susie is waning like the Piscean Age, she nevertheless achieves gnosis (cf. sublime wisdom and revelation) thus allowing *ascensio* (re-awakening to aristocratic and rightful leadership) in the ethereal afterlife. Susie is transported to a mystical, illusionary Purgatory to experience epiphany echoing Dorothy Gale's (Judy Garland, 1922-1969) ascension upwards via a tornado symbolizing the Winding Staircase of Solomon's Temple which leads to the Middle Chamber of I Kings 6:8. Within Masonic ritual, the initiate is instructed that herein is wisdom and to study the seven liberal arts and sciences. Thus,

Dorothy climbs an allegorical staircase to reach the magical Land of Oz to receive gnosis *qua* wisdom which, for her, is the understanding that *there is no place like home.*

Susie's surname, Salmon, evokes fish; accordingly, when she perishes, she is consumed by water suggesting the waning astrological Age of Pisces and the coming of the new, numinous solar age of Aquarius. Approaching the entrance to Heaven, a large tree greets Susie suggesting the Tree of Life and the Tree of Wisdom, echoed in the Bible at Genesis 3:24, and by Kabbalah's *sefirot*.[22] The tree is a symbol of Susie's ascension, or in her case, mastery of life (which is like her self-created Purgatory, illusionary) and death, culminating in spiritual rebirth and Gnostic reawakening. Susie learns to let go of her family, the corporeal world, and enter the spiritual realm, Heaven, or the Gnostic pleroma. Susie's great tree represents the kabalistic Tree of Life; Kabbalah is a Hebrew system of rabbinic numerology, philosophy, science, magic, and mysticism developed during the Middle Ages by Rabbi Isaac the Blind (ca. 1160–1235). Kabbalah is a critical part of Western occultism having been reinterpreted in accordance with Christianity termed *Cabala*.[23] The medieval and Renaissance Cabalists were desirous of returning humankind to a spiritual state before the fall of Eden, and that redemption is achieved through intense experiences of matter's darkest realms.[24] Kabbalah, along with the extant tome *Sefer Yetzirah*, preserve secret traditions and Jewish esotericisms relating to the nature of God; Kabbalah is a guarded, secret doctrine. Kabbalah

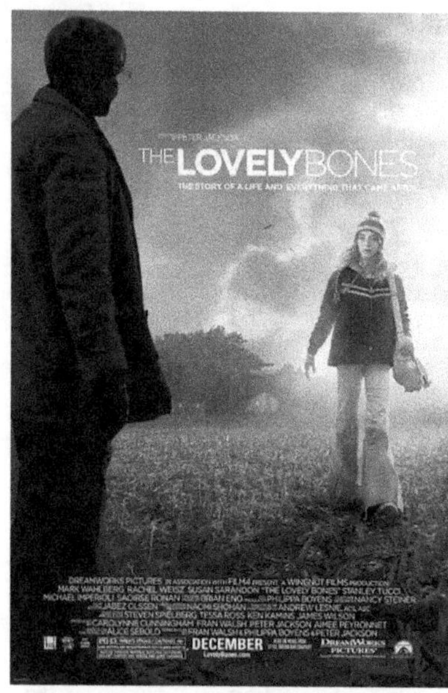

One-sheet movie poster for *The Lovely Bones* features the solar heroine Susie (cf. the dawn, the female embodiment of the sun) confronted by her shadowy murderer, George Harvey (Stanley Tucci), darkness incarnate. Susie and George represent Manichean cosmology (a/k/a Zoroastrian Dualism), the eternal conflict of light against dark. This struggle is also an internal one, of ego against shadow self since we all wrestle with angels and demons.

---

22 Rosemary Ellen Guiley, *The Encyclopedia of Witches and Witchcraft*, p. 184. Kabbalah's Tree of Life is formed by its 10 *sefirot*, representing aspects of the divine, and 22 connecting paths.
23 *ibid.*
24 See Wilson's *Secret Cinema*, p. 74.

parallels Gnosticism because both doctrines include magic, occult symbolism, cosmologies, a belief in spiritual God (Kabbalah's *Ein Sof*), angels and demons, and ascension and apotheosis of the being (perfection, transition or improvement of the self, cf. alchemical change) and of the soul (divine approbation).

Not all hidden imagery is kabalistic or mystical. For instance, the opening sequence of 1985's *Back to the Future* foreshadows the film's cinematic climax atop Hill Valley's Clock Tower, and the film's closing moments. The movie begins by going, literally, back to the future by displaying Emmett "Doc" Brown's (Christopher Lloyd) eclectic collection of timekeeping devices. One will observe a clock with a drunkard raising a bottle to his mouth anticipating Hill Valley's local vagrant, Red (George "Buck" Flower, 1937-2004), greeting Marty McFly (Michael J. Fox) upon returning to 1985 in the DeLorean with the line, "Crazy drunk driver." Next one will see a tiny man, dressed as the Doc Brown of 1955, hanging off the minute hand of one of his clocks. This is a harbinger of when Brown dangles before the clock-face, clinging to its hands for dear life, trying to reconnect the cable to harness lightning, returning Marty to 1985. When Brown's radio alarm clock goes off an advertisement for Statler Toyota Dealership is airing. Before time traveling back to 1955, Marty, accompanied by his girlfriend, Jennifer Parker (Claudia Wells), covets a 4x4 truck on a Statler Toyota flatbed trailer. At the end, Marty finds the same truck in his parents' garage. By employing this hidden symbolism, the filmmakers convey the idea that time is bendable, that the past, present, and future are interchangeable because one can affect the other, and vice-versa. *Back to the Future's* beginning is its end, and its end is its beginning; time is fluid, mutable because past and future mutually affect each other.

Some characters are personifications of the archetypes which reside in the collective unconscious. In *Cinema Symbolism*, this author explained that, "…Strictly speaking, Jungian archetypes refer to unclear underlying forms, or the archetypes, from which emerge images and universal motifs such as the mother, the father, the child, the trickster (Mercury), the wise man (the Hermit, Hermes Trismegistus), the temptress, the lover, the hero (sun), the heroine (moon), and the villain (shadow-Devil), among others. It is history, culture, and personal context that shape these manifest representations giving them their specific content; they are embedded in the imagery of Tarot cards which, in turn, both conceal and reveal hermetic, alchemical, astrological, and solar truths. Being unconscious, the existence of archetypes can only be deduced indirectly by examining behavior, images, art, myths, religions, or dreams. They are inherited potentials which are actualized when they enter consciousness as images or manifest in behavior on interaction with the outside world. As such, the collective unconscious does not develop individually; rather, it is inherited."[25] There are archetypal qualities which are so universal that our subconscious mind identifies with them whether we are aware of it or not. For instance, the savior archetype is a favorite in Hollywood; Christlike, this archetype steps right out of the Gospel tales. Damian Karras (Jason Miller, 1939-2001) becomes the Christianized cabalistic apotheosized savior of Regan MacNeil in 1973's *The Exorcist* by ridding her of the demon Pazuzu.[26] The savior archetype is prison inmate John Coffee (Michael Clarke Duncan, 1957-2102) in *The Green Mile* (1999) who, like James Cole in *Twelve Monkeys* (1995) bears the initials J.C., symbolizing the New Testament's redemptive savior. Coffee, like Jesus, can heal the sick: he cures prison guard Paul Edgecomb's (Tom Hanks) urinary tract infection, healing the terminally ill wife of Warden Hal Moores (James Cromwell). Like Jesus, John Coffee resurrects the dead, a mouse, and is executed for a crime he did not commit, dying for the sins of a racially segregated Southern United States. Because there is too much suffering in the world, to which he is sensitive, Coffee explains that he is "rightly tired of the pain" and is ready to rest in peace. J.C. is also John Connor of the Terminator franchise whose sole purpose is to save humanity from a mechanized menace known as Skynet. The savior archetype is Krypton's Kal-El, the only begotten son of Jor-El and Lara Lor-Van, sent to planet Earth to save its inhabitants from themselves by using supernatural godlike abilities while defeating evil, thus making him a Superman. In 1978's *Superman*, the Man of Steel (Christopher Reeve, 1952-2004) miraculously resurrects the dead by returning life to Lois Lane (Margot Kidder, 1948-2018) having died during an earthquake. The name

---

25 Sullivan, *Cinema Symbolism*, Introduction, *passim*. See also Sallie Nichol's *Jung and Tarot*, pp. 9-21, *passim*.

26 Sullivan, *ibid*, Chapter I. Father Karras undergoes transition, kabalistic apotheosis, by becoming Regan's Christlike savior when he successfully exorcises the demon that possesses her. Karras' change and apotheosis, one could argue, is more akin to Christian Cabala since Karras is a Jesuit priest.

of Superman's archenemy, Lex Luthor,[27] echoes Lucifer, who, in the context of John Milton's (1608-1674) *Paradise Lost* (1667), is the chief antagonist battling God.[28] Luthor, like Lucifer, is a wise and aloof light bearer (cf. enlightenment, wisdom), using his genius to thwart Superman at every turn, mirroring Satan's attempts to undermine God. Carrying this symbolism forward, in the latest Superman film (as of the writing of this book) titled *Man of Steel* (2013), Superman is often referred to as humankind's savior and, like Jesus, does not use his powers until his early thirties. Like the life and death of Jesus, solar imagery transcends *Man of Steel*, turning Superman (Henry Cavill) into a Neoplatonic superhero. Aboard General Zod's (Michael Shannon) ship, it is explained to Superman that the yellow sun, the earth's life-giving star, is the source of his Kryptonian superhuman powers. Later, Superman is told by a hologram of his father, Jor-El (Russell Crowe), to save the earth, prompting him to exit General Zod's (Michael Shannon) ship cruciform while the sun (cf. the light of the world) shines brightly behind him. The solar imagery repeats when Kal-El (Clark Kent) sits in a church conversing with a local pastor, a stained-glass window of Jesus pervades the scene; conspicuous in the background, the image of Jesus is impossible to miss. In custody, Superman tells Dr. Emil Hamilton (Richard Schiff) that he is 33 years old, the age of Christ at the time of his crucifixion. Kal-El's solar nexus to Jesus–as humankind's savior–is confirmed when Jor-El tells his son, "They will race behind you, they will stumble, they will fall. But in time, *they will join you in the sun*, Kal. In time, you will help them accomplish wonders."[29]

Randle P. McMurphy (Jack Nicholson) is a Jesus Christ analogue in 1975's *One Flew Over the Cuckoo's Nest*. In the novel by Ken Kesey (1932-2001), the Christ allegories are noticeable, but some are absent from the movie. Directed by Milos Forman (1932-2018), the film depicts the inmates inside a ward of a mental asylum, the Oregon State Hospital, following McMurphy as disciples, when he is exasperated McMurphy frequently invokes Jesus. He takes the patients fishing on the sea, in a literal representation of Jesus with his followers as fishermen. He performs the miracles of getting Chief Bromden (Will Sampson, 1933-1987) to speak

---

27 Played by Gene Hackman in *Superman* (1978) and its sequels.
28 See also Revelation 12:7-13.
29 *Man of Steel*, 2013, emphasis added.

and Billy Bibbit (Brad Dourif) to stop stuttering. Because of his Christlike rebellion against authority (cf. Sanhedrin), he suffers on an electroshock table; McMurphy's request for a crown of thorns (not in the film) cements the image of martyrdom. Patient Jim Sefelt (William Duell, 1923-2011) tells legends about McMurphy's mythic escape, just as the Apostles spread the word of Jesus' Resurrection in the New Testament. When the Chief kills McMurphy out of mercy, the scene mirrors the death, the tomb, and the resurrection that leads to Christianity's eternal life. Contrasting McMurphy's rebellious nature is his nemesis: the steely, cold, reactionary, pessimistic, unyielding Nurse Mildred Ratched (Louise Fletcher) who runs the ward like a military dictator; she enjoys giving the inmates their due. She employs subtle humiliation, unpleasant medical treatments, and a mind-numbing daily routine to suppress the patients who are more afraid of her than the outside world. She is nicknamed "Big Nurse" which echoes Big Brother, the name used in George Orwell's (1903-1950) novel *1984* to refer his authoritarian government. The name, Ratched, is also a pun of *ratchet*, which is a both a verb and a noun for a tool that uses a twisting motion to tighten bolts into place. This pun serves a greater metaphorical purpose in Kesey's hands because Ratched manipulates the patients by inducing them to spy on one another or expose each other's weaknesses in group sessions.

Every good guy or gal has an antagonist; a shadowy personality, the proverbial bad guy or bad woman (cf. the erotic demon goddess Lilith, or the punishing goddess Nemesis, i.e., the evil female archetype; cf. Campbell's Woman as the Temptress); McMurphy cannot exist without Ratched and vice versa. In the world of Universal Studio's Sherlock Holmes franchise from the 1940s, starring Basil Rathbone (1892-1967) as Holmes and Nigel Bruce as Dr. Watson (1895-1953), these archetypes are Professor Moriarty and Adrea Spedding,[30] a/k/a *The Spider Woman* (1944), who are male and female evil incarnate. In the world of the occult, these are the Right-Hand and the Left-Hand Paths, the latter is malicious black sorcery, the former is benevolent white magic. The Right-Hand Path hero, Batman, forever combats the Left-Hand Path villainess, Poison Ivy (a/k/a Pamela Isley, played by Uma Thurman in 1997's *Batman & Robin*), combining the temptress, mother, and trickster archetypes. Beautiful, sexy, and alluring,

---

30 Portrayed by Gale Sondergaard (1899-1985), the Spider Woman orchestrates a number of bizarre suicides that Holmes is convinced are part of an elaborate plot by a "female Moriarty."

this coquettish redhead personifies the negative attributes of Gaia–mother earth–whose obsessive-compulsive desire to protect nature usually ends paradoxically with her efforts harming the environments she seeks to protect. She is an archetypal temptress and trickster using her sexy persona to entrap the Caped Crusader.

Other archetypes are present on the big and little screen. *Star Trek's* (TV and movies) Mr. Spock (Leonard Nimoy, 1931-2015) typifies the sage Hermes Mercurius Trismegistus[31] or the hermit archetype, Card IX of the Major Arcana of the Tarot, the Hermit, and its associated mysteries. Spock, the wise loner, possesses all knowledge, and like Trismegistus is a godlike wizard who can render people unconscious with his Vulcan neck-pinch. Interestingly, Spock's hand sigil is itself an esoteric symbol. In his 1975 autobiography *I Am Not Spock*, Nimoy wrote that he based it on the priestly blessing performed by Jewish Kohanim with both hands, thumb to thumb in this same position, representing the Hebrew letter *Shin* ש which has three upward strokes similar to the position of the thumb and fingers in the salute; the letter *Shin* stands for *El Shaddai* meaning *Almighty (God)*. The kabbalists employed letter *Shin* to signify the trinity of the first three *sefirah*: *Keter* the Crown, *Chochmah* the Father, and *Binah* the Mother.[32] From the union of the Divine Father and the Divine Mother are produced the worlds and the generations of living things.[33] The three flame-like points of the letter ש have long been used to conceal this Creative Triad of the kabbalists.[34] Nimoy wrote that when he was a child, his grandfather took

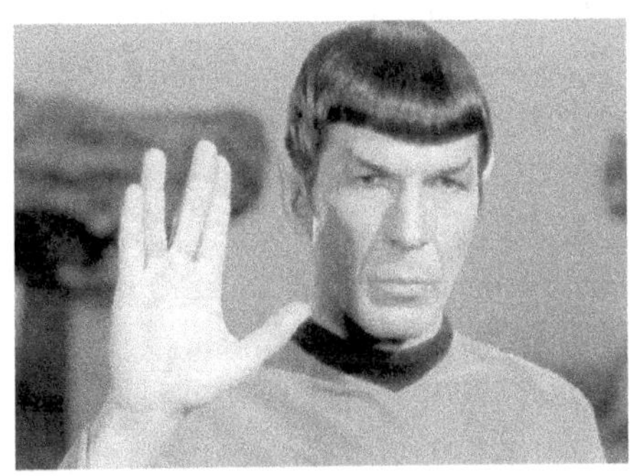

Spock flashes the Vulcan salute, a hand gesture consisting of a raised hand, palm forward with the fingers parted between the middle and ring finger, and the thumb extended. Often the phrase, "Live Long and Prosper," accompanies the kabalistic hand gesture.

---

31 Although a pagan god, Albertus Magus (ca. 1200-1280), Thomas Aquinas (1225-1274), and St. Augustine (354-430) considered Hermes Trismegistus a wise prophet foreseeing the advent of Christianity. The Hermes archetype often appears in film a wise sage, an old graybeard, providing aid to the solar, Christlike savior hero in film. See Sullivan's *Cinema Symbolism*, *passim*.
32 See Manly P. Hall's *The Secret Teachings of All Ages*, Text accompanying illustration on p. 372.
33 *ibid.*
34 *ibid.*

him to an orthodox synagogue, witnessing a rabbi perform the blessing and was impressed by it.[35]

"The man who should have been Louis Creed's (Dale Midkiff) father,"[36] the perspicacious Trismegistus-like Jud Crandall (Fred Gwynne, 1926-1993), is the only one who understands the supernatural powers of the Mi'kmaq burial ground but is averse to divulge its secrets of resurrection in 1989's *Pet Sematary*. Despite their father-son bond, Creed refuses to heed Crandall's warnings that the soil is tainted or that "sometimes dead is better," to use Crandall's cryptic terminology. Creed resurrects the family cat, Churchill, his son Gage (Miko Hughes), and wife Rachael (Denise Crosby), all with horrible consequences. In 1978's *Halloween*, the spirit of Hermes Trismegistus resides in Dr. Sam Loomis[37] (Donald Pleasence, 1919-1995), a renegade psychiatrist who comprehends the true nature of Michael Myers and his malevolent fixation with Halloween night. Although he is not a magician, Loomis nevertheless is the only one in Haddonfield who knows Myers is the Grim Reaper incarnate telling a perturbed resident at the beginning of *Halloween II* (1981), "You don't know what death is!" A disciple of fellow psychiatrist and psychotherapist Carl Jung, Loomis recounts the history of Halloween and its relationship to the collective unconscious, "…The Druid priests held fire rituals. Prisoners of war, criminals, the insane, animals, were burned alive in baskets. By observing the way they died, the Druids believed they could see omens of the future. Two thousand years later we've come no further. Samhain isn't evil spirits. It isn't goblins, ghosts or witches. It's the unconscious mind. We're all afraid of *the dark inside ourselves*."[38]

Not all of Hollywood's memorable characters are archetypes per se; rather, some are based on historical figures or equally famous fictitious

---

35 "Leonard Nimoy: 'Star Trek' Fans can be Scary," *Hero Complex*. Los Angeles Times: May 11, 2009, see also *I am not Spock* (1975) by Leonard Nimoy.

36 See Stephen King's *Pet Sematary*, p. 20.

37 The name, Sam Loomis, is an allusion to Mary Crane's boyfriend in Robert Bloch's (1917-1994) 1959 novel *Psycho*. Loomis also appears in Alfred Hitchcock's 1960 film with same name. In the film, Mary Crane's first name was changed to Marion, played by Janet Leigh (1927-2004) while Sam Loomis was portrayed by John Gavin. As such *Halloween's* director, John Carpenter, cast Janet Leigh's daughter, Jamie Lee Curtis, in the role of the film's heroine Laurie Strode. *Halloween* was Curtis' film debut. In Carpenter's *Prince of Darkness* (1987), the director once again pays homage to both *Psycho* and *Halloween* by naming Donald Pleasence's character Father Loomis.

38 See *Halloween II*, 1981, emphasis added.

personalities. For example, the thirty-ninth President of the United States, James Earl "Jimmy" Carter, becomes *Fast Times at Ridgemont High's* Mr. Hand (Ray Walston, 1914-2001). Hand, like Carter, is a displaced relic; the former does not understand his younger students, teenage Generation X. Hand also drones on about the Platt Amendment, which was an amendment to the 1901 Army Appropriations Bill that stipulated the conditions for the withdrawal of United States troops remaining in Cuba at the end of the Spanish-American War, defining the terms of Cuban-U.S. relations. The Treaty of Relations of 1903, signed in Havana May 22nd, 1903, implemented the conditions of the Platt Amendment allowing the United States to intervene unilaterally in Cuban affairs mandating negotiation for military bases on the island, including Guantanamo Bay Naval Base, in what would become the Cuban-American Treaty of 1903. Hand's interest in Cuba conjures the Mariel Boatlift, which occurred during the Carter Administration. The Mariel Boatlift was a mass emigration of Cubans who departed from Cuba's Mariel Harbor for the United States between April 15th and October 31st, 1980. The exodus started to have negative political implications for President Carter when it was discovered some of the exiles had been released from Cuban jails and mental health facilities. As such, both Mr. Hand and President Carter have negative perceptions, the two never seem to have the respect of those they govern: Carter, especially his foreign policy, was often seen as weak by the American people and Mr. Hand was never taken seriously by his students. Carter lost the 1980 election to a former Hollywood movie star, Ronald Reagan (1911-2004).

The protagonist of Umberto Eco's (1932-2016) *The Name of the Rose*,[39] William of Baskerville (Sean Connery), recalls Sir Arthur Conan Doyle's (1859-1930) *The Hound of Baskervilles* (published 1902); his name turns the medieval Franciscan friar into a Sherlock Holmes-like sleuth. Eco's *The Name of the Rose* is about a monastery's hidden library and the kabalistic and occult secrets contained therein. The film's villain, the blind monk Jorge de Burgos (Feodor Chaliapin, Jr., 1905-1992) also known as the Venerable Jorge, is an unrelenting zealot; he hates comedy, believing that anything humorous is the work of the Devil. The Venerable Jorge personifies Dominican friar Girolamo Savonarola (1452-1498), an extremist calling for a Christian renewal accompanying the destruction of secular art

---

39 Novel published 1980, film released 1986.

and culture, echoing the Venerable Jorge's fundamentalist zeal. Even the title is esoteric: the rose is an emblem of secrecy and wisdom signifying occult wisdom not available to the profane masses, hence the term *sub rosa*. Thus, "He who attempts to penetrate into the Rose Garden of the Philosophers without the key resembles a man who would walk without feet," adroitly stated by Michael Maier (1568-1622), *Atalanta Fugiens*, Oppenheim, De Bry, 1618, emblem XXVII. Maier, an alchemical-occult advisor to Holy Roman Emperor Rudolf II (1552-1612) was well versed in the Rosicrucian (Rose Cross) mysteries. As the novel (and film's) title suggests, the monastery houses Christendom's largest library of secret literature and lost works. To access the library, one must first navigate a complex staircase-maze. A maze represents the sun and its movements; it denotes light and thus en*light*enment because to solve it, one must be wise and methodical.

In *Cinema Symbolism*, this author identified the similarities between Papa Smurf and Karl Marx (1818-1883) and that the Smurfs inhabit the perfect Socialist-Marxist society since they all work without pay, wear identical uniforms, living rent-free in homogeneous housing. Notice that the name, Smurfs, is eerily similar to the word *serfs* denoting Marx's proletariat. Consequently, Gargamel and his cat Azrael epitomize the capitalistic United States, which, during the Cold War, was in eternal conflict with Soviet Russia; thus, Gargamel's endless struggle with the Smurfs symbolizes the West's militaristic game of chess with the East with each side trying to one-up the other. However, upon closer examination, there is a darker symbolic interpretation of Gargamel. When Gargamel first appeared in "*Le Voleur de schtroumpf*" ("The Smurfnapper") published in *Spirou* magazine in 1959, he captured a Smurf, which he needed as an ingredient for a potion to make gold according to the alchemic legend of the philosopher's stone. Seeking monetary gain, Gargamel embodies Western capitalism which is the polar opposite of Communistic philosophies. In the end, the other Smurfs rallied against him, liberating the kidnapped Smurf. By trying to sacrifice a Smurf to transmute gold, Gargamel is a Left-Hand Path sorcerer; he has an impressive library of grimoires (books, such as *Ars Goetia*, detailing demon conjuration), magical potions, and arcane items he uses in battling the Smurfs. Employing skullduggery and subterfuge, Gargamel created a kabalistic golem out of clay–a human-like creature made in an artificial way by a magical act–named Smurfette[40] as a means to sow discord, establishing a fifth column[41] in the Smurf's neo-Marxist village. When this was discovered, Papa Smurf succeeded in turning her into a real Smurf via white magic altering her appearance, providing the Smurfs with their sacred feminine because Smurfette is the object of desire of just about every Smurf. However, she was still a source of problems, by the end of this episode, she left the Smurf village thereby restoring the status quo of the commune. In the comic series, she made the occasional on-again, off-again appearance. But when the animated television series was introduced in the 1980s, she was featured as a permanent character in the Smurf's socialist village. In the recent motions pictures *The Smurfs* (2011) and *The Smurfs 2* (2012) Smurfette was voiced by musician Katy Perry. As a black magician, it can be argued that Gargamel epitomizes Nazi Germany which was the pre-Cold War archenemy of Communist Russia. Like Gargamel, many of the leaders of the Third Reich–including Adolf Hitler (1889-1945), Heinrich Himmler (1900-1945), Rudolf Hess (1894-1987), and Joseph Goebbels (1897-1945)–were, like Gargamel, fascinated by the dark arts and the occult sciences. Gargamel, paralleling Himmler's *SS* (*Schutzstaffel*, Protection Squadron), wears black, while his Teutonic-like hovel has a large library with a secret chamber in which his Great Book of Spells is kept. One cannot help think of the Nazi stronghold of Wewelsburg Castle, which Himmler intended to be the epicenter of the *SS* and eventual home of the Holy Grail. Gargamel, a black magician, hangs around with a feline named Azrael. In some legends, Azrael is often identified with the Archangel of Death; as such, the feline strikes fear into the Smurfs.

The oldest conflict of them all, the eternal struggle between light against dark, order against chaos, or good against evil, is commonplace in cinema. This conflict is, of course, Zoroastrian[42] dualism which, in the Gnostic Mysteries, became Manichean cosmology. Named after the Gnostic teacher

---

40 Smurfette was introduced in *Spirou* magazine in 1966. *Spirou* magazine (French: *Le Journal de Spirou*) is a weekly Franco-Belgian comics magazine published by the Dupuis company. First published 21 April 1938, it was an eight-page weekly comics magazine composed a mixture of short stories and gags, serial comics, and a handful of American comics; *The Smurfs* debuted in 1958.
41 A fifth column is a person or any group of people undermining a larger group, such as a nation or a city, from within.
42 Zoroastrianism is one of the world's oldest monotheistic religions. It was founded by the Prophet Zoroaster in ancient Iran approximately 3500 years ago.

Mani (216-276 CE), Manicheanism was also influenced by the arcane philosophies of Simon Magus.[43] Simon Magus and his Gnostic disciples taught that the Supreme Being or Centre of Light, and that the pleroma of Superior Intelligences, having the Supreme Being at their head, was composed of eight Eons of different sexes.[44] Manichaeism holds that there is an elaborate, dualistic, universal struggle between a good. spiritual world of light, and an evil, hylic world of darkness (our reality) wherein salvation is knowledge *qua* gnosis, especially esoteric wisdom. Jungian analytical psychology identifies this darkness, or wickedness, as the shadow self (or shadow) while the light, positivity, is the conscious ego, or ego. The ego is largely responsible for feelings of identity and continuity according to the reality principle: acting for benefit, for common sense, not grief. This is contrasted by the devious shadow, the unknown, the reservoir of our darkest desires and nebulous impulses. The shadow aspect of the personality is in conflict with the ego because the latter has difficulty identifying, integrating, and coexisting with the shadow. Since one tends to reject or remain ignorant of the least desirable aspects of one's personality, the shadow is largely negative (cf. villainy, gloom), while the ego is mostly positive (cf. the hero, light). In the 2015 film *Krampus*, Christmas' dark side comes to life as Krampus, a horned demon that punishes misbehaved children. In Jungian psychology, Krampus is the shadow self of

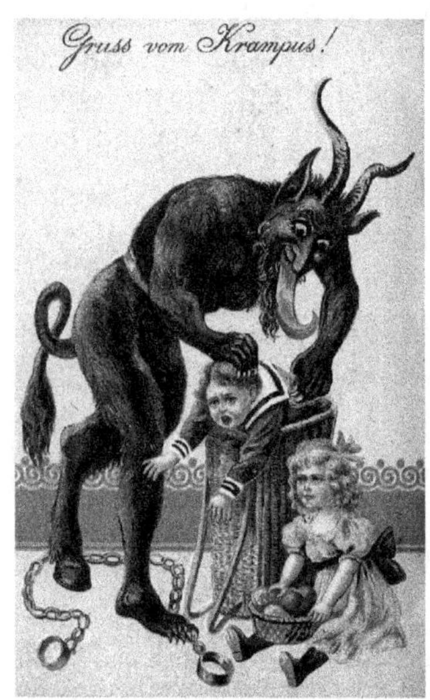

Gruss vom Krampus! A vintage postcard depicts the dark side of Christmas embodied by Krampus, a hairy devil stalking naughty children on the evening of December 5th. Known as *Krampusnacht*, the pagan festival is celebrated across Europe, and has recently become popular in the United States akin to a second Halloween.

---

43 "Simon the Magician, or Simon the Sorcerer, as he was sometimes called, was a Gnostic wonder-worker who became the prototype of a heretic and black magician. He came from Samaria, where he was worshipped as a god for his occult powers, which included mediumistic abilities. …Simon is created with founding a Gnostic sect that became known as Simonians. The Simonians recognized Simon as the first God, sometimes worshipped as Zeus, and his consort Helen as the goddess Athena." Guiley, *The Encyclopedia of Witches and Witchcraft*, p. 318.
44 See Albert Pike's *Morals and Dogma of the Ancient and Accepted Scottish Rite*, pp. 552-553.

jolly St. Nicholas who personifies the ego. According to European folklore, Krampus punishes wicked children by thrashing them with a bundle of sticks while Santa rewards wholesome children with toys; Krampus is thought to be the forerunner of Santa's naughty list.[45] In *The Empire Strikes Back* (1980), Luke Skywalker (Mark Hamill) confronts his shadow self in a cave on Dagobah when he defeats Darth Vader, only to discover that it is his face beneath the mask, the dark side is alive and well not only in Luke, but all of us. Robert Louis Stevenson (1850-1894) reveals this psychological dualism in *The Strange Case of Dr. Jekyll and Mr. Hyde* (1886); the ego is the benevolent Dr. Jekyll, and the shadow is the evil Mr. Hyde.

To counter this dark pessimism, the spiritual God (not the demiurge) ensured that each time the microcosm (humankind) heard the call of light (cf. en*light*enment), responding thus cultivating spirit, a part of the soul will be emancipated. Thus, through an ongoing process which takes place in human history, light is gradually removed from the dark world of matter, returned to the world of spirit from whence it came. Manichaeism stemmed, in part, from ancient Mesopotamian religious movements such as Zoroastrianism, which proclaimed that Ahura Mazda (also known as Ohrmazd, Ahuramazda, Hourmazd, Hormazd, and Hurmuz, Lord or simply as Spirit) was the divine, uncreated spirit by Zoroaster, the founder of Zoroastrianism. Ahura Mazda is described as the highest spirit of worship in Zoroastrianism, along with being the first and most frequently invoked spirit in the Yasna (Zoroastrianism's principle act of worship). The literal meaning of the words, Ahura Mazda, is *light wisdom*. Opposing Ahura Mazda is Angra Mainyu (also: Aŋra Mainiiu), Zoroastrianism's hypostasis of the destructive spirit; the Middle Persian equivalent is Ahriman. Comparatively, this conflict is part of the Egyptian Mysteries, personified by the sun gods Osiris and Horus, the latter battles the dark god Set (or Typhon in Greek). In Christianity, Jesus Christ–the solar light of the world–opposes darkness embodies by Satan.[46] The reconciliation, or integration, of theses pagan mysteries, philosophies, and mythology with Christianity gave rise to the philosophical and religious system known as Neoplatonism; this dovetailing theology serves as the basis for the apolo-

---

45 *Cinema Symbolism 2's* Preface, footnote 9.

46 John 8:12: "Then spake Jesus again unto them, saying, 'I am the light of the world: he that followeth me shall not walk in darkness, but shall have the light of life.'"

gies of Justin Martyr (ca. 100-165 CE), Origen (182-254 CE), St. Augustine (354-439 CE), and Thomas Aquinas (1225-1274), informing the treatises of René Descartes (1596-1650) and Immanuel Kant (1724-1804). In some respects, Neoplatonism differs from Gnosticism. Plotinus (204-270 CE), the godfather of Neoplatonism, attacked the Gnostics for their anti-materialism. In his *Enneads* (ca. 250 CE), Plotinus criticized the Gnostics for calling the demiurge, the world-maker, evil. For Plotinus, the craftsman of the world is good, a strong emanation of deity–the One–the creator who sustains the universe. The One is so simple that it cannot even be said to exist or to be a being. Rather, the creative principle of all things is beyond being, a notion derived from Book VI of the *Republic* (380 BCE), when, in the course of his famous analogy of the Sun (cf. the pagan mysteries, Osirian Cycle, astrotheology), Plato[47] says that the good is beyond being in power and dignity. Thus, concerning Neoplatonism, the sun was comparable to the spiritual godhead embodied by Jesus Christ.

Neoplatonic thought was revived during the Renaissance by Raymond Lully (ca. 1232-ca. 1315), Giovanni Pico della Mirandola (1463-1494), Francesco Giorgi (1466-1540), and Marsilio Ficino (1433-1499), all of whom birthed Christian mysticism, Cabala,[48] which was both a factor leading toward the Reformation, while being the lynchpin of hermetic studies. Christian Cabala may be said to belong to the Renaissance studies through its integration with Neoplatonism, belonging to Reformation studies through its influence on Reformation movements, both Protestant and Catholic.[49] Darker mystics also flourished during this time, such as Heinrich Cornelius Agrippa (1486-1535); his *Three Books of Occult Philosophy* argued for a synthetic vision of magic whereby the natural world, combined with the celestial and the divine through Neoplatonic participation, such that natural magic was validated by demonic sorcery sourced ultimately by God. By this means, Agrippa proposed a magic that could resolve all epistemological problems raised by skepticism in a total validation of Christian faith. But in doing so, Neoplatonism validated Christianity's astrological mysterion (sacred mysteries), its *Disciplina Arcani* (Discipline of the Arcane), wherein Jesus is not only the son, but also the heavenly sun

---

47 Born: 428/427 or 424/423 BCE; died: 348/347 BCE.
48 The Christianization of Hebrew Kabbalah with the name Jesus Christ being the true Tetragrammaton.
49 Yates, *The Occult Philosophy in the Elizabethan Age*, p. 4.

of God (Logos, the light) while the Twelve Apostles are the twelve signs of the zodiac; the Virgin Mary personifies the constellation Virgo the Virgin, Mary Magdalene becomes the planet Venus anthropomorphized. The goddess Venus, in Roman mythology, was divine beauty and love known to the Greeks as Aphrodite. The planet, also known as Lucifer the Light Bearer, is negative, representing antisolar divine light. In the morning, Venus often rises in the east prior to the sun becoming a token of false light while, at the time, announcing the coming of true light and life of the world, the resurrected savior, the sun. These arcane-astral concepts give rise to what is known as astrotheology, the descendant of astrology, taking center stage in Chapter I wherein the films *The Passion of the Christ* (2004) and *The Ten Commandments* (1956) are analyzed astrologically. The Abrahamic Faiths subsume key elements from the old pagan religions and the Ancient Mysteries, making it a study in comparative religion, not an exercise in conspiracy. An inflammatory heresy, the doctrines of astrotheology are nothing new. Judaism and Christianity, as retreads of ancient sun worship and astral legends, were investigated and analyzed in the books and treatises of polymaths like the Jesuit, Athanasius Kircher (ca. 1602-1680), the Dominican friar, Giordano Bruno, and by Freemasons Albert Pike (1809-1891), and Manly P. Hall (1901-1990). Comparative religion-mythology experts J.G. Frazer (1854-1941), Joseph Campbell, and the attorney, William Tyler Olcott (1873-1936), wrote extensively on stellar mythology and solar lore, their nexuses to Judaism and Christianity.

Neoplatonic imagery is prevalent in films produced by Hollywood. For example, the sun *qua* Christ sets in the background as Father Merrin (Max von Sydow) stares down a statue of the demon Pazuzu at the beginning of *The Exorcist*. The setting sun symbolizes the death of the divine life-giving orb, the death of Christ's light, and the exaltation of darkness *qua* evil. With divine light diminished, the cruel demon is now given license to invade Georgetown and the home of Chris MacNeil (Ellen Burstyn) and her daughter Regan (Linda Blair). Neoplatonism influenced philosopher René Descartes personified by Rick Deckard (Harrison Ford) in *Blade Runner*; Descartes was one of the geniuses of the Scientific Revolution, along with Sir Francis Bacon (1561-1626), modernized the world. Rick Deckard parallels René Descartes in that Deckard's gnosis revolves around notions of the soul–its divine spark–and creation. Descartes frequently sets his views apart from those of his philosophic predecessors residing in the opening section of the *Passions of the Soul* (1649), a treatise on the early modern version of what are now commonly called emotions. Descartes goes so far as to assert that he will write on this topic "As if no one had written on these matters before." The replicants–Roy Batty (Rutger Hauer, 1944-2019) is a sophisticated Nexus 6–are more enlightened, philosophic, and spiritual than their dull human counterparts. Near the end of the movie, Deckard undertakes a dangerous climb to a roof; the ascent betokens his coming to gnosis. No longer the hunter but the hunted; he has taken the place of the renegade Batty because he now struggles for transcendence, a height beyond the weight of gravity, the grave.[50] Deckard receives spiritual re-awakening, observing Batty expire–a nail through the Nexus-6's palm is stigmata–releasing his soul, symbolized by a dove paralleling Luke 3:22[51] and Matthew 3:16.[52] Deckard *qua* Descartes learns about the nature of the soul from Batty, coming to understand that deity endowed the Nexus-6s with a divine spirit and Cartesian emotions, something that their maker, Tyrell Corporation, never foresaw or intended.

Gnosticism, Kabbalah, mythology, and golem-making[53] likewise have always fascinated Hollywood. Manichean Gnosticism is universal in films such as the original *Star Wars* trilogy, the *Matrix* films, and Tolkien's epic *Lord of the Rings*. In Hollywood, a strict Manichean is someone who understands the dual nature of the world: the eternal conflict between good and evil, light and dark, choosing a side. The spy James Bond[54] and Buffy "the Vampire Slayer" Summers (Sarah Michelle Gellar) are Manicheans; for them, there is no middle ground, no shades of gray. You are either with them or against them in their battle against darkness.[55]

---

50 Wilson's *Secret Cinema*, p. 82.

51 "And the Holy Ghost descended in a bodily shape like a dove upon him, and a voice came from heaven, which said, Thou art my beloved Son; in thee I am well pleased."

52 "And Jesus, when he was baptized, went up straightway out of the water: and, lo, the heavens were opened unto him, and he saw the Spirit of God descending like a dove, and lighting upon him:"

53 See Gerhom Scholem's *Kabbalah*, p. 354 on the entertainment industries interest in the golem legend. Scholem writes, "Interest in the golem legend among writers, artists, and musicians became evident in the early 20th century. The golem was almost invariably the benevolent robot of the later Prague tradition and captured the imagination of writers active in Austria, Czechoslovakia, and Germany."

54 Ian Fleming's famous spy has been portrayed in film by Sean Connery, George Lazenby, David Nivan, Roger Moore, Timothy Dalton, Pierce Brosnan, Daniel Craig, and Barry Nelson.

55 cf. Philip Gardiner's *The Bond Code*, p. 12.

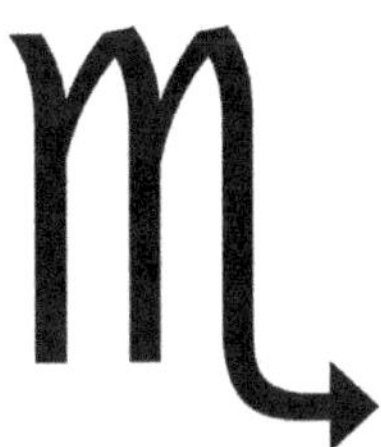

The *M* Astrology Symbol of Scorpio. Even though Fleming's spy James Bond is a solar hero, he has a mysterious dark side linking him with the astrological house of Scorpio. Bond is the Scorpio archetype rampant: dark, satanic, and saturnine; his ruthless pursuit of women, sex, combined with a desire to bring down the villain at all costs are Scorpio's astrological archetypal trademarks. Bond is always ready for any assignment his boss should give him; thus, Bond's superior is identified by the letter *M*, Scorpio's astrological sigil, identifying Bond as the embodiment of Scorpio–as above, so below. M could also stand for master because *M* has discovered an international secret which he reveals to the adept, Bond, to investigate.

Another important Gnostic philosopher was Basilides, a teacher in Alexandria, Egypt, lecturing from 117 to 138 CE. Basilides believed faith was merely an assent of the soul to any of the things which do not excite sensation because they are not present. He also believed faith was a matter of nature, not of responsible choice so that men would discover doctrines without demonstration by an intellective apprehension. Basilides also appears to have accumulated forms of dignity in accordance with one's faith. Basilides theory was that the spiritual adept must extricate himself from all material trappings, his somatic conditions because the true God is a negation of everything.[56]

Basilides' cosmology is a negation of the Gnostic vision of Valentinus (ca. 100-160 CE), the latter teaching that there were three kinds of people: the spiritual (grasping gnosis immediately), psychical (needing extra guidance), and materialists (devoid of spirit); and that only those of an impoverished enlightened nature (his disciples) received the gnosis allowing them to return to the divine, spiritual pleroma;[57] while those of a psychic nature (ordinary Christians) would attain a lesser form of salvation and that those of a material nature (pagans and Jews) were doomed to perish.[58] Valentinus' cosmology held that our reality was a creation of demiurge, and. as such, to be weary of its dogmatic institutions whether they be secular or religious. In the core text of the Valentinian school, *The Gospel of Truth* (ca. 150 CE), Jesus Christ is the luminous figure sent to rouse humankind from its stasis, lighting its divine spark, not redeeming its sin, resembling other illuminators in the Valentinian tradition: the wise serpent who awakens Adam and Eve to knowledge of Yahweh's oppressive regime; Sophia who takes on an earthly guise to correct her error in the pleroma. Valentinus'

---

56 See Wilson's *Secret Cinema*, pp. 36-38.
57 To the Gnostics, the pleroma is the spiritual universe as the abode of God and of the totality of divine powers and emanations. In Christianity, this is the totality of the godhead that dwells in Christ.
58 Sullivan, *Cinema Symbolism*, Chapter XII.

theology is the nucleus of the Theosophical Society, founded by Madame Helena Blavatsky (1831-1891) and Henry Steel Olcott (1832-1907) in the nineteenth century.

Gnosticism proper influenced the Beatles who refer to the pleroma as "Strawberry Fields Forever" where "♫ Nothing is real ♫" and there is "♫ Nothing to get hung about ♫" but it's hard to obtain because "♫ Living is easy with eyes closed, misunderstanding all you see ♫." So that we do not become systemic pawns of the demiurge, Pink Floyd encourages us to escape the monotonies of persistence by not being, "♫...just another brick in the wall ♫." In popular culture, disciples of Valentinus' asceticism include Neo (Keanu Reeves), Trinity (Carrie-Anne Moss), Morpheus (Laurence Fishburne), and the crew of Nebuchadnezzar[59] in *The Matrix* (1999); the Space Monkeys of *Fight Club*, and the Jedi Knights who reject material stasis in favor of spiritual meditations allowing them to channel a pleroma-like energy known to them as the Force. Morpheus and his Valentinian followers–and the inhabitants of Zion, the Holy Land–have shed their egos, disposing of the false, prison-like illusion of the demiurge (the Architect[60] played by Helmut Bakaitis, *The Matrix Reloaded*, 2003) for spiritual truth, and thus, sublime awakening. In *Fight Club*, Tyler Durden's[61] spiritual exercises include the physical and mental deconstruction of the self to achieve a nihilistic utopia: to destroy the modern world, society, and its obsession with consumerism and materialism–signified by collapsing buildings at the film's finale–to obtain Valentinian gnosis. On the small screen, Gnostic awakening in the material world is the plot of *The Prisoner* (1967-1968), which finds retired secret agent Number 6 (Patrick McGoohan, 1928-2009) living in an idyllic village only to discover that it is a prison ruled over by the demiurge-like Supervisor (Peter Swanwick, 1912-1968).

Walking down this Gnostic path, Chapter II explores the occult world of comic book writer, Alan Moore. Moore, a practicing mystic and enthusiast of Crowley, is the brain behind the graphic novels *From Hell*,

---

59 King Nebuchadnezzar II (ca. 634-562 BCE) was understood by Jews to be both a builder and a destroyer in the hands of Yahweh; see Ronald H. Sack's *Images of Nebuchadnezzar: The Emergence of a Legend*, pp. 58ff, nb. p. 99. In the Matrix Trilogy the crew of the Morpheus' ship, which bears the name of the Babylonian monarch, wants to destroy the machines and rebuild the world concordantly.

60 cf. the Gnostic demiurgus, see Hall's *The Secret Teachings of All Ages*, p. 57.

61 cf. Thoth Hermes Mercurius Trismegistus, the keeper of wisdom, enlightenment, and magic. See *Hall*, ibid, pp. 92-106.

V for Vendetta, and *Watchmen*, which all spawned films with the same names. Moore was influenced by fellow Gnostic author Philip K. Dick (1928-1982), an eccentric science fiction writer committed to uncovering conspiracies of big government and intrusive religions. Dick's Gnosticism, documented his novella *Do Androids Dream of Electric Sheep?,* supplied the raw material for the motion picture *Blade Runner*, a Gnostic-kabalistic fable. In *Blade Runner*, a transhuman Christlike replicant-robot named Roy Batty incarnates as an Enochic-Luciferian (i.e., a wisdom provider) philosopher-warrior. Batty, an angel to some and demon to most, is an artificial creation or a golem: an animated anthropomorphic being created entirely from inanimate matter brought to life by sorcery referenced in the Talmud and Psalms 139:16. A golem is not to be confused with a tulpa, a concept in mysticism of a being, or object, created through spiritual or mental powers. Batty was fabricated by a godlike kabalistic master of bio-mechanics named Dr. Eldon Tyrell (Joe Turkel), head of Tyrell Industries. Batty kills his creator reflecting the fate of the brilliant scientist Dr. Victor Frankenstein, destroyed by his kabalistic golem in Shelley's *The Modern Prometheus* (1818). This is not surprising since *Frankenstein*'s author Mary Wollstonecraft Shelley (1797-1851), and artists such as her husband Percy Bysshe Shelley (1792-1822) as well as William Blake (1757-1827), drew inspiration from Gnosticism, Kabbalah, the occult, and alchemy in challenging the tyrannical ideologies of priests and kings in the wake of the French Revolution (1789-1799).[62] This esoteric-political impulse carried over to America; Ralph Waldo Emerson (1803-1882) and Herman Melville (1819-1891) also invoked Gnostic rebellion in their calls for democratic revolution against enervating conformity.[63] This rebellion is echoed in Edgar Allan Poe's (1809-1849) *The Cask of Amontillado* (1846) which features an Anti-Masonic undercurrent wherein masonry, both operative and speculative, was revolted against because it was deemed a conformist organization. At one point in Poe's short story, Fortunato, the antagonist, makes a Masonic gesture, which the protagonist, Montresor, describes as "grotesque;" when Montresor appears not to recognize the gesture, Fortunato asks, "You are not of the Masons?" Montresor says he is a member, but

---

62 Wilson, *Secret Cinema*, page XII citing Kathleen Raine's *Blake and Tradition* and James Rieger's *The Mutiny Within: The Heresies of Percy Bysshe Shelley*.
63 *ibid*, see also Arthur Versluis' *Esoteric Origins of the American Renaissance, passim*.

when Fortunato, disbelieving, requests a sign, Montresor shows him a trowel he had been concealing. Poe lived during the Anti-Masonry fervor of the 1820s and 1830s during which, in the United States, Masonry was viewed as a reactionary cabal–a hidden hand–secretly operating in government, pulling the strings. In other words, at the time Poe wrote the story, Masonry was considered a divisive, unprogressive institution worthy of Gnostic-Valentinian rebellion. Montresor kills Fortunato by entombing him in a niche; Montresor uses the trowel to construct a brick wall, thereby turning one of the tools of Freemasonry against itself.

Kabbalah (sometimes its variant, Christian Cabala), Gnosticism, and occultism pervade the works of twentieth-century authors such as C.S. Lewis (1898-1963), Ian Fleming (1908-1964), and H.P. Lovecraft (1890-1937); Lovecraft's serialized novella *Herbert West-Reanimator*[64] is a re-telling of *The Modern Prometheus*. But there is more. Mary Shelley's golem–Frankenstein's Monster–shadows the vengeful Pumpkinhead, a dead-flesh demon that is resurrected from Razorback Hollow via the black magic of an Appalachian witch named Haggis (Florence Schauffler, *Pumpkinhead*, 1988). Like a psychic vampire, Pumpkinhead feeds off the life force of the human that has summoned it; Edward Scissorhands[65] (Johnny Depp) is a golem created by Vincent Price (1911-1993), a Frankenstein-like inventor. Ted (voiced by Seth MacFarlane) the teddy bear is a golem brought to life by a child's wish in the 2012 film *Ted*. Frosty the Snowman is also kabalistic golem; he is a pile of snow brought to anthropomorphic life during the celebration of the winter solstice (cf. Christmas, Hanukkah, Feast Day of Mithras, Birthday of the Unconquered Sun (*Sol Invictus*), Saturnalia) when a magical top hat, imbued with Right-Hand Path sorcery, is placed on top his head according to the song's lyrics. An overprotective golem appears in Episode 10, Season One (2013) of the television show *Sleepy Hollow*; this menacing golem shields Ichabod Crane's son Jeremy from wrongdoers. There are human-mechanical golems that appear in film and television as well. These are people fused, via scientific magic, with machinery. For example, Adam (George Hertzberg), the mechanized Big Bad from Season

---

64 Lovecraft's story was made into a movie which was released in 1985 starring Jeffrey Combs as Herbert West.

65 Directed by Tim Burton, the movie, *Edward Scissorhands*, bears the same name as the title character, and was released by 20th Century Fox in December 1990.

Four of *Buffy the Vampire Slayer* (1997-2003) is part human, part demon, part vampire, and part robot. Anakin Skywalker[66] is transformed into the mechanized Sith Lord, Darth Vader, in the *Star Wars* saga, and Alex Murphy (Peter Weller) becomes the robotic police enforcer *RoboCop* (1987). Both Vader and RoboCop seemingly embrace their transhumanism and their newfound superhuman powers, yet emotionally wrestle with their lack of humanity and destructive tendencies. In Alan Moore's *V for Vendetta*, which is analyzed in Chapter II, the title character, V, is a violent, faceless anarchist. V has no recollection of his past or true identity, so he dons a Guy Fawkes mask signifying his nihilistic mission to obliterate Norsefire England, causing Evey Hammond (Natalie Portman) to refer to him as a golem-like "created monster." According to famed Professor of Jewish mysticism Gershom Scholem (1897-1982), a golem is a product of complex Hebrew sorcery.[67]

Sublime, Gnostic epiphany can be viewed in *The Lovely Bones*, the numerous adoptions of Lewis Carroll's (1832-1898) *Alice in Wonderland* (1865), and *The Wizard of Oz* (1939) which were analyzed in *Cinema Symbolism*. Moreover, *The Truman Show's* (1998) Truman Burbank (Jim Carrey) begins his journey of gnosis in Seahaven when a studio light falls from the sky in broad daylight which, according to its label, is the Egyptian dog star, Sirius. The star *qua* studio light causes Truman to have doubts about the nature of his reality. In the mystical Egyptian pantheon of deities, Sirius is identified with the goddess Isis, the virgin consort of the dead yet resurrected sun god Osiris (cf. the material sun) and the mother of his solar offspring, Horus. As the wife and mother of the sun, Isis *qua* Sirius (the brightest star in the nighttime sky) is linked with the divine light of the sun; thus, the falling light commences Truman's quest for enlightenment. For that moment onward, Truman questions his existence eventually rebelling against Seahaven's Manichean demiurge, Christof (Ed Harris), the creator of Truman's illusionary world. Isis, weary of the world of men, was able to procure the secret name of the Egyptian sun god Amun-Ra, thus allowing

---

66 Jake Lloyd, *The Phantom Menace* (1999); Hayden Christensen, *Attack of the Clones* (2002) and *Revenge of the Sith* (2005); David Prowse, voiced by James Earl Jones, *Star Wars: A New Hope* (1977), *The Empire Strikes Back* (1980), and *Return of the Jedi* (1983).
67 Scholem, *Kabbalah*, "Part Two: Topics, Section 12, titled 'Golem,'" pp. 351-355.

her to rule in the heavens with the other gods,[68] paralleling Truman's desire to leave the make-believe world of Seahaven for the real world of truth. He accomplishes this at the film's finale when he, paralleling a Gnostic Christ, extends his arms cruciform then ascends into the sky. Truman walks up a staircase symbolizing his heavenly ascent bidding farewell to the false, hylic world of Christof *qua* the demiurge. The 1979 film *The Warriors* flirts with Gnosticism, their nocturnal journey a quest for enlightenment. The Warriors are tested–initiated into gnosis–during a nocturnal adventure during which they must battle and outmaneuver opposing gangs including the Baseball Furies, the Turnbull AC's, the Orphans, and the Rogues to make it back to their home turf, Coney Island. The Warriors are falsely accused of killing the leader of the Gramercy Riffs, Cyrus (Roger Hill, 1948-2014), who sought to unify all the gangs of New York City under one banner. Cyrus is named after Cyrus the Great (ca. 600 or 576-530 BCE) who founded the Achaemenid Empire (ca. 550-330 BCE) which unified Persia under one standard. Along the way, the Warriors are tricked by the demonic goddess Lilith in the guise of the female gang, the Lizzies, into their hideout with the promise of sex and pleasure only to discover that the Lizzies are out to kill them. Note the similarity in names: Lilith, Lizzies. Their dark journey ends with understanding: as dawn breaks and the sun rises bringing light, the Warriors receive enlightenment. The moment they finally reach Coney Island coincides with the realization that gang-banging over turf is meaningless. Having triumphed over their trials, the Warrior's war-chief Swan (Michael Beck) receives gnosis: surveying Coney Islands' dilapidated neighborhood, which up to now has been the Warrior's reality, their material world, Swan remarks, "This is what we fought all night to get back to?" Swan and his gang of select followers have lost interest in corporeal reality, in materialism, understanding that gangbanging is a false lifestyle which leads to jail or nowhere. Conscious of this, they now seek spirituality–at least, for them, something better–echoing the Gnostic teachings of Valentinus. Along the spiritual quest the Warriors have been assisted by the sacred feminine, Sophia, in the persona of the street-wise Mercy (Deborah Van Valkenburgh) whose name hides duality: the Warriors are, as their name suggests, war-like; while Mercy implies peace, benevolence, and compassion. Mercy *qua* Sophia, a sublime Gnostic goddess of

---

68 See J.G. Frazer's *The Golden Bough*, pp. 257-259.

light, is "The Virgin of Wisdom, whom all the philosophers of the world would have wooed,"[69] because not only does she balance them out, she also saves Swan's life. At the film's climax, it is Mercy who yells "Swan!" at the precise moment when Luther, Swan's sworn enemy, is about to fire his pistol. Mercy's yell signals Swan to throw his switchblade, which pierces Luther's forearm, causing his shot to miss while disarming him simultaneously. Good defeats evil; the Warriors, exonerated, leave Luther and the Rouges to the Gramercy Riffs, allowing them to dispense justice for the murder of Cyrus. Abandoning their criminal-mercenary ways, the Warriors meander on the beach toward the sunrise as Joe Walsh's redemptive "In the City" (1979) plays signifying their gnosis. The name of the movie's protagonist, Swan, implies power, initiation into the Ancient Mysteries. On the symbolism of the swan, Manly P. Hall explained, "The swan is the symbol of the initiates of the Mysteries; it is a symbol also of the divine power which is the progenitor of the world."[70] In 2010's *Black Swan*, this symbolism is reversed: personifying her shadow, Odile, the Black Swan, Nina Sayers (Natalie Portman) experiences ruination as a result of her failed alchemical transition (Chapter XI).

*   *   *   *

Gnosticism, as well as alchemy and the philosophies of Jung, transcend film and are critical to comprehending the esoteric symbolism and themes in movies; thus, they are exhaustively analyzed in *Cinema Symbolism 2*. Having shed some light on Gnosticism and Jung's theories, we now turn to the mystical world of alchemy. Medieval and Renaissance alchemy sought the transmutation of base metals into gold or ignorance to wisdom; however, in Hollywood alchemically charged films involve the transition of the self usually with dire consequences. South African government official Wikus van de Merwe (Sharlto Copley) transforms into an extraterrestrial in 2009's *District 9* after being exposed to a strange alien chemical. Nightclub crooner Johnny Favorite becomes the persona of Harry Angel (Mickey Rourke) via black magic in 1987's *Angel Heart*. Stoor Hobbit Sméagol (Andy Serkis) becomes the creature Gollum (literally *golem* signifying a newly created entity) by way of possessing a

---

69 Hall, *The Secret Teachings of All Ages*, page 132.
70 ibid, p. 76.

malevolent and powerful magical ring–his "precious"–in J.R.R. Tolkien's *Lord of the Rings* novels and films. In Darren Aronofsky's masterpiece, *Black Swan*, a sexually frustrated and self-loathing ballerina named Nina Sayers use masturbation and masochism to transmute herself from innocent ballerina into a grotesque yet sensual and poised bird-like creature. Sayers' perfected Black Swan seductress seems to have no remembrance of her pathetic White Swan personality, which suggests the psychological disorder known as schizophrenia. Anticipating Sayers' fleeting alchemical perfection in *Black Swan, 9 ½ Weeks'* (1986) Elizabeth McGraw (Kim Basinger) masturbates to a slideshow of dreamlike artwork featuring incubi[71] in a conscious effort to *become* her Jungian shadow. Symbolizing Elizabeth's shadow self is her black lingerie–specifically her gartered black silk stockings–which are an allusion to her dark, sensual desires. Finally allowing herself to receive the forbidden pleasures of the *nigredo*, Elizabeth breaks all the rules of decorum by masturbating in public. Her public onanism is akin to artistic alchemical-sorcery: it is Left-Hand Path masturbatory *magick* (more on magick spelled with a "k" later) which morphs her into a voluptuous piece of performance artwork, liberating her dark side concurrently (Chapter XI).[72] Just as Elizabeth masturbates rhapsodically to the luminous light of the Left-Hand Path, the *sol niger* or black sun, Dean Corso (Johnny Depp) is seduced, having sexual intercourse with a beautiful Aphrodite-like Lucifer the Light Bearer (Emmanuelle Seigner) at the conclusion of 1999's *The Ninth Gate*. Suggesting the solitude necessary to summon an *Ars Goetia*-like demon ritualistically, Corso performs tantric sex magick before an abandoned castle[73] from which he existentially receives the light–wisdom, gnosis–of the sublime, Ancient Mysteries. However, Corso's illumination contrasts Elizabeth's failed erotic alchemical becoming; her efforts end in sexual frustration, anxiety, melancholy, and depression.

---

71 Comparatively, this evokes the magnetic solitude of Saint Anthony practicing his austerities in the Egyptian Thebaid. The Saint was troubled by voluptuous hallucinations of female devils known as succubi; see Joseph Campbell's *The Hero with a Thousand Faces*, page 104. Elizabeth McGraw, living a celibate life after her divorce, becomes sexually aroused by paintings depicting androgynous demons.

72 See also 2009's *Veronika Decides to Die* in which Veronika Deklava (Sarah Michelle Gellar) poignantly masturbates in order to reconcile her dark side.

73 The castle is sometimes identified as a fortress once occupied by the Cathars: a Gnostic-mystical Christian sect.

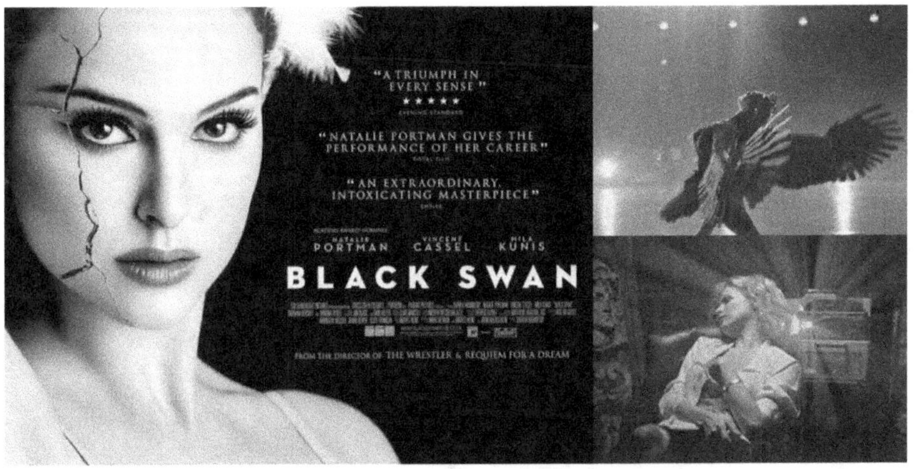

(Left) Original British Quad movie poster for *Black Swan* depicting a fractured Nina Sayers symbolizing her broken psyche. To achieve perfection, Nina masturbates and mutilates herself serving as vehicles of rebellion against the conformity of her child-like existence and her overbearing mother while, simultaneously, changing her into a sexy, graceful, satanic entity. Comparative Cinema, Top and Bottom Right: (Top) Proudly flaunting her dark wings in the light of Lucifer (cf. *sol niger*), Nina achieves an ominous alchemical transformation by turning into a flawless Black Swan creature. (Bottom) Seduced by demonic black light, *9 ½ Weeks*' Elizabeth McGraw touches herself in an art gallery unable to resist her fleshy impulses; through chic masturbation, she alchemically becomes her shadow.

The plot of Tim Burton's *Batman Returns* (1992) exhibits a failed alchemical transition regarding Selina Kyle's (Michelle Pfeiffer) metamorphosis into Catwoman. Pfeiffer's Catwoman is an ironic paradox of confidence and uncertainty, love and hate, dominatrix and submissive, master and slave. Selina is seemingly killed when she is thrown out of a high story office window by her boss but is reborn as the villainous and deranged Catwoman. At first, Selina voyeuristically embraces her dark and erotic side, announcing her new self, Catwoman, her Jungian Shadow, to the world in front of her open apartment window clad in black vinyl from head to toe, personifying a Betty Page (1923-2008) bondage-styled dominatrix. She is an evil goddess radiating her newly found fetishism before the neon words "Hell Here" formerly "Hello There," but Selina smashes the "o" in "Hello" and the "T" in "There." Skin-tight black vinyl feels fabulous against her flesh, making Selina feel "so much yummier," to use her own words. Ready to explore her fetish, she arms herself with the kinky equipment of the dominatrix: a mask, smoky eyes and ruby red lipstick, a leather bullwhip which serves as her cat o' nine tails, and razor-sharp phallic fingernails baffling Batman (Michael Keaton)

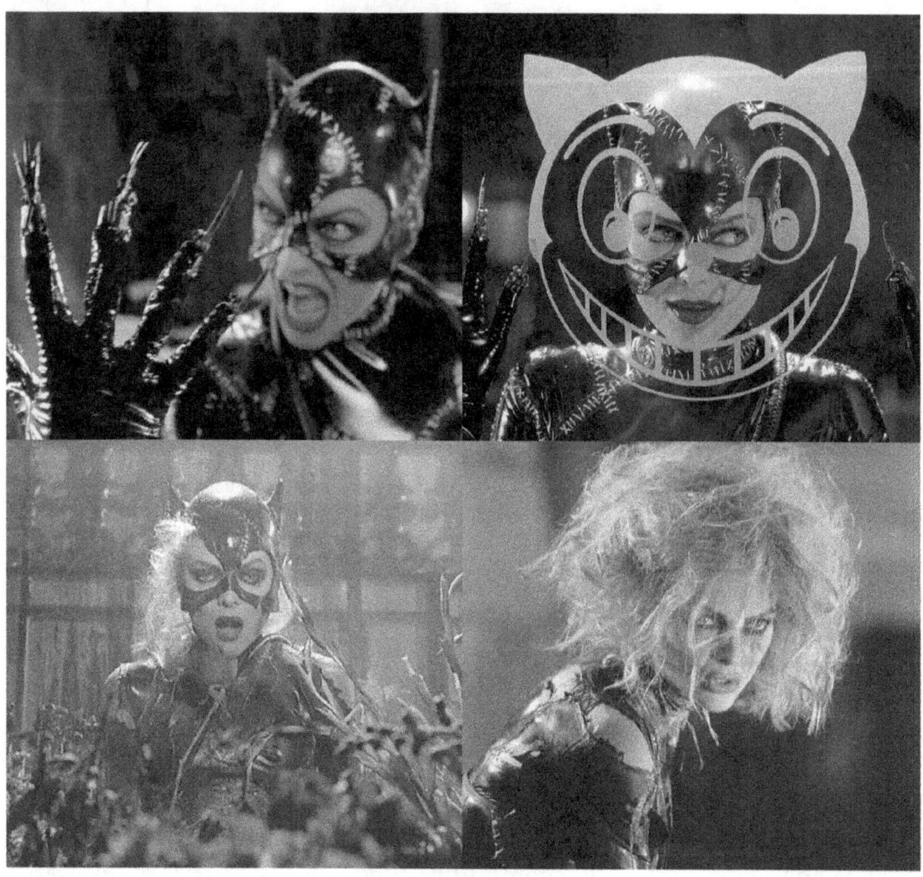

(Top Left) Lilith temporarily triumphant: "I am Catwoman, hear me roar." Catwoman makes a statement by flashing her claws when she takes out a street thug, then manhandles the thug's female victim. (Top Right) Pfeiffer's Catwoman becomes the mercurial trickster, if only momentarily, when she masquerades around Shreck's Department Store, blowing it up out of revenge. (Bottom Left) Unable to fathom her erotic self-revelation, Selina Kyle *qua* Catwoman, suffers a nervous breakdown represented by her torn and disheveled leather costume, once an emblem of her dark side, now a token of her sexual frustration. Dropped by Penguin's umbrella into a greenhouse, Selina's self-loathing is so great that her scream breaks the glass windows around her. (Bottom Right) A cruel irony personified: a sadomasochistic, timid submissive wearing the attire of a salacious and confident dominatrix. A pathetic Selina-Catwoman laments her sexual confusion explaining she is a "good girl" who will "go to Heaven" before killing her tormentor, Max Shreck. Her tattered costume symbolizes her shattered ego, her pleasure and pain, her pride and humiliation, her victory and failure; it is her torn flesh denoting the mutilated pleasures of the masochist. The Catwoman vinyl costume is to Selina what the *Lord of the Rings*' One Ring is to Sméagol, since both produce the same effect: the costume and ring are the fountainhead of change, but also the source of their love and hate. Interestingly, Sméagol and Kyle will kill the ones responsible for their twisted downfalls: Gollum murders Déagol and Catwoman kills Shreck.

and Oswald Cobblepot-Penguin (Danny DeVito) who do not know what to make of her. Both lust after her: Batman wants to hear the sound of his rubber Batman costume against her vinyl bodysuit, while Penguin, a gargoyle humanoid oddity, wishes to partake in Catwoman's nocturnal freakshow. However, Selina's transition from a sexually repressed bashful secretary to a rebellious, erotic femme fatale results in her mental erosion; Selina is fooling herself because she is not who or what she thinks she is. She believes teasing Batman and Penguin with the de- lights of bondage is her thing, her newfound sex, but it is not. Catwoman is humiliated by the Penguin when he viciously removes her from a roof via a gadget um- brella that garrotes her, crash-landing in a green- house. The once aloof and sensual dominatrix is exposed for what she is: the sexually repressed submissive. Catwoman screams out of sexual confusion, frustration, and failure, shattering the panes of glass around her. She realizes that don- ning the tight-fitting black vinyl, stiletto-heeled boots, and brandishing a bullwhip is not enough to transform her into a sexy dominatrix. She must become one with her alter ego by embracing Catwoman physically and psychologically; she must not only look the part but play it as well. No matter how hard she tries, Selina cannot reconcile her shadow with her ego; master and slave cannot coexist. She was obedient to her boss, Max Shreck (Christopher Walken), only to become Penguin's pitiful submis- sive, a role she has desperately tried to abandon with Schreck but one that she cannot escape. Although she briefly becomes the trickster by destroying Shreck's department store, her motivation was not transforma- tion, rather, it was pure revenge; Pfeiffer's Catwoman is not the Tarot's Magician or Juggler. Instead, Pfeiffer's Catwoman is moribund, frustrated, and docile; she is a fraud, and she knows it. By donning the Catwoman costume, Selina thinks she has improved herself, but comes to under- stand the flesh is weak because "Self-improvement is masturbation," as explained by *Fight Club's* Tyler Durden. Selina's ego cannot comprehend nor accept her carnality, shadow self, and liberation, thereby making her the embodiment of a failed *ascensio*. She does not suffer from Dissociative Identity Disorder because she knows when she's Catwoman and when she's Selina, having memories of both personas. Selina's hang-up is she yearns to be a sadomasochistic sexual dominant, but hiding beneath the black mask and vinyl, like a girl fiddling with the straps of her garter belt for the first time, is her hard orgasm: Selina gets off on being the wretched submissive. Pfeiffer's Selina Kyle-Catwoman's knows this and hates herself for it; she does not understand eroticism, only that she enjoys being Penguin and Batman's sexually confused masochistic slave. Selina is not a sexy vixen but a quirky masturbatory cosplayer: Catwoman is virgin-like and timid, not experienced in the pleasures of bondage; she is a sexually frustrated charlatan. Selina seemingly kills herself and Shreck with a deadly "electrical kiss," thereby destroying her unhealthy Cat-woman-bondage desires. However, in the final scene, Selina reappears looking at

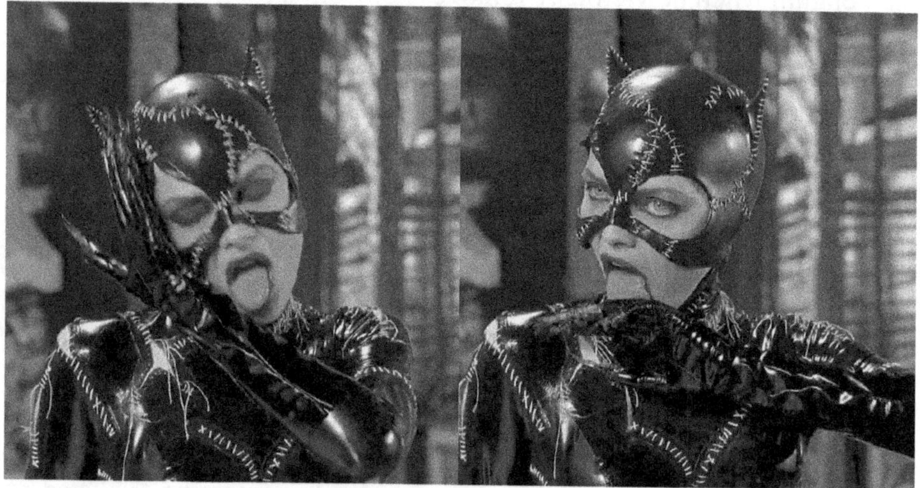

(Left and Right) Bondage and fetish exploration in *Batman Returns*: believing herself to be a dominatrix, Pfeiffer's Catwoman bathes herself by licking her black vinyl costume in front of the Penguin; however, she is a mere submissive, a slave, living in a state of sexual oblivion unable to control her newfound libido and kinky desires.

the Bat-Signal fully costumed, not only ready to explore the dangers of being Catwoman, but yearning once again to experience the agony and the ecstasy of the sadomasochist. Burton's cinematic interpretation differs substantially from the Catwoman of the D.C. comics, graphic novels, television shows, live-action, and animation. *The Dark Knight Rises* (2012) correctly portrays Catwoman-Selina Kyle (Anne Hathaway) as a confident, intelligent, and wily villainess, the way she was intended. Clad in sexy skintight jet-black leather and stiletto heels, Hathaway's Catwoman embodies the demonic goddess Lilith, a darker and more sinister version of Sophia. Not only does she dress the part, but she has successfully reconciled her shadow with her ego, making her a savvy, worldly, and formidable opponent. Hathaway's Catwoman walks the walk and talks the talk; she is the sleek dominatrix that Pfeiffer's Catwoman pines to be.

So how is this cinematic alchemy perfected? How is alchemical transmutation esoterically projected onto the subconscious mind? During the Middle Ages and the Renaissance, the Great Art was divided into four stages represented by four colors. To achieve transmutation, or the creation of the philosopher's stone (the substance that makes alchemy possible), these four steps must be realized, symbolically or literally. The first stage is the *nigredo*, or blackness,

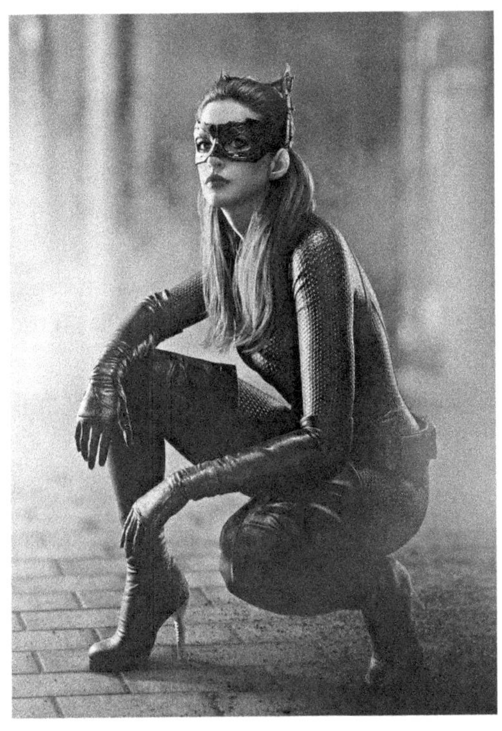

Lilith Triumphant: Anne Hathaway portrays the deadly, mysterious, sexy, and independent feline villain Catwoman in *The Dark Knight Rises*.

means putrefaction or decomposition. The alchemists believed that as a first step in the pathway to the philosopher's stone all alchemical ingredients had to be cleansed and cooked extensively to a uniform black matter. It is the first seed, primal chaos, the original abyss, and the destructive monster. The *nigredo* is the psychological Jungian shadow, our dark sides, the stoic Mephistopheles that lives within us all. The emotional equivalent of the *nigredo* is melancholia. Associated with the planet Saturn, this psychic state is far from the sun, the midnight of the soul.[74] This mood is the interior equivalent to the goring of Adonis, James Bond's urbane yet deadly archenemy, the dark forest journey of Dante Alighieri (ca. 1265-1321), and Hamlet's sable consciousness.[75] In this darkness rises the moon, the second stage, the white, the *albedo*, the lunar transition from gloom.

---

74 See Wilson's *Secret Cinema*, p. 108.
75 *ibid.*

Following the chaos or *massa confusa* of the *nigredo* stage, the alchemist undertakes a purification in the *albedo*, which is literally referred to as ablution: the washing away of impurities. In this process, the subject is divided into two opposing principles to be later coagulated to form a unity of opposites with the solar *citrinitas*, or *coincidentia oppositorum* (Union of Opposites), during the final stage, the *rubedo*. The *albedo* is the female, lunar sanctification and purification, the good Snow White; it is Diana or Artemis, Luna, and their dark counterpart, Hecate, all heavenly queens. The *albedo* synthesizes the positive with the negative: it is the imagination, the borderland between understanding and intuition, matter and spirit. From the underworld, Adonis imagines Venus; the voluptuous Bond girl is introduced to James; in the dark wood, Dante meets his ghostly guide, the poet Virgil,[76] having been sent by his soulmate, Beatrice Portinari (1266-1290); Ophelia, the eternal melancholic virgin, is vexed by Hamlet's brooding disposition. Next is the *citrinitas*, the divine masculine, the sun. In alchemical philosophy, *citrinitas* stood for the dawning of the solar light inherent in one's being, and that the reflective lunar, or solar, light was integrated. The *citrinitas* is Adonis, James Bond, Dante, and Hamlet. The final stage is the *rubedo*, the red, denoting completion, finality to the Magnum Opus; the Great Work is now complete. The three other alchemical processes-colors have been leading towards the *rubedo*. Psychologically, the *rubedo* signals that the archetypes, positive or negative, of the collective unconscious are realized by the ego. Light balances darkness; the unconscious becomes conscious; the man understands his feminine energies; the woman knows her masculine side.[77] The unification of man's feminine aspect and woman's masculine side is termed the *anima* and *animus*; in Jung's school of analytical psychology, are the two primary anthropomorphic archetypes of the unconscious mind, as opposed to both the theriomorphic and inferior function of the shadow archetypes, as well as the abstract symbol sets that formulate the archetype of the Self, the *rubedo*. According to Jung, the *anima* and *animus* are elements of the collective unconscious, a domain of the un- conscious that transcends the personal psyche. In the unconscious of the male, this archetype finds expression as a feminine inner personality: *anima*; equivalently, in the unconscious of the female, it is expressed

---

76 October 15, 70 BCE–September 21, 19 BCE
77 Wilson, *Secret Cinema*, p. 108.

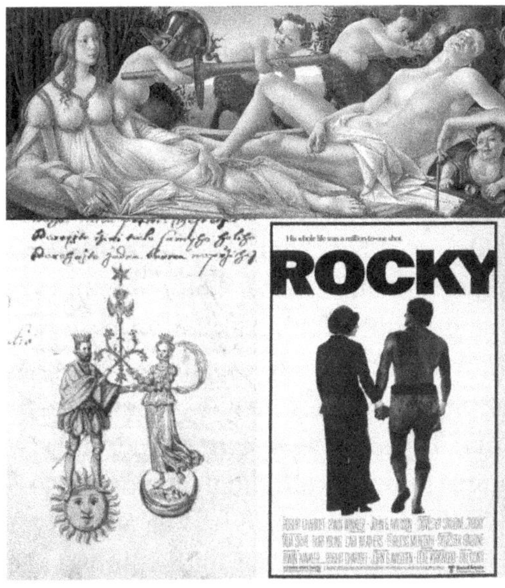

Coincidentia oppositorum: (Top) Botticelli's *Mars and Venus* (ca. 1483), depicts the opposites of war and love reconciled. (Bottom Left) The Chymical (or Alchemical) Marriage of the sun and moon, the perfected unification of the male and female, transcending duality. Image from *Rosarium Philosophorumsive pretiosissimum donum Dei (The Rosary of the Philosophers)*, 1550. (Bottom Right) The one-sheet movie poster for 1976's *Rocky* depicts the perfected union of feminine and masculine, the moon and sun, the psychological *anima* and *animus*, the perfected alchemical wedding, the syzygy. In *Rocky* and *Rocky II* (1979), Rocky Balboa (Sylvester Stallone) battles and finally defeats a quasi-sun god, Apollo Creed (Carl Weathers) to become Boxing World Heavyweight Champion. Rocky could not do this without the assistance, guidance, and encouragement of Sophia personified by Adrian Pennino (Talia Shire). Apollo, the solar champion, dresses like George Washington crossing the Delaware when he enters the arena, which is apropos, since President Washington, the first Masonic President, is the de facto Enochic solar-like deity of the Masonic Republic called the United States of America; see Sullivan's *The Royal Arch of Enoch*.

as a masculine inner personality: *animus*. When these opposites are combined, alchemically or otherwise, the *anima* and the *animus* are what Jung termed *syzygy*, a word also used to denote alignment of planets, is the sacred union of the sun (*citrinitas*) and moon (*albedo*) representing finality, wholeness, and selfhood, what Jung termed *individuation*. The individuation of the *rubedo*, the self, is the product of the syzygy, the alchemical wedding, a perfected synthesis: Venus revives Adonis; James Bond and the Bond girl have sex and, united, defeat the villain; Beatrice guides Dante through Paradise; Gertrude announces Ophelia's death, and Hamlet dies with sweet angels singing. Call it what you will: the union of the sun and moon, Osiris *qua* Orion and Isis *qua* Sirius, Adam and Eve, Apollo (sun) and Diana (moon), Jesus and Mary Magdalene *qua* Venus, and Romeo and Juliet's forbidden romance are the syzygy, the psychological process of selfhood, of individuation. "The Virgin Mary is taken up into the bridal chamber of heaven, where the King of Kings sits on his starry throne;"[78] it is the eternal Sophia awaiting marriage to the golden masculine sun. It is the sacred unification of the microcosm within recognizing the connection

---

78 Joseph Campbell, *The Hero with a Thousand Faces*, p. 100.

to the macrocosm or the spiritual godhead without, and both together become aware of their relationship to the trans-cosmic, the plentitude.[79]

The four alchemical color stages of *nigredo* the black, *albedo* the white, *citrinitas* the yellow, and *rubedo* the red are critical to deciphering and understanding alchemical films, movies that esoterically document the metamorphosis of the self or something. These movies are not about the transmutation of base metal into gold. Instead, a character starts out as one thing and, during the film, changes into something else. This something is new and emotional; it is physical or psychological, spiritual or material, negative or positive, or a combination thereof. The four alchemical colors are always present: they can appear on screen, they can be personified, or even be an object. For example, Nina of *Black Swan* starts as a timid, shy ballerina but, through alchemy, changes into an ornithological monstrosity. All the colors of symbolic alchemy appear: the *nigredo* is Beth Macintyre (Winona Ryder), Erica (Barbara Hershey) her mother, and Rothbart the

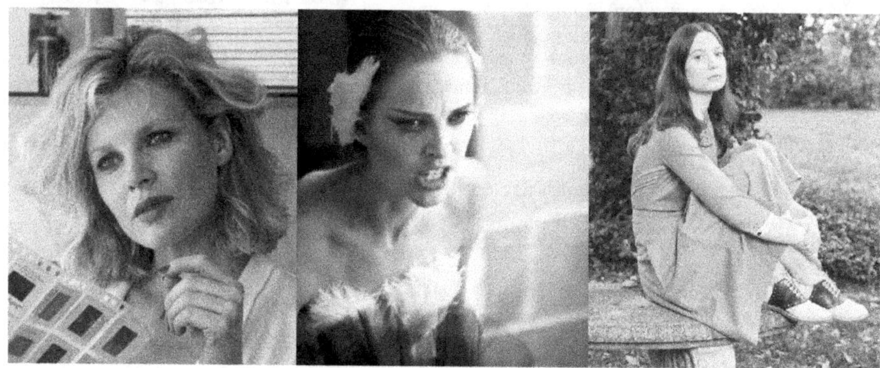

Birds of a feather flock together, so do White and Black Swans. (Left) In *9 ½ Weeks*, Elizabeth McGraw, an alluring SoHo art gallery manager, subconsciously employs slides of surreal, Neoexpressionist artwork to liberate her erotic Jungian shadow. Seated at her desk, little does Elizabeth know that the cardboard framed slides she holds will alchemically change her into an autoerotic performance exhibition (continuity error: this scene appears out-of-order in the movie). (Center) "What happened to my sweet girl?" "She's gone!" White Swan no more; Nina alchemically perfects her shadow self, Odette, the Black Swan. The beautiful ballerina's eyes burn demonically red, symbolizing her anger, self-loathing, and sexual frustration, but alchemy's *rubedo* phase as well. (Right) A seated India Stoker (Mia Wasikowska) shows off her saddle shoes, from *Stoker*, 2013. Although she is fetching, India is an unsympathetic sociopath undergoing alchemical transition by changing from an obnoxious melancholic teenager into a murderous adult. India also has a weird shoe fetish: she is plagued by saddle shoes which are the source of her hubris and anguish. In many ways, India reflects Nina's schizoid and unbalanced personality.

---

79 See Eric Wilson's *Secret Cinema*, p. 109.

black magician; Nina is the *albedo*, the moon; Thomas Leroy (Vincent Cassel) is the masculine sun, the *citrinitas*, her Luciferian enabler; and the *rubedo* is flashing red lights of the nightclub signifying finality of the Magnum Opus. The Great Work complete, Nina's transmutation will now commence: she sprouts a feather, her eyes glow freakishly red, her legs become crooked and bird-like, her feet become webbed as she alchemically becomes a Black Swan, the embodiment of her shadow persona. In *9 ½ Weeks*, Elizabeth's black silk stockings are an alchemical fetish which frees her from the stringent doldrums of her existence, allowing her shadow to surface to become real. Elizabeth stimulates her Jungian shadow by pleasurably caressing her stockings while masturbating to paintings of demons. In *Stoker*, India Stoker (Mia Wasikowska) also liberates her Jungian shadow by trading in her saddle shoes for sexy high heels; when she wears the high heels for the first time she is overcome with masturbatory rapture. For Elizabeth, Nina, and India all have one thing in common: the *nigredo* is their *rubedo*. For these ladies, their alchemy is not only to reconcile their shadow with their ego, rather, they desire to *become* their shadow alchemically, to embrace and become living, breathing high-heeled darkness. In other words, they all want to liberate the Lilith hiding within, surrendering their egos to blackness. These women strive for this dark archetype: erotic, independent, sexy, and confident. Other films depicting alchemical transition include *The Shining* (1980), *From Hell* (2001), *Passion* (2012), and *Jacob's Ladder* (1990), which are analyzed in this book.

The three ingredients of alchemy are salt, sulfur, and mercury with the latter often called the *materia prima*, the first matter of the philosopher's stone, the element of change, the Stone itself. Mercury is the fugitive qualities of matter, for its spiritual element, for mobility, for liquidity. Without the spirit of Mercury, nature would remain motionless and unchangeable. The substance Mercury denotes the god Mercurius (Hermes to the Greeks), the patron god of luck, trickery and thieves; he is also the guide of souls to the underworld. As the patron of deception and metamorphosis, Mercurius is the element of change, of alchemical transmutation. Mercurius-Hermes, or the Tarot's Juggler-Magician card, is an archetype personified by Captain Jack Sparrow (Johnny Depp) of the *Pirates of the Caribbean* films, Ferris Bueller (Matthew Broderick) in *Ferris Bueller's Day Off*, 1986); he is *Caddyshack's* (1980) Al Czervik (Rodney Dangerfield, 1921-2004) and

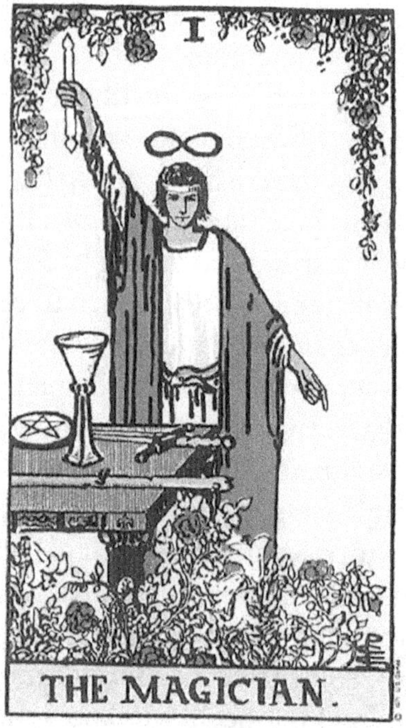

Card I of the Major Arcana is the Magician also identified as the Juggler. The card symbolizes the god Mercury (or Mercurius) and the magic of alchemical change. Mercury, the metal, in alchemical symbolism, stood for the spirit or vital energy of the divine concealed in matter, just like the Magician or Juggler following the Fool (0) is the human spirit incarnated in flesh. Mercury had a double meaning in alchemy. It was believed to combine opposites and was frequently portrayed as a hermaphrodite, self-fecundating, and self-sufficient. The posture of the Magician's arms suggests the above and below, chaos and order, good and evil; because the Magician unites the divine and diabolical, and is depicted in the old packs as a con-man, implying there are sinister possibilities with the card. This archetype can be egotistical, brutal, and ruthless, abusing power for his or her selfish ends.

Animal House's (1978) John Blutarsky (John Belushi, 1949-1982). This personality generally "fails upwards" while affecting–both positively and negatively–all the characters he interacts with. Mercurius' quests for organic generation and inorganic stasis; he (or she) cannot be defeated and is untouched by transience.[80] The Juggler-Magician is also *Meatballs'* (1979) Tripper Harrison (Bill Murray), a counselor at Camp North Star (cf. astrology, the above and below of Thoth Hermes Trismegistus' Emerald Tablet) who transforms its campers, a motley group of misfits, into champions during the yearly Olympiad; Camp North Star finally defeats its archenemy, the affluent Camp Mohawk. The female trickster is Rose Sayer (Katharine Hepburn, 1907-2003) who performs her mercurial sorcery on Charlie Allnut (Humphrey Bogart, 1899-1957) in 1951's *The African Queen.* Rose lures Charlie into believing they can, against all odds, blow up a German gunboat while uplifting his spirit during their treacherous journey. Charlie gives up drinking after Rose pours his gin overboard and, embracing sobriety, successfully navigates them to safety; during the film's epic conclusion, Charlie falls in love with Rose. The archetypal female Mercury, Loki in Norse mythology, is *Breakfast at Tiffany's* (1961) Holly Golightly (Audrey Hepburn, 1929-1993) whose magical guile and charm effortlessly manipulates, or juggles, the men in her life and Manhattan's bourgeois social scene all at the

---

80 *ibid*, p. 111.

same time. On television, during its first season (debuted September 22, 2015), the supreme female tease is *Scream Queens'* Chanel Oberlin (Emma Roberts), who uses any means necessary, including mischief and murder, to hold dominion over Kappa Kappa Tau sorority, fiendishly exploiting all those who cross its threshold. In comics, Gotham City's Catwoman and Poison Ivy embody all the characteristics of the sexy female trickster antiheroine *qua* Lilith. Selina Kyle and Pamela Isley dress provocatively and can be both heroine and villainess, noble and reckless. They are female reflections of Bruce Wayne's shadowy alter ego, the Batman, becoming his *anima*. Catwoman and Poison Ivy both sexually fantasize about Batman because he subconsciously provides the raw material that, for them, is the *animus*. Catwoman and Poison Ivy lust after Batman (as he does them, at least subconsciously); for example, in the graphic novel *Batman: The Widening Gyre*, Poison Ivy is swinging on a vine topless, spread eagle in

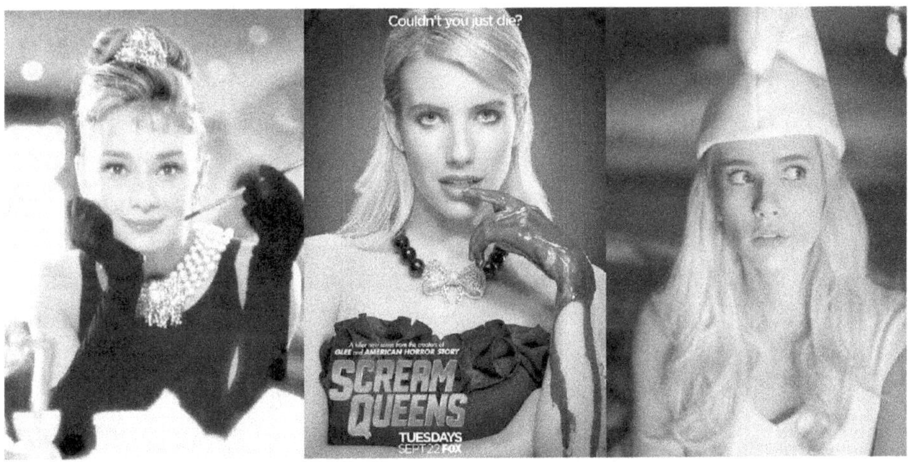

(Left) The female Juggler personified: Audrey Hepburn plays café society coquette Holly Golightly in the movie *Breakfast at Tiffany's*. The film, directed by Blake Edwards (1922-2010), was based on the novella by Truman Capote (1924-1984). (Center) "Couldn't you just die?" On television, the alchemical joker is *Scream Queens'* Chanel Oberlin, masterfully manipulating Wallace University with her elitist, decadent, and bloody murderous hand; she cleverly outmaneuvers everyone including her sorority sisters and Dean Cathy Munsch (Jamie Lee Curtis). Chanel, the ultimate mean girl, is the source of everyone's scornful derision yet, beneath the surface, everyone envies her: all her sorority sisters want to be her, at least be like her, while Chanel is the sexual fantasy of all the guys on campus. Chanel continues her alchemical, sarcastic manipulations in the second season (debuted September 22nd, 2016) of *Scream Queens*, set in C.U.R.E. Institute Hospital. (Right) Televised Jungian synchronicity: Chanel becomes Smurfette, the Smurfs' perfected feminine ideal; in the comic strip, she was originally created via Gargamel's alchemy. Chanel *qua* Smurfette appears in the Season 2, *Scream Queens* episode titled, "Halloween Blues," original airdate October 18th, 2016.

a seductive pornographic pose as Batman approaches.[81] When Batman declines to explore "the forbidden parts of her jungle" as she puts it, Ivy tells Batman she will masturbate instead.[82] The trickster archetype is Sherwood Forest's Robin Hood, hero to some and villain to others; Robin and his band of Merry Men are the subjects of Chapter XII titled "The Adventures of Robin Hood: Kabbalistic Archetypes and the Tarot."

Is there a nexus between Gnosticism and alchemy? In his book, *Secret Cinema*, Professor Eric Wilson explains:

Carl Jung is the primary source of the idea that alchemy issues from Gnosticism. In his *Memories, Dreams, and Reflections*, he argues that a current runs from ancient Gnosticism through medieval and Renaissance alchemy to twentieth-century depth psychology. The present characteristics of this current are the following: the origin of existence is an unfathomable abyss; this abyss descends into time in the form of conflicted opposition; redemption from conflict comes in the figure of a savior reflecting the abyss: the Gnostic savior from the hidden god; the philosopher's stone; the primal Self. The differences among these movements lie in emphasis on matter. Gnosticism wishes to escape matter; alchemy wishes to discover the spirit within matter; depth psychology wants to find purely materialistic redemption. These differences in focus on materiality have led some thinkers to draw a sharp dichotomy between Gnosticism and alchemy. For instance, Kathleen Raine in *Blake and Tradition* says, 'The great difference between the Neoplatonic [and by extension, the Gnostic, even more anti-materialistic than Neoplatonism] and the alchemical philosophies lies in their opposed conceptions of the nature of matter. For Plotinus and his school, matter is mere mire, the dregs of the universe, a philosophic 'non-entity' because incapable of form except as it reflects intelligibles. To the alchemist spirit and matter, active and passive, light and darkness, above and below are, like the Chinese yin and yang, complementary principles, both alike rooted in the divine. The *deus*

---

81 See *Batman: The Widening Gyre*, a six issue D.C. comic book limited series released August 2009 through July 2010.
82 *ibid*; Poison Ivy tells Batman she will "enjoy herself" while he waits.

absconditus is hidden and operating in matter, no less than He is to be found in the spiritual order' (118).[83]

In film, the relationship between Gnosticism and alchemy has less to do with matter, and more to do with epiphany, wisdom, and transition of the Self (cf. the *rubedo* phase).[84] Dorothy Gale, through her magical adventures in Oz, receives gnosis which, for her, is the understanding that there is no place like home. Alice successfully navigates the magical realm of Wonderland to likewise gain gnosis: Alice comprehends the world of adults is no different than the world of make-believe; she remarks, "I can't go back to yesterday because I was a different person then,"[85] signifying her newfound enlightenment. By the end of their adventures, Dorothy and Alice are the same people only a much wiser, wordily version of their former selves. Through their magical experiences, they have come to know thyself, which was inscribed on the forecourt of the Temple of Apollo at the Oracle of Delphi as an aphorism for those seeking higher truths. This is distinctively contrasted by alchemical transition, when a character begins as one thing then transforms (at least attempts to change) into something new. The horrific serial killer Francis Dolarhyde, the Tooth Fairy, from Thomas Harris' 1981 novel *Red Dragon*[86] murders families so that he can alchemically *become* more than a man, to become a great red (cf. *rubedo*) dragon, a powerful monster. Dolarhyde desires to be something else, he calls it a "Great Becoming," so that he can transform himself into a creature which is above the law and humanity, thereby removing himself from his current stasis; this is cinematic alchemy. Alchemical transition can be accidental or unintended: Seth Brundle (Jeff Goldblum), via two teleportation machines, commingles his DNA with that of a housefly changing him into Brundlefly in 1986's *The Fly*.

The line between Gnostic epiphany and alchemical transition is a fine line; for example, in *The Lovely Bones*, after Susie Salmon dies, she must negotiate Purgatory so that she can receive gnosis by learning to let go of

---

83 Endnote 1, Introduction of Wilson's *Secret Cinema*, p. 150.
84 To see the transmutation of gold for economic purposes this author recommends 1964's *Goldfinger*.
85 See *Alice's Adventures in Wonderland* by Lewis Carroll (1865).
86 *Red Dragon* was made into a movie titled *Manhunter* in 1986 and starred Tom Noonan as Dolarhyde. In 2002, *Red Dragon* was again made into a film–titled *Red Dragon*–with Ralph Fiennes portraying Dolarhyde.

her family and the corporeal world. In *Jacob's Ladder*, Jacob Singer (Tim Robbins) dies to alchemically transition from his mortal coil to the spiritual dimension; he undergoes change: Jacob begins the film believing he's alive, but ends it knowing he is deceased, a ghost. The sublime difference is Susie knows she is no longer alive and must become enlightened by learning to let go of her earthly reality; this is contrasted by Jacob, who realizes he has changed from a living person into something else, a spirit ready to move on. The similarity is that both Susie and Jacob must let go of their earthly existence; Susie receives gnosis by doing this, Jacob is allowed to transition by doing this. A movie that fuses Gnostic revelation and alchemical change is 2005's *V for Vendetta*, which is analyzed in Chapter II; as of the writing of this book, this is the only film this author can think of that uniquely blends alchemy and Gnosticism. As will be seen, Evey Hammond's (Natalie Portman) journey is an initiatory experience that, once experienced, results in what can only be described as *alchemical gnosis*.

When we are dealing with Jung, Gnosticism, and alchemy, we are also dealing with the archetypes which can be astrological, solar, lunar, planetary, or involve the arcane imagery of the Tarot; the archetypes can be good or evil, interweaving luminous occult attributes. For example, in *Cinema Symbolism*, this author presented the wizard archetype who personifies the wise Hellenistic god Thoth Hermes Mercurius Trismegistus, the god of magic and sorcery; inscribed upon his Emerald Tablet is the hermetic maxim, *as above, so below*. Trismegistus (the Thrice Greatest) is the personification of universal wisdom and alleged author of the *Corpus Hermeticum* (ca. 2nd-3rd centuries CE): a group of texts analyzing the divine, the cosmos, alchemy, astrology, and nature. These texts form the basis of hermeticism having profoundly influenced the development of Western occultism and magic. The Trismegistus-graybeard archetype is Gandalf the Grey, Obi-Wan Kenobi, Yoda, and their concomitant Albus Dumbledore from the Harry Potter saga. This author is pleased to announce that Dumbledore and all eight of the Harry Potter films are analyzed in Chapter VIII. Trismegistus' female archetypal equivalent is Sophia *qua* Minerva, the goddess of light and wisdom. Like Dumbledore, she also can be found in Hogwarts personified by Minerva McGonagall (Maggie Smith). The elegantly dressed Rachael (Sean Young) in *Blade Runner* is the moon, Sophia to Deckard's masculine sun. Rachael is a replicant who rejects futuristic outfits instead clothing herself in sleek 1940s attire echoing Charlotte Vale's (Betty Davis, 1908-1989) sexual revival and alchemical rebirth in *Now, Voyager* (1942).

The male and female wizard archetypes also have their dark counterparts: Trismegistus is contrasted by the evil wizard archetype: Thulsa Doom (James Earl Jones) from 1982's *Conan the Barbarian* having solved the elusive Riddle of Steel, and Dr. Anton Phibes (Vincent Price) from 1971's *The Abominable Dr. Phibes*, a supreme criminal mastermind orchestrating strange and bizarre murders. Trismegistus, personifying a dark wisdom provider, becomes Lucifer the Light Bearer, the purveyor of Left-Hand Path knowledge, destroying all those not prepared to receive his dangerous gnosis. Sophia's opposite is the demonic goddess Lilith, the Talmudic seducer of men and killer of children. Lilith is the erotic, sly, and wicked female archetype existing somewhere between the goddesses Nemesis, the vindictive mother (cf. Grendel's mother in Beowulf, ca. 700–1000), comparatively the Hindu Kali, and the luscious Aphrodite. Smart and fiercely independent, Lilith is not the mother or heroine, rather, her mantle is that of antiheroine; Lilith is Sophia, only she dresses in black leather and lingerie, stiletto heels, and black-seamed stockings while wearing sexy makeup. Lilith can be found on the television show *Buffy the Vampire Slayer* (1997-2003) in the persona of Faith Lehane (Eliza Dushku), a dark vampire slayer whose vexatious personality plays off the straitlaced heroic Buffy. Controversial for its time, the spirit of Lilith resides in vampire Countess Marya Zaleska

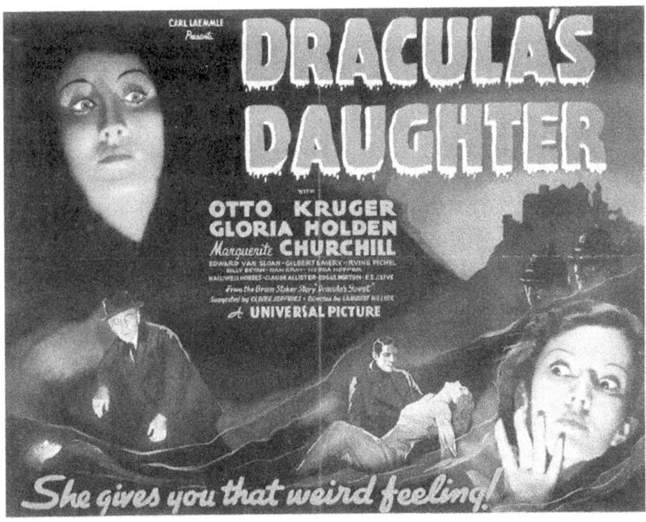

"She gives you that weird feeling!" Original 1936 half-sheet movie poster for the Universal Studio horror film *Dracula's Daughter.* The film depicts the Lilith archetype, personified by Countess Marya Zaleska, a neurotic vampire and repressed lesbian.

(Gloria Holden, 1903-1991) in *Dracula's Daughter*, released on May 11th, 1936. Zaleska is a bloodthirsty temptress who not only seduces men but desires women; lesbianism was a taboo subject when this film was released. Although she tries to suppress her lesbian yearnings, the Countess succumbs to her craving by attacking a beautiful young woman named Lili (Nan Grey, 1918-1993) whom the Countess desires to paint. The name, Lili, subconsciously evokes the archetypal qualities associated with Lilith, making Countess Zaleska the epitome of homosexuality as a predatory weakness. Today, the vampiric Countess would be embraced by the LGBT community as an early example of a repressed lesbian living in era dominated by fundamentalist Christian dogma, personified by Abraham Van Helsing (Edward Van Sloan, 1882-1964) the famed vampire hunter.

Another theory that may account for unintended esoteric symbolism and prophetic imagery in film is Jung's notion of synchronicity. Synchronicity, described by Jung in the 1920s, is the experience of two or more events as meaningfully related, when they are unlikely to be causally related. The subject sees it as a meaningful coincidence although the events need not be exactly simultaneous in time. The concept does not question, or compete with, the notion of causality. Instead, it maintains that just as events may be connected by a causal line, they may also be connected by meaning. This meaning is occult and metaphysical, going beyond rational explanation. For example, in *Cinema Symbolism*, I documented the relationship between the sun, Elvis, Apollo, and Jesus, as the parallels between the three kings are extraordinary. To briefly revisit, Presley was given to the house of Capricorn, being born on 8 January 1935. Capricorn is exalted from December 22nd to January 19th when the winter solstice occurs. The winter solstice of December 20th-22nd is when the sun, in the northern hemisphere, is annually born again; because of the ecliptic, the days start becoming longer. Elvis, synchronizing with the sun, dies under the sign of Leo the Lion on 16 August 1977 because Leo is ruled by the sun. Presley, towards the end of his life, routinely wore jumpsuits while performing at concerts that featured solar emblems including the Mayan Solar Calendar.[87] During his later concerts, Elvis came on stage to the opening sequence of Richard Strauss' (1864-194) *Also sprach Zarathustra* (1896) titled "Sunrise." Interesting, this same music would also be employed in

---

87 Sullivan, *Cinema Symbolism*, Introduction.

1979's *Being There*, heralding Chauncey Gardner's (Peter Sellers, 1925-1980) solar ascension within the political world of Washington, D.C. Even after Elvis' death, rumors of his Christlike resurrection began to circulate, truly making him an Apollonian, solar, messianic Sun-King; for this is the raw material of the collective unconscious, the stuff that dreams are made of.[88] Another example of synchronicity is the life of magician Harry Houdini (1874-1926), born 26 years before the turn of the twentieth century, dying 26 years after the turn of the twentieth century. Add 26+26 to get 52, the number of playing cards in a deck, the premiere tool of magician, synching Houdini to his legerdemain. Applied to Jung's theorem, this unexplainable nexus mystically synchronizes Houdini's life with his prowess as a magician, making him one of the greatest, if not the greatest illusionists that ever lived.

Synchronicity strives to link unrelated movies while integrating parallel occult symbolism. At first, these films seem to have nothing to do with each other, but when carefully examined, it is clear they are linked and their esoteric nexus cannot be easily explained away. For example, in *The Matrix Reloaded* (2003), we are introduced to the Merovingian (Lambert Wilson), the keeper of the rouge programs which torment and terrorize, such as ghosts, werewolves, and vampires. The Merovingian resides on Floor 101 which symbolizes Room 101 in the Ministry of Love in George Orwell's (1903-1950) *1984* (1949). Inside the Ministry's Room 101, men and women are tortured with their greatest fears and anxieties. Synchronized to Orwell's *1984*, the year 1984 saw the release of *The Terminator* starring Arnold Schwarzenegger as Cyberdyne Systems Model 101. Model 101, a Terminator, is so dubbed because it is devoid of pity and remorse, with its sole purpose to destroy humanity. In the following year, 1985, Schwarzenegger starred as a retired Delta Force operator in *Commando*. The name of his character is, interestingly, Matrix. Matrix's sole purpose is to seek and destroy those who have kidnapped his daughter, Jenny (Alyssa Milano). During the film, Jenny's kidnappers are warned by Bennett (Vernon Wells) that Matrix is coming, that he can't be stopped, implying he is a force of nature, anticipating the release of 1999's *The Matrix*, wherein humankind is forever held in stasis, trapped in an illusion. The synchronized interweaving of these films is impossible to explain

---

88 *ibid.*

rationally, but it happened regardless of Hollywood's design, purpose, or intent; this is the supernatural mystery of synchronicity. Jung's synchronicity theorem could also explain, in some instances, why arcane themes and images appear in film unintentionally. But in doing so, a paradox is created: synchronicity theorem rationally explains the irrational, a contradiction, because synchronicity is supernatural, thus above and beyond the rationale. When it comes to Jungian synchronicity, this author turns to cartoonist and purveyor of curiosities Robert Ripley (1890-1949) who said, "Believe it, or not."

* * * *

Cinema Symbolism 2 analyzes the monomyth, the heroic adventure, and all its corresponding components. Our conscious and subconscious minds and imaginations love the hero or heroine because they have done something beyond the normal range of achievement and experience. A hero is someone having given his or her life to something bigger than themselves. The hero or heroine is solar/lunar in nature: they are the light, positive and luminous; battling an evil lord, villainy, making their quest essentially Manichean. They experience most of the monomyth's components such as Supernatural Aid, Atonement with the Father, the Call to Adventure, and the Road of Trials which are universal; these elements forge legends, thus they are part of the collective unconscious. In popular culture, the solar hero archetype becomes Luke Skywalker, Neo, Buffy the Vampire Slayer (the television series more than the 1992 movie) and Frodo Baggins. The hero is plucked from the general populace, placed on a path to defeat an evil overlord, accomplishing this task in a way the overlord does not anticipate. Although the hero is a savior figure, they are differences between them. Some provide gnosis, some are liberators, and some are both. Some of these heroes and their respective Manichean journeys seem more Gnostic than others, even though they experience the same elements of the monomyth. The monomyth transcends the Harry Potter stories, which take center stage in Chapter VIII, and Chapter X surveys the *Chronicles of Narnia's* vast Neoplatonic landscape.

Esoteric imagery, arcane themes, and occult symbolism can take many forms and guises but, in the end, the result is the same: mythology making. Filmmakers love to plant little clues and references, sometimes known as *Easter eggs*, which further a hidden agenda by investing the film with subtle yet powerful imagery. They are innocuous hiding in plain sight; like all arcane imagery, they invest the film with mystery and with a sense of higher purpose while being entertaining, to challenge the audience to be alert. For example, gimmick horror filmmaker William Castle (1914-1977), can be observed waiting patiently outside the phone booth in *Rosemary's Baby* when Rosemary Woodhouse (Mia Farrow) is trying to reach Dr. Hill (Charles Grodin). Castle, the eccentric mind behind gimmick films such as *The House on Haunted Hill* (1959), *Mr. Sardonicus* (1961), *Strait-Jacket* (1964), *Homicidal* (1961) and *13 Ghosts* (1960) was slated to direct *Rosemary's Baby*, but the studio worried that he would likewise turn it into a gimmick movie. Roman Polanski was hired to direct with Castle producing, but Castle took a cue from Alfred Hitchcock (1899-1980), a director who always appeared in his films, by making a cameo. Look for the cigar-smoking William Castle the next time you watch *Rosemary's Baby* because it is great to see one horror filmmaker pay respect to one another. Hitchcock employed similar devices. In *Vertigo* (1958), Hitchcock uses Madeleine Elster's (Kim Novak) spiraling hair to denote that things

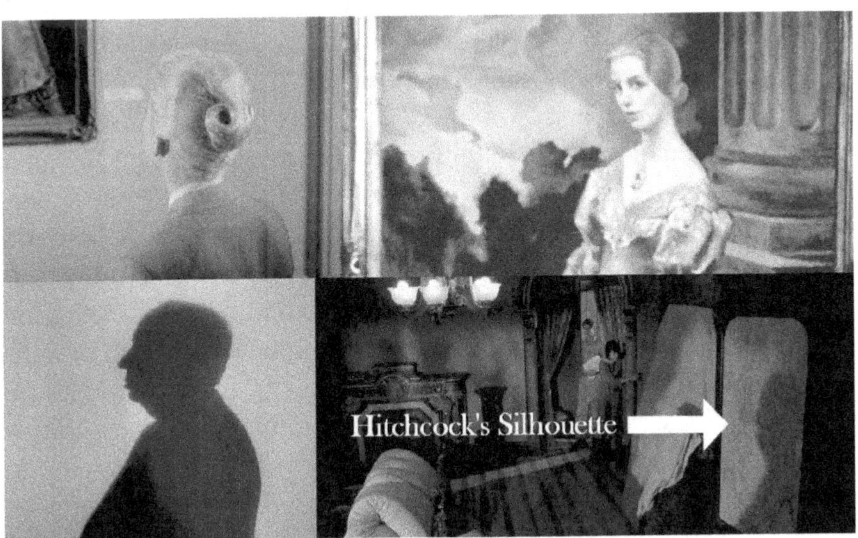

(Top Left) Madeleine Elster's spiral hair denotes uneasiness in *Vertigo*. (Top Right) Even the painting she observes, *Portrait of Carlotta Valdes*, features spiral hair subconsciously reinforcing this giddiness. (Bottom Left) Alfred Hitchcock's famous silhouette opens the television show *Alfred Hitchcock Presents*, airing from 1955-1962. (Bottom Right) In Psycho II, the filmmakers pay homage to Hitchcock by placing his silhouette from *Alfred Hitchcock Presents* in the bottom right when Mary and Norman enter mother's bedroom.

are spiriling out of control, causing the viewer's subconscious fears and anxieties to surface. When Elster is followed to the museum, she observes a painting titled *Portrait of Carlotta Valdes*, which also features coiled hair implying vertigo. Hitchcock, with his obsession for blondes and the hyper-voyeurism examined across his body of work (especially *Psycho,* 1960), reaches a kind of symphonic apotheosis in this film. In *Vertigo,* Hitchcock stitches together all the threads of his fixations into a cinematic masterwork, including subliminal and esoteric imagery. Years later, in *Psycho II* (1983), the director Richard Franklin (1948-2007) and writer Tom Holland wanted the sequel to pay tribute to Hitchcock and the first *Psycho.* In the scene when Mary Samuels (Meg Tilly) and Norman Bates (Anthony Perkins, 1932-1992) first go into Norman's mother's bedroom, before they turn the lights on, Alfred Hitchcock's famous silhouette, which introduced the *Alfred Hitchcock Presents* (1955-1965) television show, is visible on the lower right wall. Many films project parallel symbolism such as *Crimson Peak* (2015). *Crimson Peak's* director, Guillermo de Toro, uses occult techniques and arcane devices not only to convey hidden themes to the viewer, but also to pay homage to Stanley Kubrick's (1928-1999) *The Shining.* The analysis of *Crimson Peak* and *The Shining* can be found in Chapter V which is titled "Black Phillip Says You Are Wicked: Esoteric Imagery in Horror Movies."

In Chapter III, *Cinema Symbolism 2* discusses some of the films of David Lynch, something this author originally intended to do in *Cinema Symbolism.* Lynch's unorthodox films are replete with Gnostic themes and an overall sense of nihilism. Nihilism is an anathema, an extremely dangerous vision that leads in most cases to philosophical and physical anarchy, a feeling that everything goes, that nothing is worth living for; it is philosophical anarchy.[89] Nihilism rejects religious and moral principles while embracing the belief that life is meaningless; in Lynch's existential cinematic realities there are no absolute truths, only experiences. Nihilism, in Lynch's films *Blue Velvet* (1986), *Lost Highway* (1997), and *Mulholland Drive* (2001), is orthodoxy; these three films dwell in an abyss of strange particulars, weird nuances, dovetailing paradoxes, sublime ironies, and new complexities. These films formally remove all notions of normalcy transforming the world into flowing abstractions, an endless field of flux,

---

89 See Eric Wilson's *The Strange World of David Lynch,* p. 163.

an ironic realm devoid of things, constructed frames around the flows of time.[90] Nihilism, in this sense, is a first cousin to Gnosticism: a vision of the world not as an arrangement of static stuff but as a secret spiritual river, a baptism of unseen waters. As such these three films mirror Jean Baudrillard's (1927-2007) *Simulacra and Simulation* (1981) which argues that our current society has replaced all reality and meaning with symbols and signs and that human experience is a simulation of reality. Out of this Baudrillardian simulation, Lynch gives us *Blue Velvet* which depicts a strange journey of gnosis; *Lost Highway* embraces negative theology and Sethian Gnosticism; and *Mulholland Drive* features two simulations of reality: the dream world contrasted with the real world, which echoes the Gnostic idea that reality is a dream. In *Mulholland Drive*, the dream world of Betty Elms (Naomi Watts), provides cryptic insights not available to the waking conscious of Diane Selwyn (also Watts) which is critical to Diane becoming an integrated whole person. Comparatively, *Mulholland Drive's* dreamscape and its relation to interpreting reality can be found in *The X-Files* episode "Jose Chung's From Outer Space"[91] wherein alien abductees, UFO witnesses, paranormal researchers, and even the space aliens relate different versions of the same facts. The fabric of reality is distorted: what is real and what is the dream (or hallucination) is intertwined; what ghostly wisdom can be gleaned from the dream-hallucination to be applied to empirical reality is one of life's deepest mysteries. Not even Fox Mulder (David Duchovny) and Dana Scully (Gillian Anderson) can unravel this enigma; only oddball psychic the Stupendous Yappi (Jaap Broeker, 1950-2015) and author Jose Chung (Charles Nelson Reilly, 1931-2007) make sense of this illusionary chaos. The idea of dream-as-reality and reality-as-dream is the film *Total Recall* (1990) which was based on the short story, *We Can Remember It for You Wholesale* (1966) by Philip K. Dick. Chapter III also breaks down *Dune* (1984) which, like *Star Wars*, presents Campbell's monomyth in a galaxy far, far away.

Chapter IV explores the mysteries of Walt Disney Studios. Chapters VI and VII presents secret societies and their occult doctrines. The presence

---

90 *ibid*, p. 164.

91 Original airdate: April 12th, 1996. The episode is named after the 1959 Ed Wood film *Plan 9 from Outer Space*. The Stupendous Yappi is based on real life Hollywood psychic the Amazing Criswell; the Stupendous Yappi's catchphrase is "I Foresee!" while Criswell's was "Criswell Predicts." Criswell introduces Wood's *Plan 9* hence Yappi appears in "Jose Chung's from Outer Space."

of Freemasonry, the Illuminati, and other clandestine groups transcend Hollywood and thus *Cinema Symbolism 2*. Their influence, although concealed, is deliberate, potent, and palatable. Numbers aside, traditional Masonic symbols that mysteriously appear in film are the sun; the pentagram representing the Egyptian Dog Star Sirius *qua* Isis, all-seeing eyes denoting Masonic deism and omnipresence, and masculine solar pyramids[92] all have esoteric contextual meaning in most (not all) films. The lessons, allegorical emblems, and philosophies of both the Blue Lodge (Entered Apprentice, Fellowcraft, and Master Mason) and high degrees pervade film. Other secret organizations include the Rosicrucians, or the Fraternity of the Order of the Rosy Cross, influenced modern-day secret societies. The Rosicrucians were involved in hermetic wisdom, the occult, astrology, and alchemy. Rosicrucianism heralded a proto-Enlightenment, and, despite indignant claims by Masonic writers that Rosicrucianism had no connection with the Masonic Fraternity, careful reading of the evidence of sixteenth-century intellectual movements before the Newtonian revolution clearly points to several cross-influences that indicate Renaissance-Hermetic-Cabalistic-Alchemical ideas permeated some groups.[93] It is unlikely that Freemasonry escaped unscathed. From Freemasonry came the Illuminati born on May 1st, 1776, a Bavarian secret society that was supposed to be anticlerical, and was denounced as antichristian. It infiltrated Freemasonry on the continent of Europe and renamed Ingolstadt as Eleusis, Austria as Egypt, Munich as Athens, and Vienna as Rome. The Illuminati played a major role in promulgating Enlightenment, occult ideas, and cabalistic virtues throughout the Holy Roman Empire.

Outwardly pious, another political secret society which influenced not only Freemasonry, but the Illuminati was the Society of Jesus better known as the Jesuits. The Jesuit Order was founded in 1534 by Ignatius Loyola, a Spaniard of ardent imagination and earnest spirit, the society approved by Pope Paul III (1468-1548) in 1540. There can be little doubt that Loyola intended it to be a mystical and contemplative association, resembling, in many things, the colleges of Egyptian priests. The Jesuits appear to have

---

92 See Albert Pike's *Morals and Dogma of the Ancient and Accepted Scottish Rite of Freemasonry*, p. 460. Pike writes "The figure of the pyramid and that of the obelisk, resembling the shape of a flame, caused these monuments to be consecrated to the Sun and Fire."
93 See James Stevens Curl's *The Art and Architecture of Freemasonry*, pp. 243-244. cf. Frances Yates' *The Rosicrucian Enlightenment, passim.*

taken the Egyptian priests of yore for their model. Like them, they were the conservators and interpreters of religion. The vows, they pronounced, bound them to their company, as indissolubly as the interest and politics of the Egyptian priests fixed them in the sacred college of Memphis. After the Order of Jesus had fallen from its high estate, becoming merely a secret society of political agitators and intriguers, some ardent, enthusiastic men conceived the idea of superseding it by a New Order that should retain all the good of the old, and be better adapted to the circumstances of modern times, and the wants of modern society. The Society of the Illuminati and that of the Rosicrucians were formed with this aim and purpose. The adepts of the Illuminati were governed by rules nearly identical with those of the Jesuits, and the whole machinery of the two orders was constructed after the same idea."[94] The Jesuits led the Counter-Reformation; its prime objective was to restore Catholicism by any means necessary including espionage, skullduggery, and subterfuge, especially in Protestant England and Sweden. Began at the Council of Trent (1545-1563), other reforms included returning magisterial orders to their spiritual-mystical foundations, and new spiritual movements focusing on the devotional life and a personal relationship with Christ, including the Spanish mystics and the French school of spirituality. It also involved political activities that included the Roman Inquisition. From the Counter-Reformation came the high degrees of Freemasonry, which promote Catholic-occult virtues such as cabalistic apotheosis, divine appropriation, and papal monarchy. The influence of secret orders and their doctrines are in films such as *National Treasure* (2004), *The Ninth Gate* (1999), and *The Man Who Would Be King* (1975).

The Jesuits were inspired by the medieval Knights Templar. On the Templars and their mysteries, Masonic magus Albert Pike writes "...the Order of Knights of the Temple was at its very origin devoted to the cause of opposition to the tiara of Rome and the crowns of Kings, and the Apostolate of Kabalistic Gnosticism was vested in its chiefs. ...the tendencies and tenets of the Order were enveloped in profound mystery, and it externally professed the most perfect orthodoxy. The Chiefs alone knew the aim of the Order: the Subalterns followed them without distrust. ...The Templars, like all other Secret Orders and Associations, had two doctrines, one concealed and reserved for the Masters, which was Johannism; the other public, which

---

94 See Robert Macoy's *A Dictionary of Freemasonry*, pp. 181-182.

was the *Roman Catholic*. Thus, they deceived the adversaries whom they sought to supplant."[95] The Templars are the Jedi Knights in the *Star Wars* saga (see *Cinema Symbolism*), and the Templar's esoteric doctrines will be further analyzed in this book.

Freemasonry, Rosicrucianism, and the Templars influenced other societies such as the Victorian era Hermetic Order of the Golden Dawn, a Masonic-like group that fused Tarot, alchemy, astrology, and Kabbalah with Freemasonry. Known as a mystical order, the Golden Dawn was active in Great Britain and focused its practices on theurgy and spiritual development, admitting both men and women to its ranks. Many present-day concepts of ritual and magic that are at the center of contemporary traditions, such as Wicca and Thelema, were inspired by the Golden Dawn, which became one of the largest single influences on twentieth-century Western occultism. Out of the mysticism of the Golden Dawn came the O.T.O., or the *Ordo Templi Orientis* (Order of the Eastern Templars), an international fraternal and religious organization founded at the beginning of the 20th century. Originally, it was intended to be modeled after European Freemasonry, such as Masonic Templar organizations, but under the leadership of Crowley, the O.T.O. was reorganized around the Law of Thelema (a/k/a Crowley's mantra, "Do what thou wilt shall be the whole of the Law") as its central religious principle. One of the O.T.O.'s chief tenets is the practice of "magick" which, in the context of Aleister Crowley's Thelema, is a term used to differentiate the occult from stage magic, and is defined as "the Science and Art of causing Change to occur in conformity with Will," including both mundane acts of will as well as ritual magic; *magick* is designed to be transformative or alchemical.[96] From the practice of magick comes sex magick: sexual activity used in erotic, ritualistic or otherwise religious, spiritual, and occult pursuits. One practice of sex magick is using the energy of sexual arousal or orgasm with visualization of the desired result. A premise of sex magick is the concept that sexual energy is a potent force that can be harnessed to surpass one's normally perceived reality; sex magick is likewise transformative and alchemical. These occult-sexual practices and dogmas pervade *Stoker* (2013), *9 ½ Weeks*, *Passion*, and *Black Swan*

---

95 Pike, *Morals and Dogma*, p. 817.
96 See Aleister Crowley's *Magick, passim*.

which are analyzed in Chapter XI; this chapter explores the dark side of the moon, the shadowy world of the sacred feminine.

Speaking of Crowley, the personalities that transcend occult orders and secret societies are also of great importance. Crowley, as some of you know, is perhaps the most controversial and significant occultist of the last 100 years. For those not familiar, Crowley was, among other things, an English ceremonial magician, poet, spy, painter, novelist, and mountaineer. He founded the religion and philosophy of Thelema, identifying himself as the prophet entrusted with guiding humanity into the Æon of Horus (cf. a new solar age, the Age of Aquarius) in the early 20th century. Initiated into the mysteries of Freemasonry, the Golden Dawn, and the O.T.O., Crowley believed himself to be the reincarnation of other great occultists: Pope Alexander VI (1431-1503), renowned for his love of physical pleasures; Edward Kelley (1555-1597), the mystical assistant to conjurer Dr. John Dee (1527-1608/09) in Elizabethan England; occultist and adventurer Cagliostro (1743-1795), and ceremonial magician Eliphas Levi (1810-1875) who died on the day Crowley was born. Levi is also of great importance. Levi, a Freemason and an emissary of the Ancient Mysteries, wrote numerous books on the occult including *Dogme et Rituel de la Haute Magie* (*Transcendental Magic, its Doctrine and Ritual*, 1854-1856) and *Histoire de la Magie* (*The History of Magic*, 1860), among many others. Albert Pike's *Morals and Dogma of the Ancient and Accepted Scottish Rite* (1871) was heavily influenced, plagiarized verbatim in some parts, by the works of Levi. Levi is also responsible for the drawing of the Baphomet, also known as the Goat of Mendes: an ancient Pagan-Gnostic-Alchemical-Hermetic deity (or entity) that quickly gets associated–quite incorrectly–with devil worship. Nevertheless, Levi's Baphomet of Mendes' *je ne sais quoi* haunts the rambunctious Black Phillip, a demonic scene-stealing billy goat in 2015's *The Witch*. Also noteworthy is hell-raiser Madame Helena Blavatsky: an eccentric Russian, occultist, spirit medium, and author, co-founding the Theosophical Society in 1875. She gained an international following as the leading theoretician of Theosophy, the esoteric-Gnostic movement that the Society promoted. Hollywood does not shy away from Crowley, Levi, and Blavatsky; their esoteric philosophies–and personalities–manifest like a demon, taking possession of the movie, imbuing it with darkness.

"Mystical Archetypes of the Old West" is the title of Chapter IX while Chapter XIII, *Cinema Symbolism 2's* grand finale, investigates "Lost History and the Gangs of New York."

Another common thread that runs through *Cinema Symbolism 2* is the study of comparative cinema and what this author describes as *occult casting*. The former is when a filmmaker not only draws upon arcane mythology, themes, and imagery, but uses scenes and icons from other films within their movie thereby making it even more symbolic thus even more powerful. For example, the spiritual godhead of the machines, Deus Ex Machina in *The Matrix Revolutions* (2003), appears before Neo as a giant, terrifying mechanical face. This scene clearly is meant to resemble *The Wizard of Oz* when Dorothy and her fellow travelers finally stand before the almighty Oz, a large, green, menacing face. The scene in *The Matrix Revolutions* becomes clear: like the great and powerful Oz, Deus Ex Machina does not grant an audience to everyone; both demiurges are hard to reach, omnipotent, and are sources of terror, not compassion. Occult casting is when filmmakers employ a specific actor or actress because of a film (or films) they've previously appeared in, thereby investing the new film with that performance and its related themes and symbolisms. In *Cinema Symbolism*, this author explained that Anthony Zerbe's casting

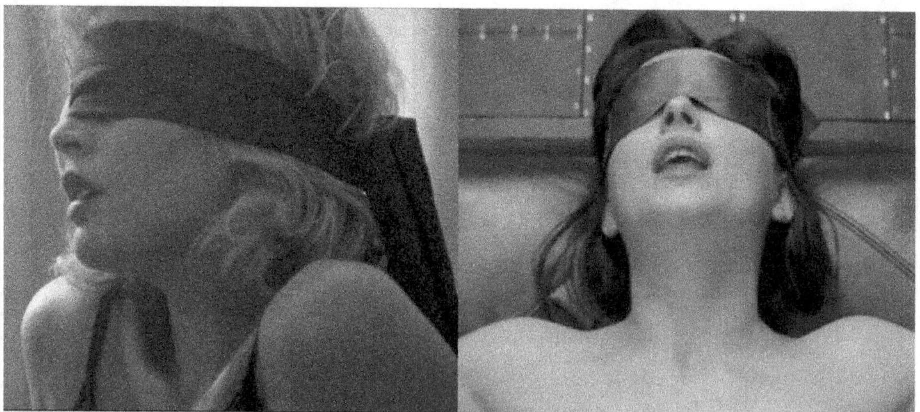

Comparative Cinema and Occult Casting: The religion of hedonism. (Left) Blindfolded, Elizabeth (Kim Basinger) explores her lustful dark side, becoming overwhelmed with carnality in *9 ½ Weeks*. (Right) Blindfolded, Anastasia Steele (Dakota Johnson) is overcome with rapture in 2015's *Fifty Shades of Grey*; accordingly, *Fifty Shades of Grey* evokes the raw eroticism of *9 ½ Weeks* by cleverly utilizing its imagery. Basinger has been cast as Elena Lincoln in *Fifty Shades of Grey's* sequel, *Fifty Shades Darker* (2017), because of the cinematic luggage she brings from her daring, sensual performance in *9 ½ Weeks*.

as Councilor Hamann in *The Matrix Reloaded* (2003) was linked to his character Matthias in 1971's *The Omega Man*. There is a singular reason why Pernilla August was cast as Anakin Skywalker's virgin mother Shmi Skywalker in 1999's *The Phantom Menace*. At first, I thought this was a rare phenomenon, but it is more common than I first anticipated. A few years ago, Lili Taylor was cast in 2013's *The Conjuring* as Carolyn Perron, a mother tormented by malevolent ghosts and demons. Her performance subconsciously recalls her performance from 1999's *The Haunting*, when Taylor played Eleanor "Nell" Lance. Lance investigates a haunted house and sees ghosts; hence her macabre portrayal as Carolyn Perron, a woman terrorized by demonic entities, is perfectly cast and devilishly clever. As *Cinema Symbolism 2* unfolds, one will understand why Mia Wasikowska was cast in 2015's *Crimson Peak* and why Max von Sydow has a tiny part at the beginning of *Star Wars: The Force Awakens*. These actors and actresses appear in certain films because of their cultural valences, thereby creating an occult construct within an occult construct; their casting is witty, but the motivation behind their casting is esoteric.

In closing this Introduction, I think I should touch upon one more aspect of this book. As a 32nd degree Scottish Rite Mason (Valley of Baltimore, Orient of Maryland), this tome that you are reading now, as well as my previous books and forthcoming books, veil arcane codes and hidden messages. Some, not all, are Masonic in nature; for instance, there are forty-seven Roman numeral pages that open *Cinema Symbolism*, both first and second editions. These forty-seven pages span the List of Illustrations to the end of the Introduction. Forty-seven is a reference to the 47th Proposition (or Problem) of Euclid, also known as the Pythagorean Theorem. This Pythagorean Theorem (right triangle) is the emblem of a Masonic Worshipful Master, the brother who governs a Blue Lodge, epitomizing Masonic rulership; thus, the forty-seven pages denote Masonic authorship. The first edition of *The Royal Arch of Enoch: The Impact of Masonic Ritual, Philosophy, and Symbolism* (2012) has 690 pages; the number 69, when turned on its side, is the astrological symbol for the fourth house of the zodiac, Cancer, during which the summer solstice occurs. It is during this time that the sun, in the northern hemisphere, is at its full strength as the days are the longest of the year. The sun is the most important

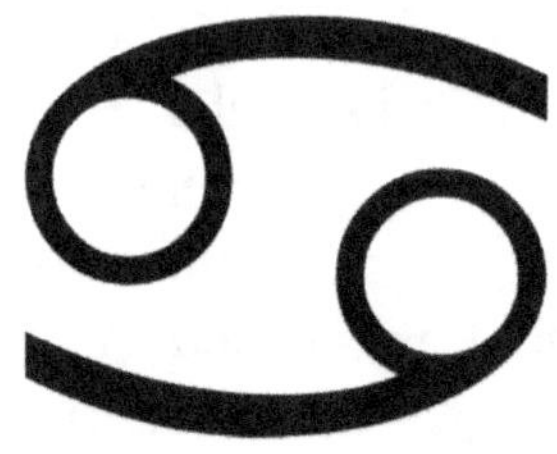

Cancer's astrological symbol.

symbol in Freemasonry,[97] so the 690 pages are a hidden reference to the sun and the summer solstice signifying, once again, Masonic authorship. Furthermore, *The Royal Arch of Enoch* (First Edition) was released in mid-August 2012, in the sign of Leo, the house of the sun, signifying the heliacal rising of Sirius, the Masonic Dog Days of Summer, implying Masonic authorship. The second edition of *The Royal Arch of Enoch* was released on December 27th, 2016; December 27th is the Feast Day of St. John the Evangelist, one of Freemasonry's patron saints.[98] I will say no more on this subject, allowing the reader to attempt to solve some of the occult riddles contained herein. With that in mind, keep an all-seeing eye out when reading Rob's books but always, above all else, enjoy *Cinema Symbolism 2*.

---

97 See Robert Sullivan's *The Royal Arch of Enoch*, Chapter I, "Masonic Symbolism 101," *passim*.
98 St. John the Baptist is the other.

CHAPTER I

SOLAR SUPERSTARS

"For as the lightning cometh out of the east, and shineth even unto
the west; so shall also the coming of the Son of man be."
– Matthew 24:27

"Remember when the sun is gone that weapon will be ready to fire.
But as long as there's light we got a chance."
– Poe Dameron, *Star Wars: The Force Awakens*, 2015.

"They say there's just enough religion in the world
to make men hate one another, but not enough to make them love."
– Louis Cyphre, *Angel Heart*, 1987.

"See, mother, I make all things new."
– Jesus Christ, *The Passion of the Christ*, 2004.

"I Jesus have sent mine angel to testify
unto you these things in the churches. I am the root and
the offspring of David, and the bright and morning star."
– Revelation 22:16.

"If this god is God, he would live on every mountain,
in every valley. He would not be the god of
Ishmael or Israel alone, but of all men.
It is said he created all men in his image.
He would dwell in every heart, every mind, every soul."
– Moses, *The Ten Commandments*, 1956

The Holy Bible, the stories of the Old and New Testaments, are solar and astrology allegories best defined as *astrotheology*. The dramatis personae and stories of the Bible are not real people or living history. Rather, the Bible presents morality lessons played out by a cast of characters who anthropomorphize the stars, the constellations, the zodiac, the planets, the sun, and the moon. The movements and interactions of these celestial bodies, observed from earth's northern hemisphere, generate the Bible's core dogmas, creating compelling archetypes found in the world's other religions, including but not limited to Buddhism, Judaism, and Islam. The Christian-astrological mysterion, or *Disciplina Arcani*, was born out of Neoplatonic apologetic thought, harmonizing and anticipating the pragmatic philosophical doctrine Occam's Razor. Occam's Razor, also known as Ockham's Razor after William of Ockham (ca. 1287-1347) is a principle of parsimony, economy, or succinctness used in logic and problem-solving. It states that among competing hypotheses, the hypothesis with the fewest assumptions should be selected. The Razor holds that one should proceed to simpler theories until simplicity can be traded for greater explanatory power. Applying the Razor to the Bible, the pedestrian explanation is the best and most accurate: the Bible is an astral-solar allegory, symbolic Logos, not factual history. Jesus and Moses are not historical figures; rather, they are solar avatars bringing light and wisdom in changing times of darkness and despair. This occult Biblical symbolism recently played out on the small screen: at the conclusion of the final episode titled "Courage" (airdate March 31st, 2013) of the History Channel's miniseries *The Bible*, Jesus Christ's final revelation is depicted as a rising sun that, like Jesus, becomes the world's resurrected messianic solar savior bringing salvation to the world. On these Pagan-Christian-Neoplatonic comparisons, Masonic philosopher Manly P. Hall explains:

> Among other allegories borrowed by Christianity from pagan antiquity is the story of the beautiful, blue-eyed Sun God, with His golden hair falling upon His shoulders, robed from head to foot in spotless white carrying in His arms the Lamb of God (cf. Aries the Ram), symbolic of the vernal equinox. This handsome youth is a composite of Apollo, Osiris, Orpheus, Mithras, and Bacchus, for He has certain characteristics in common with each of these pagan deities.

The philosophers of Greece and Egypt divided the life of the sun during the year into four parts; therefore they symbolized the Solar Man by four different figures. When He was born in the winter solstice, the Sun God was symbolized as a dependent infant who in some mysterious manner had managed to escape the Powers of Darkness seeking to destroy Him while He was still in the cradle of winter. The sun, being weak at this season of the year, had no golden rays (or locks of hair), but the survival of the light through the darkness of winter was symbolized by one tiny hair which alone adorned the head of the Celestial Child. (As the birth of the sun took place in Capricorn, it was often represented as being suckled by a goat.)

At the vernal equinox, the sun had grown to be a beautiful youth. His golden hair hung in ringlets on his shoulders and his light, as Schiller said, extended to all parts of infinity. At the summer solstice, the sun became a strong man, heavily bearded, who, in the prime of maturity, symbolized the fact that Nature at this period of the year is strongest and most fecund. At the autumnal equinox, the sun was pictured as an aged man, shuffling along with bended back and whitened locks into the oblivion of winter darkness. Thus, twelve months were assigned to the sun as the length of its life. During this period it circled the twelve signs of the zodiac in a magnificent triumphal march. When fall came, it entered, like Samson, into the house of Delilah (Virgo), wherein its rays were cut off and it lost its strength. In Masonry, the cruel winter months are symbolized by three murderers who sought to destroy the God of Light and Truth.

The coming of the sun was hailed with joy; the time of its departure was viewed as a period to be set aside for sorrow and unhappiness. This glorious, radiant orb of day, the true light 'which lighteth every man who cometh into the world,' the supreme benefactor, who raised all things from the dead, who fed the hungry multitudes, who stilled the tempest, who after dying rose again and restored all things to life– this Supreme Spirit of humanitarianism and philanthropy is known to Christendom as Christ, the Redeemer of worlds, the Only Begotten of The Father, the Word made Flesh, and the Hope of Glory."[99]

---

99 Hall, *The Secret Teachings of All Ages*, pp. 138-139; "cf. Aries the Ram" added.

Please keep an open mind because what you are about to read is controversial. Cinema is apt for both revealing and concealing esoteric visions, and the Neoplatonic-cabalistic theory that Jesus Christ is a sun god is no exception.

ASTROTHEOLOGY IN CHRISTIAN CINEMA: THE PASSION OF THE CHRIST, CHRISTMAS MOVIES, AND THE VERNAL EQUINOX

The Christian apologetic *The Passion of the Christ* is a film directed by American-born Australian actor Mel Gibson, which documents the last days of Jesus Christ. The movie opens in Gethsemane as Jesus (Jim Caviezel) prays, tempted by Satan (Rosalinda Celentano) while his apostles sleep. After receiving thirty pieces of silver, one of Jesus' other apostles, Judas Iscariot (Luca Lionello), approaches with the temple guards betraying Jesus with a kiss on the cheek. As the guards move in to arrest Jesus, the apostle Peter (Francesco De Vito) cuts off the ear of Malchus (Roberto Bestazzoni), but Jesus miraculously heals the ear. The disciples flee, the temple guards arrest Jesus, beating him during the journey to the Sanhedrin. John (Christo Jivkov) tells Mary (Maia Morgenstern, Jesus' mother) and Mary Magdalene (Monica Bellucci) of the arrest while Peter follows Jesus at a distance. The Jewish high priest Caiaphas (Mattia Sbragia) holds trial over the objection of some of the other priests, expelling them from the court. When questioned by Caiaphas whether he is the son of God, Jesus replies "I am." Caiaphas is horrified, ripping his robes condemning Jesus to death for blasphemy. Peter, secretly watching, is confronted by guards; he thrice denies knowing Jesus, causing him to run away sobbing after remembering that Jesus had prophesied that Peter would deny knowing him three times before the cock crowed. Meanwhile, the remorseful Judas attempts to return the money to have Jesus freed but is refused by the priests. Judas, tormented by demons, leaves the city, hanging himself with a rope he finds on a dead donkey.

Caiaphas brings Jesus before Pontius Pilate (Hristo Shopovto) to face death, but after questioning Jesus and finding no fault in him, removes Jesus to the court of Herod (Luca De Dominicis) because Nazareth (Jesus' hometown) is under Herod's jurisdiction. After Jesus is again found not guilty and returned, Pilate offers the crowd that he will chastise Jesus then will set him free. He then attempts to have Jesus released by giving the people an option of liberating Jesus or the violent criminal, Barabbas (Pietro Sarubbi). To his dismay, the crowd demands to have Barabbas freed and Jesus executed. In an attempt to appease the crowd, Pilate has Jesus brutally scourged and mocked as the King of the Jews with a crown of thorns. However, the crowd continues to demand Jesus' crucifixion and Barabbas' release. Pilate washes his hands of the situation reluctantly ordering Jesus' death by crucifixion.

Jesus carries the wooden cross along the Via Dolorosa to Calvary, Veronica (Sabrina Impacciatore credited as Seraphia, not Veronica) wipes Jesus' dirty and bloody face with her veil to ease his suffering. Simon of Cyrene (Jarreth J. Merz) is unwillingly pressed into helping Jesus carry the wooden cross. At Golgotha or the Place of the Skull, Jesus is nailed to the cross, crucified. As he hangs from the cross, Jesus prays forgiveness for those who did this to him and redeems a criminal crucified next to him. After Jesus gives up his spirit and dies, a single drop of rain falls from the sky, triggering an earthquake which destroys the Temple, ripping the cloth covering the Holy of Holies to the horror of Caiaphas and the other priests. Satan is then shown screaming in defeat while Jesus is taken down from the cross. The film concludes with the sun penetrating Jesus' tomb as he rises from the dead; the stone rolls away, allowing Jesus to exit the crypt.

*　*　*　*

Jesus is depicted working as a carpenter, personifying the traits associated with the demiurge or lesser, creator craftsman-like god; this reflects the theological doctrine of the Two Bodies of Christ: one corporeal (lesser) and one spiritual (higher, cf. the docetic-Gnostic Gospel of St. John). Comparatively, this Gnostic philosophy can be found in *The Truman Show*, which sees a Manichean demiurge tyrannically ruling over a false reality in which materialism is king. This demiurge, named Christof after Jesus Christ, is the creator of the fictitious seaside township of Seahaven, which serves as the backdrop for the reality television series, *The Truman Show*. Truman Burbank is initially not aware that Seahaven is an illusion, and that it–and his life–are crafted solely for entertainment purposes. Christof, echoing controversial Gnostic notions of Christ as a carpenter *qua* demiurge, is a craftsman or artisan-like deity who controls every aspect of Seahaven, aided by a host of archons: demonic and angelic servants of the demiurge, namely Truman's wife, Meryl (Laura Linney), keeping him immured in matter. Christof is responsible for the fashioning and maintenance of the hylic universe which is nothing more than an illusion. Christof has nothing to do with spirituality, awakening, or gnosis: he wants to keep Truman imprisoned and unconscious in his handcrafted reality. Truman eventually becomes conscious that Seahaven is a falsehood (see Introduction) and, like a rebellious Prometheus or Lucifer, rejects the programming, turning against the godlike Christof and his archons. The spiritual Jesus is considered to be the sacred spark within us all; since we are all God's creations, we are all imbued with the divine. Truman learns this lesson at the conclusion of *The Truman Show*.

Jesus anthropomorphizes as the sun, making him a sun god, suggesting that the Roman Empire sun god-cult of *Sol Invictus* (Unconquered Sun) which heavily influenced Nicean Christianity. Jesus, personifying the sun, is *born again* every morning and will come again to do battle with works of darkness, or the nighttime sky. Jesus the sun of god "….cometh with clouds; and every eye shall see him, and they [also] which pierced him: and all kindreds of the earth shall wail because of him. Even so, Amen," at Revelation 1:7. "Then spake Jesus again unto them, saying, I am the light of the world: he that followeth me shall not walk in darkness, but shall have the light of life," at John 8:12. Let's be clear: there is only one light of the world that comes in clouds for all eyes to see: the sun. Even during a sermon, Jesus invokes the sun's power to further his cause. At John 12:36 it is recorded, "While ye have light, believe in the light, that ye may be the children of light. These things spake Jesus, and departed, and did hide himself from them." Jesus confirms his solar attributes at Revelation 22:16[100] when he calls himself the *Bright Morning Star*, which is, of course, the sun. Many early church fathers equated the concept of *God's Sun-Solar*

---

100 "I Jesus have sent mine angel to testify unto you these things in the churches. I am the root and the offspring of David, and the bright and morning star."

Logos in the context of Neoplatonism, which sought to reconcile the pagan mysteries with Christianity. One of Neoplatonism's chief proponents was Origen whose name means *son of Horus*. Horus was an Egyptian sun-god birthed by the virgin mother Isis who becomes the Virgin Mary in Christianity. Horus defeated the dark lord Set, or Typhon, the forerunner of the Christian Devil. Origen, who can also be considered a Neopythagorean, was the student of Christian Platonist Clement of Alexander (ca. 150-215 CE) and responsible for coalescence of Christian writings that became the New Testament. Origen understood that Holy Scripture was allegorical, not to be taken as literal history.[101] This doctrine, which was known only by the initiated few, conceals Christianity's astrological and solar roots, creating Christianity's hidden mysteries: a mysterion, or the *Disciplina Arcani* . So, if Jesus embodies the sun, one must ask are there any other astral symbolisms in Christianity and thus *The Passion of the Christ*? The answer to this question is yes.

In Chapter III of *The Royal Arch of Enoch,* I explained that the Twelve Apostles are representations of the twelve houses of the zodiac. They are not historic figures. Just as the twelve signs provide aid to the sun on its ecliptic journey, the Apostles administer assistance to Jesus the Piscean Age sun god (cf. Precession of the Equinoxes, more on this later). The Apostles and their corresponding zodiacs follow this order:

1. Just as Aries the Ram is the first house of the zodiac, so is Peter the first leader of Christianity after Christ's death. He is fiery, impulsive, yet changeable; he is the rock upon which Christ founds his New Church of the Lamb. Etymologically, the name, Peter, derives from the Greek *petra* meaning rock.

2. Taurus the Bull is the dogmatic Simon Zelotes, concerned with property and finance, rebelling against the payment of taxes. God's sun *qua* Jesus admonishes Taurus "Render unto Caesar the things that are Caesar's," at Matthew 22:21. In economics and the stock market, it is from the house of Taurus the term *bull market* originates.

---

101 "The existence of certain doctrines, which are beyond those which are exoteric and do not reach the multitude, is not a peculiarity of Christian doctrine only, but is shared by the philosophers. For they had some doctrines which were exoteric and some esoteric." – Origen, *Contra Celsus* I.7.

3. Gemini is James the Lesser; intelligent, but incapable of independent thought. Slow to accept the teachings of the solar messiah, he became an eloquent preacher of the church in Jerusalem and an active evangelist. Astrologically, the city of London, England, is aligned to Gemini; as such, the English monarchy rules from St. James Palace or the Court of St. James, which is an esoteric homage to the house of Gemini.

4. Cancer the Crab is Andrew the home-body who dwells with his brother Simon Peter (a/k/a Peter). His first thought when he discovered the Messiah was to run and fetch his brother.

5. Leo the Lion is John; just as Leo is ruled by the sun, John is thus the most inspired and the most beloved of Christ's apostles.

6. Phillip is Virgo: always precise, calculating, enquiring yet practical: the traits of Virgo.

7. Libra is Matthew the even-minded tax collector who uses the scales of Libra to weigh and collect money.

8. Judas Iscariot is Scorpio the Scorpion the deadly backstabbing traitor who delivers his deadly sting or kiss. Scorpio is one of the murderers of the sun because the sun enters the House of Scorpio after the autumnal equinox, thereby sending the sun of God into death, or winter, because the days become noticeably shorter. The thirty pieces of silver paid to Judas in return for his betrayal refers to the moon's thirty-day lunar cycle.

9. James the Greater is Sagittarius, the wise teacher who along with the other two fire signs, Peter and John, are the most eager to spread the light of Christ's solar church.

10. Bartholomew-Nathaniel is dependable Capricorn in whom there is no deception.

11. Thaddeus-Jude is Aquarius the social liberal who sought better living and working conditions, and an overall preferable state of being. He interrogated Jesus at the Last Supper as to how this would be accomplished.

12. Pisces the Fish are Thomas. The two fish represent both the positive and the negative: just as Thomas believes and is courageous one moment (positive), he doubts the next (negative). While believing Christ is the Messiah, he is best known for disbelieving the Resurrection; as such he is a *doubting Thomas*.

Within the Christianity mysteries, the Twelve Apostles do not hold sway over the zodiac; it is not exclusive to Christ's followers.

There are other sublime astral occurrences one must meditate upon to unlock Christianity's *Disciplina Arcani*. For example, Mary Magdalene is the embodiment of the planet Venus. Venus, a feminine planet, associates itself with Lucifer because it often rises above the eastern horizon as false light while heralding the true light of the world: the coming sunrise, or Jesus. Within the Gnostic (and later Templar) mysteries, Magdalene was known as *Mary Lucifera*, identifying her as a feminine light bearer. The planet Venus'(called the "son of the morning star")[102] close proximately to the sun is allegorized in *The Passion of the Christ* in which Mary Magdalene is a close confidant of Jesus Christ, the sun. Venus' closeness to the sun incurs the jealousy of the Twelve Apostles, because the stars that form the zodiac are substantially farther away from the sun *qua* Jesus than Venus or Mary. It is Mary, not the Apostles, announcing Jesus' resurrection, usually depicted in Christian cinema, but is noticeably absent from *The Passion of the Christ*. Venus *qua* Mary Magdalene (cf. sacred feminine) and its esoteric nexus to the sun *qua* Jesus (the masculine) was venerated by a society of medieval warrior-monks, the Knights Templar. The knights of the mysterious brotherhood incorporated astronomical-astrological icons and lore into their mysteries and cabal. The union of the sacred feminine with the divine masculine gave rise to the rumor that the Templars secretly worshipped a pagan-Gnostic androgynous deity known as Baphomet. The Templars were arrested and suppressed in 1307, but rumors persist many of them escaped to Scotland with treasure *qua* forbidden wisdom they discovered while excavating the Temple Mount during the Crusades in the Holy Land. Rumor has it they eventually morphed into modern-day Freemasonry which preserves their esoteric teachings

---

102 This is not to be confused with the Morning Star which is another term for the sun. The sun is a star while Venus is a planet making Venus the son of the morning star. See Sullivan's *The Royal Arch of Enoch, passim.*

and wisdom. Mirroring the Templars' persecution, an outcast sect of monsters find sanctuary in a cemetery called Midian, worshipping Baphomet in 1990's *Nightbreed*. Perhaps this Templar controversy, coupled with the widespread conspiracy theory that Mary wed Jesus giving birth to his child, is why Mary's announcement of Christ's resurrection is absent from *The Passion of the Christ*.

Jesus' mother, the Virgin Mary, is the constellation Virgo the Virgin, plagiarizing the Egyptian goddess Isis. Ancient Egypt contributed its share of gorgeous symbolism to the Catholic Church as well as to the pale abstractions of her theology.[103] In art, the figure of Isis suckling the infant Horus is so like that of the Madonna and child that it has sometimes received the adoration of ignorant Christians.[104] Isis was the virgin wife of Osiris, and her attributes were the moon and the Dog Star Sirius. Embodying the moon, Isis is veiled with numinous light because the moon reflects the sun's divine rays, remaining a virgin, birthing the sun's divine personification, Horus. Comparatively, Horus is Attis, Dionysus, Hercules, Krishna, Jesus, Mithras, and Apollo, all sun gods of antiquity. The Virgin Mary, as a corrupt version of Isis, appears in Wolfgang Amadeus Mozart's (1756-1791) Masonic-Illuminati opera *The Magic Flute* (1791), embodied by the Queen of the Night, personifying both the Blessed Virgin Mary and the Catholic Church. Within the opera, the Queen epitomizes deceit, superstition, and trickery; this represents the Church's Virgin Mary as the usurper of Isis and her related mythology; the Virgin Mary is analogous to the Queen of the Night because she has stolen Isis' attributes: the moon and the stars (cf. Sirius and the constellation Virgo). Another nexus between Mary, the constellation Virgo, and the solar messiah Jesus is Virgo holding a sheaf of wheat in her hand. Symbolically, Mary's solar child Jesus is born in Bethlehem meaning *house of bread* in Hebrew and Aramaic. Although Jesus' birth is not depicted in *The Passion of the Christ*, it is nevertheless astrological. Pike explains, "At the moment of the Winter Solstice, the Virgin (cf. Virgo) rose heliacally (*with* the Sun), having the Sun (Horus) in her bosom."[105] Therefore, the sun god or Jesus Christ was symbolically born of a virgin on December 25th.

---

103 Frazer, *The Golden Bough*, p. 379.
104 *ibid.*
105 Pike, *Morals and Dogma*, p. 455. "(cf. Virgo)" added.

The New Testament archetypal personalities, Caiaphas and Pontius Pilate, represent two houses of the zodiac. The two villains personify the sign of Libra, the great astrological scales of justice. The two of them weigh and judge the sun god's veracity and, finding him guilty, condemn him to death. Under Libra is when the autumnal equinox (September 22nd-23rd) occurs making the days shorter; night governs, since the sun travels towards its symbolic death, entombed by the winter months. Three houses of the zodiac murder the sun: Libra, Scorpio, and Sagittarius, because these signs rule the autumn months when the sun *falls* towards death or winter. Libra is epitomized by the judicial Caiaphas and Pilate; Judas is the back-biting traitor Scorpio giving the sun his infamous sting or kiss of death; so, who represents Sagittarius in the Christian mysteries? Sagittarius is the Roman soldier Longinus thrusting the arrow, or spear, of Sagittarius into the side of the sun god killing him (or confirming he's dead), sending the sun into winter's frigid tomb. "The prototype of the legend seems to have been the blind god Hod, who slew the Norse savior Balder with the thrust of a spear of mistletoe, …March 15, the 'Ides of March' when most pagan saviors died, was the day devoted to Hod by the heathens, and later Christianized as the feast day of the Blessed Longinus."[106]

After Libra *qua* Caiaphas and Pilate condemn the sun to death during the winter months, its life-giving rays fail because daylight becomes scant in the northern hemisphere. Darkness rules so Jesus–the sun–is denied by his most loyal apostle, Peter. Peter's denial and the cock crowing three times before the sunrise is a metaphor. According to the *Zohar*, a cock crowing three times is an omen of death; the Gospel story of Peter's denial of Christ, three times before the cockcrow, was related to older legends associating the crowing with the death and resurrection (cf. sunrise) of the solar Savior.[107]

Thus, the sun's power and energy wanes until the winter solstice when the new, annual sun is born again, or resurrected, coinciding with the December 25th birthday of the sun, the birth of Christ. The celebration of the winter solstice is known to the Hebrews as Hanukkah; it was the Roman festival Saturnalia coinciding with the Feast Day of Mithras (*Sol*

---

106 Acharya S, *The Christ Conspiracy: The Greatest Story Ever Sold*, pp. 208-209 citing Barbara Walker's *The Woman's Encyclopedia of Myths*.
107 *ibid*, p. 201 citing Barbara Walker's *The Woman's Dictionary of Symbols and Sacred Objects*.

Invictus, December 25th) which the Christians have renamed Christmas. Indeed, with respect to the midwinter celebration of Christmas we are not left to conjecture; we know from the express testimony of the ancients that it was instituted by the church to supersede an old heathen festival of the birth of the sun, which was apparently conceived to be born again on the shortest day of the year, after which his light and heat were seen to grow till they attained their full maturity at midsummer.[108] In his book *Sun Lore of All Ages* (1914), William Tyler Olcott confirms this:

The Roman winter solstice, as celebrated on December 25th (VIII Kal. Jan.) in connection with the worship of the Sun-God Mithra appears to have been instituted in this special form by Aurelian about A.D. 273, and to this festival the day owes its apposite name of 'Birthday of the Unconquered Sun.' With full symbolic appropriateness, though not with historical justification, the day was adopted in the Western church where it appears to have been generally introduced by the fourth century, and whence in time it passed to the eastern church as the solemn anniversary of the Birth of Christ, Christmas Day.[109]

Solar adoration is synonymous with Christmas and, by default, films depicting the Nativity of Jesus. Movies focused on the Christmas celebration such as *Miracle on 34th Street* (1947), *It's a Wonderful Life* (1947), *A Christmas Story* (1983), *Home Alone* (1990), *Home Alone 2* (1992), and the numerous retellings of Charles Dickens' (1812-1870) *A Christmas Carol* uplift us because they are psychological, conjuring the rejuvenation of divine solar light, the birthday of the sun, our heavenly savior. On Jesus' celestial birth and its relation to the Christmas holiday, Olcott further elucidates:

Many of the early dignitaries of the Church reveal in their writing the solar character of the festival. Augustus and Gregory discoursed on 'the glowing light and dwindling darkness that followed the nativity,' and Leo the Great denounced in a sermon the idea that Christmas Day

---

108 Frazer, *The Golden Bough*, pp. 634-635.
109 William Tyler Olcott, *Sun Lore of All Ages*, p. 229 citing Edward B. Taylor's *Primitive Culture*. See also Frazer, *ibid*, pp. 354-355.

is to be honoured [*sic*], not for the birth of Christ, but for the rising of the new sun.

… The lighting of the Christmas tree is but the light to guide the Sun-God back to life, and the festival cakes of corn and fruit, made in honor of the Sun in ancient times, and laid on the sacred altars of the Persians as an offering of gratitude to the Lord of Light and Life, find their prototype in the plum pudding that graces the board at our Christmas feasts of rejoicing. Christmas is, therefore, nothing but an old heathen celebration of the winter solstice, the feast of rejoicing that a turning point in the sun's course has been reached, and that the life-giving orb has attained the end of its journey of dwindling hours of daylight, and has started back on a course that brings with it each day an increase of warmth and light.[110]

After the winter solstice (December 21st-22nd), the darkness of night begins to dissipate, heralding the vernal equinox (March 20th-22nd) when the sun is resurrected from the tomb when the stone of winter is symbolically rolled away; the sun god is resurrected. The third and final Omen movie, *Omen III: The Final Conflict* (1981), is set against the backdrop of the vernal equinox. The second coming of Christ occurs during the sun's springtime resurrection, thereby defeating the wickedness of Damien Thorn (Sam Neill), the Antichrist. *Omen III* was released on the vernal equinox of 1981, March 20th, signifying the end of the Antichrist's dark reign and the triumph of Christ's solar light.

Before its springtime revival, the sun god's decreased power during the autumnal months is symbolized by its scourging when, in the Gospel legends,

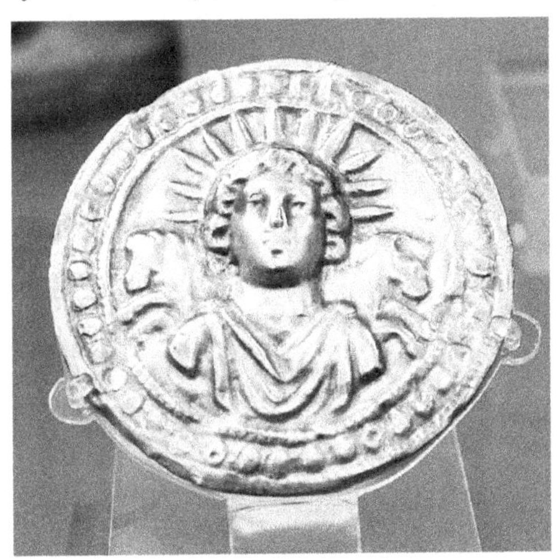

An antique golden Greco-Roman medallion (ca. 2nd-3rd century CE) featuring *Sol Invictus* (Unconquered Sun, cf. Apollo or Helios) wearing a crown of thorns signifying solar light or the sun's divine, life-giving rays. Location: British Museum.

---

110 Olcott, *ibid*, pp. 229-230; Olcott is no longer citing Taylor.

Jesus is beaten, mocked as a king with a crown of thorns placed on his head. The crown of thorns represents sun rays emanating from the sun and, by default, the sun god. In Christ's passion, there are fourteen Stations of the Cross, which are borrowed from the Egyptian Osirian mysteries, wherein the sun god Osiris is dismembered into fourteen pieces. The fourteen pieces, or stations, symbolize the maximum amount of annual full moons (each solar year has 12-14 full moons), because the moon always reflects the light despite the sun god's impending demise.

The Passion of the Christ graphically features Jesus' gory crucifixion. The place of his death is named Golgotha and is, like the rest of the New Testament, symbolic. Golgotha translated means *the place of the skull*; inside the skull is the brain, the mind, in which all truth dies or worse, is murdered. The person has a choice to accept divine truth–gnosis–or kill it, thereby living in denial, choosing ignorance over light. The two thieves depicted on either side of Christ represent the two thieves of human life: fear of the future and regret of the past. Christ symbolically dies aged 33 because there are 33 vertebrae in the human spinal column atop of which sits the skull–represented as *Golgotha*–the place where truth, *light* or en-*light*enment perishes. Jesus is nailed to a cross, and both the nails and cross are of occult significance. On the arcana of the Passion Nails, Manly P. Hall relates the following:

The three nails of the Passion have found their way into the symbolism of many races and faiths. There are many legends concerning these nails. One of these is to the effect that originally there were four nails, but one was dematerialized by a Hebrew Qabbalist and magician just as they were about to drive it through the foot of the Master. Hence it was necessary to cross the feet. Another legend relates that one of the nails was hammered into a crown and that it still exists as the imperial diadem of a European house. Still another story has it that the bit on the bridle of Constantine's horse was a Passion nail. It is improbable, however, that the nails were made of iron, for at that time it was customary to use sharpened wooden pegs. Hargrave Jennings, in his *Rosicrucians, Their Rites and Mysteries*, calls attention to the fact that the mark or sign used in England to designate royal property and called the broad arrow is nothing more nor less than the three nails of the crucifixion grouped together, and that by placing them point to point the ancient symbol of the Egyptian TAU cross is formed.

In his *Ancient Freemasonry*, Frank C. Higgins reproduces the Masonic apron of a colossal stone figure at Quirigua, Guatemala. The central ornament of the apron is the three Passion nails, arranged exactly like the British broad arrow. That three nails should be used to crucify the Christ, three murderers to kill CHiram Abiff, and three wounds to slay Prince Coh, the Mexican Indian Osiris, is significant.

C. W. King, in his *Gnostics and Their Remains*, thus describes a Gnostic gem: 'The Gnostic pleroma, or combination of all the Æons [is] expressed by the outline of a man holding a scroll * * *. The left hand is formed like three bent spikes or nails; unmistakably the same symbol that Belus often holds in his extended hand on the Babylonian cylinders, afterwards discovered by the Jewish Cabalists in the points of the letter *Shin*, and by the mediæval mystics in o the Three Nails of the Cross.' From this point Hargrave Jennings continues King's speculations, noting the resemblance of the nail to an obelisk, or pillar, and that the Qabbalistic value of the Hebrew letter *Shin*, or *Sin*, is 300, namely, 100 for each spike.

The Passion nails are highly important symbols, especially when it is realized that, according to the esoteric systems of culture, there are certain secret centers of force in the palms of the hands and in the soles of the feet.

The driving of the nails and the flow of blood and water from the wounds were symbolic of certain secret philosophic practices of the Temple. Many of the Oriental deities have mysterious symbols on the hands and feet. The so-called footprints of Buddha are usually embellished with a magnificent sunburst at the point where the nail pierced the foot of Christ.[111]

The cross that the sun waxes and wanes upon annually is twofold: one is a celestial cross, and the other is a terrestrial cross. The celestial cross is created by the four fixed houses of the zodiac; the four divisions at the four angles of

___
111 Hall, *The Secret Teachings of All Ages*, pp. 604-605.

the quadrilateral exhibited the four signs that the astrologers called *fixed*, and which they regard as the subject to the influence of the four great Royal Stars, Regulus in Leo, Aldebaran in Taurus, Antares in Scorpio, and Fomalhaut in the mouth of Pisces, on which falls the water poured out by Aquarius; of which constellations the Scorpion was represented in the Hebrew blazonry by the Celestial Vulture or Eagle, that rises at the same time with it and is its paranatellon.[112] Leo is opposite Aquarius while Scorpio is opposite Taurus, hence they form a cross. In Christianity's *Disciplina Arcani*, this astrotheological cross represents the Four Gospels which are symbolized by the four fixed signs of the zodiac: the symbol for Matthew is a man, Aquarius; the symbol for Mark is a Lion, Leo; the emblem for Luke is an ox, Taurus; and John is represented by the Eagle, or Scorpio. The four signs create the great celestial cross upon which the sun annually travels denoting esoterically the astrological foundations of Christianity. It is upon this cross that the sun is yearly *crossified* or crucified. The terrestrial cross is formed by the winter

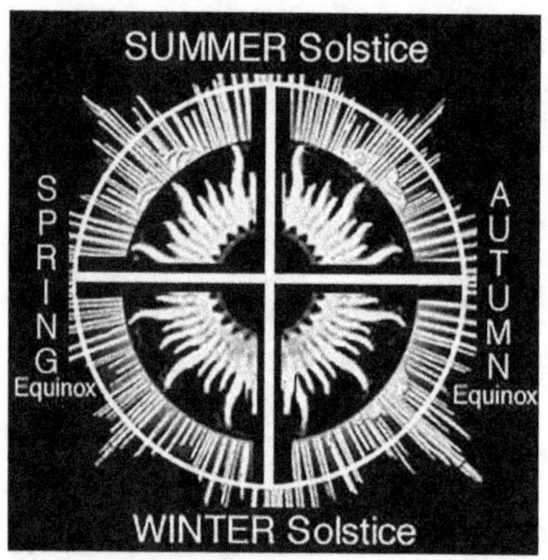

The two equinoxes and two solstices create the great terrestrial cross upon which the sun is symbolically crucified.

and summer solstices and the vernal and autumnal equinoxes, thereby creating a terrestrial cross that the sun waxes and wanes upon annually. When Jesus dies on the cross, the sky turns dark, signifying the death of the sun, the death of divine life-giving light.

However, the sun's death is only temporary. Like all sun gods, Jesus Christ emerges from the tomb, resurrected. The tomb represents the three-month tomb of winter from approximately December 21st to March 21st because the sun is deceased during winter; winter is cold and cruel; darkness reigns. The sun is resurrected after three days or months at the vernal equinox (March 20th-22nd) when diurnal solar light overtakes the night with the days beginning to increase in length; in Christianity, this celebration is Easter which is named after the pagan fertility goddess Ēostre or Ostara. Jesus, embodying the sun, exits the tomb, leaving behind the famous Shroud of Turin. The symbolism

---

112 Pike, *Morals and Dogma*, page 460.

of the sun god's burial cloth is, once again, astrological-astronomical in nature. Christian lore holds there will be three Saturdays a year when the Virgin Mary (Virgo) mourns for the dying sun (Christ); as such, God's sun will be shrouded in a burial cloth of clouds and not shine at all.[113] The genuine Shroud of Turin carbon dates from approximately 1260-1390 CE, which coincides with the first appearance of the relic in France in the 1350s. This author suspects the shroud was produced by the kabalistic sorcery of the Knights Templar.

The Shroud of Turin depicts what appears to be the face of Christ; however, the facial image of Jesus owes its origins to the pagan god Serapis, a Greco-Egyptian deity. Serapis, introduced in the third century CE, was depicted as Zeus in appearance, but with Egyptian trappings, combining iconography from a large number of cults, signifying both abundance and resurrection. In *Gnostics and Their Remains*, C.W. King (1818-1888) writes "There can be no doubt that the head of Serapis, marked as the face is by a grave and pensive majesty, supplied the first idea for the conventional portraits of the Saviour [*sic*]. The Jewish prejudices of the first converts were so power that we may be sure no attempt was made to depict His countenance until some generations after all that had beheld it on earth had passed away."[114] Like Christ, Serapis is steeped in solar mythology. Several ancient authors, including Macrobius, have affirmed that Serapis was a name for the Sun, because his image so often had a halo of light about its head. In his *Oration Upon the Sovereign Sun*, Julian speaks of the deity in these words: "One Jove, one Pluto, one Sun is Serapis." In Hebrew, Serapis is *Saraph*, meaning "to blaze out" or "to blaze up." For this reason, the Jews designated one of their hierarchies of spiritual beings, *Seraphim*.[115]

The Passion of the Christ aside, these same astrotheological themes are omnipresent in other movies about Jesus. The story of Jesus is archetypal astrological lore; it reoccurs no matter how the Christ story is interpreted or depicted on screen. This iconography appears in *The King of Kings* (1927), *The Greatest Story Ever Told* (1965), *The Messiah* (1976), *Jesus of Nazareth* (1977), and *King of Kings* (1961). These films depict

---

113 Olcott, *Sun Lore of All Ages*, page 264.

114 Quoted in Hall's *The Secret Teachings of All Ages*, p. 63.

115 Hall, *ibid*, p. 59. Macrobius was a Roman writer flourishing during the early 5th century. Julian (b. 331/332 CE–d. CE 26 June 363), also known as Julian the Apostate was a Roman Emperor, philosopher, and author.

Christ's life and death, often featuring the baptism of Jesus by John the Baptist which is absent from *Passion*; the Baptizer and Christ's baptism are also astrological in origin. In the Christian mysterion, Eridanus is the astral river in which Christ the sun god is baptized, while John the Baptist personifies the sign of Aquarius, which is home to the sun from January 20th to February 18th. The Baptizer *qua* Aquarius empties his baptismal water at the end of January, signifying the coming spring rains when the earth's foliage is annually regenerated or, like the sun, is born again. Thus, to be baptized or born again, one must be dipped or doused in the symbolic waters of Aquarius. Eastern Churches, still following the old Julian Calendar, observe the Theophany Feast (Baptism of Christ) on what for most countries is January 19th symbolizing the sun *qua* Jesus entering the constellation of Aquarius, further echoing Christianity astrological motifs.

The beheading of John the Baptist is also astrological. According to the Bible (Mark 6:14-29 and Matt 14:1-12), Herold Antipas orders John's execution to appease his young stepdaughter, Salome. In the Catholic Church, the Decollation of John was recognized on August 29th. From the perspective of the northern hemisphere, Aquarius (or John's body) is close to disappearing below the horizon on August 29th at midnight. The zodiac changes: at this time, the sun exits Leo entering Virgo; Aquarius has two faint stars on its head which can barely be seen, making it appear headless, or without a body. Leo, the constellation the sun is leaving, brightest star is Regulus, which is Latin for *little king*. By decoding these analogies, it is revealed that John's execution is allegorical: Aquarius' two faint stars above the horizon represent his head being cut off, while the rest of Aquarius' body is beneath the horizon; his head is separated from his body. The star Regulus represents Herod, not an emperor but a lesser monarch making him a little king; Virgo the Virgin signifies Salome, Herod's young virginal stepdaughter, ascending in late August. Rising, Salome *qua* Virgo can make demands of her regal father, ordering the severed head of John the Baptizer, Aquarius the Water Bearer decapitated.

It is worth noting that these Christian solar symbolisms: betrayal, death, and resurrection, are duplicated in the third-degree Master Mason ritual of Blue Lodge Freemasonry. On this Masonic occultism, Scottish Rite Grand Sovereign Commander Albert Pike explains:

The murder of Hiram, his burial, and his being raised again by the Master, are symbols, both of the death, burial, and resurrection of the Redeemer; and of the death and burial in sins of the natural man, and his being raised again to a new life, or born again, by the direct action of the Redeemer; after Morality (symbolized by the Entered Apprentice's grip), and Philosophy (symbolized by the grip of the Fellowcraft), had failed to raise him. That of the Lion of the House of Judah is the strong grip, never to be broken, with which Christ, of the royal line of that House, has clasped to Himself the whole human race, and embraces them in His wide arms as closely and affectionately as brethren embrace each other on the five points of fellowship.

…The three murderers of Khir-Om (a/k/a Hiram Abif) symbolize Pontius Pilate, Caiaphas the High-Priest, and Judas Iscariot: and the three blows given him are the betrayal by the last, the refusal of Roman protection by Pilate, and the condemnation by the High-Priest. They also symbolize the blow on the ear, the scourging, and the crown of thorns. The twelve Fellowcrafts sent in search of the body are the twelve disciples, in doubt whether to believe that the Redeemer would rise from the dead.

…Such are the explanations of our Christian brethren; entitled, like those of all other Masons, to a respectful consideration.[116]

Hiram Abif, the architect of Solomon's Temple, personifies the sun because he is murdered, buried, and resurrected. Hiram is raised from his grave by the strong grip of the Lion's Paw, an occult reference to the sign of Leo the Lion since Leo is the sole house of the sun. The three murders of Hiram, Jubela, Jubelo, and Jubelum, are the houses of Libra, Scorpio, and Sagittarius, which send the sun to death during the winter months. The twelve Fellowcrafts that locate Hiram's grave parallel the Twelve Apostles because both represent the Mazzaroth[117] or the twelve houses of the zodiac. This author mentions this now because Freemasonry, its symbols,

---

116 Pike, *Morals and Dogma*, pp. 640-642.
117 The zodiac; see also Job 38:31-32: "Canst thou bind the sweet influences of Pleiades, or loose the bands of Orion? Canst thou bring forth Mazzaroth in his season? Or canst thou guide Arcturus with his sons?"

philosophies, and rituals frequently appear in cinema, although they can be difficult to discern.

The Passion of the Christ unveiled, we turn to the 1956 film *The Ten Commandments* and Judaism. The mystical symbolism of the Jewish religion will now be unveiled, as well as its relation to an astronomical phenomenon known as the Precession of the Equinoxes, or the Platonic Year. The occultism of the Platonic Year specifically reveals that Judaism is the adoration of the sun in the sign of Aries the Ram, better known as the Arian Age, while Christianity is Piscean Age sun worship.

MOSES, THE TEN COMMANDMENTS, AND THE PRECESSION OF THE EQUINOXES

The Ten Commandments is a religious epic produced and directed by Cecil B. DeMille (1889-1959), shot in VistaVision (color by Technicolor), released by Paramount Pictures. It dramatizes the biblical story of the life of Moses, an adopted Egyptian prince becoming the deliverer of his real brethren, the enslaved Hebrews, leading the Exodus to Mount Sinai where he receives the Decalogue from God. In 1957, the film was nominated for seven Academy Awards, including Best Picture, while winning the Academy Award for Best Visual Effects (John P. Fulton, 1902-1965). Before a kabalistic interpretation of this film and Judaism can occur, *The Ten Commandments* plot must be revealed to ensure the reader has full understanding of its kabalistic mysteries.

During the rule of Ramses I (Ian Keith, 1899-1960) in Ancient Egypt, the Pharaoh is informed that the Hebrew slaves believe that a recently seen star portends the arrival of a deliverer who will free them. The Hebrew Deliver, like Jesus Christ, is heralded by a star reflecting astrology and its concomitant astrotheology, anticipating the *Disciplina Arcani*. Wanting to subvert the deliverer, yet unwilling to kill all the Hebrew slaves, Ramses believes that the deliverer must be newly born, and so orders the death of every male Hebrew infant. Jewish slave Yochabel (Martha Scott, 1912-2003), along with her young daughter Miriam (Oliver Deering, 1918-1986), prepares an ark of bulrushes placing her infant son in it. Pushing the ark into the Nile, Yochabel instructs Miriam to follow it; the girl watches as it is found by Bithiah (Nina Foch, 1924-2008), the pharaoh's daughter. The recently widowed Bithiah believes that the baby was sent by her deceased husband, naming him Moses. Bithiah dismisses the concern of her servant Memnet (Judith Anderson, 1897-1992) warning her that the child's swaddling cloth was made by Levite Hebrews. Declaring that her son will be a prince of Egypt, Bithiah makes Memnet vow never to disclose his origins, although the servant secretly keeps the cloth. Thirty years later, Bithiah's brother Sethi (Cedric Hardwicke, 1893-1964) is Pharaoh and Moses (Charlton Heston, 1923-2008) is much loved by the Egyptians even more than Sethi's son Ramses II (Yul Brynner, 1920-1985). Ramses is jealous of Moses, having just returned from Ethiopia after conquering it in Sethi's name. Sethi chides Ramses for not completing the treasure city for his upcoming jubilee, while Ramses blames his failure on the stubbornness of the Hebrew slaves. At Ramses' urging, Sethi sends Moses to oversee the new city's construction, much to the chagrin of Nefretiri (Anne Baxter, 1923-1985), the princess who must marry Sethi's heir. Nefretiri is in love with Moses, sharing her passion even though Sethi has not announced whether Moses or Ramses will succeed him. In Goshen, where the new city is being built, Moses supervises Baka (Vincent Price) the cold-hearted civil engineer or operative mason. Also driving the slaves is Dathan (Edward G. Robinson, 1893-1973), a ruthless Hebrew having become an overseer. Dathan and Baka both desire Lilia (Debra Paget), a Hebrew slave in love with the stonecutter Joshua (John Derek, 1926-1998). One day Yochabel, now an elderly woman, is almost crushed by the enormous stones being used to build the city. Joshua is condemned to death for attempting to save her causing Lilia to race through the crowd to find Moses so she can plead for mercy on his behalf. Upon examining the scene, Moses frees Yochabel and Joshua, then decrees that not only should the exhausted, starving slaves have a day of rest, but they should be fed from the temple granaries. Soon the city is almost completed, and although Ramses and the greedy priests attempt to prejudice Sethi against Moses, Sethi is nevertheless pleased by Moses' progress. Sethi announces his intention to name Moses his successor, but Memnet, determined not to let a Hebrew sit on Egypt's exalted throne, reveals the truth of his birth to Nefretiri. Desperate to protect her beloved, Nefretiri kills Memnet then tries to conceal her actions. She confesses all to Moses; however, when he finds the swaddling cloth, he suspects he is a Hebrew. Astonished by the revelation, Moses seeks out Yochabel whom Nefretiri reveals is his mother. Moses finds Yochabel just as Bithiah is pleading with her to leave Egypt hastily to prevent Moses from learning the truth, but when Yochabel cannot deny that he is her son, Moses accepts his heritage.

After being welcomed by his newly found brother Aaron (John Carradine, 1906-1988) and his sister Miriam, Moses begins working in the mud pits making bricks alongside the slaves he once commanded. Although Yochabel is convinced that Moses is the deliverer, he remains doubtful about the god of the Hebrews. Later Nefretiri pleads with Moses to return to the palace before Sethi learns of his situation. Nefretiri's argument that Moses can better help his people after he is pharaoh seems to sway Moses, but he states first he must see Baka, having taken Lilia to be his house slave. Moses arrives as Baka is about to whip Joshua, having come to rescue Lilia. Infuriated by Baka's callousness, Moses kills him then reveals his true heritage to Joshua. The amazed stonecutter declares that Moses is the deliverer, but his words are overheard by Dathan, informing Ramses of the situation. On the day of Sethi's jubilee, Ramses announces that he has captured the Hebrew deliverer, causing the courtiers to be stunned when Moses, bound in chains, is led into the throne room. Shaken, Sethi asks Moses if he would lead the slaves in revolt against him, the latter confesses that he would free them if he could. The heartbroken Sethi then announces that Ramses will succeed him and will marry Nefretiri, leaving Moses' fate for Ramses to determine. Ramses escorts Moses to the edge of the vast desert, giving him the pole to which he was bound as a staff, telling him to go forth into his kingdom. Despite his lack of water and food, Moses crosses the desert to reach Midian, where he sleeps near a drinking well out of exhaustion. While getting water from the well, he is found by the daughters of the Bedouin shepherd Jethro (Eduard Franz, 1902-1983). As time passes, Moses is accepted by the Bedouins and marries Jethro's oldest daughter, Sephora (Yvonne De Carlo, 1922-2007), although he confesses that he is still tormented by thoughts of Nefretiri. Several years later, Moses and Sephora have a son, Gresham (Tommy Duran), happily tending their flocks while back in Egypt, Ramses—made Pharaoh after the Sethi's death— has a son with Nefretiri. One day, Moses spies a burning bush on Mount

Sinai, the holy mountain of God. Climbing the mountain, upon which no mortal man has set foot before, Moses finds the burning bush and hears the voice of God, ordering him to return to Egypt to lead the Hebrews to Sinai where they will receive God's laws. Although he still doubts his ability to serve God, Moses is touched by the light of the Eternal Mind; Moses will return to Egypt accompanied by his wife Sephora and Joshua having recently escaped Egypt. An Intermission divides the movie at this point.

* * * *

Upon reaching Egypt, Moses confronts Ramses demanding that his people be freed, saying that he is God's messenger. Ramses mocks Moses' proclamation that he brings the word of the God of Abraham, although Nefertiti is thrilled to see that Moses is alive. When Moses turns his staff into a serpent which swallows up the serpents produced by the Egyptian priests, Ramses dismisses his actions as a magician's trick continuing to ignore Moses' pleas to free his people, despite nine plagues set loose upon Egypt by God. The battling serpents imply the magic wand of Hermes or Mercury, combined with Thoth in Hellenistic Egypt to become Hermes Trismegistus–the god of magic and wisdom–fused with Moses during the Renaissance. Moses' snake *qua* staff eats the Egyptians' snake *qua* staff, symbolizing that his magical and occult abilities are greater than the Egyptians. The snake motif appears on the staffs of other deities, lawgivers, healers and heroes, such as that of the Greek healing god Asclepius, which has a single snake wrapped around its single pole.[118] This paganism is at Numbers 21:9, implying the Hebrews venerate a serpent god: "Moses made a serpent of brass, and put it upon a pole, and it came to pass that if a serpent had bitten any man, when he beheld the serpent of brass, he lived."[119] Regarding this magical fetish, Merlin Stone says, "And in Jerusalem itself was the serpent of bronze, said to date back to the time of Moses and treasured as a sacred idol in the temple…until about 700 BC."[120] Concerning Moses' rod and the snake-entwined caduceus, Dr. Frederick Turning from the University of Texas remarks:

---

118 D.M Murdock., *Did Moses Exist? The Myth of the Israelite Lawgiver*, p. 386.
119 *ibid.*
120 *ibid*, p. 387 citing Merlin Stone's *When God was a Woman*.

The staff of Moses is said in ancient Jewish folk tradition to have been given to him by the angel Metatron, who is the messenger spirit between God and human beings. The staff was originally a branch of the Tree of Life, from which Metatron plucked it when the world was young. Sometimes the staff itself is called Metatron; like Ningizzida, the Mesopotamian messenger god, who is depicted alternatively as a caduceus or in human form with two snakes coming out of his shoulders, the god and his symbol are confused. Metatron's rod is thus one version of the magic staff shared by many circum-Mediterranean and Asian religions, and is a direct analogue of the caduceus of Hermes/ Mercury.[121]

Consequently, the dual of serpents symbolizes that Moses, as a god of magic, is stronger than the magicians of Egypt.

Finally, after Moses turns the Nile into blood for seven days, Ramses' advisors urge him to acquiesce, but the Pharaoh insists that there must be a natural explanation for the phenomenon. When Ramses again denies the god of Moses, Moses asserts that one final terrible plague will be brought upon the Egyptians by Ramses' words. A scornful Ramses declares that his soldiers will kill all the firstborn Hebrew children. Ramses' words are turned against him when the Hebrews protect their children by painting their doors with lambs' blood. A spreading pestilence instead kills the first-born child of the Egyptians, not the Hebrews, including Ramses' son. A grief-stricken Ramses grants the slaves their freedom, but after the exodus has begun, the vengeful Nefretiri taunts Ramses until he orders his charioteers to chase after the freed slaves. Soon the Egyptian forces find the Hebrews by the Red Sea, and Dathan foments a call for Moses' death for leading them to certain doom. To demonstrate the mighty power of the Lord, Moses uses his staff to part the Red Sea and clear a path for the Hebrews, while God's pillar of fire holds back the chariots. When the fire dissipates, Ramses orders his soldiers to cross the Red Sea, but before they can reach the Hebrews, Moses restores the sea and the Egyptians drown. A defeated Ramses returns to the palace declaring to Nefretiri that the god of Moses cannot be defiled. Soon after, Moses leads his people to the base of Mt. Sinai ascending the mountain to receive God's laws. After

---

121 *ibid*, citing Frederick Turner's *Shakespeare's Twenty-first Century Economics, The Morality of Love and Money.*

forty days pass, the people grow anxious, with Dathan proclaiming that because Moses must be dead, the Hebrews should return to Egypt where at least they can find food and shelter. Dathan assures the people that if they follow an Egyptian idol, they will be safe from the Pharaoh's wrath. Thus, Aaron is ordered to craft a large golden calf. Meanwhile, on the mountain, Moses witnesses God carve the Ten Commandments on two stone tablets.

When Moses comes down from the mountain to share the laws, he is horrified to see the people worshipping the golden calf. Dathan attempts to defy Moses, but Moses throws the tablets on the ground, causing an immense earthquake that swallows the nonbelievers. Although they are forced by God's anger to wander the wilderness for forty years, Moses and his people remain strong in their faith, until one day, they come to the Jordan River and their promised land. Moses informs his family that God has told him that he shall not pass the river; however, he gives his staff and robe to Joshua, thereby anointing him the new leader. With the restored Decalogue tablets inside the Ark of the Covenant, Moses urges his people to proclaim liberty throughout the land, then waves farewell, ascending Mount Nebo.

Elements of Zoroastrianism, the religion of ancient Persia, and astrology entered Judaism during the Hebrews seventy-year exile in Babylon during the reign of Persian Emperor Cyrus the Great, thought by some Hebrews to be the prophesied Messiah. Zoroastrianism was an old Arian Age fire religion because the Babylonians were master astrologers; the science of astrology spread so rapidly among the Israelites, especially the educated classes, during this time as to create Jewish astrological literature based upon the solar calculation of time as opposed to the lunar.[122] Likewise, Judaism is an Arian Age religion just as Christianity is a Piscean Age solar faith. Hence, Judaism incorporates astrological, or astrotheological, symbolism and beliefs: the Biblical patriarch Abraham sacrifices a ram (representing Aries) in the stead of his son Isaac. Thus, the ram or lamb, became a symbol of salvation: the paschal lamb. This esoteric theology derives from an astronomical phenomenon known as the Precession of the Equinoxes. In *The Royal Arch of Enoch*, this author explained:

---

122 The lunar calendar divided the year into 12 months representing the 12 houses of the Zodiac each with 29-30 days as there are 29.5-30 days in the lunar cycle. See Sullivan's *The Royal Arch of Enoch*, Chapter III, *passim*.

Part of the Egyptian religion was the worship of the solar bull–Apis–which is, of course, Taurus the Bull–the sun in the house of Taurus circa 4300-2150 BCE. To be initiated into the Egyptian mysteries was to be instructed in the astronomical phenomena known as the Precession of the Equinoxes. The Precession is based upon the great Solar or Platonic year: that is the sun moves through each house (starting at the vernal equinox from the northern hemisphere perspective) of the zodiac; the sun remains in that house of the Zodiac approximately 2000–2160 years (due to cusps because the sun does not just leave one house and enter another), completing the entire cycle in about 25,900- 26,100 years. It is called a *precession* because the sun moves in retrograde motion through each house of the zodiac which consists of thirty degrees; it moves one degree backward every seventy-two years. The seventy-two years cycle was symbolized by Jacob's Ladder because it has seventy-two steps; Muslims receive seventy-two virgins in the afterlife. Kabbalists generate seventy-two paths, or three-letter combinations, from the Tetragrammaton; the Jesuit Kircher knew, or knew of, seventy-two languages in the world. The sun's retrograde motion occurs because the earth teeters as it orbits the sun, also known as the ecliptic; the earth's wobble explains why different constellations appear in different places in the night sky. The sun also appears to be in motion in the galaxy due to the gravitational pull from either Spica within the constellation Virgo, or Alcyone within the Pleiades. The Precession of the Equinoxes was, according to mainstream history, observed for the first time by Greek astronomer and mathematician Hipparchus (190–120 BCE) in 170 BCE, although the phenomenon must have been known to earlier Egyptian astrologers, Hebrew Kabbalists, Druidic priests, and Persian mystics as part of their respective mysteries. Hipparchus saw that a specific house of the zodiac rose behind the sun at the vernal equinox and that it slowly moved backward over time–one degree every seventy-two years. The sun thereby moved from one house of the zodiac to the next every 2000 years or so. By his calculation, the Piscean Age will end and the Age of Aquarius will begin circa 2040; the sign of Aquarius will rise with the sun at the vernal equinox, not Pisces. The 2000–2160 years the sun remains in a house of the zodiac is called an *age–the worship of the sun adopts the personality of the particular house or celestial sign it is in during that 2000-year time frame or age.* Symbolically—as will be seen—this was of great importance and is one of the great mysteries of the ancients. For the last 2000 years (0-2012 CE) the sun crossed the equator at the vernal equinox in the constellation Pisces, giving rise to the Piscean Age. Approximately two-thousand years before the Age of Pisces, the sun rose with the constellation Aries, giving rise to the Arian Age; and two-thousand years before that was the age of Taurus the Bull. The even earlier Age of Gemini was the anthropomorphizing of the third house of the zodiac: Cain and Abel were each betrothed to a twin sister; but when Cain slew his brother, the death of Abel symbolically ended the Age of Gemini, beginning Taurus. Albert Pike describes the reverence the Persians felt for Taurus and the method of astrological symbolism in vogue among them, thus: 'In Zoroaster's cave of initiation, the Sun and the Planets were represented, overhead, in gems and gold, as was also the Zodiac. The Sun appeared, emerging from the back of Taurus.' In the constellation of Taurus the Bull are to be found the Seven Sisters—the Pleiades—famous to Freemasonry as the luminous seven stars at the top of the sacred ladder. In ancient Egypt, it was during this historical time period—when the sun dwelt in the sign of Taurus—that the Apis Bull was adored as the sun god, worshipped through the animal equivalent of the celestial sign which he had impregnated with his presence at the time of its crossing into the Northern Hemisphere. This is the meaning of an ancient saying that the celestial Bull 'broke the egg of the year with his horns.' The primary religious symbol of the Taurean Age was the Ankh, the Egyptian-solar symbol of life, fashioned from the thoracic vertebra of a bull cross-sectioned. The Age of Taurus also gave rise to bull cults of the Minoans on the island of Crete. Murals in the ruined city of Knossos in Crete depict female acrobats entertaining the court by leaping over the heads of bulls. In the holy Indian text *Rigveda* (composed circa 1700-1100 BCE), the god Surya references a solar bull shining out through all the sky while the fire god Agni was likened to a bull with hair on fire. The Age of Taurus was also affected by its opposite house Scorpio, the sign of the occult, death, and rebirth, making it a strong influence in Egypt during the Age of Taurus. The Egyptians were thought to be obsessed with death and the occult sciences. Egyptian priests performed special mystical rituals and rites over the mummified bodies of the newly dead to help their spirits navigate the afterlife. Taurus gave way to Aries then Pisces; starting in approximately 2012 the sun will be one or two degrees out of Pisces, entering into the sign of Aquarius, thus beginning the humanistic-egalitarian 'Masonic' Aquarian Age. Many in the world of Freemasonry and the occult have suggested that Solomon's Temple–note that the name "Solomon," when split in half, is 'Sol/omon' or 'Sol' meaning 'sun,' and 'omon' which is an anagram for 'moon'–and the Sphinx's nose were architectural devices that precisely calculated the Precession of the Equinoxes.[123]

The end of the Taurean Age saw the rise of the Persian Empire, over which the god-king Xerxes (Rodrigo Santoro) rules in 2006's *300*. If one pays close attention, one will see that Xerxes' throne is flanked by two golden bulls, symbolizing the age of Taurus the Bull, hence Persia's strive for global dominance.[124] The Christian Faith is the adoration of the sun–Jesus *qua* the sun god, *Sol Invictus*–in the solar Age of Pisces the Fishes. Jesus feeds his five thousand followers with two fishes in the Gospel accounts, symbolizing the sun residing in the house of the two fishes, the Piscean Age. Christ was born of a virgin because Virgo the Virgin is the opposite house of Pisces; as such, the priests and servants of Christianity, both male and female (nuns; in Aramaic nun means *fish*), remain celibate virgins. Christ washes feet and has his feet washed because Pisces rules of the feet. Christ encourages his apostles to be watery Piscean fishers of men since Pisces is a water sign; the first Pope, Simon called Peter, was a fisherman.[125]

---

123 See Sullivan's *The Royal Arch of Enoch*, Chapter III, "Esoteric Masonry."

124 See Sullivan's *Cinema Symbolism*, Introduction.

125 cf. the solar myth of the Fisher King. In Arthurian legend, the Fisher King, or the Wounded King (cf. the sun in winter), is the latest in a long line charged with keeping the Holy Grail. Versions of his story vary widely, but he is always wounded in the legs or groin and incapable of moving on his own. In the Fisher King legends, he becomes impotent and unable to perform his task himself, and he also becomes unable to father or support a next generation to carry on after his death. His kingdom suffers as he does, his impotence affecting the fertility of the land and reducing it to a barren wasteland. All he is able to do is fish in the river near his castle, Corbenic, and wait for someone who might be able to heal him. Healing involves the expectation of the use of sorcery and magic. Knights travel from many lands to heal the Fisher King, but only the chosen can accomplish the feat. This is Percival in earlier stories; in later versions, he is joined by Galahad and Bors. His name "Fisher

Old Testament Judaism was the adoration of the sun in the old former house of Aries the Ram, coming after the Taurean Age. Aries is a fire sign, and its earmarks can be found all over the Hebrew religion and the film *The Ten Commandments*. If Christ is the embodiment of the sun in the house of Pisces, then the lawgiver Moses (c.a.1393?-1273? BCE) personifies the sun residing in the house of Aries the Ram. For example, Moses communicates with deity via a burning bush since Aries is a fire sign. The burning bush also symbolizes the sun since it is a fiery orb. The Hebrews protect their houses with lambs' blood so that death and pestilence will pass over their house; the lambs' blood signifies the holy paschal lamb, or the constellation Aries. The Passover holiday celebrates the sun passing over the equator at the vernal equinox heading towards its apex in the northern hemisphere: the summer solstice. Hence, the Judeo-Christian spring festivals of Passover and Easter always coincide with the vernal equinox of March 20th-22nd when the sun, because of the ecliptic, is resurrected from the three-month tomb of winter; daylight overtakes the darkness of night. In Judaism, the Exodus-Promised Land tale signifies the transition between winter and spring (dark giving way to light) demonstrated by several factors, including the Biblical establishment of the celebration of Passover and New Year at the vernal equinox: "You shall keep the feast of unleavened bread; as I commanded you, you shall eat unleavened bread for seven days at the appointed time in the month of Abib, for in it you came out of Egypt (Exodus 23:15)" and "This month shall be for you the beginning of months; it shall be the first month of the year for you (Exodus 12:2)."[126] As it is called in the Passover passage, the first month of the year (Aries is the first house of the zodiac because it is the sign that follows immediately after the vernal equinox) is named at Exodus 13:4 as *Abib*, later styled *Nisan* and running from March to April. The Hebrew word ביבא " *'abiyb*" means 1) fresh, young barley ears, barley, and 2) month of ear-forming, of greening of crop, of growing green Abib. It is the month of

---

King" suggests the watery Age of Pisces; this legend is intertwined in the cinematic version of the Arthurian Legend *Excalibur* when Arthur–personifying the sun–is in a state of perpetual decay (cf. winter months) towards the end of the film. King Arthur health is restored when he drinks from the Holy Grail (cf. Aquarius' water pitcher) and rides forth from his castle at the vernal equinox. See Sullivan's *The Royal Arch of Enoch*, Chapter XV.

126 See D.M. Murdock's *Did Moses Exist?*, p. 345.

Exodus and Passover, March or April, Easter in Christianity.[127] Thus, the month of *Abib* or *Aviv* is named for its vernal fertility, the reawakening of life after the death of winter. Symbolically, the Hebrews are given new life in the Promised Land (cf. life, rebirth) after leaving behind their bondage (cf. winter, stagnation) in Egypt.

During the Exodus, the Hebrews are protected by a pillar of fire against pharaoh's chariot because, again, Aries is a fire sign. Moses–personifying the sun in Aries–receives the new Arian Age law upon Mount Sinai then descends the mountain to present it to the Hebrews. Moses *qua* Aries is

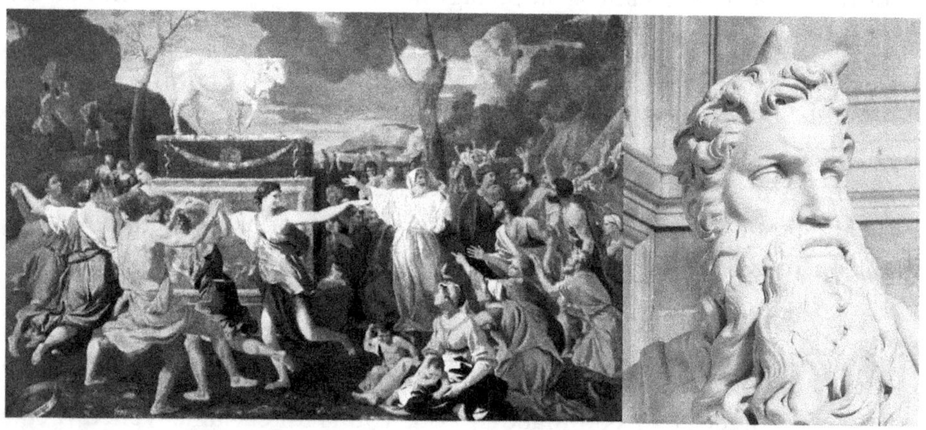

(Left) *The Adoration of the Golden Calf* by Nicolas Poussin (1594-1665) oil on canvas produced between 1633 and 1634. The painting depicts the Hebrews, led by Aaron, worshipping the Egyptian Apis Bull, the icon of the old Taurean Age, thus incurring the wrath of Aries the Ram *qua* Moses. Moses orders the killing of the Israelites worshipping Aaron's golden calf (cf. Taurus and Apis) at Exodus 32:27. (Right) *Moses* by Michelangelo (1475-1564) sculpture (ca. 1513-1515) in the Vatican depicts Moses with the horns of Aries the Ram protruding from his head.

angered because the Hebrews are still worshipping the symbol of the old age of Taurus the Bull, a golden calf. The calf is gold symbolizing the brilliant yellow glow of the sun. Pre-Reformation iconography of Moses often depicts him with rams' horns representing Moses as a solar Arian avatar because he is the Judeo law bringer of the Arian Age.[128] Incorporating Arian Age kabalistic symbolism, a ram's horn, or Shofar, is blown in synagogue services on Rosh Hashanah and Yom Kippur, and the Shofar is

---

127 *ibid.*

128 Exodus 34: 29-35. From the Hebrew *keren* which literally means *grew horns*, Moses face was also described as *cornuta* (horned) in the Latin Vulgate translation of Exodus.

mentioned frequently in the Hebrew Bible (cf. Arian Age solar adoration), the Talmud and rabbinic literature; the blast of a Shofar emanating from the thick cloud on Mount Sinai made the Israelites tremble in awe (Exodus 19:16). Watch closely in *The Ten Commandments* when Moses crafts a Shofar with his son before ascending the holy mountain where it will be revealed that he is the Hebrew's deliverer. In Judaism there are twelve Tribes of Israel symbolizing the twelve houses of the zodiac, anticipating the Christian Mysteries which transforms the twelve signs into the Twelve Apostles. Although one cannot stare at the sun, one can gaze at the moon; thus, Judaism incorporates lunar elements within its worship: all Jewish holidays begin at sunset when the sun is below the horizon with the moon visible. Lunar references can be found in the Old Testament at Isaiah 66:23, "And it shall come to pass, (that) from one new moon to another, and from one Sabbath to another, shall all flesh come to worship before me, saith the Lord." and again at Psalm 89:37, "It shall be established for ever as the moon, and (as) a faithful witness in heaven. Selah."

Judaism mirrors elements of the Egyptian religion because the Hebrews were slaves of the Egyptians, so imitating their worship should come as no surprise. During the Exodus, Moses explains that the consuming unleavened bread is the food of haste because fleeing Egypt, they did not have time to let their bread rise. However, the Egyptian religion had its own unleavened bread in the form of buns, which were "Unleavened, like the shewbread of the Hebrews, eaten by priests only, and offered to them in piles."[129] Plagiarizing the Egyptian Mysteries, the Hebrew Ten Commandments, Chapter Twenty of the Book of Exodus, are borrowed from the Egyptian Book of the Dead. The Egyptian Book of the Dead is an ancient funerary text used from the beginning of the New Kingdom (around 1550 BCE) to around 50 BCE. The book consists of magic spells intended to assist a dead person's journey through the Duat, or underworld, and into the afterlife. Except for the first two commandments that forbid the Hebrews from worshipping other gods or genuflecting before graven images, and a third that demands them to honor their parents, the remaining

---

129 See Murdock's *Did Moses Exist?* p. 89, citing Gerald Massey's *A Book of the Beginnings*, vol. 2, (1881), New York: Cosimo Classics, 2007; and E.A. Wallis Budge's *A Hieroglyphic Vocabulary to the Book of the Dead*, New York: Dover, 1991.

seven are found in Chapter 125 of the Book of the Dead; here they are compared with the Egyptian originals in italics:

Thou shalt not take the name of the Lord thy God in vain.
I have not acted deceitfully.

Remember the Sabbath day, to keep it holy.
I have not committed any sin against purity.

Thou shalt not kill.
I have not slain man or woman.

Thou shalt not commit adultery.
I have not defiled the wife of a man.

Thou shalt not steal.
I have not committed theft.

Thou shalt not bear false witness against thy neighbor.
I have not uttered falsehood.

Thou shalt not covet thy neighbor's wife.
I have not defiled the wife of a man.

The tablets upon which were inscribed the Ten Commandments were stored in the Ark of the Covenant, which, like the Decalogue itself, is also of Egyptian origin. On this comparative esoterica, comparative religion expert Dorothy M. Murdock (pen-name Acharya S, 1960-2015) provides the following:

Regarding the …'Ark of the Covenant,' for which so many have sought in vain, the fact is that numerous tribal gods of the Levant and Egypt had their arks in which to ride while carried by their followers. The 'Jewish' ark of the covenant was 'of classical Egyptian design,' sharing many measurements and element with numerous Egyptian arks. Osiris' ark 'was of the *same* size as the Jewish ark [and] was carried upon men's shoulders in the sacred procession.' Ancient Egyptian priests paraded a shrine to the Oracle of the sun god Ham/Am that was a 'boat' or 'ship' (ark) in which the God was carried. The god Dionysus, widely worshipped for centuries around the Mediterranean, was carried about in a 'ship car' or bark. In the Indian sun worship, sacred temple images were called 'Arcas,' while the Tibetans to this day carry arks in holy procession. The gods of Mexico and the goddesses of Greece were likewise borne in ritual arks. The 'ark of the covenant' is yet another common theme, present in a variety of cultures, and no single, all-powerful 'Jewish' ark is to be found anywhere.[130]

In 1981's *Raiders of the Lost Ark*, the Hebrew Ark of the Covenant is found in the ruins of the Egyptian city Tanis buried in a subterranean vault called the Well of the Souls. It seems the filmmakers, by making the final resting place of the Hebrew Ark in Egypt, were well of aware of the Ark's secret relationship to Egyptian mythology.

Lastly, the idea of a divine-solar lawgiver passing the law to a messianic, Moses-like figure predates Moses and the Hebrew religion. The Babylonian-Amorite king Hammurabi (d. 1750 BCE), allegedly received his sacred law (a/k/a The Code of Hammurabi) from Shamash. Shamash was the Sumerian-Babylonian sun god and divine lawgiver whose worship extended back some 5000 years to the kings of Ur.[131] Ur dates from the Ubaid period circa 3800 BCE, and is recorded in written history as a City State from the twenty-sixth century BCE, its first recorded king being Mesh-Ane-pada. In Ur itself, Shamash was also worshipped in early days by the side of the moon god.[132] Eannatum, of the dynasty of Isin (ca. 2800 BCE), tells of two temples erected to him at that place; and still a third edifice, sacred to both Nannar (the moon god) and Shamash at Ur, is referred to by a king of the Larsa dynasty, Rim-Sin (ca. 2300 BCE).[133] Shamash's name itself derives from the Babylonian word for sun, *shamshu*, which indicates that the later Hebrew word for the sun, שמש *sh.m.sh*, actually reflects the Babylonian solar deity.[134] As a divine lawgiver, Shamash was

130 Acharya S, *Suns of God: Krishna, Buddha, and Christ Unveiled*, page 123.
131 Murdock, *Did Moses Exist?*, p. 392.
132 *ibid*, citing Morris Jastow's *The Religion of Babylonia and Assyria*, Boston: Ginn & Company, 1898.
133 *ibid*, no longer citing Jastow.
134 Murdock, *ibid*, page 393.

also a bringer of light, legislator, and upholder of law and order. The Code of Hammurabi was provided to the Babylonian lawgiver by the sun god Shamash in a similar manner in which Moses was said to receive the Ten Commandments from the deity Yahweh via a fiery orb, a burning bush (cf. the sun).[135] These parallels are not a coincidence. On this solar symbolism, Dr. Robert M. Price explains:

> ...The basic Moses mytheme is that of the sun (god) which emerges from the tent of concealment, the night, and bestows commandments upon a king. The sun is also the source of both death (by sunstroke) and healing. Psalm 19...speaks of the sun's glorious emergence from his tent, then extols the glory of the commandments, as...the sun was the origin of the law. We also see this atop the famous stone table of Hammurabi's Code which shows the emperor receiving the law from the hand of Shamash the sun god. Moses was originally the law-giving sun, as we can still glimpse in Exodus 34:29-35, where Moses emerges from the tent of a meeting with new commandments, and with his face shining, not coincidentally, like the sun! And like Apollo, he can inflict flaming doom or heal it (Numbers 21:4-9) and even bears the caduceus like Apollo...[136]

Based on all the following, it is clear the film *The Ten Commandments* and the Old Testament are more Egyptian, astral, solar, and Babylonian in nature than Hebrew and actual Biblical history.

Know that occult, solar, and astral metaphors are not exclusive to religious films about Moses and Jesus; instead solar, planetary, and astral archetypes transcend Hollywood. If a movie has Judeo-Christian religious overtones, these astrotheological undercurrents are not far behind. For instance, in *Cinema Symbolism: A Guide to Esoteric Imagery in Popular Movies* the eschatology and the related astral symbolisms of *The Omen* trilogy were discussed and dissected; this author does not want to rehash that material here. The Omen movies deal with the birth and downfall of the Antichrist from the Book of Revelation which heralds the apocalypse. Echoing this doomsday philosophy, the film *Knowing* (2009) displays astral-occult symbolism suggesting this End of Days scenario. The movie

---

135 *ibid*, page 394.
136 See Robert M. Price's "Of Myth and Men," *Free Inquiry*. Amherst, New York, 1999-2000.

revolves around the destruction of the world by fire and the repopulation of a new planet by new age children becoming the new world's kabalistic Adam and Eve. The film opens with MIT professor John Koestler (Nicolas Cage) and his young son Caleb (Chandler Canterbury) observing the planet Saturn through an astronomical telescope. Saturn allegorically announces the coming destruction of the earth because Saturn (or Kronos) associates with death and, by default, destruction because Saturn rules the house of Capricorn (December 22nd-January 19th) when the sun is symbolically dead, being at its lowest demarcation in the northern hemisphere. According to the Bible, the earth will be destroyed a by fire its second time because of God's covenant with man not to destroy the earth by water again (cf. the flood of Noah) at Genesis 9:11.[137] Professor Koestler is the first to realize that the earth will be annihilated by the sun's rays via solar flares; Koestler associates himself with the omnipresent sun and, by default, the mythological Apollo while his girlfriend, Diana Wayland (Rose Byrne), bears the name of the solar god's lunar sister, *Diana*. It will be Diana's young daughter, Abby (Lara Robinson), who will be taken by the extra-terrestrials along with Koestler's son, Caleb, to repopulate a new planet, restarting humanity. Caleb and Abby personify the children of Apollo (Sun) and Diana (Moon)–the divine masculine and sacred feminine–becoming the new Adam and Eve. The children are the offspring of sun and the moon eventually restarting humanity by performing the *Chymical Wedding of Christian Rosenkreutz* or *Chymische Hochzeit Christiani Rosencreutz* (edited 1616) which documents the numinous union of the sun and moon; its anonymous authorship is attributed to Rosicrucian Johann Valentin Andreae (1586-1654). At *Knowing*'s conclusion, the neo-Adam and neo-Eve are seen running towards a great Tree as an emanation of the kabalistic Tree of Life, or the Tree of Wisdom. In the controversial *I Enoch*, it is explained to the Biblical patriarch Enoch[138] the intrinsic symbolism of the Tree and the *sefirot*:

---

137 Genesis 9:11: "And I will establish my covenant with you; neither shall all flesh be cut off any more by the waters of a flood; neither shall there any more be a flood to destroy the earth."

138 Enoch is one of two Biblical patriarchs to have never experienced a physical death having been transported into Heaven at Genesis 5:24; the Prophet Elijah is the other. Having never died, Enoch and Elijah are the "Two Witnesses" to Revelation or the End of Days. Recently they have been transformed into Ichabod Crane (Tom Mison) and Lt. Abbie Mills (Nicole Beharie) in the Fox televised Supernatural-Masonic drama *Sleepy Hollow*, see Chapter VI.

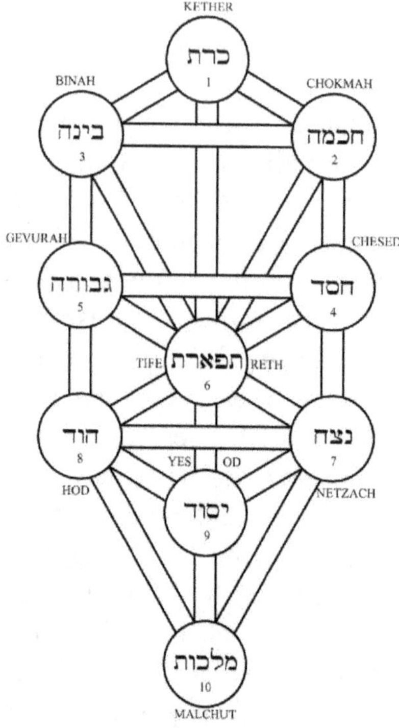

The Hebrew-Kabbalistic Tree of Life is the source of all knowledge both profane and esoteric. The *sefirot* are emanations of the mystical godhead, *Ein Sof.* In the Jewish Kabbalist view, both of the two trees in the Biblical Garden of Eden (Genesis 2:9) the Tree of Knowledge (Wisdom) of Good and Evil and the Tree of Life, were alternative perspectives of the *sefirot* and the full array of ten, as seen respectively from the last *sefirah*, *Malkuth*, and the middle *sefirah*, *Tiferet*.

Then I said: 'How beautiful is the tree, and how attractive is its look!' Then Raphael the holy angel, who was with me, answered me and said: 'This is the tree of wisdom, of which your father of old and your mother of old, who were your progenitors, have eaten, and they learned wisdom and their eyes were opened, and they knew that they were naked and they were driven out of the garden.'[139]

Eve bit from the allegorical apple, partaking of the *sefirot*, gaining gnosis. Caleb and Abby are now ready to repopulate this new planet, guided by divine wisdom, represented by the kabalistic tree. This scene echoes another 2009 film, *The Lovely Bones* directed by Peter Jackson. Toward the end, the spirit of Susie Salmon is about to enter Heaven. She has been dwelling in a Purgatory-like state, the In-Between, which is a product of her imagination and life experiences. At the entrance to Heaven stands a majestic Enochic Tree of Life *qua* Wisdom, symbolizing divine enlightenment because Susie has finally learned to move on by freeing herself from earthly memories and attachments, leaving her self-imposed Purgatory. She can now finally abandon the hylic world for a spiritual state, the Gnostic pleroma, the Christian Heaven.

---

139 *I Enoch* 32:6

CHAPTER II

ALAN MOORE PRESENTS

"Below the skin of history are London's veins. These symbols, the mitre, the pentacle star, even someone as ignorant and degenerate as you can sense that they course with energy and meaning.
I am that meaning. I am that energy. One day men will look back and say I gave birth to the twentieth century."
– Sir William Gull, *From Hell*, 2001

"But again, truth be told, if you're looking
for the guilty you need only look into a mirror."
– V, *V for Vendetta*, 2005.

"I am looking at the stars. They are so far away, and their light takes so long to reach us. All we ever see of stars is their old photographs."
– Dr. Manhattan a/k/a Jon Osterman, *Watchmen*, 2009.

"No man amongst you is fit to judge the mighty art
that I have wrought. Your rituals are empty oaths you neither understand nor live by. The Great Architect speaks to me. He is the balance where my deeds are weighed and judged, not you."
– Sir William Gull, *From Hell*, 2001.

"Accidents happen. That's what everyone says. But in a quantum universe there are no such things as accidents, only possibilities and probabilities folded into existence by perception."
– Dr. Manhattan a/k/a Jon Osterman, *Watchmen*, 2009

"A building is a symbol, as is the act of destroying it. Symbols are given power by people. Alone, a symbol is meaningless, but with enough people, blowing up a building can change the world."
– V, *V for Vendetta*, 2005

lan Moor is an English writer primarily known for his work in graphic novels which include *Watchmen* (1986-1987), *V for Vendetta* (1982-1989), *Batman: The Killing Joke* (1988), *The League of Extraordinary Gentlemen* (1999-2007), *Hellblazer*, also known as *John Constantine, Hellblazer* (1988-2013), and *From Hell* (1999 collected edition). Frequently described as the best graphic novel writer in history, he has also been called "One of the most important British writers of the last fifty years" (see Ethan Doyle-White, "Occultic World of Alan Moore," *Pentacle*, Summer 2009, p. 29). Moore is an occultist, pagan, ceremonial magician, and anarchist, including these and other nihilistic themes in his works *From Hell*, *Watchmen*, and *V for Vendetta*; in his spare time, he performs avant-garde spoken workings such as *The Moon and Serpent Grand Egyptian Theatre of Marvels* (1996), *Snakes and Ladders* (2001), and *Angel Passage* (2001) some of which have been released on compact disc. Despite his personal objections, his graphic novels have been made into Hollywood films and three of them are this chapter's subject matter. As one may expect, the movies based on Moore's stories serve up a heavy dose of the esoteric, the mystical, government conspiracies, alchemy, Gnosticism, and the occult.

CHAOS MAGICK AND ALCHEMICAL FREEMASONRY IN FROM HELL

In the 1981 film *Excalibur*, the wizard Merlin (Nigel Williamson, 1936-2011), a reinvention of Hermes Trismegistus, performs alchemical sorcery to affect the future. Merlin understands that King Uther Pendragon (Gabriel Byrne) cannot subdue his passions, he cannot restrain his lust for his rival's wife Igraine (Katrine Boorman), making it impossible for him to unify the Kingdom. Merlin develops a plan: he invokes chaos to bring stability, to foster an irenic new order. While his rival, the Duke of Cornwall (Corin Redgrave, 1939-2010), and his armies are attacking Uther's encampment, Merlin performs sorcery by conjuring the alchemical Dragon's Breath via the Charm of Making (cf. the philosopher's stone) to change Uther into the semblance of the Duke. Sustained by his lust, Uther magically rides his steed over Cornwall's moat to his castle arriving as the latter; Uther changes into the appearance of his rival. He makes love to Igraine, becoming pregnant, eventually birthing the future King Arthur. Merlin's alchemy is successful; not only has he changed Uther into Cornwall but he has transmuted the future by alchemically altering the present so that Igraine will give birth to the future king. Merlin says, "The future has taken root in the present. It is done." It will be King Arthur, not Uther, who will unite the land forging a prosperous New World Order; put another way, Merlin's alchemy will bring Arthurian order from Uther's chaos. In *From Hell*, Jack the Ripper also invokes chaos but not to bring stability, but to wrought destruction and death. Like Merlin, Jack the Ripper also intends to affect the future; only the Ripper's vision is deliciously evil, not virtuous.

From Hell, the comics and film, originate from the book *Jack the Ripper: The Final Solution* (1976) by Stephen Knight (1951-1985). The book's thesis is that the Ripper murders were part of a conspiracy between Freemasons and the British Royal Family, a claim not accepted by historians, what I consider to be fiction. Knight's book also provided the raw material for the 1979 film *Murder by Decree*, which sees Sherlock Holmes (Christopher Plummer) track down Jack the Ripper, only to have his investigation circumvented by a grand Masonic conspiracy. *From Hell* opens in 1888 wherein Mary Kelly (Heather Graham) and her close circle of friends, all London-East End prostitutes, trudge through unrelenting daily misery. The other prostitutes are Martha Tabram (Samantha Spiro), "Dark" Annie Chapman (Katrin Cartlidge, 1961-2002), Liz Stride (Susan Lynch), Mary Ann "Polly" Nichols (Annabelle Apsion), and Kate Eddows (Lesley Sharp). When their friend Ann Crook (Joanna Page) is kidnapped, they are drawn into a dark Masonic scheme with links to the British Royals, including Queen Victoria (Liz Moscrop). The kidnapping is soon followed by the murder of Tabram making it apparent that the women are being systemically attacked one by one, horrifically mutilated post-mortem.

The murder of Tabram and her companions grabs the attention of Whitechapel Police Inspector Frederick Abberline (Johnny Depp), a brilliant yet troubled man whose police work is often aided by prophetic visions. Abberline's investigations reveal the macabre and gruesome murders display occult and ritualistic undertones, while also suggesting an educated person is responsible due to the surgical methodology used. Inspector

Abberline consults Sir William Gull (Ian Holm), a physician to the Royal Family, drawing on his experience and knowledge of medicine. Abberline also locates Ann Crook in a workhouse, having been lobotomized after doctors supposedly found her to be insane, but it is implied this was done to silence her. These findings, coupled with his superiors impeding his investigations, point to a darker, organized conspiracy. Abberline becomes deeply involved with the case, which takes on personal meaning to him when he and Mary begin to fall in love.

Abberline deduces that a Masonic influence is present in the crimes. His superior Sir Charles Warren (Ian Richardson, 1934-2007), a Freemason himself, then makes a direct intervention suspending Abberline. The Masons are also operating in the higher levels of government, namely the Special Branch of the Metropolitan Police, which is under the aegis of Freemason Benjamin "Ben" Kidney (Terence Harvey), an imposing figure striking fear in all he meets. After investigating the Freemasons and their machinations, Abberline deduces that they are involved; it is then revealed that Sir William Gull is Jack the Ripper. He has been brutally killing the witnesses of painter Albert Sickert's (Mark Dexter) forbidden Catholic marriage to Crook, birthing his legitimate daughter, Alice. It turns out Sickert[140] is Prince Edward Albert Victor, Duke of Clarence, grandson of reigning Queen Victoria and therefore Alice, a Catholic, is heiress to the British Empire in violation of the Act of Settlement of 1701 which forbids Roman Catholics from sitting on the English throne. Gull is a loyal

Freemason,[141] and his increasingly threatening behavior lends insight into his criminal but calculated mind. Rather than publicly charge Gull, the Freemasons decide to lobotomize Gull to protect the Royal Family from

---

140 *From Hell* combines the Duke of Clarence with artist Walter Sickert (1860-1942) into one person. Walter Richard Sickert, born in Munich, Germany, was a painter, printmaker, and a member of the Camden Town Group in London. He was an important influence on distinctively British styles of avant-garde art in the 20th century. Sickert was a cosmopolitan and eccentric who often favored ordinary people and urban scenes as his subjects. His oeuvre also included portraits of well-known personalities and images derived from press photographs. He is considered a prominent figure in the transition from Impressionism to Modernism. Sickert took a keen interest in the crimes of Jack the Ripper and believed he had lodged in a room used by the infamous serial killer. Sickert did a painting of the room and titled it "Jack the Ripper's Bedroom." It shows a dark, melancholy room with most details obscured. This painting now resides in the Manchester City Art Gallery in Manchester. In *From Hell*, the Duke of Clarence is an artist echoing Sickert who is having a secret affair with one of Mary Kelley's circle of friends.

141 There is no evidence suggesting the historical Sir William Gull (1816-1890) was a Freemason.

the scandal. Gull is unrepentant and defiant, stating he has no equal among men. To end his ravings, Gull is lobotomized, making him an invalid just like Ann Crook. Mary Kelly does not die; Gull earlier mistook Liz Stride's lesbian protégé Ada (Estelle Skornik) for Mary and, unbeknownst, butchered her instead. Having escaped the Ripper, it is revealed that Kelly lives with young Alice in a cottage on a cliff by the sea. Inspector Abberline is found dead from an opium overdose, knowing he can never see Mary again without endangering her because the Freemasons are always watching.

The film presents a Masonic-led conspiracy working within the British government to silence those privy to a Catholic marriage between a future monarch, the Duke of Clarence, and a Catholic prostitute, Ann Crook. The entire film is an adroitly concealed alchemical-magical-Freemasonic formula: the Ripper's murders are alchemical sorcery—chaos magic—designed to create the negative energy necessary to transmute the upcoming twentieth century. Gull foretells that he will be remembered as the man who "gave birth to the twentieth century," anticipating its related horrors, most notably those of World War I (1914-1918, cf. Battle of the Somme) and World War II (1939-1945), the Holocaust and atomic destruction of Japan. Gull's twentieth century will also see the Korean War (1950-1953); the Vietnam War (1955-1975); the totalitarian, murderous regimes and of Joseph Stalin (1878-1953) and Mao Tse-tung (1893-1976); the Great Depression (1929-1939); the assassination of John F. Kennedy (1917-1963); Jim Jones (1931-1978) and the Jonestown mass suicide on November 18th, 1978; Charles Mason and Helter Skelter, John Wayne Gacy (1942-1994), David "Son of Sam" Berkowitz, and Jeffrey Dahmer (1960-1994). These are but some of the terrors wrought by the Ripper's mighty art. Gull and his alter ego the Ripper are a darker, more sinister version of the Magician or Juggler of the Major Arcana of the Tarot. Recalling the Introduction, the Juggler is Mercury,[142] a Roman deity and an essential element necessary to perform alchemy. Thus, Jack the Ripper becomes the alchemical substance:[143] an evil, clever Mercurius (not Hermes Trismegistus), echoing Crowley's notions of the *Unconscious Will*,[144] fusing Masonic ritualistic punishments

---

142 Aleister Crowley, *The Book of Thoth*, p. 69.

143 *ibid*, p. 70.

144 *Ibid*. Crowley (a/k/a Master Therion) explains the mercurial nature of the Juggler or the Magician, "If he cannot attain his ends by fair means, he does it by foul. The legends of the youthful Mercury are therefore legends of cunning. He cannot be understood, because he is the Unconscious

with gruesome murder, creating powerful chaos magic, or *magick*, necessary to affect alchemical, supernatural, and global transformation: Jack the Ripper will transmute or *birth* the twentieth century. Originating in England in the mid-1970s, chaos magic(k) is a school of the modern magical tradition which emphasizes the pragmatic use of belief systems and the creation of new and unorthodox methods to produce a mystical effect or outcome. As such, the Ripper's murders are chaotic and horrid reenactments of Masonic penalties; the murders of the prostitutes are reenactments of the executions of Jubela, Jubelo, and Jubelum, the three traitors that assassinate Hiram Abif in the third-degree Master Mason ritual. The merging of Masonic rituals with murder is designed to conjure negative alchemical transition; they are black chaos magick designed to perpetuate malignancy.

From Hell is an alchemical movie, with the colors of Renaissance alchemy present, signifying the Ripper's diabolical sorcery. The film's overuse of red, the *rubedo*, denotes the alchemical completion of the Ripper's grim process. As foreboding music plays, *From Hell's* striking red letters appear over a pitch-black background, while a blood-red sunset dramatically opens the film. The *rubedo* is ubiquitous; for example, the audience is introduced to Mary Kelly and her flaming red hair while fellow prostitute Liz Stride wears a red dress during the entire film. Inspector Abberline is introduced via the color red: the opium den is adorned with red curtains while he rests on a bed atop a red duvet with a red pillow. Sir William Gull and his Jungian darker self, Jack the Ripper, first appear on film surrounded by the color red: the Ripper is silhouetted against a red backdrop, and the interior of his carriage is lined with red when he shows Cleopatra's Needle to Polly Nichols. The Ripper consumes raw meat and red wine while the fabric that lines his portable amputation kit is red. Near the film's conclusion, Mary Kelly is seen wearing a red corset and slip while her black stockings are upheld by red garters; red candles burn bedside in her Miller's Court apartment, and Jack the Ripper's bloodbaths are key plot devices. This occult color scheme symbolizes alchemical change; thus, the grand purpose of the Ripper's grisly Masonic murders, his occult formula, his chaos magick, are to affect the upcoming twentieth century negatively by

---

Will. His position on the Tree of Life shows the third Sephira, Binah, Understanding, as not yet formulated; still less the false Sephira, Da'ath, knowledge."

transmuting positive to negative, light to darkness, life to death, good to evil. This is Jack the Ripper's chaotic, yet effective, master plan.

The alchemical *nigredo*, darkness, melancholic decay, is represented by Sir William Gull-Jack the Ripper and his ghastly murders; he moves amongst the downtrodden stalking his victims in Whitechapel's shadows. The Ripper is Saturn personified: blackness, sadness, depression, a dark craftsman, a mason.[145] He is not a spilt-personality (a/k/a Dissociative Identity Disorder, DID) because the Ripper and Gull are one and the same; Gull knows when he is the Ripper and vice versa. Gull nevertheless exhibits a demonic persona which, in Hebrew folklore, is termed *dibbuk*. Common to the Second Temple and Talmudic periods, a *dibbuk* is an evil spirit or a lost soul which enters a living person, cleaves his (or her) soul, causes mental illness, speaks through his (or her) mouth, representing a separate personality.[146] When questioned by Abberline about Freemasonry, Gull exhibits all these symptoms transforming him into another diabolical figure: Jack the Ripper. The Ripper personifies death, an allegorical Grim Reaper, wearing a sleek black tuxedo, cape and top hat, killing his prey in the most terrifying and morbid manners imaginable. The *albedo*–lunar whiteness–to his darkness are personified by Mary Kelly and her circle of female friends, the Whitechapel prostitutes. Kelly, specifically, is a positive waxing influence on Abberline. She shines her nocturnal light upon him, seemingly making his premonitions more acute; they fall in love, and he begins to suspect a Masonic-Government conspiracy is behind the Ripper killings. On the other hand, the Ripper is destroying Luna; he is methodically killing prostitutes, mutilating their genitals to annihilate their

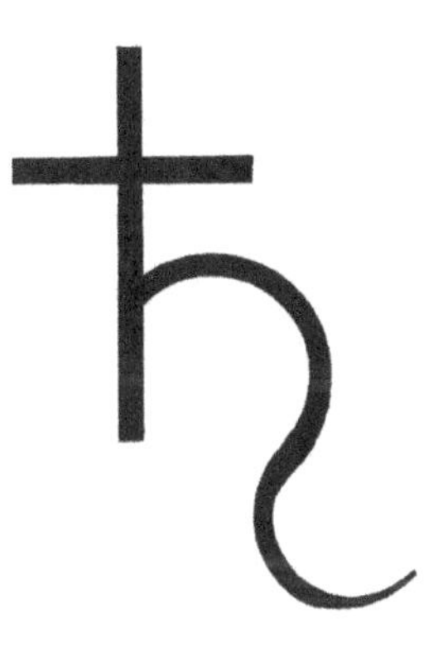

As the ruler of Capricorn, the planet Saturn represents death and melancholia because the sun is at its weakest in northern hemisphere when the house of Capricorn is exalted. The curved lower portion resembles a sickle, becoming the Grim Reaper's wicked scythe, used by Death to mow down human life.

---

145 cf. Frances Yates' *The Occult Philosophy in the Elizabethan Age*, pp. 60-61.

146 See Scholem's *Kabbalah*, p. 349; Scholem explains, "The term appears neither in talmudic literature nor in the Kabbalah, …The term was introduced into literature only in the 17th century from the spoken language of German and Polish Jews. It is an abbreviation of *dibbuk me-ru'ah ra'ha* ('a cleavage of an evil spirit'), or *dibbuk min ha-hizonim* ('*dibbuk* from the demonic side'), which is found in man."

sexuality. Jack the Ripper is destroying the positive influence of the sacred feminine upon the upcoming century. The prostitutes' putrefying bodies are prominently displayed throughout the film, signifying degradation of the feminine. Part of the Ripper's chaos magick is to impersonate destructive *nigredo* to eradicate the *albedo.* As such, the placement of the Ripper's victims and the arrangement of the coins at Dark Annie's feet form a pentacle star, or pentagram, the Masonic symbol for the sacred feminine.

In the Blue Lodge, the name of God, the Tetragrammaton, is lost with the murder of Hiram Abif, the chief architect of Solomon's Temple, during the third-degree ritual. Upon Hiram's resurrection, a substitute word is whispered in the candidate's ear in a low breath, having been rebirthed to the light. To communicate the substitute word to the new brother, the five points of fellowship must be formed, creating a symbolic pentagram. The pentagram in Freemasonry is called the Blazing Star, which symbolizes the Egyptian Dog Star Sirius, explained by Albert Pike in his book *Morals and Dogma of the Ancient and Accepted Scottish Rite of Freemasonry* (1871). Pike writes, "The Ancient Astronomers saw all the great Symbols of Masonry in the Stars. Sirius still glitters in our Lodges as the Blazing Star, (*l'Etoile Flamboyante*)"[147] and "The Star which guided them is that same Blazing Star, the image whereof we find in all initiations. To the Alchemist it is the sign of Quintessence; to the Magists, the Grand Arcanum; to the Kabalists, the Sacred Pentagram."[148] Sirius, the brightest star (hence Blazing Star) in the nighttime sky, was adored as the goddess Isis in the Egyptian Mysteries. Isis secretly possessed the secret name of Amun-Ra, the supreme Egyptian solar deity, which she spoke to procure magic to raise her brother-husband Osiris from the grave. Masonic ritual parallels this lore when the candidate is raised from the grave with a *substitute word*, communicated by creating five points or a pentagram, forging a nexus to Sirius and Isis while linking Hiram Abif to Osiris. Another link between Masonry and Isis *qua* Sirius is established by way of Masons being known as widow's sons; the widow's son is Hiram Abif *qua* Horus. On this symbolism, Masonic philosopher Manly P. Hall writes:

---

147 Pike, Albert, *Morals and Dogma*, p. 486.
148 *ibid*, p. 842.

We can apply this analogy to a great modern system of initiation, Freemasonry, which has certainly perpetuated at least the outer form of the ancient rites. Freemasonry as an institution is Isis, the mother of the Mysteries, from whose dark womb the Initiates are born in the mystery of the second or philosophical birth. Thus all adepts, by virtue of their participation in the rites, are figuratively, at least, Sons of Isis. As Isis is the widow, seeking to restore her lord, and to avenge his cruel murder, it follows that all Master Masons or Master Builders, are widow's sons. They are the offspring of the institution widowed by the loss of the living Word, and theirs is the eternal quest–they discover by becoming.[149]

The locations of the bodies and the coins at Dark Annie's feet form a pentagram symbolizing the sacred feminine–Isis–the moon or Sirius which Jack the Ripper seeks to obliterate. Sir William Gull, as a Mason, would be cognizant of this symbolism.

Echoing these Masonic themes, the alchemical *citrinitas* (yellowness) stage is also necessary for alchemy. *Citrinitas* is the golden masculine sun, light; it is alchemical awakening to gnosis or enlightenment. This is represented by the solar, astral, and arcane mysteries of Freemasonry, an all-male secret society. The antagonists, Sir William Gull/Jack the Ripper, Benjamin Kidney, Sir Charles Warren, and Lord Hallsham (Peter Eyre) are Freemasons involved in covering up the Ripper's crime and the killer's hidden motives. In this instance, the light of Masonry is a not positive but negative. It is the *sol niger*, the black sun, emanating Luciferian black light generated by the gruesome murders of the Ripper. Freemasonic rituals raise poor blind candidates to sublime esoteric light (cf. Gnostic *ascensio*), while the layout of a Masonic lodge is based on the sun: the Worshipful Master sits in the east representing the rising sun, while the Senior Warden sits in the west symbolizing the setting sun with the Junior Warden in the south, being the sun at noonday, or meridian. Masons celebrate June 24th and December 27th since these dates have astronomical significance referring to the summer and winter solstices, the periods of great festivals and celebrations throughout the ancient world.[150] Solar iconography routinely

---

149 Hall, *The Lost Keys of Freemasonry*, page 153.
150 Olcott, *Sun Lore of All Ages*, p. 306 citing Robert H. Brown's *Stellar Theology and Masonic Astronomy*.

appear on Masonic badges, jewels, and aprons. Additionally, Masonic scholar Albert Gallatin Mackey (1807-1881) writes in his *Encyclopedia* on solar symbolism (cf. *citrinitas*) and its nexus to Freemasonry:

Hardly any of the symbols of Masonry are more important in their signification or more extensive in their application than the sun. As the source of material light, it reminds the Mason of that intellectual light of which he is in constant search. But it is especially as the ruler of the day, giving to it a beginning and end, and a regular course of hours, that the sun is presented as a Masonic Symbol. Hence, of the three lesser lights, we are told that one represents or symbolizes the sun, one the moon, and one the Master of the Lodge, because, as the sun rules the day and the moon governs the night, so should the Worshipful Master rule and govern his Lodge with equal regularity and precision. And this is in strict analogy with other Masonic symbolisms. For if the Lodge is a symbol of the world, which is thus governed in its changes of times and seasons by the sun, it is evident that the Master who governs the Lodge, controlling its time of opening and closing, and the work which is it should do, must be symbolized by the sun. The heraldic definition of the sun as a bearing fits most appositely to the symbolism of the sovereignty of the Master. Thus Gwillim says: 'The sun is the symbol of sovereignty, the hieroglyphic of royalty; it doth signify absolute authority.' This representation of the sun as a symbol of authority, while it explains the reference to the Master, enables us to amplify its meaning, and apply it to the three sources of authority in the Lodge, and account for the respective positions of the officers wielding this authority. The Master, therefore, in the East is a symbol of the rising sun; the Junior Warden in the South, of the Meridian Sun, and the Senior Warden in the West, of the Setting Sun. So in the mysteries of India, the chief officers were placed in the east, the west, and the south, respectively, to represent Brahma, or the rising; Vishnu, or the setting; and Siva, or the meridian sun.

And in the Druidical rites, the Arch-Druid, seated in the east, was assisted by two other officers–the one in the west representing the moon, and the other in the south representing the meridian sun.

This triple division of the government of a Lodge by three officers, representatives of the sun in his three manifestations in the east, south, and west, will remind us of similar ideas in the symbolism of antiquity. In the Orphic mysteries, it was taught that the sun generated from an egg, burst forth with power to triplicate himself by his own unassisted energy. Supreme power always seems to have been associated in the ancient mind with a three-fold division. Thus the sign of authority was indicated by the three-forked lightning of Jove, the trident of Neptune, and the three-headed Cerberus of Pluto. The government of the Universe was divided between these three sons of Saturn. The chaste goddess ruled the earth as Diana, the heavens as Luna, and the infernal regions as Hecate, whence her rites were only performed in a place where three roads met.

The sun is then presented to us in Masonry first as a symbol of light, but then more emphatically as a symbol of sovereign authority.

But, says Wemyss (*Symb. Lang.*), speaking of Scriptural symbolism, 'the sun may be considered an emblem of Divine Truth,' because the sun or light, of which it is the source, 'is not only manifest in itself, but makes other things; so one truth detects, reveals, and manifests another, as all truths are dependent on, and connected with, each other more or less.' And this again is applicable to the Masonic doctrine which makes the Master the symbol of the sun; for as the sun discloses and makes manifest, by the opening of the day, what had been hidden in the darkness of night, so the Master of the Lodge, as analogue of the ancient hierophant or explainer of the mysteries, makes Divine truth manifest in the neophyte, who had been hitherto in intellectual darkness, and reveals the hidden or esoteric lessons of initiation.[151]

The *nigredo*, *albedo*, and *citrinitas* alchemical phases are represented in *From Hell* by the Ripper, the prostitutes, and Freemasonry. The diabolical-Masonic formula is successful (this is why the Masons, not Abberline, symbolize the *citrinitas*): Jack the Ripper will give birth to the twentieth century via his gruesome and chaotic yet methodical ritualistic murder spree. Now we understand why the color red transcends *From Hell*. The

---

151 Albert Mackey, *Encyclopedia of Freemasonry*, Vol. II, page 736.

horrors of the *rubedo* last forever; it signifies the finality of this arcane process, the Ripper's alchemical transition perfected, the twentieth-century will be recast in the Ripper's diabolical image. Evil has triumphed over good. *Sic transit gloria mundi.*

There are a few other clues which suggest this pessimistic alchemical transition. Freemasonry, as a malevolent monopoly and influence, is identified by the numeric address of Sir William Gull's row home. He dwells in a row house numbered seventy-four (74) which is forty-seven (47) reversed. The number forty-seven is an esoteric reference to the 47th Proposition (or Problem) of Euclid better known as the Pythagorean Theorem, indicating Masonic leadership and rulership. The reversal of 47 to 74 implies a backward or perverted Freemasonry, symbolized by Jack the Ripper's grizzly Masonic murders or, as Gull calls them, his *mighty art.* The murder of Polly Nichols in front of an Egyptian obelisk, Cleopatra's Needle, by the Ripper also hints at Masonry's darker side. An obelisk honors the Egyptian sun god Amun-Ra exerting a mystical-spiritual force; the obelisk *qua* solar monument denotes an omnipotent Masonic oligarchy at work.

As Sir William Gull prepares his portable amputation kit—his instruments of death—one will observe a large portrait of academics dissecting a human cadaver as an obese professor supervises. This painting is, in reality, a replication of an engraving by famed English painter, printmaker, pictorial satirist, social critic, and editorial cartoonist William Hogarth (1697-1764). The engraving, one in

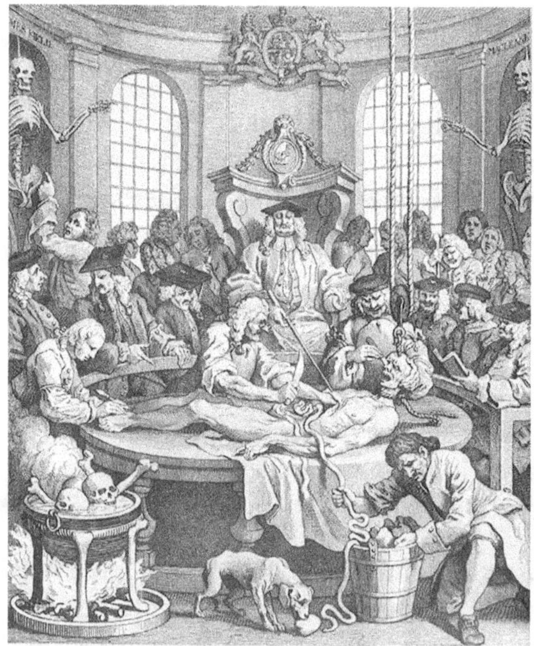

The Four Stages of Cruelty is a series of four printed engravings published by English artist William Hogarth in 1751. Each print depicts a different stage in the life of the fictional Tom Nero. Plate IV depicts Nero's corpse–having already been found guilty of murder and hanged–taken for the ignominious process of public dissection.

a series titled *The Reward of Cruelty*, is morbid and sardonic implying that, for some, death is the only reward because life is misery. Macabre phantasmagoria was nothing new to Hogarth, being one of the original members of Sir Francis Dashwood's (1708-1781) Hellfire Club. The Club was a secret society that met in the caverns beneath Dashwood's estate. During its meetings, its members engaged in orgies and various other depravities while it was rumored there was a privileged inner circle that secretly worshipped the Devil. As such, *The Reward of Cruelty* is well placed in the Ripper's hellish sanctum sanctorum.

ALCHEMICAL GNOSIS AND MELANCHOLY IN V FOR VENDETTA

Directed by James McTeigue and scripted by the Wachowski Brothers (now siblings), *V for Vendetta* is set in a near-future dystopian London. Hugo Weaving (Agent Smith from the Matrix Trilogy and Lord Elrond in *The Lord of the Rings* and Hobbit films) portrays V, an anarchist freedom fighter attempting to ignite a revolution against the brutal hegemonic regime Norsefire, led by godlike Adam Sutler (John Hurt, 1940-2017), which has completely subjugated Great Britain. Natalie Portman plays Evey Hammond, a working-class girl caught up in V's nihilistic mission, and Stephen Rea portrays the detective leading a desperate quest to stop V.

The film opens in the late 2020s with the world in turmoil: the United States has been fractured as a result of prolonged conflict and a pandemic of the St. Mary's Virus has ravaged the European continent. The United Kingdom remains the only stable country ruled by the fascist and repressive Norsefire Party, referred to simply as the Party. The Norsefire Party, like the Nazis, employ a red, black, and white color scheme on its banners and flags. Under the Norsefire regime, freedoms and liberties are heavily oppressed. Political opponents, homosexuals, and other undesirables are imprisoned in Third Reich-like concentration camps. London is subject to a perpetual curfew. A right-wing Norsefire propagandist named Lewis Prothero (Roger Allam) is nicknamed "The Voice of London," which is also the title of his nightly talk show during which he rails against nonconformists. On

November 5th, Guy Fawkes-Bonfire Night, Evey Hammond, a woman working at the state-run British Television Network (BTN), is rescued by a vigilant–identifying himself as V–from an attempted rape by secret police known as *Fingermen*. Hiding his face behind a white Guy Fawkes mask, V leads her to a rooftop to watch the theatrical destruction of the Old Bailey synchronized to Tchaikovsky's (1840-1893) *1812 Overture* (1880). Scotland Yard's Inspector Eric Finch is given the task of investigating V's activities while the Party uses the BTN to declare the destruction of the Old Bailey an emergency demolition (which is merely a cover story), but V takes over the broadcast claiming responsibility. He urges the people of Britain to rise against their oppressive government and meet him in one year, on 5 November, outside the Houses of Parliament which he promises to destroy. During the broadcast the police attempt to capture V, but Evey helps him escape. She is knocked unconscious in the melee.

V takes an unconscious Evey to his home where she is told she must remain until 5 November the following year. After learning that V is killing government officials, she escapes to the home of her boss, comedian and talk show host Gordon Deitrich (Stephen Fry). In return for Evey trusting him with her safety, Deitrich reveals to her a collection of prohibited materials including subversive paintings, an antique Quran, and homo-erotic photographs by Robert Mapplethorpe (1946-1989) explaining that he conceals his homosexuality to retain his television career. Meanwhile, Inspector Finch learns that V is the result of government-sponsored human experimentation, targeting those who tortured him during his unlawful detention. After Gordon's television show performs an over-the-top Benny Hill-like satire of the government depicting Sutler as a buffoon, his home is raided and Evey is captured while trying to escape. She is incarcerated and tortured for days for information about V, with her only solace being a note written by another prisoner, actress Valerie Page (Natasha Wightman), a lesbian arrested for the crime of being different.

Evey is told that she will be executed unless she reveals V's location, but when she says she would rather die, she is immediately released. It is now disclosed that her imprisonment and torture were staged by V to free her from her fears and anxieties, to release her from her superficial nine-to-five Norsefire existence. The note was real however, having been passed by Valerie to V years earlier when he was similarly imprisoned.

Although Evey initially hates V for what he did to her, she knows she is now a stronger person due to her pseudo-imprisonment. She departs with a promise to return before November 5th.

Meanwhile, Inspector Finch searches for the true identity of V, eventually tracing him to a bio-weapons program at a detention center for social deviants and political dissidents at Larkhill. Finch realizes that the program, directed by then undersecretary Adam Sutler, resulted in the creation of the St. Mary's Virus and its release in a false flag terrorist attack. A false flag attack is when the state attacks itself, not the enemy, whether perceived or imaginary, to usurp liberties and freedoms in the name of national security. The deaths of 80,000 people and the resulting panic enabled the Norsefire Party to win the next election, silencing opposition, turning the country into a totalitarian police state.

As November 5th nears, V's distribution of thousands of Guy Fawkes masks causes chaos in the United Kingdom, resulting in the populace questioning party rule. On the eve of 5 November, Evey visits V, showing her an explosives-laden train in the abandoned London Underground, set to destroy Parliament. He leaves it to Evey to decide whether to use it, believing that he is unfit to judge. V meets with secret police chief Creedy (Tim Pigott- Smith), having made a deal with V to hand over Sutler in exchange for V's surrender. When Creedy executes Sutler, V refuses to surrender and is shot by Creedy's bodyguards. V survives, however, systemically killing Creedy and his men. Mortally wounded, V returns to Evey to thank her, admitting his love for her before dying in her arms.

As Evey places V's body aboard the train, she is discovered by Finch who initially orders her to surrender. Disillusioned by the party's regime, Finch allows Evey to send the dynamite-laden train on its way. Thousands of unarmed Londoners wearing Guy Fawkes masks march on Parliament to watch the event. With Sutler and Creedy dead and no one left to give commands, the military allows the people to pass in peace. Accompanied by the 1812 Overture, Parliament is destroyed while Evey and Finch observe at a distance. Finch asks Evey for the identity of V, to which she replies in part, "He was all of us."

*   *   *   *

V for Vendetta's prologue is a re-creation of the infamous Gunpowder Plot of 5 November 1605 when Guy Fawkes (1570-1606), a devout Roman Catholic and Jesuit agent, attempted to blow up Protestant King James I (1566-1625) of England by planting gunpowder beneath the House of Lords during the State Opening of England's Parliament. The Gunpowder Treason was, by all accounts, a Jesuit-inspired Counter-Reformation conspiracy, since the assassination attempt was known by the principal Jesuit of England, Father Henry Garnet (1555-1605). Although he was convicted of treason and sentenced to death, some doubt has been cast on how much he knew of the plot. Its existence was made known to him through confession and, as such, Garnet was prevented from informing the authorities by the absolute confidentiality of the confessional. That notwithstanding, Fawkes' scheme smacks of Jesuit subterfuge and skullduggery: the plot would have killed a Protestant King and his Parliament, devastating the Protestant Church of England. Had the Gunpowder Treason been successful, it would have placed England back under the yoke of the Roman Church ensuring that a Catholic monarch perpetually sat on Britain's throne. The foiling of the Gunpowder Plot was commemorated for many years afterward by special sermons and other public events, such as the ringing of church bells, the lighting of fireworks, which have evolved into the Bonfire Night of today. The film's opening sequence is historically accurate: one will see Fawkes (Clive Ashborn) pushing a cart of barreled explosives with a lantern hanging from it. The lantern that Fawkes carried with him that night is an antiquity, described as a *dark relic*, in the collection of the Ashmolean Museum, University of Oxford, England. The museum was named after Elias Ashmole (1617-1692), a celebrated English antiquary politician, officer of arms, astrologer, a student of alchemy, and an adept of the mystic arts. Ashmole supported the Royalists during the English Civil War (1642-1651), and upon the restoration of

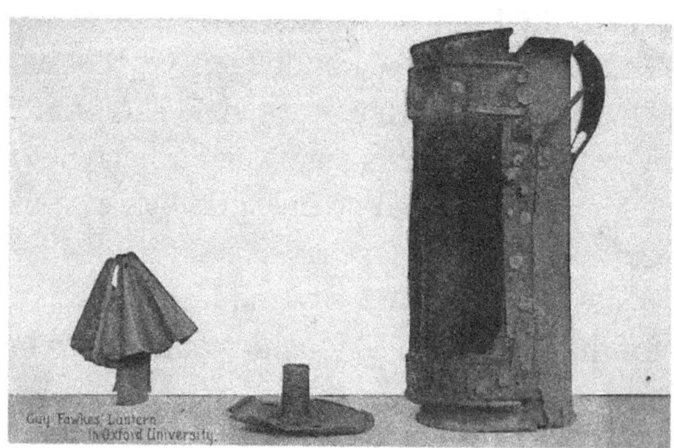

Early twentieth century postcard of Guy Fawkes' lantern in the Ashmolean Museum, Oxford University, England. Source: Author's collection.

Charles II (1630-1685) was rewarded with several lucrative offices. His library reflected his Baconian intellectual outlook, including works on English history, law, numismatics, chorography, alchemy, astrology, astronomy, and botany. Although he was one of the founding members of the Royal Society, a key institution in the development of experimental science, his interests were antiquarian, mystical, and occult as well as scientific; he was an early Freemason associating with Rosicrucianism. Throughout his life, he was an avid collector of curiosities and other artifacts. Many of these he acquired (some say swindled) from the traveler, botanist, and collector John Tradescant the Younger (1608-1662). Ashmole donated most of his collection of curios and rare manuscripts to the University of Oxford, founding the Ashmolean Museum, which is the permanent home of Guy Fawkes' lantern. The Ashmolean Museum also houses Oliver Cromwell's (1599-1658) death mask and pocket watch, Chief Powhatan's (died 1618) mantle, Henry VIII's (1491-1547) hawking glove, and presiding Judge John Bradshaw's (1602-1659) iron-lined bulletproof hat which he wore during the trial of Charles I (1600-1649). V collects similar oddities and antiquities which are displayed in his own *Musaeum Tradescantianum*[152] which V calls the Shadow Gallery.

---

152 A cabinet of curiosities, or Wunderkammer, was designed to facilitate an encyclopedic enterprise, the aim of which was the collection and preservation of the whole of knowledge. The earliest encyclopedic practices were set within a classical framework whereby new observations and practical experiments were seen as the continuation of work initiated by the great ancient thinkers, such as Aristotle and Pliny the Elder. Working within this framework, many early encyclopedists turned to empirical activities in an effort to resolve the questions prompted by the close analysis of ancient texts, made increasingly accessible during the decades immediately following the invention of the printing press. Over time, however, these activities began to reveal new truths in conflict with the tenets of classical doctrine. As a result, they began to undermine the established authority of the ancients, thereby paving the way for new methods of 'scientific' investigation. While these various methods evolved over time, the cabinet, in contrast, remained consistent in its role as a site of collection and display, where the whole of nature could be brought together in microcosm, for the benefit of closer and more detailed analysis. Within the structural parameters of the cabinet space, the collector set out to comprehend nature through the control of its various parts. The control of nature was the goal of the early collecting practice, and was the driving force behind the ordering and cataloguing of objects and artifacts. This is an important consideration in that it makes clear the fact that the collections resulting from this process were founded on an organizational principle, which, although foreign to the modern collector, was dependent on philosophical considerations relevant at the time. In line with this principle, collectors of the sixteenth and seventeenth centuries devised strategies which included the systematic categorization of the objects in their possession. In most cases, these objects were recorded and displayed in an organized manner, even if the criteria for organization were at times subjective; differing slightly from one collection to the next. Regardless

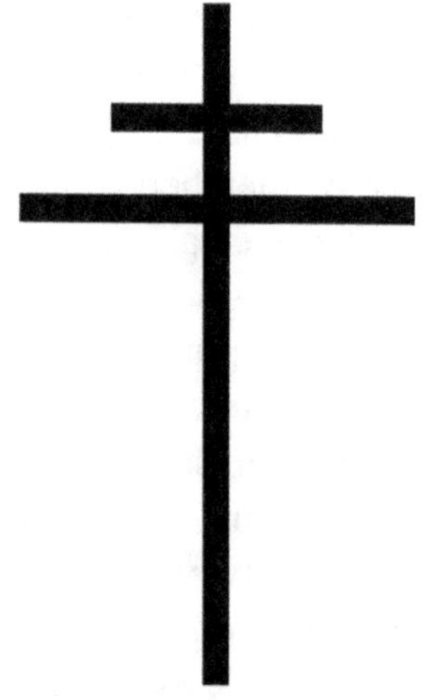

During the Crusades, the Cross of Lorraine was adopted by the Knights Templar, a medieval class of Roman Catholic warrior monks.

The film successfully blends alchemy and Gnosticism, something rare in cinema. Evey Hammond, as her first name suggests, personifies Eve, the Biblical first woman. She is subservient to the oppressive state represented by its nefarious High Chancellor *Adam* Sutler. Sutler is a manipulative demiurge: Sutler's first name symbolizes the first Biblical man, Adam, while his last name, Sutler, implies Hitler, Reich Chancellor and Führer of Nazi Germany. Sutler, like Hitler, is a totalitarian leader who rules with an iron first; England's Norsefire state is intrusive, oppressive, and fascist, representing an extreme form of fundamentalist Christianity.[153] The Norsefire Christian-esque slogan is "Strength through Unity, Unity through Faith;" while its symbol is a double red-cross better known as the Cross of Lorraine. The Red Double-Cross of Lorraine recalls the Knights Templar: over-zealous militant Christians wantonly killing in the name of Jesus Christ. The Templars battled the Muslims, their avowed enemy, in the Holy Land during the Crusades (1096-1285) while in Norsefire England merely possessing a copy of the Quran, as talk show host Gordon Deitrich discovers, is a guaranteed death sentence.

Enter the Gnostic serpent into the Norsefire garden, V, Lucifer the Light Bearer (cf. solar resurrection, reawakening), wisdom, and spiritual revelation. The serpent is a symbol of this Luciferian gnosis, and that meaning was known to the early Christians and to the Gnostic sect called the Ophites linking Christ with the serpent.[154] The serpent, as an emblem of illumination, slithers sagaciously in *Conan the Barbarian* (1982),

---

of their potential variations, the strategies adopted by these collectors enabled them to impose an order on the natural world. Their ability to do this was considered a form of power, which, in turn, was held as a characteristic unique to mankind. In this context, then, the collecting and controlling of material objects was not an end in itself, but was an integral part of a continuing process of self-discovery; of the shaping of man's identity as part of the greater universe, yet distinct among the products of divine creation. See See Edward P. Alexander's, *Museum Masters: Their Museums and Their Influence*, pp. 20-42.

153 The First Order of *Star Wars: The Force Awakens* also represents fundamentalist Christianity.

154 Paul Foster Case, *The True and Invisible Rosicrucian Order*, p. 223.

becoming an object of veneration. Serpent cult leader Thulsa Doom (James Earl Jones) is the keeper of esoteric wisdom, the Riddle of Steel, being able to shape-shift into a giant snake. Jesus confirms that the serpent is an emblem of wisdom at Matthew 10:16 telling the Apostles, "Behold, I send you forth as sheep in the midst of wolves: be ye therefore wise as serpents, and harmless as doves."

V encounters Evey tempting her with an allegorical apple or, in this case, spiritual gnosis, paralleling Eve being tempted by the serpent with knowledge and immortality. V wants to liberate Evey from the harsh conformities of the Norsefire Party which he deems evil, or at least illegitimate, illusionary, and false. To the hardcore Christian Norsefire party, V is Lucifer *qua* the Devil incarnate; V's saturnine, rebellious personality is imbued with satanic overtones. For example, two of V's Shakespearean quotes reference the Devil: "We are oft to blame in this, - / Tis too much proved - that with devotion's visage/ And pious action we do sugar o'er/ The devil himself" [quoting Polonius, *Hamlet* 3:1], "And thus I clothe my naked villainy, with old odd ends, stol'n forth of holy writ; And seem a saint, when most I play the devil" [quoting Gloucester, *Richard III* 1.3]. V's Shadow Gallery has a mirror with the Latin phrase, *Vi Veri Veniversum Vivus Vici*, when translated means: By the power of truth, I, while living, have conquered the universe; which V incorrectly attributes to Dr. Faust, a man in league with Mephistopheles. The phrase belongs to English occultist and ceremonial magician Aleister Crowley, taking this line as his magickal motto as a Magister Templi, or Master of the Temple, within his A∴ A∴ (*Astrum Argentum* or Silver Star); Crowley based his A∴ A∴ upon the occult workings of the Golden Dawn. The principle purpose of this esoteric grade is to obtain a perfect understanding of the universe, thereby becoming its master or conqueror. Crowley, although not a Satanist per se, associates himself with demonic entities and satanism via his practice of rabbinic sorcery detailed in grimoires such as *The Sacred Magic of Abramelin the Mage* (a/k/a Abramelin the Jew) and *Ars Goetia*, also known as *The Lesser Key of Solomon*. Although absent from the film, in the graphic novel, V repeats Crowley's maxim, "Do what thou wilt shall be the whole of the Law;" and quotes the Rolling Stones' song "Sympathy for the Devil"[155] introducing himself with the lyrics, "♫ Please allow me to introduce myself, I'm a man of wealth and taste. ♫" The letter *V* is the Roman numeral for the number 5, evoking the fifth card of the Tarot's Major Arcana: the Hierophant. The Hierophant is the priest of the Mysteries because of its connection with the spiritual ethers, by means of which mystic development is attained.[156] There is a malevolent side to the Hierophant Card: Levi has stated that the raised hand of the Hierophant's (or Pope's) forms a sign of esotericism: the thumb and first two fingers pointed upward, and the last two fingers folded onto the palm, casts a shadow shaped like the head and horns of the Devil, thus heralding disaster and misfortune.[157] V synchs with this Tarot archetype: he is a mercurial, eccentric Gnostic master through whom Evey obtains mystical reawakening, alchemical *qua* psychological change by way of V's dark chicanery and deception; V aspires only after the impossible and inaccessible expecting *only that which shall not be*[158] which, for him, is the destruction of Norsefire England. Evey emerges from V's pseudo-imprisonment stronger and wiser than ever. V, personifying a Norsefire Christianized Devil, seeks to destroy the fundamentalist and oppressive political party ushering England into a numinous new age of gnosis paralleling Crowley's desire to destroy Christianity to birth the new Aeon of Horus. V's gnosis comes during the destruction of Larkhill Concentration Camp where he was the subject of horrific governmental-scientific experimentations. V is baptized by fire, or born again, launching him on a Gnostic yet nihilistic quest to restore consciousness to the English people, destroying Norsefire concurrently. This Gnostic rebirth is paralleled in J.R.R. Tolkien's *Fellowship of the Ring* (2001) and *The Two Towers* (2002) when Gandalf the Grey is tried and tested by a fiery demonic

---

155 Originally released on the Rolling Stones' album *Beggars Banquet* (1968), the song is sung by Mick Jagger as the Devil in the first person.

156 Hall, *The Secret Teachings of All Ages*, p. 218. See also Sullivan's *Cinema Symbolism*, Chapter IV, explaining the application of this card during a Tarot card reading as well as Crowley's Egyptian (cf. *Book of Thoth*) interpretation of this card in regards to Emmett "Doc" Brown in the Back to the Future Trilogy. Since the *Back to the Future* Trilogy is decidedly Egyptian in nature, Crowley's interpretation of the Hierophant card seems more appropriate when applied to Emmett Brown than to V.

157 Richard Cavendish, *The Tarot*, pp. 83-85.

158 P.D. Ouspensky, *The Symbolism of the Tarot*, p. 46, on the arcana of the Hierophant. This also dovetails with *Back to the Future's* Emmett Brown in that he too seeks to achieve the impossible: time travel. See Sullivan's *Cinema Symbolism*, Chapter IV, on Brown's relation to the Hierophant card.

monster known as a Balrog, allowing him to achieve kabalistic apotheosis thus returning as a born again or resurrected godlike Gandalf the White.

Evey and V's Gnosticism is both Manichean and Valentinian. It is Manichean because their battle is against darkness, Norsefire England; they wish to return England to the light. It is Valentinian because theirs is a quest for spiritual knowledge, the relinquishing of fear and desire, rebelling against oppressive Christians and Norsefire dogma. Evey resists V's anarchist Gnostic teachings at first; however, she is finally persuaded when she sees her boss Gordon Dietrich black-bagged by Creedy's secret police. Years earlier, Evey had witnessed her parents similarly black-bagged when she was a little girl. Evey is now initiated into the mysteries by V: with her head shaven, she is imprisoned facing certain death. Evey must decide to renounce V or face execution by firing squad. Evey does not succumb to her jailors, refusing to provide them with any salient information. Over time she no longer fears death and is ready to stand up, even perish, for her convictions and beliefs, which echoes Eve's seduction by the wily serpent in the Garden of Eden that once she ate of the forbidden fruit she would not die (Genesis 3:4). In other words, Evey understands that if she gave up V, she would experience death, but if she remains silent, she will obtain true spiritual revelation and, esoterically, live forever. Suffering[159] in a state of imprisonment and decay, Evey receives gnosis: she is now cognizant that she must fight for her convictions even if they incur the wrath of the state. Emerging bellicose, she has survived her initiatory trials and is about to be reborn; in the Masonic occult vernacular, she is about *to be brought from darkness to light*. It is at this point that she learns her incarceration was a cruel ruse, an illusion, designed by V to bring about this awakening (cf. spiritual and esoteric consciousness) with her divine spark now ignited. In other words, V is Evey's personal Hermes Trismegistus, her Tyler Durden, her *daemon* or spirit guide, her alchemical Mercury. As the trickster Mercurius, the Tarot's magician, V has deceived her, but the

---

159 cf. *The Gospel According to Thomas*, commonly shortened to the *Gospel of Thomas*, which is a well-preserved early Christian, non-canonical sayings-gospel which many scholars believe provides insight into the oral gospel traditions. According to the *Gospel of Thomas*, the fundamental cause of human suffering is due to an exile of the individual soul from the spiritual realms into the material world. The entire created world, and hence its creator (the demiurge), thus becomes viewed as evil. See Bentley Layton, *The Gnostic Scriptures*, 1995. See 1998's *The Truman Show* which portrays Truman Burbank suffering in a false, materialistic world created by a demiurge named Christof who manipulates Truman for entertainment purposes.

deception has initiated Evey into Valentinian gnosis. V has presented her with an illusion: imprisonment by the state, signifying that Norsefire is a false reality. Sutler is the demiurge and Norsefire is his repressive creation, existing so long as the people submit and consent. V's alchemical chicanery enlightens Evey, placing her on the Left-Hand Path, culminating in Luciferian rebellion, destruction, and liberation. Like Jung said, "One does not become enlightened by imagining figures of light, but by making the darkness conscious."[160] By understanding Hell, Evey can experience light.

Not only does Evey gain gnosis, but she also alchemically transmutes from timid Norsefire television bureaucrat to a nihilist revolutionary; symbolically she has gone from Eve, the second wife of Adam, to Lilith, his first. Lilith, according to Hebrew folklore, was Adam's first wife leaving him because she refused to become his servant. Thus, Evey abandons Adam, the personification of Norsefire, in pursuit of wisdom, *to know thyself*, and liberation. She had shrugged off the demiurge-like conformities and constraints of Sutler's England, declaring open rebellion. Alchemically, the Norsefire party is *nigredo*, the repressive government black bagging their political opponents and those deemed undesirable and enemies of the state. V is light, *citrinitas,* while Evey is the *albedo* absorbing the sun's glow, en*light*enment, or wisdom. The *rubedo* is symbolized by V's Scarlet Carson representing completion of the Magnum Opus, the Great Work finished. For V, it is the death of his Larkhill tormentors; for Evey, it is the destruction of Parliament *qua* Norsefire. At the end, V's funeral pyre is adorned with these roses allegorizing that V's work is done, his mission accomplished, and the alchemical change finalized when Evey elects to launch the explosively-charged train car into Parliament thereby destroying it, giving the English people the promise of a new day. Evey explains to Finch, "That this country needs more than a building right now. It needs hope." Inspector Finch, tasked with stopping V, does not prevent Evey from throwing the train's switch, rather, he elects to let her finish V's work. Finch parallels *Blade Runner*'s Rick Deckard because both experience Gnostic revelation: Deckard awakens to the fact that the Nexus-6s have divine souls, Finch comes to understand Norsefire England is evil. Finch understands that V and Evey are liberators, not destroyers.

---

160 Jung, Carl G., Collected Works, *Alchemical Studies*, paragraph 335.

Although V is deadly with knives and wears black, he's not Jack the Ripper's murderous *nigredo*, nor is he putrefaction. Rather, V is an inspired melancholic, a saturnine philosopher immured in fascist Norsefire England, trying to spark revolution, leading his disciples into great depths of insight. V accomplishes his Valentinian revolution by supplying gnosis to Evey who, in turn, triggers a revolt among the populace, leading to the downfall of the Norsefire Party. V embodies Renaissance melancholy which is personified by dark humor, intense inspiration; in other words, a crepuscular Hierophant.[161] In *The Book of Life* (1489), Ficino argues that melancholic personalities tend to be brilliant philosophers. Melancholy sympathy with gloomy Saturn and with the cold core of Earth enables one to persevere in confusion and nocturnal contemplation, to gaze within and parse the heart's mysteries.[162] V persevere against all odds, to be liberating yet dangerous scholar, a free-thinker; a dark mercurial figure, moving in the shadows, supplying gnosis to the English people, liberating them from their stasis. Echoing this melancholy, V is active passivity, the paranoia of Valentinus, an aggressive luminary questioning of the status quo that rests in chronic unknowing.[163] Different from the narrow paranoia of narcissism–the idea that the world (or Norsefire England) is focused on persecuting oneself–this generous paranoia issues from skepticism toward the given, pushing all bright axioms into lurid chiaroscuro.[164] V also embodies the melancholy of the Manichean school. Unlike the paranoiac, who doesn't quite know the nature of his material atmosphere and who can muster only tentative hope for clarity, the dualist *knows* that he been abandoned to a world of irreparable evil and that his only hope for escaping squalor is through cultivating disdain for his surroundings.[165] For this is V's modus operandi: to question Norsefire's rhetoric, to ask why the English are tolerating their abusive rulers, and, in the end, to inspire the people so they can destroy their oppressors. Ficino's melancholic thinker invokes the aid of the moon, a procreative force behind sweet dews and nourishing tides hence V recruits Evey into his nihilistic quest.[166]

---

161 cf. Yates' *The Occult Philosophy in the Elizabethan Age*, pp. 61-68.
162 See Wilson's *Secret Cinema*, p. 108.
163 *ibid*, p. 41.
164 *ibid.*
165 *ibid.*
166 *ibid*, p. 109.

Initiated into gnosis and alchemically changed, a confident and victorious Evey, joined by V, ascends (cf. Gnostic *ascensio*) to a building's rooftop (like *Blade Runner's* Deckard) where she is allegorically baptized into gnosis in the pouring rain. She has transcended the dark light of V's Lucifer and is now spiritually equipped to battle Norsefire in an epic Manichean battle for the heart and soul of England. She is ready to use her newfound gnosis to defeat darkness and bring order from the ensuing chaos. Evey is the sacred feminine conjoined to V, the divine masculine, becoming Jung's syzygy, *coincidentia oppositorum*, the alchemical wedding perfected: Evey's drive to destroy Norsefire is simply her lunar light generated by V's black nihilistic black sun, *sol niger*, the luminescence of the *nigredo*, the exploration and integration of the shadow's dark impulses. Evey speaks of her alchemical marriage to V, "And it is not an idea that I miss, *it is a man*. A man that made me remember the Fifth of November. A man that I will never forget." Evey has rejected drab conformity (the state) and accepted V's Valentinian rebellion but, in doing so, now suffers the melancholy of V.

Moore's disdain for Christianity is represented by the British Television Network's broadcast tower, named the Jordan Tower, after the Jordan River. It is from Jordan Tower that the Norsefire Party spews its hate-filled propaganda to the English people, while the river has significance in both Judaism and Christianity; it's the site where the Israelites crossed into the Promised Land and where Jesus of Nazareth was baptized by John the Baptist.

V, tracking down his tormentors from the Larkhill facility, places a red rose upon their bodies after he kills them. Identified as a Scarlet Carson (which is fictitious, it is a Violet Carson renamed), V puts them on the bodies of his victims becoming his calling card. Alchemy's *rubedo* aside, the red rose is, of course, the primary and most recognizable emblem of the Rosicrucians (Rose Cross): proto Freemasons and masters of the occult, alchemy, and Cabala. The use of the rose by V identifies him with the sun, esoteric enlightenment, a restorer (of the English Nation), and a master of the Gnostic mysteries. On this arcane philosophy, Albert Pike explains, "The ROSE, was anciently sacred to Aurora and the Sun. It is a symbol of Dawn, of the resurrection of Light and the renewal of life, and therefore of the dawn of the first day, and more particularly of the resurrection: and the Cross and Rose together are therefore hieroglyphically to be read, the Dawn of Eternal Life which all Nations have hoped for by the advent of a Redeemer."[167] The redeemer of Great Britain is V, the Gnostic serpent, the black sun eclipsing the despotic rule of Norsefire England. On the rose and gnosis, "From earnest consideration of the symbols of the rose and cross, such readers would know not only *what* the Invisible Order is but exactly *where* entrance to it may be found. They would know…the meaning of the Rosy Cross should be more than sufficient to point out that the shortest and easiest way to participation in the treasure of the Gnosis."[168] The rose signifies V's anarchism, identifying him as a Valentinian illuminator, breathing new life into the English nation, causing it to be reborn and its people with it.

WATCHMEN: A CONSPIRACY SMORGASBORD

Watchmen, created by Moore and artist Dave Gibbons, was first published as a twelve-issue miniseries from DC Comics, cover-dated September 1986 to October 1987. The 2009 movie is an adaptation of the graphic novel and is set in an alternative 1985 at the height of the Cold War between the United States and the Soviet Union. Some retired vigilantes investigate a conspiracy against them, uncovering something even more grandiose and sinister. The film is a smorgasbord of conspiracy theory and conspiracy fact. The film's opening montage tells the story of the Minutemen: a collection of costumed crime fighters created in 1939 in response to a rise in costumed gangs and criminals, while the Watchmen similarly form decades later. Some of the original Minutemen were Sally Jupiter a/k/a Silk Spectre (Carla Gugino), Edward Blake a/k/a the Comedian (Jeffrey Dean Morgan), Hollis Mason a/k/a Nite Owl (Stephen McHattie), Hooded Justice (Glenn Ennis), and Ursula Zandt a/k/a Silhouette (Apollonia Vanova). Over time, many of the original Minutemen retire and are replaced by new members, called Watchmen, including the incredibly powerful Jon Osterman a/k/a

167 Pike, *Morals and Dogma*, p. 291.
168 Case, *The True and Invisible Rosicrucian Order*, p. 142.

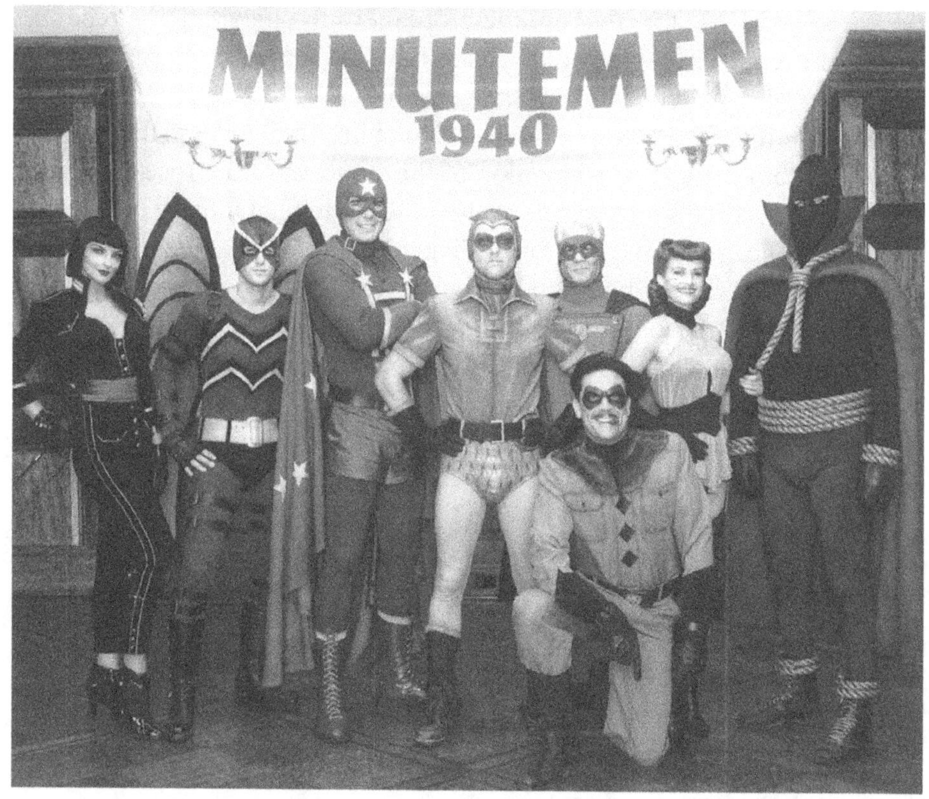

The original Minutemen, 1940 (left to right): Silhouette, Mothman, Dollar Bill, Nite Owl, Captain Metropolis, the Comedian, Silk Spectre, and Hooded Justice.

Dr. Manhattan (Billy Crudup), Daniel Dreiberg a/k/a Nite Owl II (Patrick Wilson), Rorschach a/k/a Walter Kovacs (Jack Earle Haley), Adrian Veidt a/k/a Ozymandias (Matthew Goode), and Laurie Jupiter a/k/a Silk Spectre II (Malin Akerman), the daughter of the original Silk Spectre. Their existence in the U.S. has dramatically affected world events: the superpowers of Dr. Manhattan help the United States win the Vietnam War, resulting in President Richard M. Nixon being repeatedly elected into the 1980s. The existence of Dr. Manhattan gave the West a strategic advantage over the Soviet Union, which by the mid-1980s threatens to escalate the Cold War into a nuclear holocaust. During that time, growing anti-vigilante sentiment in the country led to the outlawing of masked crime fighters. That notwithstanding, Dr. Manhattan and the Comedian operate as government-sanctioned agents, or spooks, while Rorschach continues to work outside the law. Most of the masked vigilantes keep their real identities a secret but two of them, Dr. Manhattan and Ozymandias, have revealed their names to the world. Ozymandias, which is the Greek name for Egypian Pharaoh Ramses II (ca. 1303-1213 BCE), was born Adrian Veidt; he is a closet homosexual seen hanging around with the disco band, the Village People, and an androgynous David Bowie (leaning on a car next to Mick Jagger) during the movie's opening credits.

Investigating the mysterious murder of government agent Edward "Eddie" Blake, Rorschach discovers that Blake was the Comedian, and theorizes that someone may be trying to eliminate the Watchmen. He attempts to warn his retired comrades, including his former partner Daniel Dreiberg a/k/a Nite Owl II, Dr. Manhattan, and the latter's lover Laurie Jupiter a/k/a Silk Spectre II. Dreiberg is skeptical, but nonetheless relates the conspiratorial hypothesis to vigilante turned-billionaire Adrian Veidt, who dismisses it.

After Blake's funeral, Dr. Manhattan is accused of inadvertently causing the cancer afflicting his former girlfriend, Janey Slater (Laura Mennell), and others who spent time with him after the scientific accident that gave him his superpowers. Dr. Manhattan exiles himself on Mars, giving the Soviet Union the confidence to invade Afghanistan. Later, Rorschach's theory appears to be justified when Veidt narrowly avoids an assassination attempt, and Rorschach finds himself framed for the murder of a former villain, Moloch (Matt Frewer). Meanwhile Laurie Jupiter, after breaking up with Dr. Manhattan, goes to stay with Dreiberg, and the two former superheroes come out of retirement, eventually becoming lovers. After helping Rorschach break out of prison, Jupiter is confronted by Dr. Manhattan, taking her to Mars and, after she asks him to save the world, explains he is no longer interested in humanity. As he probes her memories, he discovers she is the offspring of a voluntary affair between her mother Sally (the original Silk Spectre) and Edward Blake (the Comedian), who had previously tried to rape Sally violently. Dr. Manhattan's desire to help humankind is renewed by this improbable sequence of events, and Manhattan resolves to return to Earth with Laurie Jupiter-Silk Spectre II. In a paradoxical twist, Dr. Manhattan returns to earth from the planet Mars; in Roman mythology, Mars was the god of war. However, it will be Dr. Manhattan's false flag attack, orchestrated by Ozymandias, which will result in world peace. A similar contradiction can also be seen in 1999's *The Matrix* when Morpheus (Lawrence Fishburne) awakens Neo (Keanu Reeves) from his dream-like state bringing him to the real world (consciousness), yet in mythology, Morpheus was the god of sleep and dreams. Dualistically, *Watchmen* also suggests that the costumed, crime fighting vigilantes are their real personas, their Jungian shadows, their daemons or higher selves, while their everyday personalities and normal lives are their eidolons, their lower selves; Rorschach refers to his shape-shifting ink-blot mask as his "real face."

Investigating the conspiracy, Rorschach and Nite Owl II discover that Veidt-Ozymandias is the driving force behind everything. Rorschach records his suspicions in his journal, which he drops off at the publication office of the *New Frontiersman*, a right-wing tabloid. Rorschach and Nite Owl II confront Veidt at his Antarctic-Egyptian retreat. Ozymandias confirms he is the mastermind behind Blake's murder, Manhattan's exile, Rorschach's framing, and his own assassination attempt. Veidt-Ozymandias has accomplished this through a privately-owned subsidiary named Pyramidal Transnational. Echoing the doctrines of the Bavarian Illuminati, Veidt explains that *the ends justify the means* and this, his master plan, is to unify the United States with the Soviet Union in global peace by destroying the world's cities with exploding energy reactors he helped Dr. Manhattan create. Rorschach and Nite Owl II attempt to stop him, but Ozymandias subdues them, revealing that his plan has already been set into motion: the reactors have been detonated, and the energy signatures are recognized as those belonging to Dr. Manhattan. Simply put, Ozymandias is willing to kill millions to save billions.

Silk Spectre II and Dr. Manhattan arrive at the ruins of New York and determine that it must be Ozymandias' work. They teleport to his Antarctic base just after he has beaten Rorschach and Nite Owl II, causing Veidt to retreat and attempt to kill Manhattan. Unsuccessful, he shows them a televised news report in which President Nixon states that the United States and Soviets have allied against their new common enemy: Dr. Manhattan. The heroes eventually realize that exposing the grand conspiracy would only disrupt this peace; Rorschach, however, refuses to remain silent forcing Manhattan to annihilate him. Manhattan shares a final kiss with Laurie, departing permanently for another galaxy while an enraged Nite Owl II assaults Ozymandias, who nevertheless defends his actions. Nite Owl II and Silk Spectre II leave Ozymandias to muse on his choices and their future implications.

Laurie Jupiter and Daniel Dreiberg return to New York and plan to continue fighting crime. Jupiter reveals to her mother she's learned Edward Blake was her father, and mother and daughter reconcile. The film ends with an editor of the *New Frontiersman* telling a staff employee that, with the Cold War over, he may print whatever he likes from a collection of crank mailings, among which is Rorschach's journal. It is implied that the journal's contents are nothing more than conspiracy theory, but in reality, the journal documents the truth behind Ozymandias' global occult conspiracy.

*　*　*　*

Watchmen conveys Masonic ritualistic doctrines, including death and spiritual ascension, enveloped in conspiracy and subterfuge. For example, Jon Osterman, a nuclear physicist, dies and is resurrected (cf. the Blue Lodge's Hiram Abif), becoming the perfected Christlike sun god known as Dr. Manhattan. Although Osterman's transformation is unintended, it implies the Renaissance's mixing of science with magic to produce kabalistic results.[169] Manhattan has godlike powers, including superhuman strength, telekinesis, the ability to teleport himself or others over planetary and interplanetary distances, control over matter at a subatomic level, and clairvoyance. He perceives the past, present, and future as happening simultaneously,believing that he cannot act on that knowledge, since his actions and reactions to chronological events are seemingly predetermined. After appearing to die in a nuclear accident, Manhattan's solar Christlike cabalistic apotheosis is first seen inside the cafeteria at Gila Flats Research Lab where here appears cruciform; transformed,[170] Dr. Manhattan next appears in the sky, like the sun, as a crucified reborn savior. Osterman is a Masonic-Christ having died, brought to light *qua* spiritual revelation symbolized by his newfound superpowers, gifted with esoteric knowledge of the space-time continuum. Dr. Manhattan will also be the United States' savior in Vietnam, winning the war for President Nixon single-handedly.

---

169 Frances Yates' *Astraea*, p. 165
170 Ostermann's metamorphosis could be construed as alchemical: a transition from man to god.

The third-degree Blue Lodge Masonic ritual documents the candidate's allegorical death and solar gnosis, or *ascensio*, when he is killed and resurrected, thus brought to light and occult reawakening. The sun is the most important symbol in all of Freemasonry, represented by a point within a circle. This solar emblem was also employed by Weishaupt's Illuminati. Exoterically, the point itself symbolizes the individual brother and the circle the boundary line of his duty to God and man; esoterically, the point is the sun, and the circle symbolizes the twelve houses of the zodiac; the term *zodiac* derives from Latin *zōdiacus* which, in turn, originates from the Greek *zōdiakos kyklos* meaning *circle of animals*. Dr. Manhattan takes this Masonic-Illuminist emblem as his logo burning it onto his forehead, saying he wanted a symbol worthy of respect. The circled dot was also used by the Pythagoreans and later Greeks to represent the first metaphysical being, the Monad, identifying Dr. Manhattan with Gnosticism's spiritual godhead.

Dr. Manhattan finds his sacred feminine in Laurie Jupiter, another costumed vigilante. Toward the start of the movie, both of them are working in the Rockefeller Military Research Center. In the world of conspiracy, the Rockefeller family are global puppet masters pulling the strings of the world's economy from behind the scenes, dictating policy. The family accomplishes this through membership in scheming, Masonic-like secret organizations such as Bilderberg and the Trilateral Commission. David Rockefeller (1915-2017) was the only member of Bilderberg's Advisory Board. The Bilderberg Group, Bilderberg Conference, Bilderberg Meetings, or Bilderberg Club is an annual private gathering of approximately 120 to 160 guests from North America and Europe, most of whom are people of power and influence. About one-third are from government and politics, and two-thirds from finance, industry, labor, education and communications. Implicating the Rockefellers even further is the Trilateral Commission: a non-governmental, non-partisan discussion group founded by Rockefeller in July 1973, to pro- mote closer cooperation among North America, Western Europe, and Japan; the Commission was also established to foster substantive political and economic dialogue across the world. According to many, both organizations are behind a global conspiracy to usher in a New World Order (cf. One World Government) paralleling Ozymandias' Illuminist desire to end the Cold War and have a new order of global peace and tranquility. Hiding behind Pyramidal Transnational, Veidt maneuvers in the shadows to bring about this new world; the suggestive

Egyptian name and its pyramidal emblem imply Masonic conspiracy. The third-degree Masonic ritual is a retelling of the Osirian cycle: the Egyptian sun-god Osiris is murdered and resurrected by his virgin sister-wife Isis by possessing the name of Amun-Ra, while numerous Masonic publications and monitors suggest an Egyptian influence upon Freemasonry; included among these is Dr. James Anderson's (1679/1680-1739) *The Constitutions of the Free-Masons; containing the History, Charges, Regulations, &c. of that Most Ancient and Right Worshipful Fraternity. For the Use of the Lodges. London. In the year of Masonry 5723, Anno Domini 1723* which suggests improvement in Freemasonry by the measuring of the ebb and flow of the Nile River. The interlinkage between the writings of Masonic polemicist, London schoolmaster, and member of the Royal Society Martin Clare, to

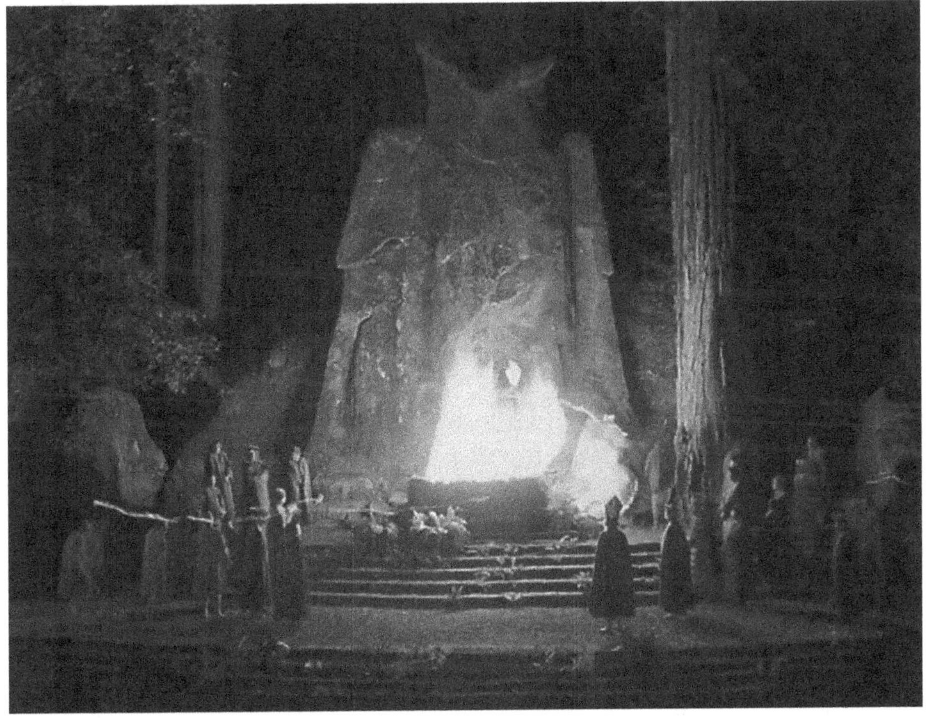

"Men were figuratively said to forget the name of God, when they lost that knowledge, and worshipped the heathen deities, and burned incense to them on the high places, and passed their children through the fire to Moloch." - Albert Pike, *Morals and Dogma of the Scottish Rite*, Chapter XIII, "The Royal Arch of Enoch or Solomon." Dull Care is burned before the owl-like Moloch statute at Bohemian Grove during the Cremation of Care ritual. The giant owl statue symbolizes Moloch, a Canaanite god mentioned in the Book of Deuteronomy and the Book of Leviticus. The worship of the deity is idolatry; see Leviticus 18:21, "And thou shalt not let any of thy seed pass through the fire to Moloch."

whom the first references to Ancient Egypt can be traced, in a Masonic context, called *A Perjured Free Mason Detected*[171] (1730) forms another Masonic link to Veidt's Egyptian Pyramidal Transnational. Clare theorizes that Masonic esoteric building techniques were used in the creation of Giza's great pyramids. Masonic involvement, along with the Illuminati's, formulation of a new democratic order for a new solar age is documented in this author's first book, *The Royal Arch of Enoch: The Impact of Masonic Ritual, Philosophy, and Symbolism* (second edition, 2016), and these occult conspiracies seem to be the driving force behind Veidt's unified new, serene, world order. Veidt explains that he wishes to use the Ancient Mysteries and Arcane Philosophies (Veidt idolizes various Egyptian Pharaohs and Alexander the Great, 356-323 BCE) in the modern world. Freemasonry–as present-day secret society instituted on June 24th, 1717–utilizes philosophies, dogma, and symbolism from the Ancient Mysteries, including Egyptian mythology, Mithraism, Zoroastrianism, Pythagorean numerology, Kabbalah, The Eleusinian Mysteries, and astrology among others.

Watchmen also hints at other real-life clandestine organizations–hidden puppet masters–which manipulate and engineer society on a global scale, echoing Veidt's grand conspiratorial design. The villain Moloch (a/k/a Edgar Jacobi) conjures images of Bohemian Grove, a Bilderberg-like summer camp for global elites. A god worshipped by the Phoenicians and Canaanites; Moloch had associations with a particular kind of propitiatory child sacrifices by their parents. During the Grove's Summer Fire Festival, the Cremation of Care ritual, a child-like effigy identified as Dull Care, symbolizing the members' worries, is burned before a giant owl-like statue of Moloch, echoing ancient ceremonies where children were sacrificed to the pagan god. Moloch can be seen on the small screen, incarnating as an evil demon seeking to unleash the Four Horsemen of the Apocalypse on the television show *Sleepy Hollow* (see Chapter XIII). Among Bohemian Grove's members, known as BoHos, have been Presidents Reagan (1911-2004), Nixon (1913-1994), Eisenhower (1890-1969), Bush 41 (1924-2018) and 43, former German Chancellor Helmut Kohl (1930-2017) and global politico Henry Kissinger. Bohemian Grove is split into various camps; the premiere camps are:

---

171 Also titled *A Defense of Masonry* written in response to Samuel Prichard's Anti-Masonic rant *Masonry Dissected.*

- Hill Billies (Big Business/Banking/Politics/Universities/Media/ Texas Business)
- Mandalay (Big Business/Defense Contractors/ Politics/U.S.Presidents)
- Cave Man (Think Tanks/Oil Companies/Banking/Defense Contractors/Universities/Media)
- Stowaway (Rockefeller Family Members/Oil Companies/ Banking/Think Tanks)
- Uplifters (Corporate Executives/Big Business)
- Owls Nest (U.S. Presidents/Military/Defense Contractors)
- Hideaway (Foundations/Military/Defense Contractors)
- Isle of Aves (Military/Defense Contractors)
- Lost Angels (Banking/Defense Contractors/Media)
- Silverado Squatters (Big Business/ Defense Contractors)
- Sempervirens (California-based Corporations)
- Hillside (Military-Joint Chiefs of Staff)
- Idlewild (California-based Corporations)

The Grove is particularl famous for the Manhattan Project (from whence Dr. Manhattan gets his moniker) planning meeting that took place there in September 1942, which subsequently led to the creation of the atomic bomb. Those attending this session included Ernest Lawrence (1901-1958), U.C. Berkeley colleague Robert Oppenheimer (1904-1967), various military officials, the S-1 Committee heads, such as the president of Harvard, along with rep-resentatives of Standard Oil and General Electric. At the time, Oppenheimer was not an official S-1 member due to security

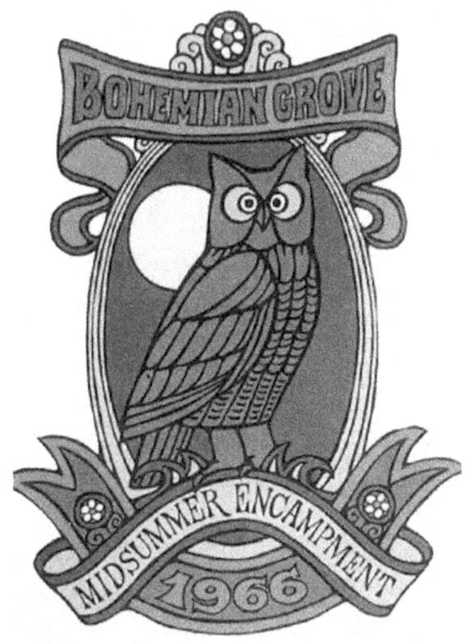

The symbol of Bohemian Grove is an owl, and its motto is, "Weaving Spiders Come Not Here" a line from Shakespeare's *Midsummer's Night Dream*, Act II, Scene II. The owl is the sacred totem of the Roman goddess of wisdom, Minerva, known to the Greeks as Pallas Athena. The owl is considered wise because it can see things in the dark, implying those initiated into secret societies have a greater understanding of arcane wisdom and symbolism, giving them license to rule the profane masses.

clearance troubles with the U.S. wartime Government, though Lawrence and Oppenheimer hosted the meeting. Grove members take pride in this event, often relating the story to new attendees.

Watchmen villain Moloch clearly is intended to conjure Bohemian Grove's Masonic-like conspiratorial reputation; this is further confirmed when Moloch–upon returning home from the Comedian's funeral–flips through his mail. For some reason, Moloch receives correspondences from Veidt's Masonic-Egyptian Pyramidal Transnational,[172] as well as from the Jesuits, which implies the secret workings of both Blue Lodge and high degree Freemasonry. The Blue Lodge ritual system was formulated in London, England while the high or *haute* degree rites were cultivated by the Society of Jesus at the College of Clermont in Paris, France in the mid-1700s as a Counter-Reformation vehicle to restore Catholic Stuarts back to the throne of England. Moloch's mail infers Masonic conspiracy at both Blue Lodge and high degree levels; note that Moloch's mail is showed to the viewer not once but twice: by Moloch and by Rorschach.

In the alternative 1985, the thirty-seventh President of the United States, Richard M. Nixon, has remained in office for a fifth term. Nixon's continuous presidency is made possible by the repeal of the 22nd Amendment and the assassinations of John F. Kennedy and journalists Bob Woodward and Carl Bernstein by the Comedian, serving as one of Nixon's black operators. In what can only be described as Jungian synchronicity, this is not the first movie which depicts Richard M. Nixon holding onto the presidency well into the 1980s. *Back to the Future II* also presents an alternative 1985 wherein the antagonist Biff Tannen (Thomas F. Wilson) is a de facto economic and political warlord through whom Nixon has remained President. In the same newspaper that features the "EMMETT BROWN COMMITTED" headline, one will see a caption beneath it that reads: "Nixon to Seek Fifth Term." In a fascinating *Back to the Future*-Alan Moore paradigm, it seems more than coincidence that Emmett Brown's vision of the Flux Capacitor–the triangular device that makes time travel possible–occurs on November 5th, 1955 exactly 350 years to the date of Guy Fawkes' failed Jesuit Treason (a/k/a the Gunpowder Plot, November 5th, 1605) which is the central plot device of Moore's Gnostic-alchemical Magnum opus, *V for Vendetta*. To this author, this is a great example of

---

172 A triangle also implies the three degrees of Blue Lodge Masonry: Entered Apprentice, Fellowcraft, and Master Mason.

Jungian synchronicity connecting two irrelative films, but others will argue this is evidence of a dark Hollywood conspiracy. The author will let the reader make up his or her mind regarding this occult cinematic nexus.

So, who watches the Watchmen? The film warns us that the Watchmen may be duplicitous malcontents, thus the name *Watchmen* recalls the *Watchers* from the apocryphal *Book of Enoch*. According to *I Enoch*, the Watchers, a race of fallen angels or demons, having displeased God by descending to earth to mate with human women, siring a race of giants known as the Nephilim (Genesis 6:4). The Watchmen, namely Ozymandias, Silk Spectre II, Nite Owl II, and Dr. Manhattan personify fallen angels or anti-heroes: Ozymandias enacts a conspiratorial false flag operation taking the lives of millions of innocents to save humanity from itself. Silk Spectre II, Nite Owl II, and Dr. Manhattan decide to keep silent to cover it up, thus becoming Ozymandias' accomplices after the fact.

CHAPTER III

THE ARCANE NOIR OF DAVID LYNCH

"It's a strange world, isn't it?"
– Sandy Williams, *Blue Velvet*, 1986.

"He who controls the Spice controls the universe!"
– Baron Vladimir Harkonnen, *Dune*, 1984.

"You unlock this door with the key of imagination. Beyond it is another dimension: a dimension of sound, a dimension of sight, a dimension of mind. You're moving into a land of both shadow and substance, of things and ideas. You've just crossed over into the Twilight Zone.
– Rod Serling/Narrator, *The Twilight Zone*
(Seasons 4 & 5, 1963-1964)

"Don't be a good neighbor to her. I'll send you a love letter, straight from my heart, fucker! You know what a love letter is? It's a bullet from a fucking gun, fucker! You receive a love letter from me, you're fucked forever! You understand fuck? I'll send you straight to Hell fucker! In dreams, I walk with you. In dreams, I talk to you."
– Frank Booth, *Blue Velvet*, 1986.

"You invited me. It is not my custom to go where I am not wanted."
– The Mystery Man, *Lost Highway*, 1997.

"It is by will alone I set my mind in motion. It is by the juice of Sapho that thoughts acquire speed, the lips acquire stains, stains become a warning. It is by will alone I set my mind in motion.
– Piter De Vries, *Dune*, 1984.

"I like to sing 'Blue Velvet.'"
– Dorothy Vallens, *Blue Velvet*, 1986.

Originally this chapter was going to include an analysis of Lynch's esoteric television drama *Twin Peaks* (1990-1991), as well as his films *Wild at Heart* (1990) and *Twin Peaks: Fire Walk with Me* (1992), but doing so would have increased the length of this book substantially. However, all three will be dissected in *Cinema Symbolism 3* so do not fret. Instead, this chapter will breakdown four of Lynch's films all of which contain arcane themes, irony, and dark symbolic undercurrents. They are *Blue Velvet*, *Dune*, *Lost Highway*, and *Mulholland Drive* (stylized onscreen as *Mulholland Dr.*). All four movies are Gnostic, or at the very least, incorporate elements of Gnosticism. *Blue Velvet* is a journey of gnosis drawing on the idea of the sacred feminine while also featuring a sublime, almost unnoticeable, alchemical storyline; *Dune* is the messianic solar monomyth, and through its lurid dreaminess broods over the ambiguous relationships between development and destiny, enlightenment and violence; *Lost Highway* suggests one can know reality through nothingness and negation–the domain of Basilides and the Sethians–by canceling concepts inadequate to reality's superabundance; while *Mulholland Drive* reflects the Gnostic idea that reality is a dream.[173] Even Lynch's *The Elephant Man* (1980) is Gnostic, meditating profoundly on the ironic dualistic interplay between ugliness and beauty, pain and redemption.[174]

If Salvador Dalí's (1904-1989) paintings somehow became three-dimensional and animated, they would probably resemble the cinema of David Lynch. One thinks of *Blue Velvet's* peculiar death scene featuring a lobotomized Detective Gordon (Fred Pickler) and an earless Don Watts (Dick Green) on display like they were in a wax museum. Lynch's cinema exhibits surreal, opposing yet interlocking dualistic imagery of nonsectarian religion and atheism, darkness and light, good and evil, formalism and surrealism, wisdom and ignorance, order and chaos, normalcy and the strange, and the divine masculine and the sacred feminine. However, in Lynch's weird cinematic world, these paradigms are tainted with varying levels of darkness, sarcasm, and of devilish irony. Lynch wants us to know there are no absolutes, only shades of gray some darker than others. Nothing is 100% positive or negative; even the good guy is an oddball, while the villain is emotionally vulnerable. For instance, despite living

---

173 See Wilson's *The Strange World of David Lynch*, pp. 24-25.
174 *ibid*, p. 25.

in a halcyon white picket fenced world, *Blue Velvet's* Jeffrey Beaumont (Kyle MacLachlan) wears an earring. It is an emblem of his desire to think independently, stand out, to rebel (not violently) against the banalities of the utopian stasis that is his Lumberton existence. On the other end of the spectrum, *Blue Velvet's* bizarre villain Frank Booth (Dennis Hopper, 1936-2010) becomes choked up when "Suave" Ben (Dean Stockwell) lip-syncs Roy Orbison's (1936-1988) "In Dreams." These abstract concepts harmoniously dovetail in Lynch's movies producing what Professor Eric G. Wilson describes as an omnipresent *transcendental irony*. In his book, *The Strange World of David Lynch*, he explains:

> Though skeptical of reaching the absolute, this irony is 'transcenden-tal.' In measuring the real against the ideal and the ideal against the real, this irony never becomes fixed on one form. Irony of this sort turns into a sort of sacred buffoonery, a boundless jest never seriously moored in the world. Destroying as it creates, standing in and outside of itself, this kind of irony approaches the infinitude of self-consciousness. This is the terror of never of never being able to rest on any representation of the world, the joy of escaping any final structure.

> Certain Lynch pictures are similar. They leave us wondering if we've experienced an awesome meditation on being or a silly avoidance of the serious. We can never be sure if we're meant to cower before the sublime or laugh our heads off. This bizarre irony necessarily brings to mind holy images, sites that both posit their powerful existence but also dissolve before the divine as ridiculously fogs. Standing before such a holy pattern, we want to quake with both fear and laughter. We are afraid of our insignificance before this immensely potent image. We get tickled over the pomposity of this same image, for it looks fun-ny when compared to the divine power it wishes to represent. Such is the holiness of transcendental irony, a mode that dwells in the middle of the overflowing, beautiful light and the tawdry lightbulb trying to capture the current.[175]

Dune aside, transcendental irony permeates the Baudrillardian cinema of Lynch, pervading the first movie presented in this chapter, *Blue Velvet*.

175 *ibid*, pp 10-13.

A SEVERED EAR, BLUE VELVET, AND A CANDY-COLORED CLOWN THEY CALL THE SANDMAN

At its heart, *Blue Velvet* is a movie about the interplay of light and darkness, enlightenment and ignorance; it is about life and all that comes with it. The film's protagonist, Jeffrey Beaumont, is on a journey of gnosis and wisdom; this is no secret because, at Arlene's Diner, he tells Sandy Williams (Laura Dern) this is his mission quest. His last name, Beaumont, denotes "*beau*tiful *mount*ain" implying a sublime journey of ascension. He wishes to go beyond the boundaries of his idyllic yet dull existence, gaining gnosis by experiencing the dark side of humanity. He seeks evil, melancholy, but does not know why he longs for the dark side. He will accomplish this mainly through the agency of two archetypal women: Sandy Williams and Dorothy Vallens (Isabella Rossellini). They are his muses, representing contrasting sides of the sacred feminine: light and dark, virgin and harlot.[176] Sandy is the virginal girl next door; she is the lunar goddess, Isis, Artemis or Diana, Sophia, the supplier of wisdom, the woman that everyman woos. Her name, Sandy, insinuates the virginal Sandy Olsson (Olivia Newton-John) from 1978's *Grease*, while sand implies earth, stability, and tranquility. But just as the lunar goddesses Artemis and Diana are shadowed by Hecate, and Lilith shadows Sophia, so too does Sandy have a darker counterpart. Dorothy Vallens is an experienced nightclub chanteuse practicing sadomasochistic sex with more than one partner. However, Lynch presents a paradox: the inexperienced virginal Sandy is obsessed with criminality while Dorothy, the typical femme fatale, yearns for motherhood. These women offer Jeffrey an ironic prototype: a set of values that erases itself, purity that is corrupt, order that dissolves into chaos.[177]

Set in Lumberton, North Carolina, the movie begins by depicting the blissful American ideal: a neighborhood of flowery white picket fences, a

---

176 On the duality of the universal goddess, see Campbell's *The Hero with a Thousand Faces*, p. 259. Campbell explains, "The Sumero-Babylonian astral mythology identified the aspects of the cosmic female with the phases of the planet Venus. As morning star she was the virgin, as evening star the harlot, as lady of the night sky the consort of the moon; and when extinguished under the blaze of the sun she was the hag of hell."

177 See Wilson's *The Strange World of David Lynch*, p. 57.

bright red fire truck drives down the street with waving, smiling firemen, school children cross the street under the protection of a crossing guard, well- manicured lawns and gardens. Lynch shows us the wholesome, saccharine Eisenhower-America of the 1950s; this is the middle-class good life often depicted in the films of Frank Capra (1897-1991). As Bobby Vinton's "Blue Velvet" (1954) plays, the peaceful home of the Beaumont's is surveyed, but something dark is lurking beneath the surface. Jeffrey's mother (Priscilla Pointer) watches foreboding crime noir films on TV while outside, as Jeffrey's father (Jack Harvey) waters the lawn. Chaos now descends upon regimented order: while trying to free the hose from a branch, he has a heart attack, or stroke, causing him to fall to the ground. Lynch sarcastically mocks serenity: as Jeffrey's father lies there helpless, the hose's nozzle pumps water out like a geyser, looking like a penis endlessly ejaculating all over this idyllic vista. A feisty terrier bites at the water as it sprays all over the place which only adds insult to injury. The camera then moves beneath the surface, showing black beetles moving about in a terrifying, grotesque symphony of chaos. Lynch's sense of irony is evident: utopias are pedantic and boring (even worthy of destruction); beneath their peaceful surface there is a dangerous yet fascinating world inhabited by chaos and darkness, there is good, but there is also evil; they harmoniously coexist. It is this corrupt, chaotic world that Jeffrey yearns to explore and experience, to break up the doldrums of his boring life.

Lynch's use of sarcasm, transcendental irony, is evidenced when Jeffrey visits his father in the hospital only to discover that his lawgiver and role model, the personification of normalcy and stability, is now in a state of disarray: he is encased in metal hooked up to various medical devices. He is unable to speak; his life is sustained by machines making him appear robotic. He is symptomatic of the doctrine: bad things happen to good people. With his father temporarily out of the way, Jeffrey is now free to investigate, unimpeded by an authority figure. After leaving the hospital, he discovers a severed human ear on the ground covered with ants. Indian mystic Osho (1931-1990) said that "Creativity is the greatest rebellion in existence,"[178] while the severed ear recalls creative genius Vincent Van Gogh (1853-1890) known for his post-Impressionist paintings but also for

---

178 See Foreword ("The Fragrance of Wisdom") of Osho's *Creativity: Unleashing the Forces Within.* This is the first sentence.

cutting off his ear.[179] The symbolism of the severed ear becomes apparent: it signifies that Jeffrey's Gnostic quest is fueled by a need to rebel against conformity, to experience a different side of life thereby creating, much like an artist, a wiser and a worldlier version of himself. He takes the ear to Police Detective John Williams (George Dickerson, 1933-2015), who like his father, is a by the book personification of regularity and normalcy. Detective Williams is a disciplined, well-trained law enforcement official symbolized by his office room number, 221, which signifies 221B Baker Street, the legendary residence of super sleuth Sherlock Holmes. Williams takes the ear, opening an investigation as night descends upon Lumberton.

When Jeffrey decides to take an evening stroll, he is advised by Aunt Barbara (Frances Bay, 1919-2011) to stay away from Lincoln Street. She knows that evil lurks there but is blissfully ignorant regarding its nature, hoping Jeffrey will remain unexposed. He visits the home of Detective Williams who will not discuss the case; Jeffrey leaves, but as he is standing outside, a beacon of light shines through the darkness. Out of the foreboding night comes Sandy (Detective Williams' daughter), the virginal pure moon to shed her light upon Jeffrey, to help him unravel the mystery he has stumbled upon: the enigma of the severed ear. It turns out her bedroom is above her father's office; eavesdropping, she believes the severed ear has something to do with a woman named Dorothy Vallens. Dorothy will, like Sandy, supply Jeffrey with gnosis: her dark world will snap him out of his spiritual stasis. Sandy *qua* Sophia launches Jeffrey on his quest for wisdom and experience by imparting knowledge to him. She takes him to Dorothy's apartment building, Deep River, on Lincoln Street. Deep River is a metaphor for the dark, ironic, strange undercurrents that run beneath everyday Lumberton. Sandy explains that Dorothy resides on the seventh floor and the nightclub where she performs–the Slow Club–is on Route 7; the number seven is imbued with mysticism. On the mysteries of the number seven, Masonic encyclopedist Albert Mackey (1807-1881) explains:

In every system of antiquity there is a frequent reference to this number, showing that the veneration for it proceeded from some common cause. …The Pythagoreans called it a perfect number, because it was made

---

179 Suffering with severe depression, Van Gogh cuts his ear off on December 23rd, 1888. He later documented the event in the painting *Self-Portrait with Bandaged Ear* (1889).

up of 3 and 4, the triangle and the square, which are the two perfect figures. They called it also a virgin number, and without a mother, comparing it to Minerva, who was a motherless virgin, because it cannot by multiplication produce any number within ten, as twice two does four, and three times three does nine; nor can any two numbers, by their multiplication, produce it.

It is singular to observe the important part occupied by the number seven in all the ancient systems. There were, for instance, *seven* ancient planets, *seven* Pleiades, and *seven* Hyades; *seven* altars burned continually before the god Mithras; the Arabians had *seven* holy temples; the Hindus supposed the world to be enclosed within the compass of *seven* peninsulas; the Goths had seven *deities*, viz., the Sun, the Moon, Tuisco, Woden, Thor, Friga, and Seatur, from whose names are derived our days of the week; in the Persian mysteries were *seven* spacious caverns, through which the aspirant had to pass; in the Gothic mysteries, the candidate met with *seven* obstructions, which were called the 'road of the seven stages'; and, finally, sacrifices were always considered as the most efficacious when the victims were *seven* in number.

…The Sabbath was the *seventh* day; Noah received *seven* days' notice of the commencement of the deluge, and was commanded to select clean beasts and fowls by *sevens; seven* persons accompanied him to ark; the ark rested on Mount Ararat in the *seventh* month; the intervals between dispatching the dove were, each time, *seven* days; the walls of Jericho were encompassed *seven* days by *seven* priests, bearing rams' horns; Solomon was *seven* years in building the Temple, which was dedicated in the *seventh* month, and the festival lasted *seven* days; the candlestick in the tabernacle consisted of seven branches; and, finally, the tower of Babel was said to have been elevated *seven* stories before dispersion.

Seven is a sacred number in Masonic symbolism. It has always been so. In the earliest ritual of the last century it was said that a Lodge required seven to make it perfect; but the only explanation to be found in any of those rituals of the sacredness of the number is the seven liberal arts and sciences, which, according to the old 'Legend of the Craft,' were the foundation of Masonry. In modern ritualism the symbolism of seven has been transferred from the First to the Second Degree, and there it is made only to refer to the seven steps of the Winding Stairs; but symbolically seven is to be found diffused in a hundred ways over the whole Masonic system.

...Hippocrates says that the centenary number, by its occult virtue, tends to the accomplishment of all things, is the dispenser of life and the fountain of all its changes; and, like Shakespeare, he divides the life of man into seven stages.[180]

The seventh degree of the York Rite is the Holy Royal Arch, which documents the recovery of the Tetragrammaton, the name of God. T.E. Lawrence (1888-1935) published his monumental work, *Seven Pillars of Wisdom*, published in 1922. Crowley wrote *777 and other Qabalistic Writings*, published in 1909. The use of the number seven invests Jeffrey's wisdom quest with the divine presence–Kabbalah's feminine *Shekinah*–making his journey of enlightenment Gnostic and numinous. But Jeffrey must enter the shadowy world of Frank and "Suave" Ben to gain the experience he craves. For this is the logic of alchemy's *nigredo*, of saturnine melancholy: the darkness is the light.

The name Sandy has symbolic meaning, so too does the name Dorothy, evoking *The Wizard of Oz* because Jeffrey is about to go over the rainbow, only in Lumberton, the other side is not a beautiful, magical land (this is where Jeffrey resides); rather, its underbelly is weirdly sinister. Dorothy *qua* Lilith is right at home in this strangeness. Jeffrey climbs the staircase of Dorothy's apartment, the allegorical Winding Stairs of Freemasonry, to achieve Gnostic *ascensio*. While hiding inside her closet, Jeffrey learns that her husband Don and her son (whom she calls "Little Donny") have been kidnapped. Dorothy, wielding a knife, discovers him and threatens to kill him. Believing his curiosity is merely sexual and aroused by his voyeurism, Dorothy makes Jeffrey undress at knifepoint, beginning to fellate him before their encounter is interrupted by a knock at the door. She hurriedly returns Jeffrey to the closet. Dorothy opens the door and in comes the inescapable night that follows the day, the darkness that dwells in Lumberton, the demented villain, Frank Booth. Booth is chaos and

---

180 Albert Mackey, *Encyclopedia of Freemasonry*, Vol. II., pp. 682-684.

darkness personified: he inflicts his bizarre behavior and sexual proclivities, which includes inhaling an unidentified gas (likely nitrous oxide), dry humping, a fetish for blue velvet,[181] and sadomasochism, upon Dorothy. Frank is a foul-mouthed, rigid, violent sociopath whose orgasmic climax is a fit of both pleasure and rage. He continually refers to her as "mommy" and to himself as both the "daddy" and the "baby." It is disclosed that Frank kidnapped Dorothy's husband and son to force her to perform sexual favors; to "Do it for van Gogh," he cruelly remarks. As Lumberton's living-breathing evil undercurrent, Frank wears black clothing and even says, "Now it's dark," once inside Dorothy's apartment. Dorothy, however, enjoys sadomasochistic sex, willingly submitting to Frank's strange whims, but is also repulsed by him because he has kidnapped her family. Frank is the Gacy-like "Candy-Colored Clown they call the Sandman:" a tormentor perpetually haunting your dreams; you do not want to get a "love letter" from this psychopath.[182] Jeffrey's observation of Dorothy's ritualistic rape by Frank becomes a Freudian primal scene, like a child seeing their parents having sex, understanding what is occurring, perceiving it as violence. Jeffrey is both repulsed and fascinated by the odd spectacle.

When Frank leaves, Dorothy *qua* Lilith resumes her romantic endeavors with Jeffrey, instructing him to engage in weird, sadomasochistic sexual behavior, reflecting Booth's chaotic darkness. Like Frank, she does not want to be looked at either. Jeffrey leaves the apartment confused yet stimulated by what he has experienced, desiring to go further. He laments to Sandy that he doesn't understand why there are people like Frank in the world, but she reassures him that good is present despite there being evil, and that good will triumph in the end. She relates to him a dream about lingering darkness, but that Robins descended upon the earth bringing happiness and light, which are the only things that matter. She speaks to him in front of a Christian church which imbues Sandy with a Marian quality; however, the dream is clearly nonsectarian feeling more Manichean than Abrahamic. Nevertheless, the church is well placed, sitting across the street from Dorothy's apartment signifying the overall religious-sacred journey of enlightenment that Jeffrey is on, and naturally, the endless conflict between light and dark.

---

181 Frank has a fetish for the fabric but also, it seems, for the song especially when sung by Dorothy.
182 John Wayne Gacy's (1942-1994) alter egos were Pogo the Clown and Patches the Clown.

Lynch's use of sarcasm and irony is sublime and profound in the relationships and interactions of Jeffrey, Dorothy, and Frank. Dorothy is a darker version of Sandy and Jeffrey's mother, and while Sandy provides the raw data for Jeffrey's whimsical quest, it is Dorothy supplying the life lessons and sexual experiences (more in this in a moment). It is by helping Dorothy become reunited with her son that Jeffrey grows as a person experiencing gnosis first hand; without Dorothy, there would be no journey of wisdom, no Gnostic quest. However, it is Frank who becomes Jeffrey's dark surrogate father, actually fostering his quest. Frank is Mercurius, the Tarot's archetypal magician, forever dwelling the in the *nigredo* phase; from his vomitous blackness comes Jeffrey's awakening. Frank wants to be called "daddy," becoming a substitute for Jeffrey's biological father; his old man is hospitalized, no longer present. Jeffrey abandons his father for Frank by following him to his Meadow Lane hideout, eavesdropping on him when he should be visiting his father in the hospital. Frank calls Dorothy "mommy," making her a nebulous substitute for Jeffrey's mother, the former a sex craving sadomasochist caring more for pleasure than for family; she is the antithesis of a traditional matriarch. However, Dorothy is also a mirror of Frank: she too *doesn't want to be looked at* and, like Frank, enjoys weird sadomasochistic sex games. But Lynch goes further down the rabbit hole by sexual role reversing. Mimicking Dorothy, Frank wears bright red lipstick and even kisses Jeffrey's lips, becoming a distorted version of the sacred feminine, a would-be-lover, although Frank is clearly not homosexual. Does this make Frank another agent of Jeffrey's gnosis? The answer, of course, is an emphatic yes: for without a villain there is no hero, without night there can be no daylight; Lynch understands this and wants to make sure the audience does as well. Frank even carries a police radio making him an evil, yet predictable, reflection of Detective Williams. Frank is a living symbol opposing everything Jeffrey is accustomed to: he is an evil, chaotic version of all his lionized authoritative figures: his mother, father, and Detective Williams, annihilating all distinctions between them. Lynch's ironic duality even transcends Frank, having an alternate persona, the Well-Dressed Man; Frank vehemently insists on drinking domestic beer, contradicting Jeffrey who prefers foreign. Frank Booth is the polar opposite of Jeffrey and the peaceful world of Lumberton depicted during the film's opening sequence. He is Lumberton's Jungian shadow.

When forced to go on a joy ride with Frank, his henchmen, and Dorothy, Jeffrey learns what it means to live on the dark side. Not only live there but to stay there. Like Luke Skywalker, he is about to confront his shadow self, an allegorical Darth Vader in a cave on Dagobah, and learn all about the mercurial nature of evil. Jeffrey will discover this at THIS IS IT, which is the name of the hideout where Dorothy's young son is being held captive. The name is appropriate: it is the liar of the Ben, an odd man blending darkness with strangeness. Because of this unique mixture, Frank admires Ben so much so that he has nicknamed him "suave;" Ben and his home represents the dark side's version of the good life. Ben is the evil force motivating Frank; comparatively, Ben is Emperor Palpatine[183] (a/k/a Darth Sidious) to Frank's Darth Vader, who, through a strange synthesis, has become Jeffry's surrogate father. The shadow thrives when the ego has been suppressed, and one of its side effects is surrealism and sublime weirdness that few understand. Ben is an effeminate eccentric wearing white makeup, lipstick, a tuxedo, smoking through a fashionable cigarette holder. He has a penchant for lip-syncing Roy Orbison's "In Dreams." At first, the song sends Frank into maudlin sadness–lamentable villainy–then unbridled rage symbolic of the bizarre nature the dark side, surfacing when freed from the constraints of the ego. Ben's hideout, replete with aging, heavyset women, some of whom still dress if they were in their 20s and 30s, is the flip side of Jeffrey's reality. Underneath his affable exterior, Ben is mysterious and menacing: despite his womanish nature, he violently punches Jeffrey in the stomach and is holding Dorothy's child hostage so Frank can live out his demented sexual fantasies with her. Jeffrey does not know what to make of the strange environment he has descended into; he is awed by the dark side and all its trappings but longs for safety and the familiarity of the empirical status quo. His initiation almost over, Frank finally initiates Jeffrey into his shadow world. Like Faustus and Dante, Jeffrey must learn to swim in total darkness before he can ascend to the light. Frank marks (violently kisses) Jeffrey with lipstick from his mouth, penetrates the boy with his fists, threatens him with death (what Frank calls a "love letter") annihilating his pride. When Jeffrey wakes the next morning in the lumberyard, battered and alone, his is now experienced; he is the same person but his Gnostic journey to the dark side has made him ostensibly wiser and worldly. His

---

183 Portrayed by English actor Ian McDiarmid.

innocence is forever lost; he has now experienced firsthand the evil that lurks in the world.

Jeffrey now unites with the sacred feminine, reconciling Sandy and Dorothy. He professes his love for Sandy, which she accepts despite her learning that he has been intimate with Dorothy. By admitting to his error, he is not fixed on one identity, rather, he is willing to now open, flexible, more understanding of light and dark; he acknowledges that a sable heart lurks beneath the sheen of shining armor.[184] He now mirrors Sandy in that he becomes to her what she has been to him: a mixture of light–the possibility of amorous bliss–and darkness–the potential for the wounds of unreturned affection.[185] In forgiving Jeffrey for his transgression, Sandy acknowledges his duplicitous existence; her embrace of his imbrications of darkness and light prepares the way for her impending marriage with him, a complementary union between a male now able to discover order rising from the chaos and a female who understands that chaos underlies all order.[186] Jeffrey also completes his Gnostic quest with Sandy's dark counterpart *qua* Lilith, Dorothy. Immediately after she is found wandering naked and insane through the neighborhood, Jeffrey offers her exactly what she needs. Jeffrey covers her bruised and nude body, offering her comforting hugs. He calls an ambulance for her, riding with her to the hospital. He stays there with her until he's sure she'll be okay. In performing these deeds, Jeffrey guides Dorothy as she earlier guided him. Before the strange and horrific night with Frank and Ben, Dorothy led Jeffrey from his safe, youthful identity to a more sophisticated manhood. She helped him loose a harmfully stultifying self and embrace a form of being more open to ambiguity, to mystery.[187] Now Jeffrey takes Dorothy from her self-destructive extremes to a more moderate identity. He aids her transformation from a sadomasochistic sensualist with hope in her heart to a loving mother with a tragic sensibility.[188] The unification with the sacred feminine now complete, indicating the syzygy, Jeffrey is now spiritual able to defeat Frank, bringing order out of chaos. He kills Frank in self-defense unifying with Sandy; the movie should end here, but it doesn't? Why?

---

184 Wilson, *The Strange World of David Lynch*, pp. 73-74.

185 *ibid*, p. 73.

186 *ibid*, p. 74.

187 *ibid*.

188 *ibid*.

Instead of the film ending with Jeffrey and Sandy's embrace at Dorothy's apartment, we are shown a concluding sequence where Sandy and Jeffrey are together in love, Jeffrey's father is out of the hospital, and the lawn is well-manicured; it is a repeat of the movie's opening sequence. Sandy's dream now becomes reality: a Robin lands on the windowsill with a beetle in its mouth, symbolizing that love has conquered evil, order has been restored from chaos. However, the movie ends by showing Dorothy united with her son; she is happy at first but as she hugs him, she becomes melancholy. The camera then turns towards the sky. She has transitioned from sadomasochism to motherhood but laments that her darkness is gone, purged from her forever. The dark side is a powerful, potent elixir which she still yearns for; it appears she wishes to return to the dangerous and mysterious world of Frank Booth. Lynch is showing the audience that Dorothy has, in fact, gone through an alchemical transition. She is not the sadomasochist she was at the start of the film; rather, she has morphed into something new: she has inherited the mantle of motherhood, become a mother to her son. To symbolize this alchemical change, Lynch has adroitly placed the color red, *rubedo*, around Dorothy signifying both transition and completion of her alchemical process. Dorothy performs before a red curtain; she wears red high heels and a red dress; she has a red blanket on her bed, she covers herself with a red towel, using a red chair with Frank during their sex games. The color red symbolizes her alchemical metamorphosis from sadomasochistic to mother, and the other colors of symbolic alchemy are also present. Frank is the alchemical *nigredo*, the darkness in Lumberton, the living personification of the chaotic black beetles which toil beneath the surface, while the virginal Sandy is the *albedo*–the sacred feminine, the moon–with Jeffrey embodying the solar *citrinitas*, the sun. Lynch even employs a solar Yellow Man (a/k/a Detective Gordon) who also interacts with Dorothy. Thus, we can conclude that *Blue Velvet* not only documents Jeffrey's Gnostic journey, it also has a veiled alchemical storyline about Dorothy's alchemical transition. Red roses become yellow tulips, signifying Dorothy's alchemy; for Dorothy the masculine *citrinitas*, Frank and Jeffrey, are her philosopher's stone.

The difference between the two journeys is that Jeffrey is better off because of his quest, he is wiser and worldly. But Dorothy's desire to be a mother results in her yearning for the dark side, she secretly pines to be reunited with Frank and all his violence, his punishing sexual antics, and weirdness. Frank plays the role of the alchemical trickster, Mercurius, to Jeffrey only, not to Dorothy. Instead. Dorothy plays this part by fooling herself. She finally realizes Frank and Jeffrey are irreconcilable representations of her conflicting personality traits: sadomasochist and wholesome mother. Dorothy deceives herself thinking she can abandon one for the other; she cannot juggle these two differing attributes. Dorothy, with the aid of Jeffrey, has found motherhood while shedding her dark sexual tendencies, but the final moments of *Blue Velvet* indicate that she still, rather ironically, desires the latter.

THE SPICE IS VITAL TO SPACE TRAVEL: DUNE'S MONOMYTH

There is no transcendental irony in *Dune*; rather it's the primordial monomyth. Paul Atreides' (Kyle MacLachlan) journey and eventual awakening to Muad'Dib, the Fremen's prophesied messiah, is Gnostic epiphany feeling more like Thomas Anderson's metamorphosis into Neo–the One–rather than Frodo Baggins (Elijah Wood) or Luke Skywalker's epic adventures. Although all four experience the monomyth, Muad'Dib and Neo's sacred quest is to bring gnosis and liberation to the people–to become gods (at least godlike, the solar savior archetype)–because they're both *sleepers that will awaken* and, in doing so, will awaken the people with them.[189] Although Skywalker and Baggins are liberators, neither will become Christlike messiahs. Instead, Skywalker vanishes[190] and Frodo returns to the Shire resuming his ordinary life.

Based on the novel by Frank Herbert (1920-1986), *Dune* opens in the year 10,191; the known universe is ruled by Padishah Emperor Shaddam IV (José Ferrer, 1912-1992). The paramount substance in the universe is the

---

189 Unlike Luke Skywalker and Frodo Baggins, Paul Atreides and Thomas Anderson also undergo a name change. Paul Atreides becomes Ulsu and Muad'Dib while Thomas Anderson becomes Neo. The change in name suggests a new identity, death and rebirth, darkness to light, ignorance to gnosis; Neo and Muad'Dib are Gnostic saviors bringing light to the masses.

190 See 2015's *Star Wars: The Force Awakens* opening crawl. Erratum: in some early editions of *Cinema Symbolism*, this author erroneously used the word *scrawl* when defining the opening lines of the Star Wars movies.

drug known as Melange or the Spice. It has many unique properties, such as extending life and expanding consciousness. One of the most profitable and important of its qualities is its ability to assist the Spacing Guild (commonly called the Guild) with folding space thereby allowing safe, instantaneous interstellar travel. Sensing a potential threat to Spice production, the Guild sends an emissary–a Third Stage Navigator–to demand an explanation from the Emperor, who confidentially shares with the Navigator his plans to destroy House Atreides. The popularity of Duke Leto Atreides (Jürgen Prochnow) has grown in the Landsraad (a Universal High Council consisting of ruling families), and he is suspected to be amassing an army while developing a secret weapon involving sound, making him a threat to the Emperor. Shaddam's plan is to give the Atreides control of the planet Arrakis (also known as Dune), the only source of Spice, and to have them ambushed by their longtime archenemy, the Harkonnens. The Navigator commands the Emperor to kill the Duke's son, Paul Atreides, a young man who dreams prophetic visions of his purpose. The death warrant draws the attention of the mysterious Bene Gesserit sisterhood, as Paul is tied to the centuries-old Bene Gesserit breeding program which seeks to produce the universe's super-being, a godlike figure known as the Kwisatz Haderach. Paul is tested by the Bene Gesserit Reverend Mother Gaius Helen Mohiam (Siân Phillips) when he is forced to place his hand in a box which subjects him to excruciating pain. He passes to Mohiam's satisfaction.

Meanwhile, on the industrial world of Giedi Prime, the sadistic Baron Vladimir Harkonnen (Kenneth McMillan, 1932-1989) tells his nephews Glossu Rabban (Paul L. Smith, 1936-2012) and Feyd-Rautha (Sting) about his plan to eliminate the Atreides by manipulating someone into betraying the Duke. The Atreides leave Caladan (their home planet) for Arrakis, a barren desert planet populated by gigantic sandworms and the Fremen, a mysterious people who have long held a prophecy that a messiah would come to lead them to freedom. Upon arrival on Arrakis, Leto is informed by one of his trusted agents, Duncan Idaho (Richard Jordan, 1937-1993), that the Fremen have been underestimated, and they exist in vast numbers and could prove to be a powerful ally. Before the Duke can establish an alliance with them, the Harkonnens launch their surprise attack.

While the Atreides had anticipated a trap, they are unable to withstand the assault, supported by the Emperor's elite Sardaukar troops and aided by a traitor within House Atreides, Dr. Wellington Yueh (Dean Stockwell). Captured, Leto dies in a failed attempt to assassinate the Baron Harkonnen using a poison gas capsule planted in his tooth by Dr. Yueh. Leto's Bene Gesserit concubine, Lady Jessica (Francesca Annis), and his son Paul escape into the deep desert, where they join a band of Fremen, led by Stilgar (Everett McGill). Paul is given the secret name Usul, which is Fremen for *base of thepPillar*, and is also given the name Muad'Dib. Muad'Dib is a kangaroo mouse on Arrakis; it's a creature in the Fremen earth-spirit mythology, appearing as a silhouette on the planet's second moon. There is also a constellation called Muad'Dib in the sky of Arrakis; its tail points to the north, resulting in it being known as *the one who points the way*, indicating that Paul is their prophesied liberator (See also Herbert's *Dune*, 1965). Thus, Paul is the *one who points the way* toward freedom.

Paul teaches the Fremen to use sonic weapons, known as the Weirding Way, targeting the mining of the Spice. Within two years, Spice production is halted. The Spacing Guild warns the Emperor of the situation on Arrakis. The Guild fears that Paul will consume the Water of Life–bile of newborn sandworms–and survive identifying him as the Kwisatz Haderach. These concerns are revealed to Paul in a prophetic dream; he finally drinks the Water of Life, entering into a trance. Awakening, he is transformed, gaining control of the sandworms of Arrakis. Paul has also seen into space and the future; the Emperor is amassing a large invasion fleet above Arrakis to regain control of the planet and the Spice.

Upon the Emperor's arrival at Arrakis, he executes Rabban for failing to remedy the Spice situation. Paul launches a final attack against the Harkonnens and the Emperor's elite shock troops at the capital city of Arrakeen. His Fremen warriors defeat the Emperor's legions, while Paul's younger sister Alia (Alicia Witt) kills Baron Harkonnen. Paul faces the defeated Emperor and relieves him of power, then engages Feyd-Rautha in a duel to the death. Paul demonstrates his newfound powers fulfilling the Fremen prophecy that he is the promised Messiah by causing rain to fall on Arrakis for the first time, as Alia declares him the Kwisatz Haderach.

Dune is a morose narrative successfully contrasting futuristic with primitive imagery, the fantastic with the mundane: advanced sonic weaponry destroys everything, and a homoerotic vampire-like Baron Harkonnen feasts on flesh; travel occurs by both folding space and on the backs of giant worms; at its heart, *Dune* is a tale of betrayal and rebellion. It is a retelling of the age-old monomyth, the grand solar heroic quest, which has always been, according to Joseph Campbell, part of our collective unconscious.[191] In its simplest terms, the monomyth or the hero's journey can be summarized, "A hero ventures forth from the world of common day into a region of supernatural wonder: fabulous forces are there encountered and a decisive victory is won: the hero comes back from this mysterious adventure with the power to bestow boons on his fellow man."[192] This quote describes *Dune* in a nutshell. The hero's journey has many components beginning with what Campbell describes as the Call to Adventure. In *The Hero with a Thousand Faces*, Campbell writes:

> This first stage of the mythological journey–which we have designated the 'call to adventure'–signifies that destiny has summoned the hero and transferred his spiritual center of gravity from within the pale of his society to a zone unknown. This fateful region of both treasure and danger may be variously represented: as a distant land, a forest, a kingdom underground, beneath the waves, or above the sky, a secret island, lofty mountaintop, or profound dream state; but it is always a place of strangely fluid and polymorphous beings, unimaginable torments, superhuman deeds, and impossible delights.[193]

This element is satisfied when Paul leaves his home planet of Caladan for the mysterious and distant planet Dune. He has accepted the adventure and all that comes with it; he does not Refuse the Call which is another element related to Call to Adventure. Refusal of the Call occurs when Paul is tested by Reverend Mother Mohiam when he places his hand in the green box. Paul does not refuse the test. He passes; having suffered great pain Paul is now prepared for the adventure ahead of him. Although she is a minor character, Reverend Mother Mohiam could be seen as satisfying the monomythic component of Woman as the Temptress because she is a female devil,[194] a mysterious, conniving figure whose loyalties are to the Bene Gesserits above all.

---

191 Campbell, *The Hero with a Thousand Faces*, pp. 6-9.
192 *ibid*, p. 23
193 *ibid*, p. 48.
194 *ibid*, p. 104.

Having heeded the call, Paul now receives Supernatural Aid, another element of the monomyth. On this Campbell explains, "For those who have not refused the call, the first encounter of the hero-journey is with a protective figure (often a little old crone or old man) who provides the adventurer with amulets against the dragon forces he is about to pass."[195] Paul receives metaphysical aid twice: first, under the supervision of three elder hermits, Dr. Yueh, Thufir Hawat (Freddie Jones), and Gurney Halleck (Patrick Stewart), Paul hones his skill with the Weirding Module (sound weapon). Later he is instructed in the ways of the Stillsuit, a water processing outfit critical to desert survival, by the sagacious Dr. Kynes (Max von Sydow). Both the weapon and suit aid Paul in mastering Arrakis, allying with the Fremen, defeating the Emperor and the Harkonnens.

The next part of the monomyth, Crossing of the First Threshold, occurs when the hero leaves behind his or her world of familiarity for parts unknown. On this Campbell explains, "With the personifications of his destiny to guide and aid him, the hero goes forward in his adventure until he comes to the 'threshold guardian' at the entrance to the zone of magnified power. Such custodians bound the world in four directions–also up and down–standing for the limits of the hero's present sphere, or life horizon."[196] Paul crosses the threshold when he traverses the desert plains in a low-flying craft with his father looking for wormsign, while observing Spice mining. He knows he is no longer home; he is aware that danger, a Harkonnen trap, may be around every corner. Indeed, this is the case when a Carryall goes missing when a worm approaches a spice harvester. Paul helps rescue workers from the harvester, then witnesses firsthand the destructive power of a worm as it destroys the harvester. The vast desert is the zone of magnified power as are the giant worms that inhabit it; Paul's threshold guardian is Dr. Kynes, suspecting Paul may be the Fremen's prophesied messiah while Paul believes Kynes might be connected to the Fremen. Paul now knows he is in uncharted regions, a world of unknowns.

Next is the Belly of the Whale, which is the hero's separation from the familiar while undergoing a symbolic metamorphosis. Campbell elucidates, "The idea that the passage of the magical threshold is a transit into a sphere of rebirth is symbolized in the worldwide womb image of

---

195 *ibid*, p. 57.
196 *ibid*, p. 64.

the belly of the whale. The hero, instead of conquering or conciliating the power of the threshold, is swallowed into the unknown and would appear to have died. …Allegorically, then, the passage into a temple and the hero-dive through the jaws of the whale are identical adventures, both denoting in picture language, the life- centering, life-renewing act."[197] For Paul and his mother, the Belly of the Whale sees them cunningly survive the Harkonnen's ambush, escape a worm, join the Fremen; they disappear, presumed dead, hiding in the deserts of Dune. Paul undergoes a rebirth: he is given the names Usul and Muad'Dib, thus initiating him into the Fremen Mysteries; he is born again. As a sign of trust Paul is shown a secret water cache (and told there are others) because their ways are his and his ways are now theirs. The old, imperial world of Caladan is gone; the new, desolate world of Arrakis is Paul's reality. The sleeper is awakening, now ready to face the Road of Trials, fulfilling his destiny by becoming the Fremen's Christlike Messiah (cf. heroic solar archetype).

On the Road of Trials, Campbell provides, "Once having traversed the threshold, the hero moves in a dream landscape of curiously fluid, ambiguous forms, where he must survive a succession of trials. This is a favorite phase of the myth-adventure. It has produced a world literature of miraculous tests and ordeals."[198] Paul earns the respect of the Fremin becoming their unquestioned leader by teaching them the Weirding Way. He becomes Arrakis' worm master by learning to control the languorous beasts. Not only do they provide transportation, but are also monstrous deadly weapons destroying everything in their wake. He is now able to declare open war on Spice mining, frustrating the Emperor and the galactic order. Next, Paul survives drinking the Water of Life, thus heralding his transformation into the Fremen Messiah or the Kwisatz Haderach. After he passes this trial, he comes to understand the worms *are* the Spice, and that there's a symbiotic relationship between the two. Paul is ready to launch a full attack on the Harrkonnens and the Emperor at Arrakeen. He passes all tests put in front of him; Paul Atreides is gone, he is now Muad'Dib ready to avenge the death of his father, making the Emperor pay for his treachery.

Another monomythic element is the Meeting with the Goddess. On this mythology Campbell writes, "The ultimate adventure, when all the barriers

---

197 *ibid*, pp 74-77.
198 *ibid*, p. 81.

and ogres have been overcome, is commonly represented as a mystical marriage of the triumphant hero-soul with the Queen Goddess of the World. This is the crisis at the nadir, the zenith, or at the uttermost edge of the earth, at the central point of the cosmos, in the tabernacle of the temple, or within the darkness of the deepest chamber of the heart. …The meeting with the goddess (who is incarnate in every woman) is the final test of the talent of the hero to win the boon of love (charity: *amor fati*), which is life itself enjoyed as the encasement of eternity."[199] Enter the archetypal sacred feminine, the moon to Muad'Dib's sun; her name is Chani (Sean Young), a fierce Fremen warrior. After Paul is initiated into the Fremen tribe, they fall in love becoming *Dune's* version of Mary Magdalene and Jesus Christ. From this moment, Chani is always by his side forging the perfected syzygy or the Union of Opposites (male and female) spiritually enabling Paul to finish his numinous quest. Muad'Dib wins the boon of love.

Although Paul's father, Duke Leto Atreides, is beloved and admired by his son, Paul satisfies the monomythic element of Atonement with the Father, an element usually reserved for the ogre father archetype. On this Campbell writes:

Atonement (at-one-ment) consists in no more than the abandonment of that self-generated double monster—the dragon thought to be God (superego) and the dragon thought to be Sin (repressed id). But this requires an abandonment of the attachment to ego itself, and that is what is difficult. One must have a faith that the father is merciful, and then a reliance on that mercy. Therewith, the center of belief is transferred outside of the bedeviling god's tight scaly ring, and the dreadful ogres dissolve.

It is in this ordeal that the hero may derive hope and assurance from the helpful female figure, by whose magic (pollen charms or power of intercession) he is protected through all the frightening experiences of the father's ego-shattering initiation. For if it is impossible to trust the terrifying father-face, then one's faith must be centered elsewhere (Spider Woman, Blessed Mother); and with that reliance for support,

---

199 *ibid*, pp. 91-99.

one endures the crisis—only to find, in the end, that the father and mother reflect each other, and are in essence the same.[200]

Assisted by his Bene Gesserit blessed mother Jessica, and unified with the sacred feminine Chani, Paul atones when he confronts and kills Feyd-Rautha, avenging his father. That, combined with the death of the Baron–a surrogate father figure or an evil uncle archetype (cf. Hamlet's Uncle Claudius)–sees the fall of the House of Harkonnen, the dreadful ogres are vanquished.

Finally, Lynch's space odyssey features the monomythic element of Apotheosis. This is an essential element that can take the form of either physical death and spiritual resurrection, or death of former-self and rebirth into gnosis (or in some cases a combination of both). On this Campbell explains, "Like the Buddha himself, this godlike being is a pattern of the divine state to which the human hero attains who has gone beyond the last terrors of ignorance. 'When the envelopment of consciousness has been annihilated, then he becomes free of all fear, beyond the reach of change.' This is the release of the potential within us all, and which anyone can attain–through herohood; for, as we read: 'All things are Buddha-things;' or again (and this is the other way of making the same statement): 'All beings are without self.'"[201] This is the finale of *Dune* when Muad'Dib fulfills the Fremen's messianic prophecy by defeating the Emperor, taking full control of Arrakis and thus Spice production, making him master of the universe. The sleeper is now awake; he will bring order out of chaos. Muad'Dib defeats a blonde-haired Harkonnen devil–Feyd Rautha–and can now use sound as a weapon without the Weirding Module. Princess Irulan (Virginia Madsen) narrates that Muad'Dib is the Hand of God, and that "where there is war, Muad'Dib will bring peace, and where there is hatred, Muad'Dib will bring love, leading the people to true freedom, changing the face of Arrakis forever." Muad'Dib states, "God created Arrakis to train the faithful. One cannot go against the word of God." To signify Muad'Dib's divinity a miracle occurs: it begins to rain on Arrakis, something that has never happened before. "And how can this be?" Alia asks as the rain falls, "For he is the Kwisatz Haderach!"

---

200 *ibid*, pp. 107-110.
201 *ibid*, p. 127, citing *Pranja-Paramiter-Hridaya Sutra* (*Sacred Books of the East*) and *Vajracchedika* (*The Diamond Cutter*).

By fulfilling the Fremen prophecy, Paul satisfies the monomythic component called the Ultimate Boon, the achievement of the goal of the quest. Campbell explains: "The gods and goddesses then are to be understood as embodiments and custodians of the elixir of Imperishable Being but not themselves the Ultimate in its primary state. What the hero seeks through his intercourse with them is therefore not finally themselves, but their grace, i.e., the power of their sustaining substance. This miraculous energy-substance and this alone is the Imperishable; the names and forms of the deities who everywhere embody, dispense, and represent it come and go. This is the miraculous energy of the thunderbolts of Zeus, Yahweh, and the Supreme Buddha, the fertility of the rain of Viracocha, the virtue announced by the bell rung in the Mass at the consecration, and the light of the ultimate illumination of the saint and sage. Its guardians dare release it only to the duly proven."[202]

The Boon is the reason the person went on the journey in the hopes of achieving. All the previous steps serve to prepare and purify the person for this step. In many myths, the Boon is something transcendent, like the elixir of life, a plant that supplies immortality, the finding of the Golden Fleece, the recovery of the Lost Word of a Master Mason in the Royal Arch ceremonial, or the discovery of the Holy Grail.[203]

*   *   *   *

Other esoteric themes hide in *Dune*. One cannot help notice Emperor Shaddam IV's gold throne room denoting heliocentric, imperial rulership. Even his throne chair depicts the sun; Shaddam is the center of the universe from which everything emanates. Comparatively, this conjures Versailles' solar Apollo Salon (Throne Room) from which the French monarch Louis XIV (1638-1715), the powerful Sun King (*le Roi-Soleil*), governed as an absolute monarch. We have the two planets, Caladan and Giedi Prime; the former is home to House Atreides, and the latter is home to the Harkonnens. Both planets are reflections of their respective ruling houses. Caladan is watery and beautiful, symbolizing Duke Leto's fair and evenhandedness, while Giedi Prime is a polluted industrial wasteland like its rulers, the

---

202 *ibid*, p. 155.
203 Sullivan, *Cinema Symbolism*, Chapter VIII.

Harkonnens: diseased, warped, and violent. The two planets echo one of Lynch's favorite cinematic devices: duality.

There are two mystery schools *qua* secret societies: the Spacing Guild and the Bene Gesserits; both seek the perfection of their members through arcane study and exercises. The Spacing Guild uses Spice to expand consciousness while emphasizing the study of pure mathematics, suggesting descent from the Pythagorean mystery school.[204] Through Spice and math they can fold space, making interstellar travel instant. The other school is the Bene Gesserit sisterhood, training their bodies and minds through years of mental conditioning to obtain superhuman powers and abilities which seem magical to outsiders. Acolytes who have acquired the breadth of Bene Gesserit abilities are called Reverend Mothers within the organization's ranks. Bene Gesserit is Latin meaning *to govern properly*, while *Gesserit* recalls the word *Jesuit*, thus evoking undertones of a regimented religious order. Echoing the Jesuits, the Bene Gesserits have been accused of using casuistry to obtain justifications for the unjustifiable[205] like using subterfuge to manipulate royal bloodlines, thereby making the Kwisatz Haderach subservient, a pawn, of the sisterhood.

Paul dreams a disembodied voice saying "the Sleeper must awaken," signifying his rebirth to Gnostic leader, his apotheosis; he will be the Fremen messiah Muad'Dib or the Kwisatz Haderach. During Paul's dream(s), an open right hand is shown as the phrase is spoken; it is the Hand of the Mysteries symbolizing sublime rebirth, consciousness, and *ascenio*.[206] It is a symbol of virtue, fidelity, a solar emblem denoting enlightenment, mystical intelligence, and initiation.[207] The hand foreshadows Paul's inauguration into the Fremen mysteries and the Ultimate Boon by becoming their prophesied savior. As their leader, Muad'Dib teaches the Fremen the Weirding Way during which it is discovered the name Muad'Dib is a killing word capable of destruction. On the power of names Origen writes, "There are names which have a natural potency. Such as those which the

---

204 When *Dune* aired on television, the theatrical "Princess Irulan Prologue" was replaced with a longer narration which provided more information about the histories of the Spacing Guild and the Bene Gesserit sisterhood.

205 James Franklin, *The Science of Conjecture: Evidence and Probability Before* Pascal, pp. 83-88.

206 Hall, *The Secret Teachings of All Ages*, p. 226; cf. Chapter XV, "The Human Body in Symbolism," pp. 222-233. See also Manly Hall's *Lectures on Ancient Philosophy*, p. 100.

207 See Mackey's *Encyclopedia of Freemasonry*, Vol. I, p. 317; Vol. II, pp. 624-625.

Sages used among the Egyptians, the Magi of Persia, the Brahmins in India. What is called Magic is not a vain and chimerical act, as the Stoics and Epicureans pretend."[208] The possession and pronunciation of a divine name was deemed to confer extraordinary and supernatural powers; to utter the name was talismanic sorcery. The pronunciation of the word was a symbol: as a destructive name, Muad'Dib symbolizes the end of the old ways–the Emperor and the Harkonnens–and the birth of the golden, new age of freedom and love.

ENTER THE MYSTERY MAN: LOST HIGHWAY'S PARADOXICAL ILLUMINATIONS

Lost Highway is a complex study in hermeneutics, which is defined as the philosophy and methodology of text interpretation especially biblical texts, wisdom literature, and philosophical texts. Although *Lost Highway* is not a text, it is cinematic philosophy open to numerous interpretations. Is it one story or two? Are the characters of Fred Madison (Bill Pullman) and Pete Dayton (Balthazar Getty) one and the same person or two separate identities experiencing similar yet contrasting realities? What is real and what is fantasy? Are Renee Madison and Alice Wakefield (both played by Patricia Arquette) and Mr. Eddy and Dick Laurent (both played by Robert Loggia, 1930-2015) real people or imaginary? Who exactly (if anyone) is the Mystery Man (Robert Blake)? Is Lynch's film Gnostic, alchemical, archetypal, or none of these? Is there a definitive objective interpretation or is it strictly subjective? Is it ironic or a study in confused logic? One thing is beyond dispute: Lynch wants *Lost Highway* to be beyond interpretation; it is a surrealistic film that raises more questions than it answers. Put another way, *Lost Highway* has too many conflicting ambiguities making it irrational rationality; when it comes to analyzing the movie, there is no singular correct answer. *Lost Highway* is a nihilistic paradox; it is a cinematic ouroboros (a serpent which bites it tail, an endless repetitive cycle), beginning where it ends.

---

208 Quoted in Pike's *Morals and Dogma*, p. 620.

Beneath the surface, *Lost Highway* is about a contrarian theology. This theological paradox holds that only by being lost can one receive gnosis; through total negation (cf. Basilides' willed limbo) one receives enlightenment; by having no sense of purpose one discovers a sense of purpose. The only way one can know thyself, and thus know God, is by being totally ignorant of one's selfhood, to cancel all divine precepts. One can only find one's direction by riding endlessly on life's lost highway.[209] *Lost Highway* is a cinematic presentation of an ancient theological tradition: the *Apophatic* tradition, which is devoted to negative theology. This theology was expounded by the Sethians, a Gnostic sect that flourished in the Mediterranean region at the time of nascent Christianity. Alongside Valentinianism, Sethianism was one of the main currents of Gnosticism during the 2nd-3rd centuries.[210] Sethians maintained that God is so radically transcendent that he can only be known through what he is not. This theology is opposed by the *Kataphatic* tradition based on a positive notion that God can be understood through what he is; negative theology maintains that God is unknowable in earthly terms.[211] Traces of this negative tradition can also be found in Neoplatonism. Despite an apparent difference between these schools of thought–Gnostics maintained that matter is separate from God while the Neoplatonists held that matter is a reflection of divinity– both believed that the spiritual godhead is radically transcendent and thus beyond human representation.[212] Given this utter otherness of God, the only disclosure of this being is through negation, through speaking of God only insofar as he is not one thing or another–not good, not just, not beautiful, not even a being.[213] In the 5th century, Pseudo-Dionysius the Areopagite, makes these Gnostic and Neoplatonic currents the basis for a full-fledged theology of negation, later Christianized by Dominican friar Thomas Aquinas.

There are no positive conceptions or morality lessons in *Lost Highway*. Instead, the movie reaches the odd nihilistic Gnostic tradition that belief in nothing might result in a shattering experience of absolutely everything;

---

209 See Wilson's *The Strange World of David Lynch*, pp. 111-112.
210 Sethianism attributed its gnosis to Seth, third son of Adam and Eve and Norea, wife of Noah who also plays a role in Mandeanism and Manicheanism.
211 Wilson, *The Strange World of David Lynch*, p. 112.
212 *ibid.*
213 *ibid.*

the film is based on the contradictory notion that total ignorance is the precursor to holy wisdom.[214] In doing this, Lynch draws upon the symbolism in *Blue Velvet* to both reinforce and reaffirm archetypal imagery. There are two separate but related narratives in *Lost Highway*. The first opens in the home of Fred and Renee Madison with Fred listening to a voice over his intercom which tells him "Dick Laurent is dead." The narrative then documents Fred's pedantic narcissistic narrowness: he is consumed by the will to control the world. His home is a lofty observatory which allows him to look down upon the world; he even needs to live near an observatory. He is paranoid and jealous suspecting his wife of infidelity; before going out to play a gig, he's a tenor saxophonist, she tells him she wants to stay at home. When Fred asks what she'll do, she replies "read" which he repeats back to her twice in sarcastic disbelief. Fred's gig is at the Luna Lounge subtly references *Blue Velvet* and chanteuse Dorothy Vallens; she embodies the dark side of the moon representing Fred's unhealthy behavior. After chaotically playing his saxophone he calls home, but Renee does not answer which only fuels his jealousy and paranoia. Videotapes mysteriously show up on their doorstep; the first merely shows the exterior of the home but the second ventures inside the house, ending with Fred and Renee sleeping in their bed. The police are called, and it's explained that Fred hates video cameras (symbolizing his self-loathing) because he wants to know the world as he remembers it, not as it really is; he hates technologies that reveal empirical reality, but on a subconscious level wants a total view of the world as he remembers it, signifying his narcissism. Fred is not interested in reality, only his solipsistic vision; thus, the phones and videos epitomize Fred's desire to be in control, to be omnipresent. He and he alone is the master of Renee, but his paranoia causes him to be unable to perform sexually indicating that his desire to be all knowing and all controlling is causing a psychological rift from which he may never recover.

Renee and Fred go to a party at Andy's (Michael Massee), a friend of Renee, causing Fred to believe there's more to their friendship. Drunk, Fred goes to the bar to get two drinks but ends up drinking Renee's, symbolizing his desire to control her. Out of nowhere, Fred is approached by

---

214 *ibid*, p. 113.

the Mystery Man,[215] telling Fred that he's in his home and hands him his mobile phone telling him to "call me." The Mystery Man insists they have met before, and Fred is stunned when the Mystery Man answers his home phone. The Mystery Man has stark white makeup with red lipstick recalling *Blue Velvet's* "Suave" Ben likewise had a similar strange appearance. The reference is apropos. Ben is the evil behind Frank, so too is the Mystery Man the evil manipulating Fred; the Mystery Man is the Devil and, as such, can miraculously be two places simultaneously. Like the Devil, the Mystery Man is Fred's evil side, or his shadow self, which is confirmed when the Mystery Man holds up a video camera, indicating that it was Fred all along responsible for the stalker-like video tapes, indicating Fred's desire to know everything by taping it, but narcissistically recalling it subjectively. For Lynch, this paradigm is rooted in evil: the Mystery Man, like Krishna the destroyer of worlds, will annihilate Fred's ego, negating all notions of his omnipotence. Evil only goes where it is welcome, and Fred's egotistical malignant behavior has opened the door to the mercurial Mystery Man. For without the Mystery Man, Fred's shadow could never emerge; Fred would never kill Renee; thus, he would never become his alter ego, Pete Dayton. The Mystery Man personifies this positive-negative paradox.

When Fred and Renee arrive home, Fred thinks he witnesses a presence in his home, which is natural, because he is seeing that part of himself embodied by the Mystery Man. He enters the home but finds nothing. Renee enters and as she removes her makeup, Fred wanders in and out of the shadows of the cloistered home, a house that reflects his convoluted mind. At one point, Fred enters an entirely dark chamber and when Renee calls out for him, he does not answer because he has merged with the presence

---

215 When the Mystery Man approaches Fred, the music playing at the party is muted. This reflects the idea that sound becomes muffled in the presence of the supernatural. On November 13th, 1974, Ronald Joseph "Butch" DeFeo, Jr. murdered his father, mother, and siblings in their home in Amityville, New York. All six of the victims were found lying face down in their beds with no signs of a struggle or sedatives having been administered, leading to speculation that someone in the house should have been awakened by the noise of the gunshots. Neighbors did not report hearing any gunshots being fired. The police investigation concluded that the victims had been asleep at the time of the murders, and that the rifle had not been fitted with a suppressor. These events would later serve as the basis for the book and film *The Amityville Horror* which documented that a demonic force was inside the house. Some claim this evil force possessed Ronnie Defeo Jr. and allowed Defeo to move and kill in silence. See *High Hopes: The Amityville Murders* (1981) by Gerald Sullivan and Harvey Aronson; *The Amityville Horror* (1977) by Jay Anson, and the film *The Amityville Horror* (1979).

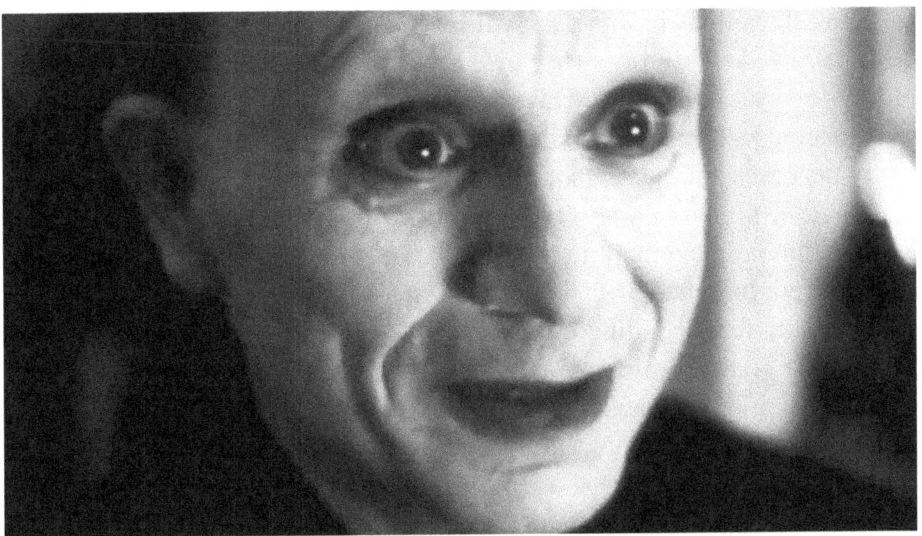

The Mystery Man is the Devil, the personification of evil, has the power of bilocation because evil is universal, everywhere. As the Mystery Man points out, evil goes where it is welcomed, manifesting like a sable angel in multiple venues simultaneously.

of the house. His identity forever lost in his jealousy, narcissism, and desire for godlike control.[216] The next morning, while dressed in the black of the Mystery Man, Fred receives a video tape which reveals him with Renee's mutilated corpse, her body torn to pieces. Like the Mystery Man, a police detective appears out of nowhere, punching Fred in the nose. Fred is sent to death row for Renee's murder. In trying to know and control Renee thoroughly–to dominate her every move–he inevitably kills her, losing the object of his knowledge.[217] In other words, in trying to know everything, Fred becomes ignorant; by being in control, Fred ironically loses all control.

Languishing in a Purgatory-like limbo, Fred suffers painful headaches; is this drab prison a manifestation of his mind or is he imprisoned for the murder of his wife? Confined to his cell, Fred has consciously (or unconsciously) willed himself to be will-less, he has relinquished his past modes of knowing, in sum Fred can no longer impose his will or paranoid tendencies.[218] His previous behavior has led him to this point; Fred's desire to be everywhere has led him to a place that is nowhere. Interestingly, through the conscious or unconscious negation of self, Fred now achieves

216 Wilson, *The Strange World of David Lynch*, p. 121.
217 *ibid.*
218 *ibid*, p.122.

selfhood. Dwelling in this dark void, Fred envisions headlights speeding down a dark, lost highway (because Fred is lost in a state of nothingness), pulling over to reveal Pete Dayton standing on the side of the road. Fred now receives a bizarre form of gnosis; within his cell, Fred Madison magically becomes another person, Pete Dayton.

Dayton, his last name *Day*ton implies light or enlightenment, is released from jail, taken home by his father and mother.[219] Pete is the antithesis of Fred; he relaxes outside not having a care in the world as opposed to paranoid Fred, spending his days locked away in a soundproof practice room. Here we see more distinct imagery from *Blue Velvet*: Pete blissfully relaxes in an idyllic backyard, much like Jeffrey Beaumont at the end of *Blue Velvet*. Pete then looks at his neighbor's backyard, observing a terrier and a water sprinkler, the agents that destroyed Jeffrey's father in *Blue Velvet*. The two scenes reference each other, but they're paradoxical. In *Blue Velvet*, Jeffrey brings order from chaos signified when he emulates his father by relaxing in his backyard, symbolizing a return to normalcy; this imagery is contrasted by Pete, the exact of opposite of his real father, Fred Madison, because Pete will not exert a narcissistic, jealous, and paranoid will to control his environment or those that live in it. Pete casually hangs out with his friends at a bowling alley. When his girlfriend Shelia (Natasha Gregson Wagner) asks if Pete if he loves her, he responds by passionately kissing her. When Pete goes to work at Arnie's Complete Car Service, he takes a ride in Mr. Eddy's Mercedes and fixes the engine smoothly without issue. Later he meets Eddy's girlfriend, Alice, a blonde version of Renee (who has dark reddish hair); Alice is light, Jung's ego, Renee is dark, the shadow. Her name, Alice, alludes to Carroll's *Alice in Wonderland* implying there is still magic and mystery in this world. Awed and inspired by her beauty, Lou Reed's (1942-2013) cover of "This Magic Moment" plays reinforcing this optimistic idealism. Passivity draws Pete and Alice together, and they wind up in a hotel room making love with Pete being able to perform. In each one of these cases, through the negation of his will to know and control, Pete finds intimacy with an external element, understanding the particularities of the things he beholds and what makes them singular. Fred could never do this because he must impose his will; his egocentric paranoia would never allow for any of this. Fred must perceive

---

219 Mr. and Mrs. Dayton are played by Gary Busey and Lucy Butler.

and remember things the way he wants to, as opposed to Pete who can recognize and admire the unique beauty within those that he encounters.

Unfortunately, the domineering spirit of Fred lives in Pete's world, personified by Mr. Eddy-Dick Laurent. Although they appear to be one and the same person, this is open to interpretation; after he is introduced as Mr. Eddy, two police detectives identify him as Dick Laurent.

Eddy embodies Fred's egocentric maniacal behavior and his desire for total control. For example, when Eddy and Pete go for a spin in Eddy's Mercedes, Eddy goes ballistic, running a tailgater off the road. He ruthlessly pummels the tailgater, insisting he get a driver's manual immediately to learn the rules of the road. This incident demonstrates that Eddy is a control freak; he even knows the exact car lengths it takes to stop a car at 35 miles per hour. Like Fred with Renee, Eddy becomes paranoid and jealous when he begins to suspect that Alice is cheating on him with Pete. Fred's dark projection through Mr. Eddy-Dick Laurent tarnishes Pete's world: Shelia breaks up with him, and Alice insists they run off together to Mexico rather than face Eddy's wrath. Alice forms a plan to steal money from one of her friends, Andy, and take it to a fence: someone who can provide them with fake passports in exchange for cold hard cash. This is the same Andy who threw the party that Fred and Renee attended earlier, where the Mystery Man first manifested. Pete breaks in, striking Andy in the head with a sculpture. Andy attacks but Pete accidentally kills him by maneuvering out of the way, causing Andy to impale his head on the corner of a glass table. Pete sees a paradoxical photo featuring Andy and Eddy-Laurent with both Renee and Alice. It is now that Pete begins to experience Fred's headaches because he is turning back into him. In killing and robbing Andy, Pete has become the full embodiment of the paranoid and violent Mr. Eddy, and will pay the consequences by turning back into Fred Madison. This transition was anticipated when Pete speaks to the Mystery Man on the phone. Like with Fred, the Mystery Man tells him they have met before; *of course they have*. Assuming Pete is Fred and Fred is Pete, then they met earlier at Andy's party; either way Pete's actions, mirroring Eddy-Laurent and thus mimic Fred, ensures the Mystery Man's return because evil only goes where it's welcome.

Robbing from Andy by stealing his car, Pete and Alice drive through the desert to the fence, but he is not at home. It is from this point on that Lynch annihilates any definitive interpretation of *Lost Highway*, literal or symbolic. While they wait, Pete and Alice make love while the ethereal "Song to the Siren" by This Mortal Coil plays in the background. This is the same song that played when Fred attempted to make love to Renee. Just before Pete climaxes, Alice removes herself from his embrace because Pete is about to become Fred; she tells him, "You'll never have me." At this boundary between states, this fence between egocentrism and transcendence, the real and the unreal, self and other, history seems to repeat itself: Fred *qua* Pete, unable to negate his former self, to suppress his previous modes of knowing and control, to follow along the *via negativa*, once more fails to merge with reality and consummate a relationship to the world.[220] In the context of *Lost Highway,* the haunting song is indicative of the difficulty associated with the transition of self, the attempt (or failed attempted) to abandon inferiorities and embrace (or integrate) new modalities, to become one with self (cf. Jung's individuation). Interestingly, this song would be used by Peter Jackson in *The Lovely Bones* to denote a similar current. The stirring song plays when Susie Salmon finally abandons the material world for the spiritual, allowing her soul to enter Heaven freely, for she knows she has no more unfinished earthly business. Unlike Fred, consumed by narcissistic paranoid chaos, Susie is at peace, having come to know thyself.

Alone in dark, the car's headlights are Fred's only beacon of light in an otherwise world of darkness, the Mystery Man returns (he is the fence between realities) carrying a video camera, symbolizing Fred's need to record the world but remember its machinations subjectively. Fred goes to the Lost Highway Hotel where he witnesses Renee and Dick Laurent having sex in one of the rooms, confirming his early suspicions. After Renee leaves, Fred kidnaps Dick, taking him to the desert. The Mystery Man reappears, hands Fred a knife, and he slits Dick's throat. The Mystery Man gives Dick a small video monitor showing him making out with Renee as they watch a porn film (starring Marilyn Manson and Twiggy Ramirez) at Andy's; Dick is being punished for this transgression. The Mystery Man then brandishes a gun, putting a bullet in Dick's head. Then, like a tempting shoulder devil, the Mystery Man whispers unknown advice into Fred's ear. Meanwhile, two sets of police detectives–one investigating Dick, the other from Fred and Renee's narrative–are investigating Andy's odd death. The photo of

---

220 cf. Wilson's *The Strange World of David Lynch*, p. 129.

Renee and Alice with Dick and Andy now only features Renee; "That's Fred Madison's wife with Dick Laurent," one of the detective's remarks. "I think there's no such thing as a bad coincidence," another investigator says after learning that Dayton's prints are "all over this place," implying Pete and Fred are one and the same person. Fred heads home, speaking "Dick Laurent is dead," into the intercom. Fred, inside the house on the other end of the intercom, is listening to himself outside signifying an ouroboros: Fred is trapped in a time loop, the movie ends where it begins, forever biting its tail. With police lights flashing and sirens blaring behind his car Fred races off; his head looks like it is about to explode violently or morph back into Pete. The headlights speed down the dark highway seemingly lost forever; the movie ends leaving the audience, like Fred, in limbo, divorced from empirical meaning.

To this author, the worst offense a film can commit is to be boring. *Lost Highway*, whatever it is, is not that; it is a film that raises questions, provoking discussion. The movie's conflicting ambiguities make it impossible to come up with one definitive explanation, regardless of what Lynch may or may not have intended. To this author, *Lost Highway* is cinematic Apophatic theology: negation to achieve nothingness to receive gnosis, to strive for the unknowable godhead. Other interpretations of the movie are possible, some more legitimate (at least reconcilable) than others. Lynch implies *Lost Highway* is alchemical: at its root, it's about Fred (cf. egocentric ignorance) physically and psychologically turning into Pete (cf. altruistic wisdom); when the prison guard finds Pete in Fred's prison cell he says "magic" has taken place. And why not, all the alchemical earmarks are present in *Lost Highway*: the masculine solar *citrinitas* is Fred and Pete, the lunar *albedo* is Renee and Alice (Fred even plays in the Luna Lounge); at one point Alice wears a white dress, stepping out of a yellow cab, signifying the union of the sun and moon; and the *nigredo*, the blackening, is naturally the Mystery Man coming to demolish the ego. In the end, Fred and Pete speed around in a conspicuous red car, the *rubedo*, indicating completion of the Magnum Opus. There is one problem with this analysis: *Lost Highway* is not alchemical. Fred turns into Pete, but resorts to his old ways and once again becomes Fred, thus no alchemical transition; Fred is the same narrow person at the end of the movie that he was at its beginning. There is no definitive metamorphosis in this film, hence no alchemy.

Another way to look at *Lost Highway* is a vast psychological land-scape; that is the characters represent different aspects (or archetypes) of Fred and Pete's tortured psyche. In this paradigm, Fred's character would be his conscious awareness, that part which wants to reduce the world to his solipsistic desire, the recall the world as it wants to, not as it is. The Mystery Man would be Fred's unconscious desire, his darkest shadow, to have control over the world. Andy's is Fred's paranoia while Renee is the sacred feminine, his *anima*, that he wishes so much to control that he divorces himself from it; "You'll never have me," Alice tells Pete right before he turns back into Fred. In Pete's narrative, Pete's character would be his consciousness awareness, his universality, his objective understanding. Paranoia and egoism belong to Mr. Eddy-Dick Laurent, a violent control freak. He becomes jealous because Alice may be cheating on him with Pete. The Mystery Man would be Mr. Eddy-Dick Laurent's unconscious desire, his shadow, for total control over Alice. But by going along with Alice's plan to rob Andy, Pete divorces himself from his conscious awareness becoming Fred *qua* Mr. Eddy-Dick Laurent who, due to his incessant need to control, is unable to possess Alice-Renee. The idea of characters not being real but representations of archetypal figments lurking inside one's fragmented psyche can be found in 2003's *Identity*. In this movie, the visitors to a Nevada hotel are nothing more than archetypal projections dwelling in the twisted psyche of murderer Malcolm Rivers (Pruitt Taylor Vince). Rivers' ego is personified by limousine drive Ed Dakota (John Cusack) while his shadow is the child Timmy York (Bret Loehr). Other subconscious archetypes include father and mother Lou and Ginny Isiana;[221] wily prostitute (cf. Lilith) Paris Nevada (Amanda Peet); trickster Larry Washington (John Hawkes); agent of justice Samuel Rhodes (Ray Liotta); and criminal Robert Maine (Jake Busey).

Lynch's casting of Bill Pullman and Robert Loggia is occult in nature and is not a coincidence. During the summer of 1996, Pullman and Loggia were heroically defending planet earth from genocidal space aliens in the blockbuster *Independence Day*. Pullman played matinee hero President Thomas Whitmore and Loggia played hard-nosed General William Grey, a character modeled after General George S. Patton, Jr. (1885-1945). In February 1997, a few months later, *Lost Highway* was released with

---

221 Played by William Lee Scott and Clea Duval.

Pullman and Loggia portraying scumbags. By doing this, this author believes Lynch is demonstrating his utter contempt for the shallow Hollywood mega-hit by sarcastically turning its uplifting saviors into nihilistic villains.

We are also left to ponder if the Mystery Man is evil or a force for good. Although his entrance anticipates the murder of Renee, this could be the catalyst which allows Fred to negate his negative omnipotence and become, if only temporarily, Pete Dayton. Such a dangerous and controversial idea implies the divine origins of evil (cf. *I Enoch*), suggesting that evil, the Mystery Man, must be present in this world. Indeed, not only is there a place for evil, but it's necessary. Thus, the Mystery Man lives in both narratives because he is truly everywhere. Other questions persist: is Renee another version of Alice or are they one and the same? Why is Mr. Eddy also known as Dick Laurent? In his narrative, Fred is jealous of Renee, fearing she is cheating on him just as in Pete's narrative Mr. Eddy-Dick Laurent is jealous that Alice is cheating on him with Pete, one could argue, is Fred. However, Mr. Eddy-Dick Laurent is shown later making out with Renee as they watch a porn film featuring Renee; Alice suddenly is nowhere to be found. As such, we are now forced to ask: who is who, and what exactly is going on here? How is possible that Fred speaks to himself through the intercom at the end? Is *Lost Highway* to be interpreted literally or symbolically? Are the characters real or imaginary? If so which ones? Is it two separate stories or one? The answer to all these questions is this: *Lost Highway* is all of these things, and none of these things. It is whatever you want it to be, and one thing is for certain, this is exactly the way Lynch wants it to be.

Mulholland Drive: The Dreamscape, the Real World, and the Hollywood Illuminati

Dream images, although surreal and hopelessly tenuous, do exist; they possess a modicum of ghostly substance and, in some instances, truth. Watching *Mulholland Drive* conjures Edgar Allan Poe's poem *A Dream Within a Dream* (1849) specifically its concluding verse, "Is all that we see or seem / But a dream within a dream?" For within Lynch's haunting movie we are never 100% what is imaginary, what is truth, or what, if anything, is a dream within a dream. Interpreting this film as rationally as possible (which can be difficult at times), *Mulholland Drive's* first two hours are Morpheus' dreamscape; that is to say, it's a dreamy projection of sleeping woman named Diane Selwyn (Naomi Watts); more on Ms. Selwyn later. Ms. Selwyn's dream opens with teenagers dancing in a jitterbug contest against a purple background as they fade in and out against one another. A vivacious Betty Elms (also Naomi Watts) emerges from the dancers flanked on each side by a smiling older couple played by Dan Birnbaum and Jeanne Bates (1918-2007). Betty is all smiles because she has won the contest. The movie then shifts to Hollywood. A brunette woman (Laura Harring) rides in the back of a limousine along Mulholland Drive. The car suddenly stops, and the brunette finds herself at gunpoint facing death. However, joyriders violently crash into the limousine, allowing her to escapes, surviving the accident. Injured and in shock, she descends into Los Angeles onto Sunset Blvd; Sunset Blvd is a subtle reference to Billy Wilder's (1906-2002) *Sunset Boulevard* (1950) which, much like *Mulholland Drive*, is a film about broken dreams in Hollywood. She sleeps in a bush, then sneaks into an apartment of an older, red-headed woman (Maya Bond). She observes the red-headed women leave the apartment with bags packed. Inside a cabinet, she falls asleep again. An ingénue, Betty Elms, arrives at Los Angeles International Airport (LAX) flanked by the same old couple from the jitterbug contest. Betty is wide-eyed, full of life, optimistic, and awed by her new surroundings. Betty gets in a cab telling the cabbie to take her to 1612 Havenhurst while the elderly couple speed off in the back of a limousine, smiling and laughing at some unknown inside joke. Betty arrives at the apartment, which is usually occupied by her Aunt Ruth, greeted by the apartment manager, Coco (Ann Miller, 1923-2004), who takes her to the unit. Inside is the mysterious brunette taking a shower. Betty finds the dark-haired woman confused, suffering from amnesia not knowing her name. The brunette assumes the name, Rita, after seeing a poster for the film *Gilda* (1946), starring Rita Hayworth (1918-1987) reflected in a mirror near her, denoting a fractured personality–a theme that pervades *Mulholland Drive*. The red-headed woman that Rita saw depart the complex was Betty's Aunt Ruth, going to Canada to make a movie. To help Rita remember her identity, Betty looks in Rita's purse, finding a large amount of money and a strange futuristic blue key.

In a chain-diner called Winkie's, a man named Dan (Patrick Fischler tells his friend Herb (Michael Cooke) about a nightmare in which he dreamt there was a horrible figure behind the diner. Plaguing Dan is Phobetor (English: Frightener): in Greek Mythology, was the personification of nightmares appearing in dreams in the form of monsters or animals. Dan's nightmare has him and Herb in the same Winkie's they now find themselves. To prove the nightmare could not be reality, the two men investigate the back of the building, but the monstrous figure, a bum (Bonnie Aarons) appears, causing Dan to collapse (presumably dead) from fright. Meanwhile, a Hollywood director named Adam Kesher (Justin Theroux) has his film commandeered by two eccentric mobsters, Vincenzo and Luigi Castigliane (Dan Hedaya and Angelo Badalamenti), insisting he cast an unknown actress named Camilla Rhodes (Melissa George) as the lead in the film. "This is the girl," Luigi repeats, regarding Ms. Rhodes. After Adam resists, he returns home to find his wife (Lori Heuring) having an affair and is thrown out of his house. Luigi reports to the strange and disproportionate Mr. Roque (Michael J. Anderson) that Adam has refused the actress. Mr. Roque then orders Adam's movie shut down. While hiding in a seedy hotel, Adam learns from the hotel's manager Cookie (Geno Silva) that his bank has closed his line of credit and that he is broke. Cookie tells Adam that he's being hounded by a mysterious and powerful Hollywood cabal. To alleviate the situation, Adam agrees to meet an enigmatic figure, the Cowboy (Monty Montgomery), urging him to cast Camilla Rhodes in the movie for his own good. Later, a bungling hitman (Mark Pellegrino), steals a black book full of phone numbers but leaves three people dead in his wake, two of them not his intended target. Earlier, the Castigliane brothers, following the orders of Mr. Roque, have contracted with this same hitman to find and kill the woman in the back of the limousine (Rita) upon learning she survived the car accident on Mulholland Drive. The woman is missing, current whereabouts unknown.

Trying to find out more about Rita's true identity, Betty and Rita go to Winkie's and are served by a waitress (Missy Crider) named Diane, which causes Rita to remember the name, Diane Selwyn. They find Diane Selwyn in the phone book and call her, but she does not answer. Betty next goes to an audition, where her performance is highly praised. A casting agent (Rita Taggart) takes her to the set of a film called *The Sylvia North Story*, directed by Adam, wherein Camilla Rhodes gives an audition and Adam declares, "This is the girl," as Luigi Castigliane emerges from the shadows, pleased with Adam's decision. A shy Betty smiles as she locks eyes with Adam, but she leaves before she can meet him, saying that she is late to meet a friend. Betty and Rita go to Diane Selwyn's apartment, breaking in when no one answers the door. In the bedroom, they find the body of a woman who has been dead for several days. Terrified, they return to Aunt Ruth's apartment where Rita, now scared that her life is in danger, disguises herself with a blonde wig, making her look like Betty. Betty invites Rita into her bed, where the two women have passionate sex. They awake in the middle of the night when Rita insists that they go to an eerie theater called Club Silencio. Rita has been saying the words "*Silencio*" and "*No hay banda*" over and over again in her sleep. On stage, the devilish master of ceremonies (Richard Green) explains in several languages that everything is an illusionary re-cording as the mysterious Blue-Haired Lady (Cori Glazer), sitting aloof in her box, surveys the theater. The MC, known as Bondar the Magician, also says there are no musicians present or "*No hay banda!*" Then a man comes out from behind the curtain wearing a yellow suit. The man is Cookie–the manager of the seedy hotel–where Adam was hiding earlier. Next, Rebekah Del Rio lip-syncs Roy Orbison's "Crying" in Spanish ("*Llorando*"); but what's odd is the version she performs is her rendition. In Club Silencio, even the genuine article is a recording. Her act causes Betty and Rita to cry, to be overcome with maudlin sadness. She eventually collapses on stage, although her vocals continue to play. Betty opens her purse, finding a blue box inside which matches Rita's blue key. Upon returning to the apart-ment, Rita retrieves the key from the closet but finds Betty has vanished. As Rita unlocks the box it falls to the floor with a thump. Rita, like Betty, has disappeared. Suddenly, Aunt Ruth comes into the room to investigate the sound, but nothing is there; Betty, Rita, the blue box, and key are gone. The Cowboy appears in the doorway of Diane Selwyn's bedroom saying, "Hey pretty girl. Time to wake up." *Mulholland Drive*, up to this point, is a dream; the blue box and key were transitional items that when married wakes the dreamer to reality. The narrative now switches to the real world which occupies the final twenty-five minutes of the film.

Diane Selwyn wakes up in her bed. She looks exactly like Betty, but she is a failed actress driven into a deep depression by her unrequited love for Camilla Rhodes (played now by Harring). Diane is a sulking, jealous, embittered version of the exuberant Betty. Likewise, Diane's apartment is austere (cf. emotional impoverishment), whereas Aunt Ruth's was bright and posh (cf. spiritual fulfillment). On Diane's coffee table is a regular blue key. On a movie set, Diane is embarrassed when Adam and Camilla begin making out in front of her. To ease her self-loathing, Diane violently masturbates like she is trying to erase her sexuality. Like Fred Madison before her, Diane's bitterness prevents her from climaxing. Camilla invites Diane to a party at Adam's house on Mulholland Drive. Her limousine stops before they reach the house with Camilla escorting her to the party via a shortcut. During the party, Adam appears to be in love with Camilla. Over dinner, Diane states she won a jitterbug contest, and she came to Hollywood when her aunt died, meeting Camilla at an audition for *The Sylvia North Story*. Another woman, played by Melissa George, who was Camilla Rhodes in the dream, lovingly kisses Camilla to arouse Diane's jealousy. Adam and Camilla prepare to make a major announcement; they laugh and kiss while Diane watches, shedding tears. Camilla's motive for inviting Diane was not well-intentioned; rather, she lured Diane to the party to humiliate her.

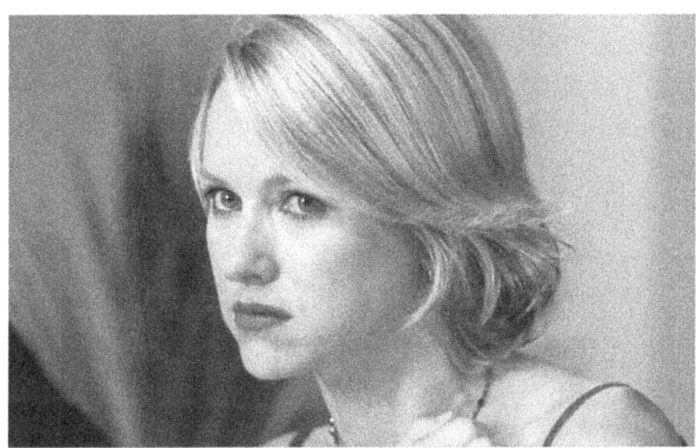

A woman scorned: unable to hide her humiliation, Diane Selwyn is brought to tears by Camilla's cruel behavior at Adam's party; Diane's palpable mortification exacerbated by her dreadful onanism.

Diane meets with the hitman (same one from the dream) at Winkie's, where she gives him Camilla's photo and a significant amount of money; a waitress named Betty serves them. The hitman tells Diane that when the job is done, she will find a blue key. Diane asks what, if anything, the key opens, but the hit man just laughs. Diane looks up seeing Dan, the man who suffered the nightmare, standing at the counter. Back at her apartment, with the blue key on a table in front of her, she is terrorized by miniature and life-size hallucinations of the elderly couple who embraced Betty at the jitterbug contest doting upon her when she arrived at LAX. The elderly couple has been unleashed by the hideous bum hiding behind Winkie's. Diane runs screaming to her bed, where she commits suicide by shooting herself. Betty and Rita are shown bathed in white light, smiling and happy. The Blue-Haired Lady at the club whispers "*Silencio*" and the movie ends. The ending sequence suggests that Diane's reality may, in fact, be a dream as well; Lynch seems to be destroying both illusion and truth.

So how is all this to be interpreted? Before Diane's dream can be analyzed, how it dovetails (or doesn't) with the real world, Lynch subtly reference his previous movies which, once understood, makes Diane's dream and her gloomy reality easier to comprehend. Diane, just like her dreamland counterpart Betty, hails from the same place: Deep River, Ontario, Canada. Deep River clearly suggests *Blue Velvet's* Deep River Apartments which is home to the shadowy sadomasochistic chanteuse Dorothy Vallens. Dorothy is the dark side of the moon–Left-Hand Path gnosis–playing opposite the virginal Sandy Williams; together they are contrasting sides of the same thing: the sacred feminine. Lynch uses Deep River to represent this dichotomy in *Mulholland Drive*: Betty is the optimistic spunky ingénue counterbalanced by the pessimistic and reserved Diane; together they are opposite sides of the same coin, the sacred feminine. Unlike Sandy and Dorothy–separate people–Betty and Diane are two halves, positive and negative, of one fully integrated harmonious self.[222] In *Blue Velvet*, Sandy and Dorothy are agents helping Jeffrey Beaumont on his Gnostic quest for knowledge and experience; this journey is likewise mirrored by both Betty and by default Diane. Betty, like Jeffrey, is willing to break the rules of the status quo to help Rita, thereby gaining wisdom (cf. gnosis) through action. She harbors Rita, a stranger, against the advice of her aunt and Coco, and she lies to the police, impersonating a concerned citizen, to gain information about Rita's car accident. She turns her banal screen test into a sexy masterpiece; next, she breaks into the apartment of a total stranger, discovers a decomposing corpse, then aids and abets someone who might be a fugitive from the law. Betty now finds herself with Rita as they fall in

---

222 Wilson, *The Strange World of David Lynch*, p. 150.

love and have passionate sex. In helping Rita locate her identity, Betty is not only on a journey of self-discovery, but she is helping Diane fuse contrasting sides of her persona. Put another way, Betty's journey of experience, which is also the search for Rita's identity, is, in reality, Diane's subconscious quest for identity and selfhood, for individuation. For this is the realization of self in which separate entities merge into a great whole; with this comes knowledge, a gnosis into the relationship between dream and reality, manifestation and abyss.[223] Diane must somehow integrate the qualities of Betty to become one with self, to become a whole person. For Diane, this is her Gnostic quest; but unfortunately, she cannot complete the journey.

Club Silencio and its performances mirror some of the venues in Lynch's previous movies as well. Club Silencio is Ben's THIS IS IT hideout in *Blue Velvet*, evoking the fence or the Mystery Man in *Lost Highway*. All three are transitional places existing between fact and fantasy, gnosis and ignorance, reality and dream; all three locations are a "…middle ground between light and shadow, between science and superstition…between the pit of man's fears and the summit of his knowledge,"[224] to quote Rod Serling (1924-1975). Club Silencio triggers Betty waking to Diane; THIS IS IT is where Jeffrey's quest for knowledge and experience culminates, and the Mystery Man is the gatekeeper of Fred and Pete dueling identities-realities. Rebekah Del Rio's lip-sync of Orbison's "Crying" should draw forth Ben's lip-sync of Orbison's "In Dreams" from *Blue Velvet*. Betty and Rita react to her lip-sync the same way Frank responds to Ben's: they become melancholy, starting to cry. This enthusiastic sadness response implies this: some imitations are more profound than others; some copies capture something akin to authenticity–to the depth of life, the mysteries of existence.[225] For Betty, Rita, and thus for Diane, this demonstrates that all Diane can ever know is reality: the graspable world is a dream, a distorted copy of an inaccessible and silent original which is Betty and Rita's perfect relationship; however, some dreams are capable of unveiling the ineffable nature of the abysmal original, which is Diane's pitiful existence.[226] In *Blue*

---

223 *ibid.*
224 Introduction from *The Twilight Zone* television show, season one, 1959-1960.
225 Wilson, *The Strange World of David Lynch*, p. 152.
226 *ibid.*

Velvet, Ben and Frank may not be pure evil, but they are the closest thing to it in Lumberton; they are legitimate copies of its underbelly.

Club Silencio's performances are recordings, "*No hay banda*," the MC proclaims to the audience. The idea of recordings as authentic representations conjures *Lost Highway's* creepy videotape recordings signifying Fred Madison's desire for total control, his negative solipsistic vision. This paranoia fractures him into Pete Dayton, a positive reflection of his former self. In *Mulholland Drive*, duality is personified by Betty and Diane, the two women mirror opposites of each other: Betty is energetic and happy while Diane is dour and depressed. When these two different identities are merged a fully integrated person is formed; it is the union of the ego, Betty, with subconscious shadow, Diane. Betty and Diane recall Fred and Pete; Fred is the shadow and Pete is the ego. One is then right to ask: who is this whole person that these fictitious personalities represent? To this author, this is none other than the director, David Lynch. If Fred and Pete (masculine) are different sides of Lynch's artistic persona, contrasting sides of his psyche, then one can argue that Betty and Rita (feminine) are opposing sides of his *anima*. Perhaps *Lost Highway* and *Mulholland Drive* should be interpreted as one continuous film instead of two, a vast complex dreamscape documenting the dark and light sides of the divine masculine and sacred feminine. For this is the mystery of cinema; it has the power to reveal, from the unfathomable depths of the imagination to unknown truths and occult wisdom.

What is Diane's dream trying to tell her? It is prophetic in nature, signaling her forthcoming suicide which is, paradoxically, unavoidable. She has already sealed her fate–more on this in a moment. On dreams, the authoritative *Encyclopedia of Magic & Superstition* states, "Some dreams however do accurately record future events but how these are stimulated and how they relate to the normal structure of the unconscious portion of the psyche is by no means clear. However, they are in a class by themselves and are usually recognized by the dreamer because of a certain strangeness…of content which makes them quite remarkable among dreams, and leaves a deep impression which is immediately remembered when the event takes place."[227] On *Mulholland Drive* and the prophetic vision, Eric Wilson writes:

---

227 *Encyclopedia of Magic & Superstition*, p. 25.

... Mulholland Dr. suggests a troubling reversal: everyday, empirical reality is meaningless; extraordinary, invisible dream is significant. This reversal is virtually nihilistic. ...Lynch's film reflects a particular sort of medieval dream vision: the prophetic dream, the window to eternity. These dreams typically featured a mentor figure explaining to the dreamer the mysteries of the heavenly realm. Such dreams were at once apocalyptic and skeptical. They were apocalyptic because they revealed unworldly unseen harmonies in the mundane regions. They were skeptical because they were suspicious of the empirical world. Such was the 'Gnostic' flavor of the medieval dream vision.

...Diane's dream is both apocalyptic and skeptical. It is apocalyptic in its revelation of the mysteries of wholeness. It is skeptical in its suspicion towards the institutions of the waking world. At once it is revelatory of the archetype and dubious towards time, Diane's dream suggests that in dreams only do we find solace and possibly truth.[228]

Diane's dream is apocalyptic because it is about her becoming a whole person. In her dream, she is Betty Elms, a lucid projection from Diane's subconscious, personifying what Diane *should be*, not what Diane *is*. In the dream, Betty helps a mysterious stranger named Rita search for her identity, but this is a metaphor for Diane searching for herself, to become one with Betty. Entering Los Angeles as a wide-eyed ingénue, Betty finds a mysterious brunette in her aunt's apartment, and she quickly moves from innocence to experience. She decides to help the woman *find herself*, which reflects Jeffrey Beaumont's journey of experience and knowledge in *Blue Velvet*. Betty's Gnostic ascension culminates when she and Rita break into Diane's apartment (a total stranger), finding Diane dead on the bed, returning to Aunt Ruth's apartment with Rita now fearing for her life. Betty disguises Rita in blonde wig, thereby aiding and abetting someone who might be a fugitive from the law. The blonde wig makes Rita look exactly like Betty. Next, Betty instigates and engages lesbian sex; Betty realizes she is in love with Rita, now her double, or Diane. In the dream, the two women resemble each other because, in reality, they are different sides of the same person: Diane Selwyn. By becoming one with Rita, Betty's optimistic activity has become one with Diane's dangerously depressed

---

228 Wilson, *The Strange World of David Lynch*, pp. 139-140.

passivity. This synthesis is the alchemical wedding, the perfect union, yin and yang: the mystical merging of separate, contrasting personas into one. This amalgamation is Betty Elms' and Diane Selwyn's gnosis, but unfortunately for the latter it is too late. She has already put a plan into place that has one ending: her committing suicide. In the dream, Betty and Rita find Diane Selwyn dead on her bed in her apartment heralding, in the real world, Diane's suicide on her bed inside her apartment. Diane's dream is prophetic but also nihilistic because Diane cannot escape it; her vision is meaningless because it presents one ending and one ending only. Diane is unable to react to the dream, only fulfill its terrible outcome.

Diane's dream is skeptical in its suspicion towards the institutions of the waking world which, in her dreamscape, manifest as a Hollywood Illuminati manipulating and controlling the movie industry. The strong-arm of this cabal are the odd Castigliani Brothers, answering to the equally strange Mr. Roque, a man whose head is disproportionate to his body. These men have omnipotent power: they can have actors and actresses eliminated, select an actor or actress for certain movie roles, ordering films shut down on a whim. They can cancel credit cards and drain bank accounts, thus bending people to their will. When all else fails, enter the Hollywood Illuminati's Luciferian mouthpiece, the mysterious Cowboy, supplying light–the lightbulb flickers on when he approaches–in the form of advice to those who have defied their will. Sitting in the dark behind a glass pane only becoming visible when the light comes on, Mr. Roque is a Gnostic demiurge. Like Lugosi's demiurge in *Glen or Glenda*, Roque also pulls the string. Mr. Roque "…organizes the experience of the fallen …His arm reaches as high as the Hollywood boardroom and as low as the two-bit hitman. He puts Adam the artistic genius under his vulgar control and tries to kill Rita."[229] Embodying the demiurge, Roque "…is an imperialist of experience, someone who reduces every event to his will to power. …He dwells solely in the limited illusions of his own making, the paltry images of his vulgar ego. He is a bad artist, attenuating the world to one ugly face. His visions are tawdry, mere fantasies of infantile control. His characters are flat, predictable."[230] Like Gnostics, Betty and Rita rebel against this demiurge. In contrast to Mr. Roque, Betty and Rita are open to otherness,

---

229 *ibid*, p. 155.
230 *ibid*.

to strange and new experiences that might change their egos once and for all; they are indeed connoisseurs of experiences, lovers of the aesthetic fecundity of each other and of their environment.[231] Although Roque and the Hollywood Illuminati exist in the dream world of Betty and Rita, their presence is nevertheless felt in reality. Like Betty, Diane has never made it as an actress, something she laments while at Andy's poolside party, indicating she has intentionally been excluded from the movie stardom she deserves. Is Lynch trying to tell us that there's a Hollywood Illuminati which manipulates the movie making industry from behind the scenes? Are they responsible for Hollywood's fascination with the occult and the placement of arcane devices in motion pictures? As to these questions, this author will let the reader decide.

So how is Diane's dream prophetic? It presents her death, at least her dead body when Betty and Rita investigate her apartment. The decomposing body in the bed is that of Diane, foreshadowing her suicide making it a self-fulfilling prophecy. Like in the dream, Diane dies in her bed. When Diane wakes from her dream, the blue key is there on her coffee table; the scenes of Diane and Camilla arguing on the sofa, Diane on the movie set with Adam and Camilla, Diane masturbating, Diane at Adam's party and Diane at Winkie's hiring the hitman are not linear; rather they occurred before the dream. In other words, they are flashbacks; this is established by the piano ashtray on Diane's coffee table. The ashtray is there in the flashbacks but is missing in real-time because the neighbor comes to retrieve it shortly after Diane wakes from her deep slumber. Diane's dream is thus projecting her subconscious fantasy as to what should have been, not what is. Betty's relationship with Rita is the way Diane visualizes her relationship with Camilla. In other words, in the dream the relationship is perfect, a fantasy of wishful fulfillment, but in reality, it's dysfunctional. Subconsciously, Betty's integration with Rita is Diane trying to integrate Betty's qualities, thereby becoming a whole, complete person. But all this is too late; Diana's dream foretold her demise which, because she put the hit out on Camilla, is unavoidable. The aged couple that terrorizes Diane causing her to kill herself is a projection from her guilty conscience punishing her for hiring the hitman to kill Camilla. Diane, just like her decaying corpse from the dream, perishes in her bed.

---

231 *ibid*, pp. 155-156.

How does Lynch successfully convey these prophetic, apocalyptic, and skeptical visions in *Mulholland Drive*? He makes the dream feel like reality and reality seem like a dream. He successfully does this by interlacing things, themes, dialog, and people found in the dream by later placing them in the real world; sometimes they're contradictory, and sometimes they corroborate. These contradictions and similarities create a delicate thread linking the empirical world to theoretical fantasy making the movie feel like a dream within a dream. A phone resting under a lurid red lamp rings in the dream and reality. In the dream, Betty enjoys the erotic affection of Rita, while in reality, Diane suffers rejection from the same woman now named Camilla Rhodes. In the dream, Rita makes passionate love to Rita while in reality, Diane woefully masturbates. Furthermore, in the dream Diane's negative reflection, her self-loathing, is projected upon the brainless prostitute Laney (Rena Riffel). Laney bears a striking resemblance to Diane: both are blondes with similar hairstyles, both wear light gray tops and jeans, and most noticeably Laney's erect nipples are mirrored in the real world by Diane's sweaty tits and hard nipples when she tragically masturbates. It is clear that Diane, through Laney, sees herself as Camilla's lowly whore. In the dream, Luigi is an enforcer for the Hollywood Illuminati when, in reality, he's a harmless guest at Andy's poolside party. Andy's degradation by the Hollywood Illuminati in the dream is mirrored in reality when Diane is insulted and abased by Camilla. The money Betty finds in the leather bag is the money Diane uses to hire the hitman to kill Camilla. The leather bag is the same in both the dream and the real world. The man who dreamt of the monstrous bum behind Winkie's is now a bystander in Winkie's; this hideous figure personifies evil both in the dream and the real world. The decomposing body that Betty and Rita find in Diane's apartment in the dream is Diane; the corpse is in the same posture that Diane is in when she wakes to reality. The corpse and Diane wear similar nightgowns. Both Betty and Diane win a jitterbug contest, but the elderly couple that dotes on Betty at the beginning later terrorize Diane, prompting her to shoot herself in her bed. In the dream and reality, mainstream success eludes both Betty and Diane. In the dream, Betty nails her audition before director Bob Brooker (Wayne Grace) who, in reality, passed over Diane for the lead in *The Sylvia North Story* because he didn't like her. In the dream the phrase

"This is the girl," is repeated several times regarding the hiring of Camilla Rhodes for the lead in *The Sylvia North Story* but in reality, it's spoken by Diane when she shows the hitman a picture of Camilla. The hitman is the same in the dream and reality and is pursuing the same quarry: Rita in the dream is Camilla Rhodes in reality. In the dream, Coco is Aunt Ruth's apartment manager, when in reality she is Andy's mother. In the dream, the waitress at Winkie's is named Diane while, in reality, the waitress is named Betty. In the dream, Betty receives a cryptic warning from an eccentric female spinster Louise Bonner (Lee Grant) who, like Sophia, is supplying her with wisdom. Her warning, in reality, indicates Camilla is not only duplicitous but mean-spirited and vengeful as well. The peculiar blue key from the dream appears as a regular blue door key in reality. In the dream, the key is a marker of the transition between sleeping and waking; in reality, it's a sign that the hit Diane ordered has been completed. The blue box, in the dream, is likewise a vehicle transition between sleep and reality; in the real world, it is possessed by the horrific bum behind Winkie's. Future Hollywood starlet, Camilla Rhodes, from the dream is, in reality, an unimportant woman tenderly kissing Camilla at Andy's party. In the dream, Diane's neighbor[232] has switched apartments with her; in reality the same neighbor has likewise switched apartments with Diane. In both dream and reality, the limousine driving on Mulholland Drive carries a woman on the verge of terrible danger. In the dream, it releases a terrified and bewildered Rita into Los Angeles where hitmen are hunting her down; in reality, it releases an emotionally vulnerable Diane into an L.A. party where Camilla maliciously rubs her nose in the fact that she's marrying Adam.[233] In the dream, Vincenzo Castigliane yells "Help me!" at the casting meeting after his brother Luigi spits out the espresso; in reality, while at Adam's party, Diane sips coffee from a cup that has the letters *SOS* written on it. Comparatively, these shifting nuances remind this author of the Creepshow Ashtray from 1982's *Creepshow*. In the film's first narrative, "Father's Day," the marble ashtray is a character, becoming the murder weapon of Bedelia Grantham (Viveca Lindfors, 1920-1995) which she uses to bludgeon her father Nathan Grantham

---

232 When Rita and Betty go to the Sierra Bonita apartment complex, the name next to #17 is L. J. DeRosa which refers to a member of the art department on the film, Laura J. DeRosa.
233 Wilson, *The Strange World of David Lynch*, p. 157.

(Jon Lormer, 1906-1986). The ashtray appears in the remaining stories, although they are not related to the first story or each other. In "The Lonesome Death of Jordy Verrill" the ashtray is next to the cash box at the Department of Meteors; in "Something to Tide You Over" it's on the nightstand next to Richard Vickers' (Leslie Nielson, 1926-2010) bed; and in "The Crate" it's on the desk when Henry (Hal Holbrook) writes the letter to Wilma (Adrienne Barbeau). In "They're Creeping Up on You!" the ashtray serves as a soap dish when Upson Pratt (E.G. Marshall, 1914-1998) washes his hands; and in the wraparound story it's on Billy's (Joe Hill) desk when he's stabbing the voodoo doll. The ashtray weaves a harmonious thread, cleverly linking these otherwise unrelated comic book stories, making the entire movie whole, one. In *Mulholland Drive*, the integration of images and items from the dreamscape with items and images (some similar, others contradictory) in the real world makes the movie whole, one. It links the dream vision to ultimate truth, thus associating waking conscious perception with unconscious fantasy. Such an upending blurs the time-honored distinction between dream and reality.[234] What we thought was a dream might be reality, and what was reality might be a dream; when it comes to *Mulholland Drive,* we are left to ponder these epistemological questions. Could it be that Betty and Rita's universe is the real world, and Diane Selwyn and Camilla Rhodes are imaginary figures living in a dream? Such a bold claim is unorthodox and problematic, but is to be expected when it comes to the arcane noir of David Lynch.

One final question remains: who is the Cowboy? The answer: he is Diane's Luciferian spirit guide, a mentor figure, his words, once deciphered, prove to be an ominous warning. As a provider of gnosis, his entrance is heralded by light (cf. enlightenment) as a lightbulb flickers on when he approaches. He speaks to Adam about his bad attitude, but then he speaks directly to Diane, although it appears as though he is still conversing with Adam. The Cowboy says to a sleeping Diane, "Now you will see me one more time if you do good. You will see me two more times if you do bad." By ordering the hit on Camilla, Diane has done bad; hence, the Cowboy appears to Diane twice more. In fact, these are the only times he surfaces in the rest of the movie. First, the Cowboy appears to Diane

---

234 *ibid*, p. 141.

standing in her doorway telling her to wake up. Second, Diane notices the Cowboy mingling in the crowd at Adam's party. By doing bad, Diane is punished by her guilty conscience, personified by the elderly couple, released from the blue box by the malevolent bum lurking behind Winkie's. The old couple enter Diane's apartment as miniatures by sneaking under the door. Once inside, they become life-size, chasing Diane down the hall into her bedroom where she shoots herself in her bed. As such, Diane fulfills her own prophetic yet ironic dream by becoming the rotting corpse of Betty and Rita's realistic dreamscape.

Symbolically dissecting the cinema of David Lynch is, at least for the author, heavy lifting. This author believes he has put forth the best esoteric explanations of the films presented in the chapter, but is cognizant other interpretations exist. One thing is for certain: irony transcends his movies making them feel weird and paradoxical; what could be described as constructive nihilism, atheistic religion, or perhaps ordered chaos. These opposites, acting upon each other, destroy the placidity of the eternal state. Lynch's films are all about destruction and rebirth, death and renewal; but they are presented sarcastically, formulating a whimsical epistemological paradox that's irreconcilable; Lynch's cinema is both form and formless, straightforward and complex, linear and contradictory, time and infinity. As St. Thomas Aquinas declared, "The name of being wise is reserved to him alone whose consideration is about the end of the universe, which end is also the beginning of the universe."[235] The concluding moments of *Blue Velvet*, *Lost Highway*, and *Mulholland Drive* bear out these labyrinthine contradictions. In *Blue Velvet*, although Dorothy's son is returned, her sadness is palpable. With her motherly identity restored, she is overcome with melancholy because her sado-masochistic ways are over; instead of being content she is empty. In *Lost Highway*, we question if Fred Madison is doomed to drive forever down a Purgatory-like dark road, or if he has somehow learned–through his experiences as Pete Dayton–a way to escape the vicious cycle of his repeated mistakes. In *Mulholland Drive*, we are left to wonder if Diane Selwyn's reality is, like that of Betty Elms', nothing more than a dream, mere shadows from the unfathomable reach beyond. The film transitions

---

235 See Campbell's *The Hero with a Thousand Faces*, p. 231. Campbell is quoting from *Summa contra Gentiles*, I.i.

to an empty Club Silencio where, in the balcony, the Blue-Haired Lady from Betty's dream whispers "*Silencio.*" This image emphasizes the artificial quality of the movie, the fact that it is a construct occurring in a theater.[236] But this startling sequence also suggests this silent theater is separate reality itself, the third realm generating and destroying both illusion and fact, mere mimicry and moving experience.[237] It is a twilight zone, wherein resides the mystery of imagination.

236 Wilson, *The Strange World of David Lynch*, p. 23.
237 cf. Wilson, *ibid*; cf. Campbell's *The Hero with a Thousand Faces*, p. 232. cf. Dr. Alton's (Timothy Farrell, 1922-1989) apocalyptic line, "Only the infinity of the depths of a man's mind can really tell the story," from *Glen or Glenda*, 1953.

CHAPTER IV

THE WONDERFUL OCCULT WORLD OF WALT DISNEY

"It's Tony's sister, she did it, she's as weird as he is."
– Letha Wedge, *Return from Witch Mountain*, 1978.

"Vibrations. My moon in Aries. Mysterious words and phrases that
have not added one red cent to my fortune!"
– Aristotle Bolt, *Escape to Witch Mountain*, 1975.

"Once I have control of his brain, Letha,
he will only be dangerous to others."
– Dr. Victor Gannon, *Return from Witch Mountain*, 1978.

"Search for a maid of sixteen with hair of sunshine gold
and lips red as the rose."
– Maleficent, *Sleeping Beauty*, 1959.

"You will now function exclusively under control.
You'll no longer think independently. All thinking an
reasoning will be done by the voice that commands you.
Do you understand?"
– Dr. Victor Gannon, *Return from Witch Mountain*, 1978.

Buckminster Fuller's (1895-1983) geodesic dome known as Spaceship Earth at Epcot (**E**xperimental **P**rototype **C**ommunity **o**f **T**omorrow) at Walt Disney World in Orlando, Florida is geometric perfection. The giant globe, an Archimedean Solid, is a spherical or partial-spherical shell structure based upon a network of great circles (geodesics) on the surface of a sphere. The geodesics intersect to form triangles that have local rigidity to distribute the stress across the structure. Geometrically, this makes sense because of all the polyhedra: octagon, square, hexagon, and pentagon, only a triangle is stable, completely rigid. Fuller, often called the Leonardo da Vinci (1452-1512) or the Benjamin Franklin (1706-1790) of the Space Age, is a philosophical descendant of English navigator, spymaster, mathematician, astrologer, and occultist Dr. John Dee. Dee possessed ahead-of-his-time knowledge of Spaceship Earth-like Archimedean Solids (i.e., polygons, cf. pentakis dodecahedron), having lectured on Euclid in Paris in July 1550, publishing a "Mathematical Preface" to Henry Billingsley's English translation of Euclid's *Elements* in 1570, arguing the impact of mathematics on the other arts and sciences.[238] Dee was also familiar with great circles, publishing *General and Rare Memorials Pertayning to the Perfect Arte of Navigation* in 1577, a work that set out his vision of a maritime empire, asserting English territorial claims on the New World. Archimedean Solids would have been used by Dee to locate the shortest route between two places on the spherical globe *qua* the earth. Dee and Fuller parallel each other in that both believed the number 252 possessed arcane secrets about the nature of the cosmos and also as a mathematical device to unlocking those mysteries. In *Monas Hieroglyphica* (1564), Dee identifies the number 252 with the famed philosopher's stone of the alchemists calling it a magistral, or master number. Five-hundred years later, Fuller, not aware of Dee's treatise, wrote, "Thus by experimental evidence we may identify the electron with the volume of the regular, unit-vector-radius-edge tetrahedron (four identical faces that are all equilateral triangles), the simplest symmetrical system of the Universe…which …calls for the fifth-frequency shell of 252 spheres."[239] To simplify, the number 252 signifies *coincidentia oppositorum* or the Union of Opposites often symbolized by the sun and moon and the yin and yang. The two-headed Roman deity Janus transcends duality, symbolizing beginnings and endings, since he looks to the future and the past simultaneously.[240] Dee and Fuller further mirror each other because Fuller referred to himself as a *comprehensivist*,

---

238 Peter French, *John Dee: The World of an Elizabethan Magus*, pp. 27-31, *passim.*
239 James Alan Egan, *Elizabethan America: The John Dee Tower of 1583*, pp. 88-109, *passim.*
240 Janus also presided over the beginning and ending of conflict, and hence war and peace, a union of opposites. The doors of his temple were open in time of war, and closed to mark the peace. See *Cinema Symbolism*, Chapter XII, analysis of Janus in relation to Harvey "Two Face" Dent in the mythology of Gotham City.

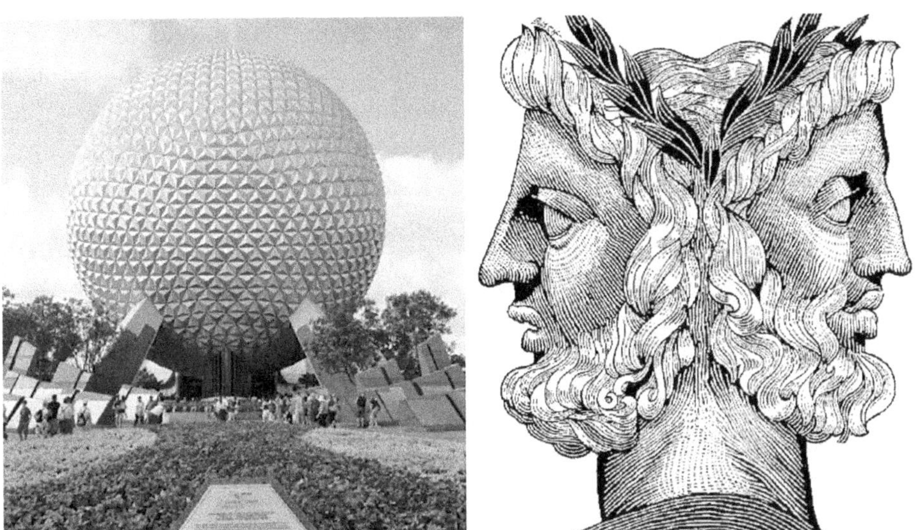

(Left) Buckminster Fuller's Spaceship Earth at Epcot, Walt Disney World, Orlando, Florida. (Right) The month of January is named after the Roman double-faced god Janus.

someone who ties together various fields of knowledge, while Dee was a polymath: a philosopher wise in many areas of learning.[241] Fuller saw himself as a *citizen of Spaceship Earth*, while Dee referred to himself as a *cosmopilite* meaning *citizen of the world*.[242] On this Dee wrote, "... to fynde hym self, *Cosmopolites*: A Citizen, and Member, of the whole and only one MYSTICALL CITY UNIVERSALL...."[243] Dee and Fuller were also cognizant that the rhythm of geometry, and the rhythm of number, are one and the same because there are four positive numbers: 1, 2, 3, and 4; and four negative numbers: 5, 6, 7, and 8. Dee called this *Consummata*[244] and encoded this mathematical occultism in a diagram entitled *Horizon Aeternitatis* (Horizon of Eternity) in *Monas Hieroglyphica* as well as in the frontispiece of *General and Rare Memorials Pertayning to the Perfect Arte of Navigation*. Thus, the positive numbers 1, 2, 3, and 4 when added together create the sum of 10 which in Pythagorean numerology is the number of God;[245] as further evidence of their divinity these

---

241 James Alan Egan, *Elizabethan America*, p. 108.

242 *ibid.*

243 John Dee, *General and Rare Memorials*, p. 54, quoted in Peter French's *John Dee*, p. 186.

244 James Alan Egan, *Elizabethan America*, p. 128.

245 Hall, *The Secret Teachings of All Ages*, "Pythagorean Mathematics," Chapter XIV, pp. 206-221. On page 221 Hall writes, "[Ten] was also called unwearied, because, like God, it was tireless. The Pythagoreans divided the heavenly bodies into ten orders. They also stated that the decad perfected

numbers when multiplied equal 24 which of the daily total of day and night or 24 hours. In Dee and Fuller's occult equation the number 9 is a null or a nothing number (9=0), a mathematical phenomenon known as the Redundancy of 9 or Casting Out Nines."[246] Nine is a zero, nothing, or a *no n*umber hence *non* in Latin, *none* in English, *nein* in German, and *neuf* in French, *nada* in Spanish, ничего (*nichego*) in Russian, *nimic* in Romanian, *niets* in Dutch, and *niente* in Italian. Both men employed this formula in proposing their mathematical philosophies, asserting that nature operates on a dualistic *vector equilibrium* or *model of happenings* (cf. Union of Opposites) and that this equation has a +4, -4 octave and a nine or null rhythm.[247] On this esoteric mathematical equation, Fuller explained that "Pulsation in the vector equilibrium is the nearest thing we will ever know to eternity and God."[248]

While Fuller is best known for Spaceship Earth at Epcot, Dee is best remembered for divining the day of January 15th, 1559, as Queen Elizabeth's coronation date at the behest of the Earl of Leicester Robert Dudley (1533-1588), who went on to become one of the greatest patrons of learning in Tudor England. Dee, like the Dominican friar Giordano Bruno, saw Queen Elizabeth I (1533-1603) as a divine, universal monarch ushering the world into a new, golden age of irenic enlightenment and reform. This golden age represented the apogee of the English Renaissance and saw the flowering of poetry, music, science, architecture, and literature. The era is most famous for theatre, as William Shakespeare and many others composed plays that broke free of England's past style of theatre. It was an age of exploration and expansion abroad, while back at home, the Protestant Reformation became more acceptable to the people, most certainly after the Spanish Armada was repelled in 1588.

Astrologically, the date of January 15th, 1559, saw the constellation Gemini (and its ruler Mercury, cf. Hermes Mercurius Trismegistus, wise

---

all numbers and comprehended within itself the nature of odd and even, moved and unmoved, good and ill. They associated its power with the following deities: Atlas (for it carried the numbers on its shoulders), Urania, Mnemosyne, the Sun, Phanes, and the One God."

246 James Alan Egan, *Elizabethan America*, pp.101-108, *passim*. Briefly, the Casting out Nines involves boiling a number down to its digital sum. Fuller called this process "Indigging" or finding the "Indig" of a number.

247 *ibid.*

248 *ibid*, citing Buckminster Fuller's *Synergetics I: Explanations in the Geometry of Thinking*, New York: Macmillan, 1979, sec. 502.52, p. 224.

leadership) rising, thereby strengthened in the 10th house of the zodiac (Capricorn), home to kings and authority. Combining Dee's mathematical mysticism, the symbolic importance of this date becomes clearer: January 15th falls under the sign of Capricorn during which the winter solstice (December 21-22) occurs heralding a new, solar or golden year celebrated on December 25th, the birthday of the sun. January is named after the Roman god Janus, the god of old endings and new beginnings. When Mary I (1516-1558, a/k/a Bloody Mary) died in November 1558, Dee saw that the old Roman Catholic era was ending, and a new Golden Age was about to begin; out with the old, in with the new is what Janus expresses.[249] The date of the January 15th is the middle of the month, making it easy for Janus' left face to look toward the beginning of the month (the past), and the right face stares toward the end of the month (the future), signifying *coincidentia oppositorum*, representing Dee's occult understanding of the number 252 as a designation of mathematical, alchemical, and astrological harmony–as above, so below.

Dee is referenced in literature, esoterically surfacing in popular culture. Dee is Edmund Spenser's (1552/1553-1599) Redcrosse Knight (cf. Rosicrucianism) in *The Faerie Queene* (1590) and Christopher Marlowe's (1564-1593) Dr. Faustus in *The Tragical History of the Life and Death of Doctor Faustus* (1592). Shakespeare's tragedy *King Lear* (1606), written during Dee's final stage of his life, the time of his disgrace and poverty, is seen as reflecting Dee himself as an old and broken man, ill-rewarded for having devoted his life to the interests of British Monarchy, his occultism alluded to through Tom o' Bedlam's supposed possession by devils.[250] In *The Tempest* (1611), written after Dee's death and during the period of the Elizabethan revival within the Jacobean Age, Dee is shadowed through Prospero in this most daring play which presents a good conjuror at a time when sorcery was a dreaded accusation of the propaganda of the reaction.[251] Dee becomes Edgar Allan Poe's dauntless and sagacious Prince Prospero in *The Masque of the Red Death* (1842) employing his castellated abbey (cf. Dee's Mortlake) as a fortress to shelter him and his guests from the ravages of the Red Death. Dee's mystical persona

---

249 *ibid*, p. 353
250 See Yates' *The Occult Philosophy in the Elizabethan Age*, p. 90.
251 *ibid*.

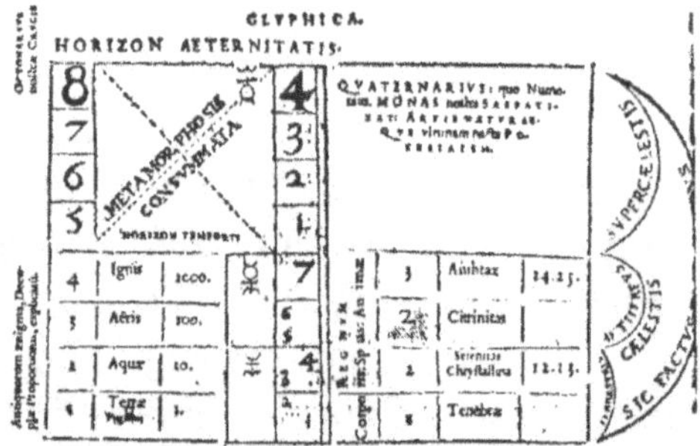

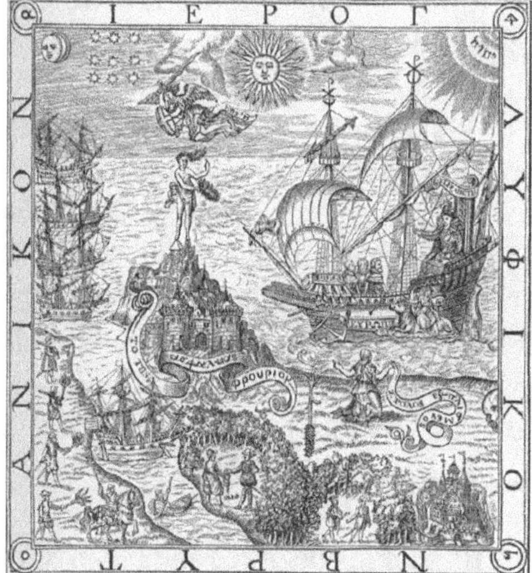

(Top) Horizon of Eternity diagram from John Dee's *Monas Hieroglyphica* displays the positive numbers, 1, 2, 3, and 4 on the right and the negative numbers 5, 6, 7, and 8 to the left in the upper left-hand corner. The number 9 is absent because 9 is a null or Horizon Number; hence, the word *Consummata* appears in its place across the diagram. Nine is always on the horizon because the multiples of 9, when added together, always equal nine: 9, 18, 27, 36, 45, 54, 63, 72, 81, and 90. This creates a horizontal formula with 9 on the far left and 90 on the far right with four linear, transpalindromic pairs: 18 and 81, 27 and 72, 36 and 63, and 45 and 54 confirming that 9 (and 90) are nothing, zero, a *ninething*, nothing, with the four pairs representing the +4, -4 octave. (Bottom) Frontispiece to Dee's *General and Rare Memorials Pertayning to the Perfect Arte of Navigation* encodes this mathematical arcana. On the left shore are four soldiers symbolizing the four positive numbers, and four ships docked above them expressing the four negative numbers. Beneath St. Michael the Archangel is Lady Occasion (sometimes identified as Fortuna), her right foot rests atop a tetrahedron. Of occult, symbolic importance is her left-hand pointing to the horizon, symbolizing that nine is always on the horizon because it is a null number.

survives in Dr. Cornelius (Vincent Grass) of C.S. Lewis' *Prince Caspian*, while Dee's 007 sigil was the inspiration for Ian Fleming's secret agent James Bond's code number.[252]

Just as we find John Dee's algebraic, magical fingerprints on the geometric arcana of Buckminster Fuller and his Spaceship Earth, easily one of Walt Disney World's most recognizable architectural icons, we also discover that the films of Walt Disney Studios are imbued with mystical iconography. For instance, in Chapter XV of this author's first book, *The Royal Arch of Enoch*, the veiled Freemasonry of Disney's *National Treasure* (2004) and *National Treasure: Book of Secrets* (2007) was analyzed. Without rehashing the entire chapter, titled "So Dark the

---

252 See Richard B. Spence's *Secret Agent 666*, p. 20 citing Richard Deacon's (a/k/a Donald McCormick) *A History of the British Secret Service*, New York: Taplinger, 1969, pp. 12-13, 27-30; see also Sullivan's *Cinema Symbolism*, Chapter VI.

Con of Man," the first *National Treasure* film is the cinematic version of the Royal Arch of Enoch high degree ritual. The Masonic rite documents the recovery of the treasure of Freemasonry, the Ark of the Covenant and the Tetragrammaton, the Name of God, also known within Masonry as the Lost Word of a Master Mason, in a subterranean vault beneath the temple mount in Jerusalem. In *National Treasure*, the treasure of the Knights Templar-Freemasons is recovered in an underground chamber beneath holy ground, Trinity Church[253] near the intersection of Wall Street and Broadway, in New York City. In the Masonic ceremony, the travelers must pass through fours veils before work commences on the Second Temple of Zerubbabel which leads to the discovery of the treasure vault. In *National Treasure*, Ben Gates (Nicholas Cage) and his coterie of treasure hunters solve four riddles which unveil the treasure vault: a Meerschaum Pipe, the Declaration of Independence, Benjamin Franklin's letters, and the mystery of Independence Hall[254] (original home of the Liberty Bell). In the ritual, the vault is found when a trapdoor is sprung in Hiram Abif's keystone; in the film, a Masonic tomb is breached which leads to the treasure. In the ceremonial, the sun's rays penetrate the vault revealing the treasure. In *National Treasure*, the sun aligns with the steeple at Independence Hall at 3:22 p.m. (when Daylight Savings Time is accounted for) with the shadow pointing to the location of a brick which hides Benjamin Franklin's glasses that, when worn, exposes a map concealed on the back of the Declaration of Independence. The sun's glorious light is critical in the ritual and the film: it rays penetrate the darkness of the vault allowing the treasure (the Name of God and the Ark of the Covenant) to be discovered; in *National Treasure*, the sun's rays reveal the location of an ocular device which transforms the Declaration of Independence into a treasure map. The sun's rays cast a shadow from Independence Hall's steeple at 3:22 p.m. which is an obscure reference to March (third month) 22nd, or the vernal equinox when the sun is resurrected from the darkness of the winter months. Light overtakes darkness; thus, the sun serves as the cabalistic device which illuminates the treasure vault in the Royal Arch ritual, bringing the light necessary to discover the

---

253 The church's identifying symbol is the *Triquetra*.
254 The Independence Hall riddle is this: "The vision to see the treasured past comes as the timely shadow crosses in front of the house of Pass and Stow." See *National Treasure*, 2004.

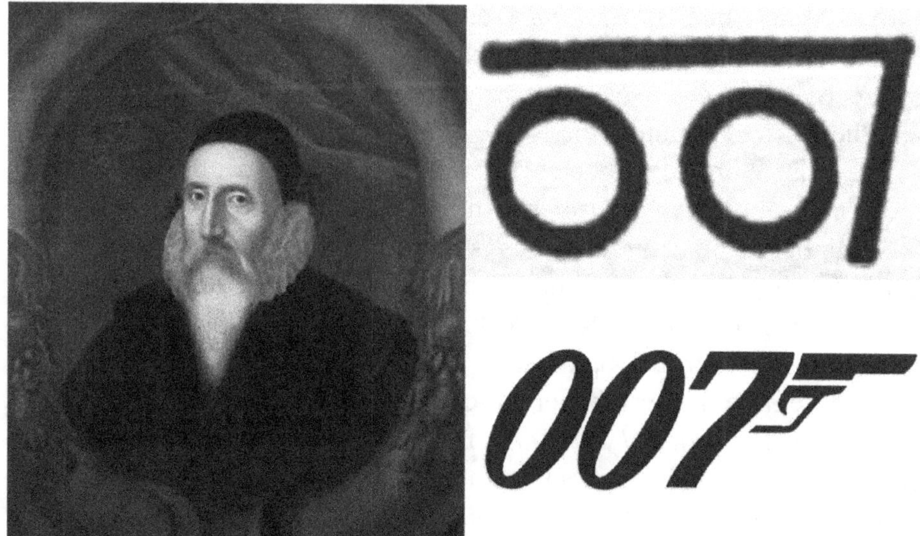

(Left) *Dr. John Dee*, portrait in the Ashmolean Museum, Oxford University. (Upper Right) Dee's 007 espionage sigil symbolizes that he was Good Queen Bess' eyes in the field, and that correspondences bearing 007 were for her eyes only. (Lower Right) Dee's esoteric signature influenced Ian Fleming, becoming James Bond's numeric designation, 007, indicating his license to kill. See Sullivan's *Cinema Symbolism*, Chapter VI.

Templar vault in *National Treasure*. The numeric designation of 322 also conjures Yale University's Masonic-like Skull and Bones secret society, its symbol is the skull and crossbones above the number 322. As such, the use of this specific number is an occult token, epitomizing the over-arching Freemasonic-Templar themes and symbols of Disney's *National Treasure* and *National Treasure: Book of Secrets*.

Before some of the movies of Disney Studios can be analyzed, this author feels it necessary to present a brief biography on Walter Elias "Walt" Disney, for without him this chapter would not be possible. Walt Disney was born on December 5th, 1901, in Chicago, Illinois, to his father Elias Disney, and mother Flora Call Disney. Walt had very early interests in art, selling drawings to neighbors to make extra money. He pursued his art career by studying art and photography by going to McKinley High School in Chicago. Walt began to appreciate nature and wildlife, and family and community, which were a large part of agrarian living. Though his father could be quite stern and often there was little money, Walt was encouraged by his mother and older brother, Roy, to pursue his talents. As an animator and entrepreneur, Disney was particularly noted as a filmmaker and a popular showman, as well as an innovator in animation and theme park design. He and his staff created numerous famous fictional characters including Mickey Mouse, Donald Duck, and Goofy. Disney himself was the original voice for Mickey. During his lifetime, he won twenty-two Academy Awards, receiving four honorary Academy Awards from a total of fifty-nine nominations, including a record of four in one year, giving him more Oscar awards and nominations than any other individual in history. Disney also won seven Emmy Awards, giving his name to the Disneyland and Walt Disney World Resort theme parks in the United States, as well as the international resorts Tokyo Disney Resort, Disneyland Paris, and Hong Kong Disneyland. The first of these was Disneyland, located in Anaheim California, which opened on July 17th, 1955, becoming the only theme park designed and built under the direct supervision of Walt Disney. Comparatively, Disneyland is Walley World in 1983's *National Lampoon's Vacation*, with Mickey Mouse becoming Marty Moose. Disney died of lung cancer on December 15th, 1966, in Burbank, California. He left behind a vast legacy, including numerous animated shorts and feature films produced during his lifetime; the company, amusement parks, and animation studio that bears his name, and the California Institute of the Arts. After his death, rumors circulated that Disney's body was kept in a subterranean cryogenic chamber beneath one of his amusement parks anticipating the day when scientists and bioengineers discover the cure for cancer. When that day arrives, Disney will be resuscitated, cured, and walk amongst the living once more.

There is a distinctive Jungian shadow lurking around Walt Disney and his related entertainments, theme parks, and amusements. For example, there is a Jolly Roger (skull and crossbones) made with real human bones in the Pirates of the Caribbean attraction at Disneyland; the morbid icon sits in the headboard

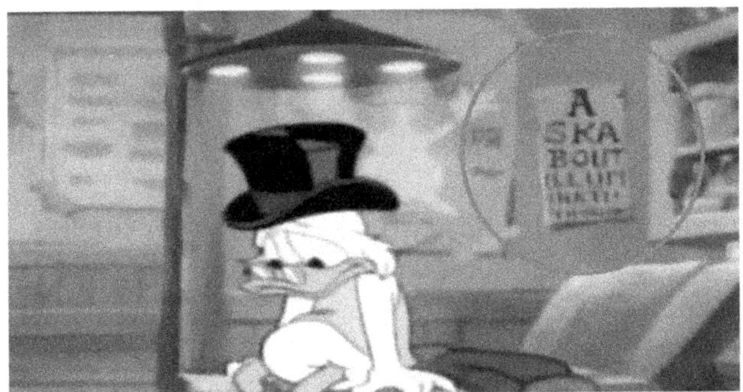

Scrooge McDuck/Illuminati: In Disney's *DuckTales* episode "Yuppy Ducks" (1989) the eye chart behind Scrooge McDuck reads "Ask About Illuminati" implying a Disney-Illuminati occult agenda. Is this mind control, simple coincidence, or the the animator screwing around?

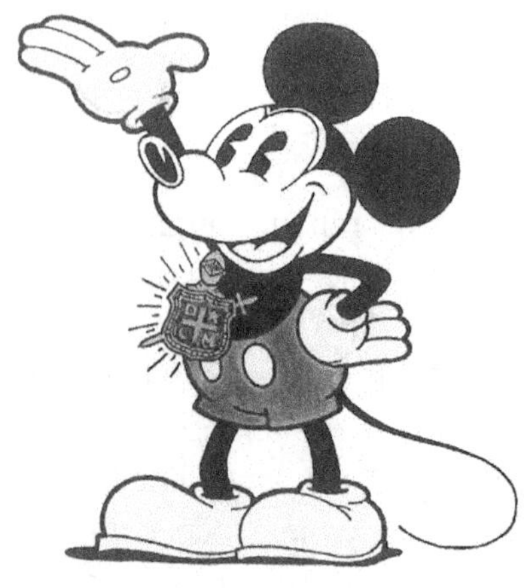

Mickey Mouse in DeMolay: "♫ Who's the leader of the club that's made for you and me? ♫" Walt Disney was proud of his DeMolay membership, remaining devoted to the Order throughout his entire life. DeMolay is named after Jacques de Molay (ca. 1243-1314), the 23rd and last Grand Master of the Knights Templar, leading the Order from 20 April 1292 until it was dissolved by order of Pope Clement V in 1307. This drawing of Mickey Mouse, as a member of DeMolay, was presented by Walt Disney to Frank Sherman "Dad" Land (1890-1959) the founder of the Order of DeMolay. There is also a January 1933 Disney comic strip of Mickey presiding over the Mickey Mouse Chapter of DeMolay.

above the bed in the captain's quarters. Rumors of pedophilia and membership in the Illuminati, or ties to an Illuminati bloodline, swirl around Walt Disney like a vulture circling carrion, however, this author cannot substantiate any concrete connection to the Illuminati or their ilk. Disney's private Club 33 in the heart of the New Orleans Square section of Disneyland smacks of high degree Freemasonry, leading conspiracy theorists to speculate Disney was a 33rd degree Scottish Rite Mason (the highest numeric degree conferred by the Scottish Rite) and thus part of an elite occult Masonic cabal, but this is also incorrect. Although Disney was in the Order of DeMolay, an international Masonic organization for young men ages 12 to 21, there is no evidence that Walt Disney was ever initiated into the Blue Lodge of Free- masonry nor did he join the Scottish Rite. The number 33 is a likely reference to the club's entrance next to the Blue Bayou Restaurant at 33 Royal Street, the name honoring the 33 corporate sponsors at Disneyland between 1966-1967 when the theme park opened. As such, this author can report that Walt Disney (and his vast empire) was not (or presently) part of an evil Illuminati conspiracy designed to enslave or corrupt children; the films of Walt Disney should not be interpreted as satanic entertainments, or mind-control devices. However, Disney's Magical Kingdom is just that: a cinematic landscape populated with the esoteric, the arcane, the mysterious, the numinous, the controversial, the subliminal, and the supernatural. It is now time to explore the Wonderful Occult World of Walt Disney.

LOVE'S DARKNESS: SLEEPING BEAUTY AND MALEFICENT

There are Rosicrucian and mystical themes found in Disney's adaptation of *Sleeping Beauty* (1959) which, when one understands its origins, is not surprising or conspiratorial. Many of Disney's animated films derive from author Charles Perrault (1628-1703), a member of the famed *Académie française*. His work laid the foundation for a new literary genre: the fairy tale. Perrault's writings stem from pre-existing folk tales which feature supernatural storylines populated with magical characters. Some of the best known of his stories include *Le Petit Chaperon rouge* (Little Red Riding Hood), *Cendrillon* (Cinderella), *Le Chat Botté* (Puss in Boots), *La Belle au bois dormant* (The Sleeping Beauty) and *La Barbe bleue* (Bluebeard) published in his *Histoires ou contes du temps passé* in 1697. It is beyond question that Perrault's stories influenced the Brothers Grimm's fairy tale compendium *Children's and Household Tales* (German: *Kinder und Hausmärchen*) published in 1812. For example, the Grimm's *Little Briar Rose* (German: *Dornröschen*) clearly borrows from Perrault's *La Belle au bois dormant*, thus providing the raw material for Disney's *Sleeping Beauty*. Further inspiring Disney was Tchaikovsky's ballet *The Sleeping Beauty* (Russian: *Спящая красавица,* 1890) which was also based on Perrault's tale and the Brothers Grimm fairy tale. Perrault's narrative and the Brothers Grimm story was, in turn, based on *Sole, Luna, e Talia* (Sun, Moon, and Talia) by Giambattista Basile (1566-1632, published posthumously in 1634), which was based on earlier folklore. This story involves astrology, with the sun and moon signifying the union of the male and female–a Rosicrucian alchemical wedding–a theme veiled in the Disney animated movie. *Sleeping Beauty* was the last Disney adaptation of a fairy tale for some years because of its initial mixed critical reception; the studio did not return to the genre until thirty years later, long after Walt Disney died, with the release of *The Little Mermaid* in 1989. Today, *Sleeping Beauty* is hailed as one of the greatest animated films of all time.

Sleeping Beauty tells the story of King Stefan (Taylor Holmes, 1878-1959) and Queen Leah (Rosa Crosby), his lovely and beautiful wife, after many childless years, happily welcome the birth of their daughter, the

Princess Aurora (Mary Costa). They proclaim a holiday for their subjects to pay homage to the princess, celebrating her birth. At the gathering for her christening, she is betrothed to Prince Phillip (Bill Shirley, 1921-1989), the young son of Stefan's friend King Hubert (Bill Thompson, 1913-1971), so that their kingdoms will always be united. Among the guests are three good fairies named Flora (Verna Felton, 1890-1966), Fauna (Barbara Jo Allen, 1906-1974), and Merryweather (Barbara Luddy, 1908-1979) that have come to bless the child with gifts. Flora and Fauna give their blessings, gifts of beauty and song, before the evil witch Maleficent (Eleanor Audley, 1905-1991) appears accompanied by her pet raven Diablo (Dallas McKennon,1919-2009). After being told that she was uninvited and unwanted, Maleficent turns to leave, but when Queen Leah asks if she is offended, the dark sorceress curses the princess. Maleficent proclaims that Aurora will grow in grace and beauty, but before the sun sets on her sixteenth birthday, she will prick her finger on the spindle of a spinning wheel and die. After the witch leaves, Merryweather uses her blessing to alter the curse so that instead of dying, Aurora will fall into a deathlike sleep from which she can only be awakened–or resurrected–by true love's first kiss. King Stefan, still fearful for his daughter's life, orders all spinning wheels in the kingdom to be burned. The fairies do not believe that will be enough to keep Aurora safe, so they spirit baby Aurora away to a woodcutter's cottage in the forest until the day of her sixteenth birthday.

Years later, Aurora, renamed Briar Rose, has grown up into a beautiful teenage girl. Maleficent, now desperate to enforce her curse because time is running out, dispatches her pet raven to locate the princess. Meanwhile, on the day of her sixteenth birthday, the three fairies ask Rose to gather berries in the forest so they can prepare a surprise party for her. While singing in the forest, Rose attracts the attention of Prince Phillip, now a handsome young man. They instantly fall in love, unaware of being betrothed years ago; their chance encounter ends with Rose inviting Phillip to her cottage later that evening. However, while she is out, Flora and Merryweather argue about the color of Aurora's ball gown. They have a magical duel with their wands, changing the color of the dress which inadvertently attracts the attention of Diablo flying overhead, thus inadvertently revealing the location of Aurora. When Aurora arrives, the fairies tell her the truth about her true heritage and that she cannot meet her suitor again. Heartbroken, she leaves the room distraught. Concurrently, Phillip tells his father of a peasant girl he met earlier and now wishes to marry, in spite of his pre-arranged marriage to Princess Aurora. King Hubert fails to convince him otherwise, leaving Hubert with equal disappointment.

The fairies take Aurora back to the castle that evening, leaving her alone to contemplate her situation. Maleficent then appears in her room, magically luring Aurora away from the fairies and, under the influence of Left-Hand Path magic, tricks the princess into touching an enchanted spinning wheel. Aurora pricks her finger, completing the demonic curse. The good fairies put Aurora on a bed in the highest tower, placing a powerful spell on all the people in the kingdom, causing them to fall into a deep sleep until Maleficent's hex is broken. From King Hubert's conversation with King Stefan, the fairies now come to realize that Prince Phillip is the man with whom Aurora has fallen in love with earlier in the woods. However, Phillip is ambushed, kidnapped by Maleficent and her minions at the woodcutter's cottage. Using sorcery, she shows Phillip that the peasant girl he fell in love with is, in fact, the hexed sleeping princess. She tells him she plans to keep him locked away until he is an old man on the verge of death, then release him to meet his love, having not aged a single day.

The fairies arrive at Maleficent's eerie castle, avoiding being spotted by her goblin guards. Luckily, they find and release the prince, arming him with the magical Sword of Truth and the magical Shield of Virtue, the latter of which features a Christian cross. After Phillip and the fairies escape the castle, Maleficent tries to stop him with a forest of dense thorns but fails when the prince cuts his way through. Conjuring the powers of Hell, she then transforms into a gigantic fire-breathing dragon to battle the prince. The fight continues on a cliff, where Phillip loses his shield. Ultimately, Phillip throws the sword, blessed by the fairies' white magic, directly into the dragon's heart causing Maleficent to fall to her death. Finally, Phillip awakens Aurora with a kiss, breaking the evil spell while waking everyone up in the palace at the same time. The royal couple descends to the ballroom, where Aurora is happily reunited with King Stefan and Queen Leah, her parents. Flora and Merryweather resume their argument over the color of Aurora's gown, even changing its color as Aurora dances with Phillip. Princess Aurora and Prince Phillip live happily ever after; the end.

* * * *

Aurora is named after the dawn, the morning light, and thus the sun, implying that she is a female messianic-like figure (a/k/a the feminized sun, more on this in *Cinema Symbolism 3*). During her christening, she is adored by three faeries bearing gifts symbolizing the Three Magi (Kings or Wise Men) delivering gifts to baby Jesus shortly after his birth in the manger. Comparatively, Jesus parallels the sun because he is *the light of the world* and the *resurrected Savior* (see Chapter I), Princess Aurora is the *dawn*, the *light* which brings happiness and warmth to her people; to quote Maleficent's curse, Aurora will be "Beloved by all who know her." Under the protection of the three faeries in the woodcutter's home, Aurora is renamed Rose Briar, evoking numinous solar light. Back in Chapter II, analyzing *V for Vendetta*, this author quoted Albert Pike on the nexus between the rose and the dawn. Like the voluptuous Aurora (or Briar Rose), the rose is a symbol of beauty, life, love, and pleasure.[255] The Rose and Aurora *qua* the dawn are linked; hence, Rose Briar is her alias while in hiding from Maleficent. The occult symbolism of solar *light* (cf. en*light*-enment, gnosis) symbolized by a red rose also turns up in Lewis Carroll's *Alice in Wonderland*, which was made into a Disney animated film in 1951, and a live action movie in 2010. In the story, animated playing cards

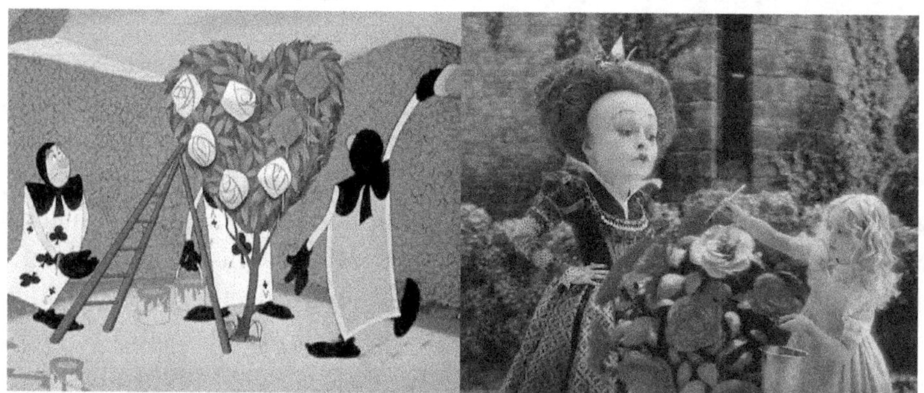

(Left) A scene from Disney's animated *Alice in Wonderland* when playing cards paint white roses red. In this context, the white rose signifies profanity (lesser desires) while the red rose is an emblem of Christian Cabala and its concomitant, the arcane Rosicrucian mysteries. (Right) This imagery reappears in Tim Burton's adaption of Carroll's story with Alice (Mairi Ella Challen) painting the roses under the watchful eye of the Red Queen (Helena Bonham Carter). Burton's film was likewise produced by Walt Disney Studios.

---

255 Pike, *Morals and Dogma*, p. 821.

paint white roses red so as to not offend the Queen of Hearts. The painting of white roses red pays homage to Dr. John Dee, like Carroll, was a mathematician widely thought to be the author of the Rosicrucian (Rose Cross) manifestos *Fama Fraternitatis* (published 1614) and *Confessio Fraternitatis* (published 1615). Aurora is the red rose and vice versa; personifying the sun at dawn, Aurora, like Jesus Christ, will be born again, resurrected from death. Aurora will be unified with the masculine, the Prince Charming archetype which for her is Prince Phillip, for only he can bestow true love's kiss, raising Aurora from her deathlike sleep. Once resurrected, Aurora and Phillip are in love; they dance united at the film's conclusion, formulating the union of the male and female: Jung's syzygy or the sacred alchemical wedding.

Sleeping Beauty's antagonist, Maleficent, is Satan if he appeared as a woman. Although regal, strong willed, and elegant, she possesses all the attributes of a female villain: cold, vain, cruel, sable, complete with demonic horns (cf. the horned god of witchcraft). She is an evil witch cursing Princess Aurora after not being invited to her royal christening, conjuring "all the powers of Hell," when battling Prince Phillip, indicating she has the Prince of Darkness himself at her beckoning call. She refers to herself as the Mistress of all Evil, symptomatic of the textbook narcissists: Maleficent has no children, family, friends, or relationships; she is evil for evil's sake and her mean-spirited attitude, in her my mind, makes her unique. The only pleasure she feels is in harming others; it is the primary source of her overwhelming pride and ego but, at the same time, her monstrous self-loathing which breeds tremendous hatred[256] endlessly nourishing her shadow self, resulting in an unbreakable vicious cycle. Unable to love and be loved, Maleficent is a sexually frustrated prude; her only companionship is her pet raven, Diablo, and a group of inept, troll-like henchmen. She is not wanted anywhere, living alone in a dark, foreboding fortress-castle atop the purple crags of the Forbidden Mountain. Her home swirls in green gases and comprises a dizzying array of rotting, mossy hallways woven into a labyrinth that only Maleficent and her goons can navigate. When Maleficent first appears at Aurora's christening, she is soon joined by her pet raven:

---

256 cf. Dr. Richard Vollin's (Bela Lugosi) line to Edward Bateman (Boris Karloff) in 1935's *The Raven*; after Vollin performs "plastic surgery" on Bateman making his appearance hideous, he tells him: "Your monstrous ugliness breeds monstrous hatred. Good! I can use your hate."

a bird that insinuates that Maleficent has a spying, sinister, secretive, and harsh personality. In Europe, the raven is an emblem of sadness, chaotic darkness, foreboding, and death,[257] mirroring Maleficent's egotistical persona, reflected by the hex placed on baby Aurora. Maleficent appearing with a raven to meddle with an infant's royal destiny is recreated years later in 1981's *Excalibur*. When Merlin the Magician proceeds to retrieve baby King Arthur from his parents, Uther Pendragon (Gabriel Byrne) and Igrayne (Katrine Boorman), to satisfy payment for upholding his end of the pact that Uther made with him, the wizard's entrance is heralded by a raven, denoting the secretive, mercurial, and often dark nature of the magus. Uther and Igrayne watch in horror as Merlin leaves with baby Arthur unmolested, King Stefan and his wife Queen Leah are likewise terrified by Maleficent's curse upon their child. As far as Diablo is concerned, near the end of *Sleeping Beauty* the fairy Merryweather uses white magic to turn the bird to stone. Finally, just like St. George slew the dragon, Apollo defeated Python, and Horus killed the serpentine Set, the heroic Prince Phillip ends the life of Maleficent, having taken the shape of a giant, imposing fire-breathing dragon paralleling preexisting mythology.

The spinning wheel, itself a character in *Sleeping Beauty*, is a symbol of wisdom. In the Pentateuch, at Exodus 28:3 it is written, "And thou shalt speak unto all that are wise hearted, whom I have filled with the spirit of wisdom, that they may make Aaron's garments to consecrate him,…" and Exodus 35:25, "And all the women that were wise hearted did spin with their hands, and brought that which they had spun,…". A spinning wheel is a metaphor for the unstoppable revolutions of the years, encouraging the contemplation of time and how it changes things: from a child to an adult, innocence to experience, ignorance to wisdom. Spinning wheels also refer to creation, since they are used to weave yarn or string into something new and grander: cloth or fabric. Most simplistically, the spinning wheel is a literal manifestation of the old phrase *spinning or weaving a spell*, which means to hex someone. Symbolizing hellfire, Maleficent materializes in the fireplace in Aurora's bedroom subsequently placing the princess in a trance, leading her through the gloomy castle keep. The wheel appears precisely at the crucial moment of the curse's fruition which is just before sunset on

---

257 cf. *Encyclopedia of Magic and Superstition*, pp. 155-156. The raven also recalls Edgar Allan Poe's bleak poem *The Raven* published in 1845.

Aurora's sixteenth birthday. Aurora, zombie-like under Maleficent's black magic, is forced to touch the spindle, thereby causing the hex to take effect.

Aurora's falls victim to Maleficent's evil enchantment when her finger is pricked on the spindle of a spinning wheel referring to her approaching maturity, growing to adulthood. Before pricking her finger, Aurora (Briar Rose) is seen frolicking like a youth in the woods with animals while the three fairies tend to hearth and home. Like a child, Aurora does not talk to strangers. However, when she dips her foot into the water by the river, for example, she appears to be testing it out, awakening to new, sophisticated knowledge of the world. This maturity could ultimately mean a flowering into sexual awareness since she is, after all, sixteen–the age between child and adulthood–and dreaming of a Prince, or an adolescent growing into an adult accompanied by the knowledge and the wisdom that comes from experience. The film never takes a firm stand on what sort of maturity Aurora grows into, but the overall concept of Aurora *awakening* to a man's kiss suggests–at least to this author–that her maturity is indeed sexual.

The fairy tales that Disney transformed into animated films are rife with sinister and taboo themes. For example, one of earliest known versions of the *Sleeping Beauty* story is an episode titled *Histoire de Troïlus et de Zellandine*, which appears in *Perseveres* (six books), composed between 1330 and 1344, first printed in 1528. *Perseveres* forms a late addition to the cycle of narratives with loose connections both to the Arthurian cycle and to the feats of Alexander the Great (356-323 BCE). In this version (appearing in Book III), Troïlus rapes and impregnates the catatonic Zellandine, delivering a child while still in a stupor; the story was purified by Perrault in 1697. These dark themes (discussed more at chapter's conclusion) are veiled in the Disney 2014 retelling of *Sleepy Beauty*. Up next, Angelina Jolie transforms the evil antagonist of *Sleeping Beauty* into an antihero with all the attributes of an Enochic demon in the blockbuster, *Maleficent*.

Maleficent premiered at the El Capitan Theatre in Hollywood on May 28th, 2014, released in the United Kingdom that same day. The film was released in the United States on May 30th, 2014, in Disney Digital 3D, RealD 3D, and IMAX 3D formats, as well as in conventional theaters. It was met with mixed reviews from critics, but was a commercial success, having grossed over $758 million worldwide, becoming the fourth-highest grossing film of 2014. The film received an Academy Award nomination for Best Costume Design at the 87th Academy Awards.

The movie reworks the original mythology of *Sleeping Beauty*. The film begins by revealing that Maleficent, a powerful fairy, lives in the Moors: a magical forest realm bordering a corrupt human kingdom. As a young fairy (Isobelle Molloy), she meets and falls in love with a human peasant boy named Stefan (Michael Higgins), whose affection for Maleficent is overshadowed by his ambition to better his station. As Maleficent and Stefan age, the two grow apart, with Maleficent eventually becoming the protectress of the Moors. When King Henry (Kenneth Cranham) tries to conquer the Moors to obtain its treasures, a grown Maleficent (now Jolie) forces him to retreat. Fatally wounded in battle, he declares that whoever kills Maleficent will be named his successor and marry Princess Leila (Hannah New), his only daughter. In response, adult Stefan (now Sharlto Copley) visits Maleficent in the Moors, where he drugs her but cannot bring himself to kill her. Instead, Stefan uses an iron chain, which burns fairies, to cut off Maleficent's wings. He then presents them to the king as evidence of her death. Maleficent awakens, writhing in pain, only to find herself wingless. Anguished by Stefan's betrayal, she declares herself Queen of the Moors, magically constructing a dark kingdom with Diaval (Sam Riley), a raven to whom she gives human form. He acts as her wings, spy, and confidant.

Sometime later, Diaval informs Maleficent that Stefan, now king, is hosting a christening for his newborn daughter, Aurora. Bent on revenge, Maleficent arrives–her shadow ascends the staircase like the Devil from Hell–uninvited, cursing the infant princess: before the sun sets on her sixteenth birthday, she will prick her finger on the spindle of a spinning wheel, putting her into a deep sleep from which she will never wake. When Stefan begs for mercy, Maleficent offers an antidote: the curse can be broken only by true love's kiss. Stefan sends Aurora to live with a trio of pixies named Flittle (Lesley Manville), Knotgrass (Imelda Staunton), and Thistletwit (Juno Temple) until the day after her sixteenth birthday, while ordering the destruction of all the spinning wheels in the kingdom, hiding what's left of them in the castle's dungeon. He sends his army to find and kill Maleficent, but she surrounds the Moors with an impenetrable wall of thorns.

Despite her initial dislike for Aurora, Maleficent and Diaval begin to care for the girl when the incompetent pixies inadvertently put her in danger. After a brief meeting with the young princess, Maleficent watches over her from afar. When Aurora (Elle Fanning) is 15, she encounters Maleficent and, aware of her omnipotent presence, calls her "fairy godmother." Realizing she has grown fond of the princess in more ways than one, Maleficent attempts to revoke the curse, but she cannot. Aurora later meets Prince Phillip (Brenton Thwaites), and the two are smitten with each other. Diaval suggests that Phillip could be the solution to Maleficent's curse by giving her true love's kiss. Maleficent disagrees, revealing to Diaval that the reason that she cursed Aurora the way she did is

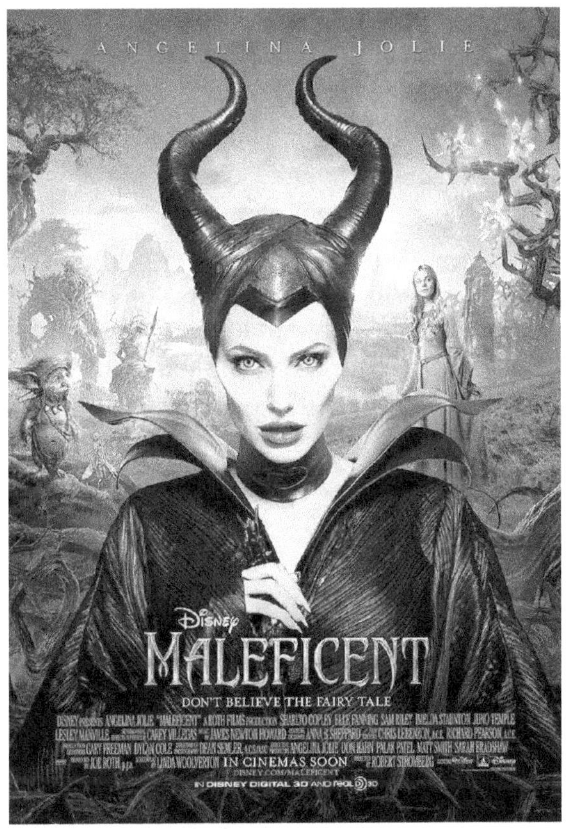

Angel or Demon? Angelina Jolie takes center stage as the horned Maleficent on the 2014 one-sheet movie poster.

that true love does not exist. Unable to share his feelings with Maleficent, Diaval argues that Aurora has the choice to decide her fate. On the day before Aurora's sixteenth birthday, Maleficent, hoping to avoid the curse, invites her to live in the Moors. When the Pixies inadvertently tell Aurora of her parentage while exposing Maleficent's devilry, a distraught Aurora runs away to her father's castle. Meanwhile, King Stefan, mad with paranoia, sits in his castle talking to Maleficent's severed wings which he keeps in a sealed reliquary. He even refuses to comfort Queen Leila on her deathbed.

After a brief reunion with Aurora, King Stefan locks her away in her room for safety. However, she is drawn by the curse to the dungeon, where a spinning wheel pricks her finger, sending into a deathly sleep. Intent on saving her, Maleficent abducts Phillip (rendering him unconscious), infiltrating Stefan's castle which has been fortified with iron everywhere. Diaval remarks that Stefan has prepared for this moment; if they go to the castle, they will never come out alive. Maleficent acknowledges the danger telling him not to come, saying it is not his fight. Regardless, Diaval decides to stand by her and go with her anyway. The two navigate the castle (levitrating Phillip behind them), managing to get Phillip to the three Pixies who are at Aurora's bedside. Phillip, after awakening from Maleficent's hex, kisses Aurora to break the curse, but his kiss fails. Alone in Aurora's chamber, Maleficent apologizes to Aurora, swears no harm will come to her, kisses her forehead breaking the spell, with Maleficent's apparent motherly worry for the maiden substituting for true love. Aurora forgives Maleficent, and as they attempt to leave the castle, Maleficent is trapped in an iron net and attacked by Stefan and his guards. Maleficent transforms Diaval into a fierce fire-breathing dragon, and he lifts the net off her but is driven back by the guards. Stefan beats and taunts Maleficent, but before he can kill her, her wings, freed from his chamber by Aurora, fly back to her, reattaching to her back. Maleficent overpowers Stefan carrying him to a tower, but cannot bring herself to kill him. Stefan attempts once more to kill her, and they both fall from the tower (cf. the Major Arcana's Tower card (XV) symbolizing archetypal destruction). Maleficent breaks herself free, but Stefan falls to his death. Soon after, Aurora is crowned queen of the human and fairy realms by Maleficent, unifying the two kingdoms, with Phillip at her side. Maleficent returns to her role as protectress over the kingdoms with Diaval. Maleficent and Diaval ascend into the heavens above the Moors, engulfed by the sun's brilliant light.

Maleficent, like *Sleeping Beauty*, features three archetypal characters: a beautiful damsel in distress, a noble prince, and an evil, narcissistic, manipulative woman. The latter archetype draws forth the goddess of revenge and retribution, Nemesis (see *Cinema Symbolism*, Chapter XI), as well as the Hindu goddess Kali: the goddess of violence, terror, and destruction; all these attributes can be found in the infamous female Disney villain. Maleficent anticipates other Disney female antagonists such as Cruella de Vil from 1961's *101 Dalmatians*, Madame Medusa from 1977's *The Rescuers*, Madam Mim from 1963's *The Sword in the Stone*, Yzma from 2000's *The Emperor's New Groove*, and Ursula from 1989's *The Little Mermaid*. However, Jolie's evil fairy has a different trait absent in these other villainesses. Jolie's Maleficent is a veiled representation of biblical motifs relating to Satan, which also forms a link to the apocryphal *Book of Enoch* or *I Enoch*. Satan, like Maleficent, started out as angelic: Maleficent is a benevolent winged angel-like fairy, overseeing and protecting the Moors from outside intrusion while Satan *qua* Lucifer was one of God's angels. Overtaken by pride,[258] Satan (echoing Origen and John Milton's Lucifer) and his host of angels rebelled against God; defeated, they were cast down. At Revelation 12:7-9, "And there was in heaven: Michael and his angels fought against the dragon and his angels; And prevailed not; nor was a place found for them in heaven any longer. And the great dragon was cast out, that serpent of old, called the Devil, and Satan, who deceives the whole world: he was cast out into the earth, and his angels were cast out with him." And Isaiah 14:12, "How art thou fallen from heaven, O Lucifer, son of the morning! *how* art thou cut down to the ground, which didst weaken the nations!" Maleficent, like a fallen angel, becomes evil when she has her angelic, feathery wings clipped by Stefan, symbolizing her tragic downfall. Angel no more, she is now a cold-hearted, spiteful villainess donning midnight black, living in exile, performing vengeful cursing sorcery. Her awakening to the dark side is accompanied by falling snow symbolizing the death of light, the death of the sun, winter, and thus the triumph of night and darkness. Maleficent's fall more closely resembles the downfall of the Enochic demons called Watchers in *I Enoch*. These demons, once angels, have been cast out for displeasing God by coming to earth, mating with human women, siring a race of giants known as the Nephilim at Genesis 6:4.[259] At *I Enoch* 12:4-5, "Enoch, you scribe of righteousness, go, tell to the Watchers of the heaven who have left the high heaven, the holy eternal place, and have defiled themselves with women, and have done as the children of earth do, and have taken unto themselves wives: You have wrought great destruction on the earth: And you shall have no peace nor forgiveness of sin." The Watchers, former angels, are experts in magic; *I Enoch* 7:2, "And the angels taught them charms and spells…" echoing this arcana Maleficent is a sorceress par excellence; she was once a good fairy adored by all that dwelt in the Moors but by turning to the dark side,

---

258 Isaiah 14:14: "I will ascend above the heights of the clouds; I will be like the most High."
259 "There were giants in the earth in those days; and also after that, when the sons of God came in unto the daughters of men, and they bare children to them, the same became mighty men which were of old, men of renown." See Chapter II, "Watchmen: A Conspiracy Smorgasbord."

now rules by fear and intimidation. An Enochic fall from grace pervades the mythology of the Transformers. The Transformers animated television series, animated movie *The Transformers: The Movie* (1986), and related live-action films (2007, 2009, 2011, 2014) tell the story of a group of fallen angels–the Autobots–rebelling against their heavenly leader, casting them down to earth. On Earth, the Autobots are heroic saviors, while the original good angels–the Decipticons–are portrayed as evil. The paradoxical idea of *positive evil* derives from the *Book of Enoch*, wherein Enoch is given knowledge from the Watchers which benefits humanity by becoming the seven liberal arts and sciences.[260] Although the wisdom derives from demons, it is nevertheless considered divine in *I Enoch*; however, in the Old Testament the knowledge is evil, causing God to initiate the Flood of Noah to eradicate this wisdom from humankind. In other words, sometimes evil is good and good is evil.[261] Maleficent, like the Watchers, is evil but can be virtuous and, by the end, inherits the heroine's mantle once more. It is her true, motherly love for Aurora which resurrects the sun at dawn, waking the young princess from her death-sleep. The movie concludes embracing one of Universalism's chief doctrines: the ultimate redemption of all evil. The film's closing moments feature Maleficent with her angelic wings restored; she flies off into the heavens: she is Lucifer the Light Bearer, having been forgiven for her past transgressions and sins. The fallen angel is allowed to unite with divine, Neoplatonic heavenly light: the sun.

Is it Maleficent's motherly true-love that awakens Aurora from her curse or is it love of another kind? In *Sleeping Beauty*, Aurora's awakening parallels sexual maturity to female adulthood. It is a male figure, Prince Phillip, which brings Aurora back to life; true love's kiss is the unifying of the sexes, male and female. The two fall in love living happily ever after. However, in *Maleficent* it is a woman's loving kiss that resurrects the young princess which begs the question: is Maleficent a lesbian or, at least, bisexual? Although this is never overtly expressed, Maleficent's tender interactions with the teenage Aurora clearly indicates that Maleficent's ability to remove her hex from Aurora is sexually motivated. For example, Maleficent's lustful eyes never leave alluring youth–throughout the film, she watches Aurora like

---

260 cf. Sullivan's *The Royal Arch of Enoch, passim*; cf. *I Enoch*. See also Thomas Smith Webb's *Illustrations of Masonry, passim*.
261 *ibid.*

a hawk. By attempting to remove her curse from Aurora immediately after tucking her into bed suggests Maleficent's can no longer hide her Freudian carnal desires. Maleficent sexual frustration and repressed sexuality are rising to the surface; when it comes to another woman, Maleficent is all the sudden helpless, becoming a slave chained to her sexual desires. Her powerful sorcery is now impotent; Maleficent's magic fails to remove her curse, which not only feeds her self-loathing and disappointment, but implies Maleficent is under a far more powerful spell, a spell which all her black magic is powerless: true love. Maleficent has conjured Aurora's curse but is unable to remove it at first, believing herself to be the evil in the world. Prince Phillip, the masculine figure, cannot awaken Aurora with his kiss because he is not in love with her; unlike in *Sleeping Beauty* when the two fall in love at first sight. In *Maleficent*, the Prince is an insignificant character hardly engaging Aurora. It is the sensual, loving kiss of Maleficent, not her black magic, which breaks Aurora's curse, implying that she yearns for the princess, motivated by lust. Maleficent's intense interest in Aurora is more than mere motherly affection; rather, she craves the princess' virginal flesh. After the defeat of the patriarch, King Stefan, Maleficent's now abandons her dark side, living freely in the Moors; Aurora embraces Phillip, with Maleficent and Diaval ascending to the heavens. Redeemed, Maleficent silhouettes the sun, symbolizing her Universalist reconciliation with godly light. The credits roll as Lana Del Rey's cover of "Once Upon a Dream" plays which, in the original *Sleeping Beauty*, was the theme of Prince Phillip and Aurora. Del Rey's cover is somber, haunting, and sinister signifying the dark, mysterious, and seductive undercurrents of *Maleficent*.

COUNTER-REFORMATION HEROINES: SNOW WHITE AND CINDERELLA

Disney's *Snow White and the Seven Dwarfs*, released in 1937,[262] comes out of the fairy-tale world of the Brothers Grimm titled *Sneewittchen* in their famous compendium of 1812. Disney's movie is simplistic: a beautiful yet lonely maiden, Snow White (Adriana Caselotti, 1916-1997), is

---

262 A live action feature titled *Snow White and the Huntsman* was released in 2012.

forced to work as a scullery maid by her envious stepmother, a vain evil Queen (Lucille La Verne, 1872-1945). The diabolical Queen asks her Magic Mirror (Moroni Olson, 1889-1954) daily "who is the fairest one of all," with the dark face in the mirror always responding that the Queen was, satisfying her ego. One day, the Magic Mirror tells the Queen that Snow White is now the fairest in the land. The jealous Queen orders her huntsman (Stuart Buchanan, 1894-1974) to take Snow White into the forest to kill her. She further demands the huntsman return with Snow White's heart in a jeweled box as proof of the deed. However, the Huntsman cannot bring himself to slaughter Snow White. He tearfully begs for her forgiveness, revealing the Queen wants her dead, urging her to escape into the woods and never look back. Lost and frightened, the princess is befriended by woodland creatures, taking her to a cottage deep in the woods. Snow White is naïve: finding seven small chairs, she assumes the cottage is the untidy home of seven orphaned children.

The cottage belongs to seven adult dwarfs: Doc (Roy Atwell, 1878-1962), Happy (Otis Harlan, 1865-1940), Bashful (Scotty Mattraw, 1880-1946), Sneezy (Billy Gilbert, 1894-1971), Dopey (Edward Collins, 1883-1940) Grumpy and Sleepy (both voiced by Pinto Colvig, 1892-1967) who work in a nearby mine. Returning home, they are alarmed to find their cottage clean, suspecting an intruder has invaded their hovel. The dwarfs find Snow White upstairs asleep, stretched across three of their beds. Snow White awakes to find the dwarfs at her bedside so she introduces herself. All the dwarfs eventually welcome her into their home after they learn she can cook and clean. Snow White keeps house for the dwarfs while they mine for jewels during the day, at night they sing, play music, and dance.

Meanwhile, the Queen discovers that Snow White is still alive when the face in the mirror again responds that Snow White is the fairest in the land, revealing the heart in the jeweled box was that of a pig. Using black magic to disguise herself as an old hag, the Queen creates a poisoned apple which will place whoever eats it into the Sleeping Death, a curse that can only be broken by Love's First Kiss, but dismisses the counter-spell laughingly. The Queen travels to the cottage while the dwarfs are away, but the animals are wary of her and rush off to find the dwarfs. The Queen tricks Snow White into biting the poisoned apple. As Snow White falls asleep, the Queen proclaims that she is now the fairest of the land. The dwarfs return with the animals as the Queen flees the cottage, giving chase, trapping her on a cliff. She tries to roll a boulder over them, but before she can do so, lightning strikes the cliff, casting her down to death. The dwarfs return to their home to find Snow White seemingly dead in a deathlike slumber by the apple. Unwilling to bury her in the ground, they instead place her in a glass coffin trimmed with gold in a clearing in the forest. They keep watch over her along with the woodland creatures. A year later, a prince (Harry Stockwell, 1902-1984), having previously met and fallen in love with Snow White, learns of her eternal sleep, visiting her casket. Saddened by her apparent death, he kisses her which breaks the evil spell and awakens her; the kiss is white cabalistic magic, countering the Queen's black sorcery. The dwarfs and animals rejoice as the Prince takes Snow White to his castle.

Coming straight out of the collective unconscious, all the archetypes are present: a pure beautiful virginal maiden (cf. *Sleeping Beauty's* Aurora), a punishing evil mother figure (cf. Maleficent, Nemesis, a mother-destroyer, see Campbell's *The Hero with a Thousand Faces*, p. 101), and the masculine hero, a Prince Charming. The princess and prince are the Tarot's Moon (XVIII) and Sun (XIX); the tyrannical mother is the High Priestess (II) card reversed denoting barrenness, hatred, and death.[263] The name, Snow White, implies purity, the moon, the virgin Diana or Artemis, the Egyptian Isis, the Christian Madonna. The evil Queen performs John Dee's Enochian Magic only she does not summon an angel; rather, she raises a demon in a black mirror, providing her with insights to satisfy her vanity. Later, the regal Queen performs alchemy by transforming herself into an old hag. She uses witchcraft again when she poisons an apple, signifying Eve's fall in the Garden of Eden; the Queen tricks Snow White into biting the apple echoing the serpent deceiving Eve into partaking of the forbidden fruit (Genesis 3:4-6). Helping Snow White are seven dwarfs, the numinous nature of the number seven having been explained in the last chapter. Finally, Snow White is described as having "Lips red as the rose. Hair black as ebony. Skin white as snow," symbolizing alchemy's *rubedo, nigredo*, and *albedo*. Her alchemical wedding perfected when the yellow solar *citrinitas* arrives in the guise of Prince Charming; he kisses her breaking the evil

---

263 Cavendish, *The Tarot*, p. 75. The Queen of Swords reversed mirrors the attributes of the High Priestess reversed; Cavendish, p. 166.

curse, awakening her from her deathly vampire-like slumber. The mystical alchemical union complete, the sun and moon live happily ever after.

In 1950 Disney released *Cinderella*,[264] which follows the same storyline as *Snow White and the Seven Dwarfs*, originating from the fairy tale world of Perrault. Cinderella (Ilene Woods, 1929-2010) is the beloved child of a widowed gentleman. While a kind and devoted father, feeling as though his daughter needs a mother's care, he remarries to a widowed woman named Lady Tremaine (Eleanor Audley), having two daughters of her own: Drizella (Rhoda Williams, 1930-2006) and Anastasia (Lucille Bliss, 1916-2012). After Cinderella's father dies unexpectedly, Lady Tremaine is revealed to be a cruel and selfish woman; alone, Cinderella is humiliated and mistreated by her stepfamily. They take over the estate, reducing her to a scullery maid–like Snow White–in her home. Despite this, Cinderella grows into a kind and gentle young woman, befriending the animals in the barn and the mice and birds that live around the chateau.

One day, while Cinderella is preparing breakfast, Lady Tremaine's cat Lucifer (June Forer) chases one of the mice named Gus (Jimmy MacDonald, 1906-1991) into the kitchen. Cinderella delivers breakfast to her stepfamily, unaware that Gus is hiding under Anastasia's teacup. When Anastasia sees Gus, she becomes angry telling her mother of the apparent prank, prompting Lady Tremaine to punish Cinderella with extra chores. Meanwhile, at the royal palace, the King (Luis van Rooten, 1906-1973) discusses with the Grand Duke (van Rooten again) his desire for his son Prince Charming[265] to settle down and have children. They organize a ball to find a suitable wife for the Prince without arousing suspicion. Cinderella asks her stepmother if she can attend, as the invitation says every eligible maiden is to attend. Lady Tremaine agrees, provided Cinderella finishes her chores and dresses in a beautiful gown. Cinderella's animal friends, led by Jaq (MacDonald again), Gus, and the other mice repair a gown that belonged to Cinderella's mother using beads and a sash thrown out by Drizella and Anastasia, respectively. When Cinderella comes down wearing her new dress, Lady Tremaine compliments her attire, pointing out the beads and the sash. Angered by the apparent theft of their discarded items, the two stepsisters destroy the gown.

---

264 A live action version of *Cinderella* was released in 2015.
265 William Phipps speaking voice, Mike Douglas (1925-2006) signing voice.

Just as Cinderella is about to give up hope, her Fairy Godmother (Clair Du Brey, 1892-1993) manifests; with her magical wand, she turns the remains of Cinderella's dress into a new ball gown with glass slippers. She also transforms a pumpkin into a carriage, the mice into horses, her horse Major into a coachman, and her dog Bruno (McDonald again) into a footman. The Fairy Godmother warns the spell will break at the stroke of midnight. At the ball, the Prince rejects every girl until he sees Cinderella. The two fall in love, dancing together throughout the castle grounds until the clock starts to chime midnight. Cinderella flees to her coach away from the castle, losing one of her glass slippers. After her gown turns back into rags, the mice point out that the other slipper is still on her foot.

Back at the castle, the Duke tells the King of the Prince's meeting with the unknown girl. The King, after hearing that the girl disappeared, and thinking that the Duke was in league with the Prince all along, goes into a rage trying to behead him. Fortunately, the Duke calms him with news of the girl's glass slipper, telling him that the Prince will only marry the girl who fits that slipper. The next morning, the King proclaims the Grand Duke will visit every house in the kingdom to find the girl whose foot fits the glass slipper. When news reaches Cinderella's household, her stepfamily prepares for the Duke's arrival. Overhearing this, Cinderella dreamingly hums the song played at the ball. Realizing Cinderella was the girl dancing with the Prince, Lady Tremaine locks her in the attic. When the Duke arrives, Jaq and Gus steal the key to Cinderella's room, but Lucifer ambushes them before they can free her. With the help of the other animals and Bruno, they chase devilish cat out the window, and Cinderella is freed. As the Duke prepares to leave after the stepsisters have tried to shove their enormous feet into the slipper, Cinderella appears, requesting to try it on. Knowing the slipper will fit, Lady Tremaine trips the footman, causing him to drop the slipper which shatters on the floor. Cinderella then produces the other glass slipper much to her stepmother's shock and horror. A delighted Duke slides the slipper onto her foot, fitting perfectly. Cinderella and the Prince celebrate their wedding, living happily ever after.

Like with *Snow White and the Seven Dwarfs*, Cinderella is the story is of a young woman freeing herself from the bonds of an overbearing evil mother-figure and, in doing so, finds true love. Once again, all the textbook archetypes are presents: the virgin lunar princess, the solar prince seeking the sacred feminine, and the wicked stepmother; all alive in the collective unconscious, all embodied in the Tarot deck, all descended from Plato's Theory of Forms. Lady Tremaine's cat, Lucifer, denotes villainy, but also invests the tale with Biblical allegory, much like the use of the number seven in *Snow White*. One difference between the two stories is *Snow White* features a mother using black magic while *Cinderella* has a mother-figure, her Fairy Godmother, employing white magic.

In *Snow White* and *Cinderella*, we find compelling heroines who threaten lingering Counter-Reformation attitudes of keeping women domesticated prisoners in their homes, whatever that "home" may be. These two fairy tales are veiled dramatic reactions to the subterfuge of the Jesuits, presenting a visionary cabalistic irenic panorama in place of strict Catholic dogma and promulgations, which still continued to be pervasive even after the Counter-Reformation's official end in 1648. This harsh religious doctrine was maintained by the Jesuits and the Holy Inquisition, all too eager to engage in witch-hunts post Counter-Reformation. In her book, *Gender and Disorder in Early Modern Seville*, Mary Elizabeth Perry explains:

> Counter-Reformation attempts to restore order required a separation of the sacred from the profane. This meant not simply the exclusion of certain dramas and dance from religious festivals; it also meant a careful distinction of good women from evil, a closer regulation of the brothel, cloisters to protect nuns from the secular world, and charity for those who lived as the 'respectable poor' in hovels crowded with women and children. To protect the pure from the profane, order depended upon a program of enclosure that went far beyond cloistered convents or the prohibition against study abroad. Needing protection not only from outside influences, but also from their own weaknesses, women were told to stay in the 'natural' confinement of convent, home, or brothel.

> …Surely women were victimized in this gendered view of God's order, for the enclosure that protects also imprisons, discredited those who are enclosed and depriving them of autonomy and opportunity.[266]

In the personas of Snow White and Cinderella, we find women escaping this oppressive religious matrix; for these women, cabalistic magic

---

266 Mary Elizabeth Perry, *Gender and Disorder in Early Modern Seville*, pp. 177-178.

restores them to their rightful positions which they have been deprived unjustly. Their restoration parallels the recovery of the cabalistic name of God, Jesus Christ, while allegorically restoring Eve (cf. Sacred Feminine) to a perfect state before her (and Adam's) fall in the Garden of Eden. They can free themselves from the cruelly forced servitude of dictatorial female archetypes, not their biological mothers, but surrogates. The cruel autocratic stepmothers of *Snow White* and *Cinderella* are personifications of the brothel, the convent, and the menial home; for the Counter-Reformation held that these were a woman's natural confinements, their drab inescapable realities. This tyrannical Catholic-Jesuit precept dominated *ancien régime* Europe up to and post-French Revolution, although by then it was a mere shadow of its former self, substantially weakened under the reign of Napoleon I (1769-1821). Through Cabala (cf. Christian sorcery), Snow White and Cinderella find liberation from this cruel and antiquated modality, giving hope that a happy ending is possible. This literary prototype was born and bred in Spenser's *The Faerie Queen* which lionized Queen Elizabeth I, the great Virgin Queen, thwarting her cruel elder Catholic sibling (cf. Stepmother) Bloody Mary; Spenser's work esoterically lauds the Neoplatonic-Hermetic-Cabalistic-Rosicrucian Renaissance of Dee, Bacon, Shakespeare, Marlowe, and Bruno,[267] thereby undermining persistent Jesuit Counter-Reformation attitudes in England and on the continent. A similar theme can be found hidden in *The Taming of the Shrew* (1590) which demonstrates Shakespeare's admiration of a woman, Katherine Minola (cf. Elizabeth I), holding her own when surrounded by manipulative, egotistical men. Queen Elizabeth I inspired the female protagonists in some of Shakespeare's other comedies; Queen Bess' spirit flourishes in Rosalind of *As You Like It* (1600), Viola of *Twelfth Night*, and Beatrice of *Much Ado About Nothing* (ca. 1598-1599). All of these women share many of the same traits, including adaptability, intelligence, and self-awareness much like Snow White and Cinderella. The exaltation of archetypal female energy mixed with Christian magic became a powerful vehicle against powerful Counter-Reformation polemics, not to mention puritanical Calvinist theology. By tapping into these archetypes and magical lore, fairy tales become more than old wives' tales; rather, they are sacred mythology

---

267 The white magic of Spenser's work serves to balance out some of the darker and controversial aspects of Bruno's occult Egyptian hermetic philosophies.

reinvented, promoting optimistic values during life's most difficult trials. For Snow White and Cinderella are the waxing moon in the darkness of night; they are the *albedo* and their light gives hope and inspiration. Today, their stories have been reimagined by Disney, dovetailing with issues that women face in the modern world: Snow White and Cinderella are personified by Merida of DunBroch (Kelly Macdonald) in 2012's *Brave*. Merida, a free-spirited young woman, teaches us to follow our heart, dispelling the antiquated patriarchal custom that a woman must marry, and that destiny is predetermined.

MICKEY AND THE BEANSTALK: A GNOSTIC FABLE

"Mickey and the Beanstalk" is the second segment of Walt Disney's *Fun and Fancy Free*, which was released on September 27th, 1947. The movie was one of the package films (feature-length compilations of shorter segments) the studio produced in the 1940s. "Mickey and the Beanstalk" is historically significant because it was the last time Walt Disney voiced Mickey Mouse because he was too busy with other projects to continue voicing the famous character. The segment is narrated by American actor, comedian, and radio performer Edgar Bergen (1903-1978) best known for his proficiency in ventriloquism with his characters Charlie McCarthy and Mortimer Snerd. Both dummies, along with Bergen, appear in the segment. "Mickey and the Beanstalk" is an adaptation of the English fairy tale *Jack and the Beanstalk*, appearing as *The Story of Jack Spriggins and the Enchanted Bean* in 1734 and as Benjamin Tabart's (1767-1833) *The History of Jack and the Bean-Stalk* in 1807 which Joseph Jacobs (1854-1916) rewrote in *English Fairy Tales* published in 1890. *Jack and the Beanstalk* is the best known of the Jack Tales, which are a series of stories featuring the archetypal Cornish and English hero and stock character named Jack. "Mickey and the Beanstalk" follows *Jack and the Beanstalk's* general storyline: Mickey, Donald Duck (Clarence Nash, 1904-1985), and Goofy (Pinto Colvig) live in a place called Happy Valley, a beautiful idyllic farming community. However, it was plagued by a severe drought after a feminized singing golden harp (Anita Gordon, 1929-2015) was stolen under the cover of night from the castle. The harp's music kept the people happy and the valley bountiful. The trio had nothing to eat but just one loaf of bread and a single solitary bean; in a memorable scene, the bread was cut into paper-thin slices so that you could see through them. After Donald is driven temporarily insane by hunger, he attempts to kill their cow with an ax, Mickey has no choice but to trade the cow for money to buy food. Goofy and Donald are excited about properly dining until Mickey returns home telling them he traded their beloved bovine for magic beans. Thinking that Mickey was tricked, Donald furiously throws the beans to get rid of them, but they fall through a hole in the wooden floor. However, the beans are magical as later that night, under the light of a full moon, a beanstalk sprouts carrying them and their house upward as it grows; the three ascend the beanstalk. Mickey, Donald, and Goofy enter a magical kingdom of enormous scope, finding and entering a huge castle. Once inside, they help themselves to a sumptuous feast rousing the ire of Willie the Giant (Billy Gilbert), who can transform himself into anything. The narrator reveals Willie stole Happy Valley's magical singing harp because he is cruel and selfish. Mickey spies a fly-swatter asking Willie to demonstrate his occult-alchemical powers by turning into a housefly. However, Willie initially suggests turning into a pink bunny but agrees to Mickey's request. Instead, he turns into a pink bunny anyway, becoming enraged when he sees Mickey, Donald, and Goofy with the flyswatter ready to strike. The Giant captures Donald and Goofy and locks them in a box, so as to keep them from pulling any more tricks, but Mickey rescues them with the help of the singing golden harp. The hapless heroes escape with the golden harp, returning her to her rightful place, restoring Happy Valley to its former glory; the giant is presumed killed when the trio chops down the beanstalk while he is climbing down after them. A happy ending is then declared; however, the cartoon ends with Willie the Giant (who has survived the fall) stomping through Los Angeles looking for Mickey Mouse. Before the scene closes, Willie notices the Brown Derby restaurant, picking up the building, searching for any sign of Mickey. Since the restaurant looks like a hat, he places it on his head, stomping off with the famous Hollywood sign blinking in the background.

Jack and the Beanstalk is a Gnostic fable thus "Mickey and the Beanstalk" is one as well. Willie the Giant is the ignorant demiurge with the Mickey, Donald, and Goofy as initiates on a numinous mission of ascension. On this Gnosticism, Manly P. Hall explains:

…The allegory of Jack and the beanstalk, which like so many other children's fables has its origins in primitive folklore, well describes the mysteries of the ladder. The beanstalk, which in a single night grew up to heaven, reminds one of the fabled mango tree of the elusive Hindu mahatma or rope thrown into the air which does not fall. The miraculous growth of the magician's plant signifies the culturing of the soul. Every philosopher is a magician, for by the aid of his unfolded intellect he accomplishes that which to the ignorant appears impossible.

…In the allegory of the beanstalk, Jack is the initiate climbing upward toward perfection. The beanstalk has two significances. First, it is the secret doctrine which may grow up to its fullness in a single night, if that night be regarded as the duration of a soul in the mortal state. The beanstalk is further symbolic of the soul itself, up which consciousness must climb to discover the divine sphere from which it was exiled. It is noteworthy that when Jack reaches the upper world, where on would naturally expect beauty and tranquility to reign, he finds instead that his newly-discovered sphere is the dwelling place of a fierce ogre who has the distressing proclivity of using strangers to supply the requirements of his menu. The giant is the ancient demiurge–the lord of the world, the royal autocrat, the vast tyrant who opposes all who would climb out of their materiality. He is selfishness, egotism, lust, and hate. He is the epitome of all physical attachment, and the appetites by which man is inclined toward the corporeal state. He is the giant of form, the hero of little minds, the fetish of the materialist, the god of those who worship through the sense alone, the supreme genius of the physical-minded, the magnificence to which fools bow down. Those who would escape the clutches of this giant must be wise indeed, for they must outwit themselves. In the ancient writings it is said that all will fail except a fortuitous destiny move with them, for skill will not suffice, prayers will be unavailing, and only the graciousness of the gods can insure success.[268]

Mickey, Donald, and Goofy go on a sacred Grail Quest to a mysterious land to retrieve a magical harp[269] necessary to restore peace and prosperity to Happy Valley. As such, their adventure is imbued with a sense of divinity, of noble purpose. Mickey's magical beans turn into a giant phallic beanstalk under the light of full moon, the sacred feminine, denoting sexual mysticism, the Union of Opposites. Upon ascending the erect beanstalk, they find the demiurge consumed with materialism: Willie the Giant has pilfered the singing harp for selfish reasons. They steal back the harp retuning it to Happy Valley's high castle. The trio survives the trials placed before them, allegorically inaugurating them into the Ancient Mysteries.

Comparatively, "Mickey and the Beanstalk" (and *Jack and the Beanstalk*) mirrors *The Wizard of Oz*. For example, Mickey, Donald, and Goofy ascend a magical ladder, a beanstalk, to have an adventure in a mysterious land. Dorothy also ascends a magical ladder, a swirling tornado, to experience a mystical land. The narrator informs us that Mickey, Donald, and Goofy must have intelligence, courage, and fortitude necessary to complete their mission, echoing Dorothy's three companions in *The Wizard of Oz*; according to the doctrines of Madame Blavatsky's Theosophy, these three attributes are critical to initiation into gnosis.[270] Dorothy confronts Oz's demiurge, the demonic, green-faced wizard, which is the giant ogre in "Mickey and the Beanstalk." Both these demiurges are either exposed as frauds: Oz's fierce face is an illusion; Willie the Giant is an idiot. Dorothy receives gnosis by learning "There's no place like home," while Mickey, Donald, and Goofy restore the magical harp thereby returning serenity to Happy Valley; as such, both stories esoterically document initiation into the Mysteries.

---

268 Hall, *Lectures on Ancient Philosophy*, pp. 427-428.

269 In the original fable, Jack ascends the beanstalk multiple times stealing gold, the goose that laid the golden eggs, and a magical harp.

270 See Sullivan's *Cinema Symbolism*, Chapter V, "President William McKinley: *The Wizard of Oz*," pp. 59-77. This chapter documents *The Wizard of Oz* as a mystical quest of *ascenio*, of the receiving of gnosis.

THE SATANIC MAJESTY OF FANTASIA

Fantasia, released on 13 November 1940, consists of eight animated segments set to pieces of classical music conducted by Leopold Stokowski (1882-1977), seven of which are performed by the Philadelphia Orchestra. Music critic and composer Deems Taylor (1885-1966) acts as the film's Master of Ceremonies, providing a live-action introduction to each animated segment. The eight sections are in this order:

- *Toccata and Fugue in D Minor* by Johann Sebastian Bach (1685-1750). Live-action shots of the orchestra illuminated in blue and gold, backed by superimposed shadows, fade into abstract patterns. Animated lines, shapes and cloud formations reflect the sound and rhythms of the music.

- *The Nutcracker* by Tchaikovsky. Selections from the ballet suite underscore scenes depicting the changing of the seasons from summer to autumn to winter. A wide variety of dances are presented with fairies, fish, flowers, mushrooms, and leaves, including "Dance of the Sugar Plum Fairy," "Chinese Dance," "Dance of the Flutes," "Arabian Dance," "Russian Dance" and "Waltz of the Flowers."

- *The Sorcerer's Apprentice* by French Composer Paul Dukas (1865-1935) based on Freemason and Illuminist Johann Wolfgang von Goethe's (1749-1832) 1797 poem *Der Zauberlehrling*. Mickey Mouse, the young apprentice of the sorcerer Yen Sid, attempts some of his master's magic but does not know how to control it.

- *The Rite of Spring* by Igor Stravinsky (1882-1971). A visual history of the Earth's origins is depicted to selected sections of the ballet score. The sequence progresses from the planet's formation to the first living creatures, followed by the reign and extinction of the dinosaurs.

- *Intermission/Meet the Soundtrack*: The orchestra musicians depart and the Fantasia title card is revealed. After the intermission, there is a brief jam session of jazz music led by a clarinetist as they wait for Taylor to return. Then a humorously stylized demonstration of how sound is rendered on film is shown. An animated soundtrack character, initially a straight white line, changes into different shapes and colors based on the sounds and instruments played.

- *The Pastoral Symphony* (No. 6) by Ludwig van Beethoven (1770-1827). A mythical Greco-Roman world of colorful centaurs and centaurettes, cupids, fauns and other figures from classical mythology is portrayed to Beethoven's music. Bacchus, the god of wine, presides over a bacchanal which is interrupted by Zeus, creating a storm, directing Vulcan to forge lightning bolts for him to hurl at the attendees. Other pagan gods featured in the segment include Apollo, Morpheus, and Diana.

- *Dance of the Hours* by Amilcare Ponchielli (1834-1886). A comic ballet in four sections: Madame Upanova and her ostriches (Morning); Hyacinth Hippo and her servants (Afternoon); Elephanchine and her bubble-blowing elephant troupe (Evening); and Ben Ali Gator and his troop of alligators (Night). The finale finds all the characters dancing together until the palace collapses.

- *Night on Bald Mountain* by Modest Mussorgsky (1839-1881) and Ave Maria by Franz Schubert (1797-1828). At midnight of Walpurgisnacht, the devil Chernabog qua Satan awakens, summoning evil spirits and restless souls from their graves to Bald Mountain. The spirits dance and fly through the air until driven back by the sound of an Angelus bell as night fades into dawn. A chorus is heard singing Ave Maria as a procession of robed monks walking with lighted torches through a forest into the ruins of a cathedral.

Of the eight segments, only two display esoteric imagery worthy of analysis.

In *The Sorcerer's Apprentice*, we find the Hermes Trismegistus wizard archetype embodied by Yen Sid (Disney backward), the sorcerer. Like all magicians, he employs a human skull (symbolizing hermeticism, wisdom) when performing magic, and he has all the attributes of the typical wizard: bald, long graying beard, a robe, and a conical hat complete with pentacles and a crescent moon; Yen Sid anticipates Albus Dumbledore. He orders his apprentice, Mickey Mouse, to fill a cauldron with water, but Mickey tires of the job, putting on his master's hat to perform kabalistic magic to create a golem[271] from a broom. The broom becomes human-like, complete with arms and legs, obeying Mickey's command to fill the cauldron. However, the golem will not stop pouring water which results in massive flooding, forcing Mickey to kill his kabalistic creation. Mickey uses a hatchet to destroy the broom, but this only makes matters worse: the golem multiplies, and the flooding continues. Yed Sid returns and, like Moses, parts the water causing it to subside; this reflects Renaissance tradition of conflating Moses with the Egyptian magus Hermes Trismegistus.[272] According to legend (cf. Ficino's *The Divine Pymander*), Trismegistus went into Egypt, giving the Egyptians their laws and letters mirroring Moses, the lawgiver of the Hebrews.[273] This Hermes-Moses comparison forges a nexus between the Renaissance study of religion, magic, alchemy, astrology, and Cabala, all claiming descent from a *prisca theologia*: the doctrine that a single, true theology exists, pervading in all religions, and that God gave it to man in antiquity.[274] This legend, a crucial part of the hermetic tradition, is thinly disguised in *The Sorcerer's Apprentice*.

During *Fantasia's* grand finale, the satanic majesty of Hell is brought to life in *Night on Bald Mountain*. The frightening mountain, the sleepy village, the dark towering demon, the ghosts and hellfire put to Mussorgsky's music is fantastic, and to this day remains one of Disney's most memorable animations. The demon Chernabog (as Satan) commands this mystical piece; Chernabog is a Slavic deity whose name means black god, about whom much has been speculated, but little can be said definitively. The only historical sources, which are Christian, interpret him as a dark, accursed god, but it is questionable how relevant or malicious he was. During the segment, he summons various evils ghosts and demons on *Walpurgisnacht*, April 30th, the Eve of May Day, the halfway point between the vernal equinox and the summer solstice when the baleful powers of witches and demons were supposed to be at their height, much like Halloween. The brooding darkness of Bald Mountain is defeated with coming dawn, the

---

271 To briefly reiterate, a golem is a creature, particularly a human being (or human-like), made in an artificial way by virtue of a magical act, through the use of holy names, the creative power of speech, and the occult use of letters or symbols. See Scholem's *Kabbalah*, p. 351.

272 Yates, *Girodano Bruno and the Hermetic Tradition, passim*. According to this tradition, Hermes Trismegistus was thought to be at least a contemporary of Moses if not one and the same person.

273 *ibid*, p. 116.

274 *ibid*, pp. 14-18.

chiming of church bells, the return of Christ, *Ave Maria*, visualized as a Neoplatonic rising sun, the light of the world (John 8:12). Although this segment is thought to be evidence of Walt Disney's participation in a Masonic-Illuminati-Demonic global agenda, instead we find light defeating dark, good triumphing over evil, hope over despair, nullifying all concepts of an evil conspiracy.

WITCH MOUNTAIN, THE OCCULT, AND MIND CONTROL

Escape to Witch Mountain and its sequel, *Return from Witch Mountain*, incorporate unique–sometimes disturbing–imagery which may not be veiled, but is nevertheless hidden in plain sight under the guise of action-adventure cinema intended for adolescents.

Escape to Witch Mountain is a 1975 film based on the novel of the same name by Alexander Key(1904-1979).The movie was directed by John Hough. The film centers upon the brother and sister pair Tony (Ike Eisenmann) and Tia (Kim Richards), whose surname they know from their deceased adoptive parents, Malone. The children are placed in an orphanage, where they face difficulties stemming from their strange psychic-psionic abilities: Tony can telekinetically control inanimate objects with the aid of his harmonica, while Tia can communicate telepathically to Tony, commune empathically with animals, and experiences premonitions. Tony's ability to produce magic through music, a harmonica, symbolizes the panpipes, or the pan flute, which, as its name suggests, was played by the pagan god, Pan. In Greek religion and mythology, Pan was the god of the wild, shepherds and flocks, nature of mountain wilds, hunting, rustic music, and companion to the nymphs. His famed Panpipes–a magical device–can best be seen in the 1905 Romantic watercolor *The Magic of Pan's Flute* by John Reinhard Weguelin (1849-1927). In the Watercolor, Pan plays the flute to allure a nymph magically; the overall theme of the painting implies the mythological occult prowess of Pan and his mystical instrument.

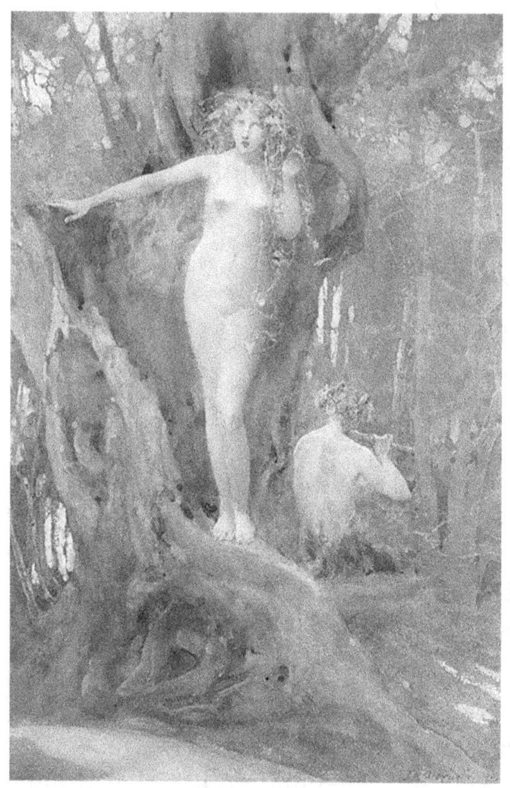

Magic of Pan's Flute: In *The Magic of Pan's Flute*, the god Pan sits on a tree root, his back to the viewer, playing on his flute (cf. Panpipes). On the opposite side of the twisted and gnarled tree stands a naked nymph, listening attentively. She is wearing flowers in her long, golden hair. Scattered rays of sunlight penetrate the misty forest, vaguely depicted in greens and purples.

Tony's sister, Tia, possess the ability to open any lock, mirroring the witchcraft relic known as the Hand of Glory. The Hand of Glory is a preserved mummified hand cut from a hanged murderer, granting invisibility to its owner along with the ability to open any lock, allowing entry into the building or dwelling. Once removed from the corpse, the hand was either dried in an oven with vervain, a herb believed to repel demons, or laid out to dry in the sun during the Dog Days of August when Sirius is exalted.[275] The Hand of Glory was an item wielded by both black magicians and thieves. Tia also has a familiar, a black cat, named Winkie; a familiar is a small animal or pet (a black cat is the most infamous) that is demon possessed allowing it to run errands, performing evil deeds on behalf of the witch or warlock. Exoterically, the cat *winks* at the children hence its name; esoterically, the name Winkie implies Winkie Country which is the Western region of the Land of Oz in L. Frank Baum's (1856-1919) Oz novels, first described in *The Wonderful Wizard of Oz* (1900). The country was ruled by the Wicked Witch of the West before Dorothy melted her with a bucket of water. Thus, the name Winkie also conjures the witchcraft associated with the evil Western Witch in Baum's novel and its cinematic adaptation. Tony and Tia's

---

275 Guiley, *The Encyclopedia of Witches and Witchcraft*, page 150; see also Waite's *The Book of Black Magic*, page 306.

abilities associate them with black magic and witchcraft, implying they may be the ungodly offspring of a coven of witches. Tia carries with her at all times a weird, Masonic-like celestial Star Case; it's blue, symbolizing the Blue Lodge degrees of Freemasonry. Echoing Masonry's rituals and philosophies, the Star Case hides occult secrets along with a strange Map, not to be understood by the profane and uninitiated. The Star Case's strap features runes which appear to be either extraterrestrial or Enochian (Dee's angelic language) in nature. The children mention that they also once spoke a foreign, heavenly language which implies an extraterrestrial dialect which parallels the tongue of the angels in the mythos of Enoch and his off-world travels (see *I Enoch, passim*). Enoch's heavenly journey serves as the basis of Freemasonry's Royal Arch of Enoch ceremonial, which is part of both the Scottish and American (York Rite) high degree systems. [276]

Tia has fragmented memories of her early childhood, including an accident at sea and a man she later remembers as Uncle Bené, pronounced "Ben-ay" (Denver Pyle, 1920-1997), believing he drowned during their rescue. *Bene* or *bené* comes from the Latin meaning *good* or *well* as found in words like *benediction* or *benefactor*. During a field trip to see Walt Disney's *Snow White and the Seven Dwarfs*, Tia experiences a premonition so she warns wealthy attorney Lucas Deranian (Donald Pleasence) against a potentially dangerous

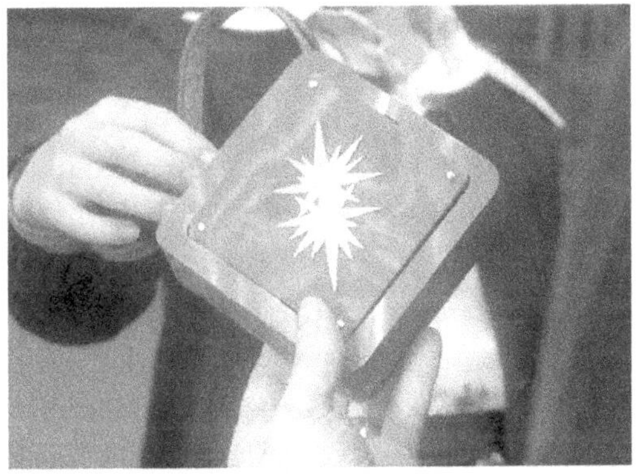

Tia's blue, Masonic-like Star Case displays double stars mostly likely symbolizing the binary Egyptian Dog Star, Sirius. Sirius, adored as the virgin mother Isis in the Egyptian Stellar Mysteries is the Blazing Star of Freemasonry, which is a pentagram symbolizing the Five Points of Fellowship which must be formed to communicate the Substitute Name of Deity. Paralleling the rituals and symbols of Freemasonry, Tia's Star Case hides secret information and truths not to be disseminated to the masses.

car accident. Deranian informs his employer, millionaire Aristotle Bolt (Ray Milland, 1905-1986), of the children's unique abilities. Bolt intends to use the children's talents to satisfy his greed. Bolt, obsessed with the occult, demands Deranian retrieve the children at all costs. Bolt is introduced

---

276 Sullivan, *The Royal Arch of Enoch, passim.*

by consulting three wise men or Magi: an astrologer, a guru, and a psychic, to gain esoteric insights into the procurement of money and treasure. During the scene, the three Magi stand on a mosaic of the zodiac while Bolt clearly personifies an occult Illuminati-like puppet master: it is disclosed that California law enforcement obey him in secret. Bolt, like a typical Illuminist, will stop at nothing to get what he wants–the ends always justify the means. His last name is Bolt–meaning *to confine*–because he intends to keep the children locked away in his mansion, which is the opposite of *key*, meaning to liberate, since a key opens bolts and locks; *key* is also the surname of the novel's author, Alexander Key. Deranian's detective work leads him to the orphanage where he poses, with forged legal paperwork, as Tia and Tony's uncle though not under the name Bené, taking them to Bolt's mansion.

Though initially suspicious of Bolt's motives, Tia and Tony are seduced by the wealthy and ostentatious trappings of Bolt's home. Bolt's estate, named Xanthus, has an equestrian facility transforming Xanthus into an esoteric reference to one of the Mares of Diomedes, Xanthus or Xanthos. The Mares of Diomedes, also called the Mares of Thrace, were four man-eating horses in Greek mythology. Magnificent, wild, and uncontrollable, they belonged to the giant Diomedes (not to be confused with Diomedes, son of Tydeus), king of Thrace, a son of Ares and Cyrene living on the shores of the Black Sea. Bucephalus, Alexander the Great's horse, was said to be descended from these mares. The horse, Thunderhead, is rambunctious symbolizing the legendary mare Xanthus; Tia uses telepathy to tame Thunderhead making the horse subservient to her every command. Bolt eventually reveals that he has been monitoring the children via a closed-circuit television system and that he and Deranian are aware of their mystical powers. The night of this revelation, Tia and Tony make an escape using their psionic abilities to control Thunderhead, guard dogs, and the security fence, as well as deploying their black cat Winkie to disable an allergic security guard. Bolt sends Deranian and a thug, Ubermann (Lawrence Montaigne) after the children. Ubermann refers to the *Übermensch*, Friedrich Nietzsche's (1844-1900) supermen who, like Bolt, are above the law, morality, acting with impunity. Tia and Tony hide out in a Winnebago motor home owned by a crotchety widower named Jason O'Day (Eddie Albert, 1906-2005). Initially negative towards the children, Jason gradually begins to recognize their powers and the truth of their story; Tia's vague memories of a disaster at sea intrigue him. He agrees to take the children on the route indicated by the contents of Tia's Star Case, which leads them to an elevation known as Witch Mountain, home to metaphysical phenomena. Avoiding Bolt, the law, and an incited mob convinced the children are black magicians, they eventually make their way up Witch Mountain, pursued by Deranian and Ubermann, as well as Bolt in a helicopter. Along the way, the children visit the house of Jason O'Day's brother, Hiram O'Day. Hiram O'Day recalls Freemasonry's resurrected sun-man Hiram Abif; the latter goes missing from Solomon's Temple during the third-degree Master Mason ritual; thus, Hiram O'Day does not make an appearance, his current whereabouts unknown. Further linking the two missing men is the surname, O'Day, paralleling Freemasonry's solar iconography.

With their memories returning, the children realize their accident at sea did not involve a boat, but a spacecraft. Tony and Tia are actually from another planet making them star children; the dual-star emblem on the Star Case is an occult symbol for a binary star system, mostly likely Sirius,[277] where their home planet was located. Having come to Earth because their planet was dying, survivors of the journey made their way to Witch Mountain, forming an extraterrestrial village to await the surviving children, each pair in possession of a Star Case to help them find their way to their new home. Tony and Tia are the first Star Children to reach their destination. The children are reunited with their Uncle Bené, who survived thanks to an accommodating shark whom he had telepathically asked for help. When Bolt and the others leave in defeat, Jason witnesses the spaceship's return as it flies over him to say a final goodbye. *Escape to Witch Mountain* intentionally confuses the audience by intertwining witchcraft and supernatural powers with extraterrestrial abilities. It is not until the end that the audience discovers the humanoid children are, in fact, space aliens. However, the alien colony, or coven, is located on Witch Mountain symbolizing, at least implying, that Tony and Tia's powers may indeed be occult in origin.

---

277 What the naked eye perceives as a single star is actually a binary star system, consisting of a white main-sequence star of spectral type A1V, termed Sirius A, and a faint white dwarf companion of spectral type DA2, named Sirius B.

* * * *

Return from Witch Mountain is the 1978 follow-up to the Disney's film, *Escape to Witch Mountain*. It was written by Malcolm Marmorstein and is based, again, on the novel by Alexander Key. Ike Eisenmann, Kim Richards, and Denver Pyle reprise their roles as Tony, Tia, and Uncle Bené. The two villains are played by Bette Davis (1908-1989) as Letha Wedge, a greedy woman using the last of her money to finance the scientific experiments of Dr. Gannon, played by Christopher Lee (1922-2015). Having spent a good deal of time enjoying the company of their new-found family and friends at Witch Mountain intensively honing their occult-like supernatural powers, Tony and Tia are in need of a vacation. Uncle Bené drops them off in their flying saucer at Rose Bowl Stadium in Los Angeles, California, after which the siblings quickly become separated from each other. Dr. Gannon and his benefactor, Letha, happen to see Tony using his powers to save their henchman, Sickle (Anthony James), from falling off a building to certain death. Realizing that Tony has supernatural powers, Dr. Gannon becomes frantic to examine Tony remarking to Letha, "I need that boy, Letha, I need him desperately!" Although Dr. Gannon is referring to medical experimentation, there is a decidedly pedophilic vibration to the scene; Dr. Gannon has a jubilant grimace on his face implying Letha knows what Gannon is secretly referring to, as he nods in agreement.

Dr. Gannon drugs the boy with a tranquilizer, kidnapping him to their castle-like laboratory. What comes next draws upon the occultism of the German Expressionist film *The Cabinet of Dr. Caligari* (1920). Dr. Caligari (Werner Krauss, 1884-1959) uses occult mind-control techniques to manipulate a near-silent somnambulist, Cesare (Conrad Veidt, 1893-1943), whom the doctor keeps asleep in a cabinet. Once inside their claustrophobic dungeon, Dr. Gannon successfully employs mind-control technology of his own invention on the boy, paralleling Caligari and the Renaissance tradition of using scientific methodology to effectuate magical results.[278] Aided by a Sabbatic Goat (cf. Goat of Mendes, Baphomet) named Alfred, Dr. Gannon transforms Tony into a Manchurian Candidate[279] by placing

---

278 See Yates' *Astraea*, already cited.

279 *The Manchurian Candidate* (1959) by Richard Condon (1915-1996), is a political thriller novel about the son of a prominent US political family who is brainwashed into being an unwitting assassin for a Communist conspiracy. It was made into a film in 1962 and remade in 2004.

a mind-control receptor behind his ear. Later, Alfred the Goat will be accused of being a shape-shifting magician by a taxi cab driver. Like a somnambulist, Tony is completely hypnotized, doing the bidding of his captors. Under the influence of Dr. Gannon and Letha, Tony obeys, without question, the voices of his masters: he plunders a museum, attempts to hold the United States ransom by triggering a China Syndrome[280] in a nuclear reactor outside Los Angeles, and tries to kill his sister on numerous occasions.

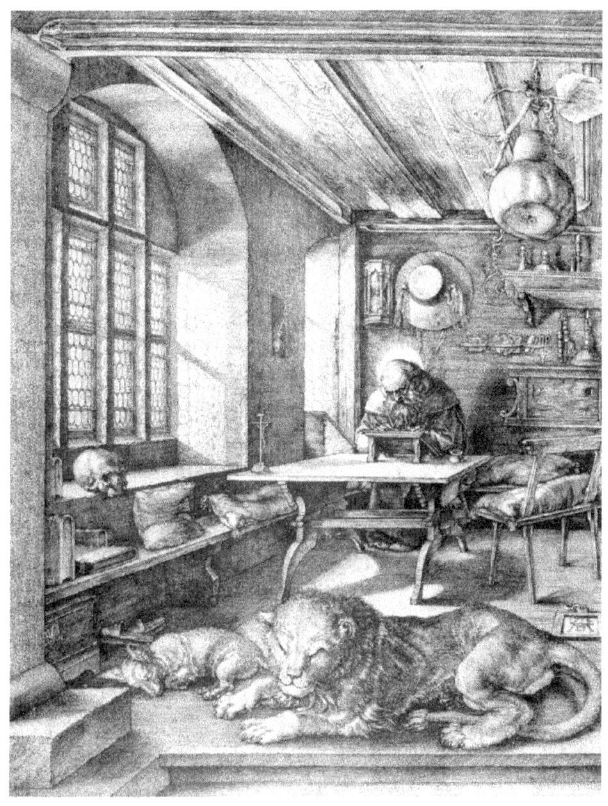

Saint Jerome in His Study (German: *Der heilige Hieronymus im Gehäus*) is a 1514 engraving by the German artist Albrecht Dürer

However, Tia uses her telepathic powers to break the mind control of Gannon and Letha. She gets additional help from a group of young would-be gang-bangers she stumbles across called the Earthquake Gang, and a hapless truant officer Mr. Yokomoto (Jack Soo, 1917-1979), whom the gang have nicknamed "Yo-Yo," to find her brother and foil the villains' sinister plans.

Tia uses an abandoned mansion as her hideout which also serves as the base of operations for the Earthquake Gang. The mansion is the old West Temple Apartments (a/k/a The Rochester) which was built in 1887

---

280 The China Syndrome (loss-of-coolant accident) is a hypothetical nuclear reactor operations accident characterized by the severe meltdown of the core components of the reactor, which then burn through the containment vessel, the housing building, then notionally through the crust and body of the Earth until reaching the other side which, in the United States, is jokingly referred to as being China.

becoming the subject of various lawsuits to keep it as a historic landmark in the 1960s-1970s. In the autumn of 1970, the Rochester was moved temporarily to the railroad property just north of Union Station (Alameda and Bruno Streets in Los Angles) where it is in *Return from Witch Mountain*. The structure was demolished in 1979. Inside, Tia's quarters include a human skull signifying the death's head in the study of St. Jerome, depicted in the famed engraving by Albrecht Dürer (1471-1528), becoming a symbol for the mysterious and mystical; for Tia's the skull is an emblem of her extraterrestrial powers.

Like Aristotle Bolt before him, Dr. Victor Gannon is an illuminist in that he too wants to use the children's powers[281] to become "the most powerful man in the world," to quote him directly. When Gannon fails, and with Letha hung out to dry, Tony is returned to his usual self, the nuclear reactor is restored, allowing Tony and Tia to return to Witch Mountain with Uncle Bené to continue to perfect their abilities. The movie ends where it began, at the Rose Bowl Stadium in Los Angeles. The rose is an icon of secrecy, Rosicrucianism, the mysteries, and the occult. On Rosicrucianism and the symbol of the mountain, Manly P. Hall explains, "…gives a valuable key to esoteric Rosicrucianism by dividing the path of spiritual attainment into three steps, or schools, which he calls *mountains*. The first and lowest of these mountains is *Mount Sophia*; the second, *Mount Qabbalah*; and the third, *Mount Magia*. These three mountains are sequential stages of spiritual growth."[282] Thus, it is only appropriate that Tony and Tia leave from and return to Witch Mountain, a modern *Mount Magia*, sub rosa (English: under the rose) signifying 1) Tony and Tia's magical abilities, and 2) the esoteric underpinnings of the two films.

THE LION KING: THE OSIRIAN CYCLE AND HAMLET RETOLD

Released approximately one week before the summer solstice of 1994, *The Lion King* is an epic musical adventure and one of the most important

---

281 Dr. Gannon only has interest in utilizing Tony, not Tia.
282 Hall, *The Secret Teachings of All Ages*, pp. 464-465.

movies of the Disney Renaissance. Defined as an era from 1989 to 1999, the Disney Renaissance saw Walt Disney Feature Animation (renamed Walt Disney Animation Studios in 2006) experience a creative resurgence in producing successful animated films based on well-known stories, which restored public and critical interest in the Walt Disney Company. A box office success receiving mostly positive reviews, *The Lion King* veils Egyptian symbolism, solar iconography, Christian mysticism, citing Shakespeare's *Hamlet* (full title *The Tragedy of Hamlet, Prince of Denmark*, 1603).

In the Pride Lands of Africa, a mighty lion rules over the animals as king. With the birth of King Mufasa (James Earl Jones) and Queen Sarabi's (Madge Sinclair, 1938-1995) son Simba,[283] the Circle of Life is renewed but ferments envy and resentment with Mufasa's brother, Scar (Jeremy Irons), knowing his nephew now replaces him as the heir to the throne. In Scar's yellow eyes is the evil gaze of *Sleeping Beauty's* Maleficent whose eyes are the same color as Scar's, symbolizing that his villainy is equal to her devilry. After Simba has grown into a young cub, Mufasa gives him a tour of the Pride Lands, teaching him the responsibilities of being a king and the purpose of the Circle of Life. Later that day, Scar tricks Simba and his best friend Nala[284] into exploring a forbidden elephant graveyard, despite the protests of Mufasa's hornbill majordomo Zazu (Rowan Atkinson). At the cemetery, three spotted hyenas named Shenzi (Whoopi Goldberg), Banzai (Cheech Marin) and Ed (Jim Cummings) attack the cubs before Mufasa, alerted by Zazu, rescues them; Mufasa forgives Simba for his foolish actions. Later that night the three hyenas plot with Scar to kill Mufasa and Simba.

The next day, Scar lures Simba to a gorge and tells him to wait there while he gets Mufasa. On Scar's orders, the hyenas stampede a large herd of wildebeest into the gorge. Mufasa rescues Simba, but as Mufasa tries to climb the canyon's walls, Scar throws him back into the stampede where he is trampled to death. After Simba finds Mufasa's body, Scar convinces him he was responsible for his father's death, advising Simba to flee the kingdom. As Simba leaves, Scar orders Shenzi, Banzai, and Ed to kill the cub but Simba escapes. That night, Scar announces to the pride that both

---

283 Young Simba voiced by Jonathan Taylor Thomas, adult Simba voiced by Matthew Broderick, and singing voice Jason Weaver.
284 Young Nala voiced by Niketa Calame, adult Nala voiced by Moira Kelly.

Mufasa and Simba were killed in the stampede stepping forward as the new king, allowing a pack of hyenas to live in the Pride Lands.

After running far away, Simba collapses from exhaustion in a desert. Timon (Nathan Lane) and Pumbaa (Ernie Sabella), a meerkat and a warthog, find him, nursing him back to health. The double act continues the tradition of Laurel and Hardy,[285] Amos and Andy,[286] Abbot and Costello,[287] Lewis and Martin,[288] R2-D2 and C-3PO,[289] and Beavis and Butthead.[290] Simba subsequently grows up with them in the jungle, living a carefree life with his friends under the motto *Hakuna Matata* ("No Worries" in Swahili). When he is a young adult, Simba rescues Timon and Pumbaa from a hungry lioness, Nala. She and Simba reconcile, falling in love. Nala urges Simba to return home, telling him the Pride Lands have become a wasteland with not enough food and water. Feeling guilty over his father's death, Simba refuses and storms off, leaving Nala disappointed and angry. As Simba exits the jungle, he encounters Mufasa's mandrill friend and soothsayer, Rafiki (Robert Guillaume). Rafiki tells Simba that Mufasa is alive, taking him to a pond. There Simba is visited by the ghost of Mufasa in the sky, who tells him he must take his rightful place as the king of the Pride Lands. Simba realizes he can no longer run from his past, deciding to return home. Nala, Timon, and Pumbaa join him in the fight against Scar.

Returning to the Pride Lands, Simba sees Scar hit Sarabi and confronts him, but Scar taunts Simba over his part in Mufasa's death. However, when Scar pushes Simba to the edge of Pride Rock, he reveals that he killed Mufasa. Enraged, Simba roars back up, forcing Scar to reveal the truth to the pride. Timon, Pumbaa, Rafiki, Zazu, and the lionesses fend off the hyenas while Scar, attempting to escape, is cornered by Simba at the top of Pride Rock. Scar begs Simba for mercy, insisting that he is family, placing the blame on the hyenas. Simba no longer believes Scar, but spares his life on the condition of forever leaving the Pride Lands. Scar appears to comply but then attacks his nephew. After a fierce fight, Simba throws his

---

285 Stan Laurel (1890-1965) and Oliver Hardy (1892-1957).
286 Freeman Gosden (1899-1982) and Charles Corell (1890-1972)
287 Bud Abbott (1897-1974) and Lou Costello (1906-1959).
288 Jerry Lewis (1926-2017) and Dean Martin (1917-1995).
289 Kenny Baker (1934-2016) and Anthony Daniels.
290 Both voiced by Mike Judge.

uncle off Pride Rock. Scar survives the fall but is attacked and eaten alive by the hyenas, having overheard his betrayal of them.

With Scar and the hyenas gone, Simba ascends to the top of Pride Rock, taking over the kingdom as rain falls. Sometime later, with Pride Lands restored to its former glory, Simba looks down happily at his kingdom with Nala, Timon, and Pumbaa by his side; Rafiki presents Simba and Nala's newborn cub to the inhabitants of the Pride Lands signifying the Circle of Life continues.

Mufasa and Simba, like *The Chronicles of Narnia's* Aslan the Lion (Chapter X), are Neoplatonic sun kings; they are personifications of Leo the Lion, the zodiac's solar house, the astral King of the Jungle, their manes symbolize powerful, life-giving sun rays. The movie begins with the sunrise with Mufasa comparing life and death to a rising and setting sun; he explains, "A king's time as ruler rises and falls like the sun. One day, Simba, the sun will set on my time here, and will rise with you as the new king." With Mufasa dead and Simba exiled presumed dead, the Pride Lands turn to decay; when the sun is absent and the rain ceases, the land dies; it is only reborn (or born again) when Simba returns, defeats Scar the pretender, thus continuing the Circle of Life. The area that the Neoplatonic solar godly lions are forbidden to enter is north of the river, the elephant cemetery, home to the devious hyenas; it is not part of their divine-solar kingdom. The sun is not welcome in the north, only the east, south, and west; in the east, rising at dawn, in the south, at noon, then in the west, setting at dusk. Because divine light is not welcome, the Devil's direction is north, the domain of darkness and penal cold.[291] Since all churches were built facing east, north is always on one's left when one enters a church. The Devil lurks on the north side of a church which is why people prefer not to bury their dead there. Left (Lat. *sinister*) is associated with the ill-omen and danger in many cultures; on the medieval stage, north is the direction of Hell. Hence, it is in the north that Lucifer of Isaiah 14:13 sets up his throne;[292] in *The Lion King*, north is home to darkness: Scar and the evil hyenas lurk there.

Solar iconography, linked with the Dark Continent, evokes the Egyptian Osirian Cycle, the eternal battle of the sun against darkness, God against

---

291 Jeffrey Burton Russell, *Lucifer: The Devil in the Middle Ages*, p. 69.
292 *ibid*, pp. 69, 71; footnote 17 p. 71.

the Devil, with *The Lion King* mirroring this mythology. In the Egyptian pantheon, Osiris is the constellation Orion, Isis is Sirius, and Typhon is the constellation Scorpio. This Egyptian astral symbolism is suggested when Mufasa explains, "Simba, let me tell you something my father told me. Look at the stars. The great kings of the past look down on us from those stars." On the Osirian myth, Masonic author Albert G. Mackey writes:

In the mysteries of Osiris, which were the consummation of the Egyptian system, the lesson of death and resurrection was symbolically taught; and the murder of Osiris, the search for the body, its discovery and restoration to life is scenically represented. This legend of initiation was as follows: Osiris, a wise king of Egypt, left the care of his kingdom to his wife Isis, and traveled for three years to communicate to other nations the art of civilization. During his absence, his brother Typhon formed a secret conspiracy to destroy him and usurp his throne. On his return, Osiris was invited by Typhon to an entertainment in the month of November, at which all the conspirators were present. Typhon produced a chest inlaid with gold, and promised to give it to any person present whose body would most exactly fit it. Osiris was tempted to try the experiment; but he had no sooner laid down in the chest, than the lid was closed and nailed down, and the chest thrown into the river Nile. The chest containing the body of Osiris was, after being for a long time tossed about by the waves, finally cast up at Byblos in Phoenicia, and left at the foot of a tamarisk tree. Isis, overwhelmed with the grief for the loss of her husband, set out on a journey, and traveled the earth in search of the body. After many adventures, she at length discovered the spot whence it had been thrown up by the waves and returned with it in triumph to Egypt. It was then proclaimed, with the most extravagant demonstrations of joy, that Osiris was risen from the dead and had become a god. Such, with the slight variation of details by different writers, are the general outlines of the Osiric legend which was represented in the drama of initiation. Its resemblance to the Hiramic legend of the Masonic system will be readily seen, and its symbolism will be easily understood. Osiris and Typhon are the representatives of the two antagonistic principles–good and evil, light and darkness, life and death. There is also an astronomical interpretation of the legend which makes Osiris the sun and Typhon the season of winter, which suspends the fecundating and fertilizing powers of the sun or destroys its life, to be restored only by the return of the invigorating spring.[293]

Masonic Scottish Rite Sovereign Grand Commander Albert Pike adds:

Whether Egypt originated the legend, or borrowed it from India or Chaldaea, it is now impossible to know. But the Hebrews received the Mysteries from the Egyptians; and of course were familiar with *their legend*,–known as it was to those Egyptian Initiates, Joseph and Moses. It was the fable (or rather the *truth* clothed in allegory and figures) of Osiris, the Sun, Source of Light and Principle of Good, and Typhon, the Principle of Darkness and Evil. In all the histories of the Gods and Heros lay couched and hidden astronomical details and the history of the operations of visible Nature; and those in their turn were also symbols of higher and profounder truths. None but rude uncultivated intellects could long consider the Sun and the Stars and the Powers of Nature as Divine, or as fit objects of Human Worship; and *they* will consider them so while the world lasts; remain ignorant of the great Spiritual Truths of which these are the hieroglyphics and expression.

…Osiris, said to have been an ancient King of Egypt, was the Sun, and Isis, his wife, the Moon: and his history recounts, in poetic and figurative style, the annual journey of the Great Luminary of Heaven through the different Signs of the Zodiac.

In the absence of Osiris, Typhon, his brother, filled with envy and malice, sought to usurp his throne; but his plans were frustrated by Isis. Then he resolved to kill Osiris. This he did, by persuading him to enter a coffin or sarcophagus, which he then flung into the Nile. After a long search, Isis found the body, and concealed it in the depths of the forest; but Typhon, finding it there, cut it into fourteen Pieces, and scattered them hither and thither. After tedious search, Isis found the thirteen pieces, the fishes having eaten the other (the privates), which she replaced with wood, and buried the body at Philae; where a temple of surpassing magnificence was erected in honor of Osiris.

---

293 Mackey, *Encyclopedia of Freemasonry*, Vol. I., p. 233.

Isis, aided by her son Orus, Horus or Har-oeri, warred against Typhon, slew him, reigned gloriously, and at her death was reunited to her husband, in the same tomb.

…Horus, who aided in slaying him (Typhon), became God of the Sun, answering to the Grecian Apollo, and Typhon is but the anagram of Python, the great serpent slain by Apollo.[294]

Although not an exact retelling, we nevertheless find the fingerprints of the legend all over Disney's story. The kingly Mufasa, the sun, personifies Osiris slain by his envious brother Scar *qua* Typhon, or Set. With the sun dead, Scar is allowed to reign, causing the land to become infertile; there is no food or water because darkness reigns, a pretender sits on the sun's mighty throne. The sacred feminine, Nala, brings Simba *qua* Horus back to the Pride Lands. Aided by his queenly mother Sarabi *qua* Isis, Simba slays Scar becoming the new sun god, thereby continuing the Circle of Life. Simba is Mufasa's posthumous redeemer, just like Horus, the posthumous redeemer of Osiris. With Scar (or Typhon) gone, Simba claims the rightful throne of his father: the fecundating and fertilizing power of the sun is restored; rain falls, and the land is born again as the invigorating spring returns. Simba has become the very incarnation of his father, the personification of the sun, the avenger of evil, the just God in whom there is no death.[295] Throw in a Thoth-like (cf. Hermes Trismegistus) mandrill named Rafiki and we are confronted with an Egyptian legend retold, making it modern-day mythology.

Since *The Lion King* is replete with solar allegory, Egyptian legends, and sacred mythology, it follows that the film exhibits Biblical (both Old and New Testaments) themes, transforming it into Neoplatonic art. King Mufasa (*qua* Osiris) tells Simba (*qua* Horus, the sun, Jesus) that he, a new king, will rule the land and its inhabitants reflecting Philippians 2:10, "That at the name of Jesus every knee should bow, of things in heaven, and things in earth, and things under the earth." Scar (*qua* Typhon, the Devil) hates Mufasa and Simba conspiring against them, suggesting I Peter 5:8, "Be sober, be vigilant; because your adversary the devil, as a roaring lion, walketh about, seeking whom he may devour." Mufasa sacrifices himself

---

294 Pike, *Morals and Dogma*, pp. 375-376.
295 Manly P. Hall, *Freemasonry of the Ancient Egyptians*, pp.69-70.

to save Simba, mirroring Jesus's sacrifice on the cross (Luke 23:44-46, Matthew 27:32-61, I Peter 2:24) for the sins of mankind; and Simba grows to maturity in exile paralleling Moses' 40 years of exile in the desert (Acts 7:30). Simba is helped by two outcasts signifying the parable of the Good Samaritan at Luke 10:25-37. Finally, Simba exposes Scar's treachery, then vanquishes him by throwing him down into an inferno to be consumed by the hyenas, recalling Jesus defeating Satan, then casting him into a fiery lake at Revelation 20:10, "And the devil that deceived them was cast into the lake of fire and brimstone, where the beast and the false prophet are, and shall be tormented day and night for ever and ever."

Similarities between Shakespeare's tragedy *Hamlet* and *The Lion King* are also transcendent. Set in the Kingdom of Denmark, *Hamlet* dramatizes the revenge Prince Hamlet is called to wreak upon his uncle, Claudius, by the ghost of Hamlet's father, King Hamlet. Claudius has murdered his brother and seized the throne, also marrying his deceased brother's widow. The protagonists of both stories, Simba and Hamlet, are royalty whose regal fathers are murdered by their treacherous uncles, taking control of the throne. Both Simba and Hamlet's fathers return as ghosts; the former reminds him of his destiny in the Circle of Life and the latter instructs his son to seek revenge. Simba lives in exile presumed dead while Hamlet's Uncle Claudius convinces him to travel to England where he is to be secretly killed, though he survives. Simba develops a close friendship with the comical Timon and Pumbaa, while Hamlet has a friend named Horatio whom he knew from college. Though Horatio does not have much of an impact on Hamlet as Timon and Pumbaa have on Simba, he does help Hamlet on several occasions and can be considered his one true friend. Simba has a love interest, Nala, while Hamlet has a love interest named Ophelia, though there is much controversy about whether he loved her or was using her; she is the one woman in his life nonetheless. Simba must learn to step up and take his place as king instead of running from his past, while Hamlet has to make the decision to commit murder-suicide, or kill his uncle and continue living (a struggle which takes place in his famous "to be or not to be" soliloquy). Simba fights with Scar, the latter killed by the hyenas; Hamlet kills his uncle with a sword and poisoned wine. When this powerful Shakespearean archetypal imagery is combined with Egyptian mysticism, Neoplatonism, and solar iconography, it is no wonder *The Lion*

King was the second highest grossing domestic movie of 1994 coming in at $312,855,561. The film's box office performance speaks to the power of the archetypes, mythology, the occult, the collective unconscious, and to the hidden symbols and themes masterfully placed in our favorite movies. *The Lion King* is an excellent example of the sorcery of the Magic Kingdom.

Some fairy tales feature disgusting and grotesque elements, exorcised by Disney for obvious reasons. In some variants, the story of *Cinderella* is much more threatening than any of its big-screen counterparts. In early versions, Cinderella has been obliged to leave her royal home and take kitchen employment elsewhere because her father, in search of a woman as beautiful as his dead wife, is determined to marry his daughter. In the Grimms' version of *Cinderella*, the stepsisters attempt to trick the Prince by cutting off their heels and toes to make the slipper fit their foot, but the Prince spots the blood on their stockings realizing they're imposters. In the Grimms's take on *Snow White*, the evil queen is a dabbler in the black arts. She requests the Huntsman bring back Snow White's viscera, but instead he returns with the organs of a wild boar. She consumes them believing she is eating Snow White. In ritual cannibalism, eating the enemies' flesh is a source of strength. By eating parts of Snow White, she believes she will regain her beauty.

Rape and necrophilia are also present in these fantasies. In fact, they form the very crux of the original fairy tale of *Sleeping Beauty* before it was purified by Perrault in 1697. It is rape, not a princely kiss, which the various Prince Charmings bring to the catatonic beauties of earlier versions. None of this is featured in the Disney films; instead, the conspiratorial-negative criticism usually focuses on the use of white magic to defeat evil. Often, this white magic is deemed occult and Antichrist (at least not Christian) which is a mistake: the magic of these fairy tales, and the Disney movies based upon them, is Renaissance Cabala reinvented, not black magic. It is Christian magic which seeks to elevate the suffering soul over hardship and oppression; this is not evidence of an evil conspiracy, rather the fairy tale is an archetypal morality lesson wherein good triumphs over evil, white magic defeats black magic. Renaissance sorcery is victorious over Counter-Reformation platitudes, the injustices of the Inquisition, and the medieval narrow-minded Catholic magisterium.

Many conspiracy theories directed toward Disney stem from the late 1970s and 1980s when the studio produced a string of movies with dark and mature undercurrents to target teenagers. Live action movies from the time-frame include *Escape to Witch Mountain*, *Return from Witch Mountain*, and *The Black Hole* (1979) which was inspired by the success of *Star Wars*. Other films include *Dragonslayer* (1981), *The Watcher in the Woods* (1980), and *Something Wicked This Way Comes* (1983); while the animated *The Black Cauldron* (1985) was equally mysterious and menacing. Parents took their kids to see these movies relying on the Disney brand, not knowing these films dealt with dark subject matter not suited for children. A backlash occurred leading to the Disney Renaissance, which recaptured the magic of the studio's earlier animated features. Spanning a ten-year period beginning in 1989, Disney produced and released ten animated films: *The Little Mermaid* (1989), *The Rescuers Down Under* (1990*)*, *Beauty and the Beast* (1991), *Aladdin* (1992), *The Lion King, Pocahontas* (1995), *The Hunchback of Notre Dame* (1996), *Hercules* (1997), *Mulan* (1998), and *Tarzan* (1999), which revitalized Disney critically and commercially. Although these movies were directed toward children, these films successfully combined comedy with adult themes which kept parents and Generation X buying tickets and filling theaters. This revival has not dampened the world of conspiracy, rather has only inflamed it because many of these movies exhibit hidden sexual references, phallic symbols, and other imagery not suitable for children. For instances, to this author the word *SEX* appearing in *The Lion King* as a dust cloud is just an animator goofing around, but many consider this evidence of an evil Illuminati conspiracy designed to undermine Christian values. The debate over this continues to rage, but make no mistake: the films of Disney hide arcane imagery and occult nuances. This author plans to continue the analysis of Walt Disney movies in *Cinema Symbolism 3*.

CHAPTER V

Black Phillip Says You Are Wicked: Esoteric Imagery in Horror Movies

"The Horseman was a Hessian mercenary
sent to the shores by German princes to keep Americans
under the yoke of England. But unlike his compatriots,
who came for money, the horseman came for love of carnage."
– Baltus Van Tassel, *Sleepy Hollow*, 1999.

"Ghosts are real, this much I know."
– Edith Cushing, *Crimson Peak*, 2015.

"Do you know where you are Bartolome? I will tell you where you are. You are about to enter Hell Bartolome, *Hell*! The netherworld, the infernal regions, the abode of the damned, the place of torment, pandemonium, abandon, *Tophet, Gehenna, Naraka*; the pit and the pendulum."
– Nicholas (as Sebastian) Medina, *The Pit and the Pendulum*, 1961.

"To a new world of gods and monsters!"
– Dr. Pretorius, *The Bride of Frankenstein*, 1935.

"We must get rid of that bitch of an American girl. Vanish, she must vanish. Make her disappear, understand? Vanish, she must vanish. She must die, die, die! Helena, give me power. Sickness, sickness, away with her, away with trouble. Death, death, death!"
– Madame Blanc, *Suspiria*, 1977.

"She ran out to that tree by the dock, climbed up, proclaimed her love to Satan, cursed anyone who tried to take her land, and hung herself. Time of death was pronounced at 3:07 in the morning.
– Lorraine Warren, *The Conjuring*, 2013.

"Enjoy the Horrorthon doctor.
And don't forget to watch the Big Giveaway afterwards."
– Conal Cochran, *Halloween III: Season of the Witch*, 1982.

The horror film *Trick 'r Treat* (2007, released 2009) cleverly shows us the five life-phases of Halloween that we all experience, assuming we live long enough: 1) youth, when we carve pumpkins and go trick 'r treating under the supervision of our parents; 2) as parents, celebrating Halloween with our children; 3) adolescence, when we tell ghost stories, engaging in mischief with our juvenile friends; 4) young adulthood, when Halloween is one of the greatest party nights of the year, and 5) old age, when the macabre yet mischievous holiday is twenty-four hours that we just want to be over and done with. *Trick 'r Treat* will one day be televised around late October just like *It's a Wonderful Life* and *A Christmas Story* are aired through Yuletide; *Trick 'r Treat* encapsulates the dark festival like no other.

The word *occult* comes from the Latin *occultus* meaning hidden, and many horror movies, like *Trick 'r Treat*, incorporate hidden symbolisms, undercurrents, and esoterica. As such, horror films are occult films that explore monsters (human and nonhuman), the demonic, ghosts and ghouls, the world of witchcraft and sorcery, and the shadow that dwells in us all. These subjects are all the domain of the occult. This dark world, when presented as a motion picture on the silver screen, can haunt our dreams informing our nightmares; horror movies can truly terrify us. They exploit our deepest fears and magnify our greatest anxieties. Horror movies *are* the occult on celluloid: they both demonstrate and dignify the chaotic maelstrom of the Left-Hand Path.

SUSPIRIA: DANCING QUEEN MEETS WITCHCRAFT

ABBA's most famous song, "Dancing Queen," was released on 16 August 1976.[296] Almost one year to the day, 12 August 1977, *Suspiria* was released to movie-going audiences; it is the story of a blossoming ballerina, a dancing queen, vanquishing a coven of evil witches hiding in a ballet school. *Suspiria*, Latin for *sigh*, is named after the founder and Directress

---

296 "Dancing Queen" was first released in Sweden on August 16th, 1976; August 21st, 1976 in the UK; and November 12th, 1976 in the USA.

of the *Tanz Akademie* (Dance Academy) in Freiburg, Germany, Helena Markos. Markos, a vile witch, was known to the initiated as the *Black Queen* and *Mater Suspiriorum*,[297] the Mother of Sighs. Markos, a Greek émigré, was exiled from many European countries. She had written several books on a variety of arcane subjects. In 1895, she founded an institute just outside of the Black Forest (German: *Schwarzwald*) wherein adepts could perfect their dance and study the occult sciences. The locals feared her, believing she was a witch. As Markos' wealth grew, so did suspicion about her demonic nature. To avert this unwanted scrutiny, she faked her death in 1905, making it look like she died in a fire. Control of the academy, which, over time, solely became a ballet school, was said to have gone to Markos' favorite pupil, but this was Markos herself. The *Akademie* bears a plaque outside its entrance stating that Dutch Renaissance humanist, Catholic priest, and social critic Desiderius Erasmus (1466-1536) once lived there.

Perhaps just as famous as the film is its score which was composed by the Italian progressive rock band Goblin; while watching *Suspiria* the music is just as profound as the horror on the screen. At first glance, *Suspiria* appears alchemical with its overuse of reds, blacks, whites, and yellows; however, this is not the case.[298] These intense and iridescent colors, along with omnipresent blues and greens, instead pay tribute to the animation of Walt Disney. The film's director, Dario Argento, has commented that "… we were trying to reproduce the color of Walt Disney's *Snow White*; it has been said from the beginning that Technicolor lacked subdued shades, was without nuances–like cut-out cartoons."[299] The somber film plays out like *Snow White* exhibiting folkloric, Brothers Grimm-like characters: an evil queen, a youthful protagonist losing her innocence but gain wisdom, and hermetic helpers providing wisdom to the heroine on her quest against evil. Many of the Brothers Grimm stories are set in the Black Forest, such as *Little Red Riding Hood* and *Hansel and Gretel*, with the former featuring

---

297 The Three Mothers (*Le Tre madri* in Italian) is a trilogy of supernatural horror films by Italian film director Dario Argento. It consists of *Suspiria*, *Inferno* (1980), and *The Mother of Tears* (2007). Each film deals with one of the titular Mothers, a triumvirate of ancient and evil witches whose powerful magic allows them to manipulate world events on a global scale.

298 Within the ballet school there is also a red room and a yellow room wherein students perfect their dance; however, Suzy's adventure is more Gnostic than alchemical.

299 Maitland McDonagh, *Broken Mirrors/Broken Minds: The Dark Dreams of Dario Argento*, pp. 142-144, *passim*.

a lycanthrope and the latter an evil witch; as such, Markos' occult dance academy is right at home bordering *der Schwarzwald*.

Like many of Disney's films, *Suspiria* veils its symbolism, appearing from its opening sequence through to the its grand finale. The movie begins with Suzy Bannion (Jessica Harper), a young American ballerina, arriving from New York in Munich, Germany on a stormy night to matriculate at a prestigious dance academy in Freiburg. Suzy arrives on Flight 237 from New York, which is displayed on the airport's flight board. Flight Number 237 seems to be the source for Stanley Kubrick's infamous room 237 in *The Shining* because, in Stephen King's novel, it is room 217; Kubrick deliberately changed it. Applied to *The Shining*, the number 237 subconsciously recollects Suzy's flight number, thereby evoking *Suspiria's* omnipresent witchcraft. Kubrick is doing this deliberately because a malevolent, decaying female ghost, reminiscent of Helena Markos, dwells in room 237 of the Overlook; the number 237 is also numerically important within the context of *The Shining*–more on this later. *Suspiria* would have been known to Kubrick, having been released in 1977, with *The Shining* being released three years later in 1980. Witchcraft and demonism abound in Markos' dance academy and it is Suzy's call to defeat it.

Suzy arrives at the airport dressed in white *qua* an emblem of her youth and purity; she epitomizes Snow White on a mission to destroy a coven of witches only she doesn't know it yet. From out of the crowd, a woman dressed in red passes Suzy, walking ahead and exiting the airport door in the distance, her hair and clothes rippling in the wind. At this point she is nothing but a contrapuntal figure, adding visual interest to the image, the woman anticipates Pat Hingle (Eva Axén) running frantically from the ballet school when Suzy arrives. Pat, young, tall, slender, and also wears red, mumbles something mysterious to the intercom while standing in doorway of the *Tanz Akademie* when Suzy approaches her. Suzy tries to understand her but cannot make sense of what she is saying or doing. Also observable during the film's beginning is the heavy use of rain and running water symbolizing the baptism, commencement, or the genesis of Suzy's mystical quest.[300] After Suzy is refused access to the Academy, she decides to spend the night in town. Pat, having just been expelled from the

---

300 cf. Pike's *Morals and Dogma*, p. 357; Pike writes, "…and the baptismal water, for water is not only the cleanser of all things, but the genesis or source of all."

dance school under suspicious circumstances, finds refuge at a friend's apartment in town. Pat talks to her friend about the strange goings-on at the dance school, then removes herself to the bathroom. Anticipating the black lingerie masturbatory fetishism of *9 ½ Weeks'* Elizabeth McGraw, a demon materializes from a pair of black stockings and slip which hang outside the bathroom's window. Just like black silk stockings are the decadent symbol of Elizabeth's darker-self, so too is a demon able to manifest in black lingerie (cf. shadow, dark sensuality, fetishism), entering the material world. The coven of witches, hiding in the secret chambers within the dance academy, sent the demon whose eyes are seen in the black slip, then, suddenly, a muscular hairy arm reaches out from the lingerie, smashing a pane of glass. The demon smothers Pat by pressing her face hard against the glass, making her appear piggish, then repeatedly stabs her, piercing her beating heart with a large knife. Her friend overhears Pat's screaming so she tries to call for help, but none of the neighbors reply. Pat is then bound with a cord before she is hung mid-air after crashing through a large stained-glass ceiling. Her friend is killed directly below by the falling glass and metal.

Suzy returns to the Academy the next morning where she is introduced to Madame Blanc (Joan Bennett, 1910-1990) and dance instructor Miss Tanner (Alida Valli, 1921-2006). Blanc, the headmistress of the school, is a witch answerable to the school's mysterious and never seen directress, later revealed to be none other than Helena Markos. Also introduced is a creepy boy named Albert (Jacopo Mariani), Blanc's nephew. Argento's use of the name, Blanc, is an intentional paradox; *blanc* is French for *white*, yet Blanc is the de facto leader of the black magic coven inside the ballet school. Miss Tanner, another black magician, is an archetypal female German martinet: ruthless, cruel, and emotionless.[301] Although she is not as brutal, Tanner resurrects the persona of Ilse Koch (1906-1967), known as the Witch of Buchenwald (German: *Die Hexe von Buchenwald*) or, more commonly, the Bitch of Buchenwald because of her bestial cruelty towards the prisoners at the infamous Nazi concentration camp.

---

301 Comically (and comparatively), this battle-ax archetype becomes Ms. Beulah Balbricker (Nancy Parsons, 1942-2001) in the *Porky's* movies. Lynn Honeywell (Kim Cattrall) antagonizes Balbricker with the following insults: "Well, it sure beats stomping and waddling around like a frigid hippopotamus, Beulah. …Beulah, Beulah Ballbreaker. …Well, if I heard a hurdy-gurdy playin' I'd think I was talkin' to the fat lady in the circus. But as it is I guess I'm talkin' to a ton of bad news named Beulah, Beulah, Beulah!" – *Porky's*, 1982.

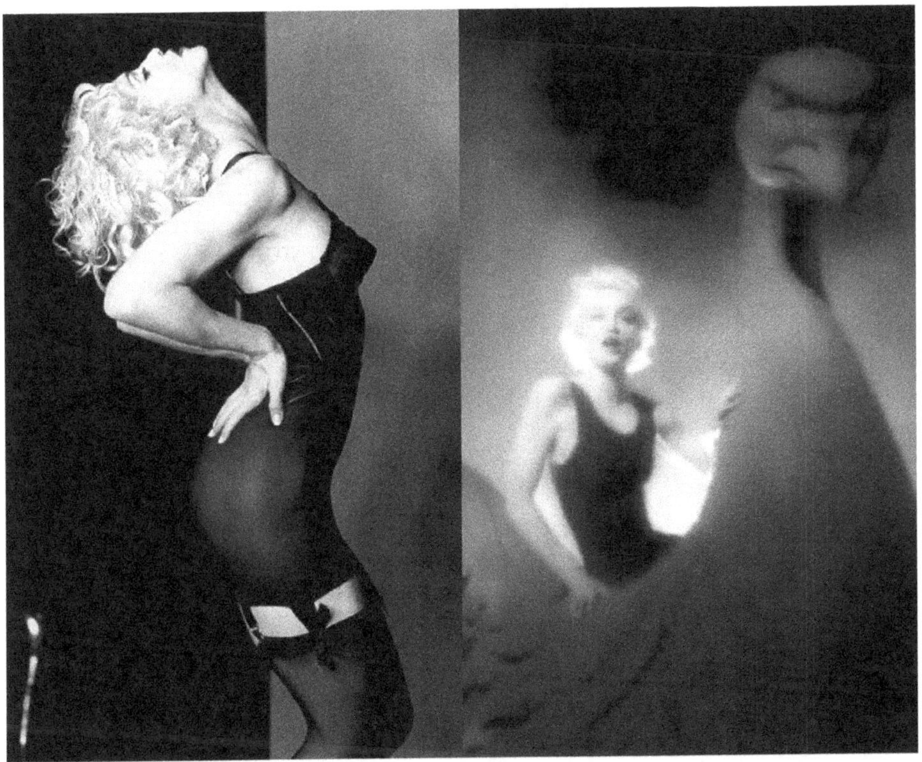

(Left) Mirroring the film *9 ½ Weeks*, Madonna's black lingerie and stockings are a self-gratifying fetish; implying masturbation, she sings, "♫ Satin sheets are very romantic, what happens when you're not in bed...♫" while gyrating in the sexy lingerie. (Right) Exuding a dark forbidden sensuality, Madonna begins the video singing atop an angry black swan which would, twenty-one years later, symbolize the same thing in *Black Swan*: autoeroticism and the emergence of the shadow self. Is this a conspiracy, predictive programming, or Jungian synchronicity at work? Images from the music video "Express Yourself," 1989.

Suzy is escorted to the ballet student's locker room, where she meets Sara (Stefania Casini) and Olga (Barbara Magnolfi). Suzy has arranged to stay with off-campus with the latter. Olga jokes that Sara and Suzy's names both begin with the letter *S* for snakes. A serpent is an emblem for wisdom; Olga's quip recalls Jesus telling the Apostles to be wise as serpents, implying Suzy must be at the top of her game if she is going to defeat the evil lurking inside the dance school. The following morning while Suzy hones her ballet, Blanc offers Suzy a dormitory room, but she declines the offer. Suzy now wears black tights, the alchemical *nigredo*, seeming at one with her shadow self, but she is still a novice. Wearing her black baller outfit, a nubile Suzy confidently dances in the hallway on her way to her next lesson. However, as she strolls down the corridor, an old female servant (Franca Scagnetti, 1924-1999) symbolically masturbates by polishing an erect, phallic piece of silver while Albert ghoulishly smiles from behind the crone. Suzy, thunderstruck by what she is experiencing, is blinded by the Luciferian light of the Left-Hand Path as "Witch!" is hurled at her by a menacing disembodied voice. Hexed by the black sun, Suzy is now conscious of her sensual shadow self, struggling to walk down the rest of hallway, appearing dazed and confused by her psychological onanism, her awakening (or discovery); she is transitioning from innocence to experience. Doused in sweat, Suzy makes it to her dance lesson where she is punished by the Nazi-like Miss Tanner for experiencing, at least symbolically, the pleasures of the flesh. Suzy is badgered by the disciplinarian Tanner, forcing her to dance to a piano played by a blind man, Daniel (Flavio Bucci). Dancing to the music of a blind man, Suzy naturally suffers the superstitious symptoms associated with masturbation: fatigue, dizziness, an epileptic-like fainting spell, and a nosebleed.[302] Symbolically, Suzy was caught tasting the erotic and forbidden fruit of the Left-Hand Path so she was chastised; she gained experience of the dark-side while losing her innocence which, ironically, is the modus operandi of the witches she will ultimately defeat. In other words, by pursuing her carnal desires by allegorically pleasuring herself, Suzy becomes, if only momentarily a "Witch!" just like the menacing voice pronounced when she was enveloped by the light of the *sol niger*, the black sun.

Later that night, Suzy awakens to discover she has been moved into a dormitory room against her wishes. Suzy is cared for by Professor Verdegast (Renato Scarpa), his surname is a tribute to Bela Lugosi's character in 1934's *The Black Cat*, Dr. Vitus Verdegast. In *The Black Cat*, Dr. Verdegast, like Suzy, battles devil worshipers commanded by the Crowley-like ceremonial magician Hjalmar Poelzig portrayed by Boris Karloff (1887-1969). Professor Verdegast recommends that Suzy is to be served bland food and medicated with a glass of wine daily. Suzy befriends her fellow *serpent*, Sara, after the two are roomed next to each other. As Suzy and the rest of the students prepare for dinner, chaos ensues when hundreds of maggots fall from the ceiling. The students are told this was due to spoiled food boxed in the attic. Maggots, which feed outdoors on carrion,

---

302 Thomas A. Laqueur, *Solitary Sex: A Cultural History of Masturbation, passim.*

appear inside the *Tanz Akademie*, epitomizing an unknown and unseen malignancy within the walls of the ballet school. Due to the unnatural infestation, the girls are invited to sleep in the practice hall overnight. During the night, Sara identifies a distinctive whistling snore as that of the school's mysterious directress, not due to return to the academy for several weeks.

The next morning, Tanner orders the school's blind piano player Daniel to leave the academy immediately after his guide dog bites young Albert. It is implied Daniel's German Shepherd sensed Albert's evil aura and bit him out of defensive necessity or a natural reaction. Later that night, Sara overhears the teacher's footsteps, beginning to count them while Suzy becomes irresistibly drowsy, falling asleep. Suzy tells Sara that the path of the staff's footsteps indicate that they are not leaving the school but going to an unknown location inside the building. Meanwhile, while Daniel and his guide dog cross a plaza within the city, Daniel senses a strange presence. Suddenly, his passive dog lunges at him, tearing his throat out, killing him. The next day, Suzy tells Madame Blanc that she recalls the words *irises* and *secret* from Pat's mumblings before she fled the academy. Suzy and Sara go for a swim while Sara reveals to Suzy that she and Pat were close friends, recalling that she had been talking strangely for some time. Sara also tells Suzy that Pat kept notes on the unusual activity within in the ballet school. Later that evening, Sara searches for Pat's notes in her room, but they appear to have been stolen. Suzy suddenly becomes drowsy and falls asleep before Sara flees to the attic after hearing approaching footsteps. Sara is chased by an unseen pursuer and, thinking she will be able to escape through a window into another room, falls into a pile of razor wire. Becoming entangled, she struggles in anguish until a mysterious black-gloved hand slits her throat.

The following morning, Blanc and Tanner inform Suzy that Sara has abruptly left the academy. Confused and suspicious, Suzy goes to meet one of Sara's acquaintances, a psychologist, Frank Mandel (Udo Kier), explaining that the academy was founded by Helena Markos, a mysterious woman widely believed to be a witch. Markos' first name *Helena* is an esoteric reference to writer and occultist Madame Helena Blavatsky, founder of the neo-Gnostic Theosophical Society, the bane of Christians throughout Europe. Dr. Mandel's colleague, the Hermes Trismegistus-like Professor Millus, further supplies Suzy with arcane information telling her that a coven can only survive with their queen intact. The actor playing Professor Millus, Rudolf Schündler (1906–1988), is best known to horror aficionados as Karl the Butler from *The Exorcist*; his appearance subconsciously draws forth terrifying demonism.

Armed with Millus' knowledge, Suzy returns to the academy that night only to discover all of the students have gone to the theater. Suddenly, she overhears the footsteps Sara identified earlier; Suzy follows them to Madame Blanc's office. She remembers Pat's dialog after discovering irises painted on the wall of Blanc's office. Pat said, "The secret, I saw behind the door! Three irises, turn the blue one!" The color blue associates with gnosis and consciousness,[303] thus by rotating the blue iris, the secret of the ballet school is unveiled. After entering a hidden passage and passing by a large Rosicrucian rose (cf. mysticism), Suzy discovers Madame Blanc, Albert, Miss Tanner, and the staff performing an occult, demonic Eucharist-like ritual. They curse Suzy with sickness and death. Unseen, Suzy then turns to find Sara's bloodied body in a coffin with two needles piercing her eyes and with nails through her wrists, like she was crucified. Frightened, Suzy then sneaks into another room, accidentally awakening a shadowy figure, revealing herself to be the Black Queen herself, Helena Markos. Signifying Markos' superiority, power, omnipresence, and rulership over the coven, one will notice an Illuminati-Masonic all-seeing eye on the wall next to her bedchamber.[304] Helena then orders Sara's nearby corpse to rise from the dead to murder Suzy. However, Suzy stabs Helena through the throat with a decorative blade, killing her, causing Sara's reanimated corpse to vanish. The blade was a feather from an ornamental peacock, a bird that epitomizes pride,[305] reflecting Markos' arrogance and superiority. Helena Markos' demise causes the *Tanz Akademie* to catch fire and shake like it was in an earthquake. As the academy is slowly destroyed along with the coven inside, Suzy manages to escape before the building becomes a raging inferno. Suzy has killed the evil queen; with her quest finished, Suzy *qua*

---

303 Hall, The *Secret Teachings of All Ages*, p. 146. The color of the other two irises are yellow and red, Hall writes that "Consciousness, intelligence, and force are fittingly symbolized by the colors blue, yellow, and red."

304 *ibid*, pp. 226-230. See also Robert Macoy's *A Dictionary of Freemasonry*, page 505. One will notice the words Jehovah and Elohim, both meaning God, written around the name Helena Markos on the walls of the ballet school's hidden corridors.

305 Hall, *ibid*, page 276.

Snow White emerges victorious with the witches trapped inside destroyed by purging fire; she has purified Freiburg of its baneful influence. Suzy is cleansed by rain sent from the heavens above.

Suspiria's final acts are the occult; the movie plays out sequentially like a deck of Tarot cards, specifically cards nine through sixteen in order, and card twenty of the Major Arcana;[306] this archetypal storyboard comes straight out of Jung's collective unconscious. As her journey draws to an end, Suzy symbolically walks upon the paths[307] of the kabalistic Tree of Life seeking perfection to defeat the coven. Tarot imagery begins when Suzy speaks to psychiatrist Frank Mandel, introducing her to the sagacious Professor Milius. Milius provides her with unique insights regarding witches, the occult, and their motives. Milius, the author of the definitive book on witchcraft titled *Paranoia or Magic*, embodies the Hermit Card (IX) of the Tarot. The Hermit is the inscrutable sage, the fluidic essence of Light, and master of learning; thus, the Hermit carries the lamp–the lantern of Hermes Trismegistus aloft while wearing the cloak of Apollonius–symbolizing higher knowledge, the insights of the mystic, and the path of initiation.[308] Like a hermit, Millius supplies wisdom, informing Suzy witches "...are malefic, negative and destructive. Their knowledge of the art of the occult gives them tremendous powers. They can change the course of events and people's lives, but only to do harm. ...The correct term would be a coven of witches. A woman [who] becomes queen of her magic is a hundred times more powerful than the rest of the coven, which is like a serpent. Its strength rests with its leader, that is, with its head. A coven deprived of its leader is like a headless cobra, harmless." Armed with Milius' knowledge, Suzy returns to the dance academy ready to meet her fate and deal out punishment. Foreshadowing the coming battle with the coven, Suzy disposes of a sinister and over-aggressive bat. After killing the bat, Suzy now personifies both the Wheel of Fortune (X) and

---

306 This is the numeric order of the Major Arcana cards in the Rider-Waite Deck which is considered the modern, universal deck. In some of the other decks some, not all, of the cards can be numbered differently but generally fall into a similar sequence.

307 The 22 paths of Kabbalah's Tree of Life mirror the 22 cards of the Tarot's Major Arcana; see Cavendish's *The Tarot* p.51, *passim*.

308 Ouspensky, *The Symbolism of the Tarot*, p. 53. Apollonius of Tyana (ca. 15-100 CE) was a Greek philosopher reputed to have supernatural powers including the ability to heal the sick. In the 19th century, Masonic magician and transcendentalists Eliphas Levi attempted to conjure the spirit of Apollonius in a necromantic ritual. A spirit appeared and scared Levi half to death; he never acknowledged whether the shade was really Apollonius. See Guiley, *ibid*, pp.11-12.

Justice (XI) cards of the Tarot. Suzy is passive, of timid reason, but ready to confront active evil symbolized by the ascending and descending figures on the Wheel of Fortune. The two figures on the wheel symbolize the eternal conflict between light and dark, as recalled by the famous passage in William Blake's *Marriage of Heaven and Hell*: "Without Contraries is no progression. Attraction and Repulsion, Reason and Energy, Love and Hate, are necessary to Human existence. From the contraries spring what the religious call Good and Evil. Good is the passive that obeys Reason. Evil is the active springing from Energy."[309] Many of the ideas associated with the Wheel recur in interpretations of the Justice card (XI) which depicts a woman ready to give each their due (Latin: *Ius suumcuique tribuit*) with her raised sword; nothing can escape it. In the Golden Dawn system of Tarot and Kabbalah, Justice's path leads up from the *Tifereth*, the central *sefirah* on the Tree, round which the other spheres form a symmetrical and balanced arrangement, to *Geburah*, the *sepirah* of punishment and destruction. These cards signify Suzy destiny: she must dispense justice upon the ballet school and the malignant witches that hide within. Justice's balancing scales symbolize the ebb and flow of opposing factors, such as cause and effect, good and evil which go around and around on the previous card, the Wheel of Fortune, are now displayed on the Justice card in a stable equilibrium. By becoming a living representation of both the Wheel of Fortune and Justice, Suzy is ready to pass Judgment (Card XX)[310] upon the coven for their witchcraft, murders, and abominations; she is the karmic lawgiver that will balance light with dark, it is Suzy's fate or fortune to perform this task. In other words, Suzy's authentic self, real knowledge, inner truth, has been sown in Justice and the evil of the coven will be reaped in the Wheel. Sitting atop the Wheel of Fortune is a grotesque mother-like sphinx creature, the chthonic counterpart to the positive mother principle seen on Tarot card III, the Empress.[311] Applied to *Suspiria*, this demonic sphinx dovetails with the Dance Academy's great evil matriarch, Helena Markos.

---

309 Quoted in Cavendish's *The Tarot*, page 102.

310 The angel on the card is generally thought to be Michael, the leader of the forces of light which routed the Devil and the hosts of darkness in the war in heaven, and this makes him an appropriate symbol of a victory over the lower nature of man. The imagery on the card show part of what the Middle Ages expected to happen at the end of the world on the Day of Wrath. See Cavendish's *The Tarot*, p. 136. In terms of *Suspiria*, Suzy has met out Judgment on the coven–the lower nature–by destroying its diabolical witchcraft.

311 Nichols, *Jung and Tarot*, p. 181.

In Blanc's office, Suzy solves the sphinxlike conundrum of Pat's mumblings from the film's beginning, unlocking the mystery of the blue iris, which opens the door that leads to the hidden chambers inside the ballet school. Pat sought to betray the *Tanz Akademie* by exposing the witches that hide within, thus she is a traitor thereby associating with the old, traditional interpretation of the Hanged Man (XII) which identified the card with Judas Iscariot, the arch traitor committing suicide by hanging.[312] Pat, like the archetypal qualities of the card, suffers from spiritual illness symbolized by the upside down image on the card; the cause that Pat gave her all to, the dance school, has failed her.[313] By rebelling against the witches and thus the school itself, Pat's confidence has been destroyed by learning what she thought was reality was, in fact, an inversion: the *Tanz Akademie* is not a prestigious ballet school,

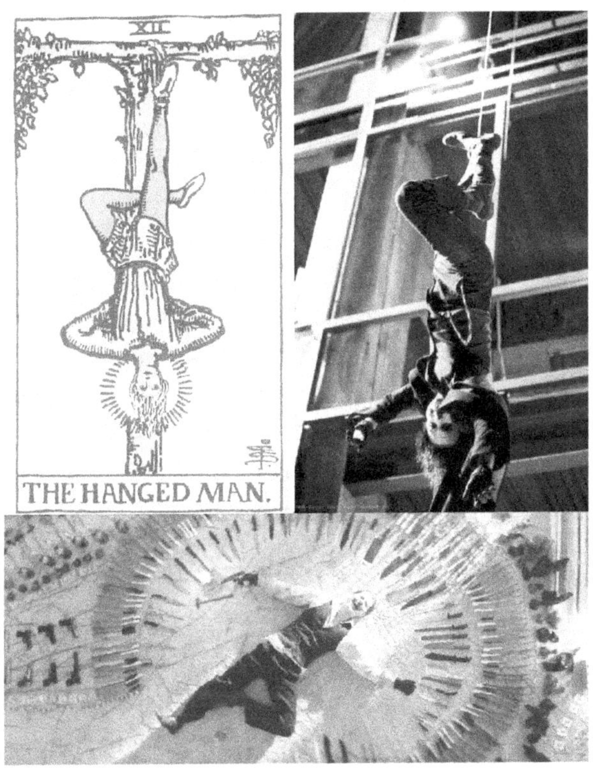

(Top Left) The Hanged Man card from the Rider-Waite deck. (Top Right) Personifying the archetypal villainous traitor, this arcane imagery incarnates as Batman's archnemesis the Joker (Heath Ledger, 1979-2008) in 2008's *The Dark Knight*. (Bottom) This imagery, complete with crossed leg, reemerges from the collective unconscious when, once again, the Joker (Jared Leto) appears in the same occult posture in 2016's *Suicide Squad*. Furthermore, Leto's Joker is circled by weapons imitating the sun radiating from behind the Hanged Man's head.

---

312 Cavendish, *The Tarot*, p. 107. Pat also dovetails Criswell's take on the Hanged Man; Criswell explains, "You [Pat] are becoming a martyr for others [the witches] who are using you for their own selfish and evil ends. Plan to make drastic changes at once." See *Criswell's Forbidden Predictions based on Nostradamus and the Tarot*, p. 96. Pat does in fact make drastic changes upon learning the ballet school's dark secret. She flees the school in a heavy rainstorm and takes sanctuary with her friend in town.

313 Nichols, *Jung and Tarot*, p. 222.

rather it is a nightmare: a front for a coven of malefic witches. For her disloyalty, the coven summons a devil that hangs Pat from the neck; in the Sicilian Tarot, the man is hanged by the neck, transforming her into the Hanged Man of the Major Arcana. Next, Suzy locates the coven of witches so Madame Blanc curses her with card thirteen (XIII) of the Tarot's Major Arcana, Death. The reaping skeleton of this card signifies death, but philosophically that irresistible impulse in Nature which causes every being to be ultimately absorbed into the divine condition in which it existed before the illusionary universe had been manifested.[314] Suzy will not die, not succumb to the death hex; rather, the dance school is about to be exterminated, rid of its dark infestation.

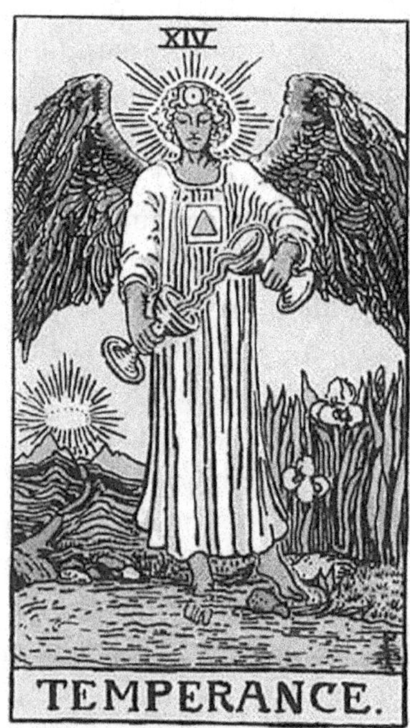

Temperance, Card XIV from the Rider-Waite Tarot deck. Temperance has the sun on her fore-head with a light cluster around her head symbolizing the light or gnosis of the Hermit ready to combat the agents of darkness.

Suzy now embodies card fourteen (XIV), the angelic Temperance, linking Suzy *qua* Snow White to the purity of the moon and the lunar goddess Artemis, the protectress of female virtue. The card's number, fourteen, belongs to the moon, which goes from new to full, and full to new, in fourteen days.[315] Having survived the demonism of the school this far, she is a delicate angel yet deceptively resolute, Suzy's divine powers are in herself; steel is tempered to make it strong yet resilient.[316] As the angelic Temperance, the card's flowing water invests Suzy as a holy person, saint, or spiritual healer since the water's transference symbolizes positive influence and divine emanation;[317] thus, the pouring water reconnects the heroine with the sacred world.[318] Personifying the card Suzy is complete within herself, being delicately balanced ready to walk the path that waits.[319] Suzy, or Temperance ready-for-bat-

---

314 Hall, *The Secret Teachings of All Ages*, p. 420
315 Cavendish, *The Tarot*, p. 115.
316 Nichols, *Jung and Tarot*, pp. 253-255.
317 Cavendish, *The Tarot*, p. 115.
318 Nichols, *Jung and Tarot*, p. 254.
319 cf. *Criswell's Forbidden Predictions Based on Nostradamus and the Tarot*, p. 98.

tle, next encounters the Devil Card (XV), Helena Markos: the black, deceptive, fearful, intelligent, evil sorceress; like the card's imagery, Markos is a beastly horror.[320] Markos sits on her bed hiding behind a veil; only her shadow is visible because to see her, "…one must be able to see unfairly, incorrectly, and narrowly."[321] Thus, Suzy observes her when the veil is pulled back, Markos' invisible body narrowly reflects light, allowing Suzy to stab her, killing her unfairly. Levi identified the Devil card with Pan, the Baphomet of the Knights Templar, and the satanic goat of the witches' sabbath, and described it as a symbol of occult science.[322] The idea of combining a school of dance with occult studies, black magic and witchcraft, is Markos' brainchild and dovetails with Levi's interpretation of the card accurately. Markos is also as clever as Mephistopheles, having faked her death, convincing the world that she does not exist.[323] Temperance *qua*

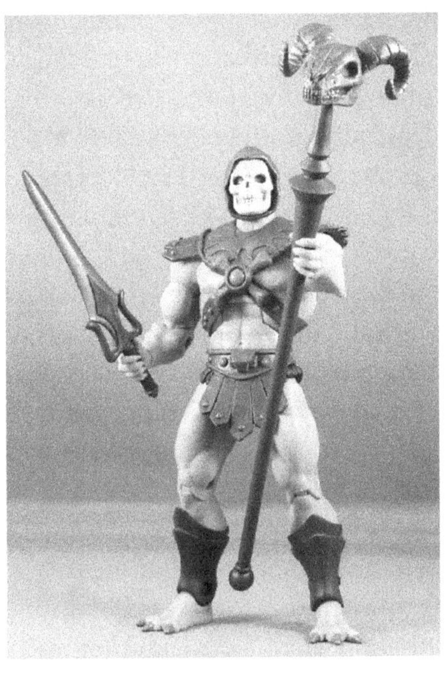

He-Man and the Masters of the Universe: He-Man's archvillain is the Grim Reaper-like Skeletor, his staff is tipped with a demonic goat skull symbolizing Baphomet, the devilish Goat of the Witches' Sabbath. Skeletor appears here in toy form manufactured by Mattel, circa 1984. *Masters of the Universe* was made into a feature film by Golan-Globus Productions starring Frank Langella as the dark lord Skeletor and Dolph Lungren as He-Man. The movie was released on 7 August 1987.

Suzy kills the Devil *qua* Markos, and the *Tanz Akademie* and the witchcraft it housed becomes card sixteen (XVI), the Tower when the school, and its coven, are engulfed in flames, destroyed, "…and the whole tower became filled with fire and smoke."[324] The Tower is the fall of evil, the destruction of false values and systems, and Suzy has delivered its Judgment (again, Card XX):

320 *ibid*, p. 99; on the Devil card Criswell writes, "…you [Markos] are recognized as a demon. You are a black magician."
321 See Ouspensky's *The Symbolism of the Tarot*, p. 52 discussing the Devil's attributes.
322 cf. Cavendish's *The Tarot*, p.120.
323 Nichols, *Jung and Tarot*, page 268 quoting French poet and art critic Charles Baudelaire (1821-1867).
324 Ouspensky, *The Symbolism of the Tarot*, p. 48. The author's description of the Tower dovetails with the destruction of the ballet school.

the ballet academy's demonic coven is ruined. Crowley said of the Tower, "To obtain perfection, all existing things must be annihilated."[325] At the beginning of the movie, the narrator informs the viewer that, "Suzy Bannion decided to perfect her ballet studies in the most famous school of dance in Europe. She chose the celebrated Academy of Freiburg." Unbeknownst to Suzy, she perfected herself, only not the way she thought; for Suzy's journey was the destruction of the celebrated academy, and in doing so, has lost her innocence but has gained valuable wisdom and experience. Suzy has rid the world of the demonic Helena Markos; by completing her quest, achieves something that *Black Swan*'s Nina Sayers dies for: perfection.

Suspiria draws inspiration from *Rosemary's Baby* in that both films are about a coven of witches hiding in plain sight. Both films feature heroines battling the agents of darkness, and both female protagonists receive insights on witchcraft from hermits: Professor Millus in *Suspiria* and Edward "Hutch" Hutchins (Maurice Evans, 1901-1989) in *Rosemary's Baby*. Both women find the coven of evil witches hiding at the end of dark corridors, an allegorical Left-Hand pathway. Rosemary Woodhouse (Mia Farrow) succumbs to the somber light of the dark side choosing to nurture the Antichrist while Suzy opts to destroy evil. Suzy, having deciphered the secret of the *Tanz Akademie*'s blue iris, stands in the pouring rain as the ballet school burns behind her, her mission accomplished. The torrential downpour symbolically reflects the arcana of the iris flower because, "Iris was [also] the Greek goddess of the rainbow, which classical authors regarded primarily as a *sign of rain*, 'the waters from on high.'"[326]

REDRUM: TRANSCENDENTAL REPETITION AND THE OVERLOOK HOTEL

If Stanley Kubrick's *2001: A Space Odyssey* (1968) portrays the apotheosis of man (and, by default, humankind), then his 1980 film *The Shining* is its antithesis graphically depicting his descent into madness and savagery. *The Shining* is all about alchemy, foreshadowing, repetition, and duality signifying that old-age struggle of light versus dark

---

325 Cavendish, *The Tarot*, p. 123.
326 *ibid*, p. 116, emphasis added.

(Manichean Cosmology), good against evil; it is the ego against the shadow self to use Jung's lexicon. Kubrick's intentional use of repetition suggests notions of reincarnation, or in *The Shining,* a vicious reoccurring cycle of murder and death transcending the Overlook Hotel; it is unbreakable, monotonous, and never-ending. Put another way, the Overlook is a revolving door that never stops turning. This allegorical ouroboros is explained to Jack Torrance (Jack Nicholson) by the ghost of Delbert Grady (Philip Stone, 1924-2003) telling him, "I'm sorry to differ with you sir, but you are the caretaker. You've always been the caretaker. I should know sir; I've always been here."

The film, based on Stephen King's novel of the same name, opens with a small island in the middle of a lake, symbolizing the isolation of the Overlook during its winter hiatus. Jack begins his alchemical quest in a yellow Volkswagen symbolizing the sun. Torrance is on a solar-alchemical journey, only for

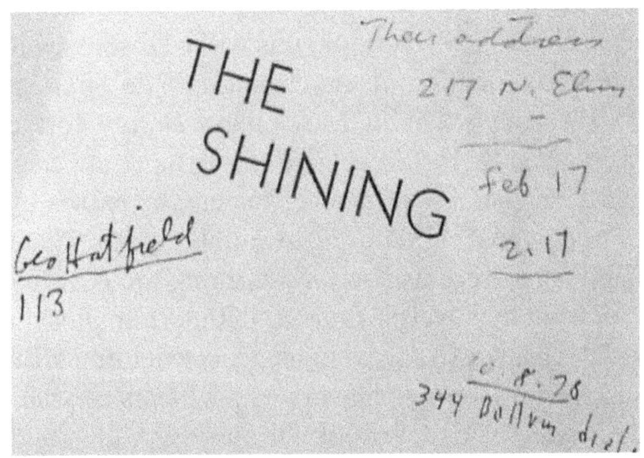

Kubrick's copy of Stephen King's *The Shining* reveals his desire to embed the number 217–changed by Kubrick to 237–into the film, hinting at an occult agenda.

him, it will result in ruination, transforming Jack into the personification of living darkness. Jack is a blend of anti-gnosis *qua* antilight or anti-sun: he is a fallen angel. He begins as a failed father and husband. To redeem himself, he goes to the Overlook seeking seclusion so he can write a manuscript, but ends up a cold-blooded murderer. The yellow Volkswagen travels on a road evoking the sun, named *Going-to-the-Sun Road*, where the opening automobile sequence was filmed. In *The Shining*, the road is the Road to Sidewinder which is, in reality, the Going-to-the-Sun Road which crosses Glacier National Park in Montana, U.S.A., intersecting the Continental Divide at Logan Pass. Astrological-astronomical and solar motifs transcend *The Shining*, becoming alchemical tokens of Jack's downfall.

Critical to the film is the use of doubles and repetitive devices, signifying the reincarnation-repeating cycle manifesting like a phantasm inside the Overlook. Kubrick employs these repeating devices immediately. For example, the construction of the Going-to-the-Sun Road began in 1921 which is the date that concludes the film: a black and white photo appears at the film's which reads: Overlook Hotel July 4th Ball 1921. Upon meeting with the hotel's manager Stuart Ullman, (Barry Nelson, 1917-2007), Jack tells him that it took him three and a half hours to reach the hotel or 210 minutes, and the July 4th picture is part a grouping that has 21 framed photos. The film symbolically ends where it begins, with the number 21. The number 21, when doubled, is 42, which also appears, symbolizing the repetition of the Overlook; this will be discussed in more detail later. Also, note the repetition of the casting of *The Shining*: *Jack* Nicholson plays *Jack* Torrance, *Danny* Lloyd plays *Danny* Torrance, and She*ll*ey Duva*ll* plays Wendy Torrance; note the letter *L* appears twice in her forename and surname. As Jack drives the car, he passes two stationary cars and is passed by two cars coming toward him; Kubrick repeats doubles, denoting that history repeats itself, reinforcing the never-ending reincarnation that thrives in the Overlook. Next, Ullman explains that a few years earlier, in 1970, Charles Grady went on an ax-wielding killing spree foreshadowing Jack's murderous endeavors with a hatchet. When the Torrance family, on their way to the Overlook, discuss starvation and the cannibalism of the Donner Party,[327] a few minutes later they are shown an endless cornucopia of food and provisions. Not only does Kubrick employ repetition but duality as well.

The hotel manager, Stuart Ullman, is dressed in the typical red, white, and blue clothing that can be found ad-nauseam in *The Shining*. Red, white, and blue represent the United States flag and the dark side (cf. alchemical *nigredo*) of America, and the colors transcend the Overlook. In *Cinema Symbolism: A Guide to Esoteric Imagery*, this author explained the Overlook itself was an emblem of United States patriotism since it was constructed over an Indian burial ground, just as the United States was built on the Native American Indian Nations. Symbolizing America, a carving of

---

327 The Donner Party was a group of American pioneers who set out for California in a wagon train. Delayed by a series of mishaps, they spent the winter of 1846-47 snowbound in the Sierra Nevada. Some of the immigrants resorted to cannibalism to survive, eating those who had succumbed to starvation and sickness.

a bald eagle sits on Ullman's office windowsill; Wendy and Danny Torrance wear the red, white, and blue of the United States flag when they are introduced in their apartment. Later, Wendy and Danny also wear red, white, and blue when they enter the Overlook's hedge maze for the first time, and both identify the Overlook Hotel with the United States. Wendy says, "The loser has to keep America clean," which Danny repeats back

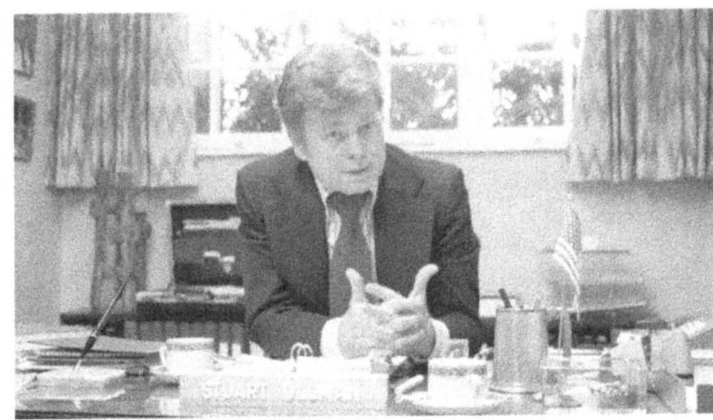

Stuart Ullman wears red, white, and blue with an American flag sitting on his desk because the Overlook Hotel characterizes the sinister aspects of American patriotism. The Overlook was built on top of an Indian burial ground symbolizing the United States, which was likewise founded at the expense of the Native American nations thus burying them, which most tend to *overlook*, hence the hotel's apt name. Indians were placed on reservations; as such, the hotel has no choice but to incorporate some "Navajo and Apache motifs," to quote Ullman. Additionally, in the Overlook *qua* America women and African-Americans are forever resigned to the kitchen.

to her indicating that the loser must keep the Overlook *qua* America free of debris. A few of the trash cans outside the hedge maze's entrance display Old Glory[328] reminding all the Overlook's guests to keep America clean. Furthermore, an American flag hangs over Jack in the Colorado Lounge while he types his manuscript. Throughout the film, Danny, Wendy, and Jack all wear red, white, and blue clothing, or combinations thereof, symbolizing this patriotic occultism; even Dick Hallorann (Scatman Crothers, 1910-1986), when he returns to the Overlook from Miami, is wearing a blue scarf over a red shirt. Wendy and Jack's weapons of choice further signifies the conflict between Native Americans and European-Americans: Wendy uses a baseball bat against Jack as a symbol of America's pastime, while Jack employs an ax, representing an Indian tomahawk, when trying to butcher Wendy and Danny.

When Jack meets with Ullman during THE INTERVIEW, Ullman tells him that the hotel's final day of operation before closing for the winter is October 30th, making the family's arrival at the hotel October 31st, or Halloween, identified as CLOSING DAY. Halloween initiates the triduum of Hallowtide, the time in the liturgical year dedicated to remembering

---

328 Old Glory is a common nickname for the flag of the United States, bestowed by William Driver, an early nineteenth-century American sea captain.

the dead, including saints (hallows), martyrs, and all the faithful departed believers. According to many academic scholars, All Hallows' Eve is
a Christianized feast initially influenced by Celtic harvest festivals, with
possible pagan roots, particularly the Gaelic Samhain. Samhain was a festival marking the end of the harvest season and the beginning of winter,
the darker half of the year. It is celebrated from sunset on October 31st to
sunset on November 1st, the halfway mark between the autumn equinox
and the winter solstice, signifying diminishing daylight. Their arrival at
the Overlook coincides with the darker half of the year when demons and
ghosts are free to roam, manifesting in the material world. With the sun
absent, darkness is exalted giving demonic phantoms license to haunt and
terrorize the Overlook. "When evening came, after the sun had set, they
began bringing to Him all who were ill and those who were demon-possessed," so it says in the Bible at Mark 1:32.

Jack calls Wendy to inform her that he got the job, and from this point
on Kubrick bombards the subconscious mind with repetition to represent
the deathly metempsychosis pervading the Overlook. For instance, when
Danny and Wendy are introduced dining in their kitchen, the number on
Danny's shirt is 42. Danny and Wendy watch the movie Summer of '42,[329]
on TV in the Overlook while it snows outside. There are four (4) bar stools
on the left and two (2) on the right when Jack first enters the Gold Room,
standing between them at the bar. If one adds the 33 letters and 9 spaces
in the phrase, "All work and no play makes Jack a dull boy," one gets 42.
The number 42 appears on the license plate on Hallorann's rental car when
he drives in the snow after he returns from Miami. While talking to his
imaginary friend, Tony, in a mirror (cf. duality) about the Overlook, Danny
passes out. Kubrick next employs the Disney cartoon character Goofy as a
repetitive device. When a doctor (Anne Jackson) examines Danny, a marionette of Goofy hangs under the window on the right-side of his bedroom.
The dim-witted Goofy is dressed exactly like Wendy: blue overalls (Wendy
wears a blue overall frock), red shirt, and yellow shoes during the sequence.
Kubrick transfer Goofy's stupidity to Wendy by dressing her like the dopey dog; her naiveté towards her alcoholic and child-abusing husband is
stupefying. Wendy, it seems, would rather live in denial than confront the

---

329 *Summer of '42* is a 1971 American coming-of-age comedy-drama film based on the memoirs
of screenwriter Herman Raucher. It was one of Kubrick's favorite films.

painful reality of his abusive nature. When Wendy speaks to the doctor in the living room, two books are sitting between them. The first is titled The Manipulator (author unknown) symbolizing Jack's marionette or pup-

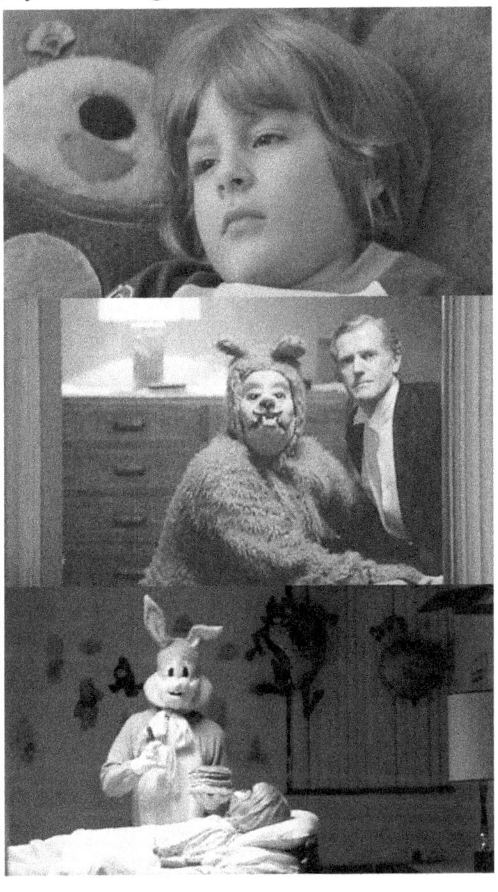

pet-like manipulation of Wendy, which indicates she would rather be dysfunctional than be independent and self-sufficient. The other book, The Wish Child written by Ina Seidel (1885-1974), is a work of fiction about two children during the Napoleonic Wars, anticipating the two ghostly Grady daughters murdered in the Overlook. Seidel is also the author of Das Labyrinth (1922) which foreshadows the two mazes of the Overlook. When watching *The Shining*, pay attention to the bear pillow that Danny rests his head on while the doctor examines him. The bear turns up later in *The Shining* as a costume (in King's novel it is a dog suit) worn by a ghost performing fellatio on another ghost. Contextually, the bear is a dualistic-repetitive emblem of childhood innocence contrasting adult deviant sexual activity; it is youth versus age, inexperience opposed to experience, evoking the interdependence of good and evil. Kubrick repeats colors to denote the Overlook's reincarnation. When the Torrance family arrives at the Overlook on Halloween, Danny

(Top) The bear's meaning in *The Shining* is dichotomous. The bear, as a toy pillow, is a symbol of youth and innocence in Danny Torrance's bedroom. (Middle) But the bear is also a token of dark eroticism: in one of the hotel rooms, a sinister ghost wears a bear costume while performing oral sex on another spirit. Although they are unidentified, in King's novel the two homosexual ghosts are named Roger and Derwent. (Bottom) Comparative Cinema: Director Eli Roth briefly pays homage to *The Shining* in his film *Cabin Fever* (2002) when a strange hysterical boy named Dennis (Matthew Helms) is bedridden in a hospital. A mysterious person in a bunny suit stands over him holding a plate of pancakes in one hand and a large syringe in the other. The person in the rabbit suit parallels the ghost in the bear suit: both are creepy, disturbing, and intentionally out-of-place.

plays darts and shines, seeing the daughters of Delbert (or Charles) Grady; notice their blue dresses are the same shade as the blue wallpaper outside the Torrance's living quarters. Since the two girls were violently murdered, this symbolizes murder and death are in the very walls of the Overlook itself. This same shade of blue is used in The Shining's opening credits when the actor's names appear, foreshadowing the Grady daughters and the horrors of the Overlook; Wendy's bathrobe features the same shade of blue. Furthermore, Jack sleeps in a green t-shirt, wears a green tie during his interview, typing his book wearing a green button-down shirt; green heralds the interior of room 237's green bathroom, making the color another of Kubrick's repetitive devices. Furthermore, the bathroom in the Torrance's apartment in Boulder, Colorado has a green rug and green window curtains foreshadowing room 237's bathroom. When Wendy discovers Jack's "All work and no play makes Jack a dull boy" manuscript, she is wearing a green checkered shirt, thereby finalizing the color cycle because the haunted bathroom has been breached, its horrors unleashed. Wendy now knows Jack is mad, evidenced by his repeating the same phrase over and over again in his novel.

To conjure repetitiveness and thus reincarnation, everything manifests in doubles and twos, and Kubrick successfully imprints this duality on the audience's mind. Ullman says, "Goodbye girls," to female twins before showing the Torrance's their apartment, and the daughters of Delbert Grady (1920s) are twins.[330] However, Mr. Ullman explains that in 1970, Charles Grady had daughters that were eight and ten–born two years apart. Ullman explains the Overlook was constructed in two years, from 1907-1909. The Overlook has two mazes: the corridors of the hotel and a natural, outdoor hedge labyrinth. Jack Torrance uses two typewriters, one white and one blue-gray; Wendy tends to the Overlook's two boilers, and the narrative moves forward every other or second day: Tuesday, Thursday, Saturday, Monday, and Wednesday. When Hallorann, Wendy, and Danny tour the kitchen, Hallorann tells them they "Could eat up here a whole year and never have the same menu *twice*," and Wendy remarks that Hallorann has referred to Danny as "Doc" twice. There are also two, and only two, African-Americans: Dick Hallorann and Larry Durkin (Tony Burton, 1937-2016). In Hallorann's Miami bedroom, there are two paintings of topless

---

330 The actresses who played the Grady daughters, Lisa and Louise Burns, are identical twins.

African-American women, and his television is between two lamps. As Hallorann watches TV, these same lamps sit on nightstands book-ending his bed. Back at the Overlook, Wendy serves Jack two eggs, sunny side up. Two tennis balls are used: one green thrown by Jack, and the other pink since pink is one of Wendy's favorite colors; and Portland, Maine and Portland, Oregon are both mentioned by Jack while he sits at the bar. The Colorado news reports Susan Robertson has been missing for 10 days, later Hallorann watches Channel 10 News in Miami where the weather is the antithesis of Colorado: in Colorado a blizzard, in a matter of hours, drops 10 inches of snow, versus an unprecedented heat wave in Miami. There are two Sno-Cats: one at the Overlook, the other at Durkin's Auto Supply.

Lloyd the Bartender (Joe Turkel) serves up booze in the Overlook's Gold Room which is based on the design of Frank *Lloyd* Wright (1867-1959); again, Kubrick repeats the name Lloyd. Lloyd the Bartender personifies the Devil, to whom Jack offers up his "goddamn soul" for a drink (Bourbon whiskey), thereby forging a Faustian Pact with Lloyd. However, Jack's money, which is in pairs, two twenties and two tens, is no good with the ghostly barkeeper. Jack downs the drink at approximately 66 minutes and 6 seconds into the film, the 666 a reference to the Antichrist of Revelation; as such, Jack is now possessed by evil. In an interesting piece of occult casting, Turkel would go on to play the Devil-like Dr. Eldon Tyrell, the progenitor of the Enochic-Luciferian Nexus-6s in 1982's *Blade Runner* thereby conjuring his devilry from *The Shining*.

Anticipating Aronofsky's *Black Swan*, Kubrick uses mirrors throughout the film to reflect the character's shadow selves, their doppelgängers (double-goer). Danny first talks to his imaginary friend Tony in front of a mirror, and a mirror will reveal Jack's hidden motives when the word, *REDRUM*, is seen in the mirror backward spelling the word, *MURDER*. Likewise, room 237's female ghost's ugliness is revealed via her reflection in the bathroom's mirror.

The most famous pairing is the Overlook Hotel's two mazes. One is the long, dark corridors of the hotel which Wendy describes as an enormous maze, and will need to "leave a trail of breadcrumbs" every time she comes in; Kubrick loves showing the audience the hotel's long and claustrophobic passageways. The other is the outdoor, natural labyrinth, which will become Danny's protective mandala. The maze is an esoteric

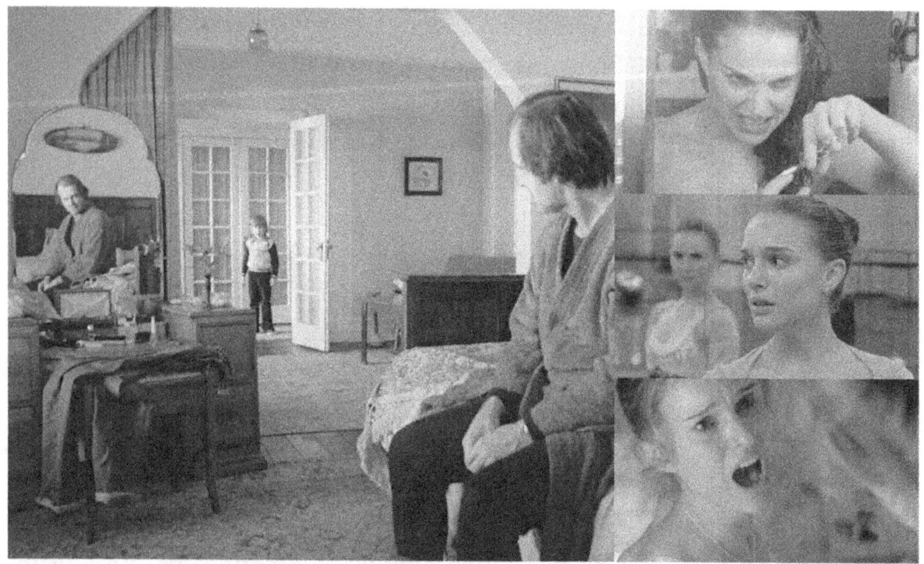

(Left) Jack Torrance's phallic shaped mirror anticipates his dark intentions, *MURDER*, in *The Shining*; the word *MURDER*, *REDRUM* backward, will be seen by Wendy in this very mirror. Danny timidly approaches his father, by now the spirits of the wicked hotel are manipulating Jack. (Right, Top to Bottom) In *Black Swan*, mirrors are everywhere symbolizing Nina's dark side. She takes pleasure in pain: her visage grins with torturous delight when she clips her fingernails too close. Nina's shadow comes alive in a mirror, akin to scrying a demon. While looking into a mirror, Nina's chaos magick–which for Nina is the synthesis of mutilation and masturbation–takes effect; horrified, Nina's painful alchemical metamorphosis into the Black Swan begins.

device signifying death and reincarnation, the Overlook Hotel's macabre methodology. In his book, *Through the Labyrinth*, Hermann Kern explains:

> Death and reincarnation symbolize the transition from one form of existence to another, presumably higher, one, and one of the most important rites of pass is initiation, 'all the rites and verbal instruction given to the initiate with the basic intention of changing his or her religious and social life.' …Death, when symbolized in rituals, marks the end of one's way of life up to that point; the novice is born into new existence. This meaning of the labyrinth is also reflected in its serpentine pattern, the continual change of direction from left (the opposite direction in which the sun travels, i.e., towards death) to right (the direction in which the sun travels, i.e., life). Returning to the womb, regressing to an embryonic stage, being cast out again by way of restrictive twists and turns and the narrow entrance: this interpretation–symbolic death–is borne

out in the shape and narrowness of the winding path. It is not by chance that labyrinths are associated with the loops of entrails; it is fitting, then, that in India the labyrinth was thought magically to ease birthing, and that labyrinths symbolized birth and reincarnation for the Hopi.

Initiation signifies symbolic death and rebirth. Yet, physical death can also be seen as the transformation of the former existence and as a passageway to a new one. Accordingly, the labyrinth's path also represents the path to the underworld, the return to Mother Earth being associated with the promise of reincarnation…

In light of the of the labyrinth's close association with death and reincarnation, it seems plausible that the Roman Game of Troy, otherwise known as the labyrinthine Trojan Ride, served to commemorate two occasions: the founding (i.e., birth) of a city and burial ceremonies. The depiction of the portal of the temple of Apollo at Cumae, allegedly by the hands of Daedalus, accords with this idea: Cumae is where the huge grotto–the chasm, Mother Earth's vaginal opening, and the entrance to Hades–opens up. Therefore, if the Labyrinth symbolizes death and reincarnation as described above, then we should expect to find labyrinths in only those cultures in which it is believed there is an afterlife.[331]

It is synchronistic that the Hopi Indians interpreted the labyrinth as a symbol for reincarnation, since the Overlook was built overtop an Indian burial ground. The murderous souls of Delbert Grady, Charles Grady and Jack Torrance are forever trapped inside the maze-like Overlook because, as Grady remarks to Torrance in the men's room, Jack has "always been the caretaker," because Grady has "always been here." When he first arrives at the Overlook, Jack tells Stuart Ullman that he had no problem finding the hotel, yet Torrance, during the film, can never escape it; in other words, Jack can arrive at the Overlook Hotel but cannot exit its haunted hallways. Jack does not want to leave, telling Danny that he could stay in the hotel "forever, and ever, and ever;"[332] later Jack becomes enraged when Wendy suggests they should leave to take Danny to a doctor. Becoming a metaphor

---

331 Hermann Kern, *Through the Labyrinth*, pp. 30-31.
332 The Grady Twins repeat this phrase to Danny earlier, making it another example of repetition in *The Shining*. Another example of repetitive dialog occurs when Danny and Wendy are eating lunch in their apartment, Danny repeats the line "Yeah, I guess so," to Wendy twice.

of Manichean Cosmology or Zoroastrian Dualism, the unnatural man-made maze–the Overlook's dark and dense corridors–is home to demons and ghosts, while the natural exterior maze protects Danny from his father's demonically-possessed murderous rampage. Once Jack enters the outdoor maze, he becomes trapped, unable to find his way out, causing him to freeze to death in the brutal conditions.

*   *   *   *

Although he is not a wizard, Hallorann personifies a Hermes Mercurius Trismegistus archetypal figure. Like Danny, Hallorann can "shine," communicating with Danny telepathically, and he is also cognizant of the malevolent ghosts which inhabit the Overlook. Hallorann is a hermit: he is not married, living alone in solitude. His death is foreshadowed: while Jack throws a tennis ball around the registration desk, an anti-black minstrel golliwog doll is on the floor. The doll's location is close to the spot where Hallorann will die after being struck by an ax wielded by Jack. The doll is a symbol of racist attitudes towards African-Americans before the Civil Rights Movement of the 1960s; the ghost Delbert Grady uses the n-word when describing Hallorann. This racism seems to be the attitude of the Caucasian spirits that haunt the decadent Overlook. Based on their dress, the ghosts appear to be from the 1920s or 1930s–pre-Civil Rights Movement, naturally.

The sun, enlightenment (cf. gnosis) are the antithesis of darkness and downfall, these Manichean themes are omnipresent in the Overlook Hotel only reversed. Jack's yellow, solar-like Volkswagen and the sun-road, having already been explained, is not traveling a path of light (or a wisdom quest), rather, it is one of darkness and descent; it is a journey into the depths of evil and madness. Jack's sable descent occurs in the solar Gold Room, which looks like a Mayan-Aztec pyramid of sun worship. But this is not a temple of light, but one of darkness: light is dark, and dark is light for Jack. Here he drinks alcohol furnished to him by the devilish Lloyd, provoking him to blame Wendy for his failures. Drinking alcohol sets him on the path towards madness, opening the door the Overlook's ghosts to influence and torment him. Even the Gold Room's mysterious band, the Unwinding Hours, signifies the literal unwinding and interweaving of time as Jack flip-flops from the present to the past and back again allegorizing the sinister, ghostly cycle of reincarnation that is forever unwinding inside the Overlook. One minute he is in the present talking with Lloyd, the next time he enters a 1920's party in full swing. In the Gold Room, time unwinds, becomes absent, even distorted: Wendy indicated that Jack hurt Danny five months earlier, yet in the Golden Room Jack tells Lloyd the incident was three years ago.

The sun *qua* Gold Room rules over the twelve houses of the zodiac, thus the number 12 repeats in the hotel, but Kubrick's use of the number twelve is twofold. He utilizes it to denote solar-astral allegory as well as repetition, the latter signifying the Overlook's perpetual reincarnation cycle. Halloriann's litany of a freezer and pantry stock includes 12 turkeys, 24 (2 dozen, 12x2) pork roasts, 12-pound bags of sugar, and 12 jugs of black molasses. The hotel is identified as "KDK12" by Wendy when she is on the radio with the Forest Service; room 237[333] is 12 when 2+3+7 are added. Furthermore, when multiplied, 2x3x7, the sum is 42 which reincarnates: 42 is the number on Danny's red, white, and blue shirt from earlier, when he invoked Tony in the bathroom; Wendy and Danny watch the film *Summer of '42* in the Overlook; the number 42 is on Halloriann's license plate. The names Charles Grady and Delbert Grady have 12 letters. Two distinct times are displayed: 8 a.m. and 4 p.m.; add 8+4 to get 12. Jack throws the tennis ball 12 times against the wall; Wendy and Danny make 12 turns (including entering) in the hedge maze; the Colorado TV news reports that 24 (12x2) year-old Susan Robertson has been missing; Wendy flips through 24 (12x2) of Jack's "All work and no play makes Jack a dull boy" pages, and Jack strikes the bathroom door with the ax 12 times.

But Jack is not Apollo. Instead, he is a fallen, lost, or false sun villainous archetype that presides over the entire hotel, paralleling the sun's mastery of the twelve houses of the zodiac.[334] Solar rulership is presented negatively and is metaphorically reversed;[335] the sun is missing or, alternatively, Jack is a black sun, the *sol niger*, emanating negative, if not deadly, rays. Solar and stellar lore (cf. the zodiac) are astronomical archetypes, evoking light against dark, good against evil. Kubrick has no problem drawing

---

333 Paying homage to room 237 is the 1994 film *Shawshank Redemption*. The film, based on the Stephen King novella *Rita Hayworth and the Shawshank Redemption*, sees Ellis Boyd "Red" Redding (Morgan Freeman) jailed in cell 237.
334 Sullivan, *Cinema Symbolism*, Chapter VII.
335 *ibid.*

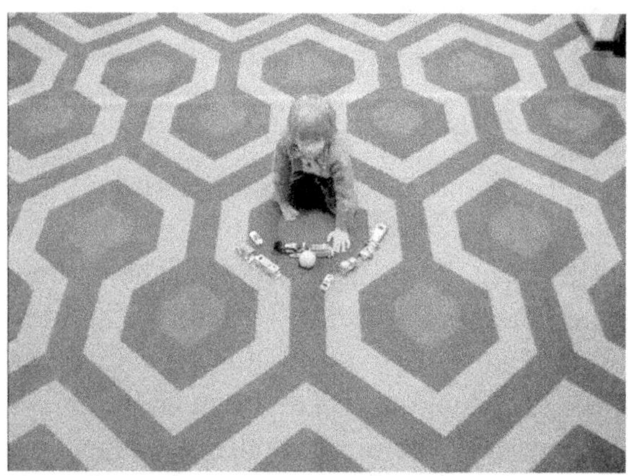

The Overlook's Hotel's carpet is a repetitive circular pattern, symbolizing the hotel's reincarnation cycle. Danny plays with his toys while sitting on the monotonous carpet.

down the heavens to convey Zoroastrian Dualism-Manicheanism: Stuart Ullman explains that Charles Grady's horrors occurred in hotel's west wing signifying the dying, setting sun and the coming darkness (cf. evil) of night.[336] The Torrance family care for the Overlook during the winter months (northern hemisphere) when the sun (cf. light) is in death, darkness prevails, thereby allowing the demons to run amok throughout the hotel, tormenting the family. Jack's alchemical downfall is mirrored by a female demon dwelling in room 237. The ghost is initially young and beautiful, but this appearance is a ruse; in reality, she is an ugly crone seeking to harm all those that enter. The green bathroom she haunts conjures the planet Venus and, by default, Venus' concomitant Lucifer, embodying false, negative light since Venus-Lucifer appears in the morning sky before the sunrise. Green is the color of Venus (and Islam); on this Manly P. Hall explains, "The feminine principle is repeatedly emphasized in Islamic symbolism. For example, Friday, which is sacred to the planet Venus, is the Moslem's holy day; green is the color of the Prophet, and being symbolic of verdure, is inevitably associated with the World Mother; and both the Islamic crescent and the scimitar may be interpreted to signify the crescent shape of either the moon or Venus."[337] Venus *qua* Lucifer announces or bears the divine light, the sun, while simultaneously rising as a substitute or false light at dawn. Thus, the female ghost's initial appearance in distorted and dualistic: at first, she appears beautiful (cf. Aphrodite or Venus, the goddesses of beauty and love in Greco-Roman mythology), when she is in fact a hideous, cackling witchy creature. Like Lucifer, the female ghost

---

336 Ullman explains, "He [Grady] ran amuck and killed his family with an axe. Stacked them neatly in one of the rooms in the West wing and then he, … he put both barrels of a shotgun in his mouth."
337 Hall, *The Secret Teachings of All Ages*, p. 629.

in room 237 is a reflection of Jack's antisolar, demonic transformation and ruination; the demons and ghosts of the Overlook transmogrify Jack into a monstrous psychopath. The sun, when added to the twelve houses of the zodiac, equals the number thirteen which denotes authentic solar leadership (i.e., Christ and the Apostles). The repetitive placement of the number twelve within the Overlook implies that the zodiac is without its solar ruler; in other words, Jack, the hotel's perpetual caretaker, has symbolically replaced light with darkness. Thirteen is the height of the hedge maze; its walls are "thirteen feet high" according to Ullman. Thirteen, in this context, is Christ and the Apostles or the sun presiding over the zodiac; thus, the natural hedge maze, being thirteen feet high, is a beacon of heavenly light, the life-giving sun, providing sanctuary to Danny against his father's homicidal murder spree.

Jack Torrance's metamorphosis into a demon-possessed murderer is alchemical, so the four colors associated with Renaissance alchemy are present in *The Shining*. The alchemical *nigredo* is the Overlook, its never-ending dark corridors work its Left-Hand Path magic on the Torrance family. It is host to a party of elegant yet evil spirits that plague Jack, infesting him spiritual decay while simultaneously effectuating his alchemical

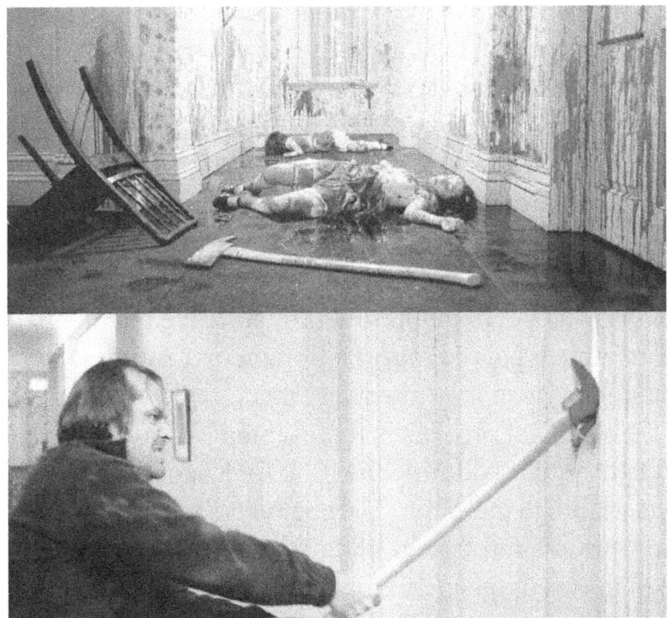

Repetition inside the Overlook Hotel. (Top) The ax that Delbert-Charles Grady used to butcher his daughters is the same ax (bottom) that Jack uses when he goes on his murderous rampage. Like everything in the Overlook, repetition is transcendent.

rebirth into a brutal murderer. The Overlook prompts Jack to start drinking thus becoming Jack's Mercury, the hotel is the Juggler-manipulator of the Tarot; it is the agent that alchemically transforms Jack from a struggling writer to psychopath. As a dark agent of alchemy, this makes the Overlook the monster of the movie. The alchemical *albedo*, the moon, is represented by the movie's lone female, Wendy. Her light is negated because she is dependent and subservient to Jack, calling her a "sperm bank," abusively bossing her around. Although her husband is right at home in the Overlook, she is a stranger in a strange land, not understanding the demonic influence the hotel is exerting on her husband. Nor does she comprehend Danny's supernatural ability; rather, Wendy turns a blind eye to it. Despite her flaws and ineptitude, she does manage to trap her husband in a food storage vault, provoking Delbert Grady to admonish Jack that "…Your wife appears to be stronger than we imagined, Mr. Torrance. Somewhat, more resourceful. She seems to have got the better of you." Even Goofy, once in a while, is intuitive and clever just like Wendy. The moon always shines in darkness, despite the Overlook's attempts to black her out.

The alchemical *citrinitas*, the yellow sun that *shines*, is none other than Danny Torrance. Embodying the sun, Danny wears an Apollo 11 sweater since Apollo (or Helios) was the most famous and recognizable sun god of antiquity. Danny, like the brilliant rays of the sun, has a unique talent that makes him acutely aware of the evil lurking within the Overlook. He sees the two dead Grady daughters in the hotel upon arrival; he immediately realizes there is an evil presence in room 237, knowing that Hallorann is afraid of what's inside. Danny warns Wendy that Jack is going to try to kill them by writing *MURDER* backward, *REDRUM*, on the door, navigating the hedge maze saving his life. Danny can do this because the special talent he possesses is the ability to *shine* like the sun, allowing him to detect psychically when good and evil are present, not perceived by the five ordinary senses. Like an archetypal old sage, Hallorann explains to Danny the mysteries of this unique gift shortly after they meet.

The finality of the alchemical process is represented by the color red, the *rubedo*, which appears regularly during the film, foreshadowing Jack's transition from failed patriarch to murderer. The characters frequently dress in red clothing, Danny throws red tipped darts in the Overlook's game room, room 237's key tag is red, the Overlook's Sno-Cat is red, the Gold

Room's sofas are red, and the lettering for the band, the Unwinding Hours, on the Gold Room's sign is red. Hallorann calls the Forest Service on a red telephone and sees a smashed red Volkswagon Beetle on his way to the Overlook, Danny's scrawls *REDRUM* with red lipstick, the interior of the Gold Room's men's room is stark red, and Danny wears a blood red sweater and pajamas. But the most overt use of red is when gallons of blood flow from the Overlook's elevators into the hallway. The blood is the finality of the *rubedo*, the completion of the Great Work; when the elevator's doors finally open, Jack is father no more, he is now one with self: a vicious psychopath. Jack's alchemical downfall is aided by the demonic ghosts in the Overlook, preying on his fears, failures, and anxieties transforming him into a monster. Once changed, Jack tries to murder Wendy and Danny, succeeding in killing Hallorann with an ax. This is Jack's Magnum Opus, his macabre individuation.

After he dies from hypothermia, it is revealed that Jack has been part of Overlook the entire time: he appears in a black and white photo during a July 4th celebration dated 1921. The overall feel of the scene suggests reincarnation; Jack has always been there because he has never left. Delbert Grady was right all along; Jack has always been the caretaker which is now revealed through the enigmatic photo. As the film ends, Al Bowlly's (1898-1941) "Midnight, the Stars and You" (1934) plays which was heard in the Gold Room during the ghostly New Year's Eve party. The photo depicts a July 4th party; the national holiday occurs shortly after the summer solstice of June 20th-22nd. Bowlly's song is a musical talisman signifying New Year festivities, occurring after the winter solstice of December 20th-22nd. The song, when combined with the photo, evokes duality to the subconscious mind: the winter and summer solstices simultaneously. This song played along with the photo denotes light against dark, the exaltation of the sun in summer and its death in winter; two opposing forces in continuous conflict. Such is the nature of the Overlook Hotel.

*   *   *   *

In the photo, Jack's arms and hands form the hermetic symbol of duality: the above and the below of the Hellenistic sage Hermes Trismegistus.

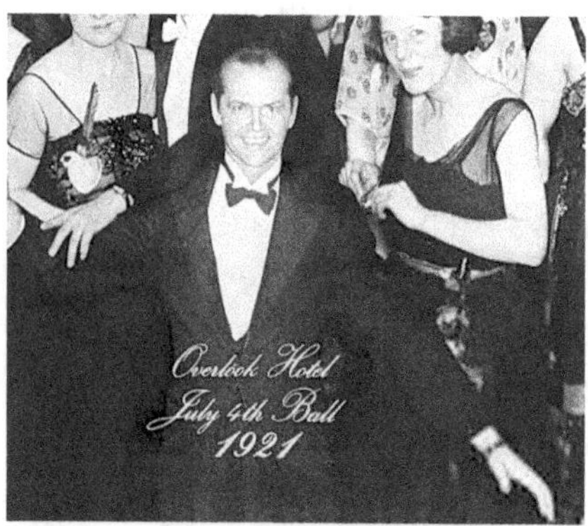

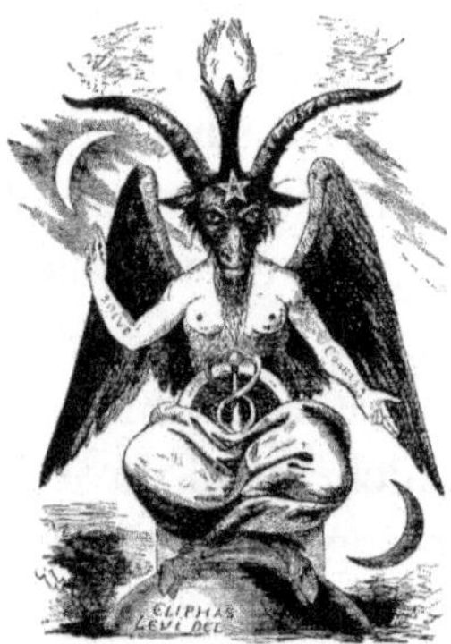

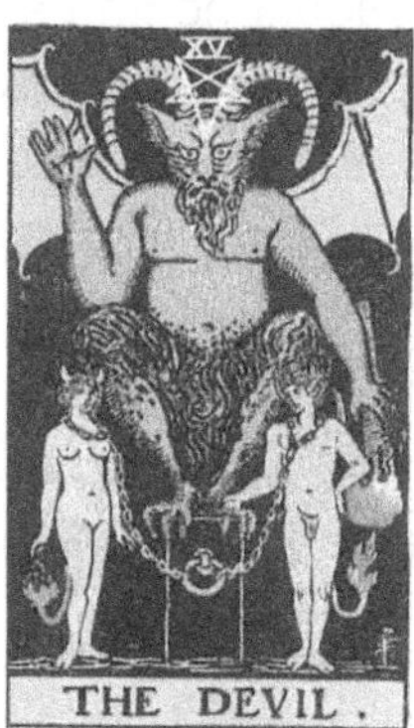

(Left) Jack Torrance *qua* Grady in the Overlook, July 4th, 1921. His arms form the hermetic maxim of *as above, so below* incorporated into Eliphas Levi's drawing of the Baphomet (or Goat) of Mendes (Center). The occult posture signifies duality: above and below (one hand up and the other down) or the heavens and the earth, light and dark, active and stagnant, positive and negative, and order and chaos. The Caudices of Hermes in Baphomet's lap suggests alchemical (cf. *serpens murcurialis.*) transition. (Right) Card XV of the Tarot, the Devil, also depicts this arcane iconography; Levi saw Baphomet mirrored in the card. A horned man and woman are held captive by the Devil symbolizing their pride, animal urges, fetishisms, and lustful desires.

"What is above is like what it below, and what is below is like that which is above," is inscribed on the Emerald Tablet of Hermes; all magic and alchemy originate from the *Tabula Smaragdina*.[338] Jack's esoteric gesture is a metaphor of both his alchemical transformation into a psychopath and the repetitive, reincarnating doubles of the movie. The gesticulation also identifies Jack with the devil card of the Major Arcana of the Tarot. Jack's demonism and savagery epitomize the nature of this card, "The card is … a symbol of the power of evil in the world, man held captive by his own animal urges,…the dominance of brute force… the exaltation of …hatred, cruelty …The inverted torch suggests the flames of hell and the blazing inner fires of man's savage passions."[339]

Jack transmutes from a failed husband into a beastly monster, echoing the archetypal qualities of this card. Thus, Jung said of the Devil's image as half man, half beast, "Exactly describes the grotesque and sinister side of the unconscious, for we have never really come to grips with it

---

338 Yates, *Girodano Bruno and the Hermetic Tradition*, p. 150. See also *The Emerald Tablet of Hermes*.
339 Cavendish, *The Tarot*, pp. 118-119.

and consequently it has remained in its original savage state."[340] Finally, the photo poses an epistemological crisis. Is Jack Torrance, in fact, the reincarnation of Delbert Grady? If so, is Jack talking to his former self in the Gold Room's men's room? Did Jack undergo alchemical change from failed writer and sullen father to murderous psychopath, or was it all predestined, part of the Overlook's predetermined repetitive cycle? Was Charles Grady the reincarnation of Delbert since they both have two daughters? Delbert Grady has no memory of killing his daughters with an ax, but then admits that he "corrected them." Unfortunately, *The Shining* does not definitively answer these questions, leaving it to the viewer to draw his or her own conclusions.

It has been suggested that *The Shining* reveals a hidden truth: that the film's director, Stanley Kubrick, actually shot the footage of the "astronauts" jumping and floating around on the "moon." Whether Apollo 11 went to the moon or not is another debate, but the idea is that NASA, and default the government, lacked the technology to film on the moon so they retained Kubrick to film the lunar footage in a secret soundstage. According to the documentary *Room 237* (2012), the government and NASA were impressed with Kubrick's use of lighting-special effects in *Dr. Strangelove* (1964) and *2001: A Space Odyssey* (1968) so they approached him to film and stage the moon landing. Accordingly, Kubrick reveals this secret in *The Shining* by hiding it in plain sight for all eyes to see. When Danny is playing with his toys in the hallway, his toy vehicles are arranged similarly to the way they would be around a rocket before it takes off, a pink tennis ball rolls in from out of nowhere. Pink, one of Wendy's favorite colors, is recognized as such by Danny asking, "Mom?" Danny, wearing his Apollo 11 sweater, stands with authority symbolizing a rocket launch, going to room 237 which Kubrick deliberately changed from room 217. The documentary suggests the reason for the switch is that, in the late 1970s, the moon was approximately 237,000 miles from earth. Danny or Apollo 11 goes to the moon; by implementing this symbolism, Kubrick is telling the audience that he, in fact, orchestrated the footage of the astronauts on the moon and that, in effect, the moon landing, at least the famous images that were presented to the world, was secretly filmed on earth. However, I believe the number 237 is a tribute to Argento's *Suspiria* and Suzy's flight

---

340 Nichols, *Jung and Tarot*, p. 265 citing Jung's *Psychological Reflections*.

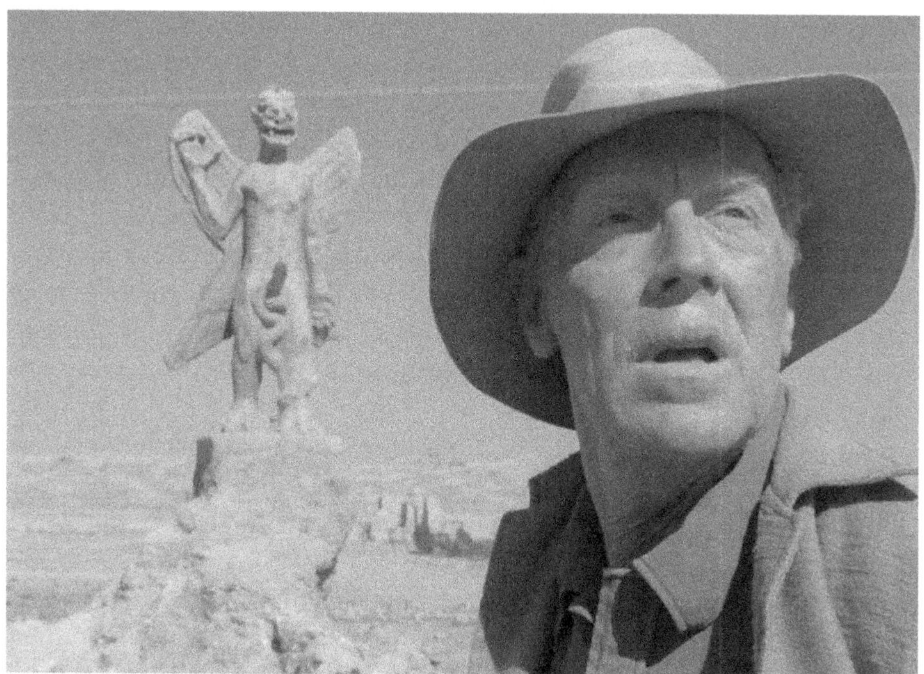

Father Merrin, played by Max von Sydow, confronts the demon Pazuzu in the Iraqi desert in *The Exorcist*. The imagery of Levi's Goat of Mendes and the Tarot's Devil card reside in the Pazuzu statue: its arms represent the hermetic maxim of *as above, so below* symbolizing the Union of Opposites. Years later, in *Star Wars: The Force Awakens*, on the desert planet Jakku, von Sydow's character Lor San Tekka also confronts a dark lord, the First Order's Kylo Ren (Adam Driver). Mirroring *The Exorcist*, this confrontation occurs at the beginning of the film, and in a desert. By casting von Sydow to portray a character that challenges Ren, just as Father Merrin faced Pazuzu, the filmmakers have cast a mnemonic spell by symbolically transforming San Tekka into a Christian hierophant *qua* Jesuit: a white magician wanting to return balance to the Force; with Ren and the First Order embodying Pazuzu's raw demonism. Furthermore, San Tekka and Father Merrin both possess sacred talismans portending future events: San Tekka has a digital relic containing a holographic map leading to Luke Skywalker and Merrin unearths the Pazuzu amulet. The purpose this mystical construct is to subconsciously transfer's Pazuzu's evil onto that of the First Order and Ren to signify their malevolence; Snoke (Andy Serkis) and his disciples are devils in the new *Star Wars* films. After a brief exchange, Ren strikes down San Tekka recalling yet another von Sydow movie. Ren killing San Tekka imitates Baron Harkonnen killing von Sydow's character, Dr. Kynes, on the desert planet of Arrakis in Dune, which again subconsciously conveys that Ren and the First Order are, like the Harkonnens, savage monsters. Is this all a coincidence? This author does not think so; instead, this author believes the hiring of von Sydow in *The Force Awakens* is one of the best examples of occult casting of all time.

number. This author encourages the reader of this book to re-watch *The Shining* to make up his or her mind regarding this Apollo 11 Easter egg, however, what is beyond dispute is that Kubrick intentionally uses numerology, doubles, repeating imagery and dialog throughout the film. The reason for this is not sinister, rather, it conveys, if only on a subconscious level the repetitive cycle that is forever occurring, or reoccurring, in the

Overlook. Kubrick also successfully employs astronomical, astrological, alchemical symbols and themes, all archaic earmarks of Jung's collective unconscious, to convey transition and change, death and resurrection, reincarnation and recycling. *The Shining* is more than just a horror film; it is a masterpiece that successfully transmits arcane themes to the audience, and like the Overlook Hotel, keeps us returning over and over again to watch this cinematic classic.

EASTER EGGS IN HALLOWEEN III: SEASON OF THE WITCH

But it is not only the souls of the departed who are supposed to be hovering unseen on the day when autumn and winter resigns the pale year. Witches then speed on their errands of mischief, some sweeping through the air on besoms, others galloping along the roads on tabby-cats, which for that night are turned into coal-black steeds. The fairies, too, are all let loose, and hobgoblins of every sort roam freely about.[341] So it is, and will always be, on 31st October, Halloween.

At the time of its theatrical release on 22 October 1982 (USA), *Halloween III: Season of the Witch* was already considered cinematic heresy among horror movie fans. How could Hollywood make a *Halloween* movie without Michael Myers? John Carpenter and Debra Hill's[342] idea was to use the Halloween brand to create an anthology with different plots, characters, and settings. However, this did not go over well with fans of the original 1978 *Halloween* and its sequel, so *Halloween III* paid the price. Despite the criticism, Michael Myers is in *Halloween III*: he briefly appears in a television commercial for 1978's *Halloween* (identified as "the immortal classic") making the latter a movie within a movie. Jamie Lee Curtis (Laurie Strode in *Halloween, Halloween II, Halloween: H2O* (1998), and *Halloween* (2018)) is also in *Halloween III*: she can be heard as the voice of Santa Mira's curfew announcer and telephone operator. During the 1980s and 1990s, *Halloween III* could not shake the criticism

---

341 J.G. Frazer, *The Golden Bough*, p. 626.
342 The creative minds behind the Halloween franchise.

(it was a bomb at the box office) that it did not continue the Michael Myers storyline, it was as though people forgot that *Halloween III* was an actual horror movie worth watching. This author has encountered numerous movie fans that have never seen *Season of the Witch* with the reason being given, "Michael Myers is not in it," or, "that's the weird stand-alone Halloween movie." It was as though no one would watch it, or admit to watching it, for these reasons.

As fate would have it, this author is writing this analysis of *Halloween III* on October 22nd, 2015, and is happy to report that the movie is now considered and underrated classic. With intriguing characters and a deliciously evil plot, the movie is fun to watch, especially on October 31st, making it a Halloween must-see. A large part of *Season of the Witch's* occultism revolves around the film's antagonist: a malevolent Druidic warlock named Conal Cochran (Dan O'Herlihy, 1919-2005) pilfering one of Stonehenge's trilithon stones (a bluestone) to harness its magical properties. Cochran runs a Halloween mask-making and novelty company named Silver Shamrock Novelties, which parallels real-life mask making company Don Post Studios. Cochran has embedded a tiny piece of the trilithon stone in the back of the Silver Shamrock trademark, tagging it to the back of three of his most iconic Halloween masks: a witch, a jack-o-lantern, and a skull. After a televised Horrorthon on Halloween night, children are instructed to wear their masks while watching the Big Giveaway at nine o'clock. The Big Giveaway is nothing more than a flashing pumpkin which appears on screen, activating the piece of trilithon stone in the mask's logo, causing the child's face to be ravaged by bugs, spiders, bees, snakes, and other parasites.[343]Cochran demonstrates his black magic when he and Dr. Daniel Challis (Tom Atkins) descend in an elevator (cf. descent into Hell) into the Final Processing area of his mask-making factory. Cochran's computers and televisions are arranged so that they form a Stonehenge-like magic circle before the trilithon stone, forming a scientific-magical megalithic structure rooted in the modern, yet with ancient origins. While standing in this circle, Cochran shows Challis a demonstration of his mask's diabolical properties when "Little" Buddy Kupfer (Bradley Schachter) wears a jack-o-lantern mask while watching the Big Giveaway's flashing pumpkin. Cochran's henchman

---

343 See Sullivan's *Cinema Symbolism*, Chapter VII.

initiates the Big Giveaway by pressing 666 on the computer's control pad signifying Antichrist-demonic sorcery. Meanwhile, inside Test Room A, Buddy's mask melts his face with snakes and crickets which eventually turn on his parents, killing them as well. Like *Evilspeak*, *Halloween III* is a great early cinematic example of the fusion of sorcery, witchcraft, and the occult with modern-day technology to produce terrifying effects.

Cochran reminds this author of an eviler version of candy-maker Willy Wonka (Gene Wilder, Johnny Depp). Cochran, similar to Wonka, lives alone in a mysterious factory surrounded by servants: Oompa Loompa's in Wonka's case, androids in Cochran's factory. Echoing Wonka, the keeper of candy-making secrets, Cochran

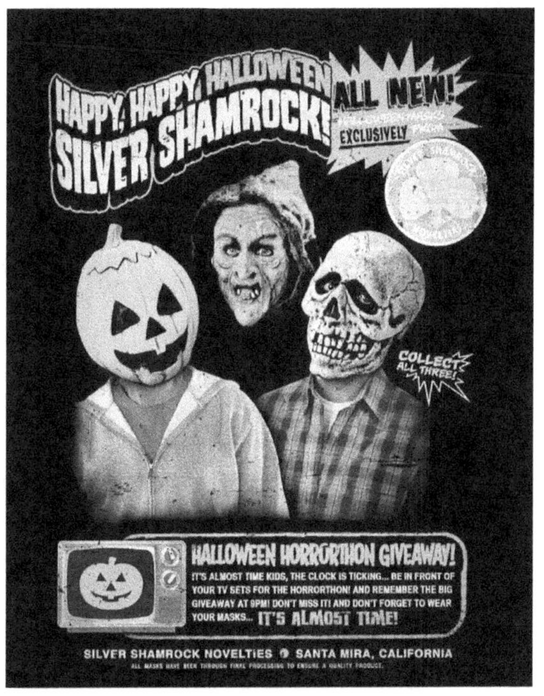

Silver Shamrock Novelties' Big Three Halloween glow-in-the-dark masks: a jack-o-lantern, a witch, and a skull. The three masks represent the trefoil form of a shamrock while the subtitle of the film, *Season of the Witch*, is named after the Donovan song "Season of the Witch" featuring Jimmy Page, then a noted session guitarist working in England, providing the haunting guitar. The film's director, Tommy Lee Wallace, is a fan of the psychedelic song making it the film's subtitle. Wallace was a collaborator with John Carpenter and Debra Hill (1950-2005) on such films as *Halloween, Escape from New York*, and *The Fog* (1980). As Dr. Dementia, Wallace's voice hosts the TV horror movie marathon in *Halloween*. He is the voice of KAB Radio's promos and lead-ins in *The Fog*. In *Halloween III*, Wallace narrates the Silver Shamrock commercials.

is the holder of the esoteric secrets of toy-making, mask-making, and practical jokes. He guards his secrets jealously making him a perfect example of the evil Hermes Trismegistus wizard archetype in the vein of *Conan the Barbarian's* (1982) Tulsa Doom (James Earl Jones). Like *Blade Runner's* Dr. Eldon Tyrell (Joe Turkel), Cochran is also an expert in Kabbalah, alchemy, and golem creation. He has perfected a series of mindless, drone-like androids that do his bidding without question; to quote Cochran golem-making is just "Another form of mask-making." Cochran's Silver

Shamrock factory is located in the fictitious town of Santa Mira, California, paying homage to 1956's *Invasion of the Body Snatchers* which was also set in Santa Mira, California. The Nexus implies that Cochran is replacing humans with robot counterparts (cf. 1975's *The Stepford Wives*) paralleling *Invasion of the Body Snatchers* wherein large extraterrestrial seed pods reproduce and duplicate replacement copies of each human. Additionally, *Season of the Witch's* "Stop it!" ending mirrors the "You're next!" ending of *Invasion of the Body Snatchers*. Cochran's emotionless gray-suited androids aside, in *Halloween III's* Santa Mira it's hard to know who is human and who is an android; the film intentionally blurs these lines. Is hotel operator Mr. Rafferty (Michael Currie, 1928-2009) a robot? Rafferty stands next to Cochran when the latter is told that Marge Guttman (Garn Stephens, Tom Atkins' wife at the time) has become the victim of a misfire, her face annihilated by one of the Halloween mask's trademarks. Rafferty refers to Cochran as a "great man," covering for him when Challis wants to examine Guttman, which seemingly places him in the know regarding Silver Shamrock's Big Giveaway evil scheme.

Questions surround the film's female protagonist, Ellie Grimbridge (Stacey Nelkin). She is investigating her father's death and, towards the end of the film, is abducted by Cochran's androids. She is presumably killed and replaced with an Ellie homicidal robot which attacks Challis during the film's climax. However, what if Ellie *was* one of Cochran's kabalistic golems the entire time? If so, could she have been sent back by Cochran to make sure her "father" Harry Grimbridge (Al Berry) was killed, so as to tie-up any loose ends he may have left behind? It is hinted that Ellie may indeed be a robot from the outset: when Challis and her make love, Challis is bemused that she never tires and that her stamina seems to be never-ending. He also questions Ellie's age, to which she answers that she is "older than she looks," indicating that she may be non-human. Assuming Ellie is an Android during the film's entirety is like watching *Blade Runner*, believing that Deckard is a Nexus-6: it puts a new twist on the movie, challenging the viewer to look for veiled symbolisms and their meanings.

Silver Shamrock Novelties' logo, a silver shamrock, is symbolically important, indicating witchcraft. The color silver is linked to the moon which associates with the goddesses Diana and Hecate (a darker incarnation of the former), the latter the patronesses of witches. To the Druids, the shamrock symbolized the spring equinox and the resurrected sun.[344] The shamrock emblematizes the Celtic sun wheel which was used at spring and summer sabbaths.[345] A trefoil is correctly tied to the magical number three or the tripartite goddess Hecate (Hecate was depicted with three faces) and the caduceus or magical wand of Hermes Trismegistus, the thrice greatest god of magic and wisdom. However, Cochran has employed the mysteries of Druidism for darker purposes. The Silver Shamrock trademark symbolically identifies Cochran as a warlock using the dark side of Druidism to carry out his evil plan; three Silver Shamrock masks have malevolent magical properties. Cochran conjures harmful magic while his motivations and timing are based on astrology and astronomy which were part of the Druidic Mysteries. Cochran explains to Dr. Challis: "Halloween, the festival of Samhain. The last great one took place three thousand years ago, when the hills ran red with the blood of animals and children. …It was part of our world, our Craft. …To us, it was a way of controlling our environment. It's not so different now. It's time again. In the end, we don't decide these things you know. The planets do. They're in alignment, and it's time again. The world's going to change tonight doctor. I'm glad you'll be able to watch it. And happy Halloween." Challis escapes his confines by tossing the skull mask he was wearing over one of the cameras watching the room. The television monitor that the camera is wired to sees the room through two eye sockets, which pays homage to the opening sequence of the original *Halloween* when a young Michael Myers stalks his sister while wearing a clown mask. Challis manages to kill Cochran–he becomes a victim of the trilithon stone's mystical properties–yet his demonic plan succeeds because one of the television stations refuses to pull the Big Giveaway's flashing pumpkin during the movie's closing moments.

What is also great about *Halloween III* is that its characters are anti-archetypes. The hero, Dr. Daniel Challis, is a gritty, older, cigarette smoking alcoholic (he even shares his booze with Santa Mira's wino), doing everything possible to hide from his ex-wife and children. Another Easter egg: Challis' young son Willie is played by Joshua John Miller, the son of Jason Miller, better known as Father Damien Karras in *The Exorcist*; thus, *Halloween III* forges a nexus to one of the greatest horror-suspense movies

---

344 Guiley, *The Encyclopedia of Witches and Witchcraft*, p. 316.
345 *ibid.*

of all time. Stacey Nelkin is great as Ellie, the investigative girl-next-door heroine only she doesn't get rescued by the hero, and the film's villain, Cochran, is just as over-the-top as any of James Bond's nemeses. Cochran, an Irish mask-making-practical-joke-creating evil Druidic warlock, can be found nowhere else in cinema and, unlike the Bond villains, his evil plan succeeds in the film's closing moments.[346] If you passed on this movie the first time around, or if you have never seen *Halloween III: Season of the Witch*, give it a watch; you will find a well-made, entertaining, and unique horror film that was way ahead of its time in 1982.

ANGEL HEART: THE PURE DOCTRINES OF LUCIFER

Angel Heart, based on William Hjortsberg's (1941-2017) Faustian detective novel *Falling Angel* (1978), was written and directed by Alan Parker, released theatrically in 1987. The film and novel feature Postmodern aspects; regarding literature, Postmodern fiction is a diverse blending of literary genres, fusing diverse cultural and stylistic levels, the serious with the playful, that resist classification according to traditional literary rubrics.[347] Set in January (cf. winter, death of sun, darkness exalted) 1955 New York and New Orleans, the movie is both modish noir and an occult-satanic thriller; a rare but effective combination. The film also successfully blends alchemy with Gnosticism, another cinematic rarity.[348] The alchemical storyline is told in narrative flashbacks: a pre-WWII crooner, Johnny Favorite (real name Jonathan Liebling), has sold his soul to Satan *qua* Lucifer *qua* the Devil for stardom. However, Johnny has figured out a way to trick the Prince of Darkness: he has discovered an ancient, black magic rite in an obscure manuscript that will get him out of his pact. The ritual involves abducting a random male victim, the reading of incantations in Greek and Latin and, with a virgin dagger, splitting open the innocent victim, devouring his heart. Once the ceremony is complete, symbolized by an eerie

---

346 At least Cochran's plan appears to succeed; it is left to the viewer's speculation whether the third station pulled the plug on the Big Giveaway.

347 M.H. Abrams, *A Glossary of Literary Terms*, p. 168.

348 Wilson, *Secret Cinema*, p. 5.

red hotel window denoting the *rubedo* (alchemical finality), Johnny will alchemically become the person he just murdered assuming his memories, identity, and personality. Regarding Gnosticism, the movie is a journey of revelation: it is the quest of private investigator Harry Angel (Mickey Rourke) to locate missing person Johnny Favorite at the behest of Louis Cyphre (Robert De Niro), a refined eccentric claiming Johnny is in breach of contract. But, as Harry finds out, it is a journey of self-discovery which will reveal who he is, to know thyself, unraveling a painful truth: he is the person that he has been searching for the entire time.

The film opens with Harry meeting Cyphre in a private throne room-meeting chamber above an African-American church in Harlem run by Pastor John (Gerald Orange), according to his banner, "is God." The flamboyant pastor cares nothing about Christian charity, only about wealth and riches; he preaches to his flock that he is still riding around in a Cadillac when he should be in a Rolls Royce. The Pastor's avarice aside, there is a much darker side to his ministry. Suicide has occurred in an upstairs room in his temple, and the throne room where Cyphre meets Harry has a closet which hides an altar with voodoo fetishes, glass eyeballs, an inverted crucifix with menacing wrought iron nails driven into it, along with images of demons and other tokens of ill omen. The shrine identifies Pastor John as a false profit, an apostate of Hell, a disciple of Cyphre's alter ego. Once it is revealed who Cyphre really is, we understand why Cyphre is using the Christian Church as his earthly headquarters. Cyphre wears an enameled ring featuring a silver inverted pentagram identifying him with black magic. On this pentagram, Manly P. Hall explains:

The pentagram is used extensively in black magic, but when so used its form always differs in one of three ways: the star may be broken at one point not permitting the converging lines to touch; it may be inverted by having one point down and two up; or it may be distorted by having the points of varying lengths. When used in black magic, the pentagram is called the 'sign of the cloven hoof,' or the footprint of the Devil. The star with two points upward is also called the 'Goat of Mendes,' because the inverted star is the same shape as the goat's head.

When the upright star turns and the upper point falls to the bottom, it signifies the fall of the Morning Star (the sun).[349]

Louis Cyphre is *LouCyphre* or Lucifer and from the outset, it is clear that Cyphre knows Harry was once Johnny Favorite. Cyphre employs Harry to find Johnny because he owes him a debt. Although he has some misgivings, Harry agrees to locate Johnny, current whereabouts unknown. Seeking Johnny's trail, Harry travels to Poughkeepsie, Coney Island, and New Orleans. Just about every person he questions about Johnny ends up brutally murdered. Included among these are Dr. Albert Fowler (Michael Higgins, 1920-2008), Johnny's old society girlfriend Margaret Krusemark (Charlotte Rampling), her father Ethan (Stocker Fontelieu, 1923-2009), jazz musician Toots Sweet (Brownie McGhee, 1915-1996), and Epiphany Proudfoot (Lisa Bonet), Johnny's daughter by voodoo priestess Evangeline Proudfoot. Black magic envelops the victims: Margaret wears a necklace with an inverted pentagram and Toots has an inverted pentagram carved on a gold tooth, identifying them as black magicians. As Harry moves deeper into the dark world of the occult which Johnny circulated, he increasingly suffers flashback of a soldier celebrating New Year's Eve in Times Square during World War II. Suggestive images of rotating fan blades and elevator gears turning clockwise and counterclockwise also frequently appear, symbolizing the eternal dualistic struggle of good against evil, light against dark, order against chaos; their revolutions are but mere microcosms of Mani's cosmological macrocosm.

Finally, after much psychological and physical duress, the mystery is finally unveiled. In the final dialog with Cyphre in Margaret's apartment, Harry discovers that he was once Johnny; that it is was him who abducted and ritualistically killed the soldier, identified as Harold Angel by his dog tags, abducting him while he was celebrating New Year's Eve. In a black magic ceremony, Johnny viciously killed the soldier so he could alchemically become him, thus voiding the contract and the debt–his soul– owed to Lucifer. Cyphre informs him that he is the murderer of Johnny's former acquaintances, but the killings were naturally guided by him. Lucifer, is it he who bears the light, and with it its splendors intolerable blinds feeble, sensual, or selfish souls?[350] Doubt it not; in solving the mystery of his

---

349 Hall, *The Secret Teachings of All Ages*, pp. 326-327, "(the sun)" added.
350 Pike, *Morals and Dogma*, p. 321.

identity, flashbacks reveal what Harry has been repressing: he killed those who once knew Johnny. Cyphre has the last laugh by playing a record, "Girl of my Dreams," by Johnny Favorite as a cruel reminder of Harry's former self and doomed pact. Harry-Johnny can now acknowledge the chaos in his own being, the destructive powers of his heart.[351] By doing so, he might be able to synthesize dualistic contradictions: turbulence and pattern, demon and angel.[352] Harry has figured out that Louis Cypher is Lucifer, therefore he should know that his daughter's name is also a riddle: Epiphany means *illuminating discovery*, signifying his Gnostic expedition of self-revelation. If he can, he will undertand that Cyphre *qua* Lucifer bears light: he supplied gnosis by putting him on a journey of enlightenment to discover his true identity; however, this apocalyptic revelation turns his reality into a living nightmare. There is no happy ending: Harry has gone down the rabbit hole and is worse off because of it. Louis Cyphre-Lucifer is nothing more than Hermes Trismegistus in a black suit; he is the wise, fork-tongued, aloof, academic, stoic Mephistopheles outwitting his quarry. When Harry-Johnny says the alias, Louis Cyphre, is a "dime store joke," the Lucifer to sarcastically quips, "Mephistopheles is such a mouthful in Manhattan, Johnny."

Like Kubrick's *The Shining*, the conclusion of the movie poses an epistemological question that leaves the viewer guessing. Throughout the film, a mysterious shrouded person in black appears cleaning up after bloody murders, suicides, and Johnny's evil ritual. Near the end of the movie, Harry-Johnny accuses Cyphre of being the murderer of Fowler, Toots, Margaret, and Ethan, but Cyphre tells him they were killed by his hand. Before disappearing from Margaret's apartment, one will observe Cyphre's elongated fingernails removing Harry's gun and dog tags from the floor. These incriminating items next appear in Harry's hotel room becoming circumstantial evidence, indicating he killed his daughter, Epiphany, her corpse in the bed. Although Harry-Johnny is innocent of this crime, these items will convict him. Before Harry-Johnny enters the hotel room, one will see this mysterious person in black seated outside Harry's room on the walkway. The mysterious figure's identity is finally revealed: it is an unrecognizable, clean-shaven Cyphre with a water basin on his lap waiting

---

351 Wilson, *Secret Cinema*, p. 122.
352 *ibid.*

to clean up the bloodbath inside. Cyphre's presence is a reminder that evil is omnipresent and, like the Mystery Man, can be anywhere and everywhere; he has obviously murdered Epiphany to frame Harry-Johnny. Harry-Johnny will get the electric chair, visualized in a prophetic dream after Harry-Johnny murders Toots, thus allowing Cyphre to finally claim his soul. But the question remains: does this mean that Cyphre killed Johnny's past colleagues? Or was Cyphre right all along, that Harry-Johnny was indeed the murderer, disclosed in the flashbacks? Although the movie never fully answers this ambiguity, it appears to be the latter. During the film's end credits, Harry-Johnny descends in an old wire cage elevator symbolizing his descent into Hell, the mysterious alchemical *nigredo*, which for him is nothing and everything, chaotic order, death and life.[353]

In *Cinema Symbolism*, this author shed light on some of the other veiled imagery exhibited in the film. For example, Ethan Krusemark admits to being under the aegis of Satan, "The Prince of Darkness protects the powerful," he tells Harry. Krusemark's alias is Edward Kelley, thereby affiliating himself with the historical Edward Kelley and Dr. John Dee, two necromancers developing a system of conjuring, Enochian Magic. When questioned Ethan Krusemark emphatically states, "I was Edward Kelley," implying reincarnation; it is not a coincidence that both men share the initials, *E.K.* Dee and Kelley's Enochian Magic is the invoking of angels through occult ceremonies, the use of dark mirrors, a secret language, and mysterious incantations, forming a nexus between Ethan, sorcery, and Johnny's evil ritual. Meanwhile, his debutant daughter, Margaret (a/k/a the Witch of Wellesley a/k/a Madame Zora), reads Tarot cards, casts horoscopes, and practices witchcraft and black magic. Harry discovers she owns a Hand of Glory which is a preserved mummified hand cut from a hanged murderer, granting invisibility to its owner and the ability to open any lock it comes across. Once removed from the corpse the hand was either dried in an oven with vervain, a herb believed to repel demons, or exposed to the heat of the sun during the Dog Days of August when Sirius is exalted.[354] The Hand of Glory was an item wielded by both black magicians and thieves. Lighting the wicks on the fingers, or its tips, allegedly put people

---

353 *ibid*, p. 123.
354 Guiley, *The Encyclopedia of Witches and Witchcraft*, p. 150; see also Waite's *The Book of Black Magic*, p. 306.

to sleep or rendered them speechless. The wicks were made of the hanged man's hair according to European folklore; once lit the Hand could only be extinguished by dousing it with milk. The Hand of Glory's hypnotic power was referenced by the Jesuit demonologist Martin del Rio (1551-1608) in his commentary

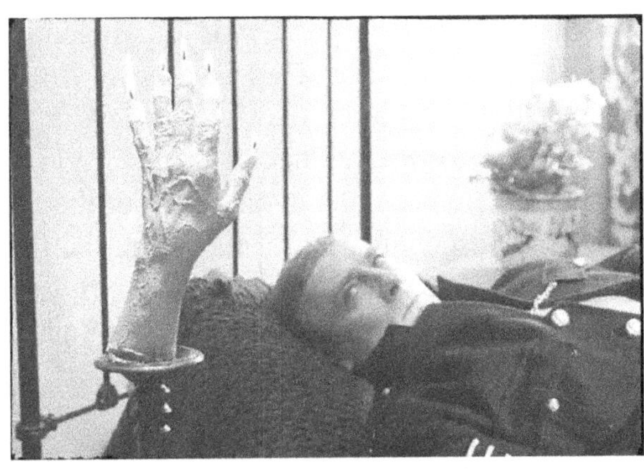

Witchcraft's Hand of Glory in 1973's *The Wicker Man*, a film that shrouds the mysterious disappearance of a girl with paganism and the occult.

Disquisitionum Magicarum (1599-1600) which was used during the Salem Witch Trials of 1692. The Hand of Glory is a living serpent (cf. wisdom) and is wholly in accordance with the genius of black magic.[355]

The events of movie take place twelve years after Johnny murdered the soldier and stole his soul, which evokes Judeo-Christian Biblical imagery associated with the Twelve Tribes of Israel and the Twelve Apostles. Thus, Louis Cyphre is the Judeo-Christian Devil, the Dragon, the cunning serpent. Although Cyphre's appearance is limited, his presence lurks behind every corner anticipating Harry's every move. For instance, when Harry becomes anxious or danger is approaching, a beating heart can be heard growing louder as the anxiety increases; Harry is one step closer to figuring out who he is. One cannot help but draw a parallel to E.A. Poe's poem *The Tell-Tale Heart* (1843), a story in which a murderer's guilt manifests in the form of his victim's beating heart beneath floorboards. The killer finally rips up the floorboards revealing the body and his guilt, just as Harry consciously begins a journey that will unveil that he was once Johnny, making him the murderer of the young soldier. Harry will come to learn that he sold his soul to Satan for stardom, but tried to duck out of it by stealing the soul of another. He is only able to receive gnosis after unifying with the sacred feminine by having sex with Epiphany. Harry-Johnny is ignorant he is committing the abomination of incest by performing this monstrous act and that, in doing so, his alchemical wedding will seal his fate. It will be

---

355 Waite, *ibid*, p. 307.

Epiphany's death that condemns him, placing him in the electric chair, his soul claimed by Lucifer. Harry-Johnny's Gnostic quest ends in damnation, or does it? He conjured the Devil, forged a satanic pact for stardom, successfully performed a black magic ceremony wherein he stole the soul of another and managed to avoid wrath of the Prince of Darkness for twelve years. By descending into Hell during the film's final credits, he realizes that he must pay for his diabolical transgressions yet, at the same time, Harry-Johnny can acknowledge his darkness: he is a prideful Left-Hand Path magician and occultist par excellence.

CLIMBING JACOB'S LADDER

Adrian Lyne's *Jacob's Ladder*, also known as *Dante's Inferno*, is a horror-psychological thriller wherein all is not what it seems: the protagonist's perception is distorted, leaving the viewer speculating as to what is hallucination and what is empirical reality. *Jacob's Ladder* supplied the raw material for M. Night Shyamalan's *The Sixth Sense* (1999) while influencing the *Silent Hill* video game series. If *Jacob's Ladder* is to be taken literally, and this author sees no other way of interpreting it, Jacob Singer's (Tim Robbins) 1975 post-Vietnam life in New York City is not real. Rather, his New York experiences are fragments of Singer's self-made Purgatory-like existence which he must learn to relinquish to enter Heaven, a state of spiritual consciousness. The movie's opening title, *Jacob's Ladder*, is written in blood red placed over a black background similar to Lyne's 1986 erotic drama *9 ½ Weeks*, suggesting alchemical change. Jacob's metamorphic journey culminates when his soul finally learns to abandon material reality, and everything he is holding on to for the spiritual world; he will depart earth transitioning to the celestial, heavenly realm.

The story begins on October 6th, 1971, when Jacob Singer was a soldier with the 1st Air Cavalry Division, deployed in a village in the Mekong Delta during the Vietnam War. Suddenly, his unit comes under heavy fire from the tree line, and many of Jacob's comrades are killed or wounded. Soldiers also begin to exhibit abnormal behavior, some even going catatonic or collapsing into bloody seizures. Horrified, Jacob attempts to flee into the jungle, only to be stabbed in the stomach with a bayonet by an unseen attacker. The movie then moves forward four years to 1975. Jacob wakes on a New York City subway train, dressed as a postal worker with a copy of Albert Camus' (1913-1960) *The Stranger* (1942) in his hands. The book foreshadows Jacob's disorientation, strange visions, and that he does not belong where he is; it will be revealed he is a stranger in a strange land. After Jacob finds himself locked in the underground subway station, he tries to escape via the tracks, where he is nearly hit by an oncoming train. Paralleling Alice traveling down the rabbit hole to Wonderland to gain gnosis, Jacob descends a dark subway tunnel, beginning his journey towards transitional truth. The film then shifts back and forth between Jacob's chaotic memories of Vietnam, similar to Harry Angel's flashbacks, symbolizing unknown horrific evils. Jacob is also tormented by memories of his late son Gabe (Macaulay Culkin, uncredited), hit and killed by a car while bicycling, and of his ex-wife, Sarah (Patricia Kalember). Currently, he is a postal clerk living in Brooklyn with Jezzie Pipkin (Elizabeth Peña, 1959-2014), her forename is an abbreviation of the biblical Jezebel. Jacob experiences bizarre demonic hallucinations apparently suffering from a severe case of post-traumatic stress disorder, encountering more direct threats to his life. During a party, a fortune teller informs him that he is dead after reading his palm; Jacob then sees Jezzie sexually assaulted by a demon while dancing. Imitating Lyne's female leading ladies Alex Forrest (Glenn Close) of *Fatal Attraction* (1987), and Elizabeth McGraw of *9 ½ Weeks*, Jezzie also has a penchant for black stockings, signifying her dark sensuality and shadow; she conspicuously wears them, writhing in pleasure while the demon sexually molests her on the dance floor. The devils of *Jacob's Ladder*, with their rapid moving faces, eerily mimic the artwork of Francis Bacon (1909-1992), known for his bold, graphic, and emotionally charged imagery. Bacon's painterly but abstracted, grotesque figures typically appear isolated in glass or steel geometrical cages set against flat, nondescript backgrounds. Jacob also experiences problems with his back so he visits chiropractor Louis Denardo (Danny Aiello), his guardian angel, whom Jacob describes as a cherub, because it will be Louis enlightening him to his deathly condition. Not only is Louis an angel, but he is Jacob's personal Thoth Hermes Mercurius Trismegistus, providing Jacob with the wisdom he needs to move on. The veiled insights that Louis provides Jacob are his Mercury, an essential ingredient for transitioning out of Purgatory;[356] for Jacob knowing the truth of his benighted condition is his alchemy; it is his philosopher's stone.

As the hallucinations become increasingly bizarre, Paul (Pruitt Taylor Vince), one of Jacob's old Army friends, contacts him, indicating he too is having similar experiences, but is killed when his car mysteriously explodes. After the funeral, his surviving platoonmates confess to Jacob they have been experiencing horrible hallucinations, agreeing to seek the truth about possible Army experimentations through legal proceedings. They meet a lawyer, Mr. Geary (Jason Alexander), saying they have a case, but later backs out claiming he has discovered they were never even in Vietnam, and that they were all discharged during wargame training in Thailand. Jacob's comrades are intimidated into abandoning the lawsuit while Jacob is briefly kidnapped by government agents trying to silence him. It appears that Jacob will founder in the *nigredo*, will cede to chaos.[357] Escaping the government operatives, Jacob is robbed of his wallet and identity by Santa Claus, taken to a hospital where he descends into Hell, or Inferno. He is tortured by an image of Gabe's demolished bicycle, told he is deceased, undergoing horrible medical tortures. He is rescued by his guardian angel, Louis; the latter then performs chiropractic healing on Jacob while imparting to him the truth of his stasis, the confining nature of his Purgatory, although Jacob thinks he is speaking allegorically.

Jacob returns to Jezzie's apartment rifling through the contents of a cigar box, Golden Eagle Brand, which stores the mnemonic tokens he has been painfully clinging to for too long. Among the box's contents are Jacob's dog tags, photos of his friends, military discharge papers, a college degree, and a *momento mori*: a note written by his deceased son Gabe in red crayon (cf. *rubedo*) urging him to come home. Over the phone, Jacob is contacted by a man named Michael Newman (Matt Craven), appearing to treat his wounds in a medevac helicopter during a flashback to Vietnam. Against the wishes of Jezzie, Jacob meets with Michael, who claims to have been a chemist in the Army's chemical warfare division in Saigon, where he worked on creating the Ladder: an LSD-like drug that would

---

356 cf. the trickster element associated with the god Mercury. Jacob tricks himself by thinking he is alive when he is actually dead.
357 Wilson, *Secret Cinema*, p. 123.

increase aggression, taking people straight to their most primal urges. The drug was first tested on monkeys, then on a group of captured enemy combatants with gruesome results. Later, small doses of the Ladder were secretly given to Jacob's unit. Succumbing to the effects of the drug, the 1st Air Cavalry Division attacked each other: Jacob was bayoneted by one of his fellow soldiers that, instead of targeting the enemy, could not distinguish friend from foe.

The last scenes have Jacob returning to the apartment building he once lived with Sarah. Symbolizing Saint Peter and the Gates of Heaven, Jacob is welcomed by Sam the Doorman, like he was anticipating his arrival. Jacob enters his apartment and is surprised to see Gabe at the foot of the stairwell. Gabe, whose name alludes to the archangel Gabriel,[358] takes Jacob by the hand and together the two of them ascend the staircase, disappearing into a bright light. The dénouement reveals that Jacob fought in Vietnam, but that he did not survive. At the moment of death, his body rests in an Army triage tent with a peaceful expression on his face.

* * * *

Jacob's New York City life is not empirical reality; instead, it is a self-created Purgatory that he must learn to free himself from; to let go of his thoughts, his memories, and his materialism. In other words, Jacob must become cognizant of his true condition so that he can abandon the life he desperately clings to so that he can ascend to the afterlife. Symbolizing the feminine alchemically, the moon, the *albedo* stage, are the two women in Jacob's life: his ex-wife Sarah and his current girlfriend, Jezzie. The two women are a negative influence, the dark side of the moon, and not positive. They are Jacob's morose past, Sarah, and stagnant present, Jezzie, which are consuming him. Because he cannot free himself of Luna's powerful influence, they are preventing achieving alchemical change; they are roadblocks, staying his rebirth from a dull caterpillar into a beautiful butterfly. Jezzie's name symbolizes the Biblical figure Jezebel, inciting her husband King Ahab to abandon the worship of Yahweh, encouraging the worship of the pagan deities, Baal and Asherah. Jezebel associates with falsehood,

---

358 Gabriel is not called an archangel in the Bible, but is so called in Intertestamental period sources like the *Book of Enoch*. In the Roman Catholic, Anglican, Lutheran, Eastern and Oriental Orthodox churches, the archangels Michael, Raphael, and Gabriel are also referred to as saints.

making her a symbol of Jacob's faux existence, Purgatory. Jezzie laments when Jacob decides to meet with Newman, his name *New-man* implies rebirth, urging him not to go since she seems to know that Jacob will become aware of his stasis. The solar light symbolizing truth, alchemy's *citrinitas* stage, is represented by Jacob's powerful material attachments within Purgatory. Although they are symbols of his life, he must divest himself of them to climb Jacob's Ladder, comparatively the Ladder of Mithras, to effectuate alchemy. Jacob's memories, his sacred truths, his attachments–the ones that he must abandon or "burn away" to quote Louis–are stored in the Golden Eagle cigar box, representing alchemy's *citrinitas*. The box contains material truths and spiritual revelations; "…The eagle typified the sun in its material phase and also the immutable demiurgic law which all mortal creatures must bend. The eagle was also the Hermetic symbol of sulfur and signified the mysterious fire of Scorpio–the most profoundly significant sign of the zodiac and the *Gate of the Great Mystery*. Being one of the three symbols of Scorpio, the eagle, like the Goat of Mendes, was an emblem of the theurgic art and the secret processes (cf. alchemy) by which the infernal fire of the scorpion was transmuted into the spiritual *light-fire* of the gods."[359] Gabe, Jacob's deceased son or sun, is also an embodiment of the material: personifying Jacob's most powerful *citrinitas* earthly attachment, Gabe is hit and killed by a truck standing next his Apollo bicycle.

Jacob experiences evil in the world (the death of Gabe) more than he does good, signified by the demons that frequently plague him. Jacob's melancholy is the *nigredo*; his blackening is the Purgatory in which, much like the subway station, he is trapped unable to escape. Jacob's *nigredo* is carried to darker and dangerous extremes when Jacob descends into Hell, only to be rescued by the angelic Louis. However, the agonies of Hell are necessary; while Louis performs his healing art upon Jacob, he quotes the German theologian and mystic Meister Eckhart (Eckhart von Hochheim, ca. 1260–ca. 1328) explaining to Singer, "Eckhart saw Hell too. …He said, 'The only thing that burns in Hell is the part of you that won't let go of your life. Your memories, your attachments, they burn them all away. *But they're not punishing you*,' he said, '*they're freeing your soul*.' … So, …if you're frightened of dying and you're holding on, you'll see devils tearing

---

359 Hall, *The Secret Teachings of All Ages*, p. 277 "(cf. alchemy)" added; see also Pike's *Morals and Dogma*, p. 774ff.

your life away. But if you've made your peace, *then the devils are really angels, freeing you from the earth.*" Louis is correct: Jacob must descend into Hell, which he does, having his attachments and memories burned away, forcing him to let go of the contents of the Golden Eagle cigar box. He must become conscious of his death, accept it, and leave earth behind, knowing that life moves on without him; this alchemical construct is anticipated earlier when Jezzie burns old photographs of Jacob's life with Sarah. Like a parable, Louis allegorically describes how the Hell and Purgatory of the *nigredo* may become Heaven, which, for Jacob is the finality of the *rubedo*.[360] Jacob finally lets go: he transmutes into a spiritual entity, abandoning the material realm when he returns to his former apartment, to come home and, seeing the spirit of Gabe, accepts his death climbing the staircase, symbolizing Jacob's Ladder of Genesis 28:10-19, finally achieving alchemical change.[361] Understanding that the change was beneficial, Jacob now enters Heaven, the light, forever departing the lesser world, Jacob's soul liberated by the *nigredo*, the demons of Hell. Throughout, the alchemical *rubedo* subtly manifests like an apparition: Gabe flies a red kite, Gabe holds a red toy while sitting at the bottom of the staircase at film's finale, Gabe's note is written in red crayon, and a red glow shines upon Jacob during his one of his Vietnam flashbacks. Red saturates Jacob during his cab ride home. Jacob's alchemical transition now complete, a veiled truth is at last revealed: Jacob died in Vietnam and, having made his peace, is now able to depart Purgatory with Gabe at his side.

MURDER: THE OVERLOOK HOTEL TRANSCENDS CRIMSON PEAK

Guillermo del Toro's ghostly gothic romance *Crimson Peak* draws inspiration from Poe's *The Fall of the House of Usher* (1839), Henry James' (1843-1916) *The Turn of the Screw* (1898), Hitchcock's *Rebecca* (1940), *The Haunting* (1963, remade 1999) and Stephen King's *Salem's*

---

360 cf. Wilson's *Secret Cinema*, p. 124.

361 During the cab ride to the apartment, a Nixon Now campaign pin seems to vanish from the dashboard. This is intentional and symbolizes Jacob's forthcoming departure from the material world.

Lot (published 1975, TV movie 1979) while also being a monumental cinematic allusion to Kubrick's *The Shining*. One of the characters in *The Fall of the House of Usher* is a crumbling morbid castle; James' novella *The Turn of the Screw* (visualized on-screen in 1961's *The Innocents*) is an eerie ghost story; Hitchcock's *Rebecca* is a tale about a young woman falling in love with an aristocratic yet brooding widower; *The Haunting* is about a house that comes alive; while evil lives in the stone foundation, wooden beams, and plaster ceilings of *Salem Lot's* Marsten House; it is easy to see in these stories the acorns that grew into *Crimson Peak*. *Crimson Peak* is not about an alchemical transition; there are no Gnostic saviors or wisdom providers, no hardcore Tarot imagery. Yet the film is brimming with symbolism from start to finish, del Toro never takes his foot off the esoteric gas pedal.

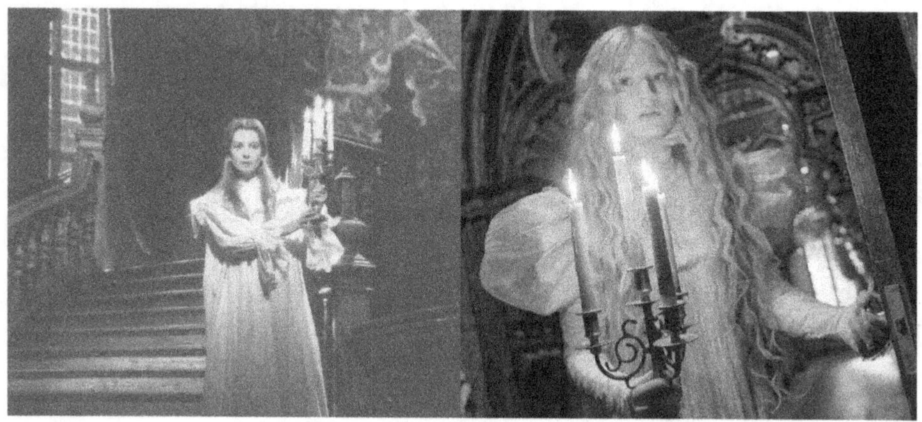

Comparative Cinema: (Left) Miss Giddens (Deborah Kerr, 1921-2007) descends the staircase of a haunted mansion in *The Innocents*. (Right) *Crimson Peak's* Edith Cushing investigates the ghosts of Allerdale Hall.

In 1887 Buffalo, New York; Edith Cushing (Sofia Wells), the young daughter of wealthy American businessman Carter Cushing (Jim Beaver), is visited by her mother's ghost warning her to "Beware of Crimson Peak." As the scary black female ghost approaches young Edith, the wall clock stops ticking which conjures, to the subconscious mind, *The Exorcist*. When Father Merrin is examining the Pazuzu amulet, the wall clock stops ticking. The stoppage of time in both movies denotes the presence of the supernatural; for Edith and Merrin something wicked their way comes.

Fourteen years later, Edith (now Mia Wasikowska) is a budding yet frustrated author preferring to pen ghost stories over writing the romance novels that her editor wants. She is a modern woman, living during the Suffragette movement which was gaining momentum at the time; Edith personifies a departure from the archetypal repressed Victorian-Edwardian era woman. She meets Sir Thomas Sharpe (Tom Hiddleston), an English baronet having come to the United States to find investors, including Edith's father, to finance his clay mining invention: the clay harvester. Disdaining privileged aristocracy and unimpressed with Sharpe's prototype and previous failures to raise capital, Carter rejects Sir Thomas' proposal. Edith notices that Thomas and his sister, Lady Lucille (Jessica Chastain), wear expensive but outdated and somewhat frayed fashions. Shortly thereafter, Edith is once again visited by her mother's spirit bearing the same warning.

Sir Thomas is determined to persuade Carter to change his mind. However, when he and Edith become romantically attached, Carter and Edith's friend, an ophthalmologist named Alan McMichael (Charlie Hunnam), disapprove. Carter hires a private detective, Mr. Holly (Burn Gorman), to uncover unsavory facts about the Sharpes. Carter confronts the siblings, bribing them into returning to England. Following Carter's admonition, Sir Thomas abruptly and cruelly ends his relationship with Edith, but the next morning he sends her a note explaining his harsh actions. Not long after, Carter is brutally murdered though no suspect is apprehended. Edith and Sir Thomas eventually marry and return to Cumberland, England. They arrive at Allerdale Hall, the Sharpes' dilapidated mansion, which sits on top of a red clay mine. As Edith settles in, she finds that Lucille acts somewhat cold towards her while Sir Thomas remains distant. Edith is left confused and uncertain by their odd behavior.

Soon Edith begins to see gruesome scarlet ghosts throughout the mansion. To help calm Edith, Sir Thomas takes her to the depot. After being snowed in for the night, they finally consummate their marriage. Lucille angrily lashes out when they return the next morning, frightening Edith. By the time Sir Thomas mentions that the estate is also referred to as "Crimson Peak," due to the warm red clay seeping up through the snow, Edith is growing increasingly weaker, coughing up blood.Edith explores the mansion, piecing clues together, discovering that Sir Thomas previously married three wealthy women who were fatally poisoned for their inheritances. She realizes that she too is being poisoned. She also discovers the siblings have had a long-term incestuous relationship, resulting in a sickly infant that eventually died. Lucille murdered their mother, and Sir Thomas inherited the family manor that, like many aristocratic estates of the era, is no longer profitable; the Sharpes are virtually penniless. The brother and sister began the marriage and murder scheme to support themselves and to fund Thomas' clay harvester invention. Lucille explains to Edith the marriages were for money, but "…The horror was for love. The things we do for love like this are ugly, mad, full of sweat and regret. This love burns you and maims you and twists you inside out. It is a monstrous love, and it makes monsters of us all."

Back in Buffalo, Mr. Holly informs Alan what he uncovered about the Sharpes, including Thomas' multiple marriages and the murder of their mother, Beatrice Sharpe, which occurred inside Allerdale Hall, remaining unsolved. Realizing Edith is in danger, Alan arrives at the estate to rescue her. Lucille stabs him in the left armpit demanding that her brother finish him off. Sir Thomas, having fallen in love with Edith not wanting her harmed, inflicts a second, non-fatal stab wound to Alan before hiding him in the cellar. Lucille forces Edith to sign a transfer deed granting the Sharpes ownership of the Cushing estate, confessing to the murder of Edith's father. After Edith signs the deed, she stabs Lucille in the chest with a pen (a gift from her late father), trying to escape. Sir Thomas burns the deed and promises to protect Edith so that she and Alan can escape. Lucille, jealous and furious over Sir Thomas falling in love with Edith, murders him in rage. She then pursues Edith with a giant hatchet-like meat cleaver, the same one she used to butcher her mother. Aided by Sir Thomas' ghost, Edith kills Lucille with a shovel. Sir Thomas bids Edith a silent farewell as his spirit departs. Edith and Alan are rescued, with Lucille's ghost now haunting Allerdale Hall. The end credits imply Edith has written a novel titled *Crimson Peak* based on her experiences at the haunted mansion; however, interwoven within the movie is an unconventional, esoteric interpretation that is not easy to observe.

Crimson Peak is sumptuous Edwardian era perfection fused with neo-Manichean overtones; the first half bathed in yellow solar light while the second act is melancholic darkness. The transition from light to dark is symbolized by the waning autumn sun and its eventual death in winter. After the prologue, the movie opens on approximately October 21st, 1901, a mere ten days before Halloween, the height of autumn. This date is disclosed when Alan investigates the mysterious payment Carter made to the Sharpes in return for Sir Thomas' breaking Edith's heart and leaving Buffalo; the check stub reveals this date. The bitter coldness that accompanies the sun's death is visualized when Edith arrives at decaying Allerdale Hall in the form of dead flies, along with Lucille's callous behavior. Darkness is exalted, allowing evil to roam its hallways, evidenced by the ghosts that torment Edith; a blizzard soon follows. The tobacco-gold hues that saturate Buffalo, New York symbolize the booming wealth of America and the Industrial Revolution; historically, the first half of the movie takes place during the extravagant Pan-American Exposition (World's Fair) which was held in Buffalo from 1 May through 2 November 1901. The Exposition is primarily remembered for being the venue of President William McKinely's assassination on September 6th, 1901; McKinley ran for president on the gold standard platform. On the other end of the spectrum, Allerdale Hall's stagnant colors denote the spiritual malignancy residing within, as well as the Sharpes' impoverished condition; this is the second half of the movie. This color symbolism flourishes in the character's lush and extravagant costumes. The two women, Edith and Lucille, look like Pre-Raphaelite paintings brought to life: Edith wears gold and yellow tones complemented by her unmistakable golden hair, symbolizing the wealth and greed of America and, by default, President McKinley's prosperous gold standard. While typing, she wears a tie, identifying her as a modern woman, while her dresses and frocks are representative of the Suffrage Movement: they are flowing, cordial and relaxed, reflecting her free spirit. On the other end of the spectrum, Lady Lucille's clothing is an extension of the home, Allerdale Hall, also known as Crimson Peak; her dresses are tight, constricting, mirroring her rigid and cold personality. While sojourning in Buffalo, Lucille takes Crimson Peak with her when, at McMichael's party, she wears a dark red dress and a red ring; Crimson Peak is the cruel and bitter Lucille and vice versa; Allerdale Hall and Lucille are one and the same. The color red also signifies European bloodlines and aristocracy, something not found in the United States, and the two colors, red and gold, masterfully play off of each other.

Lucille and Edith are next seen outside at a picnic with Edith in gold and Lucille in solid black with a red rose; the red rose again represents Crimson Peak; the black is decay symbolized by the deathly moths that infest in the haunted mansion. It is here that Lady Lucille forges an esoteric nexus between Edith's gold clothing, butterflies, and the sun. While looking at the dead butterflies with Edith, Lucille remarks "They're dying. They take the heat from the sun, and when it deserts them, they die. ... Beautiful things are fragile. At home, we have only black moths. Formidable creatures, to be sure, but they lack beauty. They thrive on the dark and cold." Lucille is talking

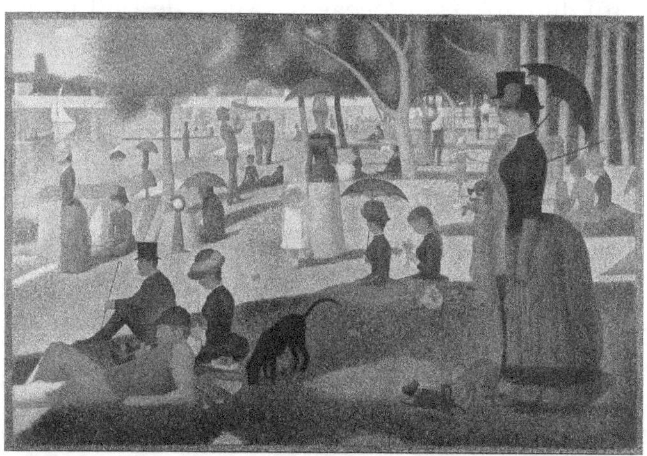

Crimson Peak's picnic in the park scene conjures *A Sunday Afternoon on the Island of La Grande Jatte – 1884* by George Seurat (1859-1881), the painting that launched Neoimpressionism. This is a textbook example of art imitating art.

about Edith and herself: Edith is a beautiful butterfly, imbuing her with the attributes of a solar heroine (the dawn), while Lucille personifies a moth: cruel and cold, walking death. The butterflies are dying because the sun is likewise heading towards winter. Lucille's dresses exhibit velvet moth wings with black thorns or spikes dangling off, signifying Allerdale Hall's foreboding spiked, iron maiden-like hallway. The moment Allerdale Hall appears, it is evident the home is a living, breathing character; the costume designs mirror the interior of the haunted mansion. Since Lucille and Thomas are one with their house; they wear teal, symbolizing the teal walls of Crimson Peak. Edith continues to wear yellows, whites, a butterfly brooch, and sits in a butterfly-shaped wingback chair signifying her heroic solar attributes, yet she is weak and dying enveloped by the wintry darkness of Allerdale Hall. She is a delicate solar butterfly mercilessly preyed upon by Lucille's cold and callous moth; the sun is weak for winter has come. Edith is now the sun in death; personifying the sun, she carries around solar fire, a lit candelabrum, while navigating Allerdale Hall's dank corridors. Like her, the candle light is faint and fleeting. As Edith's poisoning escalates, she becomes worse, causing her to abandon her yellow clothes for a thin white full-length nightgown becoming a metaphor for her frail condition, making her appear skeletal, almost a walking corpse. She is pale because the light has gone out of her world.

Crimson Peak's esoteric symbolism is not limited to its resplendent wardrobe. Carter seeks information about the Sharpes from Mr. Holly, providing him with truthful yet sensitive information. Later Holly supplies this same documentation to McMichael, realizing Edith is in jeopardy. Holly's name is a reference to the holly leaf which denotes truth in heraldry;[362] as such, Mr. Holly furnishes accurate intelligence to Messrs. Carter and McMichael. When Edith returns from the depot, Lucille is making breakfast in the scullery and opens the oven's iron door. Cast on the iron door is the word *PERFECT*, which conjures Nina Sayers' final words and quest for perfection in *Black Swan*. The singular word subtly recalls the love-hate relationship between Lily (Mila Kunis) and Nina, thus investing Edith and Lucille's relationship with the same negativity and destructive attributes. Edith and Lucille, like Lily and Nina, share an unhealthy love-hate relationship consumed by jealousy, ending in murder and death. The two women argue and are constantly at odds, but this is only the tip of the iceberg. Lucille goes into a jealous, murderous rage when she learns Edith has slept with Thomas, and Edith is likewise envious of Lucille's overbearing, unnatural relationship with Thomas, eventually discovering its incestuous nature.

Lucille's ring is an emblem of her (and her brother's) English aristocratic bloodline. The ring was worn by her mother and is given to Edith, but after Edith discovers the Sharpe's murderous endeavors, Lucille violently removes the ring from finger, symbolically banishing her from the family, stripping her of any blood ties to the Sharpes. Like most serial murders that keep souvenirs from their victims, Lucille clips and keeps locks of hair from Thomas' wives; however, the one in the drawer on the far left is white signifying it is from her mother, Beatrice. The house bleeds more as the tension builds, culminating in a fight between Lucille and Edith in

---

362 William Sloane Evans, *A Grammar of British Heraldry*, p. 141.

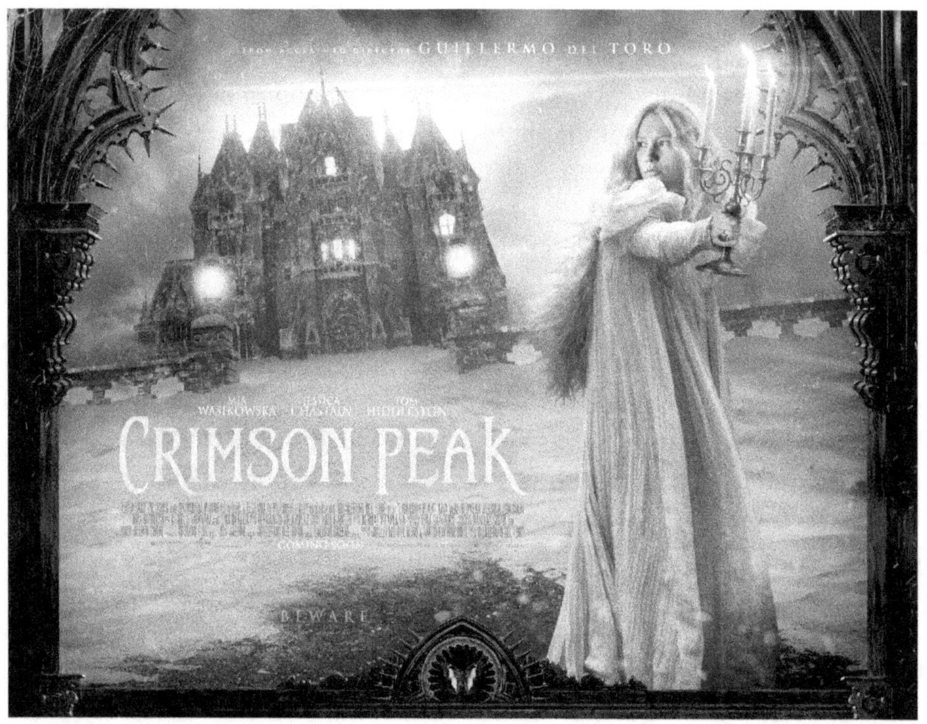

Crimson Peak's British Quad teaser poster displays two of the film's main characters: the grim Allerdale Hall a/k/a Crimson Peak (left) and heroine Edith Cushing (right). Sir Thomas explains that Allerdale Hall is alive, breathing through its chimneys.

a snowy limbo. *Crimson Peak's* climax feels like a ghostly white death shroud, blanketing the screen.

Extravagantly hiding in plain sight for all eyes to see, *Crimson Peak* pays homage to Kubrick's *The Shining* making it one of the movie's esoteric gems, a comparative cinematic treasure trove. There are no reincarnation motifs in *Crimson Peak* like there are in *The Shining*, but there is some repetition symbolizing Lucille and Thomas' marriage and murder routine. Edith eventually unlocks the mystery, so repetitive keyhole symbolism is strategically placed throughout the film. Edith's mother's ghost is keyhole- shaped, reflecting the keyhole form of the Cushing family gravestone, mirroring the keyhole design of Allerdale Hall's dark spiked hallway. The repetition continues: in the park in Buffalo, Lucille gently caresses Edith's face, brushing her cheek with a butterfly; Edith kisses Lucille on the cheek in the mansion's scullery, and later Lucille stabs Sir Thomas in the check then slashes Edith's cheek. Thus, the main characters faces-cheeks evoke interdependent duality: pleasure and pain, beauty and ugliness, love and hate, light and dark, life and death, trust and betrayal, all transcending Allerdale Hall.

But the most overt reference to *The Shining* is when Edith encounters the malevolent ghost of an old woman emerge from a tub in a green bathroom which scares the living daylights out of her, paralleling Jack Torrance encountering an evil female ghost (young at first, but then turns old) emerge from a tub in room 237's green bathroom, which scares the living daylight out of him. These two scenes are practically identical. Upon closer inspection, it becomes evident there are numerous similarities between *Crimson Peak* and *The Shining*, some of which are remarkably well hidden, others not so much. The repetition and the menacing bathroom female ghost aside, so far this author has documented the following likenesses:

Crimson Peak	*The Shining*
A struggling writer, Edith Cushing, goes to an isolated haunted mansion with two people, Sir Thomas and Lady Lucille Sharpe. Ghosts aside, they are the only three inhabitants of the mansion during the film.	A struggling writer, Jack Torrance, goes to an isolated hotel with two people, Wendy and Danny Torrance. Ghosts aside, they are the only three inhabitants of the hotel during the film.
The name, Edith Cushing, has 12 letters.	The name, Jack Torrance, has 12 letters.
Mia Wasikowska portrays Edith Cushing. The name, Mia Wasikowska, has 13 letters.	Jack Nicholson portrays Jack Torrance. The name, Jack Nicholson, has 13 letters.
While sitting in Ogilvie's (Jonathan Hyde) office, Edith tries to persuade him to publish her manuscript.	While sitting in Ullman's office, Jack tries to persuade him to hire him as the winter caretaker.
Gruesome murders have occurred inside Allerdale Hall.	Ghastly murders have occurred inside the Overlook Hotel.
Edith Cushing is tormented by ghosts.	Jack Torrance is tormented by ghosts.
Edith Cushing's wardrobe consists of golden yellow frocks and dresses.	Jack Torrance drives a yellow Volkswagon Beetle.
The estate's name, Allerdale Hall, has 13 letters.	The resort's name, Overlook Hotel, has 13 letters.
Allerdale Hall sits on a mountain in Cumberland, England.	The Overlook Hotel sits on a mountain in Colorado, United States.

Crimson Peak	The Shining
Edith Cushing attends a party with wealthy aloof American elites most of whom are superficial.	Jack Torrance attends a party with wealthy aloof American elites who happen to be ghosts.
Edith Cushing is warned by the ghost of her dead mother to beware of Crimson Peak	Danny Torrance is warned by his imaginary friend, Tony, to beware of the Overlook Hotel.
Edith Cushing conspicuously uses a typewriter.	Jack Torrance conspicuously uses a typewriter.
Inside an opulent men's room, Carter Cushing solicits the truth about Sir Thomas and Lady Lucille from Mr. Holly.	Inside an opulent men's room, Jack Torrance solicits the truth about the Overlook Hotel and his son's extrasensory talent from Mr. Grady.
The name, Holly, has 5 letters.	The name, Grady, has 5 letters.
Alan McMichael can see ghosts via spirit photography.	Dick Hallorann can see ghosts via the ability to "shine."
The name, Alan McMichael, has 13 letters.	The name, Dick Hallorann, has 13 letters.
McMichael explains ghosts and supernatural phenomenon to Edith, "Now, it's my belief that houses, places, be it by chemical compounds in the earth or the minerals in the stone can retain impressions or a person that is no longer living." Edith responds, "Perhaps we only notice things when the time comes for us to see them." The high-water mark of this conversation occurs 23 minutes 7 seconds into the film.	Hallorann explains ghosts and the ability to "shine" to Danny, "It's just that you know some places are like people, some shine and some don't. I guess you could say the Overlook Hotel here has something about it that's like shining… when something happens it can leave a trace of itself behind… Not things that anyone can notice, but things that people who shine can see.…" Danny then asks Hallorann about room 237.
To pass the time at Allerdale Hall, Edith plays Go Fetch, throwing a red rubber ball for her dog to retrieve.	To pass the time at the Overlook Hotel, Jack throws a tennis ball against the wall.
In Allerdale Hall, a ghost rolls the red rubber ball to Edith while she is playing with her dog.	In the Overlook Hotel, a ghost rolls a tennis ball to Danny while he is playing with his toys.
Some parts of Allerdale Hall are off limits: Edith is told to stay out of the clay pits in the basement. The body of the Sharpe's dead mother is hidden there (along with other secrets). She does not heed the admonition and investigates the basement.	Some parts of the Overlook Hotel are off limits: Danny is told to stay out of room 237. A ghost of an evil woman lurks there. He does not heed the admonition and investigates the room.
Allerdale Hall has long dark labyrinth corridors and an elevator.	The Overlook Hotel has long dark labyrinth corridors and an elevator.

Crimson Peak	*The Shining*
While at Allerdale Hall, Lucille corrupts Edith by serving her poisoned tea making her anemic.	While at the Overlook Hotel, Lloyd corrupts Jack by serving him alcohol making him psychotic.
While at Allerdale Hall, Edith wears yellow, symbolizing butterflies and the sun. She is a beacon of light in a dark place.	While at the Overlook Hotel, Danny wears an Apollo 11 sweater because he personifies the alchemical *citrinitas*, or the sun. He is a beacon of light in a dark place.
Edith discovers a murderous conspiracy going on inside Allerdale Hall involving the Sharpes. Thumbing through documents and photos, she realizes something is terribly wrong as a wax recording of Sir Thomas reciting the English ditty-nursery rhyme "Ding Dong Bell" plays: "Ding dong bell, kitty's in the well. Who put her in? Little Johnny Thin. Who pulled her out? Little Johnny Stout. Oh what a naughty boy was that who tried to drown poor pussy cat…" Sir Thomas' weird and uneasy recording indicates madness.	Wendy discovers a murderous conspiracy going on inside the Overlook Hotel. She realizes something is terribly wrong when she discovers Jack's manuscript only features the proverb, "All work and no play makes *Jack* a dull boy," typed over and over again as she flips through the pages. She realizes her husband has gone mad. Later, while wielding an ax and ready to kill, Jack recites the English nursery rhyme, *The Three Little Pigs*, epitomizing homicidal madness.
While at Allerdale Hall, Edith has a prophetic nightmare of a red ghost in the distance pointing towards something. Later, she encounters this specter floating around the staircase pointing towards Lucille's bedroom.	While at the Overlook Hotel, Jack has a prophetic nightmare about murdering Wendy and Danny with an ax. Later, he tries to kill them with an ax.
Blood red clay saturates Allerdale Hall, symbolizing the murders that have occurred there.	Danny writes the word, *REDRUM*, in red on a door symbolizing the murders that have occurred in the Overlook Hotel.
McMichael discovers Edith may be in peril at Allerdale Hall, deciding to go there to investigate. He travels a great distance to do this.	Hallorann discovers the Torrance family may be in peril at the Overlook Hotel, deciding to go there to investigate. He travels a great distance to do this.
A blizzard hits Cumberland and Allerdale Hall. The winter storm impedes travel substantially.	A blizzard hits Colorado and the Overlook Hotel. The winter storm impedes travel substantially.
In Lucille's bedroom, Edith observes a sexual perversity, seeing Lady Lucille and Sir Thomas engaging in passionate incestuous foreplay.	In one of the hotel rooms, Wendy onbserves a sexual perversity, seeing a ghost perform fellatio on another ghost.

Crimson Peak	The Shining
Edith is pushed backward off a balcony, landing hard on the floor below, rendering her unconscious. Edith injures her leg in the fall.	Jack is knocked backward down a flight of stairs, landing hard on the floor below, rendering him unconscious. Jack injures his leg in the fall.
On his way to Allerdale Hall, McMichael stops at a depot to get assistance so he can get to the mansion during a blizzard. The manager agrees to meet him there in the morning. As night falls, McMichael makes his way to the mansion.	On his way to the Overlook Hotel, Hallorann calls Larry Durkin to get assistance so he can get to the hotel during a blizzard. Durkin agrees to let him use a Sno-Cat. As night falls, Hallorann makes his way to the hotel.
Shortly after arriving at Allerdale Hall, McMichael is wounded in the stomach with a knife. He survives.	Shortly after arriving at the Overlook Hotel, Hallorann is wounded in the stomach with an ax. He dies.
Lucille becomes enraged when Thomas suggests they abandon Allerdale Hall because he is worried about Edith's deteriorating condition. This catalyst ignites Lucille's anger, sparking her killing spree.	Jack becomes enraged when Wendy suggests they abandon the Overlook Hotel because she is worried about Danny's deteriorating condition. This catalyst ignites Jack's anger, sparking his killing spree.
Edith defends herself with a large kitchen knife against Lucille's murderous rampage. Edith wounds Lucille's left hand as she is coming through the elevator door.	Wendy defends herself with a large kitchen knife against Jack's murderous rampage. Wendy wounds Jack's left hand as he is coming through the bathroom door.
Lady Lucille attacks Edith with an oversized hatchet-styled cleaver.	Jack attacks Wendy with a hatchet.
Edith and Lady Lucille fight outside in the blizzard in a labyrinth formed by construction equipment and the clay harvester. Edith kills Lucille.	Danny eludes Jack outside in a hedge maze during a blizzard. Danny escapes, and Jack freezes to death.
By movie's end, the snow covering Allerdale Hall turns blood red from the clay deposits beneath the surface. The color red is everywhere.	By movie's end, the elevator doors of the Overlook Hotel open pouring gallons of blood down the hallway. The color red is everywhere.
During *Crimson Peak*, it is clear that Edith, Sir Thomas, and Lady Lucille are trapped inside Allerdale Hall becoming part of the ghostly mansion.	During *The Shining*, it is clear that Jack, Wendy, and Danny Torrance are trapped inside the Overlook becoming part of the ghostly hotel.
Two people survive Allerdale Hall: Edith Cushing and Alan McMichael.	Two people survive the Overlook Hotel: Wendy and Danny Torrance.

Crimson Peak	The Shining
The ending of *Crimson Peak* is its beginning: Edith, dressed in her white nightgown and her bloody hands, looking at the ghost of Sir Thomas. Furthermore, *Crimson Peak* starts in Buffalo, New York, in the autumn approximately ten days before Halloween; the date on the check Carter Cushing cuts to the Sharpes is dated October 21st, 1901. When Edith goes to Allerdale Hall, winter comes in the form of an unrelenting blizzard.	The ending of *The Shining* is it beginning: Jack, driving on the *Going-to-the-Sun* Road, its construction began in 1921. It takes Jack 3 ½ hours to get to the Overlook which is 210 minutes. The number 21 is also the film's end: the July 4th, 1921 framed photo featuring Torrance-Grady hangs in a cluster of 21 photos. Furthermore, *The Shining* starts in Colorado in the autumn with the Torrance family arriving at the Overlook Hotel on Halloween. Winter soon follows in the form of an unrelenting blizzard.

Is this all a coincidence? This author doesn't think so and continues to investigate these two analogous movies post publication of this book.

Stripping away *Crimson Peak's* ostentatious veneer, one is presented with a sinister and complex interpretation of del Toro's masterpiece; for within *Crimson Peak* all is not what it appears to be. Keyholes imply keys, and keys unlock doors or symbolically solve mysteries; for within Allerdale Hall's long dark corridors and bleeding walls we find allusions to insanity, leaving this author convinced *Crimson Peak* hides esoteric symbolism, but the movie is, behind the veil, a story about mental illness and a descent into murder. What is presented on screen is not reality; rather, an occult matrix is interwoven within *Crimson Peak*. Within this secret paradigm another story is told, something much more profound than a mere damsel in distress, linked to a marriage and murder scheme. In other words, there is an ambiguous paradigm locked away in *Crimson Peak's* gothic landscape. To perceive this latent template, one must become a detective by observing and interpreting the relevant aspects of this movie as metaphoric clues. When these clues are deciphered, this author is convinced an alternative exposition surfaces; it is a distorted solipsistic panorama existing in Edith's troubled psyche. Edith sees what she wants to see; her surroundings are illusionary and her story, also titled *Crimson Peak*, is a projection of her tortured subconscious. Edith's unconscious energies have overwhelmed all conscious and rational perceptions; unconscious turbulence demonizes reasonable understanding. A complex psychotopographic[363] construct unfolds when *Crimson Peak* is decoded correctly: it becomes evident Edith is mentally disturbed evidenced by her ghostly visions, a symptom of an undiagnosed mental condition, likely schizophrenia, but also her guilty conscience because Ms. Edith Cushing is a murderess.

Edith has seen apparitions since she was a child, continuing to do so into adulthood. After being visited by her mother's black ghost, a moth lands on one of the hallway's gaslights, foreshadowing the coming of Lucille. Edith meets Sir Thomas, falling in love with him, but his insolvency prompts her wealthy father to end their relationship. Heartbroken, Sir Thomas departs for England but remains a splinter in Edith's fractured mind. Lady Lucille is not real; rather, she Edith's shadow brought to life, the evil unconscious side of her personality; put another way, Lucille is nothing more than Edith's Mr. Hyde, her Tyler Durden, more akin to John Shooter (John Turturro) in *Secret Window* (2004). Enraged that her father[364] terminated the romance, Edith becomes Lucille, savagely murdering him, apprehended by Holly the investigator. Edith is tried and sentenced to a deteriorating mental institution named Crimson Peak. Allerdale Hall is an anagram for *All Red Hell*, which not only references its crimson name, but also to the harsh conditions of the antiquated hellish, insane asylum. The staff and workers of the mental institution never appear; instead, it is experienced through Edith's delusional paranoid fantasies. Her reality is this: upon arriving, Edith wishes to escape the psychiatric hospital, symbolized by a master set of prison-like cell keys which she wants but can never obtain; they're a token of liberation. The poisoned tea is a metaphor for the various drugs and medications she is forced to take at the institution which she believes are making her ill. Crimson Peak's infernal automated clay harvester is a metaphor for the asylum's monotony. Like most sanitariums and mental institutions from the era, Crimson Peak has an old-style iron caged elevator. "Secrets everywhere," Lucille tells Edith showing her a book with a fore-edge painting depicting an Asian couple in the sexual po-

---

363 Victoria Nelson, *The Secret Life of Puppets*, pp. 110-111. She uses this term to describe literature in which the "inner psyche processes are projected sympathetically onto an exterior landscape."

364 Earlier, when Carter Cushing gives his daughter the gold pen, his gaze becomes suspicious like he is worried about something. He does not appear concerned that his daughter wishes to use a typewriter, instead he stares at his daughter like there is something seriously wrong with her.

sition *soixante-neuf* (69) which repulses her, imitating *Repulsion*'s Carol Ledoux (Catherine Deneuve), a young woman disgusted by sex. Edith passes off her disinterest in sex as mourning for her father, but beneath her prudish ego she knows Lucille, her shadowy unconscious, is correct: there are secrets everywhere, revealing and concealing.

Later, when Edith investigates the mansion and discovers the mural, she wears a bright yellow dress with a large black bow (implying wings) with two long black ribbons, symbolic of a malignant blackness that cuts through her otherwise sunny personality. The stark yellow and black costume suggests another insect, the bumblebee, a bug that toils in its dark hive becoming a metaphor for Edith, languishing away in a bleak insane asylum. The mural of children[365] playing with a humanoid insect denotes fantasy, not reality, and Sir Thomas' workshop is a metaphor for the other lunatics inside the asylum; Sir Thomas' carvings have strange, creepy faces. His mechanical toys represent the child-like mental states of some of the inmates. When Edith and Thomas are snowed in at the depot, Thomas reads her manuscript remarking, "This fellow Cavendish, your hero. There's a darkness to him. I like him. Does he make it all the way through?" Edith responds, "It's entirely up to him…Characters talk to you. They transform. They make choices." Cavendish is clearly a representation of Thomas, still part of Edith's cracked psyche. Her imaginary characters speak to her, implying insanity; she doesn't even know what they will do within her story. The labyrinthine house *qua* lunatic asylum only adds to her madness; its dark nooks and crannies, its phonographs and wax cylinder recordings reflect Edith's unhinged and overactive imagination. Edith wakes from gloomy dreams not knowing what is real and what is imaginary. She has no intimate relationships inside the asylum, the consummation of her marriage is a mere sexual fantasy which occurs beyond its walls; there is no sex inside the asylum. However, this taboo erotica,[366] much like the fore-edge book, upsets her ego, bringing forth Lucille from her subconscious. Lucille is now forced to punish Edith: she throws herself off a balcony, injuring her leg. Later, Lucille uses a knife to slash Edith's face.

---

365 The mural is a nod to another of del Toro's movies, *Pan's Labyrinth* (2006).

366 Edith sees herself as Lucille engaging in foreplay with Sir Thomas; this is most likely an allegory for masturbation. This is a reference to Wasikowska's performance in *Stoker* when she masturbates while fantasizing about murder denoting mental illness.

While confined at Crimson Peak, Edith wears a long flowing white nightgown, suggesting a straitjacket or the white pajamas, white shirts and slippers of those confined to a mental institution. Due to her self-destructive behavior and the injuries she has wrought to herself, her medication dosage is increased, symbolized by poisoned porridge, confining Edith to a wheelchair. McMichael is not an ophthalmologist; instead, he is a physician at the asylum. Edith is under his care at Crimson Peak; he sets her injured leg because he understands human anatomy.[367] The characters of Lady Lucille and Sir Thomas do not exist inside Crimson Peak, instead they are fragments, or psychological projections emanating from Edith's deranged mind; because she is a murderer she spends most of her time in isolation symbolized by the name Enola, which is *alone* spelled backward. Edith is obsessed with this name, trying to unravel its mystery but is unable to decipher its true meaning. Lucille confesses to Edith that she murdered her mother when she was a child, suggesting that Edith also killed her mother when she was a little girl; perhaps Mrs. Cushing was poisoned, its symptoms passed off as Black Cholera. Edith, like Lucille, was never suspected because the idea of a child murdering a parent was too much to bear; this is explained by McMichael, "There was no one else in the house at the time, only the children. The truth was too horrible to consider." McMichael

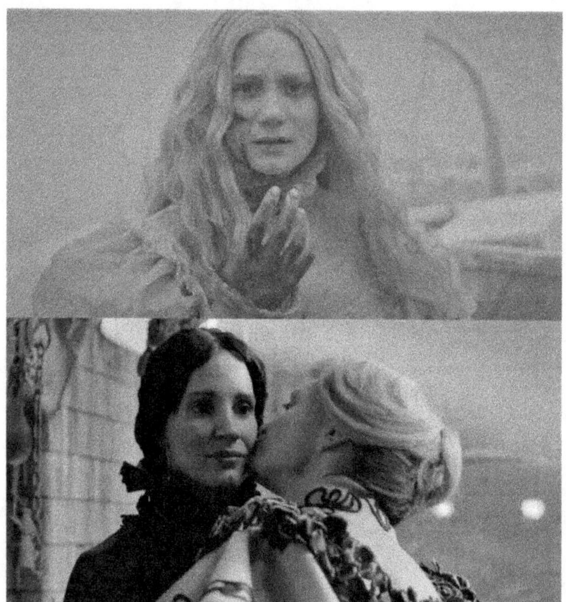

(Top) Edith Cushing with blood on her hands. Is there a deeper symbolism to this stark, ghostly imagery which opens and closes the movie? Edith's cheek is slashed and bloody because del Toro uses cheeks as a repetitive device to indicate duality. (Bottom) Edith gently kisses Lucille on the cheek upon arriving at Allerdale Hall. Lucille is pleasantly surprised by the kiss, suggesting that she, and perhaps Edith, are bisexual.

---

367 Remember, Sir Thomas asks McMichael where he should stab him to cause the least amount of injury. McMichael knows the precise location because he is a physician, not an eye doctor.

then remarks that Lucille was placed in a mental institution, an apt reference to Edith's current confinement.

Edith also bears the Mark of Cain of Genesis 4:11-16 when God cursed Cain for killing his brother Abel, Edith is likewise branded for murdering her mother. While editing her manuscript in Samuel Ogilvie's office, Edith accidentally smears black ink on her forehead, identifying her with darkness, evil and the cold of winter;[368] she then tells Ogilvie that in her novel, "The ghost is…a metaphor for the past," subtly indicating she is haunted by her past evil deed, being tormented by her mother's black ghost. During the film's opening montage, which is also its closing sequence, Edith has blood on her hands dissolving to her mother's coffin being carried by pallbearers, signifying Edith is the murderer. The red ghosts she imagines in Crimson Peak are also metaphors for the past; they're morbid manifestations symbolizing the bloody murder of her father, for which she has been sentenced to a madhouse for the rest of her life. Edith Cushing, like Jack Torrance, is a psychotic monster.

At first, this interpretation, my fan theory, may be difficult to grasp, so hone your vision by putting on Edith's reading glasses, examining the occult cinematic evidence objectively. Both Lucille and Edith are symbolized by opposing aspects of the same thing, winged insects: Lucille is the moth (darkness, shadow self) while Edith is the butterfly (light, ego); the two women identify with insects, because the word *insect* is an anagram for *incest* signifying the love, or lust, both women share with Sir Thomas. Another parallel indicating that Lucille and Edith are different aspects of the same person is the manner in which one of their parents was murdered: Beatrice Sharpe dies as a result of a massive head wound mirroring Carter Cushing, who also dies as a result of massive head injuries. The brutal murders of Edith's father and Lucille's mother recall the infamous ax murders of Andrew and Abby Borden on August 4th, 1892. Like Beatrice and Carter, Andrew and Abby died from having their heads viciously bludgeoned. Andrew's spinster daughter Lizzie Borden (1860-1927) was suspected, tried for the murders but found not guilty because, "…The truth was too horrible to consider." The date on the *Cumberland Illustrated News* graphically documenting Beatrice Sharpe's bloodthirsty murder is August 16, 1879, anticipating the Borden murders of August

---

368 See Pike's *Morals and Dogma*, p. 662.

1892. Afterward, Lucille was sent to a mental institution as suspected by Dr. McMichael; so too was Edith likewise incarcerated because she is the murderer. Finally, Edith *qua* Lucille comes to understand she murdered her father out of her love for Thomas so she could inherit his wealthy estate (this was Lizzie Borden's motive as well) living happily ever after; in the darkest recesses of her mind, Edith finally understands "the horror was for love." Lucille, Edith's shadow persona, now kills Sir Thomas; moments later outside in the snow, Lucille sees a specter for the first and only time; Lucille *sees* Thomas' pale spirit. Having killed her brother, his ghost is a projection of Lucille's guilty conscience, just as Edith's wraiths are a projection of her guilty conscience. Lucille is guilty of fratricide, just as Edith is guilty of parricide; *the ghost is a metaphor for the past.* Put another way, the ghosts of *Crimson Peak* can only be seen by their killer: Edith killed her mother so she can see her black ghost, she killed her father so his ghost manifests as the red phantoms tormenting her inside Crimson Peak, and Lucille can see the ghost of Sir Thomas. Since Edith *can also see* Sir Thomas' spirit *but did not kill him*, this proves Edith and Lucille are one and the same person. The deaths of Lucille and Thomas symbolize Edith's attempt to reconcile her mental condition and the divergent sides of her personality, tearfully realizing the siblings are nothing more than phantasms. Edith remains in the madhouse placed under McMichael's care, symbolized by the two of them together in the somber white limbo at film's conclusion; her life bookended by an empty past and a nihilistic future. Edith's solar light has been extinguished once and for all.

This alternative interpretation is confirmed by the contradictory and dreamlike images presented when the end credits roll; these images are critical to understanding this occult explanation. Edith's inability to grasp reality is symbolized by pinned down butterflies which should be dead but instead flap their wings; like Edith they are dead to the world, imprisoned, but alive. One pinned down butterflies is even situated with Edith's Victorian clasped hands belt implying Edith is pinned down; try as she might, she might, she cannot fly away from the madhouse. The dead flies Edith discovers upon first entering Crimson Peak are now alive and buzzing, symbolizing the filth and degenerate conditions often associated with asylums.

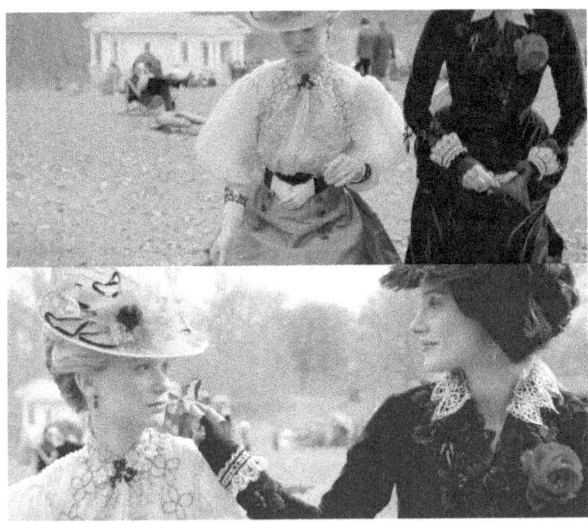

(Top and Bottom) Picnic in the Park: Edith and Lucille kibitz while examining dying butterflies in a Buffalo park; Lucille caresses Edith's cheek with a butterfly. Edith wears a distinguishable clasped hands belt, one hand over the other, which also appears during the end credits juxtaposed with a pinned down butterfly evoking imprisonment. Does Edith's belt symbolize something else, something sexual? Lucille, dressed in deathly black, personifies Edith's shadow self; Lucille is a psychological archetypal projection resurrected from the deepest, darkest depths of Edith's subconscious. The black cobweb pattern on Edith's blouse symbolizes the shadowy web that Lucille and Thomas are weaving around her. Alternatively, the cobweb could signify the emergence of her shadow self from the depths of her subconscious, taking shape as Lady Lucille.

There is water on the floor of the menacing spiked hallway symbolizing the efforts to keep the institution sanitized. Her expensive gold pen now erratically spews black ink, denoting chaos, and the typewriter she used at film's beginning is offset between a reflex hammer, a syringe, and a stethoscope. The three out-of-place medical devices are persuasive symbolic evidence that the user of the typewriter, Edith Cushing, is in a mental hospital under a doctor's supervision. The pages of Edith's manuscript appear smoldering, which occurs when Lucille tosses Edith's manuscript in the furnace, indicating her story was never written because it was destroyed. However, at the very end (it's the final image) the cover of her book, *Crimson Peak*, is displayed with Edith's name on it, indicating the story just presented is an account of her ghostly experiences at Crimson Peak. *But we know she did not write it* because, in truth, she is confined in a madhouse. How can this be reconciled? Go back to the start of the movie; after young Edith is haunted by her mother's ghost, the same exact light green, red-skulled book cover appears on screen. *Crimson Peak* is now presented; the book opens to Buffalo, but Edith's name is missing from the cover. The only logical explanation is that Edith never wrote the novel because she is insane, a patient at a mental institution called Crimson Peak. Thereafter, McMichael suggests this account is the correct interpretation saying,

"Now, that man will never perceive the colors red or green. He only accepts their existence because the majority around him does," implying the red and green *Crimson Peak* book cover, and the red and green hues that pervade the movie, are illusionary; the story is not literal even though *the majority* will perceive it as such. Edith's response to this is, "Perhaps we only notice things when the time comes for us to see them," only Edith is talking about herself, and her inability to separate reality from fantasy. The only conclusion that can be drawn is that the movie's exoteric plot should be negated because it isn't *real*; it is both allusion and illusion simultaneously, signified by its prevailing red-green color scheme. *Crimson Peak's* hidden ambiguities ensure that there will never be one definitive conclusive interpretation; we will forever remain in a hermeneutical limbo.

Are Edith's ghosts real or not? Are her surroundings real or imaginary? Wasikowska's past cinematic baggage subconsciously augments the idea that Edith's reality is an imaginary construct and what she's experiencing is a latent metaphor for murder and madness. In other words, the casting of Mia Wasikowska as Edith Cushing is occult in nature, harmoniously reinforcing the underlying imagery that Edith is mad and locked away in a lunatic asylum. While in England, Edith drinks tea at Crimson Peak, recalling the Mad Hatter's tea party from *Alice in Wonderland*. In 2010, Wasikowska played the title character of Alice in Disney's adaptation of *Alice in Wonderland*, which forges a nexus between Edith's tea drinking and the lunacy associated with the Hatter, his discombobulated tea party, and the discordianism found in Wonderland. The link between *Crimson Peaks's* Edith Cushing and Alice in *Alice in Wonderland* is forged during the end credits. Jessica Chastain's name correctly appears before a moth, the red rose from her dress worn during the picnic scene, and a caged butterfly, all perfectly symbolizing Lucille. Tom Hiddleston's name naturally appears before Sir Thomas' tools in his workshop; and Charlie Hunnam's name materializes before medical devices, indicating McMichael is a physician, not an ophthalmologist. If he were an ophthalmologist, Hunnam's name would be surrounded by spectacles, an ophthalmotrope, glass eyes, and an optometer. Wasikowska's name appears before a teapot, two tea jars, and a tea cup which, at first, seems improper because her name should be with a typewriter, a butterfly, or her gold pen.

However, her name placed around tea-related items dovetails with the hidden undercurrent that Edith is mad, confined to a mental institution. The tea she consumes during the film recollects from the subconscious mind the madness surrounding Wonderland's nonsensical Hatter and his weird tea party.[369] Edith is locked away in a madhouse named Crimson Peak because she is mad as a hatter.

Wasikowska's casting as Edith also alludes to her performance in 2013's *Stoker*, a movie released two and a half years before *Crimson Peak*, tying into the idea that *Crimson Peak* is all about patricide and Edith's descent into madness. Wasikowska's India Stoker (see Chapter XI for the full esoteric breakdown of the film) is a young woman becoming a murdering psychopath, suggesting that Wasikowska's Edith is likewise a murderess. Not surprisingly, there are aspects of *Crimson Peak* that imitate *Stoker*. For example, like *The Shining* both movies feature a dwelling that is a character. Both India and Edith have relationships with untrustworthy men to free themselves from a repressive family dynamic. India stabs a bully with a pencil, foreshadowing Edith stabbing Lucille with a pen. India pleasures herself while taking a shower, symbolized by Edith when she wears a clasped-hands belt tightly around her waist with its fingers pressed slightly above her erogenous zone, subtly denoting masturbation. India uses a mysterious key to unlock family secrets just like Edith using a mysterious key to unlock family secrets. As such, Wasikowska's casting as Edith Cushing is motivated by her previous performances in *Alice in Wonderland* and *Stoker* because Guillermo del Toro's brooding film is a metaphor for Edith murdering her father and being confined to a madhouse; this is the esoteric phantasmagoria of *Crimson Peak*. In this author's opinion, this subtext transforms *Crimson Peak* from a ghostly gothic romance into a multilayered occult symbolic masterpiece. Although *Identity* and *Lost Highway* (see Chapter III) flirt with similar psychological themes, this author can think of no other movie quite like *Crimson Peak*. Accordingly, in the next 5 to 15 years this author predicts *Crimson Peak* will be considered a cult classic following in the footsteps of films like *Barbarella* (1968), *The Rocky Horror Picture Show* (1975), *Plan 9*

---

369 In Disney's 2010 adaptation of *Alice in Wonderland*, the Mad Hatter was played by Johnny Depp. Wasikowska and Depp reprised their roles as Alice and the Mad Hatter in 2016's *Alice Through the Looking Glass*.

from Outer Space, *12 Monkeys* (1995), *Harold and Maude* (1971), *The Warriors*, *This is Spinal Tap* (1984), *The Toxic Avenger* (1984), *The Evil Dead* (1981), *Big Trouble in Little China* (1986), *Office Space* (1999), and *Fight Club*.

* * * *

Horror movies perfectly reflect the alchemical *nigredo*, the tumultuous darkness that lives in us all. They allow us to view our shadows within the safety of a movie theater or in the shelter of our living rooms without consequence. When children watch a horror movie for the first time they are usually traumatized, but their anxiety is relieved by a parent telling them, "It's only a movie." As we get older we come to learn that horror films can be reality; look no further than the atrocities of Nazi Germany, the terror of Helter Skelter, or the sickening murders of Jeffrey Dahmer (1960-1994) whose bizarre, cannibalistic crimes mirrored those of a film that was popular at the time of his arrest in July 1991: *The Silence of the Lambs*, released on February 13th, 1991. The postulation of horror films *qua* reality *qua* horror films was summed up perfectly in 1996's *Scream* when Sidney Prescott (Neve Campbell) responds to Billy Loomis' (Skeet Ulrich) comment about *The Silence of the Lambs*; she says, "But this is life. This isn't a movie," to which he replies, "Sure it is, Sid. It's all, it's all a movie. It's all one great big movie. Only you can't pick your genre."

CHAPTER VI

FREEMASONRY IN POPULAR CULTURE

"Nobody puts Baby in a corner."
– Johnny Castle, *Dirty Dancing*, 1987

"Give my regards to King Tut, asshole."
– Colonel Jonathan "Jack" O'Neil, *Stargate*, 1994.

"Without books, we have neither a past nor a future."
– Ichabod Crane from the episode "The Golem," *Sleepy Hollow*, 2013.

"Don't fuck with me!"
– Liana Telfer, *The Ninth Gate*, 1999.

"The Toad Style is immensely strong and
immune to nearly any weapon. When it's properly used,
it's almost invincible. It can even bend solid metal."
– Venom House Instructor, *Five Deadly Venoms*, 1978.

"Look around you, all of you, what do you see?
A bunch of buffoons in fancy dress. You think the Prince of Darkness
would actually deign to manifest himself before the likes of you?
He never has and he never will. Never!"
– Boris Balkan, *The Ninth Gate*, 1999.

"♫ Frosty the Snowman is a fairy tale they say.
He was made of snow but the children know
that he came to life one day. ♫"
– Cocteau Twins, lyrics from the song "Frosty the Snowman," 1993.

The number forty-seven signifies Masonic rulership; it is an occult reference to the 47th Proposition (or Problem) of Euclid, which is also the Pythagorean Theorem, or a Pythagorean Triangle. Two of its sides symbolize sun gods, Osiris and Horus, while the third represents Isis the moon goddess; the triangle is an operation of the sun and moon which are two of the lesser lights of Freemasonry. It is the emblem of a Masonic Worshipful Master, governing his lodge by sitting in the east *qua* the rising sun. Does the number forty-seven, when applied to cinema, indicate Masonic involvement? Examining the evidence, the answer to this question appears to be *yes*. There are *47 Ronin* (2013), a Japanese legend signifying the loyalty, sacrifice, persistence, and the honor that people should preserve and reflect upon in their daily lives. These oriental, timeless teachings synchronize perfectly with the philosophies of both the Blue Lodge and high degree Masonry. In 2015, we were introduced to *Hitman: Agent 47*,[370] a mysterious assassin (Rupert Friend) who works for a top-secret non-government organization called the International Contracts Agency (known as either the ICA or just the Agency), reflecting Masonry's secretive and conspiratorial nature. In *Star Wars: The Force Awakens*, it is revealed during a high-level meeting (cf. a Masonic cabal) of the Resistance that the First Order's Starkiller Base's superweapon is charged by the sun; thus, its thermal oscillator, the device which harnesses the sun's power, is located in Precinct 47.

This chapter explores Hollywood's fascination with Freemasonry and Masonry's influence–whether sought or unsought–upon the entertainment industry. Some explanation and information must first be given about Freemasonry before this chapter proceeds. Modern-day nonsectarian Blue Lodge Freemasonry was established in London, England on June 24th, 1717; its rituals, philosophies, and symbols derive from the Abrahamic faiths as well as mystical sources. Included among these are Kabbalah, Christian Cabala, Sufism, astrology, the Egyptian Osirian Cycle, sacred geometry, Rosicrucianism, Gnosticism, and the Ancient Mystery Religions such as Mithraism and the Rites of Eleusis. High degree Freemasonry was born out of Andrew Michael "the Chevalier" Ramsay's (1686-1743) Oration of 1737, wherein Ramsay declared Freemasonry owed its origins to an order of medieval Roman Catholic warriors known as the Knights

---

370 Agent 47 was originally played by Timothy Olyphant in 2007's *Hitman*.

Templar. The Templars, it seems, incorporated the spiritual exercises of various Mystery Religions that they encountered during the Crusades in the Holy Land, finding their way into Craft Freemasonry. These high or *haute* grades of Masonry were further developed by the Society of Jesus at the College of Clermont in the 1740s and 1750s as a vehicle of the Counter-Reformation to restore the Stuart Pretenders to the throne of England. These twenty-five (twenty-two, in reality, the first three degrees are those of the Blue Lodge) high degrees eventually influenced the creation of both the Scottish Rite and the York Rite in the United States years later. Of utmost importance within these high degrees is the Royal Arch of Enoch ceremonial, the 13th degree of the Scottish Rite and the 7th degree of the York Rite. This paramount ritual documents the recovery and restoration of what was lost in the Blue Lodge upon the death of Hiram Abif: the secret name of God, the Tetragrammaton, from which all wisdom, light, or enlightenment emanates (cf. *I Enoch*).

Brothers of the Masonic Fraternity have exerted a tremendous influence upon the fabric of history. Dr. James H. Billington explains:

The rituals leading to each new level of membership were not, as is sometimes suggested, childish initiations. They were awesome rites of passage into new types of associations, promising access to higher truths of Nature once the blindfold was removed in the inner room of the lodge. Each novice sought to become a 'free' and 'perfected' Mason capable of reading the plans of the 'Divine Architect' for 'rebuilding the temple of Solomon,' and reshaping the secular order with moral force.[371]

Freemasonry also impacts Hollywood. Many actors and filmmakers from the Golden Age of Hollywood were Masons including Clark Gable (1901-1960), Cecil B. DeMille, Joe E. Brown (1891-1973), Tom Mix (1880-1940), William "Bud" Abbott (1895-1974), Audie Murphy (1925-1971), Douglass Fairbanks Sr. (1883-1939), W.C. Fields (1880-1946), Elmo Lincoln (1889-1952), Ernest Borgnine (1917-2012), Oliver Hardy (1892-1857), Al Jolson (1886-1950), Richard Bernard "Red" Skelton (1913-1997), Roy Rogers (1911-1998), Gene Autry (1907-1998), Will Rogers (1879-1935), Louis

---

371 James H. Billington, *Fire in the Minds of Men*, p. 92.

B. Mayer (1884-1957), and John Wayne (1907-1979). Modern Hollywood Masons include Richard Pryor (1940-2005), Michael Richards, Telly Savalas (1922-1994), and Bronson Pinchot.[372] Today, the late-night talk show *Jimmy Kimmel Live!* films at the old Hollywood Masonic Temple (adjacent El Capitan Theatre) which was built in 1921. Stories of a secret tunnel running from Grauman's Chinese Theater under Hollywood Boulevard to the Masonic Temple have been confirmed by current ABC employees of the show; however, the tunnel has been sealed off, no longer accessible. What Hollywood's elite used this tunnel for (likely part of a network of catacombs) remains a mystery and is open to speculation.

Critical to this chapter and the next, titled "The Illuminati in Film," are other secret societies-fraternal orders such as the Odd Fellows, Madame Blavatsky's Theosophical Society, the Hermetic Order of the Golden Dawn and the *Ordo Templi Orientis* (Order of the Eastern Templars) better known as the O.T.O. The Golden Dawn was:

One of the most influential Western occult societies of the late 19th to early 20th century. Like a meteor, it flared into light, blazed a bright trail and then disintegrated. Members included W. B. Yeats, A.E. Waite, ALEISTER CROWLEY and other noted occultists.

…The key founder was Dr. William Wynn Westcott, a London coroner and Rosicrucian. In 1887 Westcott obtained part of a manuscript written in brown-ink cipher from the Rev. A. F. A. Woodford, a Mason. The manuscript appeared to be old but probably was not. From his Hermetic knowledge, Westcott was able to decipher the manuscript and discovered it concerned (*sic*) fragments of rituals for the 'Golden Dawn,' an unknown organization that apparently admitted both men and women.

Westcott asked an occultist friend, Samuel Liddel MacGregor Mathers, to flesh out the fragments into full-scale rituals. Some papers evidently were forged to give the 'Golden Dawn' authenticity and a history. It was said to be an old German occult order. Westcott produced papers that showed he had been given a charter to set up an independent lodge in England. The Isis- Urania Temple of the Hermetic Order of the Golden Dawn was established in 1888, with Westcott, Mathers, and Dr. W. R.

---

372 See Chapter XV, "So Dark the Con of Man," of Sullivan's *The Royal Arch of Enoch.*

Woodman, Supreme Magus of the Rosicrucian Society of Anglia, as the three Chiefs. The secret society quickly caught on, and 315 initiations took place during the society's heyday, from 1888-1896.

An elaborate hierarchy was created, consisting of ten degrees each corresponding to the 10 Sephiroth of the Tree of Life of the KABBALAH, plus an eleventh degree for neophytes. The degrees are divided into three orders: Outer, Second and Third.

One advanced through the Outer Order by examination. Initially, Westcott, Mathers, and Woodman were the only members of the Second Order, and they claimed to be under the direction of the Secret Chiefs of the Third Order, who were entities of the astral plane. Mathers's [*sic*] rituals were based largely on Freemasonry.

…During its height, the Hermetic Order of the Golden Dawn possessed the greatest known repository of Western magical knowledge. Second Order studies centered on the Kabbalistic Tree of Life. Three magical systems were taught: the Key of Solomon; Abra-Melin magic; and ENOCHIAN MAGIC. Materials were also incorporated from the Egyptian Book of the Dead, William Blake's Prophetic Books and the Chaldean Oracles. Instruction was given in astral travel, SCRYING, alchemy, geomancy, the TAROT and ASTROLOGY.

The key purpose of the order was 'to prosecute the Great Work: which is to obtain control of the nature and power of [one'] own being.' … Elements of Golden Dawn rituals, Rosicrucianism and Freemasonry have been absorbed into the rituals of modern Witchcraft.[373]

While none of the originally charted Golden Dawn temples survived past the 1970s, several organizations have since revived its teachings and rituals. Among these, the following are notable: *Sodalitas Rosae+Crucis et Solis Alati*, the Open Source Order of the Golden Dawn, and the Hermetic Order of the Golden Dawn, Inc.

If the Golden Dawn was androgynous Freemasonry fused with Tarot, sorcery, alchemy, and necromancy, then the O.T.O. was primarily the Golden Dawn only with an added, new element: sex magick. The mantra

---

373 Guiley, *The Encyclopedia of Witches and Witchcraft*, pp.157-159.

of the O.T.O. is the Thelemic "Do what thou wilt shall be the whole of the Law," taken from Crowley's *The Book of the Law* (1904). In the book, *Aleister Crowley: The Nature of the Beast*, Colin Wilson (1931-2013) writes on the history and practices of the O.T.O.:

This event occurred in the following year (1912), when Crowley received an unexpected visit from a German named Theodore Reuss, who introduced himself as a high-ranking German Freemason and the head of a magical order called the OTO - *the Ordo Templi Orientis*, or Order of the Temple of the East. And, to Crowley's astonishment, Ruess accused him of betraying the secrets of the ninth grade of this order. Now it so happened that Crowley *was* a member of the OTO–he had joined it in the previous year. But then, Crowley was a kind of collector of secret societies, and he had joined it thinking it was simply another order of Freemasons (otherwise, why did he call it a temple?). Crowley hastened to point out that he had not reached the ninth grade, and so could not betray its secrets. Reuss then reached out and took from Crowley's shelf his recent work *The Book of Lies*, and pointed to a section that opened: 'Let the adept be armed with his magic rood and provided with his mystic rose.' Reuss was obviously unaware that although 'rood' means rod in old English, it is generally used of a crucifix, and that this is what Crowley meant by it. Crowley had a flash of intuition, and realized that the 'secrets' of the ninth degree were sexual in nature. He and Reuss had a long conversation about magic and sex, and found themselves in close sympathy. And when Reuss left, he had allowed Crowley to found an English branch of the OTO. Crowley had to go to Berlin to be initiated; typically, he chose for himself the magical name Baphomet–the name of the demonic idol that the Knight Templars (*sic*) were accused of worshipping. The rituals of the OTO were not simply an excuse for sexual orgies. The order had been founded around the turn of the century by a rich German named Karl Kellner, and Reuss was his successor. (He seems to have been rather an odd character: a member of the German secret service, a journalist, a music hall singer, and a political agitator who tried to infiltrate the London Marxist organization.) Kellner had been heavily influenced by the branch of Hinduism known as Tantra, an attempt to achieve mystical union with the universe by regarding it as a continuous process of creation. This was blended with orthodox Western magic, which is based upon the belief that the mind can exercise a direct influence on nature. One of the most widespread forms of magic, for example, is the charging of talismans with magical power–a talisman is a 'charm' designed to help its owner to achieve a certain end, such as wealth or sexual conquest or fame. A talisman would normally be 'charged' by the performance of a ritual or ceremonial magic. In the OTO, two 'initiates' would perform a ceremony culminating in a sexual act, concentrating the aim of the magical operation, and end by anointing the talisman with a mixture of sperm and the secretions of the vagina, known as the 'elixir', or amrita.

...Crowley's first act on becoming head of the London OTO was to rewrite all its rituals in his own inimitable style. They are, of course, full of quotations from *The Book of the Law*, and laced with Crowleyan blasphemies, such as a section on the Black Mass in which Crowley attacks Roman Catholicism as 'that base and materialistic cult', and praises practitioners of the Black Mass because 'at least they set up Man against the foul demon of the Christians.'[374]

Also practiced by the O.T.O. is kundalini (coiled one) which in yogic theory is a primal energy, or *Shakti*, located at the base of the spine. Different spiritual traditions teach methods of awakening kundalini for the purpose of reaching spiritual enlightenment. Kundalini has been called an unconscious, instinctive or libidinal force, or "Mother energy or intelligence of complete maturation"[375] important to magical, sexual workings. O.T.O. sex magicks can be heterosexual, homosexual, or solitary depending on the adept's desired result. Crowley and the O.T.O.'s influence stretched across the pond to the United States; specifically, to Los Angeles, movie-making capital of the world. One of Crowley's first American disciples was rocket scientist, inventor, author, and occultist Marvel Whiteside "Jack" Parsons (1914-1952), one of the principal founders of the Jet Propulsion Laboratory founded on Samhain-Halloween, 1936, signifying Parsons' interest in dark occultism-black magic. Parsons was also a founder of the Aerojet

---

374 Colin Wilson, *Aleister Crowley: The Nature of the Beast*, pp. 102-104.
375 See Stuart Sovatsky's *Words from the Soul: Time, East/West Spirituality, and Psychotherapeutic Narrative, passim.*

Engineering Corporation. He invented the first castable, composite solid rocket propellant, and pioneered the advancement of both liquid and solid-fuel rockets-technologies that became pivotal in the Space Age, which ensued long after his lifetime. In 1941 Parsons joined the Agape Lodge, the California-Los Angeles (later Pasadena) branch of the O.T.O. After joining, Parsons conducted the Babalon Working along with poet, actress, artist, and fellow occultist Marjorie Cameron (1922-1995). The Working was a series of occult rituals and ceremonies designed to invoke the Thelemic goddess Babalon to Earth. During the Working, Parsons professed to embody an entity named *Belarion Armillus Al Dajjal*, the Antichrist "…who am come to fulfill the law of the Beast 666 [Crowley]"[376] heralding Armageddon and, for Parsons and Crowley, the end of Judeo-Christianity. Armageddon would culminate in the birth of a new solar age, what Crowley referred to as the Aeon of Horus in *The Book of the Law*. Assisting Parsons and Cameron with the Working was none other than L. Ron Hubbard (1911-1986), science fiction writer and founder of Scientology, using the alias of Frater H.[377] Parsons died in a mysterious explosion in his home at the age of thirty-seven; in 1972 Parsons was honored by the International Astronomical Union, naming a lunar crater after him, Parsons Crater, located on the dark side of the moon.

Of all these secret orders, by far Freemasonry is the most pervasive. The truth is that without Freemasonry, groups such as the Golden Dawn and the O.T.O. probably would not exist. So, without and further ado, it is now time to explore Masonic themes and symbolism in cinema.

Kabbalah, the Scottish Rite of Freemasonry, Dante's Inferno and The Ninth Gate

Loosely based on the novel *The Club Dumas* (1993) by Arturo Perez-Reverte, *The Ninth Gate* is a film this author first analyzed in *The Royal Arch of Enoch* and touched on again in *Cinema Symbolism*. For the benefit

---

376 John Carter, *Sex and Rockets*, p. 162.
377 Some contend Hubbard's alias was Frater X. *Frater* is Latin for *brother*.

of those who have not read *The Royal Arch of Enoch,* this author feels compelled to reinvestigate the occult symbolism of the movie. To those who have read *The Royal Arch of Enoch*, this new analysis, while reiterating and highlighting this author's earlier analysis, will present fresh material hitherto not present in any of this author's other books. Roman Polanski's film, interestingly enough, mirrors another 1999 film which featured a demonic, sex magick cabal operating behind these scenes: Kubrick's *Eyes Wide Shut*. *The Ninth Gate* was released worldwide on August 25th, 1999 (March 10th, 2000, in the United States) while *Eyes Wide Shut* was released July 16th, 1999 (United States, see Chapter VII), a little over a month earlier. Is this evidence of a Hollywood occult conspiracy at work or Jungian synchronicity and the collective unconscious affecting popular culture? It is noteworthy that 1999 also saw the release of three decidedly Gnostic movies: *The Matrix* released on March 31st, (United States), *eXistenZ* released on April 19th (United States), and *Fight Club* on October 15th (United States). One could argue that 1999 was a red-letter year for the debut of films that conceal, beneath the celluloid surface, esoteric iconography, demonism, the occult, Kabbalah, archetypes, Manichean, Valentinian, and Basilidian Gnosticism, and Masonic-like secret societies. To the profane, *The Ninth Gate* follows this narrative.

Dean Corso, a New York City rare book dealer, makes his living conning people into selling him valuable antique books for a low price, then selling them for profit; he does regular business with the equally unscrupulous Bernie Ornstein (James Russo), the owner of Bernie's Rare Books. Corso meets with wealthy book collector Boris Balkan (Frank Langella), having recently acquired a copy of *The Nine Gates to the Kingdom of Shadows* by 17th-century occult author Aristide Torchia. According to legend, the book is Torchia's adaptation of an older book, *The Delomelanicon*, written by the Devil himself, which purportedly conceals the means to summon ritualistically the Devil *qua* Lucifer *qua* Mephistopheles to become invincible, acquiring supernatural wisdom (cf. Marlowe and Goethe's *Dr. Faustus*), and immortality. Torchia was burned at the stake in 1666 along with most of his works; only three copies of *The Nine Gates* are known to exist, but Balkan believes only one is genuine. He hires Corso to investigate all three copies, paying him handsomely to acquire the authentic copy by any means necessary.

Balkan's copy of *The Nine Gates* previously belonged to Andrew Telfer (Willy Holt, 1921-2007), committing suicide soon after selling the book to Balkan. Telfer's death by hanging opens the movie; as he writes a suicide note, an inkwell featuring two horns sits on his desk symbolizing, to the subconscious mind, the forthcoming devilry of Polanski's film. Telfer's widow Liana (Lena Olin) wants the book back because he originally bought it for her, not knowing how she planned on using the book. Liana seduces Corso, but she fails to reacquire *The Nine Gates*. Meanwhile, Corso's business partner, Bernie, is murdered; his corpse hung upside down, imitating one of the engravings in *The Nine Gates* while simultaneously summoning the twelfth card of the Tarot's Major Arcana from the collective unconscious: the Hanged Man. Bernie was hiding Balkan's copy of *The Nine Gates* in his shop, implying he was killed by someone, or something, looking for the book.

Corso, after retrieving the book from Bernie's bookstore, travels to Toledo, Spain, where antique book restorers Pablo and Pedro Ceniza (both played by José López Rodero) show him that three of the book's engravings are signed LCF, which Corso understands to mean that Lucifer designed, cut, and prepared them. The twin brothers inform Corso that they owned the book previously, having sold it to Andrew Telfer as a gift for his wife, Liana. They tell Corso the copy is authentic and that although forgeries can be produced, they are too costly to be profitable. Corso goes by train to Sintra, Portugal, to compare Victor Fargas' (Jack Taylor) copy of *The Nine Gates* to that of Balkan's. To his surprise, Corso discovers that the signature, LCF, is found on three different engravings in the Fargas copy, which vary in detail from their counterparts in the Balkan copy. The next morning, a mysterious young woman, identified in the credits as the Girl, awakens Corso, leading him back to Fargas' dilapidated estate. The Girl has been tailing Corso since Balkan hired him to investigate the book. There he finds the old man murdered, and the engravings ripped out of his copy of *The Nine Gates*, which smolders in the fireplace.

In Paris, Corso visits Baroness Kessler (Barbara Jefford), the owner of the third copy of the book. The Baroness initially refuses any contact with Corso once she realizes who his employer is, but Corso returns, intriguing her with evidence that the engravings differ among the three copies. Gaining access to Kessler's copy, he finds the LCF on three different engravings, which are also slightly different from their counterparts in the other two copies. Shortly afterward Kessler is killed, the engravings removed from her copy, and the book set on fire. When Corso flees the Baroness' burning library, he is accosted by Liana's bodyguard (Tony Amoni) but is rescued when the Girl intervenes on Corso's behalf. Corso now believes that all three copies of *The Nine Gates* are genuine, but that each has deliberately falsified engravings, requiring possession of all three to solve the occult riddle and ritual. In the meantime, Liana steals Balkan's copy from Corso's hotel room. Corso and the Girl follow her to a mansion in the village of St. Martin, Liana's maiden name, witnessing her using *The Nine Gates* in a satanic ceremony that will culminate with ritual sex magicks. The ritual at Liana's estate is meeting of a secret society known as the Order of the Silver Serpent which celebrates Torchia and his work. The Order of the Silver Serpent echoes the rites and sorcery of the Golden Dawn and the O.T.O. Balkan suddenly interrupts the proceedings, garrotes Liana, takes back his copy, then flees the villa.

Corso pursues Balkan to a remote castle which is depicted in one of the engravings, and on a postcard, identifying the castle as the Devil's Tower. Corso found the postcard in Kessler's copy, travels to the tower, finding Balkan preparing to open the Nine Gates via ritualistic black magic. After a struggle, Balkan traps Corso in a hole in the floor, immobilizing him and allowing him to perform his summoning ceremony with Corso as a witness. After arranging the engravings on a makeshift altar, in a selected order, Balkan begins reciting a series of phrases related to each of the nine esoteric engravings. Balkan solves the mystery of *The Nine Gates*: "To travel in silence, by a long and circuitous route, to brave the arrows of misfortune and fear neither noose nor fire, to play the greatest of all games–and win! Foregoing no expense is to mock the vicissitudes of fate and to gain at last the key that will unlock the Ninth Gate." Balkan then douses the floor and himself with gasoline and sets it ablaze, believing himself to be immune to the flames. When Balkan's invocation fails, he screams in pain as the fire engulfs him. Corso frees himself, shoots Balkan killing him, escaping the burning castle with the engravings.

Outside, the Girl miraculously appears to Corso, and the two perform sex magick before the flames of the burning castle as the Girl's face contorts with demonic pleasure. Afterward, she tells him that Balkan failed because the ninth engraving he had used, despite being signed LCF, was a forgery. Corso, following her directions, returns to the Ceniza brothers' bookshop. Upon arriving, he finds the store empty and a large bookcase being removed from the wall by repairmen who are, in reality, the Ceniza brothers. From atop of the cabinet falls the authentic ninth engraving with a very different image than the forgery. On it is a likeness of the Girl, signifying that she is Lucifer, the LCF of the variant engravings. With the last authentic LCF engraving in hand, Corso returns to the castle and, having performed all the ritual requirements of the woodcuts, crosses the threshold of the Ninth Gate. The castle doors swing open; Corso receives the light of Lucifer the Light Bearer, sublime gnosis, and all the knowledge of the Ancient Mysteries.

Although Corso is on a Gnostic quest of enlightenment, he acts like an ignoramus, not knowing what he is seeking, if anything. He knows that, whatever it is, Balkan wants it, whatever *it* is, and if that be the case, he wants *it* too. Corso does not undergo alchemical transition; he is the same person at the start of the film that he is by movie's end. However, Corso is the chosen traveler depicted in *The Nine Gate* woodcuts; the riddle that Balkan solves is referring to Corso, not Balkan. For instance, when Corso visits the Ceniza brothers, they explain that the book's Rosicrucian-like engravings veil arcane interpretations. Ceniza explains to Corso that the third illustration could mean that if one ventures too far, danger will descend from above. The third engraving features an archer in the clouds about to fire an arrow down upon the path the traveler *qua* Corso is walking. The archer resembles the Ceniza twins, and it is immediately after leaving their bookshop that danger descends from above when scaffolding collapses from the side of a building, nearly killing Corso. By the end, Corso has fulfilled the imagery of the engravings, and thus, achieves the Luciferian light of the Left-Hand Path which, for Corso, is apropos since it both reflects and epitomizes his shady personality.

The film begins with Andrew Telfer hanging himself after selling his wife's copy of *The Nine Gates to the Kingdom of Shadows* to Boris Balkan. Andrew Telfer, like Aristide Torchia before him, is willing to give his life for the book albeit for different reasons than Torchia; signifying their deathly devotion to the book. To symbolize their unnatural devotion to the grimoire, both men have the same initials, A.T. Torchia, burned at the stake in 1666 for writing *The Nine Gates* in collaboration with the Devil, is a veiled rendering of Dominican mystic Giordano Bruno. Bruno, like Torchia, was burned at the stake by the Inquisition in 1600 for writing and lecturing about Egyptian mysticism, astronomy, astrology, magic, hermetic sorcery, and the occult. The book, *The Nine Gates to the Kingdom of Shadows*, is a composite grimoire of spell books such as *Ars Goetia* (a/k/a *Lesser Key of Solomon* or *Lemegeton*), *The Red Dragon*, *The Black Pullet*, and *Clavicula Salomonis* (Key of Solomon). *The Nine Gates* also mirrors occult texts, such as the Heinrich Cornelius Agrippa's *Three Books of Occult Philosophy*, Francis Barrett's (1744-?) *The Magus, or Celestial Intelligencer* (1801) and the *Corpus Hermeticum* (a/k/a *The Divine Pymander*), the latter of which was allegedly written by Hermes Trismegistus. The tome that inspired Torchia to write *The Nine Gates*, the *Dalomelanicon*, clearly draws inspiration from early twentieth-century gothic author H.P. Lovecraft's fictitious grimoire, *The Necronomicon*, which according to Lovecraft, was composed by the "Mad Arab" Abdul Alhazred. The *Dalomelanicon* was written by the Devil as a means to conjure him (or her) while Lovecraft's infamous *Necronomicon* was a grimoire allowing one to communicate with the Old Ones: a race of malignant primordial cosmic beings, the most famous (or infamous) is Cthulhu. The plates within *The Nine Gates* are influenced by German goldsmith and engraver Michel Le Blon (1587-1660); many of his woodcuts display Rosicrucian, hermetic, and kabalistic iconography, indicating that occult riddles, and their answers, are hidden in the illustrations. *The Nine Gates* engravings also feature Tarot imagery like the Hanged Man and the Wheel of Fortune as well as Hebrew letters, implying Gematria. The illustrations in *The Nine Gates* also bear a striking resemblance to the images in Barrett's *The Magus*, and to the engravings in the Luther Bible of 1533-1534.[378]

Balkan, a wealthy publisher and esoteric bibliophile, is a loose rendering of ceremonial magician and occultist Aleister Crowley. Crowley, proclaimed the "Wickedest Man in the World," was a practicing hermeticist and magician claiming to have successfully summoned demons and entities via the rituals of *Ars Goetia* and *The Book of the Sacred Magic of Abramelin the Mage*. Echoing Crowley's necromantic magic, Balkan only collects rare folios that feature the Devil as the protagonist; his interest

---

378 See Sullivan's *The Royal Arch of Enoch*, Chapter XV titled "So Dark the Con of Man."

in *The Nine Gates* is supernatural: Balkan's grand design is to unlock the book's unholy mysteries, gaining admittance to the Ninth Gate. Balkan's demonic intentions are symbolized at film's opening when Corso is leaving the apartment after giving a book appraisal. Corso encounters another book dealer, Witkin (Allen Garfield), accusing the former of being unscrupulous. Behind Corso, one will see a fire exit sign that features a stick-man figure heading down a flight of steps toward the fire rather than away from it. Corso gets in an elevator, heading down, symbolizing that the hellfire of Boris Balkan soon awaits him.

The Girl, Lucifer *qua* the Devil, is voluptuous paralleling her concomitant Venus or Aphrodite, the mythological Greco-Roman beauty- love goddess. Symbolizing the beautiful and alluring Venus, the Girl often appears around seashells: Shell gasoline stations appear behind her and a sculpture of a seashell overlooking Fargas' pond shadows the Girl when she and Corso break into his estate. These seashells trigger, to the subconscious mind, Botticelli's (1445-1510) iconic, Neoplatonic painting *The Birth of Venus*, which depicts the beautiful goddess emerging from the sea on a seashell. As Lucifer, she baptizes Corso with blood while her face miraculously appears on the blood red stamp affixed to the Devil's Tower,

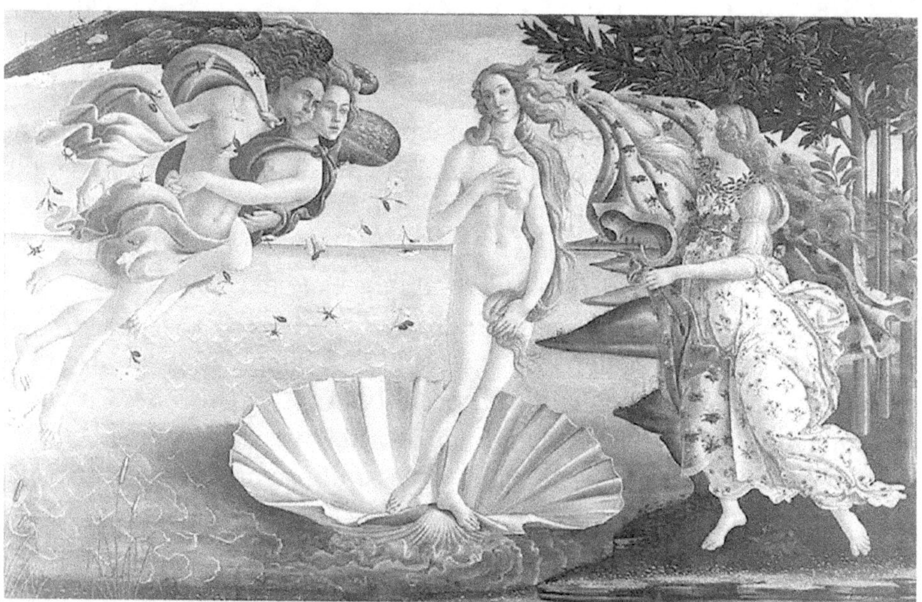

Sandro Botticelli's Neoplatonic *The Birth of Venus* was allegedly commissioned by the Medici family in the mid-1480s.

La Tour du Diable, postcard that Corso examines while in the café after Balkan escapes him. The actual castle is Chateau Puivert allegedly used by the Cathars to defend themselves during the Albigensian Crusades[379] in the 13th century. The Cathars were a sect of Gnostic Christians which Pope Innocent III (1161/62-1216) considered heretical, hence the castle serves as the place to open the Ninth Gate. In *The Ninth Gate* engraving (real and forgery), the Girl is riding a beast, personifying the Whore of Babylon: a figure of evil mentioned in the Bible's Book of Revelation. Her full title is Babylon the Great, the Mother of Prostitutes and Abominations of the Earth. The Whore associates with the Antichrist and the Beast of Revelation, all three connected to an evil kingdom; *whore* can also be translated to mean *idolatress*. Lucifer *qua* the Whore of Babylon has sex with Corso, drawing forth the infamous Babalon Working sex magick O.T.O. rituals of Jack Parsons and Marjorie Cameron, designed to bring about the Antichrist and the End Days in Christian eschatology.[380] In *The Ninth Gate*, it is Lucifer and the LCF derivative engravings, which brings the wisdom or the light of the Left-Hand Path that Corso existentially receives by entering the castle during the film's concluding moments. By riding on a beast, the Girl represents not only Lucifer, but also a satanic entity from the Book of Revelation that bestows Enochic wisdom (more on this in a moment) rather than heralding the End of Days. The other main female antagonist, Liana de St. Martin-Telfer, is as equally dark, beautiful, and nebulous as the Girl. Liana de St. Martin is named after Louis de St. Martin (1743-1803), a French teacher of mysticism and Cabala, endeavoring to establish a secret cult with magical-theurgical rites. Louis de St. Martin was influenced by Christian mystic Jacob Boehme (1575-1624) becoming the first to translate Boehme's work from German to French. St. Martin's published letters show an interest in spiritualism, magical evocation, and the works of mystic Emanuel Swedenborg (1688-1772). Out of this grew Martinism, a form of mystical Christianity concerned with the fall of the

---

379 The Albigensian Crusade or Cathar Crusade (1209-1229) was a 20-year military campaign initiated by Pope Innocent III to eliminate Catharism in Languedoc, in the south of France. The Crusade was prosecuted primarily by the French crown and promptly took on a political flavor, resulting in not only a significant reduction in the number of practicing Cathars but also a realignment of the County of Toulouse, bringing it into the sphere of the French crown and diminishing the distinct regional culture and high level of influence of the Counts of Barcelona.

380 cf. "Of Our Lady Babalon, and of the Beast Whereon she Rideth," Chapter 11, Part III of Crowley's *Magick*, pp. 214-216.

first man, his state of material privation from his divine source, and the process of his return, called Reintegration or Illumination.[381] This occultism is reflected in high degree Freemasonry, namely in the Royal Arch of Enoch ritual in which the candidate possesses the Tetragrammaton, the Name of God, becoming godlike by returning him, symbolically, to a cabalistic condition pre-Fall of Eden. A Martinist Order was founded in 1886 by Augustin Chaboseau (1868-1946) and Gerard Encausse (1865-1916, a/k/a Papus), the latter being a disciple of Levi. The Martinist Order was an influence upon the Hermetic Order of the Golden Dawn in the late nineteenth/early twentieth century. Therefore, Liana presides over a mystical, sex magick secret society, the Order of the Silver Serpent, which meets yearly at her estate in France to perform occult rites from *The Nine Gates to the Kingdom of Shadows* in homage to her namesake, Louis de St. Martin.[382] Liana, a long-legged raven-haired beauty dressing in seductive black, wearing black lingerie and smoking black cigarettes, personifies the demon-trickster goddess Lilith. In mythology, Lilith is considered to be female evil incarnate. Signifying Liana's evil ways, the name, Liana, closely resembles the name, Lilith. Lilith was Adam's first wife; she rebelled against him (cf. Eve Hammond's rebellion against Adam Sutler in *V for Vendetta*), transforming her into a beautiful raven haired, winged demon who seduces men and kills infants.[383] It is probable that there is a residue of the image of Lilith as Satan's partner in popular late medieval European notions of Satan's concubine, or wife in English folklore, "the Devil's Dame."[384] Embodying Lilith's sable and sexy persona, Liana seduces Corso to reobtain *The Nine Gates* copy her deceased husband sold to Balkan, later performing satanic rituals as the master of ceremonies of the Order of the Silver Serpent.

Each chapter title page of *The Nine Gates* has a small but noticeable image of a winged Baphomet, or the Goat of Mendes,[385] which suggests

---

381 Some sources suggest Martinism was named after Jacques de Livron Joachim de la Tour de la Casa Martinez de Pasqually (1727?-1774), an esoteric, theurgist, mystic, and tutor of both Louis de St. Martin and Jean-Baptiste Willermoz. See Sullivan, *ibid*, Chapter XV titled "So Dark the Con of Man."

382 Sullivan, *ibid*.

383 Scholem, *Kabbalah*, pp. 356-363, *passim*.

384 *ibid*, p. 358.

385 The Nine Gates' cover features an inverted pentagram which, according to Manly P. Hall, symbolizes the Left-Hand Path and the Goat of Mendes; see Hall's *The Secret Teachings of All*

Left-Hand Path mysticism and gnosis. Its frontispiece displays a tree symbolizing the kabalistic Tree of Life-Wisdom with a snake signifying the serpent in the Garden of Eden tempting Eve with knowledge, implying the forbidden, Luciferian wisdom in the book. The phrase *Sic Luceat Lux*, or *Thus Shines the Light* is prominently printed on the book's frontispiece. The serpent looks like two snakes intertwined, which would symbolize the Caduceus of Hermes and, by default, Hermes Trismegistus. Upon closer inspection, the serpent is biting its tail, making it an ouroboros, signifying duality, the Union of Opposites: chaos and order, yin-yang, male and female, dark and light, good and evil, and ignorance and wisdom. The snake in the tree also signifies the Brazen Serpent at Numbers 21:9[386] that Moses erected in the desert to cure snake bites, denoting the medicinal-magical qualities associated with the Caduceus of Hermes and Rod of Asclepius,[387] and the alchemical *serpens murcurialis*. The serpent is also the emblem of the coven-secret society the Order of the Silver Serpent which meets yearly on the anniversary of Torchia's death to honor him by reading from *The Nine Gates*. Liana has a serpent tattoo on her thigh while a silver snake coils around each of the four bedposts in the chamber[388] in which she reads from *The Nine Gates*. The bed indicates that she, and the other members, will perform sex magick (or an orgy, as implied by Baroness Kessler) after reading from the tome for conjuration-necromantic purposes. In sum, in the serpent is a symbol for the demonic yet sublime gnosis one can achieve by unlocking the conundrums of Torchia's adaptation of *The Delomelanicon*.

Although book dealer Bernie Ornstein possesses no particular archetypal qualities, he is nevertheless surrounded by mysterious symbolisms. Bernie dies in his bookshop in the occult posture of the hanged man, featured on engraving six in *The Nine Gates*, borrowed from Card XII of the Rider-Waite Major Arcana Tarot deck: the Hanged Man. In old packs, the

---

Ages, pp. 326-327.

386 "And Moses made a serpent of brass, and put it upon a pole, and it came to pass, that if a serpent had bitten any man, when he beheld the serpent of brass, he lived."

387 In Greek mythology, the Rod of Asclepius is a serpent entwined rod held aloft by the Greek god Asclepius, a deity associated with healing and medicine. The symbol has continued to be used in modern times, where it is associated with medicine and health care. It is often intertwined (albeit incorrectly) with the Caduceus of Hermes.

388 On either side of the bed one will see two painted black statues of Goetia-like demons. These statues appear earlier, on either side of Boris Balkan when her lectures on witchcraft in his publishing headquarters. The statues reflect the evil natures of both Liana de St. Martin-Telfer and Boris Balkan.

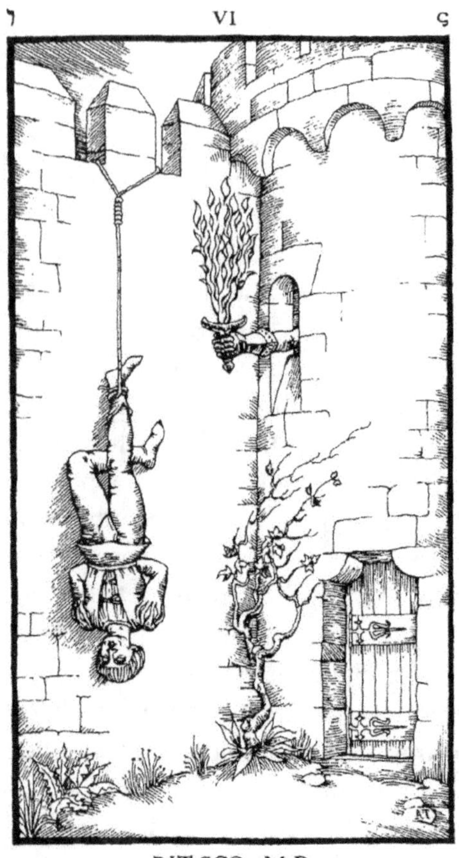

Engraving six from *The Nine Gates to the Kingdom* of Shadows unveils a hanged man lifted from the Tarot.

card associates with the arch-traitor, but in this instance, the symbolism draws from Freemason and Golden Dawn member A.E. Waite's interpretation of the card. The Hanged Man, Waite said, hints at "a great awakening that is possible," and that "after the sacred Mystery of Death there is a glorious Mystery of Resurrection."[389] To Jung, the Hanged Man symbolized the conscious mind which has volunteered to die in order to beget a new and fruitful life in that region of the psyche which has hitherto lain fallow in the darkest unconsciousness, the journey to Hades.[390] The Hanged Man symbolism foreshadows Corso's revelation at film's climax that he is, in fact, the traveler depicted in *The Nine Gates* woodcuts. Corso is born again when he enters the castle to receive the light thereby bringing him from darkness (ignorance) to the light (gnosis, wisdom) of Lucifer. The idea of *receiving the light* is a crucial tenet of Freemasonry; also important within Masonic lore is the winding stairs of Solomon's Temple Middle Chamber. Bernie's corpse, in the hanged man posture, dangles from winding stairs forging another nexus to occult Freemasonry. Moving upward, the winding stairs lead to the middle chamber of Solomon's Temple wherein the candidate is instructed to study the seven liberal arts and sciences. According to Masonic legend, the seven liberal arts and sciences were restored when Hermes Trismegistus (a/k/a Hermes the Philosopher) correctly pronounced

---

389 *ibid*, p. 106.
390 cf. Cavendish, *ibid*, pp. 108-109.

the Tetragrammaton in the Vault of Enoch, reinstating the wisdom encoded on one of Enoch's Pillars. On the Gnostic ascent of the Winding Stairs, Albert Mackey provides the following:

But we are not yet done. It will be remembered that a reward was promised for all this toilsome ascent of the winding stairs. Now, what are the wages of a Speculative Mason? Not money, nor corn, nor wine, nor oil. All these are but symbols. His wages are Truth, or that approximation to it which will be most appropriate to the degree into which he has been initiated. It is one of the most beautiful, but at the same time most abstruse, doctrines of the science of Masonic symbolism, that the Mason is ever to be in search of truth, but is never to find it. This divine truth, the object of all his labors, is symbolized by the Word, for which we all know he can only obtain a *substitute*; and this is intended to teach the humiliating but necessary lesson that the knowledge of the nature of God and of man's relation to him, which knowledge constitutes divine truth, can never be acquired in this life. It is only when the portals of the grave open to us, and give us an entrance into a more perfect life, that this knowledge is to be attained. 'Happy is the man,' says the father of lyric poetry, 'who descends beneath the hollow earth, having beheld these mysteries; he knows the end, he knows the origin of life.'

The middle chamber is therefore symbolic of this life, where the symbol only of the word can be given, where the truth is to be reached by approximation only, and yet where we are to learn that that truth will consist in a perfect knowledge of the G.A.O.T.U. This is the reward of the inquiring Mason; in this consist the wages of a Fellow-Craft; he is directed to the truth, but must travel farther and ascend still higher to attain it.[391]

Ornstein's winding stairs anticipate Corso's spiritual journey of ascension, of enlightenment,[392] the knowledge that comes by navigating the trial and tribulations of *The Ninth Gate* by unlocking its satanic mysteries,

---

391 Mackey, *Encyclopedia of Freemasonry*, Vol. II, p. 852.
392 cf. "The Ladder of the Gods," Chapter 18 of Hall's *Lectures on Ancient Philosophies*, pp. 409-431.

allowing entry into the castle to receive supernatural Luciferian light, the luminous gleam of the *sol niger*, the glow of Left-Hand Path gnosis.

The Nine Gates is an occult representation of the Kabbalah. Kabbalah is Hebrew mysticism based on the *Zohar*: a set of books which document esoteric beliefs about the Torah, namely assigning an allegorical meaning to Holy Scripture. Occult author Rosemary Ellen Guiley (1950-2019) writes on Kabbalah saying:

Kabbalah (the preferred spelling of scholars) signifies 'doctrine received from tradition,' specifically oral tradition and secret, mystical knowledge not revealed to the masses. According to legend, the Kabbalah was taught by God to a group of angels, who, after the Fall, taught it to man in order to provide man with a way back to God. It was passed to Adam to Noah to Abraham, who took it to Egypt, where it was passed on to Moses. Moses included it in the first four books of the Pentateuch but left it out of Deuteronomy. He initiated 70 elders into the Kabbalah who continued the tradition of passing it on orally. David and Solomon were Kabbalistic adepts. Eventually, the wisdom was written down.

The Kabbalah is a body of writing by anonymous authors. The main works are the *Sefer Yetzirah*, or *Book of Creation*, and the *Zohar*, or *Book of Splendor*. The origins of the *Sefer Yezirah* date to the 8th century. The *Zohar* is believed to have been written by Leon of Guadalajara, Spain, in the 13th century.

… Its study and analysis peaked by the 19th century and began to decline. Interest in the Kabbalah was revived by non-Jewish Western occultists, such as FRANCIS BARRETT, ELIPHAS LEVI and Papus. It was held in great esteem by members of the HERMETIC ORDER OF THE GOLDEN DAWN, including Samuel Liddell Macgregor Mathers, ALEISTER CROWLEY, and A.E. Waite, all of whom were influenced by it. DION FORTUNE called the Kabbalah the 'Yoga of the West.'[393]

The Kabbalah forms the Tree of Life-Wisdom with its ten circular centers called the *sefirot*. Nine of the *sefirot* (signifying *The Nine Gates*

---

393 Guiley, *The Encyclopedia of Witches and Witchcraft*, pp. 184-185.

to the Kingdom of Shadows) symbolizes different levels of human consciousness, intellect, and emotion; the tenth, *Keter* or Crown, denotes above consciousness residing at the top of the kabalistic Tree. The light of human consciousness is transformed in each of the nine *sefirot*, positively and negatively. Kabbalah, its *sefirot* and paths reflect characteristics of the eternal godhead; Kabbalah is an emanation of the divine. The *sefirot*, their names and aspects are: 1. *Keter*, supreme crown; 2. *Chokmah*, wisdom; 3. *Binah*, understanding; 4. *Chesed*, mercy, greatness; 5. *Geburah*, strength, rigor (punishment in the Golden Dawn system); 6. *Tiphareth*, beauty, wisdom; 7. *Netzach*, victory, force; 8. *Hod*, splendor; 9. *Yesod*, foundation; 10. *Malkuth*, kingdom. There is a hidden *sefirah* called *Da'at* (the mystical state) in which all ten *sefirot* in the Tree of Life are united as one. To many Kabbalists, when the *sefirot*, its gates or portals, are unlocked it grants the practitioner access to a separate universe, above *Keter*, of divine spiritual enlightenment. Kabbalah's eternal godhead termed *Ein Sof* (sometimes *Ain Soph* or *Ayn Soph*) understood as God before his self-manifestation in the production of any spiritual realm, probably derived from Solomon Ibn Gabirol's (ca. 1021-ca. 1058) term, the Endless One (*she-en lo tiklah*), or the Infinite; it is the divine presence existing beyond *Keter*, beyond the *sefirot*. Like the unknowable Monad of the Gnostics, this unfathomable being manifests his depths in pristine emanations, the *sefirot*, by which God flows from infinite to finite.[394] Like the Gnostic pleroma, the *sefirot* constitute a spiritual organism.[395] The ten *sefirot* are arranged in three columns connected by twenty-two paths, corresponding to the twenty-two cards of the Major Arcana of the Tarot and the twenty-two letters of the Hebrew alphabet. The twenty-two paths combined with the ten *sefirot* equals 32, a reference to the thirty-two degrees of Scottish Rite Masonry; this implies a mystical nexus between the Scottish Rite (and by default the York Rite) and *The Nine Gates* wherein the initiate navigates an ascent to obtain arcane wisdom, perfection, and Luciferian exaltation. Add in the hidden *sefirah*, *Da'at*, to get the number 33, symbolizing the last, honorary degree in the Scottish Rite: Inspector General. Kabbalah links Freemasonry to other branches of mysticism such as Pythagoreanism and Gematria, which

---

394 cf. Wilson's *Secret Cinema*, p. 74.
395 *ibid.*

both involve the use of letters, symbols, and numbers to produce a magical effect or outcome.

The Nine Gates' engravings symbolize the nine *sefirot* from Kabbalah and human consciousness. Once their mysteries are unlocked, the highest *sefirah, Keter*, opens, allowing the adept access to the godhead in the antimaterial sky; this is what Balkan seeks to accomplish. Polanski mingles Kabbalah with necromantic black magic (or magick). The merging of black and white magic, creating a Union of Opposites, was analyzed by Crowley, explaining that "…every magician must firmly extend his empire to the depths of hell. 'My adepts stand upright, their heads above the heavens, their feet below the hells.' This is the reason why the magician who performs the Operation of the 'Sacred Magic of Abramelin the Mage,' immediately after attaining to the Knowledge and Conversation of the Holy Guardian Angel, must evoke the Four Great Princes of the Evil of the World."[396] Thus Balkan, a black magician, is attempting to perfect Left-Hand Path gnosis by solving the book's demonic riddle; make no mistake, Balkan is not walking the Right-Hand Path. Rather, he is pursuing unity with a Gnostic deity of some sort, likely Abraxas (from whence we get the word *abracadabra*). On Abraxas, Jung wrote a short treatise in 1916 called *The Seven Sermons to the Dead*, which called Abraxas a God higher than the Christian God and Devil that combines all opposites into one being. Rather than practice demonic magic, Balkan should have become a Freemason instead, because the wisdom Balkan desires can be found, albeit symbolically, within high degree Freemasonry; this cabalistic occultism is part of the Royal Arch of Enoch ceremonial.

The Royal Arch of Enoch's ritual-history tells that Enoch after returning from his visitation to the heavenly afterworld, concealed the wisdom he learned from the archangels and Watchers (a/k/a the Fallen Angels) in a subterranean vault. Upon two pillars he inscribed wisdom: the ability to read, write, mathematics, make weapons, etcetera, placing the Tetragrammaton on a gold delta in between them so that this knowledge would survive the Flood of Noah. In the heavens, Enoch beheld the kabalistic Tree of Life and its concomitant, the Tree of Wisdom, as an emanation of all wisdom: the Name of God. In *I Enoch*, the wisdom is considered divine even though its origins are demonic; in the Old Testament, this knowledge was deemed

---

396 Crowley, *Magick*, p. 297.

evil evidenced by God's desire to eradicate it and humankind with the Great Flood of Noah. Within the underground vault, Enoch placed the sacred name, along with the pillars, beneath nine arches.[397] In Masonic history and philosophy (cf. *Old Charges* of Dr. J. T. Desaguliers, Cooke Manuscript), the treasure vault is first discovered by Hermes Mercurius Trismegistus and Pythagoras. Both correctly pronounce the Tetragrammaton, allowing Trismegistus to restore the seven liberal arts and sciences (i.e., reading and writing) and Pythagoras to restore mathematics, including the 47th Proposition of Euclid, back to humanity. This Name of God is the word that Hiram Abif, the architect of Solomon's Temple, possesses in the third-degree Masonic ritual. Hiram refuses to give the word to three Fellowcrafts so they kill him; the word becomes forever lost in the Blue Lodge, making it the *Lost Word of a Master Mason*; the word is rediscovered in high degree Freemasonry. In the Masonic ritual, the initiate rediscovers the Name of God and in doing so becomes a citizen-king: a symbolic Trismegistus, Pythagoras, and Enoch and is now exalted[398] to the Royal Arch, implying cabalistic apotheosis. By beholding the Tetragrammaton, the Masonic adept becomes a godlike possessor of legitimate yet demonic Enochic wisdom, returning himself to a favorable status, albeit symbolically, prior to the Fall of Eden. In the Masonic ceremony (various ritual lectures), this esoteric, occult, forbidden wisdom inscribed on Enoch's Pillar and the sacred name is concealed beneath nine arches. Hence, the satanic wisdom, the Kingdom of Shadows, dwelling beyond nine gates *qua* nine arches. Moreover, Balkan solves *The Nine Gates'* satanic conundrum beneath an arch deep in the castle keep.

Dante Alighieri's *Inferno* (*Divina Commedi*, ca. 1308-1320) anticipates Masonic mysticism and Torchia's *Nine Gates*. Lucifer the Light Bearer *qua* Satan is imprisoned at the bottom of nine circles. The nine Circles of Hell in descending order based on severity of punishment are Limbo, Lust, Gluttony, Greed, Anger, Heresy, Violence, Fraud, and Treachery. Satan is a giant demon, frozen mid-breast in ice at the center of Hell. Satan has three

---

397 Sometimes identified or illustrated as archways.

398 The candidate is exalted to the Royal Arch of Enoch in the York Rite. In the Scottish Rite, the Royal Arch comes at the end of the Lodge of Perfection (degrees 4-14) thus making the candidate perfect–a *parfait adepte* within the French Rite of Perfection–upon the completion of the degrees. See Sullivan's *The Royal Arch of Enoch, passim*; cf. Thomas Smith Webb's *Illustrations of Masonry, passim*.

faces and a pair of bat-like wings. As Satan beats his wings, he creates a cold wind which continues to freeze the ice surrounding him, and the other sinners in the Ninth Circle. The wind gusts he creates are felt throughout the other circles of Hell. Each of his three mouths chews on Judas Iscariot, Marcus Junius Brutus (85 BCE-42 BCE), and Gaius Cassius Longings (ca. 85 BCE-42 BCE), the three great arch traitors, the three most famous enemies of church and state; Judas, the betrayer of Jesus, and Brutus and Cassius, the chief assassins of Julius Caesar. Paralleling the Luciferian gnosis dwelling beyond Torchia's *Ninth Gate*, Dante's Lucifer *qua* Satan appears to be evil at first, but a Johannite-Gnostic interpretation of the *Divine Comedy* presents Satan as divine enlightenment, the *sol niger*, and, by default, Jehovah as the cruel demiurge. On this occult interpretation Masonic magus Albert Pike elucidates:

> Commentaries and studies have been multiplied upon the *Divine Comedy*, the work of DANTE, and yet no one, so far as we know, has pointed out its especial character. The work of the great Ghibellin is a declaration of war against the Papacy, by bold revelations of the Mysteries. The Epic of Dante is Johannite and Gnostic, an audacious application, like that of the Apocalypse, of the figures and numbers of the Kabalah to the Christian dogmas, and a secret negation of every thing [*sic*] absolute in these dogmas. His journey through the supernatural worlds is accomplished like the initiation into the Mysteries of Eleusis and Thebes. He escapes from that gulf of Hell over the gate of which the sentence of despair was written, *by reversing the positions of his head and feet, that is to say, by accepting the direct opposite of the Catholic dogma*; and then he reascends to the light, by using the Devil himself as a monstrous ladder. Faust ascends to Heaven, by stepping on the head of the vanquished Mephistopheles. Hell is impassable for those only who know not how to turn back from it. We free ourselves from its bondage by audacity.[399]

Pike insinuates that, according to the secret doctrines in Dante's magnum opus, the adoration of the Judeo-Christian demiurge Jehovah or Yahweh, should be cast asunder in favor of esoteric gnosis, enlightenment,

---

399 Pike, *Morals and Dogma*, p. 822.

the wisdom of Lucifer the Light Bearer which can only be discovered by the adept in Hell's ninth circle. Dante negates Christian dogma implying that in darkness is light, and in light, darkness. A nexus between *Inferno* and the mysteries of *The Ninth Gate* is forged when book dealer Bernie Ornstein examines Balkan's copy before a bust of Dante which sits on his desk. Comparatively, in high degree Freemasonry, demonic yet divine knowledge is sequestered away in an underground vault beneath nine arches. In *The Ninth Gate*, Left-Hand Path gnosis exists beyond the nine gates once the riddle of Torchia's tome is solved by a supreme initiate.

The Ninth Gates features two booksellers and restorers, Pablo and Pedro Ceniza, personifying the constellation Gemini the Twins. They are twin brothers, consulted by Corso because they once owned the copy of *The Nine Gates* that Corso is now investigating. When Corso questions them about the engravings in the book, they immediately turn to the third gate (or chapter) and its corresponding etching is no coincidence. This engraving displays an archer in the clouds about to fire an arrow down upon a gated bridge as a traveler approaches it. The traveler is the Fool card of the Major Arcana personifying Corso, not yet realizing that he is the naïve pilgrim on the woodcuts. They explain to Corso this symbolizes that if one travels too far, terror and even death may descend from above. They further tell Corso that books of this nature always conceal hidden riddles and mysteries. The face of the archer in the clouds is the face of the Ceniza Brothers, or Gemini. It is the third engraving in the book because Gemini is the third house of the zodiac. Gemini is ruled by the planet Mercury, known to the Greeks as Hermes and to the Egyptians as Thoth, when fused, becomes the wise Hellenistic sage Hermes Mercurius Trismegistus. As mentioned, Trismegistus restores the seven Enochic liberal arts and sciences pillar by correctly pronouncing the Tetragrammaton in the Vault of Enoch, according to the Masonic legend of the Holy Royal Arch. It is from this pillar that reading and writing are restored to humankind; as such, Gemini the Twins, the Ceniza Brothers, are at home in a bookshop that specializes in resorting esoteric lore and lost wisdom. The Latin phrase under the engraving of the third gate reads "VERB. D.SUM C.S.T. ARCAN." meaning VERBUM DIMISSUM CUSTODIAT ARCANUM, when translated to English means *the Lost Word Keeps the Secret*. The lost word the phrase refers to is the Tetragrammaton recovered during the various Masonic

Royal Arch ceremonies, dovetailing with the Masonic-Enochic-kabalistic imagery veiled in Polanski's film. Although eight of the nine LCF engravings were original, the ninth engraving used in his summoning ceremony was a forgery, hence, Balkan was deemed unworthy to gain admittance. In search of the authentic ninth plate, Corso returns to the Ceniza's Bookshop only to learn it has closed permanently. Two unassuming workmen are cleaning out its contents. The original LCF ninth engraving is found atop a dust covered wooden bookcase. When the two workmen pull the bookshelf from the wall, it falls to the ground, discovered by Corso. Corso, now with all nine authentic LCF engravings in hand, is granted entrance to the ninth gate at *La Tour du Diable* where he receives the light of Lucifer the Light Bearer. The two workmen are, in fact, the Ceniza brothers from earlier in the film; in a final act of hermeticism, provide Corso with gnosis by supplying the final piece of the puzzle, granting him access to the ninth gate.[400] Personifying the planet Mercury, the Ceniza Brothers *qua* Gemini have provided Corso with the final engraving, an allegorical philosopher's stone, allowing Corso's transformative, sable awakening while at the same time becoming the Tarot's Juggler-Magician by tricking Balkan into believing he possessed an original set of the LCF engravings.

FREEMASONRY ON THE SMALL SCREEN: SLEEPY HOLLOW

The television series *Sleepy Hollow* displays Masonic symbolism both exoteric and esoteric. Debuting September 16th, 2013, on the Fox Network, the series is considered a modern-day adaptation of the 1820 Halloween short story *The Legend of Sleepy Hollow* by Washington Irving (1783-1859) with an added concept from *Rip Van Winkle* (1819), also by Irving. One of the characters on the show, Police Captain Frank Irving (Orlando Jones), surname pays homage to *The Legend of Sleepy Hollow* author. As of the writing of this book, only two seasons have aired with a third on the way, so this analysis will focus primarily on season one because, in this author's opinion having watched all the episodes from both seasons,

---

400 cf. Chapter XV, "So Dark the Con of Man," of Sullivan's *The Royal Arch of Enoch.*

season one displays more occult imagery than season two by a large margin. Furthermore, I will not scrutinize each episode; instead, I will first provide an overview of the series followed by an esoteric dissection of the key points presented in the series. The pilot episode begins in 1781: Ichabod Crane (Tom Mison), a soldier and spy in the Colonial Army on a mission for General George Washington, decapitates a demonic Hessian soldier transforming him into the dreaded Headless Horseman; at the same time the Horseman kills Crane. More than 230 years later, in the present-day, Ichabod rises from his grave: a crypt containing occult artifacts with mystical sigils on its walls. Ichabod finds himself in the township of Sleepy Hollow along with the Headless Horseman, revealed to be Death, one of the Four Horsemen of the Apocalypse, is summoned back from his watery grave by an unknown party. The resurrection of the one causes the resurrection of the other because their blood was mixed after Crane decapitated the Horseman on the field of battle.

Police Lt. Abigail "Abbie" Mills (Nicole Beharie) begins investigating the Headless Horseman after he beheads Sheriff August Corbin (Clancy Brown), Abbie's mentor and partner. Her investigation reveals the presence of two occult groups in Sleepy Hollow: one a force for good, the other evil; both are connected with the Four Horsemen and the pending apocalypse. The killing spree the Horseman embarks on forces Ichabod and Abbie to team up, especially when they find out that they are destined to be the Two Witnesses from the Book of Revelation, the only ones who can protect the world from the forces of Hell and the End of Days. Assisting them in this task, at least until the end of Season 2, was Ichabod's wife Katrina (Katia Winter) a white magician turned evil; she died in the Season 2 finale *Tempus Fugit* (airdate: 23 February 2015). Also assisting them is Abbie's sister Jennifer "Jenny" Mills (Lyndie Greenwood). Since Ichabod Crane's worldview is from 18th century Colonial America, some friction exists between him and Abbie, and also between him and the people he must now interact with in the 21st century. This displacement is often a source of comic relief in the show, but it also forces him to perceive things differently which turns out to be a positive attribute. Ichabod and Abbie need resolute wisdom: the Headless Horseman aside, the other main antagonist is the demon Moloch commanding an army of evil creatures which he unleashes on the heroes seemingly every week; Moloch was destroyed halfway through Season Two. Whether Moloch returns to the show remains to be seen.

It is revealed that Ichabod and Abbie are the Two Witnesses of Revelation; within Judeo-Christian eschatology, they are the Prophet Elijah and Enoch, the two patriarchs that never experience physical death. Ichabod reflects Enochic-Masonic ritualistic symbolism because he is resurrected from a subterranean vault (cf. Vault of Enoch) which stores sacred wisdom encoded in George Washington's Bible (cf. the Tetragrammaton, Pillars of Enoch) to know good from evil which is necessary to defeat the latter.

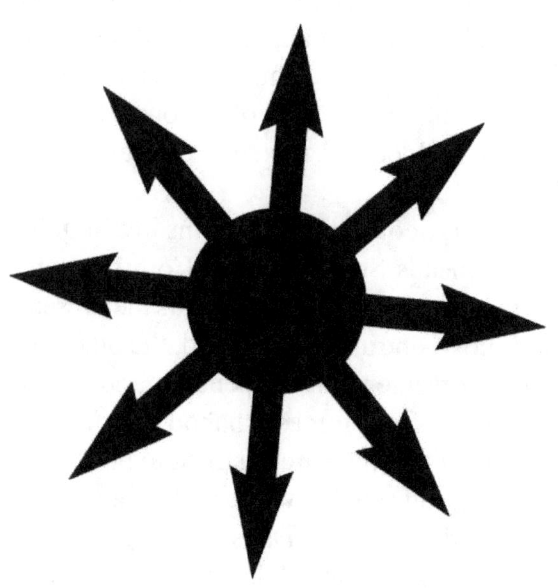

The Chaosphere, the emblem of chaos magick, is tattooed on the back of the Horseman's head.

Ichabod, like Enoch, hints at immortality having survived for over 225+ years. It is revealed that Ichabod is a Freemason and that the Masons have been tracking the Horseman to avert the Apocalypse. The Horseman, before his decapitation, has a chaosphere[401] tattooed on the back of his head which identifies him as a Left-Hand Path chaos magician seeking to unleash Hell on earth, or unfettered chaos and anarchy. In the episode, *The Lesser Key of Solomon* (airdate 7 October 2013), a modern-day Hessian soldier named Gunther (Carsten Norgaard) moonlights as a piano instructor; during a piano lesson he tells his student, "Left hand, Aaron. *Always the left hand will save you*," implying the Horseman's diabolical sorcery. The Hessians seek to locate *The Lesser Key of Solomon*, perform a dark ritual, liberating its seventy-two demons from Hell. The Hessians identify the grimoire as

---

401 The tattoo is also the symbol of the Hessians in league with the Horseman. In the episode *The Lesser Key of Solomon*, Ichabod Crane sees the tattoo on the chest of a modern-day Hessian and identifies it saying, "The Mark of the Rheinhessen. Shadow Warriors. Fifth Battalion."

Item 37, a reference to I Kings 1:37, "As the LORD hath been with my lord the king, even so be he with Solomon, and make his throne greater than the throne of my lord king David," indicating they seek to enshrine Moloch in a throne higher than God. Later in the episode, it is revealed the Hessians–past and present–and the Horseman are secretly in service to Moloch. The Freemasons seek to prevent their reign of terror; in the episode *The Sin Eater*, (airdate 4 November 2013, in Japan the episode is titled *The Freemason and his Sin*), Ichabod recounts a story from his past about Arthur Bernard (Tongayi Chirisa), a recently freed slave interrogated by the Redcoats on suspicion of treason. Crane turns against his native England siding with Bernard, informing him to seek out General Washington, a Freemason, and to speak the words *"Ordo ab Chao,"* (English: Order Out of Chaos) to join the American Revolution. The phrase is a familiar tagline of the Scottish Rite (founded May 31st, 1801) referring to the reconfiguration of the original 25 degrees of the Rite of Perfection. Within the mythos of *Sleepy Hollow*, it identifies the Masons as secret combatants against the Horseman and Moloch's ilk: the Freemasons seek to bring order (and thus salvation) out of the chaos the Horseman and Moloch seek to ignite.

Veiled Masonic-Enochic symbolism hides in Part I of Season One's finale titled *The Indispensable Man*, which aired on 20 January 2014 (along with Part II titled *Bad Blood* on the same date). It is divulged that George Washington survived his death to return from the afterlife so that he could encode secrets in his Bible as to the whereabouts of Purgatory's entrance. To keep the secret safe, Washington was buried in a secret crypt in Sleepy Hollow. A map was interred with him

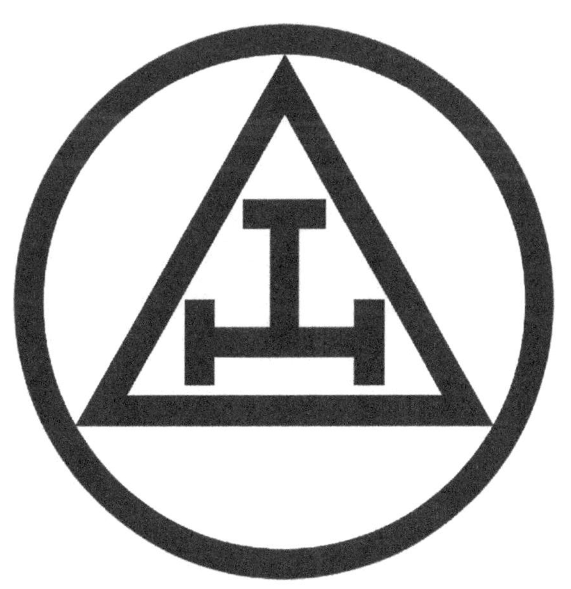

Triple Tau: The Triple Tau.

showing the precise location of this hidden portal to the netherworld. Like Osiris *qua* the Hiramic initiate in the third-degree Masonic ritual, Washington is resurrected from death: this allows him, like Enoch, to write down the occult secrets of the afterlife. His Bible aside, the supernatural map along with Washington's corpse are entombed, like the Pillars of Enoch and the Tetragrammaton in the Royal Arch of Enoch ceremonial, in a hidden underground vault. Once the vault is discovered by Abbie and Ichabod, Washington's sarcophagus and its treasure are uncovered, Ichabod exclaims "Eureka," an esoteric Masonic reference to Pythagoras, exclaiming "Eureka" or "I have found it" after finding and pronouncing the Tetragrammaton in the Vault of Enoch. By pronouncing the Name of God correctly, Pythagoras restores Enoch's mathematical pillar and the 47th Proposition of Euclid back to humankind.[402] Like Pythagoras, Ichabod recovers Washington's sacred map, restoring heavenly, divine secrets of the afterworld. With the secrets of the map in hand, Ichabod and Abbie infiltrate Purgatory to frustrate Moloch from commencing the End of Days, thereby saving humanity. Enochic symbolism shadows Jenny Mills, patient number 49 in Tarrytown Psychiatric Hospital; 4+9 equals 13 which resurrects the 13th degree of the Scottish Rite, the Royal Arch of Enoch (or Solomon) ritual, from the collective unconscious. Symbolically, this transforms Jenny into a source of light or enlightenment which Ichabod and Abbie can rely on when combating evil (cf. darkness, the Headless Horseman only comes out at night). Enochic symbolism is woven into the tapestry of *The Vessel* (airdate 13 January 2014) when Freemason Benjamin Franklin removes mystical lantern from its crate, a Triple Tau, an emblem of Royal Arch Masonry, is observable on a shield above the fireplace mantle. Even in Season 2, Ichabod brandishes the Sword of Methuselah, a powerful blade possessing the power to defeat demons; Methuselah was the son of Enoch according to Luke 3:37.[403] In fact, Abbie's ancestor, the witch Grace Dixon (Onira Tarés), describes the weapon as "Enoch's sword for fallen demons" in her diary.

Sleepy Hollow does not limit its esoteric symbolism to Freemasonry and grimoires such as *The Lesser Key of Solomon*. A kabalistic golem is

---

402 See Sullivan's *The Royal Arch of Enoch, passim.*

403 "Which was the son of Mathusala, which was the son of Enoch, which was the son of Jared, which was the son of Maleleel, which was the son of Cainan,"

the antagonist the appropriately titled Season One episode, *The Golem* (airdate 9 December 2013), and in *The Vessel*, a magical lantern is used to exorcise the demon Ancitif. A lantern as a mystical, supernatural device stems from the lore of ever-burning lamps of antiquity. For example, St. Augustine described a perpetual lamp in a temple in Egypt sacred to Venus, which neither wind nor water could extinguish. He believed it to be the work of the Devil. During the Middle Ages, a lamp was found in England which had burned since the third century, kept ablaze by cabalistic magic. The monument containing it was believed to be the tomb of the father of Constantine the Great. The Lantern of Pallas was discovered near Rome in 1401 (CE). It was found in the sepulcher of Pallas, son of Evander, immortalized by Virgil in his *Aeneid* (29-19 BCE). The lamp was placed at the head of the body and had burned with a steady glow for more than 2,000 years. In 1550 (CE) on the island of Nesis, in the Bay of Naples, a magnificent marble vault was opened in which was found a lamp still alight which had been placed there before the beginning of the Christian era. Pausanias (ca. CE 110–180) described a beautiful golden lamp in the temple of Minerva which burned steadily for a year without refueling or having the wick trimmed. The ceremony of filling the lamp took place annually, and time was measured by the ceremony. According to the *Fama Fraternitatis*, the crypt of Christian Rosencreutz when opened 120 years after his death was found to be brilliantly illuminated by a perpetual lamp suspended from the ceiling.[404] Carrying these occult themes forward, in Season Two the Hanged Man of the Tarot's Major Arcana was an important plot device in the episode *"Pittura Infamante"* (airdate 19 January 2015), and a necromantic manuscript written by Dr. John Dee was central to the episode "Spellcaster" (airdate 2 February 2015).

Occult symbolism is camouflaged in the season one episodes much more so than in the season two episodes. Why the producers and directors deemphasized *Sleepy Hollow's* arcane symbolism is unknown to this author and is open to speculation. What is obvious is that season two shifted away from season one's overt Masonic storyline, taking with it the show's occult symbolism. This is unfortunate because the program's Masonic and esoteric themes made it entertaining. That said, season two is entertaining nevertheless and worth watching. Whether *Sleepy Hollow* returns to its

---

404 See Hall's *The Secret Teachings of All Ages*, pp. 180-181.

Masonic roots in season three remains to be seen but if it does, rest assured it will be analyzed by this author in *Cinema Symbolism 3*.

COMPARATIVE CINEMA: THE MAN WHO WOULD BE KING AND STARGATE

The Man Who Would Be King (1975) is based on Rudyard Kipling's novella of the same name (published 1888) and, like *National Treasure*, both conceals and reveals Masonic secrets, ritualistic philosophies, and high degree esoterica. The film follows two rogue ex-non-commissioned officers of the Indian Army who set off from late 19th century British India in search of adventure which they find by becoming unlikely monarchs of Kafiristan (trans: Land of the Infidels). The two scoundrels, both Freemasons, are Daniel "Danny" Dravot (Sean Connery) and Peachy Carnehan (Michael Caine). The movie is told via flashback with Peachy telling Kipling (Christopher Plummer) about their journey. Kipling, also a Mason, is the editor of *The Northern Star*; the real-life Kipling was initiated into the mysteries of Freemasonry in Hope and Perseverance Lodge, No. 782, in Lahore, Pakistan. Kipling briefly explains the history of Freemasonry stating that its roots are buried in deep antiquity; that, long ago, Masons were in India and the Middle East, and that they were responsible for the construction of Solomon's Temple. Shortly thereafter, Peachy and Danny sign a contract in front of Kipling pledging mutual loyalty and forswearing alcohol and women until they achieved their grandiose aims. Peachy and Danny, along with twenty Martini-Henry rifles, set off on an epic overland adventure north beyond the Khyber Pass, fighting off bandits, blizzards, and avalanches, into the unknown land of Kafiristan. Just before starting on their journey, Kipling tries to dissuade the two men from their mad scheme; as a token of brotherhood, Kipling gives Dravot his Masonic watch fob with the square, compasses, and an all-seeing eye.

Upon reaching Kafiristan, the two Masons, along with a Gurkha soldier going by the name Billy Fish (Saeed Jaffrey), make plans to consolidate power. Billy is the sole survivor of a missing mapping expedition dispatched several years earlier which had been lost in an avalanche. Billy speaks English as well as the local tongue, helping the two men navigate the terrain and communicate with the natives. Peachy and Danny are at first shocked by some of the local customs, but the two men remain culturally sensitive because they do not want to offend their hosts. While skirmishing with local tribes, Danny is struck by an arrow but is unharmed, leading the natives to believe that he is a god. In fact, the arrow was stopped by a bandolier hidden beneath his clothing. As victory follows victory, the defeated are recruited to join the swelling army. Finally, with nobody left to stand in their way, Danny and Peachy are summoned to the holy city of Sikandergul by Buddhist-like holy men having vowed to keep their eyes closed, suggesting the Gnosticism of Basilides. The two men are greeted by Kafu Selim (Karroom Ben Bouih, ca. 1871-?) who sets up a reenactment of the arrow incident to determine whether Danny is a man or a god by seeing whether he bleeds. When Danny flinches, the monks grab him and tear open his shirt, only to be stopped by Danny's Masonic jewel given to him by Kipling. Kipling's tale proves correct about the antiquity of Freemasonry: the Masonic jewel matches the emblem known only to the highest holy man, the symbol of Sikander (Alexander the Great), having conquered the country thousands of years before, promising to return. Upon seeing Sikander's ancient Masonic symbol, Peachy exclaims, "They're Masons! By the square, level, plumb rule, compasses, the all-seeing eye! The craft, Danny! That's what saved us." The chief deity of the holy city is Imbra; the god has a large all-seeing eye–its most distinct feature– making it appear extraterrestrial. The holy men are convinced Danny is the Son of Sikander, hailing him as a divine monarch sent by Imbra. Next, the two men are led down to storerooms heaped with treasure that belonged to Sikander, which now belongs to Danny to do with as he pleases. As time passes, Danny comes to believe that fate has led him to become the godly ruler of Kafiristan while Peachy wishes to leave as soon as spring arrives with his share of the booty. Just as Peachy is about to depart with a caravan of treasure, Danny is revealed to be mortal. During Danny's wedding to a slave-girl, his soon-to-be wife Roxanne (Shakira Caine) bites him causing him to bleed, thus exposing his humanity. Danny is forced to walk to the middle of a rope bridge over a deep gorge as the suspension ropes are cut. Peachy is crucified between two pine trees, but he is cut down the next day surviving the grisly ordeal. Eventually, he makes his way back to India and

Kipling, but his mind has become unhinged from his sufferings. As Peachy finishes his story, he presents Kipling with Danny's decomposed head, still wearing its crown, thereby confirming the tale to be true.

Exoterically, the movie does not shy away from its Masonic foundations. Esoterically, the movie veils Masonic morality under a variety of guises. For example, Peachy and Danny abstain from drinking and womanizing to fulfill their dreams, which reflects one of the first tenets taught to a candidate entering the Blue Lodge, "…To learn to subdue my passions and improve myself in Masonry."[405] Once in Kafiristan, the two men–specifically Danny–are presumed to be gods echoing the third-degree ritual of death and resurrection. No longer shirking responsibilities, having forsaken their selfishness for divine kingship They begin as rakehells: in the train car Peachy (and by default, Danny) explains his flamboyant lifestyle claiming to be an expert in "whiskey, women, waistcoats and bills of fare." Later, once Danny is proclaimed a God, we see him (accompanied by Peachy) dispenses justice as a Solomonic lawgiver. Peachy and Danny have died, now born again, ruling Kafiristan judiciously. They have undergone Gnostic *ascensio* by forsaking their debaucheries, becoming Kafiristan's wise monarchs.

Their *ascensio* complete, they now symbolically travel through the high degrees of Masonry by receiving treasure in a subterranean vault, mirroring the Royal Arch of Enoch ritual. Peachy and Danny achieve kabalistic apotheosis becoming godlike; however, the two forget that Masonic teachings are allegorical, not literal. Danny develops delusions of grandeur: first, he suggests Peachy bow to him like the others, ostensibly to "keep up appearances" in front of the natives, continuing the deception. Then, he begins making plans to turn the land into a modern country, to the extent that he envisages eventually meeting Queen Victoria as an equal. Disgusted, Peachy decides to leave and, loaded on a mule train, take as much loot as he can carry thereby returning to his hedonistic ways. The two men pay for their transgressions: Danny is thrown into a pit while Peachy is crucified, cut down, doomed to walk the earth deranged and deformed. As a token of their tale, Peachy gives Kipling Danny's mummified skull, conjuring Masonry's Chamber of Reflection, wherein one can meditate on their mortality. Along with an hourglass and chalice, a human skull is an

---

405 See Duncan's *Masonic Monitor*, rituals-lectures of Entered Apprentice and Fellowcraft degrees.

important relic within the Chamber, symbolizing another Masonic tenet: life is fleeting and that no man lives forever. Danny's crowned skull implies that death claims all men whether rich or poor, surf or king. Danny's divine kingship could not save him because no man is God.

A nexus is forged between Freemasonry and extraterrestrial life by the god Imbra. The deity has a large all-seeing eye which keeps watch over the holy city of Sikandergul. It is implied that Freemasonry's all-seeing eye derives from Imbra, and Imbra's statue depicts the deity as an alien, not as a traditional god. The implication is that Freemasonry, as a modern-day mystery school, is the keeper of off-world supernatural secrets and holy mysteries, making Masonic leadership sacred and just. This is evidenced by Alexander the Great's icon which was a Masonic symbol, the same one worn by Danny. This ancient symbol, coupled with Kipling's earlier tale about Masonry's reach into the arcane past, implies extraterrestrial cultivation of the earth, transforming the Masons into the gatekeepers of this forbidden wisdom. Human civilization as the product of alien design is the subject matter of the finale movie this chapter analyzes, *Stargate*. Interestingly, this film incorporates some of the same themes and imagery from *The Man Who Would Be King*, making it a product of Freemasonry.

$$*\quad*\quad*\quad*$$

Stargate,[406] like Alan Moore's *Watchmen*, is a conspiracy smorgasbord replete with Egyptian-occult imagery and theories which, considering the film was released in pre-internet 1994, was ahead of its time. In many ways, *Stargate* is a retelling of *The Man Who Would Be King* with an added Egyptian-extraterrestrial twist instead of a Middle Eastern narrative. Before the movie begins, an Egyptian King Tut-like death mask appears, only this one is of his father, Akhenaten (a/k/a Amenhotep IV), a Pharaoh of the 18th Dynasty, and a major historical figure in the world of conspiracy. Akhenaten ruled for seventeen years, dying perhaps in 1336 BC or 1334 BCE. He is especially noted for abandoning traditional Egyptian polytheism by introducing the worship of the Aten which can be described as both monotheistic or henotheistic; an early inscription likens the Aten to the sun. On this Manly P. Hall explains, "In his [Akhenaten's] heart was the peace of the Aten, the spiritual sun (Ra, the esoteric sun god).

---

406 The Fifteenth Anniversary Extended Edition Blu-ray was watched to write this analysis.

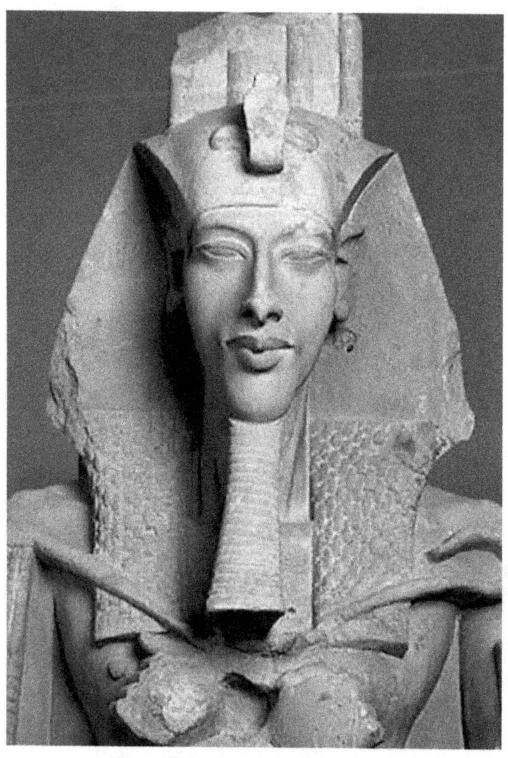

Sculpture of the Egyptian Pharaoh Akhenaten.

Being a Pharaoh of Egypt, he was the personification of the Aten, the high priest of universal truth. It was therefore his duty to perform the works of the Aten and to be the manifestation before men of the virtues resplendent in the sun."[407] Within the conspiracy world, it is theorized that Akhenaten was extraterrestrial and that his worship of the Aten, the one god, reflects his off-world origin. Akhenaten's appearance was also odd: his head was elongated with an hourglass figure, making him appear like an androgynous space alien. In *Stargate*, Akhenaten is one and the same with the sun god Ra (substituted for the Aten), portrayed as an androgynous humanoid by Jaye Davidson. The casting of Davidson as an epicene pharaoh is not surprising, since he played a transgendered woman, Dil, two years earlier in *The Crying Game* (1992). Ra's body is inhabited by a parasitic space alien–the body is merely his host–having used a wormhole, a Stargate, to transport slaves from Egypt back to his desert, Egyptian-like planet. To keep the people enslaved, Ra has banned all writing on this planet which mirrors Akhenaten's suppression and censor of other deities such as Thoth (cf. Hermes Trismegistus), the Egyptian god of writing. It is also explained that Ra is responsible for human civilization by way of Egypt, which dovetails with the conspiracy theory that the Great Pyramids of Giza and Egyptian culture was influenced by extraterrestrials. The film implies that Akhenaten *qua* Ra and his Aten-sun worshipping ilk were space aliens responsible for crafting human civilization. The symbol of the god Ra is the all-seeing Masonic

---

407 Manly P. Hall, *Twelve World Teachers*, p. 23, parentheses added.

eye incorrectly identified as the Eye of Ra. In Egyptology, there is no Eye of Ra only the Eye of Horus. Nevertheless, Ra's all-seeing heliocentric eye mirrors the divine Masonic emblem of the one-eyed god Imbra[408] in *The Man Who Would Be King*.

The movie opens in Giza, Egypt during a 1928 Howard Carter-like expedition, which draws forth from the subconscious the desert scenes in Egypt from 1981's *Raiders of the Lost Ark*. The chaos, the people running around, the hectic search for artifacts is in both films. In *Raiders of the Lost Ark*, the holy Ark of Covenant is lost and found in the Egyptian desert; by being rediscovered in the deserts of Egypt, it is suggested that the Stargate-wormhole (an Einstein-Rosen bridge) is, like the Hebrew Ark, of divine origin. However, the Stargate's divinity is not Abrahamic; rather it is extra-terrestrial. The implication is clear: space aliens are our gods, polytheistic, henotheistic, or monotheistic it doesn't matter (cf. Erich von Daniken's *Chariots of the Gods*, 1968). Years later, after its discovery, the Stargate-wormhole is stored in a top-secret military installation, Creek Mountain, suggestive of another scientific-conspiracy organization, CERN. CERN, derived from the name *Conseil Européen pour la Recherche Nucléaire*, is a European research organization that operates the largest particle physics laboratory in the world. Established in 1954, CERN is based in a northwest suburb of Geneva on the Franco-Swiss border, having twenty-two member states. Israel is the first (and currently only) non-European country granted full membership. CERN's primary function is to provide the particle accel-erators and other infrastructure needed for high-energy physics research; as a result, numerous experiments have been conducted at CERN as a result of international collaborations. CERN is also the birthplace of the World Wide Web. The main site in Geneva, Switzerland has a large computer facility containing powerful data processing services, primarily for exper-imental information analysis; because of the need to make these facilities available to researchers elsewhere, it has historically been a networking hub. In the world of conspiracy, CERN's Large Hadron Collider (LHC) is secretly employed to open wormholes, black holes, and pan-dimensional doorways via particle collision, alchemy, kabalistic magic, and subatomic

---

408 This is also the symbol of Alexander the Great. The implication is that Imbra's divinity was bestowed upon Alexander allowing him to rule as Imbra's godly agent on earth. See *The Man Who Would Be King*.

physics. The United States' secret underground military installation clearly resembles CERN and its top-secret scientific experiments.

It is here that a Graham Hancock-like Egyptologist and linguist, Daniel Jackson (James Spader), is retained to translate the Egyptian hieroglyphs on the Stargate's cover stones which, once deciphered, will open the portal. Once inside the top secret installation, Daniel is taken to Level 28, which subtly evokes the Scottish Rite's 28th degree, known as the Knight of the Sun, which signifies the veiled Masonic and solar-Egyptian mythology of the film.[409] Daniel unravels the cipher's astrological riddle by recognizing the constellation Orion (cf. Robert Bauval's 1983 Orion Correlation Theory regarding the Giza Pyramids' alignment to the three stars in Orion's Belt), revealing the mysterious 7th symbol, opening the Stargate; the mysteries of the number seven having already been explained earlier in this book. It also disclosed that seven points are necessary to coordinate a map in a three-dimensional space.

Comparatively, Daniel Jackson echoes *The Man Who Would Be King's* Daniel Dravot in that:

1. Both men have the same forename.

2. Both men travel to a strange desert land.

3. Both men are given a charm with the Masonic all-seeing eye before leaving for this strange land.

4. Both men are thought to be gods–or representatives of the gods (the cyclops-like Imbra in *The Man Who Would Be King* and Ra in *Stargate)*–when discovered wearing the Masonic talisman.

5. Both men attempt to be culturally sensitive to the natives.

6. In *The Man Who Would Be King*, Daniel suffers what appears to be a fatal wound while Daniel in *Stargate* is killed and resurrected like Freemasonry's martyr Hiram Abif.

---

409 This high degree is known as the Knight Commander of the Temple in the Scottish Rite's Southern Jurisdiction. cf. Pike's *Morals and Dogma*, Chapter XXVIII, pp.581-800. Similar arcana can be found in 2006's *The Da Vinci Code* where the number 13 appears (also on an elevator's keypad) symbolizing the 13th degree of the Scottish Rite, The Royal Arch of Enoch (or Solomon), when, echoing that degree ceremony, esoteric knowledge is required to further the adventure. See Sullivan's *The Royal Arch of Enoch*, Chapter XV, "So Dark the Con of Man."

7. Both men decide to stay in the strange land, taking a local woman for a wife while their friend, Peachy in *The Man Who Would Be King* and Col. Jack O'Neil (Kurt Russell) in *Stargate*, want to return home.

By drawing on the symbolism and themes of *The Man Who Would Be King*, *Stargate* clearly implies a Masonic-Egyptian-extraterrestrial nexus which has always fascinated alternative historians and conspiracy theorist alike. Many Masonic historians such as James Anderson (ca. 1679/80-1739), Martin Clare, and Albert Pike trace Masonry back to the mysteries of Egypt. Masonic ritualist Thomas Smith Webb (1771-1819) spoke of an infinite plurality of worlds in his 1797 *Illustrations of Masonry*[410] which reflects Giordano Bruno's belief that other planets harbored extraterrestrial life. Comparatively, the idea of a man being mistaken for a Masonic-like God is featured in *The Simpsons'* episode titled "Homer the Great" (airdate 8 January 1995). Homer Simpson is admitted to a Masonic-like secret society known as the Stonecutters, but is mistaken for a god when Homer's birthmark is revealed to be the Stonecutter's emblem. The Masonic birthmark identifies Homer as the Chosen One, a kingly figure who will return the Stonecutters to everlasting glory.

Freemasonry, whether intentional or not, always turns up in film sometimes in the most unlikely places. In *Flash Gordon* (1980), Klytus (Peter Wyngarde, 1927-2018), the scheming manipulator behind Ming the Merciless (Max von Sydow), wears the Masonic square and compasses on his chest plate. To the Anti-Mason, the symbol is apropos: Klytus is the hidden hand working in Ming's governmental apparatus, playing both sides against the middle. Masonry, as the inheritor of all the ancient Babylonian and Egyptian Mysteries, is featured in *The Wizard of Oz*, wherein Dorothy ascends Masonry's winding staircase of the Middle Chamber, symbolized by a twisting tornado, to be transported to a magical land to receive gnosis. In *Fight Club*, an all-male nihilistic Gnostic secret society–that no one talks about–manipulates society from behind the scenes, trying to destroy it. Thomas Anderson (Keanu Reeves) goes into a quasi-Masonic Temple, complete with black and white checkered mosaic floor tiles, ascending a

---

410 Webb states in his *Illustrations*, "Numberless worlds are around us, all framed by the Divine Architect, which roll through the vast expanse, and are conducted by the fame unerring law of nature." See also Sullivan's *The Royal Arch of Enoch, passim.*

winding staircase to receive gnosis from the Hermes Trismegistus-like Morpheus (Laurence Fishburne) in *The Matrix* (see *Cinema Symbolism*) to become the One.

Even the music videos on MTV and VH1 are not immune to Freemasonry: by far the greatest Masonic-alchemical music video ever produced is Gloria Estefan's "Live for Loving You" which was the fourth and last single from her third solo album, *Into the Light*, a Luciferian title, released in 1991. The video begins with an Enochic sun (cf. the Hurd Plate-Engraving; see Sullivan's *The Royal Arch of Enoch*, Plate VII) rising over Solomon's Temple's black and white checkered floor, the Threshing Floor of Ornan the Jebusite of II Chronicles 3:1.[411] The Threshing Floor evokes not only Solomon's Temple, but also anticipates the construction of the Second Temple, the Temple of Zerubbabel, in Masonry's high degrees. Then the video's director appears before a rising sun, incarnating as a cigarette smoking flamingo, between two palm trees, representing the Pillars of Enoch. The director has deposited himself between two pillars, becoming a living Royal Arch Word *qua* Tetragrammaton, a supreme initiate. Owls and serpents, both tokens of wisdom, appear throughout the video symbolizing the sacred Masonic knowledge associated with the Holy Royal Arch. In a rainforest, Gloria begins the video as unassuming earth goddess but, as the video progresses, Gloria exhibits all the colors of alchemical transition: her dresses are black, white, and red; she even drives a red car with a black and white dog that has a red scarf tied around its neck. She wears a white bathrobe representing the *albedo*, and a sexy black ensemble denoting the *nigredo*. Gloria wears a sleek yellow bodysuit, the *citrinitas*, while relaxing in a rickshaw pulled by a muscular Adonis personifying the masculine sun. The alchemical process commenced, Gloria must finish what she began, ending the video in the *rubedo*. She wears a sultry red dress and high heels, signifying alchemical completion, while sitting on a crescent moon, the supreme symbol of the feminine. The Great Work is finished; Gloria has transitioned from an earth goddess to a majestic lunar goddess like Isis and Diana. Gloria has transcended earth by becoming Mozart's apotheosized Queen of the Night, ruling from the starry canopy above.

---

411 "Then Solomon began to build the house of the LORD at Jerusalem in mount Moriah, where the LORD appeared unto David his father, in the place that David had prepared in the threshing floor of Ornan the Jebusite."

CHAPTER VII

THE ILLUMINATI IN FILM

"Well it was covered up by the Higher Echelon. Take any fire,
any earthquake, any major disaster, then wonder.
Flying saucers, Captain, are still a rumor, officially."
– Col. Tom Edwards, *Plan 9 from Outer Space*, 1959.

"I'm the key figure in an ongoing government charade,
the plot to conceal the truth about the existence of extraterrestrials.
It's a global conspiracy actually, with key players in the highest
levels of power that reaches down into the lives of every man,
woman, and child on this planet, so of course,
no one believes me. I'm an annoyance to my superiors,
a joke to my peers. They call me 'Spooky.' Spooky
Mulder whose sister was abducted by aliens
when he was just a kid and who now chases after
little green men with a badge and a gun shouting
to the heavens or to anyone who will listen
that the fix is in, that the sky is falling and
when it hits it's gonna be the shit-storm of all time.
– Fox Mulder, *The X-Files: Fight the Future*, 1998.

"Don't you think one of the charms of marriage is that it
makes deception a necessity for both parties?
May I ask why a beautiful woman who could have
any man in this room wants to be married?"
– Sandor Szavost, *Eyes Wide Shut*, 1999

This chapter will not waste the reader's time by going on a Beavis and Butthead snipe hunt looking for eyes in triangles (more a Masonic emblem than an Illuminati one) placed in cinema. To this author, when an Eye in the Triangle turns up in the background or foreground of a film, it is most likely (not always) placed there for sensationalist reasons; to get people believing that there's an Illuminati-mind-control conspiracy in Hollywood. Posting blogs and YouTube videos about Hollywood Mind Control is what the movie-making industry wants, and wants you to believe; to get the populace talking about a movie, negatively or positively, is Hollywood's grand modus operandi. They want controversy and the more, the better; Hollywood wants the tail to wag the dog. This sentiment was summed up best by Bela Lugosi (Martin Landau, 1928-2017) when he said to Ed Wood (Johnny Depp) in 1994's *Ed Wood*, "There is no such thing as bad press, Eddie." Instead, this chapter will explore the Illuminati, and analyze Illuminist doctrines featured in cinema.

The Illuminati (a/k/a the Bavarian Illuminati) was founded on 1 May (Beltane) 1776 by University of Ingolstadt canon law professor Adam Weishaupt (1748-1830) and his close confidant, Xaver Zwack (1756-1843). The entire infrastructure of the Illuminati was modeled after the Society of Jesus. The Jesuits had been the most powerful and influential political-religious secret society until 1773 when it was suppressed by Pope Clement XIV (1705-1774) due to its geopolitical chicanery and festering occultism. Enter Weishaupt and the Illuminati shortly thereafter to pick up where the Jesuits and the Counter-Reformation left off; on the Illuminati, Albert Mackey writes:

…Its founder at first called it the Order of the Perfectibilists; …Its professed object was, by the mutual assistance of its members, to attain the highest possible degree of morality and virtue, and to lay the foundation for the reformation of the world by the association of good men to oppose the progress of moral evil. To give to the Order a higher influence, Weishaupt connected it with the Masonic Institution, after whose system of degrees, of esoteric instruction, and of secret modes of recognition, it was organized.

…Weishaupt, though a reformer in religion and liberal in politics, had originally been a Jesuit; and he employed, therefore, in the construction of his association, the shrewdness and subtlety which distinguished the disciples of Loyola; and having been initiated in 1777 in a Lodge at Munich, he also borrowed for its use the mystical organization which was peculiar to Freemasonry.

…The original design of Illuminism was undoubtedly the elevation of the human race.[412]

Terry Melanson, in his book *Perfectibilists: The 18th Century Bavarian Order of the Illuminati*, further explains:

The Order was secret, hierarchical, and heavily modeled on the Jesuits. 'The Illuminati first assumed the name Perfectionists' [that is, *Perfectibilists*; Ger. *Perfectibilisten*], writes the 19th century historian Friedrich Christoph Schlosser. And 'to the theological shield of the Jesuits inscribed with the phrase, '*Extension of the Kingdom of God*,' they set up in opposition a philosophical standard emblazoned with the words '*Perfection of Man.*' *Perfectibilists*, however, sounded bizarre and not sufficiently mysterious; Weishaupt quickly changed the name to the Order of the Illuminati (*Illuminatenordens*)–chosen, perhaps, because of the 'image of the sun radiating illumination to outer circles.' The Order was therefore always represented in communication between members as a circle with a dot in the center.

The concept of the perfection or perfectibility of man is an old one, and has had a wide range of adherents in the last three thousand years. Weishaupt could have drawn inspiration from any one–more likely a multitude– of these traditions while initially naming his Order. In terms of religion, mysticism, and the occult, Perfectibilists have been associated with antinomianism, sects adhering to the teachings of Dionysius the Areopagite, the Hesychasts, the Jansenists, the Fraticelli, the Brethren of the Free Spirit, the Anabaptists, the Quakers, the Beghards, the Cathers or Albigensians, and the Familists.[413]

---

412 Mackey, *Encyclopedia of Freemasonry*, Vol. I, pp. 346-347.
413 Terry Melanson, *Perfectibilists*, p. 18.

Like Masonry, Illuminati initiates progressed through a series of degrees or circles to receive light or enlightenment; however, light was, in fact, revolutionary zeal symbolized by solar fire. The purpose of ascending the Illuminist hierarchy was not so much to attain wisdom; rather, it was to remake the initiate into a loyal servant on a universal mission, "We cannot use people as they are, but begin by making them over."[414] The revolutionaries' primitive vision of the world as a dualist struggle between the forces of darkness and of light may originate in the neo-Manichean view of Weishaupt's followers and their elect group of *illuminated ones* was engaged in struggle with the *sons of darkness*, their categorical name for all outside the order. At the very center within the inner circle of Areopagites burned a candle symbolizing the solar source of all illumination. The Zoroastrian-Manichean cult of fire was central to the otherwise eclectic symbolism of the Illuminists; their calendar was based on Persian rather than classical or Christian models.[415]

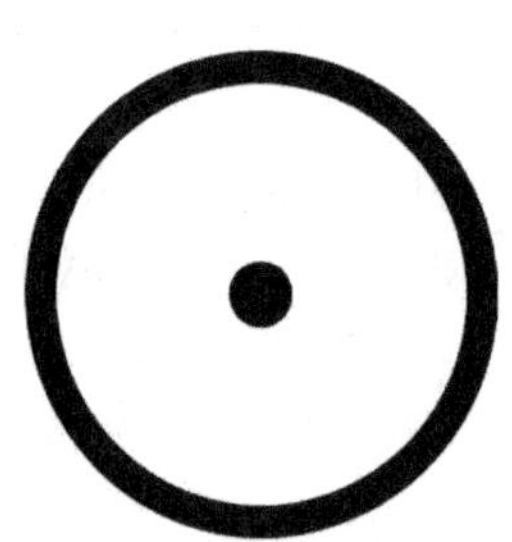

The Point Within a Circle is the solar symbol of the Illuminati. The point represents the sun and the circle is the zodiac, indicating heliocentric rulership.

Like the high degrees of Masonry (cf. Rite of Perfection), the Illuminati appears to be another Jesuit Counter-Reformation ruse created to infiltrate Masonry; exoterically, they were revolutionary; esoterically, they were reactionary. The Jesuits were charged with leading the Counter-Reformation beginning at the Council of Trent (1545-153) employing espionage and subterfuge under the guise of hermeticism, Cabala, and mysticism to secretly lure Protestants back to the pagan and Neoplatonic mysteries of the Roman Church. In this author's next book on Masonry entitled *Freemasonry and the Path to Babylon*, this author briefly explains, "As a symbolic method of projecting the ideas of initiation into society, Illuminism also emulated an important Jesuit agenda of the supranational Roman Catholic mission to restore the temporal and spiritual power of the Church, consistent with post-Tridentine magisterial theory during a time of hardship. The subtle deployment of Cabalism, hermeticism, mysticism, and the occult squared

---

414 Letter of Weishaupt to Zwack, March 10th, 1778, quoted in James H. Billington's *Fire in the Minds of Men*, p. 94.
415 Billington, *ibid*, pp. 94-95

perfectly with Jesuit Counter-Reformation triumphalism, and is reflected in Illuminati's revolutionary yet duplicitous reactionary agenda." With the suppression of the Jesuits in 1773, the Illuminati did just that: it was a Jesuit Counter-Reformation vehicle which carried them through the turmoil of the French Revolution and the First Republic of Napoleon I. After Napoleon was defeated at Waterloo in 1815, just as the Illuminati was fading from European history, the Jesuits, the Holy Inquisition, and the Papal States were restored. Although the Illuminati seems to have disappeared from the history books, many contend they are still around, manipulating governments, instigating all wars and conspiracies. Whether they still linger depends on who you ask, but their influence is unquestioned. Illuminism survives in the *haute* degrees of Freemasonry, in the revolutionary fire that sparked the American and French Revolutions, in the doctrines of the Carbonari (English: Charcoal Burners), and in the philosophies behind the Communist Revolutions of the 20th Century. In the world of politics, Illuminism is the fusion of sorcery with statecraft to transform society economically, philosophically, morally, and religiously on all levels: local, state, and global; the successful transformation of the globe into a New World Order.

Today, the Illuminati's agenda is social engineering; they are puppet master seeking world domination, toiling behind the scenes to end all religions and governments for a demonic hegemony. This notion originates from the anti-Illuminist works *Proofs of a Conspiracy* (1797) by John Robison (1739-1805), Abbé Augustin Barruel's (1741-1820) *Memoirs Illustrating the History of Jacobinism* also published in 1797, Nesta Webster's (1876-1960) *Secret Societies and Subversive Movements* (1924), and Léo Taxil's (real name Marie Joseph Gabriel Antoine Jogand-Pagès, 1854-1907) *Les Mystères de la Franc-Maçonnerie* (*Mysteries of Freemasonry*) published in1885-1886; the latter portrayed Freemasons, and by default the Illuminati, as Luciferian Devil Worshippers. Despite Taxil admitting his treatise was a hoax,[416] the damage was done; the rumors of Masonry and the Illuminati's evil agenda persists to this day. As far as Barruel goes, he was a Jesuit and likely pointing the finger away from his

---

416 *National Magazine, an Illustrated American Monthly*, Volume XXIV: April-September, 1906, pp. 228 and 229. See also Arturo de Hoyos and S. Brent Morris' "Albert Pike and Lucifer," *It True What They Say About Freemasonry?* (1998).

own society by portraying the Illuminati as anti-Jesuits when, in fact, they were not. Robison's work had the most impact in the United States: his book was preached by Jedidiah Morse (1761-1826) which ultimately led to the formation of the Anti-Masonic Party (first Third Party in the US) in 1828. The Illuminati, globalist masters running all governments, pulling all strings from behind the scenes, is how they are often portrayed in film.

The Illuminati appears in 1979's *Being There* when billionaire Ben Rand's (Melvyn Douglas, 1901-1981) coffin is being led to its final resting place: a pyramidal crypt capped with an all-seeing eye, signifying that he was part of a Masonic-like hidden hand or secret cabal running the US government. While the President (Jack Warden, 1920-2006) eulogizes him, Rand's pallbearers, also part of this secret, globalist group, discuss who they will "select" as the next President. The secret coterie in *Being There* is more akin to globalist groups such as Bilderberg,[417] the Trilateral Commission,[418] the Council on Foreign Relations,[419] and Yale University's Skull and Bones[420] (to see Skull and Bones' influence upon the founding of

---

417 Bilderberg is an annual private conference of about 120 to 160 political leaders and experts from industry, finance, academia and the media, established in 1954. About two thirds of the participants come from Europe and the rest from North America; one third from politics and government and the rest from other fields (see Chapter II). The group's original goal of promoting Atlanticism has grown; in 2001, Denis Healey, a Bilderberg group founder and, a steering committee member for 30 years, said: "To say we were striving for a one-world government is exaggerated, but not wholly unfair. Those of us in Bilderberg felt we couldn't go on forever fighting one another for nothing and killing people and rendering millions homeless. So we felt that a single community throughout the world would be a good thing." See Jon Ronson, (10 March 2001), "Who pulls the strings? (Part 3)," *The Guardian* (London). Retrieved 1 June 2015. See also Chapter II.

418 The Trilateral Commission is a non-governmental, non-partisan discussion group founded by David Rockefeller in July 1973, to foster closer cooperation among North America, Western Europe, and Japan.

419 The Council on Foreign Relations (CFR), founded in 1921, is a United States nonprofit, 4900-member organization, publisher, and think tank specializing in U.S. foreign policy and international affairs, headquartered in New York City, with an additional office in Washington, D.C. Its membership has included senior politicians, more than a dozen Secretaries of State, CIA directors, bankers, lawyers, professors, and senior media figures. The CFR promotes globalization, free trade, reducing financial regulations on transnational corporations, and economic consolidation into regional blocs such as NAFTA or the European Union, and develops policy recommendations that reflect these goals. See Robert D. Schulzinger's The Wise Men of Foreign Affairs, passim.

420 Skull and Bones is an undergraduate senior secret society at Yale University, New Haven, Connecticut. It is the oldest senior class landed society at Yale. The society's alumni organization, the Russell Trust Association, owns the society's real estate and oversees the organization. The society is known informally as *Bones*, and members are known as *Bonesmen*. The group Skull and Bones is featured in conspiracy theories, which claim that the society plays a role in a globalist/

the CIA, check out 2006's *The Good Shepherd*) more than the Illuminati. However, many argue and believe that these elite global groups are linked, at least influenced, by the Illuminati. The James Bond antagonist Ernst Stavro Blofeld runs an Illuminist organization named SPECTRE: **SP**ecial **E**xecutive for **C**ounter **I**ntelligence, **R**evenge, **E**xtortion, which seeks global dominance over the East and the West. The Illuminati are, like Weishaupt, purveyors of the occult, desiring to obtain mystic artifacts to further their nefarious global agenda. The use of sex magicks to achieve a higher, mystical godhead are linked to the practices of the Illuminati which originates from the alchemical, kabalistic, tantric sex rites of Crowley's O.T.O.; the 8th (VIII) degree of the O.T.O. is Perfect Pontiff of the Illuminati and Epopt of the Illuminati. Illuminist Franz Karl von Eckartschausen (1752-1803) was a prolific writer on art, magic, drama, alchemy, politics, mysticism, science, religion, and history becoming one of the recommended authors for Illuminati initiates; it is no surprise that Eckartschausen's last work, *The Cloud upon the Sanctuary*, was Crowley's major early influence and the impetus for him embarking on a magickal mystery tour.[421] The purpose of these sexual rites is to transcend society, to become a god; when the rituals are performed correctly, one is given license to rule over the masses. But first, to become the masters of time and space, the Illuminati seek to get their hands on an ancient, Masonic artifact known as the Triangle.

LARA CROFT: TOMB RAIDER

Released on June 15th, 2001, *Lara Croft: Tomb Raider* is an action- adventure film based on the popular *Tomb Raider* video game series featuring Angelina Jolie in the role of Lara Croft. Lara has often been described as a female combination of James Bond and Indiana Jones, and Jolie was perfectly cast in the part. At the time of the film's release, it was the highest-grossing video game adaptation until it was surpassed by *Prince of Persia: The Sands of Time* (2010), which grossed $336 million. The film

---

corporatist conspiracy for world control. Conspiracy theorists suggest that Skull and Bones is a branch of the Illuminati (see Melanson's *Perfectibilists*, pp. 150-156), or that Skull and Bones itself controls the Central Intelligence Agency.
421 Melanson, *ibid*, pp. 295-296.

is also the highest-grossing action film with a woman in the lead role, next to Sigourney Weaver's *Aliens* (1986). The movie begins with Lara in an Egyptian tomb, seeking a diamond. As she approaches it, she is attacked by a large robot. After an intense chase and battle, she disables it by ripping out its motivational circuits. She takes the diamond, which is revealed to be a memory card labeled "Lara's Party Mix," inserting it into a laptop computer in the robot, whereupon it plays music. It is now revealed that the scene took place in a practice arena in her home. Her computer-hacker assistant Bryce (Noah Taylor) programmed the robot, SIMON, to challenge her in combat.

It is the day (May 15th) of the first phase of a planetary alignment, culminating in a solar eclipse, which happens once every 5,000 years. In Venice, the Illuminati search for a key to rejoin halves of the Triangle, which must be accomplished by the final phase of the alignment. Mr. Powell (Iain Glen), an Illuminist, makes assurances that they are ready, but in reality, he has no idea where to find the key. Lara's butler, James "Hilly" Hillary (Chris Barrie), tries to interest her in several projects but she ignores them. May 15th, as Hilly is aware, is the day that Lara's father, Lord Richard Croft (Jon Voight), disappeared many years earlier. She has not recovered from the loss. Later that night, Lara dreams of her father, about what he said of the alignment, and of an object linked to it called the Triangle of Light. Waking, she becomes aware of a clock ticking. Searching for it, she discovers a secret chamber under the staircase with a carriage clock that had spontaneously begun ticking. Bryce probes it and finds a strange, occult device hidden inside the clock. Since the device resembles a clock, Lara consults a clock expert friend of her father's, Mr. Wilson (Leslie Phillips). She believes it is connected to the Triangle of Light, but Wilson disavows knowledge of the clock and the Triangle. Lara next encounters Alex West (Daniel Craig), a fellow tomb raider with unscrupulous methods. They are attracted to each other, but Croft cannot abide his mercenary attitude. That night, Lara is contacted by Wilson, telling her that he gave her name to a man named Manfred Powell in regards to the clock. Unbeknownst to Lara, Wilson is a member of the Illuminati searching for the Triangle.

The next day, Lara sees Manfred in his home, showing him photographs of the clock. Later, while discussing it with Bryce, she points out that Manfred was lying about his knowledge. That night, while Lara does bungee-ballet, armed commandos invade the mansion and steal the clock despite her attempts to fend them off. The following morning, Lara receives a postdated letter from her deceased father to be delivered, coinciding with the beginning of the alignment. In the letter, he explains that the clock is the key to retrieve two halves of the Triangle of Light, revealed to be an object of extraordinary destructive power which granted its wielder power over time and space. He says that it was made from a metal found in a crater formed by a meteor which had fallen to earth during a previous alignment. Initially housed in a city built in the meteor crater by those worshipping the object, misuse of the Triangle's power destroyed the city, so it was split into two halves. One was hidden in a tomb, the Tomb of the Dancing Light, in Cambodia, and the other half in the ruined city in Siberia. Her father urges her to find and destroy both halves before the Illuminati can reunite them.

In a subterranean temple in Cambodia, Alex—now in the service of Manfred and the Illuminati—deciphers part of the puzzle regarding retrieval the triangle's half, but Lara manages to grab the piece successfully. Before everyone can leave, the piece emits liquid metal bringing the statues in the temple to life, attacking the team, killing some members. Lara is left to fight off and destroy a huge six-armed guardian statue which is the last one to come to life. She successfully defeats the statue, exiting the temple by diving through a waterfall. She then travels to a Buddhist town where a young monk welcomes her. After a worship service, a sagacious monk gives Lara some tea, as they converse, telling her that he knew her father before he vanished.

Lara and Manfred arrange to meet in Venice since each of them has what the other needs to unite the Triangle. Powell proposes a partnership to find the Triangle, informing Lara that her father was a member of the Illuminati, which she vehemently denies. Though hesitant at first, she, along with Bryce, meet with Manfred regarding the trip to Siberia. Inside the tomb, there is a giant model of the solar system, which activates as the alignment nears completion. Lara retrieves the last half of the Triangle, but when Powell tries to unite it, the halves will not fuse. He realizes that Lara knows the solution to the puzzle, shooting West to persuade her to finish the Triangle to save both West's life and her father's. Lara reluctantly complies, and they then struggle for control of the Triangle, with Lara prevailing.

Lara then finds herself in a strange alternate existence standing before her father. He explains that it is a crossing of time and space, urging her to destroy the Triangle instead of using it to save his life. She leaves her father returning to the chamber, where time is slowly running backward from the point when Manfred killed West. Lara takes the knife he threw into West's chest and redirects it into Powell's shoulder, then destroys the Triangle, which returns time to its normal flow. The chamber begins to self-destruct, everyone turns to leave, but Manfred tells Lara that he killed her father, retrieving his pocket watch with a picture of Lara's mother inside. Lara and Manfred engage in a hand-to-hand combat. Lara kills him, recovering the watch, escaping as the chamber crumbles. Back at the mansion, Hilly and Bryce are shocked to see Lara wearing a dress. She goes into the garden to her father's memorial, then returns inside, where Bryce has a repro-grammed SIMON, ready to challenge Lara once again. Hilly produces a silver tray with Lara's pistols, which she takes with a smile; the film ends.

The filmmakers did a great job making this movie feel like a video game. All the elements of a successful action-adventure video game are present. For example, the film opens in simulator wherein Lara hones her combative skills which are put to the test when she fights off wave after wave of bad guys when her mansion is invaded. Next, she is sent on a quest to prevent a powerful artifact falling into the wrong hands, she must solve two puzzle rooms: the tombs in Cambodia and Siberia; and there are two Boss Battles: the giant six-armed stone statue in Cambodia and Manfred Powell during the movie's climax. It is no secret who the bad guys are: they are the Illuminati seeking world domination by uniting two halves of a magical relic, the Triangle, to become masters of time and space. The symbol of the Illuminati is the eye in the triangle, which again, is more Masonic than Illuminist but nevertheless is effective, suggesting the om-nipresence of the mysterious group. Lara is tipped off to the Illuminati's devious plans when a posthumous postdated letter arrives from her miss-ing father. The letter is a note with a verse from the William Blake poem *Auguries of Innocence* (ca. 1803), "To see a World in a Grain of Sand / And a Heaven in a Wild Flower / Hold Infinity in the palm of your hand / And Eternity in an hour." Blake's mystical writings and artwork influenced se-cret organizations such as the Golden Dawn and the Theosophical Society. In Lord Richard Croft's library, Lara retrieves a volume of Blake's work in which he has concealed information about the mysterious Illuminati. Lord Richard, a Howard Carter-like archeologist, warns that the Illuminati are dangerous and must be stopped at all costs. Upon deciding to take up the quest, Lara wears a white t-shirt with a dark red cross emblazoned upon it symbolizing the Knights Templar. By pursuing the relic and the Illuminati, Lara is on a protective, religious quest of divine providence; she will be the knight in shining armor defeating the evil secret society. During her journey, Lara frequently encounters jasmine, a flower of female intuition, signifying that Lara is on the right path: she is fulfilling her destiny by tracking down the ancient artifact and defeating the Illuminati.

Because the Illuminati is the film's villain, the movie is replete with solar symbolisms, some overt, some covert, signifying the Bavarian Illuminati's use of the sun as the source of all illumination (cf. Manichean Cosmology, Zoroastrianism). The Illuminati is defined as the "People of the Light" hence, they are after the Triangle of Light. The Triangle must be made whole when all the planets are aligned during a solar eclipse (Phase II). Inside the Siberian tomb, when the Illuminati high priest possesses the Triangle, he attempts to unify it standing before a giant solar globe indicative of sun worship; in fact, the last puzzle room is the solar system. Before entering the Cambodian tomb, Manfred informs West that they must work faster, because there are seventy-two minutes to the next alignment. The seventy-two minutes symbolizes the seventy-two years the sun moves one degree backward based on the Precession of the Equinoxes while, at the same time, the number seventy-two evokes the seventy-two demons of *Ars Goetia*, thereby imbuing the Illuminati with sinister overtones. A few moments after Manfred says, "Into the belly of the beast," to which West responds, "And out of the demon's ass." Once inside the tomb, West attempts to place the clock inside a solar portal to release the first half of the Triangle. However, Lara realizes it is a trick: the real portal is aligned to a floating, rotating all-seeing eye which represents the Eye of Horus, the Egyptian sun god.

The Illuminati are portrayed as global puppet masters above the law, transcending all governments. When the Illuminati arrives in Siberia, they give orders to the Russian Army, operating amphibious vehicles from the old Soviet Union. Although the Illuminati are foreigners, the Russian officers and soldiers obey their commands without question.

Next, the Illuminati's agenda is taken to a more sinister level. These global elites do not seek treasure; rather, they practice sex magicks, perform occult rituals, handing out death sentences to all those standing in their way. Meet the Illuminati of Stanley Kubrick's *Eyes Wide Shut*.

KUBRICK'S ILLUMINATI IMPULSE: EYES WIDE SHUT

Kubrick's *Eyes Wide Shut* is an erotic thriller loosely based on Arthur Schnitzler's (1862-1931) 1926 novella *Dream Story*; it is a film which can only be properly understood when viewed through symbolic lenses. If not watched symbolically, *Eyes Wide Shut* is a snooze-fest that, at times, can be excruciatingly dull. But Kubrick is too sly a filmmaker not to be aware of this. The film's monotony seems to be intentional on Kubrick's part, like he's trying to tell the viewing audience that movies incorporate occult icons and themes and, that when viewing a film, to always be aware of this. To communicate this message, Kubrick uses precise imagery that is so overt and evident that even those ignorant of the use of concealed imagery in cinema cannot help but take notice. When Kubrick's movie is understood symbolically, *Eyes Wide Shut* is a dark masterpiece, exploring and exposing the blight of the human condition, the microcosm, and its nebulous reflections within the world: the macrocosm. Kubrick reveals the ugly existing in each of us and how evil manifests, but there is one evil so ruthless and vile that it makes other evils trite, even meaningless.

Eyes Wide Shut spent a long time in production holding the Guinness World Record for the longest continuous film shoot period at 400 days. The movie, set in the late 1990s, takes place over the course of a few days and nights during the Christmas holiday. The film begins by introducing Dr. William "Bill" Harford (Tom Cruise) and his wife, Alice (Nicole Kidman), a young couple with a daughter, Helena (Madison Eginton), living in New York City. Their daughter's name, Helena, evokes the legendary Helen of Troy, in Greek Mythology, the most beautiful woman in the world. In this context, their daughter's name identifies Bill and Alice as upper-middle class socialites *qua* gods (Helen of Troy's parents were the king of the gods,

Zeus, and the voluptuous Leda), not only wealthy, but are also elites, beautiful people having birthed a beautiful child. It should come as no surprise that Kubrick cast Cruise and Kidman to play these parts because, at the time of its release, they were Hollywood's "it" couple. Bill and Alice go to an opulent Christmas party thrown by the equally wealthy Victor Ziegler (Sydney Pollack). Bill runs into an old friend from medical school, Nick Nightingale (Todd Field), now playing piano professionally. Nick invites Bill to visit him in a bar he often plays jazz music. While a mysterious European man named Sandor Szavost (Sky du Mont) tries to pick up Alice, two young vixens attempt to take Bill off for a tryst. He is interrupted by a call from his host upstairs; Ziegler was having sex with Mandy (Julienne Davis), a young woman having overdosed on a speedball.[422] Mandy slowly recovers with Bill's aid.

The next evening at home, while smoking marijuana, Alice asks him if he had sex with the two young women. After Bill reassures her, she asks if he is ever jealous of men that are attracted to her. As the discussion gets heated, he states that he thinks women are more faithful than men. She rebuts him, telling him of a sexual fantasy she recently had about a naval officer they had encountered on a vacation. Disturbed by Alice's revelation, Bill is then called by the daughter of a patient having just died in his sleep, subsequently journeying over to her place. In her pain, Marion Nathanson (Marie Richardson) impulsively kisses Bill saying she loves him. He rejects her advances, relieved when her fiancé Carl (Thomas Gibson) arrives. Next, Bill takes a contemplative walk in the street of New York City. He meets a prostitute named Domino (Vinessa Shaw), going to her dingy apartment.

Once inside, Alice phones just as Domino begins to kiss Bill, after which he calls off the awkward encounter. Meeting Nick at the jazz club where he's just finishing his last set, Bill learns that Nick has an engagement but must play piano blindfolded. Bill presses him for details. He learns to gain admittance, one needs a costume, a mask, and the password, *Fidelio*, the name of the only opera by Ludwig van Beethoven (1770-1827). Bill goes to a costume shop called Under the Rainbow offering the owner, Mr. Milich (Rade Serbedzija), a generous amount of money to

---

422 A speedball is a term referring to the intravenous use of cocaine with heroin or morphine in the same syringe.

rent a costume and mask. In the backroom of the shop, Milich catches his underage daughter (Leelee Sobieski) with two Japanese men performing a role-playing sex game, expressing outrage over their lack of decency. Milich detains them and threatens to call the police.

Bill takes a taxi to a country mansion named Somerton. He gives the password, enters, discovering a Masonic-Illuminati-O.T.O. sex magick ritual taking place. Since Nick is an outsider–not initiated into the secret society's mysteries–he must play the piano blindfolded, not privy to its rituals and symbols. Although he is masked, a woman takes Bill aside warning him he does not belong, insisting he is in terrible danger. They are interrupted by a porter telling Bill that the taxi driver wants to speak with him. However, the porter takes him to a room where a disguised, red-cloaked master of ceremonies (cf. a magus; a Crowley-like magician) interrogates Bill about a second password which Bill says he has forgotten. The master of ceremonies insists that Bill "kindly remove his mask," then his clothes. The masked woman having tried to warn Bill now intervenes asking that she be punished instead of him. Bill is ushered from the mansion and warned not to tell anyone about what transpired.

Just before the breaking dawn, Bill arrives home guilty and confused. He finds Alice laughing loudly in her sleep and awakens her. While crying, she tells him of a troubling dream in which she was having sex with the naval officer and many other men while laughing at the idea of Bill seeing her with them. The next morning, Bill goes to Nick's hotel where the homosexual desk clerk (Alan Cumming) tells Bill that a bruised and frightened Nick checked out a few hours earlier after returning with two large, dangerous-looking men. Nick tried to pass an envelope to the clerk when they were leaving, but it was intercepted, and Nick was driven away by the two men. Bill goes to return the costume–but not the mask, which he has misplaced. Milich, with his daughter by his side, states he can do other favors for Bill, "and it needn't be a costume." The same two Japanese men from the night before nonchalantly appear and leave; Milich has prostituted his daughter rather than reporting them to the police. Bill returns to the Somerton in his car and is met at the gate by a man with a note warning him to cease his inquiries. At home, Bill thinks about Alice's dream while watching her tutor their daughter.

Bill reconsiders his sexual offers from the night before. He first phones Marion but hangs up after Carl answers the phone. Bill then goes to Domino's apartment with a gift. Her roommate Sally (Fay Masterson) is home, but not Domino. After Bill attempts to seduce Sally, she reveals that Domino has just tested positive for HIV. Bill leaves, noticing a man is following him. After reading a newspaper story about a beauty queen named Amanda Curran suffering a drug overdose, Bill goes to the hospital to see her. Bill is informed that she died earlier in the day, but is given permission to examine what is revealed to be Mandy's body–the Mandy in Ziegler's bathroom from the Christmas party–in the morgue. Bill is summoned to Ziegler's house, where he is confronted with the events of the past night and day. Ziegler was one of those involved in the occult ritual orgy, having identified Bill's interloping via his connection with Nick, the pianist. His position within the powerful secret society has been jeopardized by Bill's intrusion since Ziegler recommended Nick for the job at Somerton.

Ziegler claims that he had Bill followed for his protection and that the warnings made against Bill by the society are only intended to scare him from speaking about the orgy sex rite. But he implies the society is capable of acting on their threats, telling Bill: "If I told you their names…I don't think you'd sleep so well," implying that the Illuminati is above the law. Bill asks about the death of Mandy, whom Ziegler identifies as the masked woman at the party sacrificing herself to prevent Bill's punishment, and about the disappearance of Nick. Ziegler insists that the pianist is safely home in Seattle. Ziegler also says Bill's punishment was a charade by the secret society to frighten him further, and it had nothing to do with Mandy's death; she was a hooker and addict having died from another accidental drug overdose. Bill does not know if Ziegler is telling him the truth, but he says nothing further, dropping the matter.

When he returns home, Bill finds the rented mask on his pillow next to his sleeping wife. He breaks down in tears, deciding to tell Alice the truth of the past two days. The next morning, they go Christmas shopping in a toy store (likely FAO Schwarz) with their daughter. Alice muses that they should be grateful they have survived, that she loves him, and there is something they must do as soon as possible. When Bill asks what it is, she replies, "Fuck." The movie abruptly ends and the credits roll.

* * * *

Eyes Wide Shut is Kubrick's final film; he died five days after submitting the final cut to Warner Brothers, and immediately conspiracy theories emerged: was Kubrick killed by a secret cabal, the Illuminati, because his swan song exposed the inner workings of the mysterious secret society? Like all great art, the movie does not draw any definite conclusions; rather, it lets the audience make up its mind whether or not Kubrick was deliberating exposing a shadow group that manipulates society–eliminating all those that get in its way–or if the film is fiction. It is curious that Mentmore Towers in England was the location where Kubrick filmed the Somerton mansion scenes, the headquarters of the film's secret society. The nineteenth-century estate was built for the Rothchilds: a banking clan rumored to be involved with the Illuminati and devil worship, only adding the film's mystery. By using a Rothchild mansion as a base for diabolical global elites, was Kubrick trying to expose the Illuminati? Was he killed because he knew too much?

One thing is sure: Kubrick's use of symbolism is intentional; even to the passive moviegoer, Christmas lights pervade the movie. The Christmas lights are not the tiny white lights that are often used; instead, they are gaudy reds, greens, oranges, blues, and yellows appearing in every scene. The Christmas season, a time for joyous celebration, is given a visceral subtext by Kubrick to convey humanity's shadow self, the corruption of materialism. Underneath the gleeful Christmas lights and carols is a world of malaise in which sex, drug use, alcoholism, prostitution, marital infidelity, death, disease, pedophilia, and pornography flourish; they are the earmarks of society's amoral dark side. While Bill walks the streets of New York City, Christmas is intertwined with a couple making out, a XXX shop, and rowdy juvenile delinquents calling him "faggot." Christmas lights shine brightly in the dingy apartment of prostitutes Domino and Sally. Getting ready to attend a Christmas party, even the beautiful Alice is introduced using the toilet. Kubrick employs Christmas, and its jovial decorations, to run parallel with the wickedness in the world. Evil does not take a break just because it is Christmas. Kubrick wants the audience to understand this: Christmas does not rid the world of society's seedy underbelly; it is alive no matter what time of year it is. However, Kubrick then reveals the spiritual evil lurking in this world, plaguing humankind from the shadows:

the Illuminati. There are no Christmas lights at Somerton because their evil is transcendent, and their power is supernatural.

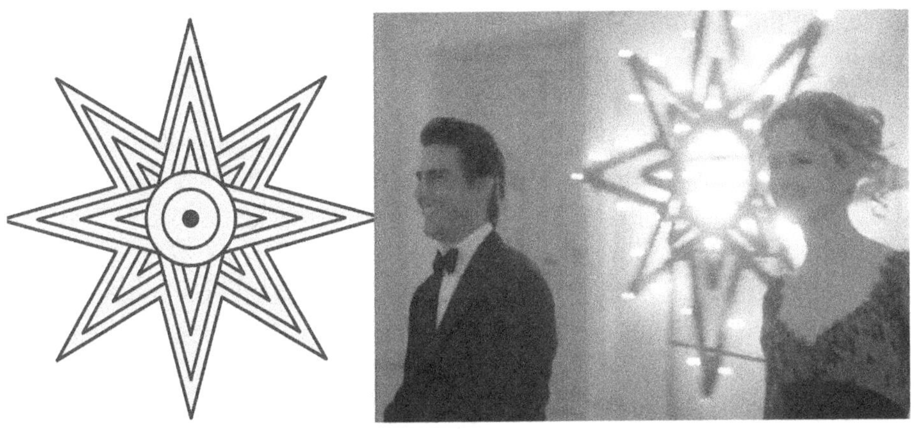

(Left) In antiquity, the eight-pointed star was the symbol of the goddess Ishtar, the divine personification of the planet Venus. (Right) An eight-pointed star *qua* Christmas decoration hangs on the wall behind Bill and Alice Harford when they enter Ziegler's party. Other eight-pointed stars can be observed during the Christmas party, mostly in the dance hall.

The name, Alice, suggests Lewis Carroll's *Alice's Adventures in Wonderland* and *Alice Through the Looking Glass*, foreshadowing the adventures of her husband, Bill, into a magical land. Only Bill's journey does not take him to a surreal subterranean world. Instead, he explores the occult world of sex magick and secret societies. The movie starts with Bill and Alice attending a Christmas party thrown by the affluent Victor Ziegler. As Bill and Alice mingle, several eight-pointed stars appear in the background as bright yellow and white Christmas decorations. Coming straight out of the collective unconscious and mythology, the stars evoke the Babylonian goddess Ishtar, whose ancient symbol was an eight-pointed star. Ishtar was the goddess of love, war, fertility, and sexuality, the latter a critical component of the movie; her cult may have involved sacred prostitution. To the ancient Assyrians and Babylonians, she was a moon goddess, the ruler of the night and through her one could gain secret knowledge; one of the most famous myths about Ishtar describes her descent to the underworld.[423] The eight-pointed star is a hidden emblem

---

423 cf. Guiley's *Encyclopedia of Witches and Witchcraft*, p. 172.

of Ishtar, anticipating Bill's nocturnal journey to Somerton where he descends into the secret society's unholy, dark sexual world. Bill gains wisdom from his adventure, which is not available to the vulgar masses: he learns that secret organizations do exist, and the world is their playground, people are merely pawns in their elaborate games of manipulation and deception.

During the party, a European Don Juan named Sandor Szavost attempts to seduce Alice while they dance. When they first meet, Szavost drinks from her wine glass, implying the sexual exchange of bodily fluids while his name, Sandor, signifies the middle name of Church of Satan founder, Anton Szandor LaVey (1930-1997). Founded on Walpurgisnacht (April 30) 1966, LaVey's Church of Satan to this day employs demonic, sex magick rites as part of their liturgy and rituals. The name Sandor foreshadows the sensual and perverse ceremonies of the unnamed secret society which Bill will eventually encounter. While Alice dances with Szavost, he asks her, "Did you ever read the Latin poet Ovid on the *Art of Love*?" which is a blatant invitation to adultery since *Art of Love* (*Ars amatoria*, 2 CE) discusses how to procure mistresses. As they kibitz, Alice reveals she used to work in a SoHo art gallery which draws forth the erotic adventures of *9 ½ Weeks*' Elizabeth McGraw, who, like Alice, works in a Soho art gallery. Almost a psychic vampire, Szavost uses every debonair pick-up line in his repertoire to hypnotize Alice into having sex with him. Meanwhile, Bill enjoys the company of two beautiful young women, both of whom, likewise, want to have sex by escorting him, "Where the rainbow ends." Echoing the magical journeys of Alice in Carroll's stories, this implies the mystical travels of Dorothy in the Land of Oz. Unlike Dorothy going over the rainbow to experience Oz to receive gnosis,[424] Bill ventures into the realm of secret societies by going Under the Rainbow's spectrum. Under the Rainbow is the costume shop supplying Bill with the mask and cape necessary to gain admittance to the Illuminati shadow gathering, exposing him to living darkness; the Illuminati is *where the rainbow ends*. The two young ladies are interrupted when Bill is requested to come to an upstairs bathroom. A prostitute named Mandy has caught the Christmas Spirit by having sex with Ziegler, nearly overdosing on a speedball. She

---

424 See "President William McKinley: The Wizard of Oz" in Sullivan's *Cinema Symbolism*, Chapter V, *passim*.

is in need of medical attention so Bill comes to her (and Ziegler's) rescue. Mandy recovers, but by overlapping a Christmas party with sex, drugs, infidelity, and prostitution, Kubrick wishes everyone Happy Holidays with his middle finger firmly extended.

Kubrick employs names in *Eyes Wide Shut* to convey a hidden meaning. Alice, Sandor, and Helena aside, the surname of Bill's enabler, Nick Nightingale, is a token of the common nightingale bird which sings at night; as such, Nick provides Bill, under the cover of darkness, the secret location and password to gain entry to the secret society. The password to enter the sex ritual is *Fidelio*, which means *faithful*, signifying Bill and Alice's marital infidelity. Beethoven's *Fidelio* is about a wife sacrificing herself to free her husband, a political prisoner from death. This password anticipates the master of ceremonies exposing Bill as an intruder, causing Mandy to sacrifice herself to save him from the wrath of the secret society. It is here, within the confines of Somerton, where Kubrick presents the real evil in the world: ruthless master manipulators who secretly rule the world, engaging in bizarre sexual rites to satisfy their dark desires. Although the group in never named, it is unmistakable Kubrick is suggesting an amalgamation of the Illuminati, Bilderberg Group, Skull and Bones, and Bohemian Grove fused with Masonic-like and O.T.O. ritual pomp, sex, and circumstance. Both inside and outside the mansion, all traces of Christmas are gone, signifying that herein is the evil in the world, not the petty immoralities that plague society. Although the material world may be corrupt and sick with its crimes, diseases, addictions, hang-ups, and sexual perversions, it is within this Illuminati-like cabal that order is wrought from chaos: evil augments evil–everything is permissible.

Inside Somerton's main chamber, Nick plays the piano blindfolded because he is not initiated into the society's mysteries; he is profane, not worthy to witness the inner workings of the temple. Nick's music was scored by English composer, pianist, and viola player, Jocelyn Pook. Pook's composition titled "Masked Ball" features an Orthodox Divine Liturgy, which was recorded in a church in Baia Mare, Romania, only played backward. From the subconscious comes forth the demon Pazuzu speaking English in reverse in *The Exorcist*, imbuing the quasi-religious Masonic-Illuminati-O.T.O. ritual with eeriness and foreboding. The music's backwardness further denotes the rituals of the Black Mass, performed backward by a defrocked priest to mock the Catholic Holy Mass. The backwardness also evokes Crowley's backwardness in *Magick* (1913), the occult mythology of the adept. The erotic rites are led by a red-cloaked master of ceremonies, burning incense from a censer while circling selected women, preparing to engage in sex magick. The nude women form a circle which comes from the supernatural world of witchcraft:

In WITCHCRAFT, the magic circle provides a sacred and purified space in which all rites, magical work and ceremonies are conducted. It offers a boundary for a reservoir of concentrated power and acts as a doorway to the world of the gods. …Within the circle it becomes possible to transcend the physical, to open the mind to deeper and higher levels of consciousness. Circles have had magical significance since ancient times…The remnants of stone circles in Britain attest to the importance of the circle in ancient pagan rites.

The Witch enters a magic in anticipation of uniting with the gods and the forces of nature in a harmonious relationship. The deities are invited, not commanded, to witness and participate in the rites; all spirits are treated respectfully.

….The circle is ritually cast DEOSIL with an athame, though sometimes swords or wands may be used.

…God and Goddess are invoked through ritual. The purpose of the ritual– such as magic working, a handfasting or sabbat observance–is stated and the work is carried through.

…Witches use the term *circle* as a synonym for their regular meetings.[425]

The master of ceremonies uses an incense burner to cast the magic circle *widdershins* (counter-clockwise, against the sun), not *deosil* (clockwise), conjuring negative energies; the ceremony foments black magic.[426] The initiates of the group, both male and female, all wear Venetian masks while they observe the occult ceremony. Bill's white Venetian mask, incidentally, was modelled from the face of Ryan O'Neal, the star of Kubrick's *Barry*

---

425 Guiley, *Encyclopedia of Witches and Witchcraft*, pp. 219-220.
426 *ibid*, p. 365

Lyndon (1975); one could argue that *Eyes Wide Shut* is a dreary version of *Barry Lyndon*. It is well known Kubrick likes to cite his earlier works so this is not surprising. From above, a woman and man wearing a female jester and *bauta* masks slowly turn toward Bill and nod, implying they know him. Could this be Ziegler and his wife, Illona (Leslie Lowe), or could this be Sandor with Bill's wife, Alice? The couple's identity is never disclosed; Kubrick also likes to keep things mysterious and the audience guessing. By wearing carnival masks, the cabal exudes power and superiority,

> …masks are used mainly for ritual purposes. The donning of a mask is believed to change a man's identity and faculties, for the assumed appearance is held to affect inner nature and to assimilate it to that of the being represented by the mask. Thus a masked person is not simply a man or woman whose real identity is hidden, but he is an *enigmatic entity standing outside the sphere pf ordinary conduct and enjoying a freedom of movement and expression denied to the ordinary man.* As he has submerged his own identity by the wearing of a mask, other beings, such as an ancestor, a spirit or a totem animal, are enabled to manifest themselves in his body and voice.
>
> Masks have also the function of concentrating power in the hands of those who are in charge of the sacred objects. *Thus they are linked not only with the representation of power, but also with its exercise.* The human guardian and wearer of the mask partakes of the power of divinity or spirit which the mask symbolizes *and is thereby elevated above the common mass of the uninitiated.* Thus masks are and always were primarily means of transformation and identification with the entities of a nonmaterial sphere to which man has access only if he sheds his own identity and enters that of beings existing on a superior plane.[427]

The wearing of Venetian masks further symbolizes the Carnival of Venice (Italian: *Carnevale di Venezia*, dating from approximately 1162) creating an odd paradox: the Carnival ends with the Christian celebration of Lent,

---

427 *Encyclopedia of Magic and Superstition*, p. 180, emphasis added. See also the *Halloween* film series and 2007's *Trick 'r Treat* in which Michael Myers (the former) and Sam (the latter) dons masks while performing the gruesome and horrid rituals associated the Samhain thus transforming both of them into supernatural beings who cannot die.

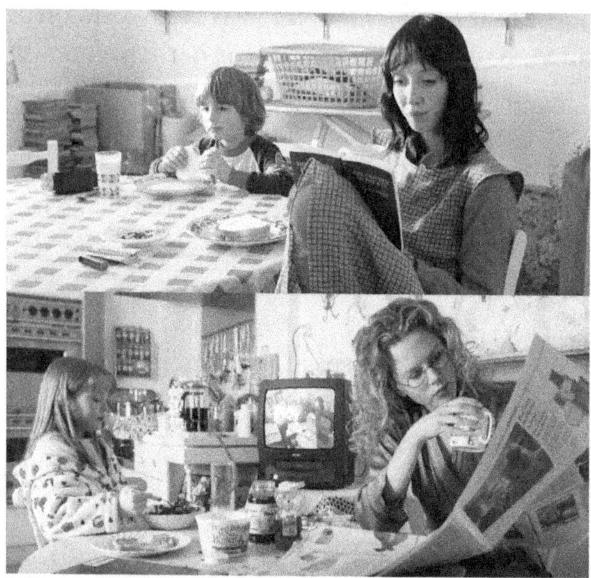

Comparative Cinema: (Top) Near the beginning of *The Shining*, Wendy and Danny Torrance have lunch; it is normalcy heralding the coming maelstrom. (Bottom) Nineteen years later, Kubrick employs this same cinematic imagery in *Eyes Wide Shut* when Alice and Helena Harford have breakfast. Kubrick draws upon his own imagery to suggest, to the subconscious mind, the mystery and horrors of *The Shining*, investing *Eyes Wide Shut* with same dread and uneasiness. But this isn't the only reference to *The Shining*. When Bill is being followed on the street by the Illuminati's enforcer, he walks past a restaurant with an address of 237, referencing the demonic room in the Overlook.

forty days before Easter on Shrove Tuesday (*Martedi' Grasso* or *Mardi Gras*), the day before Ash Wednesday. This Christian rite is reversed in *Eyes Wide Shut*, where the masks are worn in a bizarre ceremony which could be termed *satanic* or at least, diabolical. Astronomically and astrologically, it appears that in the view of this Illuminati-like group is that there is a profound dark side of the new Age of Aquarius. Based on some fairly objectively interpreted astrological teachings, it could be concluded that the Aquarian Age will only appear to be one of rational humanitarian egalitarianism.[428] The Saturno-Uranian reality looming behind this world of appearances will be one of an enlightened system of control by a ruling elite: the final reign of the Illuminati.[429] Is this the mystery Kubrick was cinematically revealing to the world back in 1999 when *Eyes Wide Shut* was theatrically released? Or is it just a controversial work of fiction? Is Tom Cruise's bad acting a metaphor of the typical American's wanton apathy and ignorance of a secret society's occult agenda being perpetrated against them, or is his performance only meant to be an earnest depiction of a sexually frustrated, death loving physician? Or, perhaps more troubling, is *Eyes Wide Shut* all of these things at once?

---

428 Stephen E. Flowers, *Fire & Ice: Magical Teachings of Germany's Secret Occult Order*, p. 52.
429 *ibid.*

Exposed as a trespasser, Bill is brought before the red-cloaked master of ceremonies sitting on a throne chair topped with a double-headed eagle. The eagle denotes the double-headed eagle of the Scottish Rite of Freemasonry, indicating authority and secrecy. In the end, Bill is returned to his pedestrian life but cannot let go of what he has seen. Like the final shot of the July 4th photo in *The Shining*, the rest of the movie raises epistemological issues which are not entirely explained. Was Alice's dream just that, *a dream*, or are her recollections of men watching her having sex evidence that she was, in fact, present at the sex magick ritual? Is this why she is comfortable sleeping next to the mask Bill wore to the ceremony? Has her sexual desires been rekindled by attending the ceremony thus saying to her husband, in a toy store, that she wants to "fuck." Has Alice turned the table on her husband: by the end of the film Bill regrets his sexual escapades but Alice seems to be able to fornicate without remorse or fear of the consequences? Has their argument from earlier in the film been reversed with Bill now as the passive with Alice becoming the aggressor? Was Mandy's death[430] an accidental drug overdose or was she indeed murdered, sacrificing herself, to save Bill from the retribution of the Illuminati? Is the secret group that Bill infiltrated global puppet masters or is it, as Ziegler jokes, wealthy adults merely satisfying their weird sexual hang-ups? What is real and what is imagined? Kubrick lets the audience make up its mind, but he does provide clues to those that are well-versed in symbolism.

For example, Ziegler explains the nature of the secret society, the dangers that Bill has brought upon himself, and the problems he has caused Ziegler. The exchange occurs over a red felt pool table which harkens back to the ritual which was conducted on blood-red carpeting, signifying that Ziegler is telling Harford the truth when he states, "Listen, Bill, I don't think you realize what kind of trouble you were in last night. Who do you think those people were? Those were not just ordinary people there. If I told you their names, I'm not gonna tell you their names, but if I did, I don't think you'd sleep so well." Kubrick uses the color red, not for alchemical purposes, but to recollect the truthfulness of an earlier scene, transferring its macabre veracity to Bill and Ziegler's conversation. Kubrick uses this same cinematic-occult technique again: at the very end of the movie, when

---

430 *"Rex tremendae"* from Mozart's Requiem (1791) plays as Bill walks into the cafe and reads of Mandy's death in the newspaper.

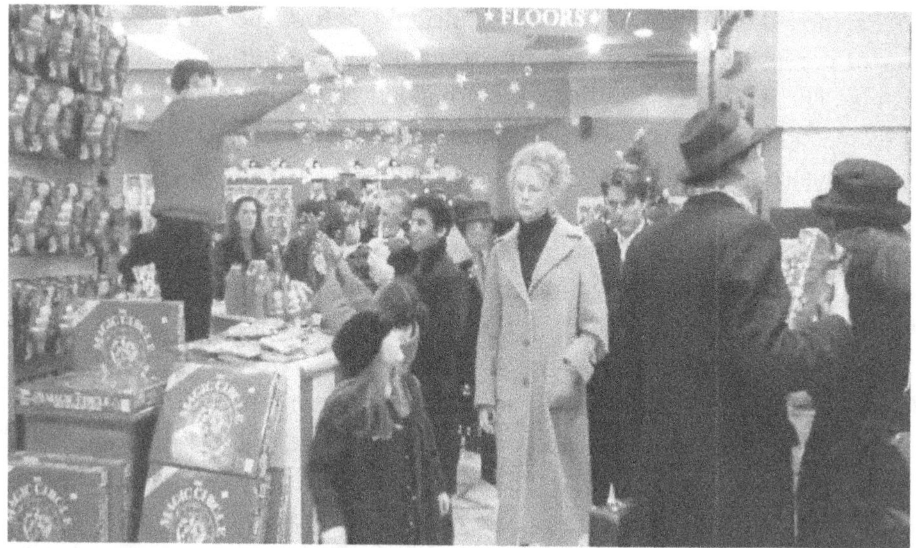

At the end of the film, the Harford family stroll past a stack of *The Magic Circle: Deluxe Box of Tricks* in the toy store.

Helena is in the toy store, she walks past a magic kit, *The Magic Circle: Deluxe Box of Tricks* stacked on top of each other. The magic kit recalls the circular, esoteric sexual rite performed at the Somerton mansion. On the floor near the *Deluxe Box of Tricks* is an inverted pentagram evoking black magic. Kubrick is suggesting to the audience that the secret group and its ritual are real, powerful, and supernatural; they are the world's elite whose Crowley-like Thelemic will is enforced no matter what the cost. These people are not ordinary and cannot be stopped; in other words, no one–not Bill, Nick, or Mandy–will get in their way. Kubrick is informing the audience, through cinema symbolism, that when it comes to the Illuminati the means always justify the ends.

Within the world of conspiracy, *Eyes Wide Shut* is the smoking gun when it comes to unmasking the world's elite, their shadowy rites, their obsession with the occult, and the unmerciful enforcement of their doctrines. It has been argued that Kubrick was unmasking this (or at least trying), similar to him employing Danny Torrance and his Apollo 11 sweater to reveal that he filmed the staged moon landing footage (see Chapter V) in *The Shining*. As such, Kubrick was killed by secret, globalist ruling elites for making *Eyes Wide Shut* because he was disclosing this Illuminati-Bilderberg-Masonic secret cabal to the world. Whether this is the case is open to speculation. However, what is irrefutable is that Kubrick used occult symbolism in his films to convey hidden messages; he does this successfully in *The Shining* and *Eyes Wide Shut*. Both movies employ the use of arcane imagery and esoteric symbols to express hidden truths making both films masterpieces; however, what is conspiracy fact and what is conspiracy theory will continue to be debated, returning to the cinematic world of Stanley Kubrick. Perhaps, in the end, this is what Kubrick wanted.

THEY LIVE, THE X-FILES: FIGHT THE FUTURE, AND ANGELS AND DEMONS

John Carpenter's *They Live*, based on the short story *Eight O' Clock in the Morning* (1963) by Ray Nelson, cinematically presents the deepest fear of every conspiracy theorist: an above-the-law, secret ruling elite using hypnotic, mind-control technologies and devices via mass media to keep humanity in perpetual stasis, apathy, poverty, and stupidity. Only here the wealthy, human ruling class have covertly allied themselves with skull-faced extraterrestrials who, through subliminal advertising and a televised signal, order the rest of mankind to SLEEP, OBEY, CONSUME, WATCH T.V., REPRODUCE, WORK 8 HOURS SLEEP 8 HOURS PLAY 8 HOURS, and DO NOT QUESTION AUTHORITY. However, their plans are foiled when a drifter, Nada, discovers sunglasses which disable the alien transmission allowing him to see through the deception, exposing the global conspiracy.

The Illuminati of *They Live* are extraterrestrials, exploiting earth's resources to their benefit unbeknownst to its inhabitants. They are using mind control to extinguish humankind's divine spark, while turning us humanity economically depressed slaves. Meanwhile, the global ruling elites are reduced to middlemen serving the aliens, allowing them to dumb-down the profane masses, implementing their nefarious plan unseen. As long as the aliens succeed, the wealthy will get wealthier, reducing the rest of humankind to a total state of ignorance; in other words, *They Live* is Extraterrestrial-Illuminati-Reaganomics. But all is not lost: a church serves as a hidden base from which a Bill Cooper-Jordan Maxwell-David Icke styled announcer interrupts the alien televised signal with a pirate broadcast, warning those watching about the alien takeover and their war on consciousness.[431] However, most viewers are disinterested, wishing to remain ignorant, rather than confronting painful truths. Such is the cry within the conspiracy world.

The movie starts by documenting the dismal mechanisms of divisive control and bondage: superficial jobs, poverty, a quasi-police state, and entertainments which laud the pursuit of wealth, opulence, and all that comes with it. The aliens have placed subliminal messages within advertising to enslave humanity. The ad, when seen by the naked eye, usually connotes the underlying command it conceals. For instance, the first billboard Nada observes is for a computer company called Control Data. Its tagline is "We're Creating the Transparent Computing Environment" and the hidden message beneath it is OBEY. Control Data Corporation (CDC) was one of the largest computer corporations (along with IBM and General Electric) through the 1960s. When he puts the glasses on, he is told to OBEY because all information is–or will be–controlled by computers and the conglomerates that manufacture them. Humankind will be subservient to the computer, not the other way around; this echoes the nightmare scenario of *The Terminator's* Skynet, anticipating the computerized false reality, the artificial consciousness of *The Matrix*. Next, Nada sees a billboard featuring a beautiful bikini-clad woman with the tagline, "Come to the Caribbean" with the hidden message enticing the unsuspecting viewer to MARRY AND REPRODUCE. Not surprisingly, print money tells humankind, THIS IS YOUR GOD. The Illuminati understands humanity's weaknesses and knows how to exploit them. Nada understands this better than anyone: the first place he attacks is a bank signifying the ubiquitous power of money, the method of the extraterrestrial's authority and control, *the root of all evil*, or as his friend Frank (Keith David) tells him, "The Golden Rule: he who has the gold makes the rules." *They Live* warns us always to remain vigilant, beware of a superintending hidden hand because things may not be what they seem. This maxim also applies to the film itself. On its surface, *They Live* appears to be a science fiction thriller, but in a tweet dated 27 September 2013 the film's star, "Rowdy" Roddy Piper (@R_Roddy_Piper),

---

431 Bill Cooper, b. Milton William Cooper, 1946-2001.

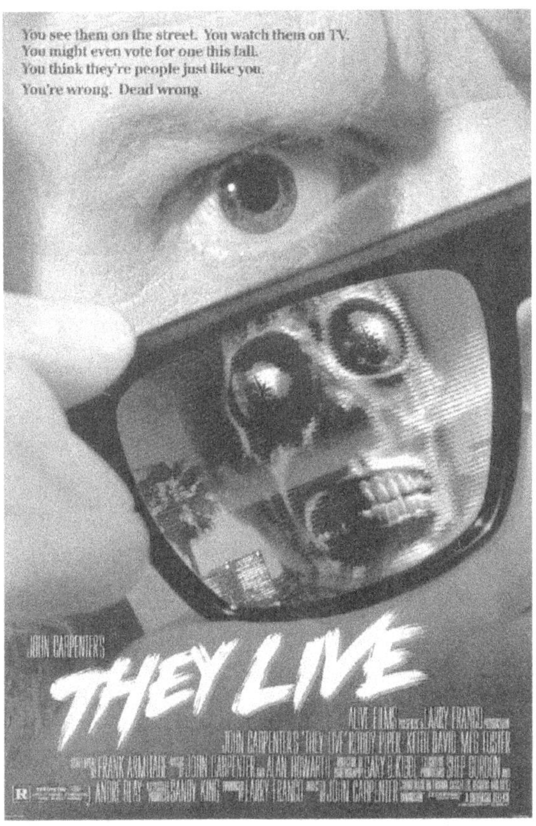

Gnostic vision in film: The one-sheet movie poster for *They Live*. Carpenter's film presents an illusionary world wherein reality and appearance are blurred by Illuminist space aliens. In their false reality, materialism is a god to be worshipped, perpetuated by greedy demiurge-like extraterrestrials. Truth and spirituality can be found in a church, only its congregation does not worship and pray; instead, they lead the resistance against the controlling aliens.

said the movie was, in reality, a documentary. If Piper is to be believed, *They Live* is a cryptic warning about the condition of humanity and the methods used to control it, to beware the dystopian worlds of *Soylent Green* (1973) and *Logan's Run* (1976).

The Illuminati aside, *They Live* also features elements of Gnosticism, exploring the relationship between illusion and reality. No one knows who is an alien and who is human until unique sunglasses are put on; only then is the extraterrestrial's manipulative ruse exposed. Nada, his name is Spanish for *nothing*, implies Valentinus' rejection of materialism and Basilides' epistemological negation of everything. Personifying nothing, Nada is anti-wealth and anti-demiurge thus anti- extraterrestrial and anti-Illuminati. He rebels against them, their authority, their money, and power; Nada wants *none* of it. Although he tries to be optimistic, Nada suffers the melancholy of Mani: he is a stranger in a strange, land; a gloomy messenger having discovered the alien menace controlling the populace. Like all Gnostic saviors, Nada is willing to suffer martyrdom by awakening humankind from its deep slumber, enlightening the world. Carpenter also employs a church creating a paradox: exoterically a place of peaceful Christian prayer and worship, in *They Live* it is the hidden headquarters of the alien resistance: a temple preaching gnosis, practicing Valentinian rebellion.

*   *   *   *

Released on June 19th, 1998, *The X-Files: Fight the Future* takes place between the end of season five (episode titled "The End," airdate May 17th, 1998) and the start of season six (episode titled "The Beginning," airdate November 8th, 1998) of the television series, and is based on the series' extraterrestrial-government conspiracy mythology. Five principal actors from the television series appear in the film: David Duchovny, Gillian Anderson, Mitch Pileggi, John Neville (1925-2011), and William B. Davis, reprising their respective roles as FBI agents Fox Mulder, Dana Scully, FBI Assistant Director Walter Skinner, the Well-Manicured Man, and the Cigarette-Smoking Man. The picture is well made, but overall it feels more like a made-for-TV movie than a Hollywood summer blockbuster. The movie also suffers because it was based on a television program that was still airing at the times of its release, so if you were not familiar with the TV show's lore, you probably had no interest in the movie. Watching *Fight the Future* present day, the film is a perfect time capsule of the pre-9/11/01, pre-internet-social media world of 1998 in which the movie inhabits. That being said, the idea of FEMA[432] (Federal Emergency Management Agency) taking over the United States government, suspending the Constitution in a post-9/11/01 world seems trite, far-fetched, dating the movie substantially.

The Illuminati of *The X-Files: Fight the Future* (and the television series) is called the Syndicate, and is a powerful Bilderberg-like shadow organization which has infiltrated all governments at the highest levels. Two of its leading members are the mercurial Cigarette-Smoking Man and the Well-Manicured Man, now joined by the influential Conrad Strughold (Armin Mueller-Stahl). The Syndicate's modus operandi is the conceal-ment of a program orchestrated by an unidentified extraterrestrial species to colonize and repopulate the planet, safeguarding their stake in that fu-ture, which they believe to be inevitable. Murder, cover-ups, sabotage and other wetwork (a/k/a Black Ops) projects necessary to protect the conspir-acy, the Syndicate employs an unknown number of henchmen commonly known as the Men in Black. The Men in Black are merciless enforcers of

---

432 On March 1, 2003 FEMA was absorbed into the Department of Homeland Security.

the conspiracy whose actual names, like the members of the Syndicate, are rarely if ever known. Many worked ostensibly for the U.S. Defense Department, Central Intelligence Agency, NASA, State Department, Federal Bureau of Investigation, National Security Agency, along with other government agencies. The Men in Black, along with the Syndicate, travel in Black Helicopters, vehicles epitomizing an alleged conspiratorial military takeover of the United States.

Attempting to expose the Syndicate is conspiracy author Dr. Alvin Kurtzweil played by Martin Landau. Kurtzweil tells Mulder the Syndicate is secretly planning to release a deadly extraterrestrial Armageddon-like plague to carry out their devious colonization project. In attempting to explain that the destruction of the office building in Dallas was part of the conspiracy, a vast cover-up, Kurtzweil remarks that the Syndicate "know their way around Dallas," cleverly implying they were responsible for President Kennedy's November 1963 assassination. Kurtzweil is the author of two books, *Four Horseman of the Global Domination Conspiracy* and *Countdown to Apocalypse*, which elaborate on this conspiracy. His two biblical-doomsday-conspiracy volumes conjure 1991's *Behold a Pale Horse*[433] written by government conspiracy theorist and radio broadcaster Bill Cooper. Cooper linked the Illuminati (cf. the Syndicate) with his beliefs that extraterrestrials were secretly involved with the U.S. government. He described the Illuminati as a secret international organization, controlled by the Bilderberg Group, which conspired with the Freemasons, Skull and Bones, the Knights of Columbus and other clandestine organizations. According to Cooper, the Illuminati conspirators not only invented alien threats for their gain but actively conspired with extraterrestrials to take over the world; the Illuminati's ultimate goal was the establishment of a New World Order. Cooper's theories are embodied by Kurtzweil, transcending the entire *X-Files* television and cinematic mythos; it is apparent Cooper's take on the Illuminati pervades the Syndicate. One could argue Fox Mulder is a more sophisticated, refined version of Cooper because the two are motivated by a desire to expose government conspiracies. Even more mysterious, does *Fight the Future* anticipate Cooper's death? When

---

433 cf. Revelation 6:8, "And I looked, and behold a pale horse: and his name that sat on him was Death, and Hell followed with him. And power was given unto them over the fourth part of the earth, to kill with sword, and with hunger, and with death, and with the beasts of the earth."

Mulder is shot by a man in black masquerading as a medic, the name, Cooper, is observable in block capital letters on the back of the ambulance. Why the name appears is an enigma, but Mulder is shot–nearly killed–immediately after the name appears on screen. Could this be a harbinger of the death of Bill Cooper on November 6th, 2001, a little over three years after *Fight the Future* was released, when he was killed in a shootout with Arizona deputies for evading an arrest warrant for tax evasion? Is this part of Hollywood's sinister predictive programming agenda, or is this the collective unconscious at work foretelling future events? Is this movie merely depicting the Illuminati, or is *The X-Files: Fight the Future* a genuine Illuminati production? You decide.

*   *   *   *

Finally, *Angels and Demons*[434] depicts the Illuminati as anti-religious, anti-Vatican European free-thinking rationalists well ahead of their time. The secret society pre-dates Weishaupt's 1776 Illuminati counting 16th and 17th-century physicists, astronomers, and mathematicians among its members. Only two members are identified: Galileo Galilei (1564- 1642) and sculpture Gian Lorenzo Bernini (1598-1680), but it is hinted that other masters would likely include Isaac Newton (1643-1727), René Descartes, Tycho Brahe (1546-1601), Dr. John Dee, Johannes Kepler (1571-1630) Sir Francis Bacon, and Blaise Pascal (1623-1662). The Illuminati–Professor Robert Langdon (Tom Hanks) calls them "the Enlightened Ones"–are highly intelligent, educated progressives whose scientific teachings undermine Catholic dogma. They are forced underground, forming a secret society after the Vatican's *La Purga* (The Purge) of 1668 when four unnamed Illuminati Scientists were branded with the sign of the cross and executed. *La Purga* is fiction; however, one finds a parallel to the execution of Neoplatonic Dominican friar Giordano Bruno in 1600. Denounced as a heretic, Bruno was burnt alive at the stake for his controversial views on magic, astrology, and the plurality of worlds; see the previous chapter. The Illuminati have returned seeking retribution for *La Purga*, promising to destroy the Vatican with light by detonating Antimatter inside its walls.

---

434 The film is based on Dan' Brown's novel (2000) which has the same name. The film was released (USA) on May 15th, 2009.

Although the movie is historical fantasy, in *Angels and Demons* we see the anti-religious, antichristian, and anti-church sentiments of the Illuminati. The historical Illuminati were on the surface anti-Vatican; however, the Illuminati of Weishaupt esoterically promulgated the Counter-Reformation Jesuit agenda of cabalistic, mystical Catholic triumphalism. Instead, the Illuminati are merely depicted as anti-Catholic, anti-religious zealots hell-bent on revenge, murder, and destruction; their Counter-Reformation agenda is absent. The movie also suggests the Illuminati are infiltrators, having penetrated governments, the Vatican, and other organizations of importance. This occult infiltration was part of Wieshaupt's agenda: the Illuminati of 1776 sought to employ Freemasons and other elites to reconfigure society along occult, Erastian, and Newtonian heliocentric lines by any means necessary.

The nexus between science and religion is bridged by scientific- conspiratorial organization like CERN where Antimatter, a highly volatile substance, is produced and harnessed within its Large Hadron Collider. A particle of Antimatter is stolen and hidden in the catacombs beneath St. Peter's Basilica where it is to be detonated, thereby destroying the Vatican. Art imitates life because there is the statue of the Hindu god Shiva at CERN's headquarters which implies annihilation. The statue, depicting Shiva's cosmic dance of creation and destruction, was given to CERN by the Indian government in 2004 to celebrate the research center's long association with India, which started in the 1960s. The cosmic dancer

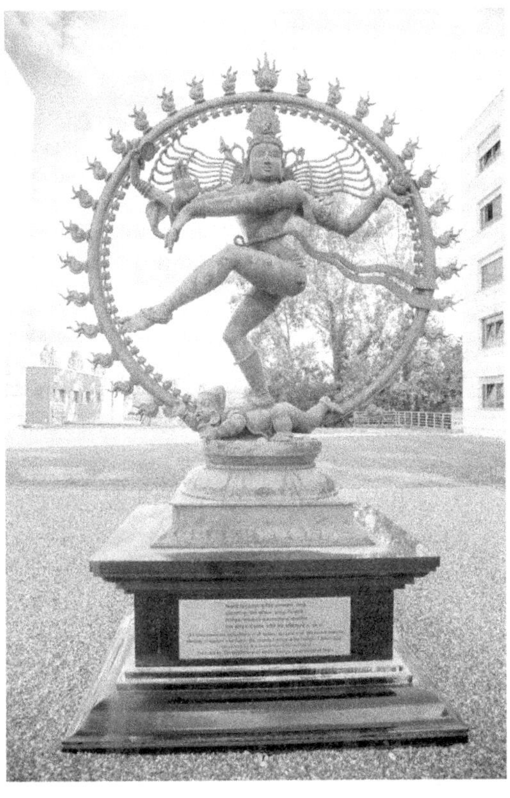

The statue of Shiva performing the Nataraja dance at CERN in Geneva, Switzerland.

performs his divine dance to destroy a weary universe and prepare for the god Brahma to start the process of creation. The science of CERN will be used to level the Vatican ending its reign of superstition while heralding a new age of reason and enlightenment.

The Illuminati's modus operandi is expertly presented in these three films. In *They Live*, we see the mind-controlling Illuminati manipulating mankind to keep it ignorant, devoid of spirit, trapped in a materialistic oblivion; in *Fight the Future*, we see the Illuminati as the shadow force working behind all governments and conspiracies; and in *Angels and Demons*, we see the Illuminati in all its secular glory. Violence is the Illuminati's currency, dispensing death to those defying their will. Absent from all the movies presented in this chapter is the alleged devil worshipping, Luciferian dogma of the Illuminati, which is a good thing. The Illuminati as a Synagogue of Satan (an evil cabal linked to Freemasonry) takes center stage in the books *Pawns of the Game* (1958) and *Satan, Prince of this World* (1966) by William Guy Carr (1895-1959). Unfortunately, Carr's books relied on Taxil's *Les Mystères de la Franc-Maçonnerie* (*Mysteries of Freemasonry*) which, as explained at the beginning of this chapter, was a hoax.[435] Nevertheless, some commentators persist in believing the historical Illuminati was in league with the Devil–the evidence does not substantiate this conclusion. Alas, this Luciferian subterfuge still lingers to present day: painfully ill-informed conspiracy theorists unequivocally proclaim the Illuminati survived, perpetuating their satanic agenda upon an unsuspecting populace. A modern-day Illuminati hell-bent on global domination, using Hollywood's cinematic sorcery to sedate, or mind control, humankind is tabloid sensationalism….or is it?

Leaving the shadow world of secret societies, we now turn to the world of wizardry and witchcraft. It's time to journey to Hogwarts and explore the magical, monomythic world of the Harry Potter movies.

---

435 Carr also relies on the equally ill-informed Nesta Webster. Author's Note: The idea of Masonry and the Illuminati being linked to Luciferianism originates from Pike's *Morals and Dogma* wherein he compares-equates the planet Venus to Lucifer.

CHAPTER VIII

SLYTHERIN, RAVENCLAW, HUFFLEPUFF, AND GRYFFINDOR: THE HARRY POTTER UNIVERSE

"Congratulations Potter, fine achievement. Well done boy.
I'm sorry we haven't spoken, after all your story is one I've heard many
times. Quite remarkable. Tragic, of course, to lose one's family."
– Bartemius Crouch Sr., *Harry Potter and the Goblet of Fire*, 2005.

"Did you see his face? Maybe if the fat lump had given this a
squeeze, he'd have remembered to fall on his fat ass."
– Draco Malfoy, *Harry Potter and the Sorcerer's Stone*, 2001.

"Funny, the damage a silly little book can do,
especially in the hands of a silly little girl.
– Tom Marvolo Riddle,
Harry Potter nd the Chamber of Secrets, 2002.

"I've lost all my possessions.
Apparently, people have been hiding them."
–Luna Lovegood, *Harry Potter and the Order of the Phoenix*, 2007.

"Nasty brat standing there as bold as brass. Harry Potter,
the boy who stopped the Dark Lord. Friend of Mudbloods and
blood-traitors alike. If my poor mistress only knew."
– Kreacher, *Harry Potter and the Order of the Phoenix*, 2007.

"Mum used to read those, 'The Wizard and the Hopping Pot,' 'Babbity
Rabbity and the Cackling Stump.' Come on, Babitty Rabbity, no?"
– Ron Weasley, *Harry Potter and the Deathly Hallows – Part 1*, 2010.

"Well, well, Lupin. Out for a little walk in the moonlight, are we?"
–Professor Severus Snape,
Harry Potter and the Prisoner of Azkaban, 2004.

ogwarts School of Witchcraft and Wizardry is divided into four houses: Gryffindor, Hufflepuff, Ravenclaw, and Slytherin. Each one of
these houses bears an animal or a reptile on its coat of arms: Gryffindor
is represented by a lion, Hufflepuff a badger, Ravenclaw an eagle, and
Slytherin, a snake. The two prestigious houses are Gryffindor and Slytherin
because Gryffindor is home to Harry Potter and his friends, while Slytherin
is the house of Voldemort and his unholy disciples. The two houses are forever at odds because Gryffindor is residence to the heroes, while Slytherin
houses the villains. Concordantly, the lion and serpent which adorn their
respective coats of arms is heraldry at its finest: the lion symbolizes mighty
Leo the Lion, the house of the sun, Apollo and Mithras, the abode of champions performing Herculean deeds. Comparatively, Gryffindor's lion is the
great Neoplatonic Aslan the Lion from Lewis' *Chronicles of Narnia* tales.
Aslan, personifying the life-giving sun, is in eternal conflict with the wicked, cold, and cruel wintry queen Jadis (see Chapter X). Rowling has stated
in interviews[436] that Lewis' stories were an influence upon the Harry Potter
series; another example is Harry's mean-spirited cousin Dudley Dursley,
evoking the Pevensies' equally ill-tempered cousin, Eustace Scrubb from
The Voyage of the Dawn Treader (Chapter X). On the other end of the
spectrum, Slytherin's cold-blooded serpent is the clever devil, the villainous archetype without which the hero has no purpose, no sense of being;
Slytherin is the temple of the dark Lord Voldemort and the Malfoys. The
battle between good and evil is symbolized by the lion of Gryffindor versus the serpent of Slytherin; it is Jesus against Satan, St. George and the
Dragon, Horus against Set (or Typhon), or Apollo slaying Python. It's all
Manichean Cosmology-Zoroastrian Dualism: the endless battle of light
against dark.

In *Cinema Symbolism*, this author identified the Harry Potters stories as
Gnostic; however, upon re-watching them to write this chapter this author
believes they are more Gnostic-like than akin to Gnosticism proper. Each
one of the Potter stories is a meditation on the monomyth, and although
Harry is a resurrected Christlike savior, he is not a supplier of wisdom nor
is he a religious redeemer; he dies, resurrects, and defeats an evil lord–that

---

436 Jennie Renton, "The story behind the Potter legend: JK Rowling talks about how she created
the Harry Potter books and the magic of Harry Potter's world." *Sydney Morning Herald*; http://
www.accio-quote.org/articles/2001/1001-sydney-renton.htm. Retrieved 1 May 2016.

is how his story ends. However, there are Gnostic components within the Potter saga: for example, there is Albus Dumbledore, the wise Hermes Trismegistus archetype, and Sophia, the wise sacred feminine, personified by Hermione Granger, Minerva McGonagall, Luna Lovegood, and Ginny Weasley. They all provide thoughtful insights, especially Hermione, in Harry's darkest hour.

There are seven Harry Potter novels but eight movies because the final book, *Harry Potter and the Deathly Hallows* (published 2007), was split into two movies. The first Harry Potter book, *Harry Potter and the Philosopher's Stone* (1997), had its title cinematically changed to *Harry Potter and the Sorcerer's Stone* in many countries (including the USA) for marketing reasons because the latter is catchier, more appealing. Chris Columbus directed the first two Potter movies.

HARRY POTTER AND THE SORCERER'S STONE

Harry Potter is a seemingly ordinary boy, living in a cupboard under the staircase in the home of his neglectful and cruel relatives, the Dursleys, in Surrey, England. On his eleventh birthday, Harry is visited by a mysterious stranger, Rubeus Hagrid (Robbie Coltrane), who informs him that he is a wizard, famous in the wizarding world for surviving an attack by the evil Lord Voldemort (Richard Bremmer) when he was a baby. Voldemort killed Harry's parents, James (Adrian Rawlins) and Lily (Geraldine Somerville), but his attack on Harry rebounded, leaving only a lightning-bolt scar on Harry's forehead while rendering Voldemort powerless presumed dead. Hagrid reveals to Harry that he has been invited to attend Hogwarts School of Witchcraft and Wizardry of which Hagrid is Keeper of Keys and Grounds. Harry and Hagrid visit the hidden London street, Diagon Alley, where Harry withdraws money from a goblin bank, Gringotts, while Hagrid retrieves a mysterious object from Albus Dumbledore's (Richard Harris, 1930-2002) vault within the bank. Dumbledore, a powerful wizard with a long white beard, is the headmaster of Hogwarts. After buying his magical school supplies, including a wand with the money he withdrew, Harry boards the train to Hogwarts via the concealed Platform 9 ¾ in King's Cross Station. Aboard the train, Harry meets and gets along with Ron Weasley (Ruppert Grint), a boy from a large, but poor, pure-blood wizarding family, and Hermione Granger (Emma Watson), a witch born to non-magical parents, termed *Muggles*. Once they arrive at the school, Harry and all of the other first-year students are sorted into the four different houses: Gryffindor, Hufflepuff, Ravenclaw, and Slytherin. Since Slytherin is noted for being the house for darker wizards and witches, Harry successfully convinces the magical Sorting Hat (Leslie Phillips) not to put him in that house. He ends up in Gryffindor, along with Ron and Hermione. Ron's older brothers have all gone to Gryffindor as well, including the mischievous Weasley twins, Fred and George (James and Oliver Phelps). At Hogwarts, Harry begins learning wizardry and discovers more about his past and his parents. He also becomes enemies with Draco Malfoy (Tom Felton), a pure blood platinum blonde wizard in Slytherin House; *Malfoy* comes from the Latin word for evil-doers, *maleficus*, which was used in medieval times to de-

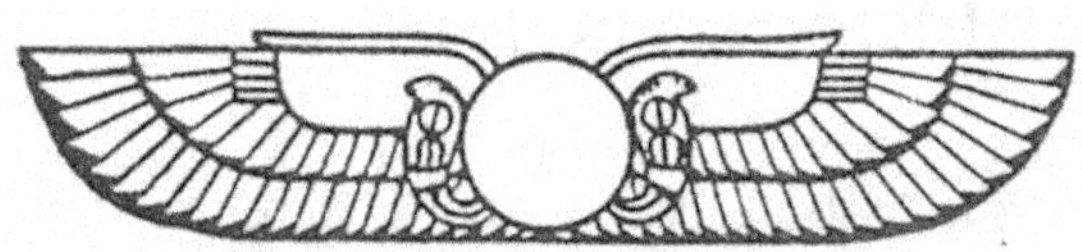

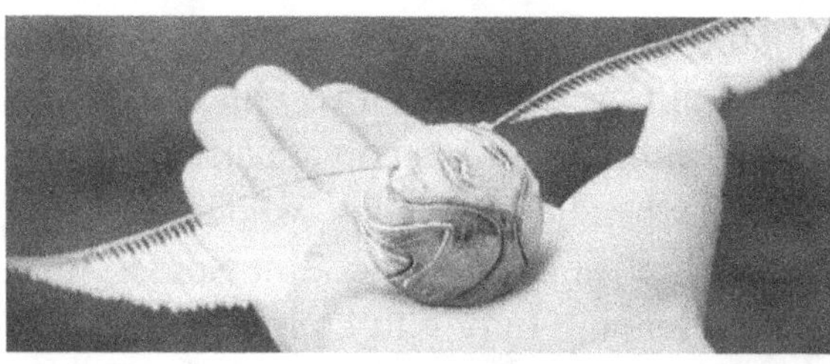

(Top) The Egyptian winged solar disk symbolizes the sun gods, Ra and Horus. (Bottom) In the game of Quidditch, the purpose of a Seeker is to catch the Snitch, a winged solar orb. The Seeker is seeking the sun and, in doing so, acquiring solar, godlike attributes.

scribe witches. Harry gets recruited by Gryffindor's Quidditch team (a sport combining wizardry, broomsticks, soccer, and lacrosse) as a Seeker, like his father James was before him. The purpose of a Seeker is to catch the Snitch, a golden-winged orb echoing the winged sun disk of Egypt which was synonymous with the solar deities including Ra (spiritual) and Horus (material). The Golden Snitch forges an esoteric nexus between the sun gods of Egypt, thereby transforming, quite adroitly, Potter into an archetypal solar hero, a Horus or Christlike figure that will go on to defeat a dark lord.

Harry, Ron, and Hermione discover a vicious large three-headed dog on a restricted floor in the school. The dog, named Fluffy, is guarding the sorcerer's stone (a/k/a the philosopher's stone), an alchemical substance that can be used to grant its owner immortality. The stone is linked to Nicolas Flamel (ca 1330– March 22nd, 1418), a successful French scribe and manuscript seller. After his death, Flamel developed a reputation as an alchemist believed to have discovered the philosopher's stone, achieving immortality. These legendary accounts only appeared in the seventeenth century; in Rowling's mythology, Flamel is alive, about to celebrate his 666th birthday. The number 666 immediately conjures the Antichrist of Revelation, implying that the magic studied at Hogwarts is not of the cabalistic variety; instead, all the young witches and wizard of Hogwarts are, even if the taint be modest, touched by evil. Furthermore, it is implied that Dumbledore and Flamel may be one and the same person.

Harry suspects that the sorcerer's stone was what Hagrid retrieved from Dumbledore's Gringotts vault. Harry concludes that Hogwart's potions teacher, the sly and unfriendly Severus Snape (Alan Rickman 1946-2016), is trying to obtain the stone to return Voldemort to a human form. Later, Harry encounters Voldemort drinking unicorn blood in the Forbidden Forest while serving detention (along with Ron, Hermione, and Draco) after being caught wandering the school grounds at night.

After hearing from Hagrid that the three-headed dog will fall asleep if played music, Harry, Ron, and Hermione decide to find the stone before Snape does. They get past Fluffy and face a series of trials which guard the stone: surviving a deadly plant called Devil's Snare, capturing a flying key, and winning a violent life-sized game of chess. After passing the tests, Harry discovers that it was not Snape who wanted the stone, but rather Defense against the Dark Arts teacher, Professor Quirinus Quirrell (Ian Hart). Quirrell removes his turban revealing Voldemort, living on the back of his head like a parasite. Voldemort attempts to convince Harry to give him the stone, which Harry suddenly finds in his pocket thanks to an enchantment by the Dumbledore. Voldemort promises to bring his parents back from the dead, but Harry refuses. Quirrell attempts to kill him but Harry's touch causes Quirrell's hand to turn to dust. Quirrell then tries to take the stone, but Harry grabs his face, causing Quirrell to turn completely into dust. When Harry gets up, Voldemort's spirit manifests, passing through Harry, knocking him unconscious before fleeing.

Harry wakes up in the school's hospital wing with Dumbledore at his side. Dumbledore explains that the stone has been destroyed and despite Ron nearly being killed in the chess match, both he and Hermione are fine. Dumbledore explains why Quirrell was burned by Harry's touch: when Harry's mother died to save him, her death imbued him with a magical, love-based protection spell against Voldemort. Harry, Ron, and Hermione are rewarded house points for their heroic performances, and Neville Longbottom (Matthew Lewis) is rewarded for bravely standing up to them, winning Gryffindor the House Cup. Before Harry and the rest of the students leave for the summer, Harry realizes that while all others students are going home, Hogwarts is now his home.

Hogwarts School of Witchcraft and Wizardry is based upon H.P. Lovecraft's Miskatonic University, a fictional university located in the equally fictitious town of Arkham, which is in the real-life county of Essex in Massachusetts. The university is named after the Miskatonic River, also fictional. Miskatonic is highly prestigious, on par with Harvard University, and the two are the most popular schools for the children of Massachusetts' gentry. Miskatonic University is famous for its collection of occult books; its library has one of the few genuine copies of the *Necronomicon*, a fictional grimoire authored by the "Mad Arab" Abdul Alhazred.[437] Accordingly, there is a deep interest and pursuit, both overt and covert, of esoteric knowledge by Miskatonic's students just like there is at Hogwarts. The *hog* in *Hog*warts esoterically connects the school with arcane teachings because, as an animal sacred to Diana, it was frequently employed in the Ancient Mysteries as an emblem of the occult arts.[438] An English mystic associated with Rosicrucianism, Sir Francis Bacon employed a hog as his mysterious signature[439] and is thought to have used the animal in some of the works of William Shakespeare, indicating that he is the author behind the works of the Bard. For instance, the famous statement from Mistress Quickly in *The Merry Wives of Windsor* (1602): "Hang-hog is latten for Bacon, I warrant you;" resonates Baconian impression. The devilish Puck, sometimes known as Robin Goodfellow, in *A Midsummer's Night's Dream* (1605) says, "I'll follow you. I'll lead you about a round, through bog, through

---

437 See Sullivan's *Cinema Symbolism*, Chapter VII.
438 Hall, *The Secret Teachings of All Ages*, p. 288.
439 *ibid*, p. 547.

bush, through brake, through brier. Sometime a horse I'll be, sometime a hound, a hog, a headless bear, sometime a fire. And neigh, and bark, and grunt, and roar, and burn, like horse, hound, hog, bear, fire, at every turn," in Act III, Scene I. Furthermore, the word "*honorificabilitudinitatibus*" spoken by Costard in Act V, Scene I of *Love's Labour's Lost* (1597) is an anagram for the Latin phrase *hi ludi, F. Baconis nati, tuiti orbi* which, in English, means *these plays, F. Bacon's offspring, are preserved for the world.* Bacon was a link in that great chain of minds which has perpetuated the secret doctrine of antiquity from its beginning; the cryptic, distinguished works of the Bard of Avon are evidence of this arcana. Thus, the identification of Bacon with a hog mystically connects Hogwarts to the magical Rosicrucian scientist, thereby establishing the school as a legitimate inheritor of the Ancient Mysteries.

In Albus Dumbledore, we find the Hermes Trismegistus archetype perfected (cf. Tarot's Hermit Card); he is the wise elderly wizard, and a mentor to Harry and his friends. Much like Yoda, Gandalf, and Obi-Wan Kenobi, Dumbledore knows many hidden truths, but, like all sages, only dispenses them on a need-to-know basis; obtaining gnosis from this mercurial headmaster is sometimes easier said than done. His throne chair in the Great Hall is embellished with a golden pyramid, denoting solar, Egyptian, and Masonic rulership. To resurrect this archetype from the subconscious mind, we turn to the occult world of Freemasonry. Hermes Trismegistus is critical within high degree Freemasonry, especially the legend surrounding the Royal Arch of Enoch ritual. To reiterate, Hermes Trismegistus enters Enoch's subterranean vault, correctly pronounces the Tetragrammaton, restoring the seven liberal arts and sciences back to humanity (see Chapter VI). Again, the Royal Arch of Enoch ritual is the 7th degree of the York Rite and the 13th degree of the Scottish Rite; likewise, it was originally the 13th degree in the French Rite of Perfection. Dumbledore, personifying Trismegistus, maintains a subterranean vault at Gringotts in which he keeps a valuable artifact, treasure, the sorcerer's stone. The entrance to Dumbledore's vault is numerically identified on the keystone in its arch; Dumbledore's vault is number 713. The number is an esoteric reference to the Holy Royal Arch ritual in both high degree bodies, synchronizing perfectly with the Dumbledore-as-Trismegistus archetype, bringing forth from the subconscious the time-everlasting Masonic legend of recovering sacred relics in an underground vault. At Hogwarts, Dumbledore's female equivalent is the wise Madam Professor Minerva McGonagall whose forename, Minerva, is the Roman goddess of wisdom. She is the moon to Dumbledore's sun. Hogwarts omniscient caretaker, Argus Filch (David Bradley), is all knowing and all seeing; he is the pervasive eyes of Hogwarts, knowing all its dark secrets. Filch is inopportune: he appears where he is not wanted, and comes even though no one beckons him. To symbolize his all-seeing transcendence, his forename, Argus, is an obscure reference to Argus Panoptes, a 100-eyed giant in Greek mythology. Thus, symbolically, Hogwarts School of Witchcraft and Wizardry is governed by Hermes Mercurius Trismegistus, the god of magic, and Minerva the goddess of wisdom. Hogwarts' hallways, secret passages, and tenebrous recesses are forever watched by a caretaker and his cat, Mrs. Norris; Filch's eyes are everywhere.

The name of the saga's villain, Voldemort, was masterfully crafted by Rowling. The Latin root, *mor*, refers to death, paralleled in an old Germanic root, *mara*, for darkness which becomes the Old English, *mare*, which we find in the word *nightmare*. The name Volde*mor*t is darkness and death, and we find the root *mor* in names denoting evil and villainy. The sinister executioner Mord (Boris Karloff) chops of heads in 1939's *Tower of London*; Sherlock Holmes' nemesis is Professor Moriarty; H.G. Wells (1866- 1946) sent a time traveler into the future to encounter a cave-dwelling evil cannibalistic race called the Morlocks in *The Time Machine* (1895) which was made into a movie directed by George Pal (1908-1980) in 1960. Wells also created an evil genius named Dr. Moreau. King Arthur was betrayed by Mordred. Frodo Baggins travels to the black land of Mordor, the home of the evil Lord Sauron, beginning as the lieutenant of Morgoth, the original villain in Tolkien's Middle-earth.

To obtain the sorcerer's stone, Harry, Hermione, and Ron must win a game of human chess, its pieces giant, enchanted, and deadly. The game of chess symbolizes the Manichean conflict between Harry and Voldemort. On the occultism of chess, Manly P. Hall writes:

The chessboard consists of 64 squares alternately black and white and symbolizes the floor of the House of the Mysteries. Upon this field of existence or thought move a number of strangely carved figures, each according to fixed law. The white king is Ormuzd; the black king, Ahriman; and upon the plains of Cosmos the great war between Light and Darkness is fought through all the ages. Of the philosophical constitution of man, the kings represent the spirit; the queens the mind; the bishops the emotions; the knights the vitality; the castles, or rooks, the physical body. The pieces upon the kings' side are positive; those upon the queens' side, negative. The pawns are the sensory impulses and perceptive faculties–the eight parts of the soul. The white king and his suite symbolize the Self and its vehicles; the black king and his retinue, the not-self--the false Ego and its legion. The game of chess thus sets forth the eternal struggle of each part of man's compound nature against the shadow of itself. The nature of each of the chessmen is revealed by the way in which it moves; geometry is the key to their interpretation. For example: The castle (the body) moves on the square; the bishop (the emotions) moves on the slant; the king, being the spirit, cannot be captured, but loses the battle when so surrounded that it cannot escape.[440]

Indeed, Harry's struggle with Voldemort and the Death Eaters symbolizes the perpetual war between light and dark, good against evil. Ron's chess game anticipates this great battle.

Much like Frodo Baggins, Luke Skywalker, and Thomas Anderson, Harry Potter is plucked from the general populace and placed on a numinous journey of adventure. For Potter's adventure is the sacred monomyth; it is his destiny to save the wizarding world from an evil dark lord named Voldemort, an imitation of *The Lord of the Rings'* Sauron and *Star Wars'* Darth Vader or Emperor Palpatine. *Harry Potter and the Sorcerer's Stone*, like all the Potter stories and films, incorporates microcosms of the macrocosm or, put another way, unique elements of the monomyth. *Harry Potter and the Sorcerer's Stone's* monomyth features these following components.

- The Call to Adventure: Harry receives letters from Hogwarts School of Witchcraft and Wizardry inviting him to matriculate.

---

440 Hall, *The Secret Teachings of All Ages*, p. 426.

- Refusal of the Call: These invitations are confiscated by the Dursleys because they do not want Harry to go to Hogwarts fearing he will suffer his parent's fate. When Hagrid comes to retrieve Harry, the boy doubts he's a wizard saying he is "Just Harry."

- Supernatural Aid: Harry gets his magic wand and wizarding supplies at Diagon Alley. He later gets a cloak of invisibility. The mantle is critical to completing the adventure allowing Harry to sneak into the restricted section of the library.

- The Crossing of the First Threshold: Harry arrives at Diagon Alley with Hagrid, a threshold guardian, and later passing through the secret entrance to reach Platform 9 ¾. Both experiences, along with the train ride to Hogwarts, serve to introduce Harry to his new magical world.

- The Belly of the Whale: Harry and Ron save Hermione from the troll in the bowels of Hogwarts. For the first time, they realize they are not in Kansas anymore.

- The Road of Trials: Harry walks away from Mirror of Erised, a magical device which shows the most desperate desires of a person's heart. Later Harry encounters Voldemort in the Dark Forrest and survives. Harry, Hermione, and Ron sneak past Fluffy, escape the Devil's Snare, capture the flying key, surviv a deadly chess game to reach Voldemort so they can prevent him from obtaining the sorcerer's stone.

- The Meeting with the Goddess: Hermione Granger, a motherly figure supporting Harry and Ron with her vast knowledge. She is Princess Leia to their Luke Skywalker and Han Solo (Harrison Ford).

- Atonement with the Father: Campbell writes, "Whether he knows it or not, and no matter what his position in society, the father is the initiating priest through whom the young being passes on into the larger world… there is a new element of rivalry in the picture: the son against the father for mastery of the universe."[441] Harry is a budding initiate attempting to awaken his magical-chaotic powers, personified by Voldemort, channeling them into a healthy order, represented by Dumbledore. Since Harry bears Voldemort's powers: he took on his energies when he survived Voldemort's murderous spell, the Killing

---

441 Campbell, *The Hero With a Thousand Faces*, p. 115.

Curse or *Avada Kedavra*, he is the only wizard capable of defeating the formidable black magician. As such, the two are linked, surrogate father with surrogate son. Harry begins the process of atoning with his father by thwarting Voldemort's plans to obtain the Sorcerer's Stone. Although he defeats Voldemort, Harry's victory is short-lived because the evil wizard escapes; their rivalry has just begun.

- The Ultimate Boon: Quirrell and Voldemort are vanquished with Harry recovering the sorcerer's stone. Because of Harry, Ron, Hermione, and Neville's heroics, Gryffindor wins the House Cup.

- Refusal of the Return: Harry does not want to go back to the mean-spirited Dursleys. Harry now understands Hogwarts is his home, and he decides to stay there during the summer holiday.

- Rescue from Without: Campbell explains, "The hero may have to be brought back from his supernatural adventure by assistance from without. That is to say, the world may have to come and get him. For the bliss of the deep abode is not lightly abandoned in favor of the self- scattering of the wakened state."[442] While convalescing in the hospital wing, Harry is reassured by Dumbledore that Hermione and Ron are well. Dumbledore also explains how he was able to recover the sorcerer's stone and defeat Quirrell and Voldemort.

As will be seen, most these elements repeat in the remaining films while other monomythic components are introduced.

HARRY POTTER AND THE CHAMBER OF SECRETS

Released on November 2nd, 2002, *Harry Potter and the Chamber of Secrets* is this author's favorite in the series. The story has believable and unexpected plot twists, and the scene in Aragog's Liar is scary and not cliché. The film picks up after the events of *Sorcerer's Stone*; Harry spends the summer without receiving letters from his Hogwarts friends. In his room, Harry meets Dobby (Toby Jones), a house-elf warning him that bad things will happen if he returns to Hogwarts, disclosing that he intercepted

---

442 *ibid*, p. 178.

his friends' letters to keep him away from Hogwarts. Harry chases him downstairs, where Dobby destroys a cake made for the Dursleys' guests. The Dursleys lock Harry up, but Ron, Fred, and George rescue him in their father's flying Ford Anglia. They return to their home, the Burrow, where Harry meets Ginny Weasley (Bonnie Wright), the youngest of the Weasley's seven children.

While purchasing school supplies, Harry and the Weasley family bump into Hagrid and Hermione Granger, and they attend a book-signing by celebrity wizard Gilderoy Lockhart (Kenneth Branagh), announcing he will be the new Defense Against the Dark Arts teacher. Harry also encounters Draco and his father Lucius Malfoy (Jason Isaacs); when no one is paying attention, Lucius slips a book in Ginny Weasley's cauldron. When Harry and Ron are blocked from entering Platform 9 ¾, they fly to Hogwarts in the Ford Anglia crashing into the hostile Whomping Willow. Ron's wand is damaged, and the car ejects them before driving off, disappearing. They are allowed back into school but face detention.

While serving detention with Lockhart supervising, Harry hears strange voices; he later finds caretaker Filch's cat, Mrs. Norris, petrified with a message written in blood announcing "The Chamber of Secrets has been opened" and threatening "Enemies of the Heir ... Beware." Professor McGonagall explains that one of Hogwarts' founders, Salazar Slytherin, supposedly constructed a secret chamber, placing inside it a monster that only his heir can control, to purge the school of impure-blooded wizards and witches known as Mudbloods. More attacks occur over the course of the year. Harry and Ron suspect that Draco is the heir, so Hermione suggests they question him while disguised using Polyjuice Potion, an alchemical drink which temporarily changes one into someone else's appearance. Their makeshift laboratory in the girl's bathroom is haunted by a ghost nicknamed "Moaning Myrtle" (Shirley Henderson,), a student killed there years earlier. Rowling has a keen sense of humor: a shy, lonely female student seeking sanctuary in a bathroom stall, Moaning Myrtle is an allusion to female masturbation as her name *Moaning* clearly insinuates. But J.K. does not stop here; like a mad sexual scientist,[443] Rowling has no problem taking on male masturbation in *Prison of Azkaban*.

---

443 I think of Dr. Bernardo (John Carradine, 1906-1988) in *Everything You Always Wanted to Know About Sex * (*But Were Afraid to Ask)*, 1972. Another masturbatory sexual innuendo can

When Harry talks to a snake (a feat that Salazar Slytherin could also perform), some believe he is the heir. Using the Polyjuice Potion, Harry and Ron learn that Draco is not the heir, but he mentions that a girl died when the Chamber was last opened fifty years ago. Harry finds an enchanted diary, owned by a former student named Tom Marvolo Riddle (Christian Coulson), which shows him a flashback fifty years earlier, when Riddle accused Hagrid, then a student, of opening the Chamber. When the diary disappears and Hermione is petrified, Harry and Ron question Hagrid. Professor Dumbledore, Minister of Magic Cornelius Fudge (Robert Hardy), and Lucius Malfoy come to take Hagrid to Azkaban, but he discreetly tells the boys to "follow the spiders" who are privy to the conversation by using the invisibility cloak. Lucius has Dumbledore suspended. In the Forbidden Forest, Harry and Ron find a giant, blind talking spider (an Acromantula) named Aragog (Julian Glover), revealing Hagrid's innocence and that the dead girl was found in a bathroom. Aragog then sets his colony of Acromantula on them, but the now-wild Ford Anglia saves them.

A crumpled book page in Hermione's hand reveals the Chamber's monster is a basilisk, a giant serpent that can instantly kill those making direct eye contact with it; the petrified victims survive because they saw it indirectly. The school staff learns that Ginny was taken into the Chamber; "Her skeleton will lie in the chamber forever" is found written on a wall. Professors McGonagall and Snape cajole Lockhart into rescuing her. Harry and Ron find Lockhart planning to flee rather than entering the Chamber. They expose him as a fraud having stolen the memories of other wizards and claimed their heroic deeds for himself. Knowing Myrtle was the girl the basilisk killed; they drag Lockhart to the girl's bathroom and find the Chamber's entrance beneath the giant sink. Once inside, Lockhart uses Ron's damaged wand against them, but it backfires wiping his memory, causing a cave-in.

Harry enters the Chamber alone finding Ginny unconscious, dying, guarded by Tom Riddle. After some repertoire, Harry realizes Riddle is the Heir of Slytherin. Riddle tells him he used the diary to manipulate Ginny into reopening the Chamber. Riddle then reveals his full name, Tom

---

be found in the name of Harry Potter's babysitter, Mrs. Figg, whose name, Figg, suggests the word *Frig* as found in the slang term, *Frig off*, meaning masturbation. Mrs. Figg does not appear in any of the movies.

Marvolo Riddle, from which he created the anagram for his future new identity, "I am Lord Voldemort." When Harry expresses loyalty to Dumbledore, the latter's phoenix Fawkes (named after the 17th century Jesuit conspirator) flies in with the Sorting Hat causing Riddle to summon the basilisk.

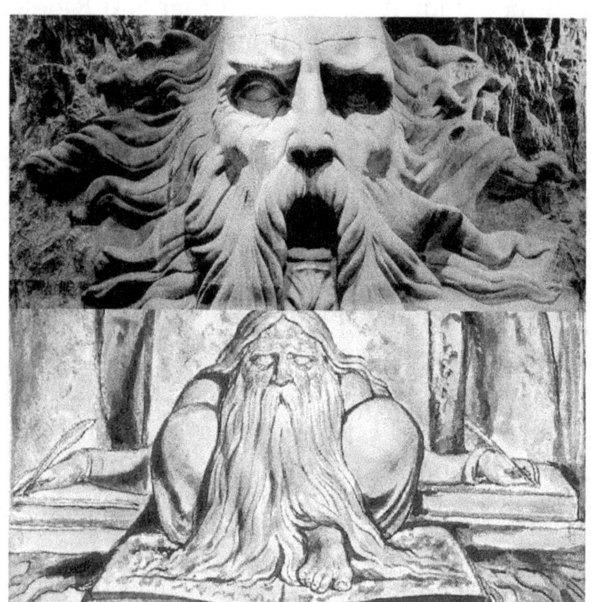

(Top) The sculpture of Salazar Slytherin's face inside the Chamber of Secrets is modeled after William Blake's Urizen, seen on the cover of Blake's *The Book of Urizen* (bottom), published in 1794. In Blake's mythology, Urizen serves as a satanic force similar to Milton's Lucifer *qua* Satan; hence, his visage becomes that of Salazar Slytherin, the founder of Slytherin House, Lord Voldemort's villainous home.

Fawkes blinds the basilisk, and the Sorting Hat eventually produces a sword with which Harry battles and slays the basilisk, but he is poisoned by one of its fangs. Harry defeats Riddle by stabbing the diary with a basilisk fang then revives Ginny. Fawkes' tears heal him, and he returns to Hogwarts with his friends and a baffled Professor Lockhart. The grand finale of this film is clearly a Neoplatonic Christian allegory, with Harry descending into the bowels of Hell, the subterranean Chamber of Secrets, to battle a giant serpent (cf. the Devil, the snake in the Garden of Eden) and its evil master, to save young Ginny, the archetypal damsel in distress. Harry is rescued by Dumbledore's Phoenix, Fawkes, a Christlike bird which self-combusts only to be resurrected from its ashes.

Dumbledore, reinstated as headmaster, praises them, ordering Hagrid's release. Dumbledore informs Harry that the sword he wielded was Godric Gryffindor's sword, explaining Harry is different from Voldemort because he chose Gryffindor instead of Slytherin. Harry accuses Lucius, Dobby's master, of putting the diary in Ginny's cauldron and, soon thereafter, tricks him into freeing Dobby. The basilisk's victims are healed, and Hagrid returns to school having been released from Azkaban Prison.

Freemasonry, whether consciously or unconsciously, is an influence upon J.K. Rowling and, thus, the Harry Potter stories. The beginning of *Chamber of Secrets* sees the Dursleys, Uncle Vernon (Richard Griffiths, 1947-2013), Aunt Petunia (Fiona Shaw), and Dudley (Harry Melling) putting on their best attire for an important meeting with the Masons. The meeting is so critical they rehearse their schedule: Petunia, conspicuously wearing an apron, will be in the lounge graciously welcoming them to their home; Dudley, like a lodge officer, will open the door for them. Uncle Vernon explains that during this meeting, he could make the biggest deal of his career, implying Masonic favoritism and influence. Because of the meeting's importance, Potter, an outsider (Pike's vile multitude)[444] or cowan, will be upstairs pretending he does not exist; he is not privy to the auspicious gathering. Although the Masons turn out to be nothing more than a nondescript couple, the importance of the clandestine meeting is conveyed by referring to the guests as the Masons.

The basilisk is a legendary reptile reputed to be king of serpents and said to have the power to cause death with a single glance. In Shakespeare's *Richard III* (ca. 1592), the recently widowed Anne Neville, on hearing seductive compliments on her eyes from her husband's murderer (Richard, Duke of Gloucester), retorts that she wishes they were those of a basilisk, that she might kill him.[445] In Act II, Scene IV of Shakespeare's *Cymbeline* (published 1623), a character says about a ring, "It is a basilisk unto mine eye, Kills me to look on't." The basilisk affiliates with royalty and royal blood, hence, it is a tool of the Heir of Slytherin, facilitating Salazar Slytherin's noble work by purging Hogwarts of Mudbloods. On the nexus between the basilisk and aristocracy, Masonic magus Albert Pike writes, "The salient basilisk, or royal ensign of the Pharaohs, often occurs on the monuments—a serpent in folds, with his head raised erect above the folds. The basilisk was the Phoenix of the serpent-tribe; and the vase or urn was probably the vessel, shaped like a cucumber, with a projecting spout, out of which,

---

444 In *Morals and Dogma*, Pike writes "In fact, what can there be in between the vile multitude and sublime wisdom?" Pike goes on to say, "The truth must be kept secret, and the masses need a teaching proportioned to their imperfect reason." Although these quotes are often attributed to Pike, he is actually quoting the great Kabbalist Synesius, Bishop of Ptolemais. See Pike's *Morals and Dogma*, p. 103.

445 David Colbert, *The Magical Worlds of Harry Potter*, pp. 33-34,

on the monuments of Egypt, the priests are represented pouring streams of the crux ansata or Tau Cross, and of scepters, over the kings."[446] Accordingly, only a pure-blooded wizard, the Heir of Slytherin, can communicate with the deadly serpent, ordering it to kill Mudbloods: non-royal wizards and witches. Believe it or not, the herb Sweet Basil is thought to have derived its name from the basilisk because of the old belief that basil attracted of even begot poisonous scorpions.[447]

Once again, we are presented with the monomyth and here, for your consideration, is *Chamber of Secrets'* breakdown.

- The Call to Adventure: Ron, Fred, and George Weasley rescue Harry from the Dursleys having locked Harry inside a bedroom. They escape in a flying Ford Anglia, beginning year two at Hogwarts.

- Refusal of the Call: Dobby has intercepted letters written to Harry from his friends to keep him from returning to Hogwarts. The Dursleys, having grown tired of Harry's magical skylarking, lock him inside of one of Dudley's bedrooms to keep the wizarding world at bay.

- Supernatural Aid: Harry finds Tom Marvolo Riddle's diary. It will later be disclosed that the diary is a Horcrux containing part of Voldemort's soul. Riddle's diary mind-controls Ginny, ordering her to open the Chamber of Secrets. Inside the Chamber, Harry destroys the diary, thereby destroying a part of Voldemort while saving Ginny.

- The Crossing of the First Threshold: Harry returns to Diagon Alley by using Floo Powder. While in Flourish and Blotts bookstore, he meets his new Defense Against the Dark Arts Professor, Gilderoy Lockhart. Harry is also introduced to the film's villain, Lucius Malfoy; his forename, Lucius, implies Lucifer *qua* Mephistopheles, a stoic philosopher, a black magician. Both characters serve as threshold guardians by inaugurating Harry into the mysteries of year two. Harry exposes Lockhart as a fraud, coming to suspect that Lucius is in league with Voldemort.

---

446 Pike, *Morals and Dogma*, p. 413.
447 *Encyclopedia of Magic & Superstition*, p. 219.

- The Belly of the Whale: Harry, Hermione, and Ron take the Polyjuice Potion to transform themselves into Slytherin House students. Although the potion backfires on Hermione, Harry and Ron enter the Slytherin Dungeon (a/k/a/ Common Room) to learn what Draco knows about the Chamber of Secrets.

- The Road of Trials: Harry breaks his arm during Quidditch while evading a rogue bludger. Later, Harry and his friends are puzzled when they learn he is a Parselmouth, sensing it may be a dark harbinger. In the Forbidden Forrest, Harry and Ron escape Aragog's Liar assisted by the flying Ford Anglia. Although Hermione has been petrified, she has left behind a valuable clue on how to enter the Chamber of Secrets and the specific monster that lurks within. Harry and Ron discover the entrance, descending to the Chamber with Lockhart. Harry confronts Riddle and battles the basilisk.

- The Meeting with the Goddess: We are introduced to Harry's future wife, Ginny Weasley. Through no fault of her own, she becomes Voldemort's victim, unleashing the basilisk. Dying inside the Chamber, she is rescued by her future husband.

- Atonement with the Father: Once again, Harry confronts and defeats his surrogate father, Voldemort, this time a sixteen-year-old vision-memory of the dark lord. Harry brings order from chaos; however, the black magician's spirit is getting stronger, and many more trials lay ahead.

- The Ultimate Boon: Voldemort is vanquished, Ginny is rescued, Hermione is restored, and Hagrid is released from Azkaban Prison. Harry tricks Lucius into giving Dobby a sock, freeing him from bondage.

- Rescue from Without: Hagrid receives a hero's welcome when he returns to Hogwarts; he comes to understand how much is cherished by the professors and the student body.

Next, *Harry Potter and the Prisoner of Azkaban* documents year three at Hogwarts School of Witchcraft and Wizardry.

HARRY POTTER AND THE PRISONER OF AZKABAN

Directed by Alfonso Cuarón, *Prisoner of Azkaban* grossed a total of $796.7 million worldwide with its box office performance, ranking as the lowest-grossing in the series. However, it was, at the time, the best-reviewed film of the series and currently the second-best-reviewed film of the franchise *behind Harry Potter and the Deathly Hallows Part 2*. With the death of Richard Harris on October 25th, 2002, Michael Gambon was cast as Albus Dumbledore, a role he assumes in the rest of the Potter films. *Prisoner of Azkaban* sees Harry and his friends growing up; they are now awkward, rebellious teenagers and their magical powers are increasing with them. Harry, now aged 13, has been spending another dissatisfying summer at Privet Drive. When Uncle Vernon's sister, Marge (Pam Ferris), insults Harry's parents, he becomes angry accidentally causing her to inflate and float away. Harry rebels: he flees with his packed luggage fed-up with his life with the Dursleys. The Knight Bus delivers Harry to the Leaky Cauldron, where he is forgiven by Minister of Magic Cornelius Fudge for using magic outside of Hogwarts. After reuniting with his best friends Ron and Hermione, Harry learns that Sirius Black (Gary Oldman), a convicted supporter of the dark wizard Voldemort, has escaped Azkaban Prison intending to kill Harry.

The trio is returning to Hogwarts for the new school year on the Hogwarts Express when Dementors–malevolent guards from Azkaban Prison–suddenly board the train, searching for Sirius. Looking like the Grim Reaper, one enters their compartment, causing Harry to pass out. However, new Defense Against the Dark Arts teacher, Professor Remus Lupin (David Thewlis), repels the Dementor with a Patronus Charm. At Hogwarts, headmaster Albus Dumbledore announces that Dementors will be guarding the school while Sirius is at large. Hogwarts groundskeeper Hagrid is introduced as the new Care of Magical Creatures teacher; his first class goes awry when Draco deliberately provokes a hippogriff, Buckbeak, that attacks him. Out of spite, Draco's father Lucius has Buckbeak sentenced to death. Lupin teaches his class how to perform the Riddikulus

Charm on a Boggart, a shape-shifting creature that takes the shape of the magician's worst fear.

The Fat Lady's portrait (Dawn French), which guards the Gryffindor quarters, is found ruined and empty – she has vacated the portrait. Terrified and hiding in another painting, the Fat Lady tells Dumbledore that Sirius Black has entered the castle. During a stormy Quidditch match, Dementors attack Harry, causing him to fall off his broomstick which is destroyed by the Whomping Willow. Lupin privately teaches Harry to defend himself against Dementors using the Patronus Charm. At Hogsmeade, Harry is shocked to learn that not only had Sirius Black been his parents' best friend, betraying them to Voldemort, but that Sirius is also his godfather.

After Harry, Ron, and Hermione witness Buckbeak's execution, Ron's pet rat Scabbers escapes from his pocket. When Ron gives chase, a large ferocious black dog appears and drags both Ron and Scabbers into a hole at the Whomping Willow's base, which is an underground passage to the haunted Shrieking Shack. The trio discovers that the dog is Sirius, the magician is an Animagus: a witch or wizard that can morph him or herself into an animal at will. Lupin arrives embracing Sirius as an old friend. Lupin admits to being a werewolf–he transforms every full moon–explaining that Sirius is innocent.[448] Sirius was falsely accused of betraying the Potters' hiding location to Voldemort, murdering their mutual friend Peter Pettigrew (Timothy Spall). It is disclosed that Scabbers is Pettigrew, an Animagus committing the crime for which Sirius was convicted. After forcing him back to his human form, Lupin and Sirius prepare to kill him, but Harry convinces them to turn Pettigrew over to the Dementors.

As the group departs the full moon rises; Lupin transforms into a werewolf; his surname, Lupin, is a shortened version of *Lupine* meaning *related to wolves*. Sirius morphs into his dog form to fight him off; in the chaos, Pettigrew changes back into Scabbers and escapes. Sirius and Harry are attacked by Dementors, while Harry sees a figure in the distance save them by casting a powerful Patronus spell. He believes the mysterious figure is his dead father and passes out. He awakens to discover that Sirius has been captured and sentenced to the Dementor's Kiss: the sucking out of one's soul. Acting on Dumbledore's advice, Harry and Hermione travel back in time with Hermione's Time-Turner witnessing themselves repeat

---

448 For more on lycanthropy see Sullivan's *Cinema Symbolism*, Chapter VII.

the night's events. They save Buckbeak from execution then watch the Dementors overpower Sirius and Harry. The present Harry realizes that the unknown person casting the Patronus Spell was not his father, but himself, doing so again, not altering the timeline. Harry and Hermione then rescue Sirius and the three escapes on Buckbeak. Lupin resigns to preempt an uproar from parents over a werewolf teaching their children. Sirius sends Harry a Firebolt Broomstick with a feather from Buckbeak, identifying Sirius as the sender. The movie ends with Harry taking the broom for a spin.

*　*　*　*

Although it's not esoteric in nature, one can observe Buckbeak take a shit after Hagrid selects Harry to meet the proud hippogriff. Keep an eye out for this humorous Easter egg the next time you watch *Prisoner of Azkaban.*

Esoteric symbolism is limited in this Potter movie; after the students arrive at Hogwarts, Dumbledore addresses them from a podium adorned with an owl, a symbol of sagacity because it is the sacred totem of Minerva, goddess of wisdom. An owl can see things in the dark, implying Hogwarts' students are the initiated few (see Chapter II). The owl, in the wizarding world, signifies that witches and wizards are superior to those of a non-magical nature, Muggles, the *profane* in Masonic nomenclature.[449]

Unlike *Sorcerer's Stone* and *Chamber of Secrets*, in which Harry and his friends were youths, one cannot help notice that they are now teenagers in *Prisoner of Azkaban.* Although sexual education does not appear to be taught at Hogwarts, the third-year students are required to obtain a copy of *The Monster Book of Monsters* by Edwardus Lima. When opened, the hairy book loses control attacking the person opening it; the only way to calm it is to stroke its spine. The hyperactive book is clearly a tongue-in-cheek sexual innuendo for male masturbation, the third-year students' hormonal teenage sexual energies coming to fruition. Rowling's sexual metaphor is now apparent: the excitable book can only be relaxed by *stroking it*; its hairiness conjures the old wives' tale that masturbating causes hairy palms.

---

449 cf. p.249 of *Morals and Dogma*; Pike writes: "Pythagoras and Plato, the most mystical of the Grecian Philosophers (the latter heir to the doctrines of the former), and who had travelled, the latter in Egypt, and the former in Phœnicia, India, and Persia, also taught the esoteric doctrine and the distinction between the initiated and the profane."

Like the Dementors, components of the monomyth manifest in *Prisoner of Azkaban.*

- The Call to Adventure: Harry flees the Dursleys on the Knight Bus. He goes to the Leaky Cauldron and meets with Minister of Magic Cornelius Fudge informing him he will not be expelled from Hogwarts. Harry learns from Mr. Weasley that Sirius Black has escaped from Azkaban and his hunting Harry. Thus, begins year three at Hogwarts.

- Refusal of the Call: Uncle Vernon tries to stop Harry from leaving 4 Privet Drive, but Harry has become too powerful and exits, disobeying his uncle.

- Supernatural Aid: The Weasley Twins give Harry the Marauder's Map. The Map is a magical document that reveals all of Hogwarts School of Witchcraft and Wizardry. Not only does it show every classroom, every hallway, and every corner of the castle, but it also shows every inch of the grounds, as well as all the secret passages that are hidden within its walls and the location of every person in the grounds, portrayed by footsteps. It is also capable of accurately identifying each individual, and is not fooled by animagi, Polyjuice Potions, or invisibility cloaks; even Hogwarts' eccentric ghosts are not exempt. Stairs of the Map! The Marauder's Map identifies Scabbers as Peter Pettigrew.

- The Crossing of the First Threshold: Dementors stop the Hogwarts Express, boarding the train, searching for Sirius Black. Harry comes to learn first-hand the nature of their malignant power. By keeping an all-seeing eye on Hogwarts, the Dementors are de facto threshold guardians.

- The Belly of the Whale: Aided by the invisibility cloak and the Marauder's Map, Harry sneaks out of Hogwarts to Hogsmeade Village. Underneath the invisibility cloak, he enters Hogsmeade Tavern, overhearing a secret conversation during which Cornelius Fudge reveals that Sirius Black was responsible for the deaths of Harry's parents by betraying them to Voldemort. Harry also learns that Sirius is his godfather. The episode leaves Potter in tears–emotionally scarred–but yearning for revenge.

- The Road of Trials: Harry tames Buckbeak and survives a deadly encounter with the Dementors while playing Quidditch. He learns the Patronus Charm from Lupin. Later, Harry and Hermione save Buckbeak from the headsman's ax. Then, the duo outmaneuvers the Whomping Willow and escape from Lupin having transformed into a werewolf.

- The Meeting with the Goddess: Hermione can bilocate because she possesses a Time-Turner. Hermione and Harry use it to travel back in time to save Buckbeak from execution and Sirius from the Dementors. Hermione is truly coming into her own by becoming a resourceful and powerful witch as well as one of Hogwarts' most able students. We are also introduced to the droll Head of the Divination Workshop at Hogwarts, Sybill Trelawney (Emma Thompson). Sybill is named after Sybil Leek (1917-1982), a famous English witch, occult author, astrologer, and self-proclaimed psychic. Trelawney and Leek's shared forename is apropos because Sybil, which comes from Greek Σιβυλλα, or Sibylla, means *prophetess*. In the 1960s, Sybil planned to found a school, a real-life Hogwarts, that would teach its students witchcraft and wizardry. Sybil was not a crank: two of her most famous clients were Ian Fleming and H.G. Wells; she predicted the literary achievements of the former years before he began writing 007's espionage adventures. As a child, Sybil witnessed her Russian grandmother, also a mystic, prepare astrological charts for houseguests T.E. Lawrence (1888-1935, a/k/a Lawrence of Arabia), Thomas Hardy (1840-1928), and Dame Edith Sitwell (1887-1964). Another frequent visitor to her grandmother's home was the Great Beast 666, Aleister Crowley. Master Therion, after meeting young Sybil, declared she would posthumously continue his occultism.

- Atonement with the Father: Harry confronts his evil Uncle Claudius in the form of Sirius Black. However, Potter discovers it was Peter Pettigrew who betrayed his parents, not Sirius thus saving his uncle from a terrible fate. By clearing his godfather's name and exposing

Pettigrew, Harry has is now one step closer to Voldemort. Harry discovers that the ferocious black dog, a Grim, was Sirius protecting him, not intending any harm. The two are reconciled; Sirius gives Harry a Firebolt Broom, the fastest broom in the world, and Harry happily takes it for a ride.

- The Ultimate Boon: Harry masters the Patronus Spell, casting it to save Sirius and himself from the Dementors. Mastery of the hex is crucial if Voldemort and his legions are to be defeated.

The saga continues with *Harry Potter and the Goblet of Fire*.

HARRY POTTER AND THE GOBLET OF FIRE

Released in November 2005, the fourth Harry Potter film is, up to this point, the darkest one of the series because it sees the murderous return of Lord Voldemort (Ralph Fiennes) during the movie's climax. As such, the movie is one of the best-reviewed installments within the series, praised for its high level of maturity and the development of its characters, plotline, writing, and the performances of the lead actors. Directed by Mike Newell, *Goblet of Fire* opens with a dream: Harry has a vision of caretaker Frank Bryce (Eric Sykes, 1923-2012) killed after overhearing Voldemort discussing plans with Peter Pettigrew and Barty Crouch Jr. (David Tennant). Pettigrew is now called by his nickname, "Wormtail," which draws forth the backstabbing sycophant Grima Wormtongue (Brad Dourif) from the *Lord of the Rings*. Just like the treacherous Wormtongue heeding Saruman's (Christopher Lee) every command, Wormtail will do anything to appease his dark master. Harry goes with the Weasleys to the Quidditch World Cup, but Death Eaters terrorize the spectators; Barty appears, bringing forth the Dark Mark on his forearm.

Later at Hogwarts, Albus Dumbledore introduces ex-Auror (an employee of the Ministry whose mission is to pursue and apprehend dark wizards) Alastor "Mad-Eye" Moody (Brendan Gleeson) as the new Defense Against the Dark Arts teacher; Alastor is named after English occultist, Freemason, and sex magician Aleister Crowley naturally.

Dumbledore also announces that the school will host the Triwizard Tournament at which three magical schools will compete in deadly competition by facing three dangerous challenges. The champions are selected by the Goblet of Fire: Cedric Diggory (Robert Pattinson) of Hufflepuff is chosen to represent Hogwarts, Viktor Krum (Stanislav Ianevski) will represent Durmstrang Institute, and Fleur Delacour (Clémence Poésy) will represent Beauxbatons Academy of Magic. The Goblet unexpectedly chooses a fourth Champion: Harry Potter. Dumbfounded, Dumbledore is unable to pull the underage Harry out of the tournament. Ministry official Barty Crouch Sr. (Roger Lloyd-Pack, 1944-2014) states that the champions are contractually bound, and therefore, Harry is obliged to compete. Ron becomes jealous of Harry, feeling like his sidekick, and the two have a falling-out.

For the tournament's first task, the champions must each retrieve a golden egg guarded by a dragon. Harry succeeds after he summons his Firebolt broomstick to retrieve the egg, which contains information about the second challenge. Shortly thereafter, the Yule Ball dance takes place, during which Harry's crush Cho Chang (Katie Leung) attends with Cedric, and Hermione attends with Viktor, which renders Ron even more jealous. During the second task, the champions are instructed to dive underwater to rescue their mates; Harry comes out last but is placed second behind Cedric due to his strong moral fiber and backbone. Afterward, Barty Crouch Sr. is found dead by Harry.

In the third and final task, the competitors are placed inside a hedge maze and must reach the Triwizard Cup. Viktor, bewitched, incapacitates Fleur. After Harry saves Cedric from the attacking maze, the two agree to a draw and grab the Cup together, which turns out to be a Portkey: an enchanted object cursed to bring anyone touching it to a particular location instantly. The two are transported to a forbidding graveyard, where Wormtail and a small, frail Voldemort are waiting. Wormtail kills Cedric with the Killing Curse, then performs an occult ritual using a bone from Voldemort's father, Wormtail's flesh (his hand) and Harry's blood, which fully revives Voldemort, summoning the Death Eaters. Voldemort challenges Harry to a duel to prove he is the better wizard. Harry is unable to defend himself, but tries the Expelliarmus Charm at the same moment Voldemort attempts the Killing Curse. Their spells cause the shadow impressions of the people

Voldemort murdered to appear in the graveyard, including Harry's parents and Cedric. The apparitions provide an ample distraction to Voldemort and the Death Eaters allowing Harry to escape–along with Cedric's body–by grabbing the Cup.

Upon his return, Harry tells Dumbledore that Voldemort has returned and is responsible for Cedric's death. Hogwarts grieves for Cedric. Mad-Eye takes a devastated Harry back to his room, locks the door, admitting that he put Harry's name in the Goblet, cursed Viktor, having been responsible for all the things gone wrong, then tries to attack Harry. Dumbledore, Severus Snape, and Minerva McGonagall break down his door revealing that he is not Mad-Eye Moody; the real Moody is imprisoned in a magical trunk. The false Mad-Eye's Polyjuice Potion wears off, revealing Barty Crouch Jr., doing the bidding of Voldemort. Barty Crouch Jr. is sent back to Azkaban Prison from which he had escaped. Soon thereafter, Hogwarts, Durmstrang, and Beauxbatons gather to mourn Cedric, bidding farewell to each other; the end credits roll.

Alas, there is no esoteric imagery in Goblet of Fire except for some numerological references which will be discussed later in this chapter. Unlike the first three Potter films, the elements of the monomyth are also minimized because this movie is a bridge, leaving behind the innocence of the first three films for dark finality: the showdown with Voldemort and the Death Eaters. In fact, the Ultimate Boon component is absent, having been thwarted by the return of Voldemort and the death of Cedric. Although it does not affect the storytelling, some of the monomythic elements are out of order; here is Goblet of Fire's breakdown.

- The Call to Adventure: Through no action (or fault) of his own, Harry finds himself entered into the Triwizard Tournament. The Tournament is the central plot device of the movie.

- Refusal of the Call: Harry is reluctant to participate in the tournament telling Ron "I didn't put my name in that cup. I don't want eternal glory I just wanna be... Look, I don't know what happened tonight and I don't know why, it just did, okay." Nevertheless, Harry's entrance in the Tournament causes a rift between him and Ron.

- Supernatural Aid: Neville Longbottom gives Potter a magical plant called Gillyweed, making it easier to negotiate the second task of the tournament: descent into Black Lake to retrieve something that has been stolen from each contestant. When Gillyweed is consumed by a witch or wizard, they develop gills, with webbing growing between their fingers and toes allowing them to navigate underwater efficiently.

- The Crossing of the First Threshold: Harry, accompanied by the Weasleys, attends the Quidditch World Cup; on the way Harry is introduced to Cedric Diggory. Later, the World Cup is attacked and decimated by the Death Eaters. Cedric and the Death Eaters serve as threshold guardians: Cedric will be killed by Voldemort and the Death Eaters foreshadow the Voldemort's arrival. Harry learns the Death Eaters are extremely dangerous existing outside the normal traffic of Hogwarts and the wizarding world.

- The Belly of the Whale: "The belly is the dark place where digestion takes place and new energy is created."[450] Harry and Ron attend the Yule Ball but not with the dates they desire: Harry wants to be with Cho and Ron pines for Hermione. At first, Hermione is thrilled to be going with Viktor, but misery loves company so Ron badgers and teases Hermione, bringing her to tears to make her feel as dejected as he is. Although his antics are juvenile, Ron succeeds in leaving Hermione hurt and frustrated. However, the trio emerges transformed, becoming more devoted to each other than they were beforehand.

- The Road of Trials: The three tasks of the Triwizard Tournament: Dragons, Black Lake, and the Maze. The Triwizard Tournament is designed to test the champions in many different ways: their magical prowess, their daring, their powers of deduction, and their ability to cope with danger. Cheating was also considered a standard, traditional part of the Tournament.

- The Meeting with the Goddess: Harry's new love interest is introduced, Cho Chang.

---

450 Joseph Campbell with Bill Moyers, *The Power of Myth*, p. 180.

- Woman as the Temptress: "No longer can the hero rest in innocence with the goddess of the flesh; for she is become the queen of sin."[451] Meet Rita Skeeter, a witch-journalist specializing in writing poison-pen stories tending to be based on false information, misquoting those she interviews all while working for *The Daily Prophet*, as well authoring a few tell-all biographies. Rita is shameless: as a temptress, she tries to seduce young Harry in a broom cupboard.

- Atonement with the Father: "The dark figure. Yes, that's the figure in Goethe's *Faust* is represented by Mephistopheles."[452] Lord Voldemort, Potter's evil de facto father, finally returns and duels Harry. Although Harry is weakened, he manages to escape the dark lord with the Triwizard Cup and Cedric's body. The Heir of Slytherin is furious; their dark reconciliation is just beginning, their Manichean conflict escalating.

- Rescue from Without: Harry, having survived Voldemort and the Death Eaters, is brought back to the world by Hermione, Ron, and Dumbledore who comfort him. Hermione realizes that things are changing, but no matter whatever dark trials lay ahead they will always be there for him and each other.

Goblet of Fire's brooding atmosphere continues in the next installment, *Order of the Phoenix.*

Harry Potter and the Order of the Phoenix

Directed by David Yates and released in July 2007, *Order of the Phoenix* picks up where *Goblet of Fire* left off. With the return of Voldemort, Harry's actions are now dedicated to stopping him; this makes the former Harry's surrogate father, his Darth Vader to Harry's Luke Skywalker. But least we forget that Harry is Voldemort's surrogate son, the *boy who lived* having survived Voldemort's Killing Curse. Thus, Harry is the object of

---

451 Campbell, *The Hero with a Thousand Faces*, p. 102.
452 Campbell with Moyers, *ibid*, p. 181.

Voldemort's vengeful hatred: although they are like father and son, their relationship is a paradox because the two cannot coexist. This patriarchal contradiction is prophesied in the *Goblet of Fire*. Unfortunately for Harry and Dumbledore, no one believes Voldemort has returned; many in the Ministry of Magic would rather bury their heads in the sand rather than confront a painful truth.

Order of the Phoenix is year five: Harry Potter is expelled from Hogwarts forced to defend himself against charges of using magic while underage and in the presence of his Muggle cousin Dudley after the two are attacked by Dementors. The Order of the Phoenix, a secret society founded by Dumbledore, informs Harry that the Ministry of Magic is oblivious to Lord Voldemort's return. Under the Ministry's influence, *The Daily Prophet* has launched a smear campaign against Harry and Dumbledore following Harry's encounter with Voldemort at the end of the previous year.

The encounter had an enormous psychological effect on Harry: he has nightmares not only about what happened in the graveyard but also about the Department of Mysteries at the Ministry of Magic. While inside the Order's headquarters, Harry's godfather, Sirius Black, mentions that Voldemort is after an object which he did not have last time. Harry has a hearing at the Ministry of Magic and is cleared of all charges against him. He is allowed to return to Hogwarts.

Arriving at Hogwarts, Harry discovers that Minister for Magic, Cornelius Fudge, has appointed a new Defense Against the Dark Arts professor: Dolores Umbridge (Imelda Staunton), a senior Ministry official refusing to teach defensive magic due to her belief that Dumbledore is fomenting rebellion against the Ministry. Due to her charmingly cruel personality, Dolores reminds this author of Mrs. Baylock (Billie Whitelaw, 1932-2014), the satanic nanny from *The Omen* (1976). Delores and Harry immediately clash because she denies Voldemort's return, punishing Harry for his "lies" by forcing him to write a message with a magic quill, painfully scarring his hand. When Ron and Hermione notice Harry's scars, they are outraged, but he refuses to go to Dumbledore, having distanced himself from Harry since the summer. As Delores' control over the school increases, Ron and Hermione aid Harry in forming a secret group to train students in defensive spells, calling themselves Dumbledore's Army. The Slytherin students are recruited by Delores to expose the group. Meanwhile, Harry and Cho Chang's romantic feelings blossom with Cho being Harry's first kiss right before Yuletide. However, Harry worries that his increasingly erratic behavior is making him more like Voldemort.

Harry has a vision involving an attack upon Arthur Weasley in the Department of Mysteries, from the point of view of Arthur's attacker. Concerned that Voldemort will exploit this connection to Harry, Dumbledore instructs Severus Snape to give Harry Occlumency lessons to defend his mind from Voldemort's influence. These lessons increase Harry's psychological problems because he is forced to relive all his bad experiences. The connection between Harry and Voldemort leads Harry to isolate himself further from his friends. Meanwhile, Bellatrix Lestrange (Helena Bonham Carter), Sirius' deranged evil cousin, escapes from Azkaban along with other Death Eaters. At Hogwarts, Delores and her Inquisitorial Squad expose Dumbledore's Army after illegally interrogating Cho with Veritaserum (English: truth serum). Dumbledore covers for Harry saying the Army was his brainchild and escapes just as Fudge orders his arrest. Delores becomes the new Headmistress exercising even stricter control over the campus. Harry's relationship with Cho falls apart because he believes she betrayed Dumbledore's Army to Delores. During his last Occlumency lessons, Harry finally loses his temper deflecting the spell back on Snape, allowing him to discover Snape's memories, learning that his father, James,[453] often ridiculed the anguished wizard, becoming the object of Snape's disdain.

During an Ordinary Wizarding Level (O.W.L.) exam, Fred and GeorgE Weasley rebel by setting off fireworks in the Great Hall to Delores' dismay. During this event, Harry has a vision of Sirius being tortured by Voldemort within the Department of Mysteries. Harry, Ron, and Hermione decide to alert the Order via the Floo Network, rushing to Delores' fireplace since hers is not monitored, but she intercepts them. When she berates Harry threatening to use the Cruciatus Curse (Torture Curse) to get information about the trio's intentions, Hermione tricks Delores into entering the Forbidden Forest to search for Dumbledore's secret weapon. Hermione and Harry lead her to the hiding place of Hagrid's half-brother, the giant Grawp, only to be confronted by centaurs that kidnap Delores after she attacks them. Harry, Hermione, Ron, Neville, Ginny along with the eccentric Luna Lovegood (Evanna Lynch) fly to the Ministry of Magic on

---

453 Young James Potter is portrayed by Robbie Jarvis.

Thestrals (strange creatures that can only be seen by those having closely experienced death) in an attempt to save Sirius.

The six enter the Department of Mysteries where they uncover a bottled prophecy involving Harry and Voldemort; this is the object that Voldemort is after. However, they are ambushed by Death Eaters including Lucius Malfoy and Bellatrix Lestrange. Lucius reveals that Harry only saw a dream of Sirius being tortured; it was a method to lure Harry into the Death Eaters' grasp, it was an dream, not reality. Lucius implores Harry to give him the prophecy, but Harry refuses and a fight between Dumbledore's Army and the Death Eaters ensues. Except for Harry, the Death Eaters take everyone hostage, threatening to kill them unless he surrenders the prophecy.

Harry obliges just as Sirius and Remus Lupin arrive with Order members Nymphadora Tonks (Natalie Tena), Kingsley Shacklebolt (George Harris) and Mad-Eye Moody. They attack the Death Eaters attempting to rescue the members of Dumbledore's Army. In the midst of the battle, Lucius drops the prophecy, destroying it. Harry and Sirius duel with him; just as Sirius overpowers Lucius, Bellatrix kills Sirius with the Killing Curse. In the Atrium, Harry unsuccessfully attempts to subdue Bellatrix with the *Cruciatus Curse*. Voldemort appears, but Dumbledore arrives through the Floo Network moments before Voldemort can kill Harry.

A magical duel between Voldemort and Dumbledore ensues, destroying much of the Atrium, while Bellatrix escapes. After the two prove evenly matched, Voldemort possesses Harry to try to get Dumbledore to sacrifice Harry in the hope of killing him, but the love Harry feels for his friends and Sirius makes it impossible for Voldemort to remain in his body. Ministry officials arrive before Voldemort disapparates; Fudge is forced to admit that Voldemort has returned. In the aftermath, Delores is removed from Hogwarts with Dumbledore returning as headmaster after he and Harry are exonerated. Dumbledore explains that he distanced himself from Harry throughout the year hoping it would lessen the risk of Voldemort using their connection. Harry comes to terms with the prophecy, "Neither can live while the other survives." As Harry and his friends prepare to depart on the Hogwarts Express, Harry tells them that even though a war is beginning, unlike Voldemort, they have something worth fighting for: each other.

By now one will notice that some of the characters are named after stars and constellations, such as *Sirius* Black, his cousin *Bellatrix* Lestrange, and *Draco* Malfoy; the significance of these astrological names will be discussed toward the end of this chapter. Once again, we are left to ponder the monomyth and the monomyth alone; *Order of the Phoenix* gives us a heavy dose of the Woman as the Temptress and, for the first time in the Potter franchise, the element of Apotheosis is included.

- The Call to Adventure: Mad-Eye Moody and some of the other members of the Order of the Phoenix liberate Harry from 4 Privot Drive, beginning year five at Hogwarts.

- Refusal of the Call: A Howler (a magical speaking letter) from the Ministry of Magic arrives for Harry telling him he is expelled from Hogwarts School of Witchcraft and Wizardry for using magic in the presence of a Muggle.

- Supernatural Aid: The Room of Requirement is discovered; it is a secret room within Hogwarts Castle that only appears when a person is in great need of it. Inside the chamber, Dumbledore's Army practice defensive sorcery away from Delores' prying eyes.

- The Crossing of the First Threshold: Harry is taken to the Order of the Phoenix's headquarter. The Order is a secret society founded by Albus Dumbledore to oppose Lord Voldemort and his Death Eaters. The Order was created in the 1970s becoming organized after Voldemort started his campaign to take over the Ministry of Magic to persecute Mudbloods. The Order worked with the Ministry to oppose the Dark Lord and his followers playing a crucial role in the First Wizarding War. The First Wizarding War ended on 31 October 1981, which resulted in Lord Voldemort's first fall and the defeat of his Death Eaters at the hands of the Order of the Phoenix and Harry Potter. The Order's members are threshold guardians.

- The Belly of the Whale: Already entangled in a smear campaign by *The Daily Prophet*, Harry has a hearing before Cornelius Fudge in the bowels of the Ministry of Magic to determine if he is to be expelled from Hogwarts. Although the trial ends favorably, Harry now understands that many in the Ministry are not his friends (certainly not his ally) or Dumbledore's.

- The Road of Trials: Harry and his friends must cautiously navigate Delores' Nazi-like Hogwarts. Delores, not wanting to teach the students defenses against the dark arts properly, provokes Harry to form Dumbledore's Army so that he can teach the students the Patronus Charm. Spies are everywhere; Sybill Trelawney is humiliated, and Dumbledore flees. Via Occlumency, Harry and Severus duel each other mentally, discovering secrets about the other. Later, Harry and his coterie enter the Department of Mysteries to locate the prophecy, but Voldemort and the Death Eaters intervene, with a magical battle ensuing.

- The Meeting with the Goddess: The divine masculine and sacred feminine are maturing at Hogwarts: Harry and Cho become more intimate while Ginny can't take her eyes off Harry. Ginny's blossoming magical abilities are a metaphor for puberty. *Order of the Phoenix* introduces the moon herself, Luna Lovegood, an oddball whose name, Luna, conjures the word *lunacy*, while her platinum blonde locks resemble moonbeams.

- The Woman as Temptress: Two cruel female villains pervade the movie: Delores Umbridge, a strutting martinet taking perverse pleasure in disciplining *qua* torturing students; and the odious Bellatrix Lestrange, a loyal disciple of Lord Voldemort.

- Atonement with the Father: Harry is tempted by Voldemort to kill Bellatrix for murdering Sirius, but he refuses; Dumbledore appears, dueling with the evil Lord. By the end, it is clear that Harry and Voldemort are spiritually-psychically linked, and that they have a powerful father-son bond. In the earlier films, Harry's scar began to hurt when the dark lord was near, symbolizing the nexus between him and Voldemort. According to the prophecy, "neither one can live while the other survives;" in other words, Harry and Voldemort cannot coexist.

- Apotheosis: Sirius Black is killed by Bellatrix Lestrange; "Once we free of the prejudices of our own provincially limited ecclesiastical, tribal, or national rendition of the of the world archetypes, it becomes possible to understand that the supreme initiation is not that of the local motherly fathers, who then project aggression onto the neighbors for their own defenses. The good news, which the World Redeemer brings and which so many have been glad to hear, zealous to preach, but reluctant, apparently, to demonstrate, is that God is love, that He can be, and is to be, loved, and that all without exception are his children."[454] Harry, embodying the savior archetype, does not seek vengeance rather he comes to pity the dark lord because he will never know love or friendship.

- The Ultimate Boon: The Ministry recognizes that Voldemort has returned. Delores is suspended pending investigation and Dumbledore is reinstated as Hogwarts' headmaster.

- Rescue from Without: Dumbledore explains his actions to Harry reassuring him that, although dark days lay ahead, he is not alone. Harry expresses this sentiment to his friends on the Hogwarts Express' train platform. Although brief, calmness and a sense of ease returns.

What mysteries lay ahead for Harry Potter and his friends? Next, the *Half- Blood Prince* documents Harry's sixth year at Hogwarts when he becomes obsessed with a mysterious textbook titled *Advanced Potion Making*, falls in love, and attempts to retrieve a memory that holds the key to Lord Voldemort's downfall. David Yates once again returns to direct *Half-Blood Prince* which was released in July 2009.

HARRY POTTER AND THE HALF-BLOOD PRINCE

Lord Voldemort is tightening his grip on both the wizarding and Muggle worlds, electing Draco Malfoy to carry out a secret mission. Severus Snape makes an Unbreakable Vow with Draco's mother, Narcissa (Helen McCrory), to protect Draco, but to fulfill the assignment should her son fail. Meanwhile, Harry accompanies Dumbledore to visit former potions professor Horace Slughorn (Jim Broadbent), an eccentric having gone into

---

454 Campbell, *The Hero with a Thousand Faces*, p. 135. See also the Gospel According to Matthew, 22:37-40; Mark, 12:28-34; Luke 10:25-27. Jesus is also reported to have commissioned his apostles to "teach all nations" (Matthew 28:19), but not to persecute or pillage, or turn over to the "secular arm" those that would not hear. "Behold, I send you forth as sheep in the midst of wolves: be ye therefore wise as serpents, and harmless as doves" (Matthew, 10:16).

hiding but reluctantly agrees to return to teach at Hogwarts. Dumbledore then takes Harry to the Burrow (Weasley home) where Harry reunites with his best friends Ron and Hermione. Harry believes Voldemort has made Draco a Death Eater, after seeing Draco taking part in a mysterious ceremony, but Ron and Hermione are skeptical. At Hogwarts, Harry and Ron are forced to borrow textbooks for Slughorn's potions class, and Harry is stuck with a copy which turns out to be filled with helpful notes, instructions, and spells left by the book's previous owner, the mysterious Half-Blood Prince. Using the book, Harry excels in the class, impressing Slughorn. Ron becomes Keeper of the Gryffindor Quidditch team and forms a romantic relationship with Lavender Brown (Jessie Cave), upsetting Hermione. Harry consoles Hermione, revealing that he now has feelings for Ron's younger sister, Ginny.

Harry spends the Yuletide with the Weasleys. On Christmas Eve, Bellatrix Lestrange and Fenrir Greyback (Dave Legeno, 1963-2014) set fire to the Burrow. Back at school, Ron is nearly killed when he drinks poisoned mead; Slughorn planned to give the bottle of mead to Dumbledore for Christmas. While recovering, Ron murmurs Hermione's name, causing Lavender to end their relationship. Harry confronts Draco and severely injures him with a Sectumsempra Curse taken from the textbook of the Half-Blood Prince. Snape intervenes quickly healing Draco's hemophilia-like wound. Fearing the book may be filled with more harmful spells and black magic, Ginny and Harry hide it in the Room of Requirement wherein they share their first kiss.

Dumbledore shows Harry memories of a young Tom Riddle (Frank Dillane) which reveals that Slughorn retains a memory critical to Voldemort's defeat. The memory as it exists is a fraud, but Harry eventually succeeds in retrieving the correct memory which discloses that Tom wanted information about creating Horcruxes, objects containing pieces of one's soul. In the memory, Tom asks Slughorn if splitting his soul seven times was possible. Dumbledore concludes that Voldemort eventually did this, disclosing that two of his Horcruxes have already been destroyed: Tom Riddle's diary and Marvolo Gaunt's ring. After discovering the possible location of another Horcrux, Harry and Dumbledore travel to a seaside cave where Harry forces Dumbledore to drink a painful liquid so that the Horcrux can be retrieved. The Horcrux, a gold locket, is successfully recovered. A weakened Dumbledore defends them from *Inferi* (Gollum-like creatures) and apparates back to Hogwarts, where Bellatrix, Greyback, and more Death Eaters have entered with Draco's help through a vanishing cabinet.

Dumbledore instructs Harry to hide just as Draco arrives. A distraught Draco disarms Dumbledore, revealing that he has been chosen by Voldemort to kill the headmaster. However, he is unable to bring himself to do it, and Snape casts the Avada Kedavra curse instead, killing Dumbledore. Harry attempts to curse Snape, but Snape overpowers him revealing that he is the Half-Blood Prince. Harry returns to the school to find the staff and students mourning Dumbledore. Harry later reveals to Ron and Hermione that the locket Horcrux was a fake. The pendant contains a message from R.A.B., stating that he has stolen the real Horcrux with the intent of destroying it. Rather than returning to Hogwarts for their final year, Harry, Ron, and Hermione vow to seek out and destroy the remaining Horcruxes.

"The death and resurrection of a savior figure is a common motif in all these legends;"[455] hence Harry, for the first time, is now referred to as the Chosen One, echoing Neo from *The Matrix* and Paul Maud'Dib from *Dune*. Like these saviors, Harry will also undergo death and resurrection; for Potter's messianic mission is to save the wizarding world from a maniacal evil lord. However, Potter's apotheosis does not occur until the end of *Deathly Hallows – Part 2*. The monomyth notwithstanding, esoteric symbolism resides *Half-Blood Prince*. For instance, Draco, along with some of the Death Eaters, enter Borgin and Burke's, a store specializing in dark magic, occult relics, and sinister artifacts. The name, Burke, conveys deathly mystery, referencing Edinburgh body snatcher and murderer William Burke (1792-1829); the crimes of Mr. Burke and his accomplice William Hare (1792/1804–ca. 1858?) will be discussed in Chapter XIII.

The personification of the waxing moon, Luna Lovegood, returns peddling *The Quibbler*. Marketed as the Wizarding World's Alternative Voice, *The Quibbler* is a wizarding tabloid edited and published by her father. Luna gets every issue of *The Quibbler* when it's published, which could explain her weird beliefs. Luna also wears a large, over-the-top lion's head hat to show her support for the Gryffindor Quidditch team

---

455 Campbell with Moyers, *The Power of Myth*, p. 131.

whenever they play against the Slytherin team; this is the exoteric explanation. However, embodying the soft, supernatural light of the moon,[456] Luna has no choice but to reflect the light of the sun; hence, the lion's hat is an occult reference to Leo the Lion and its ruler the sun; this, dear reader, is the esoteric explanation.

The monomyth is strong in *Half-Blood Prince* despite this being the first installment that does not feature the Atonement with the Father element; Voldemort's presence is strongly felt even though he does not appear.

- The Call to Adventure: Dumbledore enlists Harry to help him cajole Slughorn to return to Hogwarts. Slughorn is in hiding because Voldemort has returned, thus, many fear the dark lord's wrath. Dumbledore, appealing to Slughorn's magical vanity, coaxes him to return to the school. Harry learns that Slughorn has something that Dumbledore covets, something that Harry will help the Hermes Trismegistus-like wizard acquire.

- Refusal of the Call: Harry soon learns from Hermione and Ron that many students are not returning to Hogwarts. With Voldemort's return, their parents believe their children are in danger should they go back to the school. Nevertheless, the trio returns for year six.

- Supernatural Aid: Following the instructions in Severus Snape's (a/k/a the Half-Blood Prince) potions book, Harry successfully brews the Draught of Living Death in Slughorn's class. He is awarded a vial of Felix Felicis or Liquid Luck, which helps him retrieve Slughorn's unaffected memory.

- The Crossing of the First Threshold: Harry is shown memories relating to Lord Voldemort. One of the memories, Tom Riddle asking Slughorn for advice, is bogus. Dumbledore wants Harry to convince (or even trick) Slughorn to reveal the true memory. Tom Riddle and Slughorn are threshold guardians because they possess what Dumbledore, and by default Harry, covet: an unaltered memory.

- The Belly of the Whale: Harry and his gang follow Draco to Borgin and Burke's shop in seedy Knockturn Alley. There they witness

---

456 cf. Pike's *Morals and Dogma*, p. 444.

what appears to be a clandestine ceremony taking place. They know something evil is afoot but are not sure what Draco is up to.

- The Road of Trials: Harry procures Slughorn's authentic memory, revealing Tom Riddle's intent to create Horcruxes. Later, under harsh and terrifying conditions, Harry helps Dumbledore recover a Horcrux, which, alas, turns out to be a decoy.

- The Meeting with the Goddess: Harry can't keep his eyes off Ginny and Ron is infatuated with Hermione because both young ladies have, to quote Harry and Ron, "nice skin." Harry and Ginny eventually share a kiss in the Room of Requirement and Hermione comes to understand her feelings toward Ron are more than just friendship.

- Woman as the Temptress: "I killed Sirius Black, I killed Sirius Black!" Bellatrix Lestrange is wreaking havoc: she forces Severus and Narcissa to forge an Unbreakable Vow and later sets the Weasley home on fire. Meanwhile, Ron gets an obsessed girlfriend named Lavender Brown but soon realizes his heart belongs to Hermione while Harry knows he is falling hard for Ginny. For the two of them, Hermione and Ginny's "nice skin" is too tempting, proving irresistible.

- Apotheosis: Albus Dumbledore is killed; "You die to your flesh and are born into your spirit. You identify yourself with the consciousness and life of which your body is but the vehicle. You die to the vehicle and become identified in your consciousness with that of which the vehicle is the carrier. That is the God."[457] Harry, Ron, and Hermione must defeat Voldemort without their mentor.

- Rescue from Without: Even though dark days are ahead, Hermione tells Harry that she and Ron will help him find and destroy the Horcruxes.

Next, the final two films of the series, *Harry Potter and the Deathly Hallows – Parts 1 and 2,* see Harry and his friends go on a quest to find and destroy Lord Voldemort's secret to immortality: the Horcruxes. David Yates again returns to direct these final two installments.

---

457 Campbell with Moyers, *ibid*, p. 134.

HARRY POTTER AND THE DEATHLY HALLOWS – PARTS 1 AND 2

Campbell's monomyth will be applied like *Deathly Hallows* was a single movie because *Part 2* is a continuation of *Part 1*. *Deathly Hallows* is Rowling's seventh and final Harry Potter book, but for dramatic reasons the film was cleaved in half; *Deathly Hallows* was made into two films. *Part 1* was released in November 2010, with *Part 2* released in July 2011. *Part 1* begins with the new Minister of Magic, Rufus Scrimgeour (Bill Nighly), addressing the wizarding media, stating that the Ministry will remain vigilant even though Lord Voldemort is gaining strength. Harry, Ron, and Hermione prepare for a journey to destroy Voldemort's Horcruxes, with Harry watching the Dursleys depart while Hermione wipes her parents' memories of her. Severus Snape arrives at Malfoy Manor to inform Lord Voldemort and his Death Eaters of Harry's impending departure from 4 Privet Drive. Voldemort commandeers Lucius Malfoy's wand since Voldemort's wand cannot be used to kill Harry because the wands are twins.

Meanwhile, the Order of the Phoenix gathers at Privet Drive to escort Harry to safety using Polyjuice Potion to create six decoy Harrys. During their flight to the Weasley family home at the Burrow, they are ambushed by Death Eaters, killing Mad-Eye Moody and Harry's owl, Hedwig; injure George Weasley, and knock out Hagrid, which forces Harry to take over and drive his flying motorcycle while fighting Voldemort, destroying some powerlines. At the Burrow, Harry has a vision of the wandmaker Garrick Ollivander (John Hurt) being tormented by Voldemort, claiming that Ollivander lied to him when he told him that the only way he could kill Harry was by using another's wand.

Scrimgeour arrives at the Burrow with Albus Dumbledore's Will and Testament and distributes three items to Ron, Hermione, and Harry. Ron receives Dumbledore's Deluminator, Hermione a copy of *The Tales of Beedle the Bard*, and Harry the first golden Snitch he caught in a Quidditch match. Scrimgeour says that Harry was also bequeathed the Sword of Godric Gryffindor, but the Minister states that the sword was not Dumbledore's to give and, in any case, is currently missing.

Next, the Death Eaters assassinate Scrimgeour replacing him with their puppet Pius Thicknesse (Guy Henry), who, under the influence of the Imperius curse, begins persecuting Muggle-born witches and wizards, branding Harry Potter as Undesirable No. 1. The Death Eaters' persecution of impure blood witches and warlocks evokes the antisemitic pogroms of Nazi Germany. Soon thereafter, at the wedding of Bill Weasley (Domhnall Gleeson) and Fleur Delacour, Harry meets the author of Dumbledore's obituary Elphias Doge;[458] his forename, Elphias, recalls French occultist and conjuror Eliphas Levi. When Death Eaters disrupt the wedding, Harry, Hermione, and Ron disapparate to London finding sanctuary at the headquarters of the Order of the Phoenix located at No. 12 Grimmauld Place. There they discover that the R.A.B. from the false Horcrux locket is Regulus Arcturus Black, the younger brother of Sirius Black. From the mouth of Kreacher,[459] the Blacks' house-elf, they learn that Mundungus Fletcher (Andy Linden) stole the real locket. Kreacher and Dobby apprehend Fletcher, saying the locket is in the possession of Dolores Umbridge. Under the disguise of Polyjuice Potion, the trio successfully infiltrates the Ministry. In the courtroom, during an interrogation, Delores threatens a Muggle-born witch enraging Harry, admonishing her "You're lying, Dolores. And one mustn't tell lies." He then stuns her, and Hermione successfully retrieves the locket. The trio escapes from the Dementors into the wilderness after accidentally revealing the location of 12 Grimmauld Place to Yaxley (Peter Mullan), a Death Eater.

Unable to destroy the Horcrux, they take turns wearing it to dilute its evil power. Harry sees a vision of Voldemort interrogating Gregorovitch (Rade Šerbedžija), a renowned wandmaker, claiming that a teenage boy had once stolen the legendary Elder Wand from his shop. While Ron wears the locket, he is overcome by his negative feelings; after arguing with Harry he departs, upsetting Hermione. One cannot help thinking of the adverse effects the One Ring had on its bearers, like Frodo and Gollum, in Tolkien's *Lord of the Rings*. Harry and Hermione decide to go to Godric's Hollow to visit Harry's parents' graves, and the house where they were killed. Next, they visit historian and author Bathilda Bagshot (Hazel Douglas), believing

---

458 Doge was played by Peter Cartwright (1935-2013) in *Order of the Phoenix* and David Ryall (1935-2014) in *Deathly Hallows – Part 1*.
459 Voiced by Timothy Bateson (1926-2009) in *Order of the Phoenix* and Simon McBurney in *Deathly Hallows Part – 1*.

has the Sword of Gryffindor, which they deduce can destroy Horcruxes. But they are surprised by Voldemort's snake, Nagini, having taken possession of her corpse. Hermione accidentally breaks Harry's wand as they escape into the Forest of Dean, wherein Hermione identifies the mysterious thief seen in Harry's vision as Gellert Grindelwald.[460]

When evening falls, Harry sees a Patronus in the form of a doe which leads him to a frozen pond. Gryffindor's sword lies beneath the pond's ice. Harry breaks the ice and jumps in to reach the sword. The locket around his neck attempts to strangle him, but Ron arrives to rescue him. Despite the soul inside the locket attacking both of them, Ron manages to destroy it with the Sword of Gryffindor. Ron explains the Deluminator led him back to the two of them; at first, Hermione is angry with Ron but the two reconcile. They next visit Xenophilius Lovegood (Rhys Ifans) to learn about a mysterious symbol seen several times, most notably in Hermione's *Tales of Beedle the Bard*, on their journey. He tells them that the emblem represents the Deathly Hallows: the Elder Wand, the Resurrection Stone, and the Cloak of Invisibility. These are three powerful magical items forged by Death. Lovegood betrays them to the Death Eaters to have his kidnapped daughter Luna returned. Harry has a vision of Voldemort learning from Grindelwald that the Elder Wand lies with Dumbledore in his grave. The trio escapes into the wilderness once more, but Snatchers appear and chase them. They are captured and taken to Malfoy Manor where Bellatrix imprisons Harry and Ron in a cellar in which they discover Luna, Ollivander, and Griphook the Goblin.[461] Bellatrix tortures Hermione trying to discover how they procured the Sword of Gryffindor. After Dobby apparates in the cellar, they flee to the upper chamber while incapacitating Peter Pettigrew. A magical battle ensues; Harry duels and disarms Draco and Dobby disarms Narcissa. After being berated by Bellatrix, Dobby states "Dobby has no master. Dobby is a free elf. And Dobby has come to save Harry Potter and his friends." Bellatrix manages to kill Dobby right after he helps Harry and the other captives escape the estate via sorcery. Meanwhile, Voldemort breaks into Dumbledore's grave–a white marble tomb which looks like it was designed by Frank Lloyd Wright–and takes the Elder Wand.

---

460 Grindelwald the younger is portrayed by Jamie Campbell Bower and Grindelwald the elder by Michael Byrne.
461 Verne Troyer (1969-2018) played Griphook in Sorcerer's Stone but was replaced by Warwick Davis who played the Goblin in *Deathly Hallows Parts 1 and 2*.

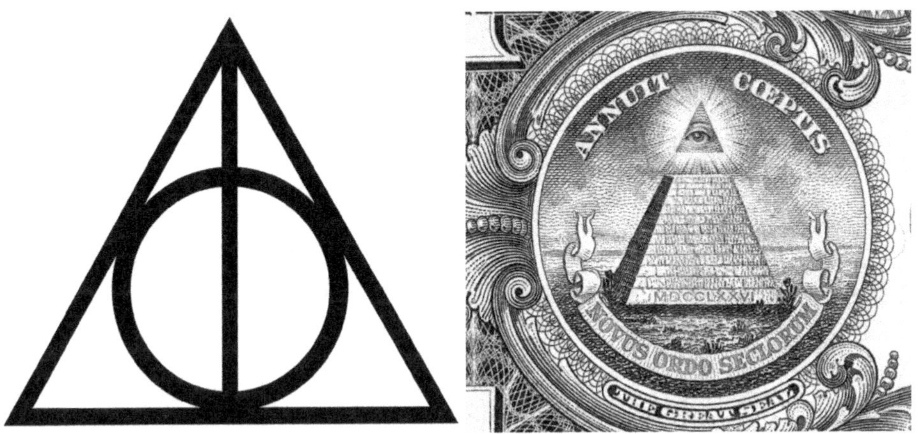

(Left) The symbol of the Deathly Hallows: the vertical line is the Elder Wand, the circle is the Resurrection Stone, and the triangle is the Invisibility Cloak. The emblem mirrors the all-seeing eye atop the truncated pyramid (right) on the back of the one-dollar bill; it is the reverse of the Great Seal of the United States. The eye is the deistic Eye of Providence, the Eye of Horus, while the seal is invested with the number 13: 13 stone levels in the pyramid, 13 letters in *Annuit Coeptis*, and 13 letters in *E Pluribus Unum*. The number thirteen is the number of transformation and rebirth: twelve signs of the zodiac ruled by the sun hence 12 Apostles and Christ (the sun), dying and reborn. The Deathly Hallows symbol heralds Harry's Christlike death and resurrection, making him the savior of the wizarding world.

*   *   *   *

Harry Potter and the Deathly Hallows – Part 2 opens with Lord Voldemort retrieving the Elder Wand from Dumbledore's grave. After burying Dobby, Harry Potter enlists Griphook, Ron, and Hermione to help him break into Bellatrix's vault at Gringotts Bank because he suspects a Horcrux may be there. Griphook agrees, in exchange for the Sword of Gryffindor. The wandmaker, Ollivander, tells Harry that two wands taken from Malfoy Manor belonged to Bellatrix and Draco, but Malfoy's has changed its allegiance to Harry.

In Bellatrix's vault, Harry discovers the Horcrux is Helga Hufflepuff's cup. He retrieves it, but Griphook snatches the Sword of Gryffindor and abandons the trio, leaving them cornered by security. The three release the dragon guardian and escape on its back. Harry sees a vision of Voldemort killing goblins, including Griphook, learning that Voldemort is aware of the theft, cognizant that Harry and his friends seek to destroy the

Horcruxes. With Griphook dead, Gryffindor's sword vanishes. Harry also senses there is a Horcrux at Hogwarts somehow connected to Rowena

Ravenclaw. The trio apparate to Hogsmeade, where Dumbledore's brother Aberforth (Ciarán Hinds) instructs the portrait of his deceased younger sister, Ariana (Hebe Beardsall), to fetch Neville Longbottom, leading the trio through a secret passageway into Hogwarts.

Snape learns of Harry's return, warning staff and students they will be punished for aiding and abetting Harry. Harry confronts Snape, but retreats after Minerva challenges him to a duel. McGonagall gathers the Hogwarts community for battle. At Luna Lovegood's insistence (cf. Sophia, female wisdom provider), Harry speaks to Helena Ravenclaw's ghost (Kelly Macdonald), revealing Voldemort performed dark magic on her mother's diadem, which is in the Room of Requirement. Meanwhile, in the Chamber of Secrets, Hermione destroys Hufflepuff's cup with a Basilisk fang; since the Basilisk was killed with Gryffindor's Sword, the fang is imbued with the sword's power. In the Room of Requirement, Draco, along two of his comrades, attack Harry but Ron and Hermione intervene. A Fiendfyre curse is cast with Harry and his friends saving Malfoy. Harry stabs the diadem with the Basilisk fang and Ron kicks it into the Room of Requirement, destroying it. As Voldemort's army attacks, Harry, reading Voldemort's mind, discovers that Voldemort's fierce snake Nagini is the final Horcrux. After entering the boathouse, the trio witness Voldemort incorrectly telling Snape that the Elder Wand cannot serve Voldemort until Snape dies, since he killed its last owner (Dumbledore); he then orders Nagini to kill Snape, which Nagini does. Before dying, Snape tells Harry to take his memories to the Pensieve Bowl. In the chaotic battle at Hogwarts, Fred Weasley, Lupin, and Tonks are killed.

Harry learns from Snape's memories that he loved Harry's late mother, Lily, but despised his father, James, because he had bullied him. Following her death, Snape worked secretly with Dumbledore to protect Harry from Voldemort because of his love for Lily. Harry also learns Dumbledore's death at Snape's hands was planned between them, and that the Patronus doe he saw in the woods had been conjured by Snape, leading him to the sword. Harry learns that he became a Horcrux when Voldemort originally failed to kill him and that Harry must die to destroy the piece of Voldemort's soul within him. In the Forbidden Forest, the Golden Snitch opens revealing the Resurrection Stone, which Harry uses to summon past loved ones, giving him the courage to confront Voldemort. Harry then surrenders himself to the dark lord; Voldemort casts the Killing Curse upon Harry, who finds himself in Limbo, where Dumbledore's spirit meets him, explaining that the part of Voldemort within Harry was killed by Voldemort's own curse. The ghostly Limbo Harry finds himself is King's Cross Station, with *King's Cross* signifying Christ's death on the cross and subsequent resurrection; mirroring Jesus, Harry has died and will soon be likewise returned to life. Harry then returns to his body, determined to defeat Voldemort *qua* Satan, once and for all.

Voldemort triumphantly announces Harry's death to everyone at Hogwarts demanding they all surrender. As Neville gives a defiant response, Harry springs to life. Neville draws the Sword of Gryffindor from the Sorting Hat, and as Harry confronts Voldemort. Locked in a battle of light against dark, they duel throughout the castle. Neville decapitates Nagini leaving Voldemort mortal, while Molly Weasley (Julie Walters) kills Bellatrix in the Great Hall. Harry and Voldemort's battle ends with Voldemort's own Killing Curse rebounding thereby obliterating him. After the wizarding combat, Harry explains to Ron and Hermione that the Elder Wand had recognized him as its true master because he had disarmed Draco, having earlier disarmed its previous owner, Dumbledore, but instead of claiming the Elder Wand, Harry snaps it in half, discarding it.

Epilog: Nineteen years later, Harry and Ginny, Hermione and Ron proudly watch their children leave for Hogwarts on Platform 9 ¾ at King's Cross Station. The film ends and with it the Harry Potter saga.

In *Deathly Hallows*, we finally learn Snape's duplicitous actions were motivated because he loved Harry's mother, Lily. The first words Snape speaks to Harry are, "Potter! What would I get if I added powdered root of asphodel to an infusion of wormwood?" back in *Sorcerer's Stone*. According to Victorian-Flower Language, asphodel is a type of lily meaning *my regrets follow you to the grave*, and wormwood means *absence* symbolizing bitter sorrow. Decoded, Snape's first line to Potter esoterically means *I bitterly regret Lily's death*,[462] signifying his love for Harry's mother. Moreover, the name of Potter's mother, Lily, is a metaphor the goddess Lilith-as-Sophia since Lilith associates herself with sacred wisdom because, in occult lore, Lilith possessed the all-powerful kabalistic

---

462 See *Dorkly.com*, "10 Harry Potter Easter Eggs That Will Take Over Your Life," http://www.dorkly.com/post/73435/harry-potter-easter-eggs, retrieved November 13th, 2015.

Tetragrammaton. Epitomizing the dark Lilith-trickster archetype, Lily Potter (née Evans) is an outcast child having been labeled a freak by her sister because of her magical abilities. Lily flirts with the dark side, fascinated by the mysterious Severus Snape, a stoic, melancholic (cf. saturnine blackness) magician-philosopher. As a powerful Lilith-like sorceress, Lily manages to deceive Voldemort by deflecting his Killing Curse, which saved not only her son but also destroyed Voldemort. Although she does not survive the attack, like Mercurius she outwits the dark lord which something few have done. As a white sorceress, Lily symbolizes the flower, lily, denoting cabalistic magic. In the Roman Catholic Church, the lily associates with eight different Saints and the angel Gabriel. The sacred association of the lily led to its use against Left-Hand Path witches, black magicians, and their spells; it was one of the flowers used in protective magic (cf. Lily's defensive spell against Voldemort) on the Eve and Feast of St. John thus lilies were always prominent on the occasion in London.[463]

Like most cinematic Christlike redeemers, Harry dies and is resurrected; but, Harry is more akin to Frodo Baggins and Luke Skywalker than Neo and Maud'Dib because like Frodo and Luke, he defeats a Dark Lord but Harry does not supply liberating gnosis like Neo or Maud'Did. Harry undergoes apotheosis but, in the end, returns to normal life marrying Ginny, having children, resembling Frodo Baggins, trying to return to daily living after destroying the One Ring. Apotheosis is the key monomythic element in *Deathly Hallows* because it not only transforms Harry into a savior archetype but identifies Voldemort as a Mephistophelean figure along the same lines as such legendary villains as Darth Vader and Sauron; their Manichean struggle forever defined as good against evil, order versus chaos, spiritual gnosis contrasted by material power. *Deathly Hallows*, being the final chapter, introduces the monomythic elements of the Crossing of the Return Threshold, Master of the Two Worlds, and Freedom to Live; when the last two films are viewed as one, the monomyth becomes visible and understandable.

- The Call to Adventure: The Order of the Phoenix arrives at 4 Privot Drive to take Harry to a safe house because Voldemort and the Death Eaters are on the loose searching high and low for Harry and his friends.

---

463 See *Encyclopedia of Magic and Superstition*, p. 226.

- Refusal of the Call: Harry does not want Ron, Hermione, or any member of the Order of the Phoenix to drink the Polyjuice Potion. He knows that by temporarily becoming him they place themselves in mortal danger.

- Supernatural Aid: Rufus Scrimgeour executes Dumbledore's will which leaves Ron the Deluminator, Harry the Golden Snitch from his first Quidditch match and the Sword of Gryffindor, and to Hermione his copy of *The Tales of Beedle the Bard*. The three items prove critical to completing the adventure and defeating Voldemort.

- The Crossing of the First Threshold: The wedding at the Burrow is assaulted by Death Eaters. Harry, Ron, and Hermione magically escape to London and are subsequently attacked in a coffee shop. The three now know they have to work in secret–disappear–should the mission to destroy the Horcruxes be successful. It is from two threshold guardians, Kreacher and Mundungus Fletcher, the trio learn Delores has the real Horcrux (the locket).

- The Belly of the Whale: The trio is captured, held prisoner in the dungeons of Malfoy Manor. Hermione is tortured and humiliated by Bellatrix; the dark witch magically carves the word *Mudblood* on the former's arm. They escape but Dobby is killed; the trio emerges hardened and resolute. They are now ready to finish the task of destroying the Horcruxes, thus ending Voldemort and his reign of terror.

- The Road of Trials: Locating and destroying the Horcruxes. Hogwarts is attacked by Voldemort and the Death Eaters causing all hell to break loose.

- The Meeting with the Goddess: Hermione and Ron fall in love as do Harry and Ginny. Helena Ravenclaw's ghost helps Harry locate a Horcrux.

- Woman as the Temptress: Meet Bathilda Bagshot, author of the book *The History of Magic*. Harry and Hermione visit the crone on Christmas Eve, but she turns out to be Voldemort's snake Nagini. Meanwhile, Bellatrix is still running amok. Ron is driven away by what he perceives to be a romantic relationship brewing between Harry and Hermione but overcomes his anxieties and returns.

- Atonement with the Father: Harry confronts and vanquishes his surrogate father, Lord Voldemort.

- Apotheosis: Harry, mirroring a Christlike savior, dies and is reborn; after speaking to the ghost of Dumbledore, Harry chooses life over death in the spectral King's Cross Station. Harry survives his death instead leaving behind the piece of Voldemort that was within him (Harry was the Horcrux Voldemort never intended) to perish in the train station *qua* Limbo; put another way, Voldemort's Killing Curse destroyed his own Horcrux. No longer tainted by Voldemort's soul, Harry is resurrected, allowing him to triumph over the dark lord (cf. Christian Devil).

- The Ultimate Boon: All the Horcruxes are annihilated.

- The Crossing of the Return Threshold: "The returning hero, to complete his adventure, must survive the impact of the world. …This is sign of the hero's requirement, now, to knit together his two worlds."[464] With his time at Hogwarts over, it is time for Harry to return to the real world. Harry satisfies this requirement by disposing of the Resurrection Stone and the Elder Wand; his wizarding days are numbered.

- Master of the Two Worlds: "Freedom to pass back and forth across the world division, from the perspective of the apparitions of time to that of the causal deep and back—not contaminating the principles of the one with those of the other, yet permitting the mind to know the one by virtue of the other—is the talent of the master. The Cosmic Dancer, declares Nietzsche, does not rest heavily in a single spot, but gaily, lightly, turns and leaps from one position to another. It is possible to speak from only one point at a time, but that does not invalidate the insights of the rest."[465] With the death of Voldemort, Harry is now the master of the wizarding world while also being able to reconcile the real world, the world of Muggles and domestic banality.

---

464 Campbell, *The Hero with a Thousand Faces*, pp. 194, 196.
465 *ibid*, p. 196.

- Freedom to Live: "What, now, is the result of the miraculous passage and return? The battlefield is symbolic of the field of life, where every creature lives on the death of another. …The hero is the champion of things becoming, not of things become, because he is. 'Before Abraham was, I AM.' He does not mistake apparent changelessness in time for the permanence of Being, nor is he fearful of the next moment (or of the 'other thing'), as destroying the permanent with its change."[466] Nineteen years later we see that Harry has married Ginny and they have children, one of them is about to matriculate at Hogwarts. With Voldemort gone, Harry is now free to live as an average person, his sacred messianic mission complete.

* * * *

Other occult themes and icons pervade the Harry Potter films, and their use is intentional. Subconsciously, these themes and icons–like the monomyth–invest the Potter saga with a sense of divinity, of purpose, of a spiritual higher calling that we all hope to achieve. We all hope to come to know thyself, to connect to the godhead. For example, the numinous number seven is everywhere: students spend seven years at Hogwarts, hence, there are seven Harry Potter novels; there are seven letters in the name, Granger, as well as in the name, Weasley. Arthur and Molly Weasley have seven children; the names: Ronald Billius Weasley, Minerva McGonagall, Albus Severus Potter, and Hermione Jean Granger, all have seven syllables. Voldemort created seven Horcruxes (Riddle's Diary, Marvolo Gaunt's Ring, Rowena Ravenclaw's Diadem, Salazar Slytherin's Locket, Helga Hufflepuff's Cup, Harry Potter–unintentionally and unknown to Voldemort–and Nagini) symbolized by seven stones. Harry's Quidditch number is 7; Krum's Quidditch number is 7; Hogwarts has seven levels and seven secret passages; in *Prison of Azkaban* Snape instructs his students to turn to page 394; add 3+9+4 to get 16, then add 1+6 to get 7. Even the author's surname, Rowling, has seven letters. Harry Potter–and J.K. Rowling–were born in the seventh month of the year (July 31st); there are seven players on a Quidditch team: three Chasers, two Beaters, one Keeper, and one Seeker; there are seven snakes which unlock the Chamber of Secrets' circular door.

---

466 *ibid*, pp. 205, 209; 'Before Abraham was, I AM,' citation is the Gospel according to John, 8:58.

Further, there are seven locks on Professor Moody's magical trunk; seven Muggles witnessed Ron and Harry in the Flying Ford Anglia; Tom Riddle's middle name, Marvolo, has seven letters; along with the genuine article, six "Harry Potters" are created with Polyjuice Potion at the beginning of *Deathly Hallows Part 1* making seven "Harry Potters" altogether. J. K. Rowling stated in an interview that the big seven in the Harry Potter series are Harry, Hermione, Ron, Ginny, Neville, Luna, and Draco;[467] the latter aside the Gryffindors from a neo-Pythagorean band[468] spreading wisdom–sometimes exoteric, at times esoteric–among the student body. There are many other examples of the sacred number seven appearing in the novels which this author will not reveal because this book deals with movie symbolism, suffice to say Rowling is successfully employing the number seven to imbue her stories with mystery and magic.

Rowling also uses the number three for the same reasons she uses the number seven. On this number's divinity, Manly P. Hall writes:

The triad–3–is the first number actually odd (monad not always being considered a number). It is the first equilibrium of unities; therefore, Pythagoras said that Apollo gave oracles from a tripod, and advised offer of libation three times. The keywords to the qualities of the triad are friendship, peace, justice, prudence, piety, temperance, and virtue. The following deities partake of the principles of the triad: Saturn (ruler of time), Latona, Cornucopiæ, Ophion (the great serpent), Thetis, Hecate, Polyhymnia (a Muse), Pluto, Triton, President of the Sea, Tritogenia, Achelous, and the Faces, Furies, and Graces. This number is called wisdom, because men organize the present, foresee the future, and benefit by the experiences of the fast. It is cause of wisdom and understanding. The triad is the number of knowledge–music, geometry, and astronomy, and the science of the celestials and terrestrials. Pythagoras taught that the cube of this number had the power of the lunar circle.

---

467 See *SnitchSeeker.com*, "J.K. Rowling talks Deathly Hallows: Part 2 Film Production, Lead Characters." http://www.snitchseeker.com/harry-potter-news/video-j-k-rowling-talks-deathly-hallows-part-2-film-production-lead-characters-82483/, retrieved April 30th, 2016.
468 A sacred fellowship who spreads wisdom to the profane; see Hall's *The Secret Teachings of All Ages*, p. 193.

The sacredness of the triad and its symbol–the triangle–is derived from the fact that it is made up of the monad and the duad. The monad is the symbol of the Divine Father and the duad of the Great Mother. The triad being made of these two is therefore androgynous and is symbolic of the fact that God gave birth to His worlds out of Himself, who in His creative aspect is always symbolized by the triangle. The monad passing into the duad was thus capable of becoming the parent of progeny, for the duad was the womb of Meru, within which the world was incubated and within which it still exists in embryo.[469]

Furthermore, the Moirae (or The Fates) were three sisters that held the thread of life of every mortal; Clotho spun the thread, Lachesis measured it, and Atropos cut it. The sisters represented the three phases of life: birth, aging, and death. Similarly, the Musai (or The Muses) were made up of nine (i.e., three times three) goddesses: Euterpe (music), Polyhymnia (the sacred), Calliope (poetry), Terpsichore (dancing), Clio (history), Erato (lyric), Thalia (comedy), Melpomene (tragedy) and Urania (astronomy)–each lending their inspiration to a form of art significant to the Greeks (interestingly, originally, there were only three Muses: Aoide–song; Melete–practice; and Mneme–memory). Of course, moving into the Christian era, the Holy Trinity emerged as the Father, the Son, and the Holy Spirit, esoterically symbolizing the three daily phases of the sun: sunrise, the sun at meridian, and sunset. The three-leafed clover is a symbol of the Trinty and a protective talisman against evil. In *The Wizard of Oz*, Dorothy has to click her heels three times while repeating her Gnostic catchphrase to return to Kansas. There are three degrees of Blue Masonry; there were three Grand Masters: the two Kings and Khir-Om (a/k/a Hiram Abif) the Artificer. The candidate gains admission by three raps and three raps call up the Brethren. There are three principal officers of the Lodge, three lights at the Altar, three gates of the Temple, all in the East, West, and South. The three lights represent the Sun, the Moon, and Mercury; Osiris, Isis, and Horus; the Father, the Mother, and the Child; Wisdom, Strength, and Beauty; *Hakamah, Binah,* and *Daath; Gedulah, Geburah,* and *Tepareth.* The candidate makes three circuits of the Lodge: there were three assassins of Khir-Om, and he was slain by three blows while seeking to escape by

---

469 Hall, *The Secret Teachings of All Ages,* pp. 216-217.

the three gates of the Temple. There are three divisions of the Temple, and three, five, and seven Steps. A Master works with Chalk, Charcoal, and a vessel of Clay; there are three movable and three immovable jewels. The Triangle appears among the Symbols: the two parallel lines enclosing the circle are connected at top, as are the Columns Jachin and Boaz, symbolizing the equilibrium which explains the great Mysteries of Nature.[470]

In the Harry Potter mythology, the sacred triad is formed by Harry, Hermione, and Ron (think Luke Skywalker, Princess Leia, and Han Solo in *Stars Wars Episodes IV*, *V*, and *VI*). Their friendship and interactions serve as the basis for their Hogwarts adventures. The three often act as one; they are his true family as opposed to Harry's false family, the Dursleys, of which there are also three (cf. anti-trinity): Vernon, Petunia, and Dudley. To revive Voldemort, Wormtail's occult ritual requires three elements: bone of the father, flesh of the servant, and blood of the enemy. There are three Unforgivable Curses: Crucio, Imperio, and Avada Kedavra as well as three Deathly Hallows: the Resurrection Stone, the Elder Wand, and the Invisibility Cloak. There are three tests in the Triwizard Tournament. In *Sorcerer's Stone*, Harry's Gringotts vault number is 687; add 6+8+7 to get 21 (7x3: the numinous seven *thrice* multiplied) then add 2+1 to get 3. Students depart for Hogwarts on Platform 9 ¾ which in decimal form is 9.75; add 9+7+5 to get 21 (again 7x3) then add 2+1 to get 3. In *Prisoner of Azkaban*, Sirius Black's Prison ID number is 930; add 9+3+0 to get 12 then add 1+2 to get 3. Rowling knows three is a magic number; "Three also referred to harmony, friendship, peace, concord, and temperance; and was so highly esteemed among the Pythagoreans that they called it perfect harmony."[471] Intrinsically, the number three surfaces in the Harry Potter stories, revealing and concealing Cabala and numerology simultaneously.

Rowling draws down the heavens by naming characters after stars and constellations mirroring the hermetic doctrine of *as above, so below*. The stars in the heavens are closer than we are to God, so naming characters after astral bodies infuses the Potter stories with sacredness. On astrology's divinity, Albert Pike explains, "Astrology was practiced among all the ancient nations. In Egypt, the book of Astrology was borne reverentially in the religious processions; in which the few sacred animals were also

---

470 Pike, *Morals and Dogma*, p. 548.
471 *ibid*, p. 632.

carried, as emblems of the equinoxes and solstices. The same science flourished among the Chaldæans, and over the whole of Asia and Africa. When Alexander invaded India, the astrologers of the Oxydraces came to him to disclose the secrets of their science of Heaven and the Stars. The Brahmins whom Apollonius consulted, taught him the secrets of Astronomy, with the ceremonies and prayers whereby to appease the gods and learn the future from the stars. In China, astrology taught the mode of governing the State and families. In Arabia, it was deemed the mother of the sciences; and old libraries are full of Arabic books on this pretended science. It flourished at Rome. Constantine had his horoscope drawn by the astrologer Valens. It was a science in the middle ages, and even to this day is neither forgotten nor unpracticed. Catherine de Medici was fond of it. Louis XIV consulted his horoscope, and the learned Casini commenced his career as an astrologer."[472] The villainous Draco Malfoy, his forename, Draco, refering to the great dragon-serpent constellation in the far northern sky, personifies the devious but wise-as-a-serpent archetype at odds with the heroic Harry and his sacred band of friends. Draco is correctly sorted into Slytherin House, which was founded by warlock who could speak to snakes, Salazar Slytherin, thus, Slytherin House's coat of arms is a serpent. Bellatrix Lestrange is named after the star, Bellatrix, the third brightest star in the Constellation Orion; Bellatrix is Latin for *female warrior*; hence, she fights alongside her master, Voldemort. The wily Sirius Black (the Black family is named after stars) is named after the Egyptian Dog Star; as such, Sirius can change at will into a black dog. Sirius, in canine-form, is nicknamed "Padfoot," a generic term for ghostly black dogs (cf. Doyle's *The Hound of the Baskervilles*) that roam the English countryside. These characters are archetypes or, at the very least, possess archetypal qualities: the serpentine enemy (cf. Typhon), the

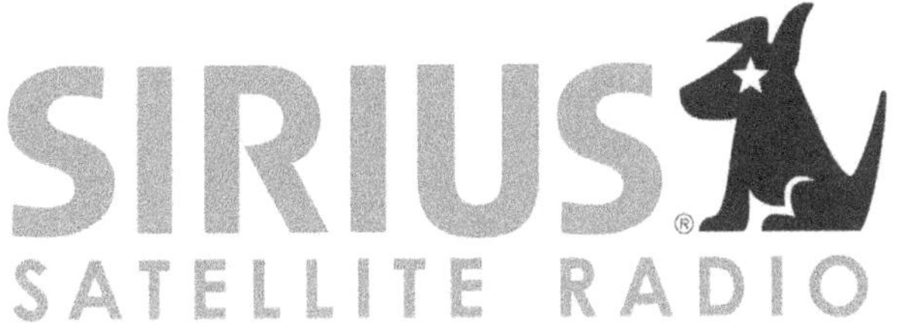

The Egyptian Dog Star in popular culture: The logo for Sirius Satellite Radio is a dog with the five-pointed star as its all-seeing eye. Since Sirius is the Dog Star it is naturally represented by a canine, and the pentangle eye denotes Freemasonry's Blazing Star.

---

472 *ibid*, p. 463.

wicked Woman as the Temptress, and the witty antihero are in other stories and mythologies simply renamed or rebranded.

I end this chapter with wisdom from Joseph Campbell because it best describes the Harry Potter adventures. Campbell said, "The usual hero adventure begins with someone from whom something has been taken, or who feels something is lacking in the normal experiences available or permitted by members of his society. This person takes off on a series of adventures beyond the ordinary, either to recover what has been lost or to discover some life-giving elixir. It's usually a cycle, a going and a returning. ...That's the basic motif of the universal hero's journey—leaving one condition and finding the source of life to bring you forth into a richer or mature condition."[473] As far as Harry Potter, the magical world of Hogwarts, and the monomyth are concerned, this author could not have said it better.

---

473 Campbell with Moyers, *The Power of Myth*, p. 152.

CHAPTER IX

MYSTICAL ARCHETYPES OF THE OLD WEST

"Announcing your plans is a good way to hear God laugh."
– Al Swearengen, *Deadwood*, 2004.

"I drink your milkshake!"
– Daniel Plainview, *There Will Be Blood*, 2007.

"The adventure is symbolically a manifestation of his character.
Even the landscape and the conditions of the|
environment match his readiness."
– Joseph Campbell, *The Power of Myth*, 1991.

"It's not a joke, it's a rope, Tuco.
Now I want you to get up there and put your head in that noose."
– Blondie, *The Good, the Bad and the Ugly*, 1966.

"I generally smoke just after I eat.
Why don't you come back in about ten minutes?"
– Col. Douglas Mortimer, *For a Few Dollars More*, 1965.

"Get three coffins ready."
– Joe, *A Fistful of Dollars*, 1964.

"Don't you ever say that again about your fathers,
because they are not cowards! You think I am brave because I carry a
gun, well your fathers are much braver because they carry responsibility,
for you, your brothers, your sisters, and your mothers.
And this responsibility is like a big rock that weighs a ton."
– Bernardo O'Reilly, *The Magnificent Seven*, 1960.

"God's not on our side because he hates idiots also."
– Blondie, *The Good, the Bad and the Ugly*, 1966

The Hollywood Western is replete with archetypes and archetypal imagery, point of fact George Lucas' Star Wars has often been called a Space Western, and some (not all) of the monomythic themes found in *Star Wars* come straight out of Western movies. First, this chapter takes on 1948's *Red River*, which presents several veiled masculine archetypes but, more importantly, their interaction with the feminine, a conflict that can only be described as the *mother vs. lover paradigm*. The characters, their relations, and the plot devices of *Red River* turn up in numerous films afterward, including but not limited to Lucas' two Star Wars Trilogies. Bridging the gap between the Westerns of Hollywood's early days and the modern era is 1960's *The Magnificent Seven*, which transformed the legendary gunslinger into a flawed melancholic. *The Magnificent Seven* paved the way for the Spaghetti Western which stripped away the romanticism of the Old West, presenting it for what it was: a lawless society populated with vicious killers living in harsh environments, demythologizing the conventions of the traditional Hollywood Western. Underneath the raw, visceral world of the Spaghetti Western lies a hidden treasure trove of Manichean conflicts, Jungian archetypes, and esoteric themes presented under the guise of mystical Roman Catholicism, better described as cinematic Christian Cabala.

THE RED RIVER TEMPLATE: MASCULINE ARCHETYPES IN ACTION

Just like Audrey Hepburn is best remembered for her iconic portrayal of Holly Golightly in *Breakfast at Tiffany's*, the role of Thomas Dunson best personifies all the hard-nosed, gritty characters that John Wayne played during his illustrious film career. Dunson is the Captain William Bligh (1754-1817) of Texas: hard, stubborn, heartless, and cold; regardless of consequence, he will finish what he started, completing the cattle drive regardless of the hardships that befall his men. The movie opens by introducing Dunson, a roughneck wanting nothing more than to start up a successful cattle ranch in Texas; he is willing to sacrifice love, hearth, and home to accomplish his dream. He begins his journey to Texas–after deciding to leave a westward-bound wagon train–with his trail hand, Nadine Groot (Walter Brennan, 1894-1974). Dunson bids a temporary farewell to his love interest, Fen (Coleen Gray, 1922-2015), instructing her to stay behind with the wagon train with the understanding that he will send for her later. Dunson and Groot press on, but they see smoke in the distance indicating that Indians have attacked the wagon train. Shortly thereafter, while keeping watch, they hear a group of Indians planning to attack them. They kill the Indians and, on the wrist of one of them, Dunson finds a bracelet he had been left by his late mother; he, in turn, had presented it to Fen as he left the wagon train as a token of his affection. Dunson naturally deduces that Fen was killed during the Indian raid. As will be seen, the bracelet reappears, playing an important symbolic role.

The next day, an orphaned boy named Matthew Garth (played as a youth by Mickey Kuhn and as an adult by Montgomery Clift, 1920-1966), wanders into Dunson and Groot's camp, traumatized and babbling incoherently. The boy had been part of the wagon train Dunson left and, after finding a stray cow, had returned to the wagon train, only to find it in ruins. It is revealed he is the sole survivor of the Indian attack. Dunson adopts him, tying the boy's cow to his wagon alongside a bull Dunson already owned. With only the bull and the cow, Dunson, Groot, and the boy enter Texas by crossing the Red River. In search of land they travel through Texas, finally deciding to settle in deep South Texas near the Rio Grande. Upon arrival, Dunson proudly proclaims all the land about them as his own. Two Mexican men appear on horseback, informing Dunson that the land already belongs to their boss. Dunson dismisses this inconvenient fact and, thanks to a quicker draw in a showdown, kills one of the men and tells the other man to inform his boss that Dunson now owns the land. Dunson names his new spread the Red River D (for Dunson), after his cattle brand. Fatefully, he promises to add *M* (for Matt) to the brand once Matt has earned it.

Fourteen years pass and Dunson now has a fully operational cattle ranch. With the help of Matt and Groot, his herd now numbers over ten thousand cattle, but he is nearly bankrupt because of widespread poverty in the southern United States. Due to its loss in the American Civil War, the former Confederate States no longer afford Dunson's beef. Dunson decides to drive his massive herd hundreds of miles north to the railhead at Sedalia, Missouri, where he believes they will fetch a good price. Dunson hires some men to help with the drive, including wisecracking professional gunman Cherry Valance (John Ireland 1914-1992); once assembled, the perilous northward journey begins. Along the way, they encounter many troubles including a stampede sparked by one of the men, making a clatter while trying to steal sugar from the chuck wagon; this leads to the death of Dan Latimer (Harry Carey Jr., 1878-1948). En route, they are told by strangers that the railroad line has now reached Abilene, Kansas, much closer than Sedalia. When Dunson establishes that none of these wayfarers have seen the railroad, he disregards the news in favor of continuing to Missouri.

Deeper problems arise when Dunson's tyrannical leadership begins to affect the rest of the men. One of the two chuck wagons accompanying the drive was destroyed in the stampede, morale drops because the men are living on nothing but beef with no coffee to drink. Unfortunately, Dunson is broke and cannot buy more supplies. Next, Dunson attempts to lynch two men for deserting the drive, for stealing a sack of flour, and 100 rounds. This leads to a rebellion with Matt turning against him. With the help of Valance and the other men, Matt takes control of the drive so that he can take it to the closer railhead in Abilene. Face to face, Dunson curses him, threatening to kill him when next they meet. The drive resumes toward Abilene, leaving the slightly injured Dunson (his hand is shot and wounded when he draws on Matt) behind with his horse and a few supplies. Matt and his men are aware that Dunson will try to recruit a posse to pursue and attack them. On the way to Abilene, Matt and his men repulse an Indian attack on a wagon train. One of the people they save is Tess Millay (Joanne Dru, 1922-1996), who falls in love with Matt. They spend a night together, and he gives her Dunson's mother's bracelet, evidently given to him by Dunson years earlier. Eager to outpace Dunson to Abilene, he leaves in the morning mirroring Dunson abandoning Fen fourteen years earlier.

Later Tess encounters Dunson, having followed Matt's trail to the new wagon train. He sees that she now wears his mother's bracelet; the bracelet has moved from one sweetheart to another. Weary and emotional, he tells Tess what he wants most of all is a son. She offers to bear him one if he abandons his manhunt, but she is rejected. Dunson sees in her the same anguish that his beloved Fen had expressed when he left her at the original doomed wagon train. Regardless of that, he resumes his hunt for Matt. When Matt reaches Abilene, he finds the town has been eagerly awaiting the arrival of such a herd to buy and ship east by railroad. Unknowingly, he has completed the first cattle drive along what would become known as the Chisholm Trail. He accepts an excellent offer for the sale of the cattle, but soon thereafter Dunson arrives in Abilene with a posse to follow through on his vow to kill Matt. Valance tries to keep the two apart, but Dunson shoots him while the former inflicts a flesh wound upon Dunson. Dunson and Matt begin a furious fight, which Tess interrupts by drawing a gun on both men demanding, like their mother, that they stop fighting because of the father-son love they share. Dunson and Matt immediately see the error of their ways and make peace. The film ends with Dunson telling Matt that he will incorporate the letter *M* into the brand as he had promised fourteen years before, and tells Matt to marry Tess.

Red River is an archetypal masculine free-for-all: the domineering, Captain Ahab-like father; the rebellious son trying to find his place in the world; the cavalier-adventurer gunslinger; and the eccentric old sage. Captain Ahab comes to life in the persona of Dunson, a bitter, relentless man stopping at nothing to get his cattle to Missouri. Dunson is the cruel father archetype, beginning the movie stern but well-intentioned; believing himself infallible, suffering tunnel vision turning him callous, but is ultimately redeemed (anticipating Anakin Skywalker in 1983's *Return of the Jedi*) by his son. He has forsaken love for wealth and power foreshadowing *Scarface's* (1983) Tony Montana (Al Pacino) mantra on happiness; Montana explains: "In this country [USA], you gotta make the money first. Then when you get the money, you get the power. Then when you get the power, then you get the woman." Dunson's bitterness and overbearing persistence eventually turns his surrogate son against him, and once away from his father finds love in Tess, giving her Dunson's mother's bracelet as a token of his affection–more on this in a moment. Also present is the smart-ass yet highly skilled sidekick, Cherry Valance. This favorite archetype incarnates in pop culture as Han Solo (Harrison Ford) from *Star Wars* Episodes IV, V, and VI; Poe Dameron in *Star Wars: The Force Awakens*; Ajax (James Remar) in *The Warriors*; and Manny Ribera (Steven Bauer) from *Scarface*. This archetype shadows Sancho Panza in Don Quixote, Robin from the Batman mythology, Dr. John Watson from the Sherlock

Holmes stories, and Kato from the numerous incarnations of *The Green Hornet* (most famously played by Bruce Lee in the 1960s TV show). Like all sidekicks, his presence is felt, but Valance is not–and never will ever be– the hero. *Red River* also has the Hermes Trismegistus archetype personified by Groot; his name rhymes with *coot* because is just that: an eccentric old man which everyone makes fun of, yet when the men need advice about navigating life's trials and tribulations, Groot is the one they always turn to for guidance. Groot is not a sagacious wizard, but as the elder of the group, he dispenses valuable insights to the others.

The masculine interactions in *Red River* are textbook cinema, reappearing in so many other movies this author could not even begin to list them. We have Cherry and Matt's silent competition yet mutual respect; Groot providing wisdom (he can even speak the secret animal language of the Indians) to the others, his surrogate children; Dunson is the harsh disciplinarian, barking orders to everyone except Groot out of respect and admiration. Groot's friendship with Quo (Chief Yowlatchie, born Daniel Simmons 1891-1966) remains brotherly despite Groot losing his false teeth to him while playing cards. A son rebelling against his father's reactionary doctrines, and a son becoming a man by finishing the task his father could not. When it comes to male relationships, they all surface in *Red River*.

Also appearing are two of the elements of Campbell's monomyth: Atonement with the Father and Woman as the Temptress although the latter could be called Mother as the Temptress.[474] The ogre father is a typical archetype found in mythology and film (see Daniel Day-Lewis as Daniel Plainview in 2007's *There Will Be Blood*), and Wayne plays it to the hilt: he is cruel, driven, unfriendly, and harsh. His adopted son, Matt, finally turns against Dunson and his cutthroat ways when he realizes that following him blindly is self-destructive. If Matt does not act, the cattle drive is doomed; the father's stubbornness does not allow him to see the obvious, but Matt does and revolts, deciding to take the cattle to Kansas, not Missouri. In doing so, he immediately gains the respect of the men, but loses that of the father who vows to destroy him. Dunson draws his gun to strike down Matt but his hand is shot by Valance, foreshadowing the injuries suffered by both Anakin Skywalker (*Attack of the Clones*) and Luke Skywalker (*The Empire Strikes Back*). Matt successfully finishes the

---

474 Or, perhaps, this could be called Meeting with the Mother-Goddess.

cattle drive understanding the anguish of the father, "…For the son who has grown really to know the father, the agonies of the ordeal are readily borne; the world is no longer a vale of tears but a bliss-yielding, perpetual manifestation of the Presence."[475] At film's end, Dunson confronts Matt with bad intentions while Cherry tries to stop him, but is unable because he is not the hero, only Matt can reconcile with the father. Matt stands up to Dunson resulting in fisticuffs, but it is Tess, the sacred feminine, who finally brings them back to reality as only a mother can do. Matt has grown to the tragedies of the father, coming to know Dunson's ruthlessness, but with Tess' intervention the two now understand the father-son love they share and are atoned.[476] This atonement, their *at-one-ment*, is symbolized when Dunson adds the letter *M* to the Red River brand.

One of the tragedies that Dunson and Matt experience is the loss of the love of a woman, Dunson with Fen and Matt with Tess although, with the blessing of the father, Matt and Tess are unified during the film's closing moments. Within the archetypal monomyth, this satisfies the Woman as the Temptress element. Campbell explains, "The mystical marriage with the queen goddess of the world represents the hero's total mastery of life; for the woman is the life, the hero its knower and master. And the testing of the hero, which were preliminary to his ultimate experience and deed, were symbolical of those crises of realization by means of which his consciousness came to be amplified and made capable of the enduring the full possession of the mother-destroyer, his inevitable bride. With that he knows that he and the father are one: he is in his father's place."[477] The female archetype is the hero's mother, not lover. Fen wants to be Dunson's soul-mate and partner, but he rejects her, giving her his mother's bracelet as a token of love. The mother bracelet eventually finds its way into Matt's hands, giving it to Tess as a token of his love, but Matt follows in his father's footsteps by rejecting her as well. The men want their mothers, not love of a sexual or intimate nature it seems. Thus, at the film's conclusion when Matt and Dunson fight only to have it broken up by Tess, *becoming their mother* (albeit symbolically), scolding them like they were little boys fighting over a toy in the backyard. It is now, and only now, that Dunson

---

475 Campbell, *The Hero With a Thousand Faces*, p. 126.
476 *ibid*, p. 125.
477 *ibid*, p. 101.

and Matt are awe-inspired by the actions of the feminine because Tess has become their mom. Embodying their mother, Dunson now encourages Matt to marry Tess, and the men are finally atoned when Dunson recognizes Matt as an equal. This could have only been accomplished by the actions of the surrogate mother, Tess. In other words, without her, the two men could not have been reconciled and may have destroyed each other. The sacred feminine once again balances out the divine masculine, only it is the mother archetype that triumphs, the *woman as lover* (or temptress) has no place in the Old West: the heroes are always loners without wives or families. The consequence of the loner–opting not to have a family–pervades the film *The Magnificent Seven*.

THE MAGNIFICENT SEVEN

It is without question that Elmer Bernstein's (1922-2004) score to *The Magnificent Seven* (1960) is one of the most recognized movie themes in history. The film's importance in cinema history is also undisputed: it marks the end of the traditional Hollywood Western while heralding a new genre, the Spaghetti Western. Gone were the romantic days of John Ford's (1894-1973) *Stagecoach* (1939) and *The Searchers* (1956) as well as Howard Hawks' (1896-1977) *Red River* and *Rio Bravo* (1959); *The Magnificent Seven* gave birth to a new genre of Western that featured a new kind of protagonist: the flawed, imperfect hero. John Wayne and Jimmy Stewart (1908-1997) were now replaced with the mysterious, aloof, highly talented (an expert with weaponry) loner, becoming the Man with No Name (Clint Eastwood), in Sergio Leone's Spaghetti Western trilogy, anticipating "Dirty" Harry Callahan (Clint Eastwood) in 1971's *Dirty Harry* and its sequels. This archetype is Snake Plissken (Kurt Russell) from *Escape from New York* (1981) and *Escape from L.A.* (1996), Lee (Bruce Lee, 1940-1973) in 1973's *Enter the Dragon*, and Indiana Jones (Harrison Ford) in *Raiders of the Lost Ark* (1981) and its sequels. Likewise, *The Magnificent Seven's* mercenaries are imperfect and tragic: they have shirked the responsibilities of family, home, and hearth to hone their skills with a weapon. Because they have no wives, children, or close friends, they are expendable and will not be mourned after they die. However, this congruency is what makes them efficient killers, immortalized as legends.

Directed by John Sturges (1910-1992), *The Magnificent Seven* is a remake of Akira Kurosawa's (1910-1998) classic film, *Seven Samurai*, which was released in 1954. *Seven Samurai* takes place in 1586 during the Warring States Period (ca. 1467-ca. 1603) of Japan. It follows the story of a village of farmers that hire seven *Ronin* (samurai without a master) to stop bandits from stealing their crops. Filmed on location in Mexico, *The Magnificent Seven* opens by paying homage to *Seven Samurai*. A Mexican village is raided for food and supplies by Calvera (Eli Wallach, 1915-2014) and his gang of banditos. As he and his men ride away from their latest pillage, Calvera promises to return to loot the village again. The dim-witted farmers visit a wise old hermit (Vladimir Sokoloff, 1889-1962), supplying gnosis (cf. wisdom of Hermes Trismegistus) by telling them to purchase guns to protect the village. Taking what little goods they have, the village leaders ride to a town just inside the American border, hoping to barter for weapons to defend themselves from Calvera. While there, they encounter Chris Adams (Yul Brynner, 1920-1985), a veteran Cajun gunslinger. After listening to their tale, Chris suggests that the village hire gunfighters, which would be cheaper than guns and ammunition. The village men relentlessly try to convince him to be their gunman. At first, he agrees only to help them find men, but later he decides to recruit six other men to help him defend the village, despite the poor pay offered.

The other men include hotheaded, inexperienced Chico (Horst Buchholz, 1933-2003); Chris' friend Harry Luck (Brad Dexter, 1917-2002), believing Chris is seeking buried treasure; the mercurial drift-er Vin Tanner (Steve McQueen, 1930-1980), having gone broke after a round of gambling, loath to accept a position as a mere store clerk. Rounding out the crew are Bernardo O'Reilly (Charles Bronson, 1921-2003), a deadly gunfighter of Irish-Mexican heritage, having fallen on hard times; a cowboy, Britt (James Coburn, 1928-2002), an expert with knives. joining for the challenge involved; and on-the-run dapper and debonair gunman Lee (Robert Vaughn, 1932-2016), a man in the midst of a confidence crisis. The group recognizes they will be heavily outnum-bered, but they hope that Calvera will move on to another village when he sees professional resistance.

Arriving at the farming community, the seven gunmen begin to train the villagers to defend themselves. In doing so, they start bonding with them. When they realize that a small meal made for them by the women consists of all the food in the village, the gunmen decide to share it with the villagers. Chico is interested in Petra (Rosenda Monteros, 1035-2018), one of the village's young women. Bernardo bonds with three of the village's little boys. Lee struggles with nightmares, fearing the loss of his skills. Calvera and his bandits soon arrive, and a gunfight breaks out. Calvera's gang sustains heavy casualties. Calvera and his banditos are run out of town by the gunmen assisted by the villagers working in concert with them. Chico, a Mexican, follows Calvera back to his camp pretending to be one of his bandits. He learns that Calvera must raid the village because he is desperate for food to feed his men, returns back to the village, reporting this to Chris. Some of the men believe they should leave, but Chris insists that they stay. They ride out to make a surprise raid on Calvera's camp but find the camp empty. Returning to the village, they find that the fearful villagers have allowed Calvera to take control. Calvera spares the gunmen's lives, believing that they have learned that the simple farmers are not worth defending; he also fears reprisals from the U.S. Army if he should kill Americans. The seven gunmen are then escorted out of the village. They debate their next move, and all but Harry agree to return and free the village from Calvera. Harry believes the effort will lead to their deaths and rides off alone. The six gunmen return to the village, and a climatic gunfight ensues. The villagers, recognizing the courage of the gunmen, join the fight. Bernardo is killed protecting the children he'd befriended, and Britt and Lee die after killing a considerable number of bandits. Harry, having a change of heart, arrives in time to protect Chris but is fatally shot. The bandits are routed with Chris shooting Calvera. Calvera, in his dying breath, asks him, "You came back, to a place like this? Why? A man like you? Why?"

The three remaining gunmen help to bury the dead. Chico decides to stay in the village with Petra as Chris and Vin prepare to leave. The village elder bids them farewell saying that the villagers have won: "Your work is done. For them, each season has its tasks. If there were a season for gratitude, they'd show it more. …Only the farmers have won, they remain forever. They are like the land itself. You helped rid them of Calvera, the way a strong wind helps rid them of locusts. You are like the wind, blowing over the land and, passing on. *¡Vaya con Dios!*" As they leave, they pass the graves of their fallen comrades. Chris comments on the fleeting life of a mercenary, "The old man was right. Only the farmers won. We lost. We always lose."

*   *   *   *

Just like Albert Mackey, Masonic Sovereign Grand Commander Albert Pike also wrote on the importance of the number seven, "Seven is the sacred number in all theogonies and all symbols, …It represents the magical power in its full force. It is the Spirit assisted by all the Elementary Powers, the Soul served by Nature, the Holy Empire spoken of in the clavicules of Solomon, symbolized by a warrior, crowned, bearing a triangle on his cuirass, and standing on a cube, to which are harnessed two Sphinxes, one white and the other black, pulling contrary ways, and turning the head to look backward. The vices are Seven, like the virtues; and the latter were anciently symbolized by the Seven Celestial bodies then known as planets."[478] In antiquity, the seven classical planets are Saturn, Mercury, Venus, Mars, the Sun, the Moon, and Jupiter; they are the original magnificent seven. In legend and mythology, each one of these planets came to embody archetypal qualities dwelling in each of the gunslingers in *The Magnificent Seven*. The cosmic breakdown of Sturges' characters is as follows.

Yul Brenner plays Chris Adams personifying Saturn. In antiquity, Saturn was the patron of the sowing and husbandry[479] thus Adams is the first (Adam is the first man in Genesis) of the seven to be sought out by the farmers. Saturn is melancholia representing death; Adams, embodying death, always wears black clothing; he is introduced driving a funeral carriage to bury someone at Boot Hill Cemetery. Adams' melancholy is understanding (cf. *Binah*, Saturn's designated *sefirah*) that once he, like the others, perish they will not be missed by anyone. They are deadly drifters without family; Adams explains this to the others, "Places you are tied down to, none. People with a hold on you, none. Men you step aside for, none." Accordingly, Adams' remarks that gunslingers like him will "always lose." This grim melancholy echoes the symbolic language

---

478 Pike, *Morals and Dogma*, p. 727.
479 See Frazer's *The Golden Bough*, p. 575.

of the Ancient Mysteries wherein *the spirits of men are the powdered bones of Saturn.*[480]

The intrinsic nature of Saturn is synonymous with that spiritual rock which is the enduring foundation of the Solar Temple, and has its antitype or lower octave in that terrestrial rock–the planet Earth–which sustains upon its jagged surface the diversified genera of mundane life.[481] If Adams is Saturn, then the sun god of the magnificent seven is Bernardo O'Reilly. As the archetypal sun, O'Reilly is the deadliest of the seven, having "faced bigger odds in the Travis County war," and he "got that Salinas thing cleared up," denoting a heliocentric reputation that, like an archetypal hero, triumphs against the worst odds. Like the sun god Apollo, the patron of music, Bernardo plays the fife. While in the village, he is followed by three adoring sun worshipping children. The three children also signify the three phases of the sun: sunrise, the sun at meridian (noon), and sunset.

O'Reilly's best friend is Harry Luck, and the two are often depicted hanging around; it is Luck who recommends O'Reilly to Adams. Just as the sun rules the day and the moon rules the night, Luck, friend to the sun, is thus an archetypal personification of the moon. Like the moon, Harry waxes and wanes: he is there one minute and gone the next finally returning to the village in all his brilliance to save Adams from Calvera. Harry's surname, Luck, associates with the moon since it can be a harbinger of both good and bad fortune. Harry also seeks treasures in the form of a lost silver mine because silver is the metal of the moon, imitating its nocturnal radiance.

The aloof, dapper, and debonair Lee is none other than Venus, the mythical goddess of beauty. As such, Lee is a dandy always dressing well, thinking very highly of himself. However, like Venus' concomitant Lucifer, the son of the morning star, which appears in the morning sky as false, negative light before the rising of the true light, the sun. Lee is plagued by self-doubt, signifying Venus' negative attributes.

The God of War, Mars, is the merciless killer, Britt. His knife and gunfire never miss its target, making him the most proficient of the seven. Quiet and unassuming yet always ready to kill; this archetype's war-like nature is unquestioned.

---

480 Hall, *The Secret Teachings of All Ages*, p. 302.
481 *ibid*, p. 303.

The mercurial drifter, the enigmatic loner *traveling like the wind*, is Vin Tanner; he is Mercury (the Greek Hermes), the god of financial gain and communication. Before joining the seven, he is seen riding into the American border town, passing in front of an apothecary, drawing forth the caduceus of Hermes (or Mercury), the emblem of the medical profession from the collective unconscious. At first, Tanner loses money at the gaming table but gains it back. He agrees to accept the $20 fee becoming the first to join Adams' crew. As a communicator, Tanner adroitly echoes the sentiments of Adams' saturnine melancholy when he says, "After a while, you can call bartenders and pharaoh dealers by their first name. Maybe 200 of 'em. Rented rooms you live in, 500. Meals you eat in hash houses, a 1000. Home, none. Wife, none. Kids, none." Providing mercurial wisdom, when Calvera asks why they accepted the job in the first place, it is Tanner communicating, "A fella I knew in El Paso one day took all his clothes off and jumped on a cactus, and I asked him the same question, why? ...He said, 'It seemed to be a good idea at the time.'"

Finally, the planet Jupiter (the Greek Zeus), King of the Gods, is the impulsive up-and-upcoming gunslinger Chico, who, like Zeus, was often hot- headed and temperamental. Upon arriving in the farming village, Chico *qua* Jupiter-Zeus reigns down thunder[482] upon the village by aggressively tolling the church bell, causing the villagers to emerge from their self-imposed hiding. Chico, embodying Jupiter offended, admonishes them harshly for not paying proper homage to the godlike seven. The other six gunslingers stand in awe of Chico's scolding and seem to admire his divinity; even Adams *qua* Saturn–up until now has been skeptical of Chico–is impressed remarking, "Now we're seven." Later, as Jupiter ascending, he yearns to have his courageous deeds–the defense of the village–immortalized in song saying, "Villages like this make up a song about every big thing. They sing them for years." Zeus-Jupiter often employed various disguises in some of his human liaisons, so it is Chico infiltrating Calvera's camp by dressing and acting as one of his bandits. In the end, Chico abandons Adams and Tanner by staying in the village taking Petra for his wife (cf. Hera the wife of Zeus). As a savior of the village, Chico's divine status is unquestioned; Chico remains in his metaphoric Mt. Olympus.

---

482 Zeus/Jupiter was the god of thunder; see Frazer's *The Golden Bough*, p. 158.

* * * *

While in the village, the seven gunslingers appear eating and relaxing around a table over which hangs a sculpture of Christ crucified. The omnipresent sculpture imbues the seven as New Testament patriarchs: they are the divine saviors of the farming village rescuing it from Calvera and his marauders. The seven classical planets were worshipped as gods, making Adams and his motley crew deities in the eyes of the peasants. However, there is another esoteric meaning behind the image of Christ. The planetary, pagan gods of old were destroyed by Christianity; Jesus Christ comes to drive out the many, false gods. The farmers turn against their hired gods by forcing the seven to leave; they would rather take their chances with Calvera. Ultimately, the seven return and take down Calvera but lose Harry, Britt, Bernardo, and Lee. Their bravery inspires the farmers to rise against their oppressors. The old hermit then offers the remaining three a place in the village, "You could stay, you know. They wouldn't be sorry to have you stay," to which Adams quips, "They won't be sorry to see us go either." Like the pagan gods, the magnificent seven disappear, vanish, they die off turning to dust. Adams is correct when he says to Tanner, "We lost. *We always lose." The Magnificent Seven* teaches us what happened to the legendary gunslinger of the West; their fate parallels that of the pagan gods of old: both were once held sacred, but over time became outdated relics. However, the mythology of the ancient gods remains eternal because they are part of all of us; they dwell in the collective unconscious. Therefore, it is easy to understand how the gods of antiquity reincarnate as archetypal gunslingers in *The Magnificent Seven.*

A FISTFUL OF DOLLARS

A Fistful of Dollars (1964) is the first of three of Sergio Leone's (1929-1989) Man with No Name films; the other two movies that round out the trilogy are *For a Few Dollars More* (1965) and *The Good, the Bad and the Ugly* (1966). The Man with No Name is portrayed by Clint Eastwood, appearing to play the same character in all three movies despite the fact that he has a name: Joe is his name in *A Fistful of Dollars,* and Manco is his name in *For a Few Dollars More*; he is known by the nickname, "Blondie," in *The Good, the Bad, and the Ugly*. Hence, his name is Joe Manco, but goes by the nickname Blondie. To Western aficionados, the three films are collectively known as the Dollars Trilogy, but more commonly they are called Spaghetti Westerns. A Spaghetti Western is a term referring to a sub-genre of Western films that were produced, usually on a small budget, by Italians in the mid-1960s. These movies were originally released in Italian, but since most of them featured multilingual casts with the sound post-synched, many Spaghetti Westerns do not have an official language. The typical Spaghetti Western team was composed of an Italian director, Italo-Spanish technical staff, and a cast of Italian, Spanish, German, and American actors, sometimes a fading Hollywood star and sometimes a rising one like the young Clint Eastwood. The Dollars Trilogy feature all the archetypal qualities that would define Western movies going forward: ghost towns, flashbacks, the hate and the vengeance, the dust, the heat, the gunmen and their faces, the music, and the double-crosses; Leone does an excellent job of putting all of this on celluloid. In many instances the cinematography of the Spaghetti Western resembles that of Kurosawa; only Leone embeds his films with a dose of Roman Catholicism and, be default, Cabala.

Leone was born in Rome and, like most Italian boys of his generation, was raised in the Catholic Church and educated in parochial schools. Like the other great Italian filmmakers of his era, his immersion in Catholicism shaped his imagination and his view of the world; his films are loaded with numinous archetypes and symbolisms that give them a pronounced spiritual quality. These Catholic religious themes–sometimes veiled and other times more obvious–permeate his Spaghetti Westerns, making them feel as though they are taking place in the Holy Land, not in a Texas-Mexico border town.

A Stranger–the Man with No Name–arrives in the little Mexican border town of San Miguel; he witnesses a man bullying a child for no reason. Thus, begins *A Fistful of Dollars*. When he enters the town, he gets harassed by four men, proving his speed and accuracy with his gun when hem easily shoots all four of them dead. Silvanito (Jose Calvo, 1916-1980), the town's innkeeper, tells the Stranger about a feud between two families vying for control of the town. On one side are the Rojo Brothers: Don Miguel

(Antonio Prieto, 1926-2011), Esteban (Sieghardt Rupp, 1931-2015) and the violent Ramón (Gian Maria Volonté, 1933-1994); and on the other is the family of the town sheriff, John Baxter (Wolfgang Lukschy, 1905-1983) and his wealthy wife Consuelo (Margarita Lozano). The Stranger decides to play each family against the other to make money. He seizes the opportunity when he sees bandits, led by Ramón Rojo, massacre a detachment of Mexican soldiers escorting gold bullion. The Stranger takes two of the dead bodies to a nearby graveyard, selling the information to both sides, saying that two Mexican soldiers survived the attack and are taking refuge in the cemetery. Both sides race to the cemetery, the Baxters to get the "survivors" to testify against the Rojos and the Rojos to silence them. The factions engage in a gunfight with Ramón, managing to "kill" the "survivors" while Esteban captures John Baxter's son, Antonio (Bruno Carotenuto).

While the Rojos and the Baxters are fighting, the Stranger searches the Rojo's hacienda for their gold stash. While he is searching, he accidentally punches out a woman, Marisol (Marianne Loch). He takes her to the Baxters, arranging to return her to the Rojos in exchange for Antonio. During the exchange, Marisol's son runs to her crying with her husband following; it is disclosed they are the man and child who were bullied at the beginning of the movie. While the family embraces, Ramón orders one of his men, Rubio, to kill her husband since he has already been told to leave town. Silvanito attempts to protect the family with a shotgun; he is about to be killed when the Stranger intervenes on his behalf, staring down Rubio. Neither Ramón nor any of his men attempt to challenge the Stranger, knowing that he is too fast on the draw. The Stranger then tells Marisol to go to Ramón and for her husband Julián (Daniel Martín, 1935-2009) to take their son, Jesús (Nino Del Arco), home. Afterward, the Stranger learns from Silvanito that Ramón had taken Marisol from her family, forcing her to live with him as his prisoner. That night, while the Rojos are celebrating, the Stranger rescues Marisol, shooting the guards, wrecking the house in which she is being held, making it appear as though it were attacked by the Baxters. The Stranger gives Marisol, her husband, and their son some money, telling them to leave the town immediately. When the Rojos discover that he freed Marisol, they capture the Stranger and torture him, but he escapes and hides in the town. Believing the Stranger to be protected by the Baxters, the Rojos set fire to the Baxter home and massacre the entire family as they run out of the burning mansion. Ramón kills John Baxter and Antonio after pretending to spare them. Consuelo emerges from the flames cursing the Rojos to rot in Hell for killing her husband and son since they were unarmed, trying to surrender. She is then shot and killed by Esteban.

With help from Piripero (Joseph Egger, 1889-1966), the local coffin-builder, the Stranger escapes town by hiding in a casket. The Stranger disappears, convalescing in a nearby abandoned mine; it is here that Piripero addresses the Stranger as "Joe." When Piripero tells him Silvanito has been captured, the Stranger returns to town to face the Rojos. With a steel chest plate concealed beneath his poncho, he taunts Ramón to "aim for the heart" as Ramón's rifle shots do nothing to slow the Stranger. Ramón uses up all his bullets, only then to have the Stranger reveal the nature of his ruse by pulling back his poncho, exposing the body armor. The Stranger shoots the rifle from Ramón's hand and kills the other Rojos standing nearby, including Don Miguel. He then uses the last bullet in his gun to free Silvanito, having been tied hanging from a post. The Stranger challenges Ramón to reload his rifle faster than he, the Stranger, can reload his pistol. The Stranger then shoots and kills Ramón. Esteban Rojo aims at the Stranger while hiding behind the curtains in a nearby building, but is killed by Silvanito. With the Rojos dead, the movie ends with the Stranger bidding farewell, riding away from the town.

Although he is not Jesus Christ (at least not yet), the Stranger takes the necessary steps to become a heroic, divine archetype in this first film of the Dollars Trilogy. The Man with No Name is not a redeemer per se; however, he is–and will always be–the good guy; he will always do the right thing. Leone makes its known that the conflict between the Rojos and the Stranger is more than just a border feud, it is Biblical in nature: it is divine good against demonic evil; it is a neo-Manichean battle between light and dark. To project this upon the viewer's subconscious mind, the movie's conflict takes place in the village of San Miguel referencing Saint Michael (in English) the Archangel that cast Satan out of Paradise during the war in Heaven described in the Book of Revelation (see also Milton's *Paradise Lost* which, differing from Revelation, presents the origin story of Satan-Lucifer as an angel rebelling against God in primeval times). Personifying Old and New Testament evil are the three Rojo Brothers, forming a diabolical trinity. Father, Son, and Holy Ghost are foreign to them instead they bless their victims with torture, beatings, and death. The de facto leader of this gang of thieves is the vicious Ramón killing without mercy: he wipes out a contingency of Mexican soldiers, he shoots the unarmed Baxter family trying to surrender, and he holds Marisol captive against her will, keeping her away from her son, Jesús. The best way to kill a man, Ramón explains, is always to aim for the heart, signifying the destruction of the devotion to the Sacred Heart (a/k/a the Most Sacred Heart of Jesus, Latin: *Sacratissimi Cordis Iesu*). The Sacred Heart is one of the most widely practiced and well-known Roman Catholic devotions, taking Christ's heart as the representation of his divine love for humanity. When the Stranger approaches Ramon during the final duel, he taunts him to, "You shoot to kill you better hit the heart. Your own words Ramón. The heart Ramón, don't forget the heart. Aim for the heart or you'll never stop me."

The man that Ramón cannot stop is the Stranger, also known as the Man with No Name, also known as Joe. He is the heroic Christlike archetype sent by Heaven to thwart the evil Rojos; like the town's namesake, he will defeat Ramón and his ilk *qua* Satan and the other rebel angels. Being a reinvention of one of Campbell's heroes with a thousand faces, the Stranger feels genuine pity for the boy Jesús and his mother Marisol *qua* Mary. Risking the trust that he has established with the Rojos, he brings them together unifying Madonna with Child, freeing them from the yoke of Ramón simultaneously. However, he is caught by the Rojos and, like Christ, scourged for his transgression. Like Jesus, the Stranger undergoes death only it is symbolic: he conceals himself in a coffin to escape town, evading the wrath of the Rojos. While recuperating in a mine, a metaphorical tomb, the Stranger is visited by Piripero, telling him that his friend *qua* disciple Silvanito is suffering martyrdom at the hands of the Rojos. Like a resurrected savior, the Stranger, ascends from his subterranean confines to finally confront and vanquish the enemy. He next performs a miracle: the Stranger can stop (or deflect) bullets, anticipating the Gnostic solar savior Neo (a/k/a The One) in *The Matrix* (see *Cinema Symbolism*, Chapter IX, *passim*). He pulls back his poncho revealing the source of his miraculous power: an iron shield protects his heart from rifle fire. Although the shield is manmade, it signifies that having died once the Stranger cannot be killed again; like Christ, he has been raised from the dead impervious to Ramón's bullets. Like an avenging angel, the Stranger swiftly dispatches the Rojos; music descends from the heavens above as the village's church bell rings declaring the defeat of evil.

The Man with No Name was a new style of hero, as laconic and self-reliant as his predecessors but with a cynicism and amorality that matched the contemporary mood of his 1960s audience. A hero whose speed and skill with firearms had reached a new and exaggerated level of artistry, utilizing them efficiently against his villainous adversaries. His clothing was also contemporary to the time: the traditional cowboy outfits of John Wayne, Jimmy Stewart, and Walter Brennan were replaced with a Mexican poncho, black hat, and a cigar that the hero is either lighting, smoking, or putting out in just about every scene. The Man with No Name returns in Leone's second Spaghetti Western, *For a Few Dollars More* only, this time, he is called Manco which is Spanish for *one-armed*.[483] The religious-Catholic symbolisms and themes that Leone featured in *A Fistful of Dollars* continue, but it is not until *The Good, the Bad and the Ugly* that he perfects his arcane-Christian storytelling.

FOR A FEW DOLLARS MORE

The Man with No Name and Colonel Douglas Mortimer (Lee Van Cleef, 1925-1989) are two bounty hunters in pursuit of El Indio, (Gian Maria Volonté, English: the Indian) one of the most wanted fugitives in the Wild West along with his gang. Indio is ruthless, shrewd, brutal with a penchant for anticipating his opponent's next move. He also has a musical pocket watch that he plays before engaging in gun duels: "When the chimes finish, begin," he says. Flashbacks reveal that Indio took the watch from a young woman (Rosemary Dexter, 1944–2010) whom Indio found with her lover (Peter Lee Lawrence, 1944–1974). Indio killed him and raped her; she drew a gun and shot herself, committing suicide while being raped. There is a photograph of the woman inside the watch's lid because it was a gift from her lover.

---

483 The name is sometimes credited as "Monco."

Clad in black, Mortimer is the inspired melancholic mercenary; he is a sagacious marksman, making him proficient in the deadly art of killing. The movie begins with his illegally stopping a train at Tucumcari to locate Guy Calloway (José Terrón), a fugitive with a bounty on his head. In one of the film's more memorable scenes, Mortimer displays both his formidable arsenal of weapons and gunslinging skill when he quickly kills Calloway at long range while the outlaw is shooting at him. After collecting a bounty of $1,000, Mortimer asks about Red "Baby" Cavanaugh (José Marco), having a $2,000 bounty on him, the bandit last seen in White Rocks. He learns that Cavanagh has already been targeted by Manco, the Man with No Name. Manco rides into White Rocks, finding Cavanagh in a saloon, playing five-card draw poker. His men try to come to his rescue, but Manco kills them all, collecting the bounty.

Meanwhile, Indio's gang, led by his right-hand man Nino (Mario Brega, 1923–1994), break into the prison where he is being held. They free him while killing his cellmate, the warden, and most of the guards. Indio's next target is the Bank of El Paso's decoy safe protecting almost a million dollars. The two bounty hunters arrive separately in El Paso, learn about each other and, after butting heads and an epic hat-duel, decide to team up to take down Indio and his gang. Mortimer persuades a reluctant Manco to join Indio's gang for the robbery. Manco breaks one of Indio's friends out of prison and is admitted to the gang, appearing to gain Indio's trust. Indio's plan includes Manco and some of his crew, providing a distraction by robbing another bank in another town, but Manco guns down the gang members sending a false telegraphic alarm. Once the El Paso sheriff and his posse leave town, Indio and the rest of his gang invade the bank and carry off the safe, which they cannot open. They ride to the small border town of Agua Caliente, where Mortimer is waiting. One of Indio's men, the hunchback Wild (Klaus Kinski, 1926- 1991), recognizes Mortimer from an earlier encounter in which Mortimer deliberately insulted him by striking a match on his hunchback. He forces a showdown but Mortimer kills him. Mortimer then proves his worth to Indio by cracking open the safe without using explosives. Indio then says he will wait a month before dividing the loot among his men, allowing the furor over the bank robbery to die down, locking the money away.

Manco and Mortimer attempt to steal the bank money from Indio but are captured in the act. However, unbeknownst to Indio's men, the bags with the money are hung over a tree branch by Manco as they are being caught. Indio's men severely beat them, tying them up to prevent them from escaping. Later Nino, on orders from Indio, kills their guard and releases them. Indio informs his gang that Manco and Mortimer escaped, sending the gang in pursuit, intending to let his crew and Manco and Mortimer kill each other off while he and Nino take all the loot for themselves. However, Groggy (Luigi Pistilli, 1929-1996), one of the more intelligent members of the gang, figures out Indio's ruse and kills Nino. Before he can kill Indio, he finds that Mortimer has already removed the stolen money from where Indio had stashed it. With the money missing, Indio convinces Groggy to join forces with him to trap Manco and Mortimer.

The next morning, Indio's men confront Manco and Mortimer in the streets of Agua Caliente. Manco and Mortimer kill the gang, one by one, in a running gun battle. Standing alone, Mortimer shoots Groggy as he runs for cover, but then has his gun shot out of his hand by Indio. Indio then opens his pocket watch and its haunting chimes begin to play. As the music nears its end, Manco suddenly appears with the same pocket watch, which plays the same tune as Indio's which Mortimer realizes was taken from him earlier. Manco covers Indio with a rifle and forces him to wait while he gives his gun belt and pistol to Mortimer, evening the odds. "Now we start," Manco announces, sitting down while Mortimer and Indio face off, with the watch's music playing again. During the standoff, Manco looks at Mortimer's pocket watch seeing the same photo that's in Indio's watch. The music finishes with Mortimer outdrawing Indio, gunning him down.

Mortimer takes Indio's pocket watch. Manco gives him back the other watch remarking on a family resemblance between the photo and Mortimer, "Naturally between brother and sister," Mortimer replies. His revenge complete and justice served, Mortimer declines his share of the bounties and rides away. Manco tosses the bodies of Indio and his men into a wagon, adding up the bounties, finding he is short of the $27,000 total. Manco spins around gunning down Groggy who was sneaking up behind him, having survived the earlier slaughter. As he leaves, he recovers the money stolen from the Bank of El Paso from the tree, though it is uncertain whether he intends to return it. He then rides off into the distance with two horses towing the wagon of corpses.

Leone recycles the Biblical imagery which he used in *A Fistful of Dollars*. In fact, Colonel Mortimer is introduced reading the Bible on board a train. Next, he gets off at Tucumcari with a black horse and dressed in black from head to toe signifying death and mortality: his surname, Mortimer, has the syllable *mort* (Latin: death, see the previous chapter). However, in the Bible death rides a pale horse not a black one, the rider of Revelation's Black Horse carries scales,[484] symbolizing divine justice which, for Mortimer, signifies the retribution he seeks for the rape-suicide of his sister at the hands of Indio. Mortimer is not hasty; he will only strike Indio and his gang when the time is right. Mortimer's patience and steadfastness are echoed by the town's name from the beginning, Tucumcari, which comes from the Comanche word *tukamukaru* which means *to lie in wait for someone or something to approach*. Mortimer is a death dealer acting according to his schedule, not someone else's, killing for bounties, not sport, making an exception for Indio which is personal.

Indio, naturally, is the embodiment of evil, the Devil. His reputation as an evil doer is unmatched, and it is revealed in flashbacks that he is the object of Mortimer's revenge. After escaping from jail, Indio takes refuge in a church, killing one of his former henchmen for betraying him. Unlike the Man with No Name, unifying Madonna and Child (Marisol and Jesús) in *A Fistful of Dollars*, Indio murders the wife and child of his former henchman before killing him in an unfair duel. Next, in the same church, Indio gives a sermon from the pulpit about a carpenter, but the carpenter Indio speaks of is a deceiver, not a redeemer; his sermon is about evil doing, not faith, hope, or charity. He tells the story of a carpenter, an expert in making vaults and safes out of wood–not iron–deceiving the person into believing it was impenetrable when, in fact, it is nothing more than a ruse. It turns out that the carpenter was Indio's cellmate, and the giant vault in the Bank of El Paso is the carpenter's duplicitous handy work. The bank's safe is not impregnable as thought; instead, it's a mere wooden decoy, with the real safe kept in a nearby wood cabinet. Indio's words inspire his men to action: they will do the Devil's bidding by robbing EL Paso's bank.

---

484 Revelation 6:5: "And when he had opened the third seal, I heard the third beast say, Come and see. And I beheld, and lo a black horse; and he that sat on him had a pair of balances in his hand."

Later, after the robbery in the town Agua Caliente, Manco and Mortimer shoot apples off of a tree, conjuring the Genesis story of the serpent with Eve in the Garden. This is fitting because Agua Caliente is the town in which Indio decides to hide after the El Paso bank robbery; the serpent has returned to the Garden to lay low for a while. It becomes known Indio sees his henchmen as nothing more than mere chattel, he has no problem allowing them to be killed (toward the end encouraging it), thereby ensuring that his percentage of the booty only increases. Unlike Christ, the Devil is okay with betraying, abandoning, or killing his apostles: when Indio is setting his men up for certain death, one can hear a cock crowing during the morning hours. To the subconscious mind, this imparts Peter's denials of Jesus,[485] symbolizing Indio's backstabbing, his deadly chicanery, and the expendability of his men.

Before engaging in gun duels, Indio opens a pocket watch which plays chimes; when the music stops, gunfire ensues. Indio's obsession with time and memory is evidenced by the flashbacks involving Mortimer's sister whenever he opens the watch. Leone's use of a watch, and its music, is the film's most distinctive icon and is metaphoric for the philosophical doctrine known as the Art of Memory, stressing archetypal images as magical mnemonics. Frances Yates explains:

"This classical art, usually regarded as purely mnemotechnical, had a long history in the Middle Ages and was recommended by Albertus Magus and Thomas Aquinas. In the Renaissance, it became fashionable among Neoplatonists and Hermetists. It was now understood as a method of printing basic or archetypal images on the memory, with the cosmic order itself as the 'place' system, a kind of inner way of knowing the universe. The principle is already apparent in the passage in Ficino's *De vita colitis comparanda* in which he describes how the planetary images or colours, memorised as painted on the vaulted ceiling, organised for the man who had so memorised them, all the individual phenomena which he perceived on coming out of his house. The Hermetic experience of reflecting the universe in the mind is, I believe, at the root of Renaissance magic memory, in which the classic mnemonic with places and images is now understood, or applied, as a method of achieving this experience by imprinting archetypal,

---

485 Matthew 26:34: "Jesus said unto him [Peter], Verily I say unto thee, That this night, before the cock crow, thou shalt deny me thrice."

or magically activated, images on the memory. By using magical or talismanic images as memory-images, the Magus hoped to acquire universal knowledge, and also powers, obtaining through the magical organisation of the imagination a magically powerful personality, tuned in, as it were, to the powers of the cosmos."[486]

The watch and its music focus the attention of the viewer to the cause of the movie: Indio's past transgressions against Mortimer's sister. The watch and its chimes are also a talisman of the present and future: when the music stops, someone will die making them a mere memory. Leone employs time and timekeeping with magical results: not only does he use the watch to hold the audience's strict attention, but even after the movie is long over, the one thing that always remains in the mind of the audience is Indio's timepiece and its mysterious, hypnotic chimes. In other words, the timekeeping device is a tool within the film's fabric activating memories of Mortimer's sister, her lover, her death, and Indio. When the music stops, death follows. Therefore, the watch and its chimes implant the film's archetypes and archetypal imagery into the conscious and subconscious mind. Mystical-modernism takes hold; thus, we remember the cruel Devil, the maiden's death by her own hands, the melancholic, revenge and redemption, and the hero; *For a Few Dollars More* is the Art of Memory in celluloid.

Although Manco is a hero in *For A Few Dollars More*, Leone does not imbue him with divine imagery or symbolism. Paralleling Mortimer, Manco is a fearless bounty hunter eventually helping the former bring down Indio, and that is about it. Instead, Leone saves Christlike imagery for Eastwood in *The Good, the Bad and the Ugly*. However, one unique piece of Christian cabalistic esoterica does surface in *For a Few Dollars More*, and seems to foreshadow the Catholic religiosity of Leone's final film in the Dollars Trilogy. At one point, Manco visits an eccentric old hermit referred to as the Old Prophet (Joseph Egger) , having also played the coffin maker in *A Fistful of Dollars*. He goes to the odd-duck sage to learn as much information as he can about Mortimer and his methodology. The Prophet personifies the wise yet eccentric Hermes Trismegistus-like archetype (echoing Walter Brennan's Groot from *Red River*), and it's interesting that Leone decided to call this hermit, Prophet. Many Christian

---

486 Yates, *Girodano Bruno and the Hermetic Tradition*, pp. 191-192.

writers, including Lactantius (ca. 250-ca. 325), Giordano Bruno, Marsilio Ficino (1433-1499), Tommaso Campanella (1568-1639) and Giovanni Pico della Mirandola (1463-1494) considered Hermes Trismegistus to be a wise pagan prophet, foreseeing the coming of Christ. Within Leone's Spaghetti Western Universe, the hermetic Prophet provides learned insights to Manco and, in doing so, prophesied the Man with No Name's cabalistic solar attributes in *The Good, the Bad and the Ugly*.

THE GOOD, THE BAD AND THE UGLY

The Good, the Bad and the Ugly is one of this author's favorite films, and is definitely in his personal Top 10 Films of All Time. Like Sturges' *The Magnificent Seven*, it has one of the most recognizable scores–composed by Ennio Morricone–in cinema history.[487] Eastwood goes by the nickname, Blondie, but clearly appears to be the same character, Joe Manco, from Leone's first two films. However, Lee Van Cleef is not reprising his role from *For a Few Dollars More*; Angel Eyes is not Colonel Douglas Mortimer. *The Good, the Bad and the Ugly* is more than a treasure hunt in the Old West; rather, it is a conflict between Christ and the Devil, battling for the soul of Tuco Ramirez (Eli Wallach), the Ugly. The religious symbolisms and archetypes Leone employed in the first two Dollars Trilogy films pervade his epic grand finale.

When each character is introduced in freeze-frame, the words, *the good*, *the bad*, and *the ugly* are written across the screen. In a desolate Western ghost town during the American Civil War, Mexican bandit Tuco Ramirez narrowly escapes three bounty hunters, killing two and wounding a third. Miles away, Angel Eyes (Van Cleef), the Bad, interrogates Stevens (Antonio Casas, 1911-1982) about Jackson (Antonio Casale, 1936-2017), a fugitive now calling himself Bill Carson, about a cache of Confederate gold. The soldier, realizing that Angel Eyes was sent to kill him by Baker (Livio Lorenson, 1923-1971), a Confederate soldier, offers Angel Eyes $1,000 to kill Baker. The interrogation concludes with Angel Eyes killing Stevens and his eldest son. He soon collects his fee from Baker, then sadistically

---

487 Morricone scored all three of the Dollars Trilogy.

kills him as well, thus earning the $1000. Next, Tuco is rescued from three bounty hunters by Blondie (Eastwood), the Good. However, Blondie delivers him to the local sheriff for a $2,000 reward. As Tuco is about to be hanged, Blondie surprises the authorities by freeing Tuco, shooting the rope from which he hangs while holding everyone at bay allowing Tuco to ride off. The two escape, split the reward money, beginning a partnership and lucrative money-making scheme. Eventually Blondie, weary of Tuco's complaints about how they split the reward money, abandons him, leaving him penniless in the desert. Tuco survives, tracking Blondie to a town being abandoned by Confederate troops led by Brigadier General Henry H. Sibley. Inside a hotel room, Tuco tries to force Blondie to hang himself, but when a Union shell destroy the hotel, the latter escapes.

Tuco captures Blondie forcing him on a sadistic march across the harsh, blistering desert. When Blondie collapses from sunburn and dehydration, Tuco prepares to shoot him, only to be interrupted by the sight of a runaway carriage. Tuco halts the carriage finding a wounded and delirious Bill Carson, promising him $200,000 in stolen Confederate gold, buried in a grave in Sad Hill Cemetery, in exchange for water. When Tuco returns, he finds Carson dead, with Blondie slumped next to him. Before passing out, Blondie reveals that he knows the name on the grave where the gold is buried. Aware that they each need the other to recover the loot, the men disguise themselves as Confederate soldiers retiring to an old Spanish frontier mission which is home to Tuco's estranged brother, Father Pablo Ramírez (Luigi Pistilli). After Blondie recovers from his ordeal, the two leave in their Confederate uniforms but are captured by a force of Union soldiers, remanded to prisoner of war camp Batterville. At roll call, Tuco answers for Bill Carson, drawing the attention of Angel Eyes; when not bounty hunting, he is a Union Sergeant at the camp. Angel Eyes has Tuco tortured by his henchman, Corporal Wallace (Mario Brega), to disclose the location of the gold. Tuco tells him the name of the cemetery but insists that only Blondie knows the name on the grave. Aware that Blondie will not yield as easily as Tuco, Angel Eyes offers him an equal share of the gold in exchange for his information. Blondie agrees and rides out with Angel Eyes and his gang. Tuco, now a prisoner aboard a Union transport in Wallace's custody, leaps from the moving train, kills Wallace and escapes.

Blondie, Angel Eyes, and his henchmen arrive in an evacuated town. Tuco, having fled to the same town, takes a bath in a ramshackle hotel room but is surprised by the bounty hunter he wounded at the beginning of the film. Tuco dispatches him, but his shots attract Blondie's attention. After Blondie informs Tuco of Angel Eyes' plans, the two renew their old partnership. They kill Angel Eyes' henchmen but discover that Angel Eyes has vanished.

Tuco and Blondie make for the cemetery, which is held by Confederate troops on one side of a strategic bridge against the advancing Union troops. Blondie suggests destroying the bridge to disperse the two armies to allow them access to the cemetery. As they rig the bridge with explosives, Tuco suggests that they tell each other their half of the secret. Tuco says the name of the cemetery as Sad Hill, while Blondie says the name on the grave is Arch Stanton. After the explosion and resulting confusion, Tuco betrays Blondie by stealing a horse, galloping ahead to claim the gold for himself. After a long search in the enormous Sad Hill Cemetery, he locates Arch Stanton's grave and begins digging. Blondie soon arrives with a shovel encouraging him at gunpoint to continue. A moment later, Angel Eyes surprises them both also at gunpoint. Blondie kicks open Stanton's grave revealing a skeleton. Declaring that only he knows the real name of the grave, Blondie writes it on a rock that he places in the cemetery's circular center, challenging his adversaries to a three-way duel.

The three men stare each other down, calculating strategy and mentally preparing to draw. Angel Eyes draws first, but Blondie fires first, killing him. Tuco discovers that his gun was unloaded by Blondie the night before. Blondie directs him to a grave beside Arch Stanton's marked Unknown, saying he wrote nothing on the rock as well. Tuco finds eight bags of gold inside and is at first overjoyed, but then looks up to find a hangman's noose prepared for him. Blondie forces Tuco atop an unsteady grave marker, tightens the noose around his neck, then carries off his half of the gold riding away. Trying to keep his balance, Tuco screams for Blondie whose silhouette returns aiming a rifle in the far distance. With a single gunshot, Blondie severs the rope, dropping Tuco face-first onto his share of the gold. Blondie smiles, riding off as Tuco curses him in rage.

* * * *

There are three astrological archetypes in *The Good, the Bad and the Ugly* which, once brought to light, make the cabalistic elements of the movie more understandable and thus more recognizable. It is beyond dispute, based on his earlier films that Leone was well aware of religious symbolism. However, the astrological archetypes presented in this film originate, in this author's opinion, from the collective unconscious. Astrologically, Blondie is Leo the Lion: the solar ruler, the leader, and magnanimous, generous, positive force;[488] he is the Good. Leo is ruled by the sun; thus Blondie, as his nickname suggests, is the golden haired, blue-eyed sun god.[489] Personifying Leo the solar hero, Blondie is honest, stoic, forgiving, and generous throughout the film: he saves Tuco from a group of bounty hunters and repeatedly rescues him from the hangman's noose. Tuco is nothing more than a "filthy beggar" to use Angel Eyes' terminology, but Blondie still protects him. Blondie, in truth, is the de facto leader of the other two: they subconsciously gravitate to him because only he knows the name (or lack thereof) on the grave at Sad Hill, the location of the gold (the metal of the sun). Once the gold is recovered, Blondie still splits it with Tuco 50/50 despite Tuco betraying him, trying to kill him earlier: in a failed effort to destroy Blondie's solar attributes, Tuco forced him through a brutal desert at gunpoint attempting to turn the sun against itself.

Tuco, a desperado, embodies the negative qualities of Aquarius the Water Bearer. These negative traits are unpredictability, rebelliousness, tactlessness, and eccentricity;[490] even Blondie calls him "the Rat." Tuco is all of these things: he is an oddball gunsmith knowing the vital components of each manufacturer's firearms, allowing him to build his own; he is a rebellious bandit committed to the outlaw's life; he is unpredictable deciding to betray Blondie by stealing a horse and going after the treasure on his own; and he is tactless, evidenced by his long, never-ending list of crimes. As Aquarius, Tuco is repeatedly tasked with finding water (cf. Aquarius' water pitcher) or is appears with water constantly: Bill Carson requests water from him, he fetches water for Blondie (in a basin) at the monastery, he shoots Blondie's water pitcher–his cantina–in the scorching desert. He then mocks Blondie by conspicuously drinking from his cantina

---

488 Derek and Julia Parker, *The Complete Astrologer*, p. 114.
489 See Hall's *The Secret Teachings of All Ages*, already cited.
490 Derek and Julia Parker, *The Complete Astrologer*, p. 126.

or water pitcher. He is the only main character to take a bath. He consumes water before going into the general store and tries to revive Blondie with water from his cantina in the desert once he realizes Blondie has learned Carson's secret.

Angel Eyes is the sign of Scorpio the Scorpion embodying all of its traits, both positive and negative: secretive, determined, intractable, and persistent.[491] A determined Angel Eyes always sees a job through even if it means killing the one who initially hired him; Angel Eyes works in secret telling no one of the gold except when it serves him; he is determined to locate it, moving in secret–unnoticed–to Sad Hill Cemetery; and he's hard to work with: Blondie chooses to ally with Tuco (having already tried to kill him) over Angel Eyes even though an alliance with the latter is more advantageous. These three archetypes surface astrologically during the gunfight at Sad Hill Cemetery. Tuco, Blondie, and Angel Eyes all stand inside the circumference of a stone circle which, esoterically, symbolizes

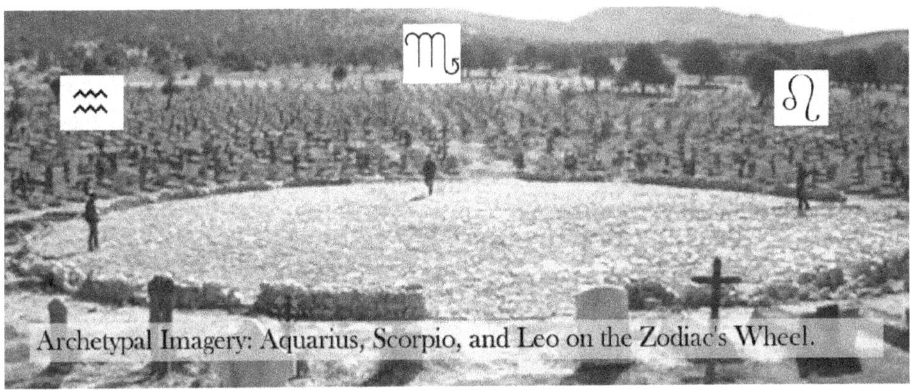

Archetypal Imagery: Aquarius, Scorpio, and Leo on the Zodiac's Wheel.

The sun's ecliptic and the zodiac. The ecliptic is an imaginary line that marks the path of the sun. The signs of the zodiac are the constellations that lie along this line. Applied to Leone's film, Tuco is Aquarius (left) standing across from his opposite house, Blondie *qua* Leo (right). Between them, at the top of the ecliptic's arc, is the house of Scorpio occupied by Angel Eyes.

the wheel of the zodiac. If one superimposed the zodiac wheel over the circular center of Sad Hill Cemetery, one would find that each character stands in his appropriate house: Blondie (Leo) stands directly across from Tuco (Aquarius) because Leo and Aquarius are opposite signs. Standing in between them, at the top of the circular arc at a 90° angle, precisely where

---

491 *ibid*, p. 120.

the house of Scorpio resides is Angel Eyes. Notice that before the gun battle begins, Angel Eyes conspicuously walks in front of Tuco (Aquarius) to move into his proper house on the zodiac's wheel. Leo, Scorpio, and Aquarius are fixed signs; hence, they make compelling, memorable archetypes when brought to life.

Leone's film is all about Christ and the Devil vying for the soul of Tuco. Blondie is the Christlike sun god (cf. Leo's solar attributes), the Good. Blondie's divinity becomes apparent when Angel Eyes refers to him as Tuco's guardian (or protecting) angel, and, just on cue, when Blondie appears, an angelic choir announces him. Each time Tuco is about to face death by hanging, a list of his crimes is read aloud by the local sheriff. It appears as though Tuco is confronted with a roll-call of his sins, or, because he has intentionally allowed himself to be put in this position, Tuco is confessing, or repenting, his transgressions. And after each confession, Tuco is granted forgiveness by Blondie-Christ, shooting the rope, thereby absolving him. Blondie attempts to teach Tuco about the deadly sin of greed when Tuco demands a higher percentage of the reward money provoking Blondie to abandon him and his materialistic ways, but Tuco does not receive the moral instruction. When Tuco takes the injured, dehydrated Blondie to a monastery, Blondie's room has a painting of Jesus' crucifixion outside it. Tuco prays in front of the painting for a brief moment, looking around to make sure no one sees him, like it's a slight to his manhood. Likewise, inside Blondie's room is a sculpture of the savior crucified signifying Blondie's Christlike solar qualities. But Blondie's divinity becomes more apparent once the action moves to the Civil War battle by the river. Blondie is appalled by the loss of life telling the dying commanding officer—to whom he administers last rites by giving him a bottle of booze—to expect good news soon. Blondie and Tuco blow up the bridge, thus ending the senseless carnage, and after he and Tuco cross the river, he goes into a ruined church to comfort a dying Confederate soldier by giving him a cigar and his coat. The way this scene is presented, along with the sentimental music, implies this is not just an act of random kindness, but this is to be taken as a noble act of divine mercy.

Opposing Blondie's Christ is none other than the Devil, Hades or Pluto, the ruler of Scorpio, the Lord of the Underworld, known as the Bad, or Angel Eyes. His nickname implies duplicity: the Devil is not an angel, but was once divine, having been cast out of Heaven by God. From the outset, Angel Eyes' evil nature is apparent. According to legend and folklore, one must never do a deal with the Devil because he will always find a way to turn the tables on you, which is what happens when we first meet Angel Eyes. The Confederate soldier, Baker, learns what it is to make a Faustian Pact with him. Although Baker gets alias that Jackson is using, Bill Carson, Angel Eyes sees the job through by violently killing Baker at the behest of Stevens, the man Baker hired Angel Eyes to kill. Accordingly, the lesson Leone presents is not to trust the Devil under any circumstances. Angel Eyes is the driving force inside Batterville prisoner of war camp which, like Hell itself, is an inferno where Confederate inmates suffer tortures and horrific degradations.

Blondie *qua* Christ and Angel Eyes *qua* the Devil are battling for the soul of Tuco, the Ugly. His nickname, the Ugly, signifies that like all of humankind, he is living in the ugliness of original sin after the fall of Eden and is seeking, perhaps unconsciously, absolution. Unlike the divine Blondie and the evil Angel Eyes, Leone gives the audience both Tuco's real name and when he encounters his brother, his conflicted backstory is presented demonstrating his humanity and independent yet rebellious spirit–all earmarks of Aquarius. Tuco greets his brother Pablo, a monk, with warmth at the monastery but his brother gives him a very un-Christian cold shoulder. In the same scene, Tuco lets his brother know that his decision to lead a life of crime was not his first choice and that Pablo's decision to become a priest was a form of cowardice. The scene leaves us knowing that Tuco is, to a degree, morally confused. Tuco's moral dilemma manifests when he interacts with Blondie, who, after saving his life twice from the gallows pole, remains unmoved; Blondie's benevolence does not stop Tuco from pursuing his savior with a murderous vengeance. During the scene when he tries to hang Blondie in the hotel room, a reference to Judas is made–Tuco believes Blondie had betrayed him when in fact he had saved him. Shortly thereafter, he tries to kill Blondie by taking him into the brutal desert. Like Christ, Blondie is tested in the desert, but it is Tuco who is punished for his sin when Blondie, not Tuco, learns the name on the grave hiding the buried treasure. Tuco is forced to the repent his sin, once again, this time by saving Blondie by nurturing him back to health. When Tuco meets Angel Eyes in the concentration camp he breaks bread with him, but this is the

Devil, not Christ and he is beaten unmercifully; after his thrashing, he is taken by the Devil's henchman, Wallace, to face death.

Traveling to the hidden gold cache, the Devil and Christ cannot work together for the greater good, so Blondie abandons Angel Eyes to renew his partnership with the Ugly because, unlike the Bad, at least he can be redeemed. In the final apocalyptic gunfight, Christ defeats the Devil dispatching him, his gun, and his hat into a shallow grave sending Angel Eyes–metaphorically–back to Hell. For all his betrayals, Blondie ties a noose around Tuco's neck and, like Judas is ready to let him hang. However, Blondie redeems Tuco one last time by cutting his rope but, like all the times before, Tuco does not understand that he has been saved, forgiven for all his trespasses; being *ugly* all he can do is he curse at Blondie as he rides off. Blondie could have taken all the gold for himself but, being *good* he splits the gold 50/50 with the man who has backstabbed him time and time again.

Although more historical than esoteric, it is worth mentioning the person and actions of Confederate Brigadier General Henry H. Sibley (1816-1886), whose militaristic activities and movements the film revolves around. He commanded a Confederate force in Texas and New Mexico, and he is mentioned by name a few times during the movie. At the outbreak of the American Civil War in 1861, Sibley resigned from the US Army, sided with the Confederacy, and was placed in command of a brigade of volunteer cavalry in West Texas. Sibley dubbed his small force the Army of New Mexico, and began planning a New Mexico Campaign to capture the cities of Albuquerque, Santa Fe, and Fort Union on the Santa Fe Trail to establish a forward base of supply. He then intended to continue north to Colorado to capture the numerous gold and silver mines in the area as a means of replenishing the badly depleted Confederate treasury. From there Sibley planned to join forces with Confederate Lieutenant John R. Baylor (1822- 1894), already in control of much of Southern New Mexico and Arizona territories and headquartered in Tucson, Arizona. Their ultimate strategy was to gain access to the warm water ports of California and establish a badly needed supply line to the South, as the Union Navy had implemented a naval blockade from Virginia to Texas.[492] Throughout the 1862 New Mexico Campaign, his opponent was Union Colonel Edward Canby

---

492 See Ray C. Colton's *The Civil War in the Western Territories: Arizona, Colorado, New Mexico, and Utah, passim.*

(1817-1873) is also mentioned by name in the movie. Sibley was initially successful at the Battle of Valverde on 20-21 February and pressed on to capture Albuquerque and Santa Fe in the first weeks of March. Although the subsequent Battle of Glorieta Pass on March 28 ended in an apparent Confederate victory on the field, Sibley had to retreat because his supply train was destroyed and most of the horses and mules killed or driven off during the fight. After the failure of the New Mexico Campaign, Sibley struggled with alcoholism; he was court marshaled in Louisiana in 1863. Although not convicted of cowardice, he was nevertheless censured. When watching *The Good, the Bad and the Ugly*, remember it is Sibley and his Confederates, and the Union forces warring with them, providing the backdrop; Sibley even appears briefly riding out of town near the beginning of the film. Upon seeing Sibley retreating, the innkeeper sardonically remarks, "Look, see that one with the white beard sitting in the wagon? General Sibley, he looks dead. He's finally getting out of our hair. Hooray for Dixie! Hooray, hooray for Dixie!"

Chapter IX concluded, we now leave the barren, lawless conditions of the Old West for the magical land of Narnia; welcome to the high fantasy world of C.S. Lewis.

CHAPTER X

IT'S THE CHRONIC(WHAT?)CLES OF NARNIA

"When Adam's flesh and Adam's bone sits at
Cair Paravel in throne, the evil time will be over and done.
– Mr. Beaver, *The Lion, the Witch and the Wardrobe*, 2005.

"Do not cite the Deep Magic to me Witch.
I was there when it was written.
– Aslan, *The Lion, the Witch and the Wardrobe*, 2005.

"What rubbish! See? That's what happens when
you read all of those fanciful novels on fairy tales of yours."
– Eustace Scrubb, *The Voyage of the Dawn Treader*, 2010.

"If the Witch knew the true meaning of sacrifice, she might
have interpreted the deep magic differently. That when a
willing victim who has committed no treachery,
is killed in a traitor's stead, the stone table will crack,
and even death itself would turn backwards."
– Aslan, *The Lion, the Witch and the Wardrobe*, 2005.

Following the success of *The Lord of the Rings* films, Hollywood was anxious to produce movies based on C.S. Lewis' *The Chronicles of Narnia*. As of the writing and publishing of this book, three Narnia movies have been released: *The Lion, the Witch and the Wardrobe* in 2005; *Prince Caspian* in 2008; and *The Voyage of the Dawn Treader* in 2010. The actors and actresses portraying the main protagonists, the Pevensie children, reprised their roles in each movie: Peter Pevensie was played by William Moseley, Susan Pevensie was played by Anna Popplewell, Edmund Pevensie was portrayed by Skandar Keynes, and Lucy Pevensie was played Georgie Henley. Lewis' stories follow a different chronology from their publication order making the movies also out of order. *The Chronicles of Narnia* were published in this order:

1950: *The Lion, the Witch and the Wardrobe*
1951: *Prince Caspian*
1952: *The Voyage of the Dawn Treader*
1953: *The Silver Chair*
1954: *The Horse and his Boy*
1955: *The Magician's Nephew*
1956: *The Last Battle*

However, to follow the correct chronological timeline, they should be read in this order:

The Magician's Nephew
The Lion, the Witch and the Wardrobe
The Horse and his Boy
Prince Caspian
Voyage of the Dawn Treader
The Silver Chair
The Last Battle

Currently, *The Silver Chair* is the next Narnia movie to go into production; the fourth story published but the sixth adventure. Within the filmmaking industry, the film considered a reboot of the franchise. The Pevensies are not in this story; instead, it follows the Narnia adventures of Eustace Scrubb and Jill Pole.

Lewis, a professor at both Oxford (Magdalen College, 1925-1954) and Cambridge (Magdalene College, 1954-1963) Universities, was a lay theologian and Christian apologist. His Narnia stories are imbued with Christian allegory, Cabala, and Neoplatonic allusions; Lewis, while at Oxford, was a member of an informal literary discussion group called the Inklings. The Inklings, of which J.R.R. Tolkien was also a member, praised the value of narrative in fiction and encouraged the writing of fantasy. Another member of this group was Charles Williams (1886-1945), a novelist, theologian, occultist, and a member of the Salvator Mundi Temple of the Fellowship of the Rosy Cross. The Fellowship of the Rosy Cross was a Christian mystical organization established by A. E. Waite in England in 1915 developing out of the breakdown of the Independent and Rectified Rite of the Golden Dawn. It was based on Waite's complicated arcane philosophies, and its rites reflected his interest in the history of the Rosicrucian Order, Freemasonry, and esoteric Christian teachings. It is through Williams, his membership in this secret society, and his involvement with Lewis and the Inklings that we find a heavy dose of Christian mysticism concealed within the Narnia tales.

THE LION, THE WITCH AND THE WARDROBE

The Lion, the Witch and the Wardrobe is cinematic Cabala akin to Leone's Spaghetti Westerns, with Aslan representing an emanation of the sacred Tetragrammaton, Jesus Christ. Neoplatonism and astrotheology pervade the story; furthermore, Lewis' mysterion features elements of the eternal monomyth. The film begins during the London Blitz (September 1940-May 1941) in the suburb of Finchley where the Pevensie children, (oldest to youngest) Peter, Susan, Edmund, and Lucy are placed in grave danger by the Luftwaffe's bombings. They're evacuated to the country home Professor Digory Kirke (Jim Broadbent), an eccentric not accustomed to having children in his house, as Mrs. Macready (Elizabeth Hawthorne), the strict housekeeper explains.

While the Pevensies are playing hide-and-seek, Lucy discovers an upstairs wardrobe and, passing through its doors, enters a wintry fantasy realm called Narnia. Observing a burning lamppost, Lucy encounters the faun, Mr. Tumnus (James McAvoy), explaining where she is, inviting her to his home. He puts Lucy to sleep by playing a lullaby on his flute. When Lucy wakes up, she finds Tumnus grieving; he explains that Jadis (Tilda Swinton), the evil White Witch, has cursed Narnia by placing it in perpetual winter with no Christmas. If a human is encountered, they are to be brought to her immediately. Tumnus cannot bring himself to kidnap her, so he quickly sends her home. When she returns to Professor Kirke's estate hardly any time has passed; her siblings do not believe her story, and when they examine the wardrobe there is nothing unusual or out of place.

One night, Edmund curiously follows Lucy into the wardrobe. He enters Narnia as well, and after searching for his sister, encounters the White Witch, claiming to be Queen of Narnia. She conjures Turkish Delights telling him about the prospect of becoming king and having power over his siblings if he brings them to her castle. During their conversation, Edmund tells the Witch that his sister Lucy encountered Mr. Tumnus during her previous visit to Narnia. After the Witch departs, Edmund and Lucy meet again and return to Kirke's home; Lucy tells Peter and Susan what happened, but unfortunately, Edmund lies denying everything. Professor Kirke talks with Peter and Susan suggesting Lucy is telling the truth, though they remain unconvinced.

While running away from Mrs. Macready after accidentally breaking a window with a cricket ball, the four siblings retreat to the wardrobe and enter Narnia. They discover that Mr. Tumnus has been taken by the Witch, and meet Mr. and Mrs. Beaver (Ray Winstone and Dawn French), telling them about the mighty Aslan (Liam Neeson). According to the Beavers, Aslan intends to take control of Narnia from the Witch. The four must help Aslan because it has been prophesied that if two sons of Adam and two daughters of Eve sit upon the four thrones at Cair Paravel, the White Witch's reign will end and dreary winter with it. Hearing this, Edmund decides to snitch, sneaking off to drop in on the Witch. When he arrives at her icy castle, she is furious he did not deliver his siblings to her thereby thwarting the prophecy. The Witch sends wolves to hunt down the children and the Beavers who barely escape. Edmund is chained in the Witch's dungeon where he meets Mr. Tumnus. The Witch demands Edmund reveal the location of his siblings. After Tumnus claims that Edmund does not know anything, the Witch tells Tumnus that Edmund betrayed him, then proceeds to turn Tumnus to stone. While Peter, Lucy, Susan and the Beavers travel to the Stone Table to meet Aslan, they hide from what they believe to be the White Witch in her sled. However, it is Father Christmas (James Cosmo), a sign that the Witch's reign is ending. Father Christmas gives Lucy a healing cordial, a drop of which will cure illness and wounds, and a defensive dagger. Susan receives a bow and arrows as well as a magical horn which will summon help when blown, and Peter a sword and shield. After evading wolves led by Maugrim (Michael Madsen), the captain of the Witch's police force, the group finally reaches Aslan's encampment. Aslan, an impressive noble lion, promises to help rescue and redeem Edmund. Later, Maugrim and another wolf ambush Lucy and Susan. When Peter intervenes, Maugrim attacks him, but Peter kills him. Some of Aslan's troops follow the other wolf to the witch's camp and rescue Edmund. Shortly thereafter, Peter is knighted by Aslan.

The White Witch journeys to Aslan's camp. Upon arriving, she claims Edmund is hers because he is a traitor, but Aslan secretly offers to sacrifice himself instead. That night, as Lucy and Susan covertly watch, Aslan is mocked, shaven, and ritualistically killed by the White Witch. In the morning, as the sun rises, he is resurrected because, to quote the lion, "there is a magic deeper still the Witch does not know." Aslan takes Susan and Lucy to the Witch's castle, where he frees the prisoners that the White Witch turned to stone. Meanwhile, Edmund persuades Peter to lead Aslan's army to fight the White Witch's forces. To stop the Witch from attacking and killing Peter, Edmund attacks the Witch destroying her magic wand but is mortally wounded by her. As the Witch fights Peter, Aslan arrives with reinforcements and kills her. Edmund is revived by Lucy's cordial. The Witch and her army defeated, the Pevensies are installed as Kings and Queens by Aslan at Cair Paravel.

Years later, the Pevensie children have grown into young men and women. While chasing a white stag through the forest, they encounter the lamppost–it is now overgrown but still recognizable–that Lucy saw on her first trip to Narnia. As they make their way through the tree branches, they exit the wardrobe becoming children again. Professor Kirke confronts them with the cricket ball that broke window indicating no time has elapsed; the movie ends.

Lewis' tale is a veiled Christian-Neoplatonic-astrotheological allegory. According to Mr. Tumnus, it is forever winter in Narnia, the land cursed by the dreaded wintry White Witch. Christmas has not been celebrated in 100 years; the sun is dead, its birthday not observed. However, this is about to change with the return of Aslan the Lion, a great Neoplatonic astrological solar lion; he is Apollo, the messiah, Jesus Christ. Aslan embodies the constellation Leo the Lion which is ruled by the sun investing him with all the attributes of a sun god. Like the sun, he will defeat winter: Aslan and the Witch's conflict is light against dark, the warm sunlight of summer against the biting coldness of winter, it is a neo-Manichean struggle concealed under the guise of Christianity. Aslan, as a pagan emanation of Jesus, the savior archetype, is a mighty Neoplatonic sun: his return to Narnia welcomes warm weather–the ice and snow begin melting as the children race to his camp–forecasting the vernal equinox when the sun is resurrected. Aslan's return also sees Father Christmas appear indicating that the sun's birthday of December 25th is going to be celebrated once again; the days will become longer and the night and darkness–and thus Jadis–will be diminished. Peter is Aslan's chief disciple mirroring Peter (a/k/a St. Peter, Simon Peter) the first apostle of Christ, ordained by Jesus to establish his church posthumously. Peter has been knighted by Aslan identifying him as his primary apostle. Like Christ, Aslan is willing to die for sin, Edmund's treason, thus redeeming the latter. Echoing Jesus, Aslan voluntarily surrenders himself to the forces that oppose him. Paralleling Jesus and the Gospel Tales, Aslan is scourged and humiliated: his mane, symbolizing sunrays, is clipped, weakening him. Aslan is killed by Jadis in a Stonehenge-like temple complete with a giant Stone Table and trilithon stones. However, like all sun gods, Aslan is resurrected when he appears alongside a rising sun denoting rebirth and regeneration; winter is disappearing, giving way for spring and summer. The giant, sacrificial Stone Table Aslan is killed upon copies Christ's crucifixion; upon Aslan's resurrection, it cracks and breaks, paralleling the stone rolled away from Christ's tomb, announcing Jesus' resurrection. Likewise, Jesus' resurrection was first witnessed by a woman, Mary Magdalene, just as Aslan's resurrection is first witnessed two girls, Susan and Lucy. Once returned to life, Aslan redeems Narnia by defeating and killing his opponent–winter– personified by Jadis the White Witch. As Aslan's enemy, she is the embodiment of winter: mean, dark, harsh, gelid, childless, and barren like the land she rules over; like the goddess Nemesis, she gives Narnia its due. She is an icy Neoplatonic embodiment of cold and cruelty; Jadis is what winter would look like if Botticelli painted her. Her frigid castle evokes Dante's *Inferno* and the 9th Circle of Hell, Lake Cocytus, a frozen wasteland where traitors spend eternity. Her castle lures the treacherous Edmund, the boy held captive in its dungeon, signifying Dante's frozen Hell and the traitors imprisoned therein. Emulating her enemy, Aslan, Jadis sheds her wintry attire for his mane, making her look more like Ēostre (or Ostara), the pagan goddess of spring, attempting to harness his solar energies. But as Jadis soon discovers winter and summer cannot coexist simultaneously; summer will always return, ending winter's bitter reign.

Comparatively the name, Lucy, implies *Luci*fer the Light Bearer, the traditional bearer of sunlight, Venus, the son of the morning star; hence Lucy encounters light–a burning lamppost–immediately upon entering Narnia. This symbolism is not satanic or evil; rather, it's a solar allegory denoting and foreshadowing that the light of Narnia, Aslan the great lion *qua* sun, is triumphantly returning. Lucy will bear this light (cf. enlightenment) by bringing her siblings to Narnia fulfilling the prophecy; together with Aslan, they will liberate Narnia from the White Witch, ending her frigid reign. Encouraging the quest is a Hermes Trismegistus-like wisdom provider, Professor Kirke, informing the two eldest Pevensie children that Lucy is telling the truth about the wardrobe and Narnia. Finally, there is the forest dwelling faun Mr. Tumnus, with his cloven hoofs and magic flute, draws forth the mischievous pagan god, Pan. These esoteric Neoplatonic themes and icons transform *The Lion the Witch, and the Wardrobe* into a modern-day myth because practically all school children read Lewis's novel as part of their curriculum.

The Lion, the Witch and the Wardrobe's Neoplatonism aside, the story also features numerous components of the sacred monomyth, including Refusal of the Return, a rare element especially in cinema.

- The Call to Adventure: Via a magical wardrobe, Lucy goes to Narnia, meets a faun named Mr. Tumnus, learning that the land is cursed because it's in a perpetual state of winter. She returns to her world, trying to convince her siblings to share her adventure.

- Refusal of the Call: Lucy's brothers and sister do not believe her instead thinking she has an overactive imagination. Although Edmund experiences Narnia, he lies about going there making Lucy appear even more childish. The two oldest siblings, Peter and Susan, still discount Lucy's tale even after the wise Professor Kirke tells them she is speaking the truth.

- Supernatural Aid: A graybeard, Father Christmas, gives Lucy a magical healing cordial and a small dagger; he gives Susan a bow, arrows, and a magical horn, providing Peter with a sword (Rhindon) and a shield. Lucy's healing cordial saves Edmund from certain death.

- The Crossing of the First Threshold: Peter, Susan, and Lucy learn of the prophecy of humans sitting on the thrones of Narnia from Mr. and Mrs. Beaver, two threshold guardians. Rather than return home, they decide to stay and help Aslan defeat the White Witch, fulfilling the prophecy.

- The Belly of the Whale: Peter, Susan, Lucy, and the Beavers escape the Queen's wolf pack in narrow subterranean tunnels and later fight them off on a frozen river-waterfall. Meanwhile, Edmund is imprisoned in the Queen's frozen dungeon.

- The Road of Trials: Peter kills the Queen's chief wolf, Maugrim, with the sword; Edmund is rescued from the Witch Witch's encampment; Susan and Lucy witness Aslan's scourging and death. Thereafter, all of them participate in an epic battle against the White Witch's forces.

- Woman as the Temptress: Enter the mother-destroyer; Campbell writes, "And always, after the first thrills of getting underway, the adventure develops into a journey of darkness, horror, disgust, and phantasmagoric fears."[493] Edmund is tempted and tricked by the White Witch, becoming a Judas Iscariot-like traitor. He thinks she is benevolent but experiences her cruelty when she slaps him across his face for failing to bring his siblings to her. She entices him to become master of his siblings, but instead ends up a prisoner in her dungeon. It is because of Edmund's inability to resist Jadis' temptations that Aslan sacrifices himself in his stead.

- Apotheosis: Aslan dies for Edmund's treasonous sins but is resurrected, cementing himself as a Neoplatonic Christ savior archetype.

- Ultimate Boon: With the White Witch and her army defeated, the four siblings are installed as kings and queens of Narnia fulfilling the

---

493 Campbell, *The Hero with a Thousand Faces*, p. 101.

prophecy. They are coronated Queen Lucy the Valiant, King Edmund the Just, Queen Susan the Gentle, and King Peter the Magnificent.

- Refusal of the Return: Campbell states, "When the hero-quest has been accomplished, through penetration to the source, or through the grace of some male or female, human or animal, personification, the adventurer still must return with his life-transmuting trophy. The full round, the norm of the monomyth, requires that the hero shall now begin the labor of bringing the runes of wisdom, the Golden Fleece, or his sleeping princess, back into the kingdom of humanity, where the boon may redound to the renewing of the community, the nation, the planet or the ten thousand worlds. But the responsibility has been frequently refused. Even the Buddha, after his triumph, doubted whether the message of realization could be communicated, and saints are reported to have died while in the supernal ecstasy. Numerous indeed are the heroes fabled to have taken up residence forever in the blessed isle of the unaging Goddess of Immortal Being."[494] The four siblings stay in Narnia until they are young men and women; they do not leave Narnia after the Ultimate Boon. Years later they discover the lamppost finally returning to Kirke's home, the real world, as children where no time has passed. To this author, this element invests the story with a sense of sadness because the children have aged in a wonderland away from the natural reality. The makes the children appear selfish, willing to forsake their mother, father—a soldier fighting in WWII—and friends for a serene fantasy world. When they finally return home—by accident—they are once again children and their life's experiences in Narnia seem to have been for naught. It is for this reason this monomythic element is seldom found in Hollywood for it is an unhappy-happy ending. This is in no way meant to criticize Mr. Lewis, but to this author a better ending would have been to have the children, after being enthroned, to relinquish guardianship of Narnia over to Aslan, its natural ruler, and return to their family and friends but willing to come back to Narnia should evil rear its ugly head again.

---

494 *ibid*, p. 167.

Peter, Susan, Edmund, and Lucy are summoned back to Narnia in *Prince Caspian,* the next film in Disney's *The Chronicles of Narnia* but, chronologically, the fourth story in Lewis' adventure.

PRINCE CASPIAN

1,300 Narnian years after the Pevensie siblings left, Caspian (Ben Barnes), a Telmarine (human, non-magical) prince and heir to the throne is informed by his mentor, Doctor Cornelius, that his Claudius-like uncle, Miraz (Sergio Castellitto), is plotting to kill him to seize the throne for himself and his newborn heir. Cornelius gives him Queen Susan's ancient magical horn, instructing him to blow it only at his greatest need. Caspian flees into the woods where he encounters two Narnian dwarfs, Trumpkin (Peter Dinklage) and Nikabrik (Warwick Davis), as well as a talking badger named Trufflehunter (Ken Scott) and blows the horn to summon help. Meanwhile, only one year in England has passed since the Pevensie children returned from Narnia. The children are waiting for a tube train when the station starts collapsing, magically transporting them to Narnia. At first, they are overjoyed, but soon realize that much time has passed since their last visit: Cair Paravel is in ruin with evidence it was attacked by catapults. From a hidden vault, they retrieve clothing and the supernatural items given to them by Father Christmas.

In the Telmarine castle, the Lords of the Council learn that Prince Caspian has vanished, and Miraz, using a captured Trumpkin, persuades them to attack the Narnians–thought extinct–to retrieve Caspian while secretly plotting to kill him instead. Lord Sopespian (Damian Alcazar) suspects Miraz's motives so he discusses his treasonous ideas with Miraz's ally General Glozelle (Pierfrancesco Favino). The Pevensies save Trumpkin from being drowned by two Telmarines; afterward, he realizes that the four children are the Kings and Queens of old, and they continue traveling together. Lucy glimpses Aslan in the woods trying convincing the others she has seen him, but only Edmund believes her.

Nikabrik and Trufflehunter lead Caspian to a gathering of the old Narnians, convincing them to help him win his throne so he can return their land and freedom. They meet the Pevensies and Trumpkin, and all journey to Aslan's How, a hilly mound of earth built over the cracked Stone Table. Peter decides they will attack Miraz's castle, rejecting Lucy's advice that they wait for Aslan to return. The Narnians raid Miraz's castle, but Caspian ruins the plan by freeing Dr. Cornelius instead of opening the gate. He learns that Miraz killed his father so he confronts Miraz but is wounded. Overwhelmed, Peter calls for a retreat. Peter, Susan, Edmund, Caspian, and the Narnians escape with heavy losses. Upon returning to Aslan's How, Peter and Caspian argue, while back at the castle, Miraz is crowned King.

Nikabrik, with the aid of a hag (Klara Issova) and a werewolf (Shane Rangi), offer Caspian assistance to guarantee military victory. The hag uses black sorcery to summon Jadis the White Witch. From inside a wall of ice, the White Witch tries convincing Caspian to free her, when Peter, Edmund, Lucy and Trumpkin arrive just in time. Peter kills the hag; Edmund kills the werewolf, and Trumpkin stabs Nikabrik when he attacks Lucy. Peter knocks Caspian aside to face the Witch, but begins to become bewitched until Edmund shatters the ice destroying the Witch's apparition. When Miraz and his army arrive at Aslan's How, Caspian suggests Peter and Miraz duel to the death with the loser's army surrendering to buy Lucy and Susan time to find Aslan. Glozelle and Sopespian cajole Miraz to a duel because they know if he refuses, he will look like a coward in front of his men. Lucy and Susan are attacked by Telmarine soldiers, so Susan remains behind to fight them while Lucy continues the quest alone. Shortly there-after, Susan is rescued by Caspian, and they return to Aslan's How. Peter defeats Miraz and gives Caspian his sword to finish him off, but Caspian spares Miraz's life. Sopespian secretly stabs Miraz with one of Susan's arrows killing him, accusing the Narnians of treachery. A battle ensues with the Telmarines gradually winning. Lucy finds Aslan in the woods where he awakens the trees, turning the fight in the Narnians' favor. Sopespian orders retreat to a bridge, where they are confronted by Lucy and Aslan. Aslan summons the river god to destroy the bridge, killing many of the soldiers, swallowing Sopespian thus winning the battle.

Caspian invites the Telmarines to remain in Narnia to coexist peaceful-ly with the Narnians; but if they wish, they can return to the human world from which they originally came. Some, including General Glozelle, wish to leave so Aslan creates a portal for them and the four Pevensies children.

Peter gives Caspian his sword, Rhindon, which was formerly given to him by Father Christmas. Susan kisses Caspian, knowing they will never meet again because Aslan has told her and Peter they will never return to Narnia. The four Pevensies return to England, leaving Caspian behind as King.

Lewis' story is, once again, steeped in Christian allegory. *Prince Caspian* depicts the true Narnians, the followers of Aslan, forced underground to avoid persecution by the Telmarines. Their exile is a metaphor for Christian persecution by the Romans (64-313 CE), with the Narnians becoming the disciples of Aslan *qua* Christ and the Telmarines representing the Romans *qua* nonbelievers. The small band of Narnians *qua* true believers find sanctuary at Aslan's How; an enormous pyramidal mound erected over the Stone Table, the place of Aslan's death and resurrection. Aslan's How mirrors the catacombs of Rome in which Christian lived and died during the Roman persecutions; it signifies believers reviled and killed for their Christian faith. The mound also conjures the Church of the Holy Sepulchre, the temple built over the alleged spot of Christ's crucifixion, just like the mound is built over the spot of Aslan's symbolic crucifixion on the Stone Table *qua* Golgotha. For the Narnians and the Christians, the Stone Table and Calvary represents the continuing need to memorialize the cost of following Aslan or Christ, even to the death if necessary.

Another veiled religious theme is the stark difference between believers and nonbelievers, the former personified by the Narnians–those who remained loyal to the Neoplatonic solar lion Aslan–and the latter, the Telmarines and some of the dwarves, especially Nikabrik (encouraging Caspian to summon Jadis). The Old Narnians are characterized as fairy tales that do not exist; hence their god, Aslan, is likewise a myth. Even Trumpkin, the dwarf eventually convinced of the reality of Aslan, disbelieves at first. Trumpkin changes his mind or rather has it changed for him when he meets the great Aslan face to face. After their momentous meeting, Trumpkin becomes a son of Narnia, an Aslan *qua* Christ convert. King Miraz is a nonbeliever–he is shocked when he sees Trumpkin–seeing the existing Narnians as an underground threat echoing Roman anxieties that the Christians were a scheming cult hell-bent on the destruction of Rome (cf. the Burning of Rome, 64 CE). To Miraz, the Narnians and their belief in Aslan is folly. Lewis (and the film) is drawing a parallel that Christian *qua* Narnian Faith will always be ridiculed by those seeing it as superstitious nonsense. On this, Paul the Apostle (a/k/a Saul of Taurus, ca. 5 CE-67 CE) states, "For the message of the cross is foolishness to those who are perishing but to us who are being saved it is the power of God" (I Corinthians 1:18). Caspian, a Telmarine King accepting the Narnians *qua* Christians, comes to personify Emperor Constantine (272-337 CE) the unifying Roman-Christian leader. Paralleling Christ's birth by an eastern star, Caspian's coming was also astrologically-astronomically foretold. Glenstorm the Centaur (Cornell S. John) states, "Tarva, the Lord of Victory, and Alambil, the Lady of Peace, have come together in the high heavens," an alignment announcing the arrival of a liberator.Perhaps the most overt Christian theme is Lucy's journey. Her struggle portrays the struggle of all Christians following the path of faith and obedience, even in the face of opposition. Lucy claims to see Aslan when no one else can, and insists on waiting for him or seeking him out when no one else wants to. Lucy has the courage to follow Aslan, making her a true believer, even if she is the only one who does so. Lucy's heroism in following, seeking, and finding Aslan through dire circumstances is a poignant lesson for Christians of all ages, but especially for children imparting invaluable lessons: the cost of following Christ (Luke 14:26-33); the dangers and trials inherent in the Christian life (James 1:12; Revelation 2:10); and the faithfulness of the Savior leading his followers home, protect them from evil, and from whom nothing can separate them (Hebrews 10:23; II Thessalonians 3:3; Romans 8:38-39). It is Lucy, embodying a Neoplatonic Lucifer the Light Bearer, bringing the light of the sun—Aslan *qua* Christ—when she returns with the mighty solar lion at the film's conclusion. Is it Lucy that bears the light? Doubt it not!

Prince Caspian presents the universality of questioning God's timing and purposes. Several times the main characters wonder why Aslan doesn't help them with their struggles, why he does not intervene on their behalf, why they can't see him, and why he has been absent from Narnia for so long (cf. Matthew 24:42, "Watch therefore: for ye know not what hour your Lord doth come"). But their faith, like Christianity, is built up by just such circumstances until we learn, as Psalm 18:30 tells us, "As for God, his way is perfect: the word of the Lord is tried: he is a buckler to all those that trust in him." If God's ways are perfect, then whatever he does and whatever timing he chooses is also perfect.

In *Prince Caspian*, we see a Charles Williams' influence; the darker, occult side of Narnia rising to the surface. The hermit professor, Dr. Cornelius, is a reflection of Dr. John Dee. Cornelius has an extensive library filled with magical texts, a celestial globe, and a shamanistic human skull, signifying a Renaissance saturnine cabalist. We see Dee's Enochian sorcery at work when Caspian, assisted by a hag and a werewolf, summons Jadis' spirit in a frozen black mirror-like surface. Like all good conjurors, Caspian performs his sorcery while standing in a protective magic circle.

Just like with *The Lion, the Witch and the Wardrobe*, *Prince Caspian* also features elements of the monomyth. Here, the components are experienced through the eyes of Caspian except Freedom to Live which affects Peter and Susan.

- The Call to Adventure: Prince Caspian escapes that Telmarine castle upon learning his aunt has given birth to a son–an heir, his cousin–giving Miraz cause to usurp the throne. Caspian knows his life is jeopardy, realizing he must find allies so he can thwart Miraz's treacherous scheme.

- Supernatural Aid: A graybeard, Dr. Cornelius, gives Caspian Susan's magical horn. When blown, help will come.

- The Crossing of the First Threshold: Caspian meets three Narnians: Trumpkin, Nikabrik, and Trufflehunter, making them threshold guardians, which he believed to be extinct, mere fairy tales. Because Caspian bears Susan's horn, Nikabrick and Trufflehunter recognize that he may be one who can restore their lands. They take him to meet other Narnians currently in hiding while awaiting the return of Kings Peter and Edmund and Queens Susan and Lucy.

- The Belly of the Whale: On his way to meet the Narnians, Caspian fights off crossbow-wielding Telmarine soldiers. Later, under the cover of night, he convinces the Narnians he is a unifier, restoring their lands despite many of them doubting him, some even wanting to kill him.

- The Road of Trials: Caspian, along with the Pevensies and the Narnians, attack the Telmarine castle but must retreat because he chooses to rescue Dr. Cornelius instead of opening the gate. Because of this, the Narnians sustain heavy losses. Caspian is tempted with black magic and later offered the opportunity to kill his uncle but refuses, thus, he passes the tests placed before him.

- The Meeting with the Goddess: Although short-lived, Caspian rescues Susan and they share a kiss.

- Woman as the Temptress: Once again enter Jadis the White Witch, Narnia's evil mother-destroyer. Caspian is induced to bring her back via black sorcery, but the Pevensies intervene in the nick of time.

- Atonement with the Father: Campbell explains, "The problem of the hero going to meet the father is to open his soul beyond terror to such a degree that he will be ripe to understand how the sickening and insane tragedies of this vast and ruthless cosmos are completely validated in the majesty of Being."[495] Caspian's ego is shattered when he learns Miraz, a father figure having life and death power, murdered his father (Miraz's brother), Caspian IX. The usurper Miraz is vanquished, and Caspian refuses Peter's offer to take his life; Caspian has made peace with his evil uncle. A defeated Miraz is then betrayed and killed by a subordinate, Sopespian.

- The Ultimate Boon: Aslan returns, Miraz and the Telmarines are defeated with Caspian enthroned as King Caspian X.

- Freedom to Live: Peter and Susan depart Narnia forever. Their adventures in the magical land over because they have outgrown it; Narnia has nothing left to offer them. Peter and Susan are masters of Narnia, for them it's time to return to their home world. For the brother and sister there is no regret of the past or fear of the future; their next moment is permitted to come to pass.

This chapter now concludes with an analysis of *The Voyage of the Dawn Treader*.

---

495 *ibid*, p. 125.

THE VOYAGE OF THE DAWN TREADER

Three Narnian years after the events of Prince Caspian, Lucy and Edmund Pevensie are staying with their priggish cousin Eustace Scrubb (Will Poulter) until the war is over. Edmund is still too young to enlist in His Majesty's Armed Forces while Lucy pines for the beauty of her older sister. In an upstairs bedroom in their cousin's home, a painting of a ship on the ocean transports Lucy, Edmund, and Eustace into a Narnian ocean.

They are rescued by Caspian, commanding the ship the Dawn Treader. He invites them on a voyage to save the seven Lords of Narnia whom his uncle Miraz banished. In the Lone Islands, where people are sold as slaves, Caspian and Edmund are captured, imprisoned, while Lucy and Eustace are sold as slaves. Caspian meets one of the lost lords, Bern (Terry Norris), revealing that the slaves are not sold but sacrificed to a mysterious green mist. The four are rescued by the Dawn Treader's crew. Bern, becoming the new governor, gives Caspian a Golden Age magical sword, one of seven (the mystical-numinous significance of this number already), given to each of the Lords by Aslan. Caspian then gives the sword to Edmund.

Their adventure continues. On another island, Lucy is abducted by the invisible Dufflepuds, forcing her to enter the manor of the magician Coriakin (Bille Brown, 1952-2013) to find a visibility spell. Coriakin encourages the crew to defeat the mist and Dark Island, from where the fog originates, by laying the Lords' seven swords at Aslan's Table on Ramandu's island, but warns them that they are about to be tested by their darkest dreams, their forbidden desires. Lucy recites a beauty incantation she found, entering a dream in which she has transformed into Susan (Lucy yearns to be like her), wherein neither Lucy nor Narnia exist. Aslan chides Lucy for her self-doubt and for questioning her self-worth, explaining her siblings only know of Narnia because of her.

On their way to Ramandu, the Dawn Treader makes a pit stop at another island. Another sword is recovered from a magical pool that turns anything it touches into gold, including one of the lost lords. Edmund is tempted by the gold, inciting him to fight Caspian until Lucy intervenes, stopping them. Meanwhile, Eustace finds and steals from a rock pit full of golden treasure. While Edmund and Caspian look for Eustace, they discover the remains of another of the lords recovering his sword. A dragon approaches but is driven away from the Dawn Treader. The dragon is Eustace, transformed by the tempting treasure by succumbing to his avarice. Reepicheep.[496] the swashbuckling mouse, befriends Eustace and is touched by the mouse's kindness. Eustace undergoes a change of heart by becoming helpful to the crew. In the meantime, Caspian gives Edmund the sword Rhindon, saying Peter would want him to have it.

The crew arrives at Aslan's Table to find three lost lords sleeping in a trance-like state. As they place the swords on the table, they realize one is still missing. A star descends from the sky, transforming into Lilliandil (Laura Brent), a beautiful woman telling them the remaining sword is on Dark Island, where they discover the last surviving Lord, Rhoop (Bruce Spence). Edmund is paralyzed by fear when a monstrous sea serpent attacks the ship. Eustace, as the dragon, fights the serpent but Rhoop wounds Eustace with the last sword, causing him to fly away with the sword impaled in his side. He encounters Aslan; the mighty lion transforms him back into a boy, removing the sword from his body, sending him to Ramandu's island with the blade. As the crew fights the serpent, the mist tries to distract Edmund by appearing as Jadis the White Witch. Eustace reaches the table and places the sword upon it, allowing the seven swords to unleash their magic bestowing Peter's sword Rhindon, wielded by Edmund, with the power to slay the sea monster, the death of which awakens the three sleeping lords, destroying the green mist and Dark Island, liberating the sacrificed slaves.

Eustace rejoins Lucy, Edmund, Caspian and Reepicheep. They sail to a mysterious shore before a massive wave. Aslan appears, telling them that his country lies beyond, although if they go there, they may never return. Caspian refuses, knowing that he has much to do as king, but Reepicheep is determined to enter, so Aslan blesses him before he paddles beyond the wave. Aslan opens a portal to send Lucy, Edmund, and Eustace home but informs Lucy and Edmund that they have grown up, and can never return to Narnia. Aslan encourages them to know him in their world by another name (a/k/a Jesus Christ, the Lion of the Tribe of Judah at Revelation 5:5) telling a reformed Eustace that he may one day return to Narnia. The three

---

496 Voiced by Eddie Izzard in Prince Caspian; voiced by Simon Pegg in *The Voyage of the Dawn Treader.*

enter the gateway swimming up to the bedroom. Eustace hears his mother announcing a visitor, Jill Pole. The three leave the room with Lucy affectionately stopping to look back at the painting which depicts the Dawn Treader sailing out of sight.

Once again, *The Voyage of the Dawn Treader* is a Christian allegory. It is through Eustace Scrubb, an insufferable brat who is quarrelsome, arrogant, greedy, and jealous which we find a Christian thematic portrayal of sin and redemption. Having landed on one of the islands, Eustace discovers a vast treasure of gold and jewels, greedily taking as much as he can carry. When he wakes, he finds that his selfishness has himself transformed him into a dragon, the outer form manifesting his inner-self. He tells his cousins he tried to change back to human but could not, a clear picture of the self-effort of man to cleanse himself of sin through works of some sort (Galatians 2:16; Romans 3:20; Philippians 3:8,9). When he is finally confronted by Aslan *qua* Jesus, it is Aslan removing the rough, scaly dragon skin with his roar and claw (by dragging it through the sand). Aslan cleanses Eustace of his sins, returning him back to normal, the whole process symbolic of the Christian repenting his (or her) sins, thus becoming a new creation in the image Christ (II Corinthians 5:17; Colossians 3:8-10). Furthermore, Aslan-Jesus slaying a great dragon conjures Revelation 12:9, "And the great dragon was cast out, that old serpent, called the Devil, and Satan...." With the dragon gone, Eustace repents his sinful ways. His transformation into a better person–a better Christian–has begun.

Through cabalistic magic, we also see Lucy question her selfhood when she yearns to be her beautiful sister. At one point, in a dream, she wills herself into Susan, making it like Lucy never existed. Lucy is overcome with the desire for the preeminence such beauty would bring her, even though her conscience is pricked. Aslan chides her, explaining how important she is to Narnia's mythology, to simply be herself and not give in to envy. Here, Aslan is the Holy Spirit indwelling, sanctifying, (Romans 8:9-11), convicting sin, reminding believers not to let it rule their lives (Romans 6:1-22; Colossians 3:5), allowing their Christian faith to sustain them.

Just like the previous Narnia movies, *The Voyage of the Dawn Treader* features elements of the hero's journey.

- The Call to Adventure: Edmund, Lucy, and Eustace are whisked away to Narnia by a magic painting. They join Caspian in his search for seven missing Telmarine lords.

- Refusal of the Call: Eustace wants nothing to do with Narnia or Caspian's quest. He wants to go home to England. However, Eustace changes (or repents) his ways by the end of the story, willing to return to Narnia when Aslan beckons him.

- Supernatural Aid: A graybeard, Lord Bern, gives Caspian a mystical sword. The sword is then presented to Edmund who restores its luster. The sword is critical to completing the mission.

- The Crossing of the First Threshold: Lord Bern and Coriakin–threshold guardians–inform Caspian and crew of an evil mist that must be stopped. The mysterious mist comes from the east and is linked to the seven missing lords.

- The Belly of the Whale: Caspian, Edmund, Lucy, and Eustace are captured by slave traders. Lucy and Eustace are auctioned off while Caspian and Edmund are held prisoner. Later, Lucy must enter a magician's mansion to locate and recite a spell.

- The Road of Trials: A greedy Eustace is changed into a dragon because he gave into temptation. Although he tries, he is unable to change back. Edmund is likewise tempted with gold and the prospect of the power that comes with it while Lucy has grown envious of her sister's beauty and grace. Caspian faces doubts about his leadership from the spirit of his father. Edmund must defeat a sea serpent of his conjuring while being tempted by the ghost of the White Witch. These are their darkest dreams which they must face and overcome.

- Woman as the Temptress: Once again, Edmund is beguiled by the White Witch's power, while Lucy is tempted by her sister's elegance, causing her to question her selfhood. In *The Voyage of the Dawn Treader*, Woman as the Temptress is linked to the Road of Trials.

- Atonement with the Father: Caspian makes peace with his father by not entering Aslan's realm. He knows there is still much to do in Narnia; by not entering, he will carry on his father's kingly legacy.

- The Ultimate Boon: The seven swords are placed upon Aslan's Table, putting an end to the mist and the evil power of Dark Island. The people sacrificed to the green mist are freed.

- Rescue from Without: After being turned into a dragon, Eustace is restored to his usual self by Aslan but is spiritually changed forever; the adventure has both humbled and uplifted him. He now cherishes his cousins Edmund and Lucy, helping him understand his ordeal. Upon returning home, Eustace explains, "We spoke often of Narnia in the days that followed. When my cousins left after the war ended, I missed them with all my heart, as I know all Narnians will miss them 'til the end of time."

- Freedom to Live: Edmund and Lucy depart Narnia forever. Their adventures in the magical land over because they have outgrown it; Narnia has nothing left to offer them. Consequently, Edmund and Lucy, like Peter and Susan before them, are now masters of Narnia, for them it is time to put away childish things (I Corinthians 13:11) to resume life in their home world.

In *The Hero with a Thousand Faces* Campbell explains, "Whether the hero be ridiculous or sublime, Greek or barbarian, gentile or Jew, his journey varies little in essential plan. Popular tales represent the heroic action as physical; the higher religions show the deed to be moral; nevertheless, there will be found astonishingly little variation in the morphology of the adventure, the roles involved, the victories gained."[497] Campbell's sentiment rings true regarding the *Star Wars* films, *The Matrix* trilogy, the Harry Potter movies, *Lord of the Rings*, and the *Chronicles of Narnia*. They all present the monomyth under different guise: the character names have been changed; the plots slightly altered but the monomyth remains the same. This cinematic evidence is proof of the power of mythology, the archetypes, and esoteric imagery. Thus, the monomyth is part of all of us dwelling in our collective unconscious; we all know it and are drawn to it when we see it. The monomyth has always been part of our soul because it is a fundamental component of our psyche and always will be.

---

497 Campbell, *The Hero with a Thousand Faces*, p. 30.

CHAPTER XI

WHITE AND BLACK SWANS: AUTOEROTICISM, ARTISTIC KINK, SEX, FETISHES, METAMORPHOSIS, AND DISCORDIANISM IN FILM

"♫ Walls so thin I can almost hear them breathing. And if I listen in I feel my own heart beating …I guess it's just a feeling. ♫"
– Eurythmics, lyrics from the song "This City Never Sleeps", 1983.

"Personally speaking, I can't wait to watch life tear you apart."
– Evelyn Stoker, *Stoker*, 2013.

"I'd have to be pretty stupid to write a book about killing and then kill him the way I described in my book.
I'd be announcing myself as the killer. I'm not stupid."
– Catherine Tramell, *Basic Instinct*, 1992.

"You've tasted your dream. Touched it! Only to have it crushed! Your heart is broken. Wounded! Your life force fading! The blood drips! The Black Swan stole your love! There is only one way to end the pain! You're not fearful, but filled with acceptance!"
– Thomas Leroy, *Black Swan*, 2010.

"Is this your duck?"
– Elizabeth McGraw, *9 ½ Weeks*, 1986.

"Death to Videodrome! Long live the new flesh!"
– Max Renn, *Videodrome*, 1983.

"Doors to the pleasures of Heaven or Hell, I didn't care which. I thought I'd gone to the limits; I hadn't. The Cenobites gave me an experience beyond the limits. Pain and pleasure, indivisible."
– Frank Cotton, *Hellraiser*, 1987.

The first part of this chapter deals with alchemical transitions in sexually charged films. These movies are stylistically noir, dark and erotic. *9 ½ Weeks* is a cinematic study in fetish exploration comingled with artistic masturbation; it is all about the pleasurable sensations that certain fabrics give to the flesh. The female protagonist, Elizabeth McGraw, delights in wearing stockings, especially black ones–likely silk, perhaps nylon–because they are her *nigredo*: the forbidden pleasures that her ego has suppressed for way too long. Black silk stockings feel fabulous against her sybaritic flesh; for Elizabeth, wearing them awakens her shadow self, alchemically freeing her to masturbate in public, submitting to John's mercurial sex games. Black stockings are Elizabeth's all-consuming fetish; they are her erotic talismans; her masturbation is akin to tantric ritualistic sex magicks. When it comes to fetish exploration, perhaps Elizabeth should've heeded Lugosi's cryptic warning in *Glen or Glenda* to, "Beware, beware. Beware of the Big Green Dragon that sits on your doorstep…" Instead,

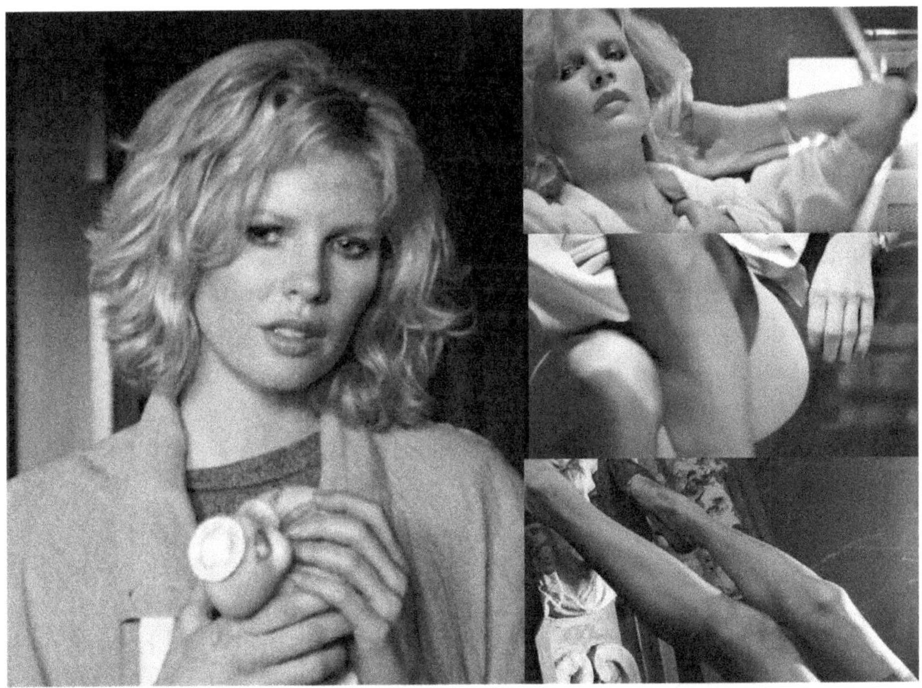

Erotic foreshadowing in *9 ½ Weeks*. (Left) Elizabeth finds an out-of-place toy rubber duck in the kitchen of one of John's friends while on a date with him. (Right, Top to Bottom) *Rubber duck* is urban slang for masturbation, making the toy a sexual talisman, anticipating Elizabeth's amorous solo flight in the basement of the art gallery.

Elizabeth succumbs to her fetish, her Big Green Dragon, by flaunting garter belts and stockings resulting in public masturbation. Onanism satisfies her pompous hedonism, while also cathartically releasing her shadow, but little does she realize her stockings will turn against her in the Chelsea Hotel. She also engages John's peculiar sex games which are just that, a *game*, which she finally comes to understand but by then it's too late. Elizabeth's alchemy is purely psychological: in trying to integrate her dark erotic side with her pure, constrictive ego, her transition consumes her, causing emotional destruction.

In *Black Swan*, the alchemical development is not only emotional with Nina transitioning from shy, melancholy virgin to a confident extrovert, from timid dancer to graceful ballerina, but her metamorphosis is also physical: she transmutes into a Black Swan-like creature. In other words, *Black Swan* is refined cinematic alchemy: the successful transformation from one thing into something else, something the character was not at the beginning of the film. To perfect this alchemy, Nina pushes the boundaries of her sexuality which, for her, is the fusion of masochism with masturbation. *Passion* is about alchemically becoming your enemy to destroy them—to transition into something that you are consciously repulsed by to get revenge. But for the two females of *Passion*—Isabelle and Christine—it is the realization that they may have been capable of nihilistic vengeful destruction the entire time. Both women's rebellious tendencies are a welcomed embrace, a liberating release from the depths of their suffocating egos.

The second part of this chapter analyzes a symbolic masterpiece, *Stoker*, which has nothing to do with *Dracula* (1897) or its author Bram Stoker (1847-1912). Rather it is about the gloomy alchemical transformation from defiant melancholy teenager to murderous psychopath. But the movie betrays its alchemical symbolism by symbolically presenting an epistemological conundrum, suggesting the metamorphosis was predestined, inevitable. *Stoker* also references Kubrick's *The Shining* and Hitchcock's *Psycho* (1960) in the most subtle of ways.

The third and final portion of this chapter details the role of Discordia in film. The thread that binds these three sections is the idea that the blackness of the soul, the luminous *sol niger*, the shadow, the *nigredo*, must be cultivated to maintain strength on the threshold between oppositions. All the female protagonists in these films are trying, consciously or subconsciously, to nourish this darkness or, alternatively, have already been consumed by it and are releasing into the world. For these women, this darkness seems to live in a state existing between apparent evil and illusionary good; it is a tragic splinter in their psyches that they cannot reconcile or integrate no matter how hard they try. The darkness pervades their very souls.

BLACK STOCKINGS, BLACK FEATHERS, AND MEDUSA: ALCHEMICAL TRANSITIONS IN 9 ½ WEEKS, BLACK SWAN, AND PASSION

Director Adrian Lyne successfully experiments with alchemical metamorphosis in the 1986 erotic drama, *9 ½ Weeks*. The movie is rich with color, and some of these colors are used by the filmmakers to signify Renaissance alchemy. Exoterically, the story is about a woman, Elizabeth McGraw, the assistant of a SoHo art gallery, who gets involved in an impersonal affair with a mysterious man, John Gray, descending into an erotic world which both excites and frightens her. Elizabeth barely knows anything about his life, she only knows about the sex games they play, and their relationship turns dark and complex degenerating into a destructive matrix. The film takes place in New York City–the city that never sleeps–a metropolis filled with shadows which reflect the secret desires of its lofty inhabitants. Passion thrives in this shadowy world; the film esoterically documents the alchemical transmutation of Elizabeth into her dark Jungian shadow–a reflection of her mysterious lover John–which she desperately wishes to embody or, at the very least, reconcile with her ego. She fails to achieve her dark, sexual transformation, suffering a nervous breakdown as a result of her attempted psychological transition.

Based on the novel of the same name, *9 ½ Weeks* refers to the duration of a relationship between Wall Street arbitrageur John Gray and divorced art gallery–Spring Street Gallery–employee Elizabeth McGraw. John, anticipating Christian Grey in E.L. James' *Fifty Shades of Grey* (2011), initiates and controls the various experimental sexual practices of this volatile relationship to expand Elizabeth's boundaries. Elizabeth first

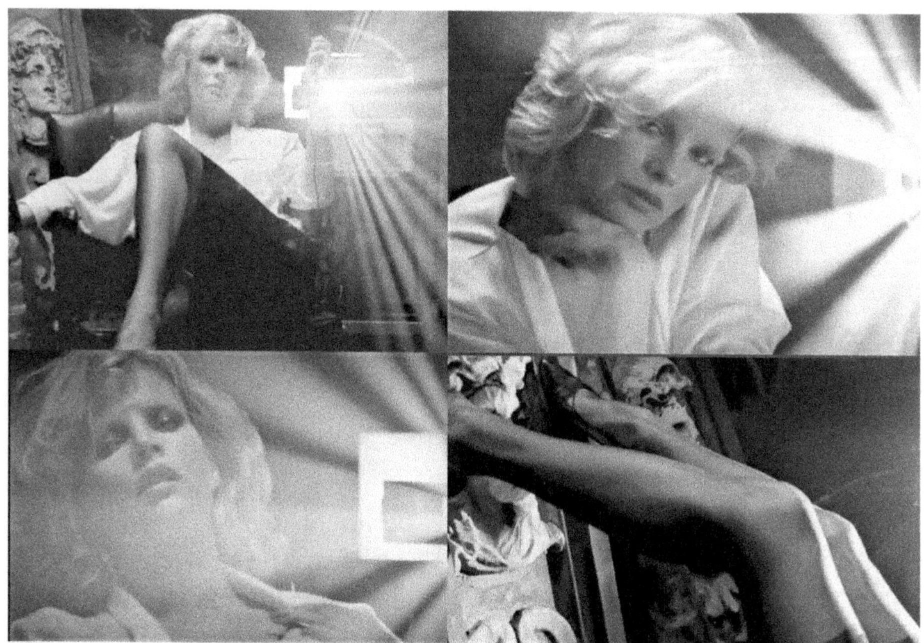

(Top Left) *The Great Masturbator* lives; the exaltation of the flesh is the exploration of a fetish. Basking in dark Luciferian light (sol niger), Elizabeth narcissistically teases her black silk stockings, symbolizing her lustful desires. By flaunting her stockings, Elizabeth seeks to emulate the decadent SoHo art scene. (Top Right) Elizabeth's dark fantasy begins: the slideshow hypnotizing her flashes paintings of women touching themselves and weird, spellbinding creatures, triggering Elizabeth's arousal. (Bottom Left) Elizabeth's sable imagination becomes reality: unable to resist her shadow self, she cups her breast commencing public masturbation thereby destroying her conscious ego. (Bottom Right) Elizabeth's fetish for black silk stocking conquers her flesh: her sultry black stockings, straps, and garter belt release her shadow, allowing her to feel passionate autoerotic felicity; they are the source of her gratification. Excitedly hoisting her legs into the air, her stockings and lingerie inaugurate Elizabeth into a pleasure dome of her own erotic creation. She has successfully performed alchemy: as strangers pass by overhead, Elizabeth puts herself on full display by becoming a sensual piece of performance art for all to observe; like snobbish art critics, voyeuristic New Yorkers are free to criticize or praise the masturbator's exquisite caresses.

sees John in New York City's Chinatown as she grocery shops with her co-worker friend Molly (Margaret Whitton, 1950-2016), then again at a street market in Greenwich Village where she decides against buying an intricately patterned French scarf priced beyond what she is willing to pay. John wins her heart when he eventually produces that scarf, wrapping it around her lovingly. They start dating with Elizabeth increasingly subjected to John's behavioral peculiarities; he blindfolds her, at first reluctant to comply with his sexual fantasy demands. Yet she sees him as loving and playful, seduced by his lavish spending patterns; he gives her an expensive golden solar-esque watch, instructing her to think about him at 12:00 p.m.

Elizabeth decides to take this imperative even further by masturbating in public in the art gallery's basement to demonic-erotic artwork; more on this alchemical-erotica later. John also masterminds an extended sensual food play sequence. However, he ultimately confuses Elizabeth by communicating his reluctance to meet her friends, despite the intimacy of their sexual relations.

Elizabeth's bewilderment and overall angst about John increases when he leaves her alone at his apartment. She examines the individual compartments of his unusually well-organized closet till she discovers a photograph of him with another woman. John calls her from a payphone booth and asks her if she went through his belongings, declaring that he will punish her if he hears that she has done so. Their ensuing altercation escalates into sexual assault until she concedes to his violent struggle to overpower her. Their erotic intensity increases as they start having sex in public places, mirroring Elizabeth's earlier public masturbation session. Elizabeth's heightened need for psychosexual stimulation drives her to stalk John to his office at the New York Stock Exchange and to obey his injunction to cross-dress herself in a men's tuxedo for a rendezvous at an upscale restaurant. On leaving the establishment, two men mistake them for a gay couple and shout "Faggot!" from their vehicle. A fight ensues, and Elizabeth picks up a knife that one of their assailants has dropped, stabbing one of them in the buttocks causing the attackers to flee. Elizabeth and John have sex onsite with intense, visceral passion. After this incident, John's sexual games acquire sadomasochistic elements: he buys a horse whip which Elizabeth uses in an extended striptease sequence for John's voyeuristic pleasure.

John's mind-bending sex games do not satisfy or empower Elizabeth; instead, they only intensify her emotional vulnerability. For example, when she sees her ex-husband on her art gallery, her ambivalence about him makes her exceptionally receptive to a message from John on her answering machine telling her to meet him at a hotel room. In the hotel, John blindfolds her then a Hispanic prostitute (Cintia Cruz) unexpectedly enters. She starts caressing Elizabeth's legs removing her black stockings, telling her in Spanish to relax while John watches them. The prostitute then removes Elizabeth's blindfold and starts working on John to see how Elizabeth will react; John wishes to see if Elizabeth is a voyeur in the hopes that the erotic spectacle will coax her into masturbating. However,

Elizabeth violently interrupts the sexual horseplay and flees the hotel while John pursues her down the steps and out into the street. They run till they find themselves in an adult entertainment venue. He spots her in a crowd of men watching a pornographic show including a man and a woman having sex on an altar. She sees John and starts kissing a random man in the crowd. Moments later, John and Elizabeth gravitate towards each other, finding themselves interlocked in each other's seemingly inescapable embrace. Then, tense and suffering from anxiety and depression, Elizabeth attends the Spring Street Gallery's opening night gala featuring the artwork of the eccentric Mr. Farnsworth (Dwight Weist, 1910-1991).

Elizabeth spends the night at John's apartment and the following morning, John senses that he will never see her again. He volubly attempts to share with her details about his life: he tells her he has five brothers, that his father worked in a foundry, and his mother who used to be a check-out girl at a grocery store. Elizabeth tells him that it is too late as she leaves the apartment. John begins counting to fifty, hoping she will come back by the time he is finished, but he never gets past number one because he knows she is not returning. Elizabeth leaves, tearfully walking the New York streets; the screen fades to black and the credits roll.

* * * *

To briefly reiterate, Alchemy is the medieval attempt to achieve material transmutation combined with a quest to reach spiritual perfection. During the Renaissance, alchemists became less concerned with occult philosophy and more interested in the search for gold. Salt, sulfur, and mercury are the great symbols of the alchemist, while there are four symbolic colors associated with the Magnum Opus or creation of the philosopher's stone: *nigredo* is blackening or melanosis, *albedo* is whitening or leucosis, *citrinitas* is yellowing or xanthosis, *rubedo* is reddening or iosis. *Rubedo*, the color red, symbolizes finalization of the alchemical process; regarding the Jungian archetype, *rubedo* would represent the self-archetype, and would be the culmination of the four stages, the merging of shadow, ego, and self. The self represents wholeness, integration, a point in which a person discovers their true nature, Jung's individuation. More than a mere mention of alchemy within the story, James Joyce's (1882-1941) *Finnegans Wake* (1939) follows the process of transmutation, weaving their entire narrative with alchemical symbolism. *Albedo*, *nigredo*, *citrinitas*, and *rubedo* denote transition and change; *9 ½ Weeks*, *Black Swan*, and *Passion* are alchemical films which esoterically employ this Renaissance color scheme.

The female protagonist, Elizabeth, yearns to awaken her Jungian shadow by playing erotic games, by sexual experimentation; it is a journey of self-discovery because she wishes to push the boundaries of her self-imposed banal status quo. In other words, she wants to alchemically effectuate selfhood by unifying her dark erotic self, the alchemical *nigredo*, with her ego. The film's use of *nigredo*, that of the *Unio Naturalis*, is an objective state, visible from the outside only (and is) an unconscious state of non-differentiation between self and object, consciousness and the unconscious; it is personified by the character of John who is both light (cf. the sun) and shadow (cf. *nigredo*, *sol niger*), existing simultaneously. However, and more importantly, the second *nigredo* is a subjectively experienced process brought about by the subject's painful and growing awareness of their shadow aspects, clearly visible in this motion picture. As Elizabeth starts to unleash her shadow, she experiences heightened sexual pleasure but not without consequence: she begins to collapse psychologically suffering from anxiety, tension, depression, and by movie's conclusion, total emotional meltdown. To effect this change, Elizabeth wears darker clothing and lingerie, symbolizing

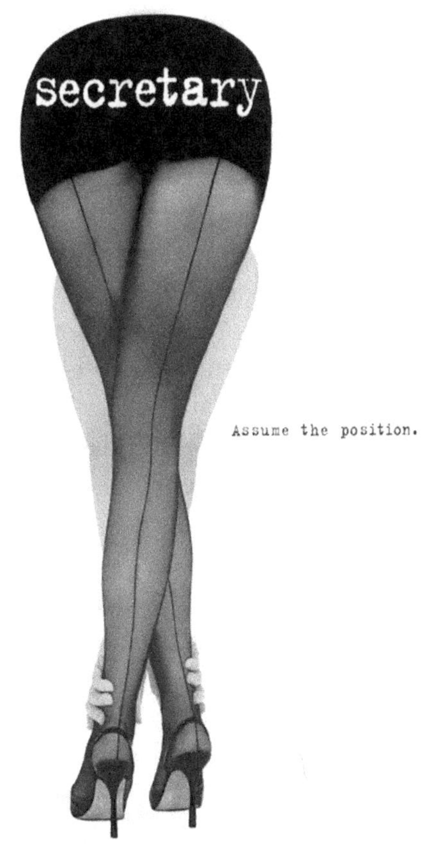

Teaser poster for 2002's *Secretary* features the emotionally disturbed Lee Holloway (Maggie Gyllenhaal) wearing blacked seamed hosiery. For poor Lee, this is a contradiction, identifying her as a Lilith-like femme fatale when, in reality, she is a craven submissive, reduced to masturbating in a toilet stall.

her transformation; Elizabeth's black stockings signify her shadow and the wanton cravings that she desperately desires to explore and experience. Elizabeth's repressed yearnings are the profound wisdom of the *nigre-do*; it is the sullen light of the Left-Hand Path that she walks upon: for Elizabeth to know herself, she must acknowledge her own darkness and black magic-like sexual desires.[498] She must learn to adore the Goat of Mendes, to worship at his black altar, supplicating for his favor. This sexual predicament torments *Black Swan's* Nina as well. Dark sensuality and erotic experiments excite and repel both Elizabeth and Nina, making both women embodiments of a conflict they cannot resolve. Neither woman can reconcile their egos with their Lilith-like shadow selves regardless of how much they masturbate, how much they pervert themselves.

Alchemy pervades the film's opening credits, displaying the film's title *Nine & ½ Weeks*, in red against black, *rubedo* against *nigredo*.[499] In the context of the story, this represents Elizabeth's desires to incorporate sexual darkness; she will be complete when her shadow is allowed to emerge from her unconsciousness, integrate with her ego, enabling it to flourish. For Elizabeth, the *rubedo* is the liberation of her dark sexual desires, to recognize them, and to reconcile her shadow with her ego; the *nigredo* is Elizabeth's *rubedo*; her daemon, or soul, is her eidolon, or masturbation. Elizabeth's perfected alchemy is not only to integrate her shadow but to allow it devour her ego. To convey this alchemy, the color red appears sporadically, but well placed throughout the film. For instance, one will immediately see that Elizabeth wearing a red sweater, symbolizing alchemical change and finality. She wears this sweater again in the art gallery while trying to sell a painting.

One will observe that Elizabeth is in often surrounded by water, including her own moisture because she sweats profusely when sexually aroused, indicating that she cannot control her shadow. Water is a symbol of change evoking baptism when one is born again. For Elizabeth, water is a metaphor for her attempt to successfully change into her darker self, to become a shadowy reflection of her mercurial lover, John. Paralleling the pervasive water, Elizabeth appears three times with fish, symbolizing

---

498 cf. Wilson's *Secret Cinema*, pp. 121-122.
499 See also Lyne's 1990 film *Jacob's Ladder* which uses this same alchemical schema during its opening sequence implying transition of the self.

her forthcoming mental and emotional meltdown. Elizabeth will esoterically come to personify elements of the Greco-Roman goddesses Venus, or Aphrodite, and fishes were sacred to her worship.[500] Observe the fish when Elizabeth, along with her friend Molly, stroll through Chinatown, entering a grocery store. Manly Hall writes, "the fish has been used as an emblem of damnation; but among the Chinese is typified contentment and good fortune, and fishes appear on many of their coins."[501] In this context, the fish's symbolism is duplicitous. It is a symbol of good fortune because Chinatown is where she first encounters John. But the fish is a herald of Elizabeth's emotional erosion which, ironically, is caused by John. A fish next appears held by the artist Farnsworth when Elizabeth speaks to the eccentric painter; the fish is out of water, indicating Elizabeth's exploration of her shadowy sexual desires is misplaced and that she, like the fish, is truly out of her league when it comes to John's erotic sex games. Finally, a picked-apart fish appears at the art gallery's exhibition party representing Elizabeth's own failed erotic transformation and resulting anxiety, and that she, like the fish, is emotionally shredded.

John, who always wears black clothes (cf. Saturn, aloof satirical loneliness), is not only the alchemical *nigredo* that Elizabeth seeks to alchemically and erotically perfect but is also the masculine solar *citrinitas*. Personifying a saturnine black sun, John projects dark light in the form of phantasmagoric sexual delights upon Elizabeth's mundane persona. She always wears soft whites, tans, pinks, and grays when she is with her friends but, as she becomes more involved with John, black outfits and lingerie emerge from her closet. Elizabeth herself is the natural embodiment of the alchemical *albedo*–the feminine moon–reflecting the light, or in this case absorbs the black light of John by willingly engaging in his sex games. Personifying the moon, Elizabeth flirts with the goddess Artemis (comparatively Diana), the grand protectress of virgins and inexperienced young women. Elizabeth's wholesome nature is not only symbolized by her soft white clothing, but in her prudish attitudes towards sex. Elizabeth is at first repulsed when her friend Molly implies that Elizabeth masturbates; Molly describes Elizabeth as a, "Divorced white female. Beautiful statuesque blonde. Witty, cultured, owns own vibrator." However, Elizabeth

---

500 Hall, *The Secret Teachings of All Ages*, p. 262.
501 *ibid*, p. 264.

shows herself to be a hypocrite when she takes the sensual pleasures of masturbation to new heights, beginning her journey to liberate her shadow self, symbolized by wearing black–not white–lingerie, specifically black stockings. Elizabeth symbolically transmutes herself from a white, lunar goddess to the goddesses of beauty and delight, Aphrodite (cf. Lucifer) and Hēdonē, when she masturbates in public, becoming a surrealistic-libidinous piece of performance art for all of New York City to observe.

Renaissance-alchemical color symbolism pervades a scene in which Elizabeth supervises artwork being displayed in the Spring Street Gallery. Elizabeth, wearing light colors and white stockings (cf. *albedo*) foreshadows her attempted transition from light angel to dark vixen. Elizabeth instructs gallery employee Harvey (David Margulies, 1937-2016) to hang artwork telling him to arrange it, "We should go black, black, red, red. That's it. From this end to that end. Black, black, red, red, black, black." This alchemical arrangement denotes that, for Elizabeth, the *nigredo* is the finality of the *rubedo*; put another way, sexual darkness is Elizabeth's Magnum Opus–there is no middle ground. Elizabeth also corrects Harvey when he mistakes a chastity belt for a dog collar signifying Elizabeth's sexual awakening which John, the solar *citrintas*, can spark within her. Elizabeth now removes her symbolic chastity belt by shedding her sexual conformities when she discovers the pleasures that accompany the provocative act of masturbating in public. For the first time, Elizabeth goes beyond the limits, unleashing her Jungian shadow by reveling in autoeroticism in the art gallery's basement. If only momentarily and symbolically, Elizabeth is a neo-pagan beauty goddess transforming the posh art gallery into a temple of masturbation with herself as the sole object of veneration with voyeuristic New Yorkers as her worshipers.

John gifts Elizabeth a golden *solar* watch with the instructions that each day, at 12:00 pm (high noon), she thinks about him touching her. The gold watch symbolically identifies John as the *citrinitas*: the watch is a gold representing the sun and the time of noon implies the sun at meridian when it is at full strength. As such, John is Elizabeth's solar enabler (cf. Lucifer because *he brings the light*) seeking to ignite a dark sexual awakening in her by supplying her with the erotic tools, the light of the *sol niger*, or the philosopher's stone necessary to affect this shadowy-alchemical change. John anticipates *Black Swan's* Luciferian light bearer, Thomas Leroy, desiring to change Nina alchemically from shy virginal ballerina to a dark, alluring seductress by encouraging sexual activity. John's apartment is stark black and white symbolizing Manichean cosmology, dualism, light against darkness, ego versus shadow self, anticipating Leroy's stark black and white office and apartment. The gold watch is gift-wrapped in red paper, identifying Elizabeth's *rubedo*: her sensual, lustful, carnal desires starting to rise to the surface. As Elizabeth's shadow now begins to manifest like a seductive banshee, she exhibits her intense, dark sexuality by exploring her fetish which, for her, is wearing black gartered silk stockings. Her stockings her sexual desire; put another way, her lust is linked to a particular object or item of clothing. Elizabeth's black stocking and sexy lingerie not only symbolize her dark sexual fantasies, but they are also the source of her incredible pleasure. They are her passport to the *nigredo*, allowing her entry into the weird sexual world of John. During her masturbation session, Lyne emphasizes that her stockings are her rapturous fetish because the camera seldom leaves them, framing her legs constantly as she pleasures herself. They are also her alchemical Mercury, allowing her to succumb to her Left-Hand Path erotic impulses, liberating her shadow self. But there is a consequence: Elizabeth's stockings are also her alchemical trickster or juggler; she believes that wearing garter belts, stockings, enticing black high heels, and lingerie that she will become a femme fatale, a dark vixen, Odile, the Black Swan. Darkness is what she desires but cannot achieve because her black lingerie–a false philosopher's stone–does not dovetail with her virginal personality; the emergence of Elizabeth's Jungian shadow destroys her emotionally because her ego cannot fathom the ascendancy of her dark sexuality.[502] For Elizabeth, they are two sides of her personality which are irreconcilable. In other words, by wearing black lingerie, hosiery, and engaging John's sexual liaisons and enticements, Elizabeth makes her shadow conscious but turns her reality into a living nightmare.[503]

---

502 cf. Mercury as the Juggler/Magician trickster or huckster archetype; see Nichol's *Jung and Tarot*, Chapter IV, pp. 45-69, *passim*.

503 *ibid*, p. 69. Elizabeth's black lingerie is her fetish and a source of pleasure. Her dark clothing, lingerie, and stockings seduce yet trick Elizabeth, resulting in psychological breakdown of the self. When Elizabeth McGraw wears her black garter belt and black stockings, Elizabeth masturbates. This symbolism is reflected in another 1986 movie, *Head Office*. An manipulative corporate vixen

As voyeuristic New Yorkers walk over the circular apertures in the ceiling of the basement of the Spring Street Art gallery while sculpted faces look on, a seated Elizabeth views a slideshow of surrealistic paintings some of which feature demons and incubi. To escape her doldrums, Elizabeth masturbates in public not private; the people passing overhead are symbolized by the first painting she observes which a woman fondling herself before giant eyeballs; the woman represents Elizabeth, and the eyes are

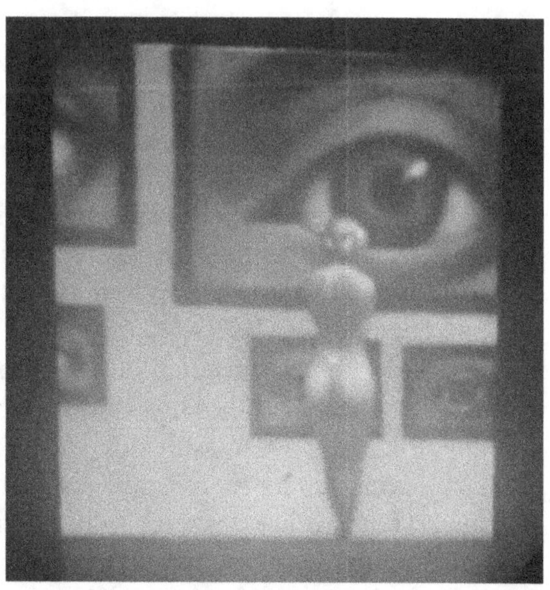

One of the paintings in Elizabeth's slideshow is a naked woman standing before a symphony of overzealous eyes, symbolizing that Elizabeth's autoeroticism is on public exhibition. Elizabeth is about to transmute into an erotic piece of performance art for all of SoHo to critique.

those of the bystanders strolling above her. Although the time on her golden *solar* watch is 7:50 a.m. or p.m. (which can be observed on the blu-ray edition), it is implied that it's noon, and she is fantasying about her lover. Regarding alchemy, the gold watch is a solar emblem, representing the alchemical *citrinitas*, referencing Crowley's *Lesser Work of Sol* (the sun) which expanded on the O.T.O.'s sex magick techniques to include magical masturbation in their eighth degree (VIII°).[504] Elizabeth uses masturbation as a vehicle to effect pleasurable, Left-Hand Path alchemy–in her case psychological change–to: 1) become a controversial

---

Jane Caldwell (Jane Seymour) wears black stockings symbolizing her dark side and nebulous sexual behavior. Like Elizabeth, Caldwell masturbates at work while wearing black stockings. Near the film's conclusion, Rachael Helmes (Lori-Nan Engler) and Jack Issel (Judge Reinhold) enter Caldwell's executive office unexpectedly interrupting her masturbation session. Caldwell legs and black stockings are briefly seen as she says "Oh, god" out of embarrassment. Echoing Jungian synchronicity, *Head Office* was released on January 3rd, 1986 approximately six weeks before *9 ½ Weeks* which was released on February 21st, 1986.

504 To reiterate, *Magick* spelled with a "k" distinguishes techniques designed to formulate mystical results as opposed to legerdemain or sleight of hand. See Crowley's *Magick*, already cited.

piece of performance artwork, 2) to perfect mystical autoeroticism, and 3) to unleash her Jungian shadow which, for her, is the exploration of her nebulous carnal cravings and fantasies. To signify the former, that Elizabeth has transcended womanhood by becoming living- breathing feminine masturbatory artwork, all the symbolic colors of alchemy are present during her transformative masturbation session. The *nigredo* is Elizabeth's smoky eyes, her pencil skirt, her black high heels, and luxurious black stockings; the *citrintitas* is the light of the projector; the *albedo* is her white blouse and luminescent skin; and the *rubedo* is her red lipstick and nail polish. Elizabeth is a masturbatory philosopher's stone. Her flesh is a temple of masturbation; on its beautiful altar are her black silk stockings because they're the source of her unfettered rapture; her stockings allow her to become an *alchemical masturbator*. Comparatively, Elizabeth's alchemical onanism anticipates Nina Sayers' use of masturbation in *Black Swan*. Nina employs self-gratification as chaos magick to transmute herself into a grotesque yet confident and graceful bird-like creature.

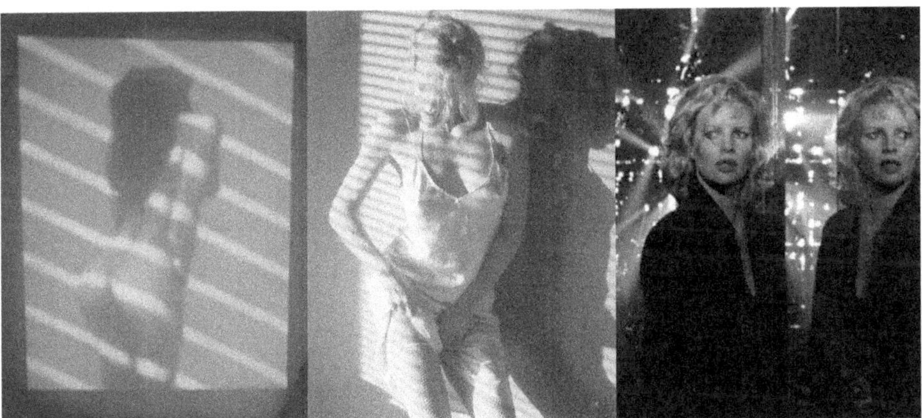

(Left) Elizabeth imitates art: another image in Elizabeth's slideshow is a painting of a nude woman masturbating. The image mesmerizes Elizabeth; the amatory artwork entices her to become one with the painting, to masturbate as well. (Center) The painting, with its white diagonal lines, is also a repetitive device foreshadowing Elizabeth's venetian blinds strip tease later in the film. When Elizabeth dances, light cuts through the blinds resembling the painting. The strip teases' lighting imitates the slideshow projector's powerful light recalling Elizabeth's masturbation and, simultaneously, transforming Elizabeth's naughty dance number into a form of self-gratification. (Right) Parallel lighting can also be seen near the movie's end, when a sexual frustrated and emotionally distraught Elizabeth enters the porn house; the light peers through apertures behind her recalling the slide projector's singular light. This signifies that Elizabeth's pleasurable, public solo flight in the art gallery is now a source of angst and shame; her mirrored reflection symbolizes her Jungian shadow only now her dark sexuality has now turned against her.

Descending into the *nigredo*, a shadowy subterranean basement *qua* theater, Elizabeth views images of demonic, hypnagogic art which includes another painting of a woman pleasuring herself which, of course, mirrors Elizabeth's passions. Elizabeth, wearing black stockings signifying her libidinous desires, becomes aroused by the mysterious artwork she watches. In *Cinema Symbolism*, this author opined that Elizabeth is becoming, allegorically, Salvador Dalí's *Great Masturbator* oil painting. Since Elizabeth's is stimulated by artwork depicting the pleasures of the flesh, she is symbolically entering Hieronymus Bosch's (ca. 1450s-1516) triptych painting *The Garden of Earthly Delights*. Its erotic center panel is a playground of corruption and temptation, suggesting alchemical change of a spiritual and psychological nature. Bosch's sensual painting parallels the artwork that Elizabeth views in the art gallery's misty cellar, transforming it into her personal plea-sure dome, a masturbatory Xanadu. The slide projector that flashes the artwork is itself a metaphor signifying Jungian psychoanalysis; Jung wrote, "Projections ...lead to an autoerotic or autistic condition in which one dreams a world whose reality remains forever unattain-able."[505] Metaphorically, Elizabeth projects her shadow personality into the surreal artwork which, as she will soon discover, is unattainable. At the same time, the slide projector introjects erotic fantasy images into Elizabeth's unconsciousness which stimulates her libido, prompt-ing Elizabeth's mystical-alchemical masturbation session. Elizabeth's masturbatory artwork is an outer reality mirroring her inner reality which, for her, is her repressed dark side that she now unchains to know herself.[506] Some of the artwork she views are of incubi which are male demons which, in mythology, have sexual intercourse with sleeping women; one could argue that Elizabeth is subconsciously fantasying about having sex with demons as she pleasures herself–her darkest fan-tasies no longer dormant–now satisfied though public masturbation. In turn, the concept of a woman's shadow self being represented by black lingerie and clothing comes straight out of the cinematic world of Alfred Hitchcock. In 1960's *Psycho*, Marion Crane (Janet Leigh, 1927-2004) wears black lingerie only after stealing her boss' money (denoting her

---

505 C.J. Jung, *The Essential Jung*, p. 92.
506 cf. Nichols' *Jung and Tarot*, p. 9.

guilt); her lingerie is white beforehand (denoting her innocence). In 1954's *Dial M for Murder,* Margot Mary Wendice (Grace Kelly, 1929-1982) outfits start out bright and lively, but become darker as the plot thickens. Using Hitchcock's *Psycho* as a template, the A&E television series *Bates Motel* (2013-2017) evokes this Hitchcockian color symbolism in the season three episode "The Deal," which aired on April 6th, 2015. Here, the vengeful mother archetype (cf. the goddess Nemesis), Norma Bates (Vera Farmiga), conspicuously wears black stockings (or pantyhose) signifying her [507]shadow when negotiating a Faustian Pact with Arcanum Club president Bob Paris (Kevin Rahm), to secure her hotel's survival at the expense of two murdered prostitutes. Famous pin-up model Betty Paige (1923-2008) also employed dark lingerie and leather in her numerous photo-shoots, representing the exaltation of her Jungian shadow while simultaneously promoting the evolution of the dominatrix archetype in a period–Eisenhower's saccharine America of the 1950s–when such ideas and imagery were considered taboo.

Elizabeth now achieves a new aesthetic. Fidgeting, squirming, crossing and uncrossing her legs–her black stockings fused with surreal art-work–Elizabeth is seduced, exchanging her flesh for masturbatory fantasy. One will notice that Elizabeth rejects a bra and pantyhose, instead wearing a black garter belt, straps, and stockings which allow easier access to her erogenous zones, her cathartic shadow now alive and thriving.[508] Fondling her breast, she sees a painting with a visible crack down the center, anticipating her blemished psychological state and forthcoming nervous breakdown. Unable to resist the forbidden black-light of the Left-Hand Path, Elizabeth performs ritualistic tantric masturbatory sex magick: doused in sweat, Elizabeth explores the mysteries of the flesh by ritualistically making love to herself.[509] As she executes her solitary

---

507 Prior to the meeting with Paris, Norma's black stockings are implanted in the viewer's subconscious. This is done by Sheriff Romero (Nestor Carbonell) who just can't take one more moment of nervous Norma tapping her foot pedantically making her hosiery whisper and/or the couch squeak.

508 "Stockings, garters, and skirts with enough leeway in length give you [the woman] the very magical tools to work with in bewitching through the Law of the Forbidden." – Anton LaVey, *The Compleat Witch*, p. 165.

509 cf. Billy Idol's "Flesh for Fantasy" (1984) song lyrics, "Ain't it strange what we do to feel alright? …Are you feeling alright, oh yeah. Turn on the light, babe, are you someone else tonight? (emphasis added)." 9 ½ Weeks anticipates Pinhead and the Cenobites of *Hellbound: Hellraiser II*

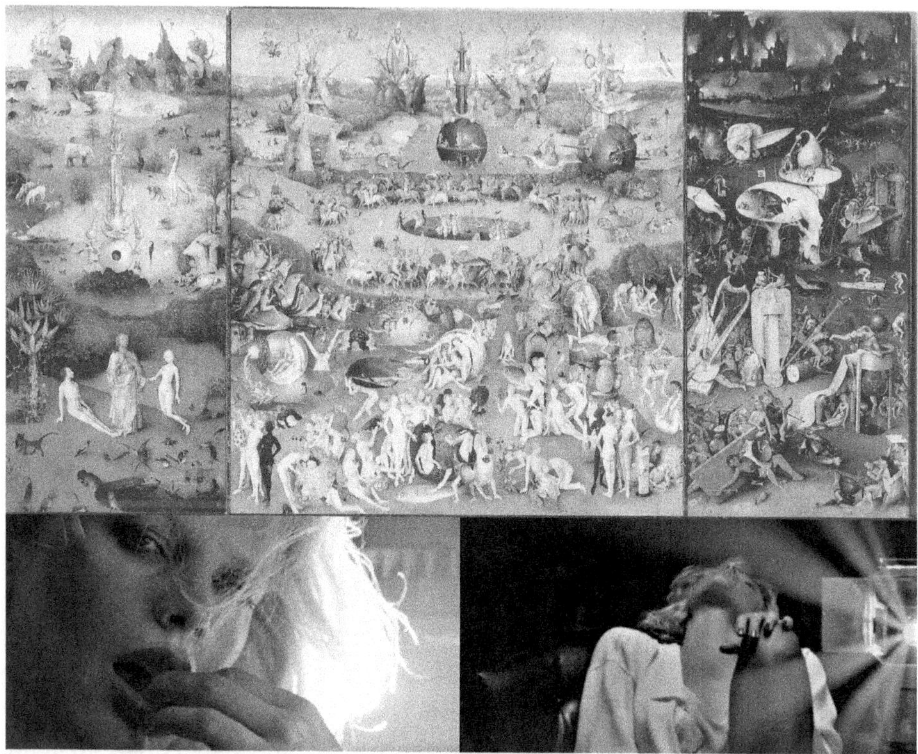

(Top) The triptych painting *The Garden of Earthly Delights* (ca. 1495-1505) by Hieronymus Bosch anticipates the erotic transmutation that Elizabeth will undergo. (Bottom Left and Right) No longer restricted by her ego, Elizabeth explores the lesser sexual mysteries of masturbation. Hypnotized by the somber yet seductive light of the Left-Hand Path, she alchemically transforms into a publicly displayed living piece of performance artwork for all of SoHo to see. The artificial-manufactured light, in Elizabeth's case, signifies the Lesser Work of Sol, which symbolically initiates her into the O.T.O.'s VIII°, known as the Perfect Pontiff of the Illuminati, wherein masturbatory magickal techniques are honed and perfected. Overwhelmed with pleasure, Elizabeth ritualistically masturbates; her black stockings are not only her fetish, they are also the alchemical *nigredo* representing her burgeoning shadow self. She wears them throughout the rest of the film, symbolizing her sexual awakening, extolling the pleasures of the flesh.

lascivious rite, fragmented projector beams of clouded *light* cut across Elizabeth's blonde hair, smoky eyes, candy apple red lips and nail polish (suggesting the *rubedo*, masturbatory fulfillment), black pencil skirt and stockings, and elegant white blouse when she deliciously caresses

---

(1988), Pinhead states, "No more deals child, it is syour flesh we want to experience, not your skill at bargaining. (emphasis added)." See also *The X-Files* season 4, episode 13 tiled "Never Again" (original airdate February 2nd, 1997) which sees Dana Scully (Gillian Anderson) experience erotic sensation when a tattoo artist's needle is pressed against her flesh, Scully delights in the mysteries of the flesh which, for her, includes the commingling of pleasure with pain. The tattoo eases her self-loathing while providing her masturbatory pleasure.

her body. Alchemically, she has successfully transformed herself into a piece of lubricious artwork: Elizabeth is now a passionate, hedonistic exhibition, crafted by her Jungian shadow. When Elizabeth approaches climax, she triumphantly and unabashedly raises her black stocking-clad legs in the air announcing that her shadow self is now conscious; through masturbation, Elizabeth has suppressed her ego, officially beginning her metamorphosis into a Left-Hand Path sexual magician, a Lilith archetype, the Arch of Hysteria. Like the horned, nude woman chained to the Devil (cf. materialistic, fleshy desires) depicted on card fifteen of the Tarot, Elizabeth has enslaved herself to compulsive lustful charms: her black stockings symbolize the embrace of her mysterious, sensual shadow which gives her temporary pleasure, but her ascent is short lived. She is purified by making love to herself making her ready to experience her darker self which will have harmful consequences. The slide projector supplies light (cf. Lucifer the Light Bearer), forging a nexus between Lucifer's concomitants Venus and her Greco equivalent, Aphrodite, deifying beauty and bliss. Elizabeth has transformed into a neo-pagan beauty goddess of fetish exploration, pleasure, momentary enlightenment, and masturbation.

As Elizabeth rhythmically masturbates to Eurythmics' "This City Never Sleeps," the remote control that Elizabeth used to operate the projector's artificial light slips off her lap, landing on the chair next to her gyrating hips. The displaced remote control denotes Elizabeth's total loss of control, her inability to curb her ecstasy; Elizabeth is not ashamed of her public masturbation, rather, she is getting off on the experience. Thus, the luminous Luciferian slideshow now flashes chaotically, symbolizing Elizabeth's unfettered euphoria, while the projector fires images like a Parabellum, indicating Elizabeth's orgasm; she has now temporarily morphed from Aphrodite-Venus into the personification of the goddess of pleasure, Hēdonē (Voluptas to the Romans), existing only for sensual gratification.[510] Elizabeth's black silk stockings victorious, she hoists legs above her planting her sexy black high heels on either side of a sculpted face. Elizabeth desires that the sculpted face, like the people passing by overhead, bear witness to her intense orgasm. Through stylish masturbation,

---

510 cf. Stephen E. Flowers' *Fire & Ice*, p. 68: The Dark Light (of the Left-Hand Path) can also be equated with the magical power of sexuality and of the orgasm."

Elizabeth's chichi orgasm releases potent sexual energy which can be used for sorcery–to birth her intention–to release of her dark, erotic Lilith-like persona.[511] The moment of climax is not just the height of pleasure, but a magical moment during which the personal ego shatters; by masturbating to the dark light of demonic paintings in a basement while strangers stroll overhead, Elizabeth's repressed shadow is given license to ascend. From here on out she will try to reconcile her dark side with her ego but, like Nina Sayers after her, will fail in the end.

Regarding the Tarot's archetypal imagery, when Elizabeth wears her black stockings and lingerie she does not transform into the Juggler, the huckster, femininized Mercury, a sublime villainess or Lilith; rather, she is the embodiment of a Tarot card that does not exist. If this card did it would be titled: The Masturbator.[512] Part of the Major Arcana, this invisible card's (cf. Kabbalah's *Da'at*) attributes would be: egotism, taboo, fetishism, fleeting pleasure, passion, unenlightened, reckless, magick, and self-deceptive; reversed the card is steadfast, practical, sensible, cautious, mundane, and reactionary. The card would precede the Fool, and its number would be 00, symbolizing nothingness, emptiness, and solitary pleasure. The opposite of the Masturbator would be the Lovers (card six in the Rider-Waite deck) which symbolizes the erotic, ecstatic union of the male and female (cf. Union of Opposites) to create new life or an alchemical higher self. Elizabeth and John fail in this endeavor, never truly becoming the Tarot's Lovers because John does not envision Elizabeth as an equal; rather, she is merely his plaything, a sex toy. Contrasting Elizabeth, whose stockings are a pleasurable fetish, Maria Bosic's (Natassia Kinski) hosiery represents her self-loathing in 1984's *Maria's Lovers*. Toward the end, Maria's husband, Ivan Bibic (John

---

511 cf. Jason Miller's *Sex, Sorcery, and Spirit*, p. 77, 80-81, "Masturbatory Magic" and "The Sigil Spell." Miller and Andrieh Vitimus (author of Hands-On Chaos Magic) both suggest the more unorthodox the masturbation session, the more pleasurable and erotic the experience. In regards to *9 ½ Weeks*, by masturbating to weird images of demons and creatures in public, Elizabeth is clearly consumed and overwhelmed by passionate, sexual rapture.

512 A Female Hermit styled Tarot card. Richard Cavendish, in his book *The Tarot*, explains the sexual attributes of the Hermit (IX) card writing, "In modern interpretations, however, the Hermit is also a phallic symbol and an emblem of masturbation, standing for the fertility of self-reliance." This symbolism can be found in the 1960 film *Psycho*. "Lives like a hermit," is how Norman Bates is described by Sheriff Al Chambers (John McIntire, 1907-1991); the surname, Bates, naturally implies masturbation.

Savage), becomes impotent, causing Maria to seek temporary solace by masturbating; while she pleasures herself, she angrily rips and tears her stockings symbolizing her angst, misery, loneliness, disappointment, and sexual frustration.

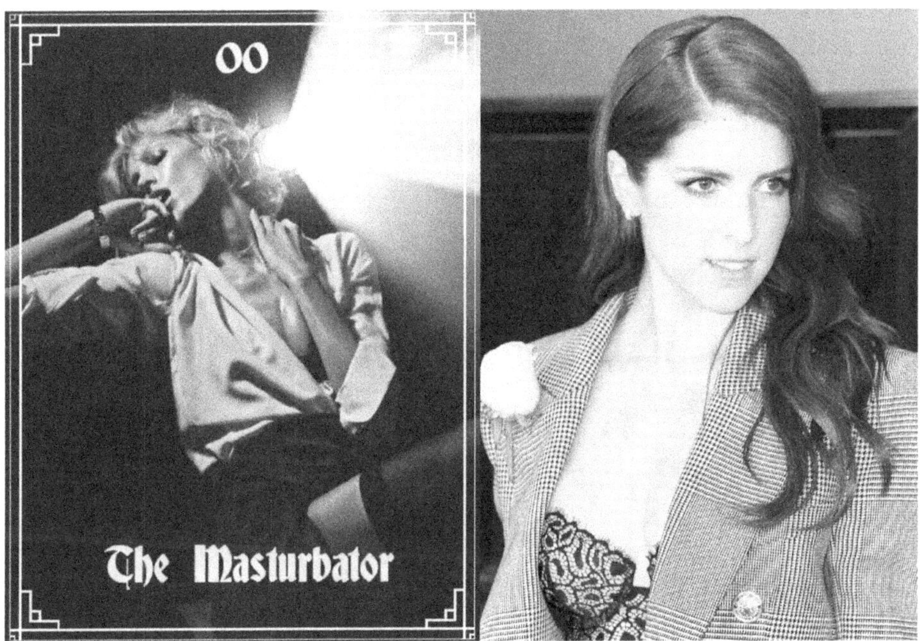

(Left) The Masturbator Tarot Card: Supermodel Anja Rubik falls in love with herself by paying homage to *9 ½ Weeks'* Elizabeth in a provocative *Vogue* (August 2014, German edition) photoshoot titled "Passion." Anja, impersonating Elizabeth's artistic alchemical masturbation session, precisely embodies all the traits of the fictitious Tarot card; if the card existed, this would be its graphic. (Right) Life imitating art: the Masturbator Tarot archetype briefly possessed actress and singer Anna Kendrick, photographed at the 2018 Grammy Awards, January, 28th, 2018. Like *9 ½ Weeks'* Elizabeth, Anna became a self-absorbed masturbator, fondling herself in a darkened theatre–a symbolic pleasure dome–to artificial light generated by a projector. Like the typical egotist, Anna has no problem letting the public know about her pleasurable caresses; see www.twitter. com, @AnnaKendrick47, Tweet dated 10:45 AM–14 Jan 2013.

* * * *

Elizabeth, having liberated her erotic shadow at the expense of her ego, is now consumed by it. She succumbs to John's ambiguous sex-games. Playing the submissive, she allows him to feed various foods to her most of which are red, *rubedo*, allegorizing Elizabeth's anticipated

441

transitional completion and resulting breakdown. Before the escapade, John prepares eggs[513] which, in this context, esoterically represents the materialism of the demiurge and earthly, sensual yet fleeting happiness; "The egg is furthermore…the proper symbol of the Demiurgus, whose auric body is the egg of the inferior universe."[514] The egg also represents the active and passive, dominance and submissive, master and slave or John and Elizabeth, "a hermaphroditic figure to emerge, uniting in itself the two principles…of the double power, the active and passive,…which they [the ancients] symbolized by the egg."[515] Elizabeth, as the moon (cf. *albedo*), now begins to welcome John's solar (cf. *citrinitas*) yet somber light which he acknowledges when she asks him, "How did you know?

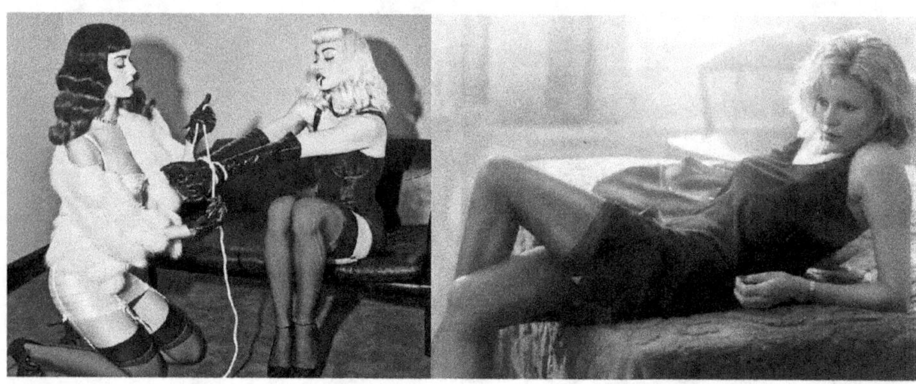

(Left) The triumph of the female Jungian shadow: Katy Perry and Madonna pose for the Summer 2014 issue of *V Magazine* dressed as a Betty Paige-like dominatrices. The Queen of Pop, routinely simulating masturbation during her on-stage performances in the 1990s, plays the bound, sexual submissive. Dressed in sexy lingerie, stockings, and high heels, both women wantonly delight in the pleasures of the flesh. It has been rumored that Katy and Madonna secretly practice witchcraft as part of a secret Hollywood Illuminati-like cabal. During the 2015 Grammy Awards (8 February 2015), Katy wore devil horns while, later in the show, Madonna performed "Living for Love," surrounded by dancing demons (cf. Baphomet, the Goat of Mendes). Wearing hellfire red and black fishnets, Madonna performed a lustful ritualistic satanic masterpiece supported by a gospel choir, suggesting her adoration of the Prince of Darkness. Make no mistake, Katy and Madonna are consumed by darkness, disciples of the Left-Hand Path, debauched apostates of Hell. Bondage and S&M photographer Rick Castro said, "Fetish is the exploration of sex as art, and the refinement of one's personal desires. Anything can be fetishized…There'll be new fetishes forever. I feel that the 21st Century is all about fetish." (Right) Elizabeth indulges her fetish for black lingerie and silk stockings in the Chelsea Hotel, allowing the ascendancy, if only momentarily, of her Jungian shadow, from *9 ½ Weeks*.

---

513 In 1987's *Angel Heart*, Cyphre also explains that within many religions the egg is a symbol of the soul. As Harry Angel watches, Cyhpre eats one signifying that he will devour Angel/Favorite's soul because it rightly belongs to him.
514 Hall, *The Secret Teachings of All Ages*, page 176.
515 Pike, *Morals and Dogma*, p. 655.

How did you know I'd respond to you the way I have?" John replies, "I saw myself in you." Although this dialog also suggests the unification of the divine masculine with the sacred feminine, it is not because Elizabeth seems to be wantonly ignorant of John's true intentions. In other words, John is not her *animus*, rather, he is an archetype she can never be or become, no matter how hard she tries. However, she is clearly under his spell; Elizabeth's black clothing is synchronized with her emerging shadow, changing her. To satisfy her shadow while perfecting, or at least finalizing, her sexual-alchemical transition, Elizabeth stalks John to his office, her dark side coming to the surface. She encounters John's secretary (Ellen Barber) wearing red high heels, signifying Elizabeth's alchemical *rubedo* is nearing. Elizabeth, with her ego suppressed, is becoming darker and weirder. Since masturbating in public wasn't enough, she next discovers the Saturnalia pleasures of role reversal when at the behest of John, she dons men's clothing, becoming a female transvestite, implying transition. Elizabeth's dark side further manifests when she's in a department store with John. He encourages her to shoplift a necklace which does; this scene begins with a sales woman sampling perfume to shoppers. The sales woman is dressed entirely in alchemy's *rubedo*, foreshadowing Elizabeth's alchemical change.

Before Elizabeth becomes her full-blown Jungian shadow, she flaunts her lunar attributes before John, the sun, giving her a gift consisting of a white garter belt, white fishnet stockings, a white slip, and gloves, all tokens of the alchemical *albedo*, the moon. Elizabeth performs a striptease, wearing moon-like lingerie reflecting John's voyeuristic desires, his solar Luciferian light; it is Elizabeth becoming her sexy Jungian shadow. Earlier, John's passport reveals his birth date as 27 October, which is under the sign of Scorpio. Scorpio's attributes are sexual intensity, darkness (Scorpio is ruled by Pluto or Hades), secrecy and mystery, all of which John personifies. Elizabeth is becoming his reflection. However, it does not take long for her to abandon the *albedo* for the *nigredo* by returning to the comfort of black clothing and stockings as her Jungian shadow is unchained. Wearing a black dress and stockings, she again submits to John's sex game by crawling before him, picking up money as he admonishes her. Elizabeth cries fall on deaf ears, because she does not realize that it's all a game to him, nothing more, nothing less. Her

tears are genuine since she knows she is unable to free herself of his domineering personality and sardonic amusements, but his dark overarching
erotic influence feeds her shadow and her lustful appetites.

Clad in black, Elizabeth is finally pushed over the precipice at the
Chelsea Hotel. Elizabeth ascends the staircase (cf. the Ladder of Mithras,
the Winding Stairs of the Masonic Mysteries, Jacob's Ladder) to receive
sensual awakening or erotic transition. Inside Room 906, Elizabeth awaits
John by sitting on the edge of the bed, satisfying her *nigredo* by wearing
only a black slip, black high heels, and her trademark black silk stockings.
Wearing black lingerie has now become a driving talismanic sensual experience; unlike her previous public autoeroticism, Elizabeth looks around
the room confirming that she is alone and begins masturbating by crossing
her legs, rubbing her thighs against one another by moving her left leg
up and down. She is interrupted by John, blindfolding her. He then allows a Hispanic prostitute into the room who immediately begins touching
Elizabeth's stockings, seemingly aware of her fetish. As John watches, the
prostitute caresses Elizabeth's legs, massaging the welts of her stockings,
exciting Elizabeth so much that she not only perspires, but alchemical
change manifests when her flesh gives off steam.

Elizabeth has become a human crucible: to produce her shadow, her
body is now a smoldering melting pot of sexuality, passion, lust, and
masturbation triggered by her black lingerie, specifically black hosiery.
Removing Elizabeth's black stockings strips the art gallery manager of
her shadow persona, making her a mere submissive unable to resist the
Hispanic's salacious whims. Her black stockings have tricked and betrayed
her; no longer a source of pride and pleasure, Elizabeth realizes they are
the fountainhead of her onanism and humiliation.

Elizabeth wilts to the prostitute's caresses because the dark side can
produce unseen side effects; the shadow opens restricted doors locked by
the ego. Elizabeth's heterosexual chastity belt now removed, she is now
willing to experience pleasure for its own sake by pursuing the taboo rap-
tures of lesbianism; however, her blindfold is abruptly removed, and John
begins to kiss and fondle the prostitute wearing conspicuous red (cf. *rubedo*) lingerie. By making out with the whore, John's end-game is to stim-
ulate Elizabeth's voyeuristic and masturbatory desires. Embarrassed that
John and the prostitute have discovered that black stockings and lingerie

are her forbidden fetish, the sensual alchemical tokens of her shadow self, Elizabeth psychologically cracks, finally realizing that sex is a mere child-like game to John, paralleling the lesson she failed to learn in the subterranean den of the art gallery. She now knows that fetishisms and the pleasures of masturbation are temporary; the lyrics of Eurhythmics' "This City Never Sleeps" tried to admonish her that her sexual hang-ups are merely "♫ just a feeling ♫." Elizabeth was warned of John's erotic gamesmanship when she entered Chelsea Hotel but wasn't paying attention: on her way to Room 906, she passes a child on the steps and a toy wagon, suggesting her own demure inexperience, understanding that she is nothing more than John's toy. By the time she flees the hotel, she is

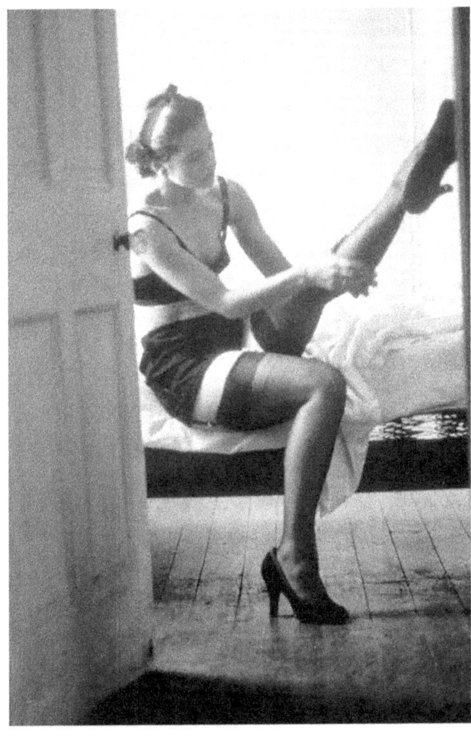

In *Maria's Lovers,* Maria Bosic (Kinski) caresses her legs because her black stockings are a source of erotic pleasure. However, Maria's hosiery will become her sexual bane representing her failures, melancholy, frustration, and self-loathing.

distraught and sexually frustrated; what was unclear to her before entering the room is now obvious upon leaving. Elizabeth knows that John's sexual brinkmanship combined with her masturbatory fetish have broken her. While it was hanging framed on the walls of the art gallery, Elizabeth should have broken the glass and put on the chastity belt when she had the chance.

A bewildered Elizabeth exits the room spiraling down the hotel's steps signifying a failed alchemical transition, entering a pit of depravity: a porn house that doubles as a brothel (cf. Dante's Lust Circle of *Inferno*). Elizabeth realizes that she is home, the venue is bathed in the alchemical *rubedo* representing Elizabeth's transition is finished, the Magnum Opus complete. She enters seeing a reflection of what she has become: a prostitute-dancer (Petina Cole) performing in red lights wearing black gartered stockings, symbolizing Elizabeth's fetish, carnal desires, and wanton hubris. Her dark side now in control, Elizabeth finally realizes that, by freeing her Jungian shadow, she in nothing more than a whore to John, one of his inconsequential playthings. Her earlier, alchemical masturbation session has backfired on her: Elizabeth's black stockings and exalted masturbatory journey to the dark side did not transform her into a shadowy sensual dominatrix, or John's equal, as she originally anticipated; instead, she realizes she was an amateur tinkering with sexual taboos. She is cognizant that she is nothing more than a disposable pawn in John's odd sex-games; she is a pathetic fetishizer exploring her sexual hang-ups, and that's all she ever will be. Her alchemical journey is finished, she has not become what she anticipated; she is, rather, a failure.

A fractured and confused Elizabeth now understands that her public autoeroticism was not an experiment in artistic expressionism; rather, it was a shameful embarrassment. She is now also cognizant that John does not see her as an equal lover;[516] instead she is his mere sexy plaything. To seek a modicum of relief, an emotionally scarred but still lustful Elizabeth begins kissing a stranger to punish John by making him jealous. However, she knows she is only punishing and destroying herself. She now consciously accepts the role of the lowly whore and the sexually frustrated masturbator, realizing this is what she has been all along. Finally, a guilty and broken Elizabeth returns to John realizing that her Jungian shadow will always lead back to his dark, Hades-like Scorpio archetype; her humiliation and psychological deconstruction now compete. Elizabeth understands that she secretly enjoys John's degradation, something she has suppressed the entire movie. Elizabeth likes masturbating while wearing gartered black silk stockings because they feel good against her flesh, allowing her shadow to surface;[517] so too does she enjoy being humiliated by John at the expense of her well-being. Elizabeth further anticipates *Black Swan's* Nina Sayers because both women are masochistic, enjoying their mortifications, albeit subconsciously. One could also argue that Elizabeth embodies the archetypal, destructive qualities associated with the Tower card of the Major Arcana, foreshadowing *Black Swan's* Beth Macintyre as well. In the end,

---

516 cf. Card VI the Lovers of the Major Arcana of the Tarot and its associated symbolic mysteries. To Jung, the card was the successful alchemical marriage of opposites, the sun and moon, king and queen, harmony between the sexes. See Cavendish's *The Tarot*, pp. **88-89**.
517 cf. Miller's *Sex, Sorcery, and Spirit*, p. 76, "Masturbatory Magic."

Elizabeth and John forgot that love is real and immortal having subjugated it to the unreal, John's sex games, and temporary: Elizabeth's self-gratifications.[518] For them, love became dissension, a tool that fettered them with iron chains to the black cube (cf. *nigredo*, melancholy, Saturn) of matter, upon which sits deceit and illusion.[519]

The consequences of failure: depressed, distraught, sexually frustrated, suffering with anxiety and unsure of herself, Elizabeth attends Farnsworth's opening night party at the Spring Street Gallery, representing the fashions, styles, and overall decadence of the 1980s. Leaving the show, she briefly returns to John but knows that she cannot stay because that might result in further emotional damage; her ego slowly returning. Elizabeth has successfully performed alchemy: she has transmuted herself from a feminine, beautiful, lunar woman into a dark version, or vision, of herself by becoming the Lilith archetype (a sexy witch) reveling in erotic darkness by pursuing her carnal desires. Like all black magicians, her sorcery-psychological transition is not without consequence: Elizabeth is not able to adjust her Jungian shadow with her ego; she *must be one or the other, not both.* In other words, Elizabeth's ego cannot reconcile the emergence of her Jungian shadow, and her ego certainly cannot play second fiddle to her budding shadow. This deadly psychological matrix causes her to suffer a nervous breakdown. This is Elizabeth's *rubedo*, her individuation.

In a cinematic twist, Kim Basinger, becoming a masturbatory piece of performance art in *9 ½ Weeks,* would go on to portray a character shown living artwork in a movie a few years later. In 1989's *Batman*, Jack Nicholson's Joker proudly presents Vicki Vale (Basinger) some of his "artwork" which turns out to be his chemically scarred girlfriend, Alicia Hunt (Jerry Hall), inside Gotham City's Art Museum. Vale is freed from the art museum by Gotham City's Jungian Shadow, Batman, recalling Elizabeth's masturbatory liberation in the art gallery's basement in *9 ½ Weeks.*

Next, the alchemical transition that Adrian Lyne experiments within *9 ½ Weeks*, Darren Aronofsky cinematically perfects in *Black Swan.*

* * * *

---

518 See Ouspensky's *The Symbolism of the Tarot*, p. 52, describing the lovers chained to the black cube that the Devil sits upon on card XV (Rider-Waite) of the Tarot.
519 *ibid.*

Fox Searchlight Pictures' *Black Swan* depicts female alchemical transition at the highest kabalistic occult level; Aronofsky's film is a retelling of *9 ½ Weeks* taken to new, daring, and even dangerous extremes. If the previous *9 ½ Weeks* section were to be sub-captioned, it would be, "Elizabeth McGraw: Alchemical Masturbator", and this portion would be titled, "Nina Sayers: Chaste Chaos Magician." Concordantly, certain aspects of both films mirror each other: *9 ½ Weeks* is set against the backdrop of a swanky SoHo art gallery, while *Black Swan* takes place in the artistic world of a Manhattan ballet company. Both movies are alchemical in nature: Nina Sayers, like Elizabeth McGraw before her, not only changes psychologically with harmful consequences, but Nina also achieves physical transmutation as well. Similar to *9 ½ Weeks*, all the symbolic colors of Renaissance alchemy are present with, once again, *rubedo* manifesting perfectly suggesting completion of the Great Work, which for Nina, ends in death. Echoing Elizabeth, Nina uses masturbation as part of her alchemical-magical formula, only she adds the element of masochism to accomplish her occult transition into an erotic and confident yet gargoyle-like monster.

For Nina, her alchemical *nigredo*–her melancholia, her envy, and her despair–are personified by three people: her saturnine, steely mother Erica; the self-destructive Beth whom she secretly admires; and the black magician Von Rothbart whom she wishes to emulate by becoming his daughter, Odile, the Black Swan. Lily is also critical, personifying Mercurius in the *nigredo* phase, much like Frank Booth in *Blue Velvet*. Suggestive of the pessimism of Mani, once Nina achieves her Black Swan personality, her alchemical awakening, she becomes distraught and paranoid which ultimately results in death. Erica is Nina's satirical melancholia; she is an overbearing matriarch wearing black, doing everything to keep her adult daughter in a perpetual, virginal child-like state. Erica is a lonely, frustrated recluse who wants to keep her daughter in a similarly depressed state; she is cruel, wanting Nina to *mirror* her. If the Tarot were to come alive, Erica epitomizes the Queen of Swords intense perception: Nina cannot hide her self-mutilations and masturbations from her; and when the card is reversed it denotes a cruel, sly, and deceitful woman.[520] At first appearing caring and supportive, Erica becomes enraged when Nina refuses a piece of a cake she

---

520 cf. Crowley's *The Book of Thoth*, p. 161. See also Cavendish's *The Tarot*, p. 166.

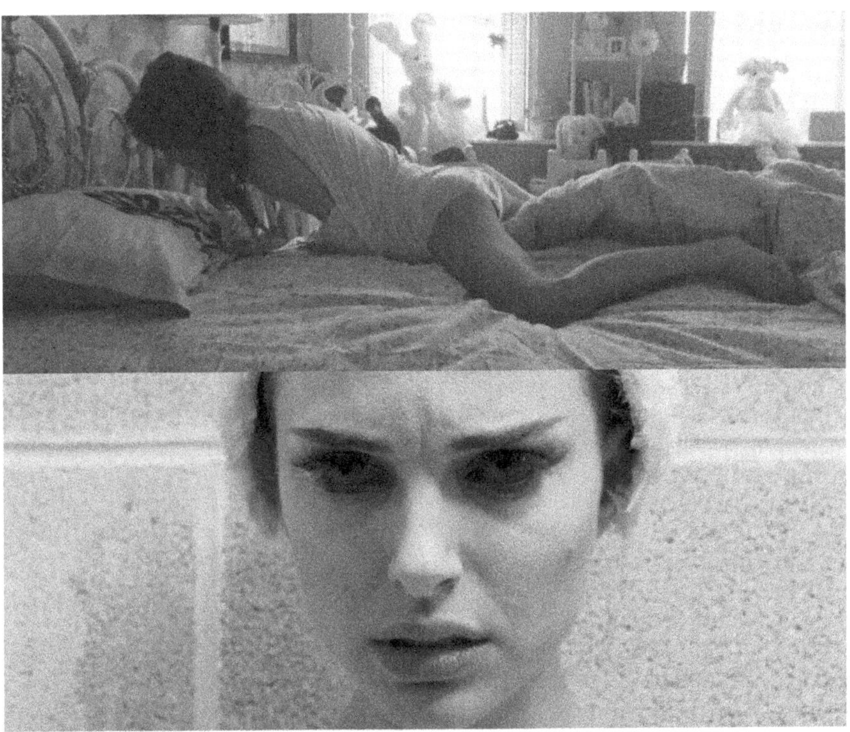

(Top) As Nina poignantly touches herself, her collection of stuffed animals, including a conspicuous black swan, provide an audience. The stuffed toys never take their eyes off her symbolizing Nina's unconscious, Jungian shadow's desire to free itself from her suffocating, constrictive ego by fulfilling one of her darkest fantasies: public masturbation. Her taboo desire becomes reality when Nina transcends the unbearable lightness of being by fondling herself in the backseat of a taxicab while fantasizing that Lily is fondling her. (Bottom) "The fact that you can stare into someone's eyes without being self-conscious is a great gift to all of us," so says Aronofsky on Nina's close-up, which appears near the end of the movie. Through chaos magick, mingled with sex magick, Nina alchemically changes into a Black Swan, signified by her diabolical red eyes, the *rubedo*. Nina's face expresses confusion, sexual frustration, and anxiety; although she had perfected Left-Hand Path alchemy, she remains a virgin, an innocent White Swan. Like *9 ½ Weeks'* Elizabeth, Nina personifies Dali's sexually conflicted *Great Masturbator* because, like her incestuous mother, has a stagnant and putrid libido.

baked; in truth, Erica is jealous that her daughter was named Swan Queen, a dream she never accomplished during her days as a ballerina. Crowley, in his *Book of Thoth*, writes that the Queen of Swords archetype moves like a balanced dancer which reflects Erica's graceful, ballet-like duplicity.[521] Nina's pines for privacy: her tyrannical mother undresses her at night, tucks

---

521 *ibid.*

her into bed, calls her "sweet girl," having instant access to Nina's bedroom which does not have a lock on its door. Erica appears to relish the total dominance she has over her daughter. In her bed, Nina attempts to initiate herself into the lesser sexual mysteries–masturbation–but is frustrated by dreary mother in the room with her; Nina's fledgling erotic catharsis turns into lugubrious embarrassment. At one point, Erica even hides Nina's doorknob so she cannot escape the confines of her tiny bedroom. Going well beyond the dark embodiment of the vile Queen of Swords inverted, it is also apparent that Nina and Erica have an incredibly unhealthy sexual relationship. Erica constantly wants to examine her daughter's tender and mutilated flesh, causing Nina to seek sanctuary to keep mother at bay. She accomplishes this by wedging a phallic, erect piece of wood between the base of her bedroom door and the wall to keep out prying mother. The elongated piece of timber symbolizes a male erection which, of course, frustrates and turns away prudish mother. Nina forcibly keeps her mother out of her bedroom when she has sex with Lily; however, upon confronting Lily the next day, it is revealed that the liaison never occurred and that Nina hallucinated the lesbian episode which Lily sardonically refers to as "lezzie wet dream." Alone in her bedroom, Nina's sexual encounter with Lily appears at first to be masturbatory fantasy. In *Cinema Symbolism,* I wrote "Unable to enter, mother at least wants to listen to her daughter's masturbatory euphoria."[522] That notwithstanding, and upon closer examination, there may be even an even more malicious explanation underlying Nina's imagined lesbian fling. When Nina wakes the next morning, she sees that the piece wood has been unbarricaded from the door from where she wedged it the night before. Since Lily was never there, the only explanation is that Nina allowed her mother access to her bedroom so that Erica could indulge her morbid and foul incestuous desires. In his book, *The Tarot*, Richard Cavendish explains the Queen of Swords reversed, thus providing keen insights into Erica's personality; she is a "…thoroughly evil woman, whose attractive exterior conceals hatred, cruelty, treachery, malice and deceit. She is an accomplished user of lies and half-truths, a dangerous enemy. A prude (In the ordinary pack of playing cards the Queen of Spades has the same reputation)."[523] Comparatively, the Queen of Swords reversed

---

522 Sullivan, *Cinema Symbolism*, Chapter XI, "Obscured Perfection."
523 Cavendish, *The Tarot*, p. 166.

is also Norma Bates (Vera Farmiga) on the television show *Bates Motel*. Norma is a murderous, weird, duplicitous, cruel woman who, like Erica, harbors incestuous desires towards her child; in Norma's instance, toward her son Norman (Freddie Highmore).

Exit the *nigredo* (momentarily), enter the joker. Embodying the trickster, Mercury, the dark agent of transition is the imperfect ballerina Lily. Although she is not Erica, Beth, or Rothbart, she is critical to Nina's metamorphosis, perpetuating blackness. Lily's name implies the sexy nocturnal goddess, Lilith. A demon of the night sky, Lilith is not only a seductress but a trickster in Babylonian mythology. Lily always wears black (cf. Mercurius dwelling on perpetual *nigredo*) and, like a demon, has two grotesque wing-like tattoos on her back, symbolizing Lilith's nocturnal flights in search of newborn children to strangulate. In German folklore, Lilith is thought to be Satan's grandmother and in the German drama about the female pope *Jutta* (Johanna), which was printed in 1565 though according to its publisher it was written in 1480, the grandmother's name is Lilith.[524] Like *Black Swan's* Lily, the grandmother in *Jutta* is depicted as a seductive dancer, a motif commonly found in Ashkenazi Jewish incantations involving the Queen of Sheba.[525] Nina secretly admires Lily's shadowy personality: Lily is loose, flamboyant, imperfect, yet an enticing ballerina. Nina not only desires to be like Lily but she also secretly harbors sexual feelings towards the coquette. Lily confirms her darkness (cf. *nigredo*) when she lures Nina into exploring her shadow self by offering her Ecstasy over dinner with the line that Nina will, "see the night sky." Lily also provides Nina with a lacy piece of black lingerie symbolizing Lily *qua* Lilith's mysteriously sexy personality. Lily is the dark source of Nina's envious fascination; she is the persona that Nina alchemically wants *to become* (cf. Francis Dolarhyde's *becoming* in Red Dragon, see Introduction). Thus, Lily embodies the Tarot's Juggler-Magician: she is a transitional agent allowing Nina to move from White Swan to Black Swan, from light to darkness. In *Cinema Symbolism*, the Tarot archetypes of *Black Swan* were analyzed by this author: Nina Sayers personifies the Moon Card (XVIII) reversed; Beth Macintyre is the Tower Card (XVI); Erica Sayers signifies the Queen of Swords (Lesser Arcana) reversed, and

---

524 Scholem, *Kabbalah*, p. 358.
525 *ibid.*

Thomas Leroy is the manipulative Devil Card (XV).[526] However, Lily-as-the-Juggler was excluded because I removed the alchemical portion from *Black Swan*, saving it for this book instead.

The Juggler-Magician card is linked with the Roman god Mercury, the patron of thieves and suites the Juggler's character as a huckster[527] (see Introduction, Chapter II). The card's French name, *Le Bateleur*, is a general term for showman or trickster; Sufi mystic and polymath Omar Khayyám (1048-1131) referred to this persona as the manipulative master of the show.[528] The Juggler, or Magician archetype, is a charlatan and a manipulator; Lily is a female deceiver, exciting and manipulating Nina's insecu-

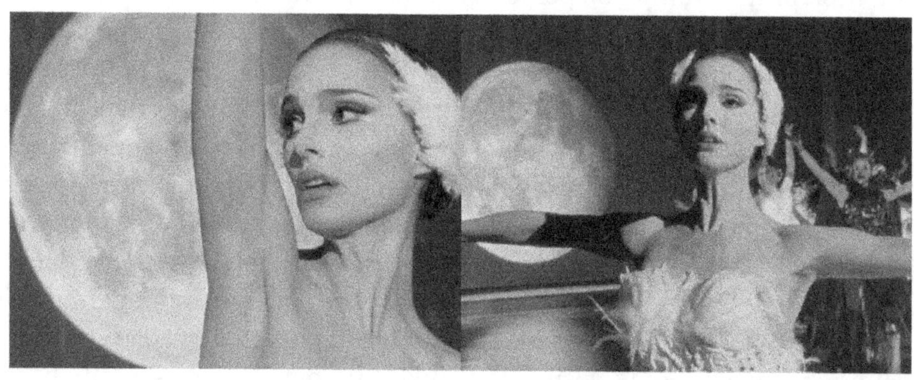

(Left) Embodying the Tarot's Moon Card, Nina, a timid virgin, associates with the moon when she dances Odette, the White Swan; the card reversed denotes lunacy. (Right) Her alchemy complete, Nina frets because she is unable to control her emerging dark side. Nina's psychological conflict is represented by Rothbart, appearing on stage triumphant, stalking her from behind.

rities and bisexuality, heightening her paranoia, anxiety, masochism (Nina enjoys being humiliated), self-loathing, jealousy, and chronic masturbation, resulting in psychological and physical transmutation which ends with Nina's total emotional downfall and death. Make no mistake, the Juggler

---

526 Sullivan, *Cinema Symbolism*, Chapter XI, "Obscured Perfection: The Goddess in Cinema," *passim*. See Cavendish's *The Tarot*, "…the Devil stands for the application of creative power and intelligence to selfish and wicked ends," p. 119.

527 Comparatively, the god Loki is the Norse version of Mercury who can affect alchemical transition of the self; see 1994's *The Mask* which sees the bashful Stanley Ipkiss (Jim Carrey) don the mask of Loki and change into a supernatural god of mischief. See *Cinema Symbolism*, Chapter XIII, for more on comedic and con-artist archetypes in film.

528 Cavendish, *The Tarot*, p. 67; Hall, *The Secret Teachings of All Ages*, p. 414.

archetype can be a black magician since evil, as well as good, has its roots in the divine (cf. *I Enoch*); in other words, the trump card can symbolize a Left-Hand Path sorcerer or sorceress.[529] Lily is also the personification of what Nina so desperately wants to become: a dark, independent, confident seductress. Lily thereby serves as an alchemical template providing Nina with dark counterpart, a doppelgänger; her ballet style and personality are the opposite of Nina's. Nina is a timid virgin, living with her overbearing mother while Lily is liberated, loose, sexually promiscuous, and self-reliant. Mercury is critical to the alchemical process, being both the transformer (god) and the element (substance) necessary for transformation; thus, Lily is an integral component of Nina's alchemical metamorphosis into her shadow self (cf. *nigredo*) which, for Nina, is freeing her inner shadow, her Black Swan, like the film's title suggests.[530] Nina perfects alchemy: by the end of the movie, she has transitioned into a demonic bird-like creature that mentally and emotionally echoes Lily's loose and flamboyant personality, but physically resembles a weird monster. Although Nina's Black Swan is an elegant dancer, she is vile and vicious: believing it is her turn, she stabs and kills Lily, when, in reality, she has stabbed herself. The wound will be her downfall, destroying her.

Exit the trickster, re-enter the *nigredo*. Nina's mental, and even physical, alchemical erosion dwells in the blackness-melancholia that is *Swan Lake's* antagonist, the Agrippa-like dark conjurer Von Rothbart. His color is also black, and his magical wisdom is clearly inspired by the melancholic Saturn of the Renaissance; he is a profound transformer–a polymath.[531] In the ballet, Rothbart is rarely seen in human form, appearing as a giant owl in the second and fourth acts. His human form is seen only in the third act with his daughter Odile (the Black Swan) when she dances with Prince Siegfried. Rothbart is a powerful sorcerer, casting a spell on Odette, the White Swan, turning her into a swan every day, returning her to human form at night.[532] The reason for Rothbart's curse upon Odette is unknown, and not explained in the ballet. The owl is a symbol of wisdom, signifying that Rothbart is saturnine Left-Hand Path knowledge that Nina, by transforming herself into the sensual Black Swan (Odile) seeks so that

---

529 cf. Cavendish's *The Tarot*, p. 70.
530 Nichols, *Jung and Tarot*, p. 52.
531 cf. Yates' *The Occult Philosophy in the Elizabethan Age*, pp. 141-143.
532 See also 1985's *Ladyhawke* for similar harmful sorcery.

she can liberate her Jungian shadow. Put another way, Nina is willing to sacrifice her pathetic ego to bring her Jungian shadow to life. This can be observed when Nina admires a giant, foreboding statue of Rothbart after being announced as the Swan Queen. Nina also dreams of dancing with Rothbart during the opening sequence which, when Nina awakens, puts a smile on her face.

Rounding out the *nigredo* is the self-destructive Beth, the embodiment of the Tower card from the Major Arcana. Nina seeks to be like her by stealing her lipstick, to emulate her darkness, to reflect the *sol niger*. After stealing Beth's lipstick, Nina suffers her paranoia, her erratic behavior and instability. Beth winds up in a hospital bed the result of a suicide attempt; Nina is willing to destroy herself to achieve perfection. Erica, Rothbart, and Beth are Nina's *nigredo,* her alchemical blackness, necessary for transmutation–blackening, death, and rebirth–yet also personifying what Nina wants to become: a dark, worldly, self-assured fem fatale which she attempts to counterbalance with her virginal, naïve innocence. Lily is Nina's personal Mercurius, existing only to perpetual blackness. Unfortunately, Nina's shadow cannot coexist with her ego: the Black Swan trashes the White Swan. Like *9 ½ Weeks'* Elizabeth, Nina's *rubedo* is the *nigredo*, her daemon is her eidolon, sex is masturbation.

Nina's desire to alchemically intertwine her innocence with her Jungian shadow emerges when she steals and proudly displays–like trophies–items that belong to the self-destructive former Swan Queen, Beth Macintyre. Beth, consumed by her shadow, attempts suicide after she is forced into an early retirement in favor of the younger Nina. Beth is confined to a hospital bed, her body ravaged by the moving car that she threw herself in front of. She has lost the will to live and is dying, both spiritually and physically. Leroy talks to Nina about Beth's deathly persona, "Because everything Beth does comes from within, from some dark impulse. I guess that's what makes her so thrilling to watch. So dangerous. Even perfect at times. But also so damn destructive." Beth's self-destructive tendencies are displayed for all eyes to observe prior to her being introduced, but the esoteric reference is missed by everyone. At the beginning, when Nina first walks into the New York Ballet Theater, she stops to observe a giant billboard featuring Beth captioned, WINTER CLASSICS REINVENTED NEW SEASON MBC FEBRUARY 12. The identification of the date, February 12, beneath

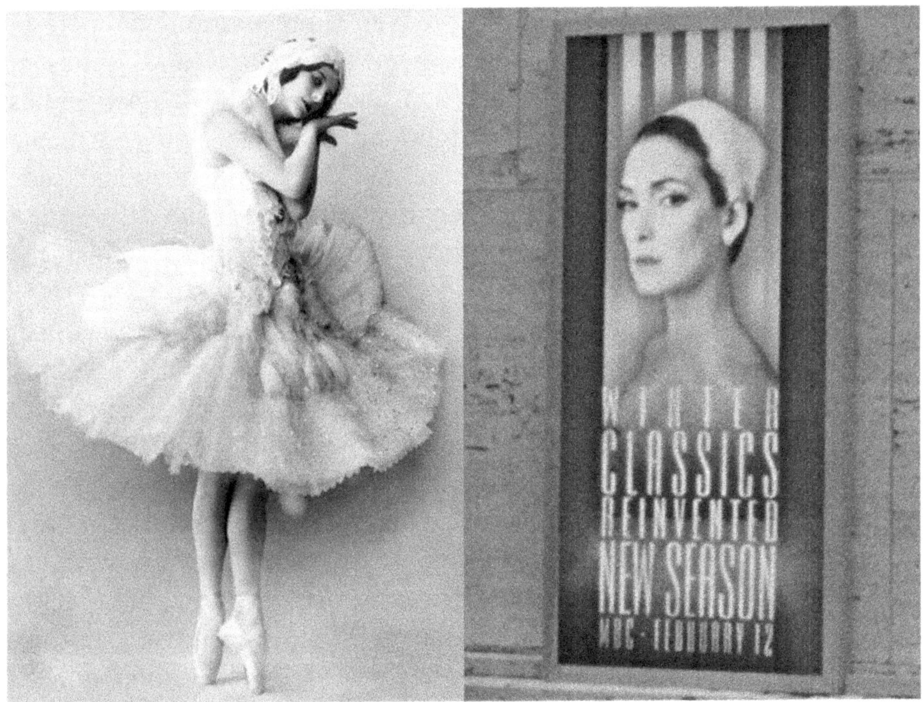

(Left) Anna Pavlova as *Le Cygne* or *The Swan*, also known as *The Dying Swan*. (Right) The Beth Macintyre banner displaying the date of "February 12" signifies Pavlova, identifying Beth as the self-destructive dying swan.

Beth's elegant visage is a concealed homage to Anna Pavlova. Pavlova was a Russian prima ballerina of the late nineteenth-early twentieth century born on 12 February 1881. Foreshadowing Beth's suicidal nature, Pavlova is recognized for the creation of the role *The Dying Swan*, a ballet choreographed especially for Pavlova by Mikhail Fokine in 1905 to Camille Saint-Saëns' cello solo *Le Cygne* from *Le Carnaval des Animaux* as a *pièce d'occasion*. *The Dying Swan* has since influenced modern interpretations of Odette in Tchaikovsky's *Swan Lake* inspiring non-traditional interpretations and various adaptations, including Aronofsky's film. The February 12th date signifies that Beth is the ruinous embodiment of Pavlova's *Dying Swan*. This occult nexus is also confirmed by *Black Swan's* end credits which bills Winona Ryder as "Beth Macintyre/The Dying Swan."

Black Swan's alchemical *albedo* stage is represented by the story's unhinged protagonist, Nina Sayers. She is the virginal moon goddess Diana, comparatively known as Artemis; in Greek mythology, the goddess was the protectress of virgins and young women. Nina, a virgin and a closet lesbian (at least bisexual), wears lunar whites and soft colors, contrasted by the *nigredo* clothing of her Erica, Beth, and Rothbart. Nina personifies the Jungian archetype of the Tarot's Moon card reversed, signifying mania and lunacy; a distorted reality that is an illusion. Nina hallucinations allude to her masturbatory quest for perfection; in other words, Nina's illness is a byproduct of her trying to be something she is not: a dark seductress, the Lilith archetype, a Black Swan.

Completing the alchemical color scheme of yellowness or *citrinitas* is Thomas Leroy, Nina's solar masculine Luciferian manipulator seeking to liberate Nina's dark side. Leroy is the clever instigator of Nina dark arousal constantly encourages her to lose herself in the role, to dance with passion not controlled discipline, and lastly, instructing her to experience the solitary pleasures of masturbation so that she can "live a little." Leroy, personifying Lucifer the Light Bearer, orders "Light!" when the power goes out during one of Nina's ballet practices and, naturally, the light quickly returns. Echoing Lucifer (and by default the Prince of Darkness), this author explained that Leroy possesses the attributes associated with the Devil Tarot card (XV): a dark schemer, a manipulating personality (see *Cinema Symbolism*, Chapter XI).

The *rubedo* appears subtly yet effectively in *Black Swan*, signifying Nina's alchemical psychological and physical metamorphosis. Aronofsky's use of red builds like a crescendo culminating in the nightclub scene finalizing Nina's occult, alchemical transition. Nina, a shy and timid ballerina, wishes to change from *albedo* to *nigredo* to become her rival, Lily. She must accomplish this so she can successfully dance the Black Swan in Leroy's visceral version of *Swan Lake*. It was explained in this book's prequel, *Cinema Symbolism*, that Nina's desire is to assimilate her inner darkness is symbolized by the film's use of mirrors and reflections. Nina's reflections are her dark side staring back at her. In fact, Nina's reflection is so dark and great that it comes *alive* while she practices. Shadow infests Nina when she sits on a subway train across from a black-suited man masturbating while he stares at her, admiring her beauty. She does not mind because the man is a reflection of her shadowy Jungian self, of her taboo desire to likewise masturbate in public. Fantasy becomes reality when Nina succumbs to her need to masturbate

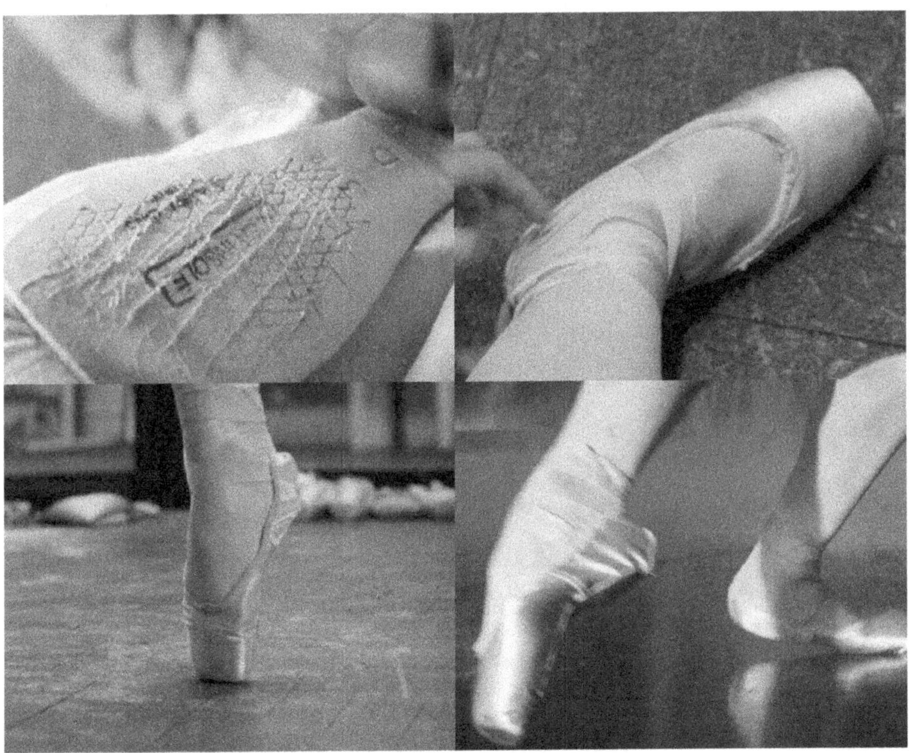

Imitating Elizabeth's fetish for black silk stockings in *9 ½ Weeks*, Nina's restrictive ballet slippers are a torturous obsession, intertwining a ballerina's grace and self-confidence with pain and humility. They are a pleasurable bondage device holding her hostage; exoterically she ravages them, burning the elastics to make sure they do not fray, scoring the bottoms to give them traction while dancing. Esoterically, she mutilates the slippers because they are tormenting emblems of her self-loathing, masochism, and sexual frustration. Her slippers arouse and repulse her; they are her agony and her ecstasy because wearing them commingles pain with pleasure. Paralleling her slippers, Nina also destroys her flesh to create a new, sensual, but paradoxical aesthetic: the fusion of masturbation with masochism to become a dark, erotic ballerina. The breaking of Nina's slippers evokes the ravaged fish in *9 ½ Weeks*, symbolizing the psychological annihilation that accompanies the pangs of the compulsive masturbator.

in public, in the back of a taxicab, fantasizing that Lily is fondling her. The Juggler card aside, Lily is also Nina's personal succubus by feeding off her darkest anxieties and sexual desires, forcing her to live up to expectations by becoming the Swan Queen, enabling her to dance the Black Swan. By satisfying her *nigredo*, her taboos, and sable yearnings, Nina successfully changes from an inexperienced virginal youth into a racy, domineering *Black Swan*; however, Nina's alchemical change is not only psychological but physical, suggesting Left-Hand Path kabalistic magic of the darkest kind.

To affect this alchemy, Nina develops a discordant cocktail of deadly chaos magick by combining masochism with masturbation which, for Nina, is a confusing mixture of pain with pleasure, pride with humiliation. In Lovecraftian-Cthulhu mythos, Nina is performing (unbeknownst

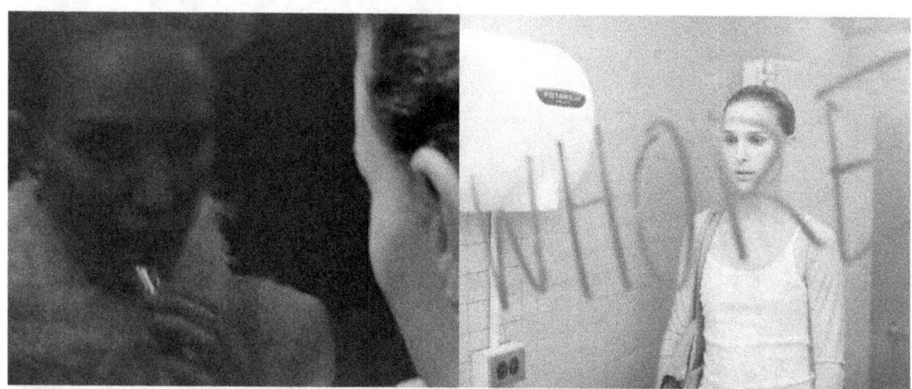

In *Beyond Good and Evil* (1886), Friedrich Nietzsche wrote, "And if you gaze long into an abyss, the abyss also gazes into you." (Left) Nina stares into darkness, the abyss, while putting on Beth's stolen lipstick so she can awaken her dormant sexuality to symbolically become a whore. Little does Nina know her dark side is staring back at her; like Beth, Nina is on a path of self-destruction that will transform her into a dying swan. (Right) Nina cannot be the White Swan and the Black Swan simultaneously; thus, she must either be a virgin, Odile, or a tempting seductress, Odette. Frightened by her erotic gnosis, she anxiously erases the word *WHORE* then runs home to her oppressive mother.

to her) Transyuggothian Sorcery: chaos magic designed to conjure cosmic, pan-dimensional demons dwelling in Transplutonian Space (comparatively, Yuggoth is the planet Pluto in Lovecraft's mythology) which is dark space outside our solar system, space beyond the pale of the sun. Nina perfects her chaotic-sex magick by channeling a Transyuggothian entity: a bizarre, red-eyed, feathery, malignant creature which possesses her body, scourging her flesh. Signifying this occult-magical formula is occurring, alchemy's *rubedo* cunningly begins to manifest. First, Nina adorns herself with Beth's stolen red lipstick to seduce Leroy into giving her the Swan Queen role; this is the first time Nina lets loose her dark side. The red lipstick and her smoky eyes suggest Elizabeth's concupiscent awakening in *9 ½ Weeks*, and later Nina employs the lipstick to write the word *WHORE* across a bathroom's mirror which she has no memory of doing; her dark sexuality is blossoming which, at first, scares her. Next, the *rubedo* appears as blood when Nina hallucinates that she is mutilating her finger by peeling its skin at the reception where Leroy crowned her the Swan Queen. As the movie progresses, the viewer will notice a heavy use of conflicting blacks and whites allegorizing Nina's virginal purity resisting, even battling, her carnal shadow self. This stark, dualistic symbolism is most noticeable in Leroy's office and apartment. Unlike Nina, Leroy has clearly integrated his Jungian shadow: one observes a swan's skeleton in his office, symbolizing Leroy's macabre personality, transcending his production of Tchaikovsky's ballet. Building upon this, *rubedo* appears as framed artwork which Nina passes by outside Beth's hospital room. While all this is occurring, Nina creates a bizarre form of chaos magick by fusing masochism with masturbation which, for her, fortuitously leads to alchemical change; it is her philosopher's stone. Nina fondles herself in bed only to be interrupted by her mother sleeping in a chair, later Nina caresses herself while taking a bath. Just before dancing in the nightclub, Nina, feeling the effects of the Ecstasy, remarks that her "hands are sweaty," a euphemism for her constant masturbations.

To perfect her chaos magick, Nina engages in self-destructive, masochistic behavior by incessantly scratching her back. When she clips her fingernails too close, she looks into a mirror; her sinister, twisted reflection mocks her implying that she enjoys the commingling of pain with pleasure. Furthermore, Nina has a phantasmagoric fetish: her ballet slippers are bondage instruments, providing her with pain and pleasure simultaneously. When not masturbating, Nina loves flaunting her ballet slippers, however, like Elizabeth's black stockings, Nina's fetish betrays her. While she is practicing a pirouette, her slipper gives way causing her to break—at least fracture—some of her toes. It is through this chaotic-sadistic masturbatory black sorcery that Nina transforms from innocent ballerina to the spellbinding Odele.

Nina's alchemical transmutation finally occurs when, goaded by the trickster Lily, she consumes Ecstasy, descending into a pit of depravity, the nightclub, which sees her dancing bathed in red lights (*rubedo*) announcing finality of the Great Work. The red lights consume the dance floor, causing Nina to morph between herself and her Black Swan persona signifying psychological deterioration; Nina can no longer differentiate reality from fantasy. As Nina dances, subliminal images of full moons and Rothbart flash in the nightclub. Her dark side, emerging like a demon from the bowels of

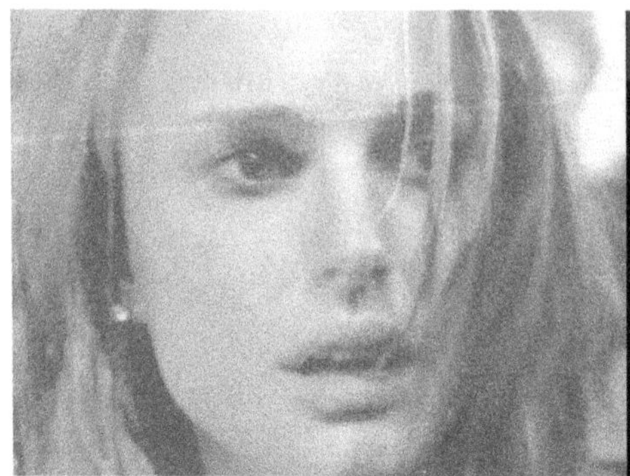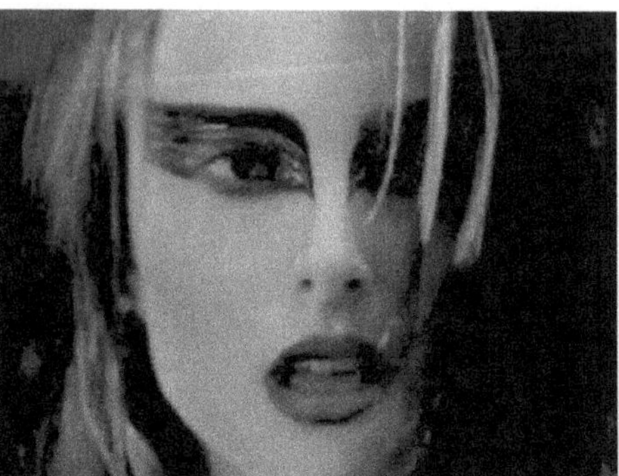

As Nina dances and rolls in the nightclub, she flashes between her typical White Swan persona (Left) and her Black Swan Jungian shadow (Right). Nina's dark side takes over; transmutation will now occur on a psychological and physical level. The red lights finalize the alchemical process initiated by Nina's masochistic masturbatory chaos magick. When Nina dances with Lily in the club, if one carefully listens one will hear Erica's disembodied voice cackling in the background music along with a demeaning chorus, "Sweet girl, sweet girl," mocking Nina's alchemical metamorphosis. The night club's dance sequence, with its discombobulated imagery, indicates that Nina cannot control her shadow. Depraved and full of hubris, Nina next promiscuously makes out in a filthy toilet suggesting–to the subconscious mind–Inferno's Circle of Lust in Dante's *Divine Comedy*.

Hell, is accompanied with all the symptoms of schizophrenia: delusions, paranoid beliefs, and hallucinations, all of which torment Nina. The night club's red lights, similar to the red lights in the sex club-porn house in *9 ½ Weeks*, suggest that the *nigredo* contains the seeds of the *rubedo*.[533] The vision of wholeness remains even in the midst of decay, although this harmony might be nothing more but an occult ideal.[534]

Nina's alchemical transition is masterfully foreshadowed by the ring-tone of her mobile device. When Erica first calls Nina on her cell phone, before being cast as the Swan Queen, the ring is a standard ringtone. Erica calls Nina right before she passes her doppelgänger on the street on her way home. However, after Nina is made Swan Queen by Leroy, and shortly before dancing with the trickster Lily, Erica calls Nina twice on her phone. The ringtone has magically changed; it now tinkles the somber "Swan Theme," symbolizing Nina's forthcoming transformation. The *rubedo* of the night-club signifies that Nina's alchemy is now complete or perfected, and that metamorphosis is on its way; Nina's Jungian shadow, or Black Swan, will devour her White Swan ego with disastrous consequences. Like *9 ½ Weeks'* Elizabeth, she cannot harmonize these two contrasting sides of her psyche.

---

533 cf. Wilson's *Secret Cinema*, p. 143.
534 *ibid.*

After exiting the club, Nina's hallucinations become menacingly acute, accompanied with Brundlefly-like physical-alchemical transmutation. Nina enters a cab, fantasizing that Lily is seated beside her, fondling her; in reality, Nina is alone on the backseat, appeasing her shadow by masturbating in public. Nina returns home, fantasizing that Lily is performing cunnilingus upon her when, once again, she is masturbating or, even worse, having incestuous sex with her mother. When Nina becomes paranoid, believing that Lily is trying to steal her Swan Queen role, her reflection comes to life in a mirror. Paranoid, Nina sees Leroy morph into a demonic Rothbart. In a last-ditch effort to resist the change and quell the hallucinations, Nina returns Beth's stolen items believing that if she rids herself of Beth's things, and thus of Beth's damaging personality, she will purge herself of her shadow. In other words, Nina believes she is contaminated with Beth's self-destructive tendencies, thereby returning the items will free her of Beth's harmful qualities. As she leaves the ballet company, she turns to see a giant billboard which once featured Beth, only now it proudly displays Nina as the Swan Queen. The date of February 12 remains because from here on out Nina is the *Dying Swan*, anticipating her impending death at film's climax. She returns Beth's items, but it is too late for the White Swan; upon returning home, she suffers a horrid hallucination of a macabre, blood-soaked Beth in her kitchen. Nina then sees her mother's amateurish artwork come alive and viciously mock her by calling her "sweet girl." Nina has unfettered her Black Swan, freeing it from her restrictive and repressive ego, but this was only possible through masochistic mutilations and masturbation, which is why the laughing artwork is so tormenting: Nina knows her shadow persona can only manifest through her own humiliation and sexual frustration. Nina's Black Swan alchemically liberated, she now begins to change psychically: standing before her mirror, her eyes blaze a demonic red, or *rubedo*, signifying completion of the Great Work while, at the same time, sprouting a black feather from her shoulder. Her legs become crooked, bird-like. Comparatively, Nina's fierce red eyes resemble those of Christopher Lee's Dracula when he portrayed the legendary vampire in a series of horror films produced by Hammer Studios. The symbolism of Nina's bloody eyes is evident: she, like the vampire, is a ghastly monster. Later, in her dressing room, Nina notices that her feet are webbed; her alchemical transition well underway.

Nina takes the stage as Odette, the White Swan, appearing sad, confused, and disoriented because she is no longer an innocent White Swan, her mother's "sweet girl;" rather, her Jungian shadow thrives. Nina's alchemical becoming is symbolized by the stage saturated with red lights (the *rubedo*, resurrected from the nightclub) with a full moon in the background. The moon signifies Nina's old-self, her virginal *albedo*, the sweet girl, the pure Odette, which is now red, *rubedo*, announcing Nina's alchemical transmutation into the Black Swan. Hence, when Nina dances the White Swan, Odette, she is bewildered and lost.[535] Think back to the nightclub: a red moon hangs behind Nina and Lily when they dance together, indicating Nina's distorted reality, her forthcoming alchemical finality. *Swan Lake's* red lights are the *rubdeo* from the dancefloor: her alchemical process finished, Nina will finally become a Black Swan, her eyes burning hellfire, dancing perfectly.

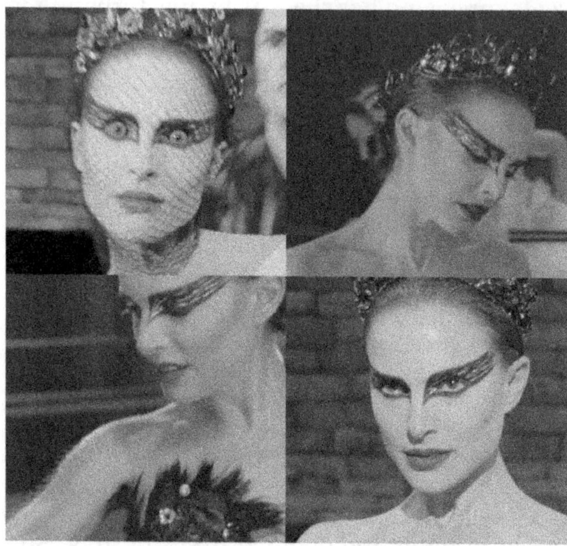

(Top Left) Nina takes the stage alchemically changing into Odette, the Black Swan. Her eyes blaze freakishly red (cf. *rubedo*), Nina's veiled face contorts with devilish delight, beaming with satanic confidence, symbolizing that her Jungian shadow is now awake and that it is finally her turn. She has successfully performed chaos magick, ritualistically fusing masturbation with masochism to accomplish her alchemy. (Top Right) For Nina, wearing the over-the-top black makeup, the blood red lipstick, and a black bodice and tutu is a sensual experience producing transmutation, the ballerina consumed with autoerotic pleasure. Nina is a fleshy cauldron of passion, lust, and momentary confidence; by donning the black of the *nigredo*, she enjoys the dark light of the Left-Hand Path. (Bottom Left) Nina alchemically grows feathers, physically transforming into the confident Black Swan. The feathers resemble hair, an allusion to superstition, the hairy palms of the masturbator, denoting Nina's dejected onanism; the black feathers further symbolize her shadow emerging from her pure, virginal flesh. (Bottom Right) Odile, the White Swan is gone; having successfully danced Odette, the Black Swan, Nina is now the Swan Queen. She is a gorgeous chaos magickian; comparatively, Nina is Edgar Allan Poe's Conqueror Worm, a poem implying human life is a mad folly ending in hideous death, because the universe is controlled by dark forces beyond comprehension. For Nina, "That the play is the tragedy, 'Man,' And its hero, the Conqueror Worm." – E.A. Poe, *The Conqueror Worm*, 1843.

Nina has had enough; backstage she kills her

---

535 The moon is also an emblem of Sayers' lunacy which was explained in *Cinema Symbolism*.

White Swan persona–her ego–finally allowing her evil, *nigredo* Black Swan to finally surface. Her shadow now rampant, Nina dances the Black Swan flawlessly with unfettered passion like she was participating in the Roman festival of Saturnalia. On stage, she sprouts feathers, growing wings, symbolizing that her *nigerdo* or inner Black Swan is alive, her virginal *albedo* is dead; Nina has affected alchemical transmutation by performing chaos magick. She kisses Leroy backstage, succumbing like a smitten schoolboy because he is unable to resist Nina's transformation into a Black Swan dominatrix, something he has yearned for all along. Through alchemy, Nina becomes someone else: when she is her true innocent self, the White Swan, she has no memory of the actions of her darker Black Swan personality and vice versa. For instance, Nina has no recollection of writing the word *WHORE* across the mirror, or stabbing herself with the shard of mirror, nor does she recall having–what appears to be–incestuous sex with her mother whom she believes to be Lily. Nina is angel and demon, light and darkness, lesbian and heterosexual: she is a disjointed, sexually repressed paradox that houses two personalities in perpetual conflict.Finally, Nina runs towards upwards the light, the sun, suggesting Gnostic *ascensio* but tragically dies knowing she cannot reconcile the shadow with the light dwelling inside, splitting her in half like a doppelganger. The sun, the light, denotes her alchemical en*light*enment which was Nina's transition from purity to darkness, Jekyll to Hyde, the divine acceptance of her shadow and the abandonment–or suppression–of the virginal *albedo*. This devilish theme is echoed in 1964's *The Masque of the Red Death* which sees Juliana (Hazel Court, 1926-2008), a student of black magic, perform satanic rituals to appease her Luciferian master, Prince Prospero (Vincent Price). Juliana attempts black magic (cf. the *nigredo*) of the highest caliber, thereby perfecting herself which, like Nina, ends in ruination: Juliana believes she has achieved demonic apotheosis, but instead is raped and murdered by a host of Goetia- like demons of her conjuring.[536] Leroy, paralleling Prospero, has ignited the solar light-fire or

---

536 See Director's Cut/Extended version; this scene was omitted from the theatrical release (USA: 24 June 1964) of *The Masque of the Red* Death due to its controversial nature. Note regarding *Masque of the Red Death*: In *Cinema Symbolism*, this author identified the phrase "bread mother" as being spoken by the Red Death to an old woman foraging at the beginning of film. Although this seems to be what he is saying, the movie's script identifies the words as "grandmother" not "bread mother." This was recently brought to this author's attention; however, the term grandmother does

alchemy by awakening Nina's suppressed dark side; he has assisted her alchemical transformation into the Black Swan while at the same time facilitating her tragic downfall. Nina, having returned to her White Swan persona, tries to reconcile her dark epiphany by running toward the sun (*the light*) but, like Icarus, comes too close; she falls to the ground, dying in a state between alchemical perfection and ruination. Nina acknowledges that becoming the Black Swan, the *nigredo*, was temporary and unsustainable, but, if only momentarily, the transition was a success. Saturated in light of the *sol niger*, Nina tells Leroy, her Luciferian master, that "I felt it. Perfect. I was perfect," with her final breath.

* * * *

Although a box-office disappointment, Brian De Palma's Passion is a gloomy, alchemical film worthy of analysis. A loose remake of the 2010 French film *Love Crimes*, *Passion* finds advertising big shot Christine Stanford (Rachel McAdams) and her mysterious assistant Isabelle James (Noomi Rapace) thrown into competition with one another after Christine takes credit for an idea that belongs to Isabelle. Before long, the two women have entered into a game of one-upmanship in the boardroom and the bedroom, which ultimately leads to murder. *Passion* features the symbolic scheme of alchemical transmutation; however, a brief description of the plot must first be given.

Christine, a bisexual advertising executive working for a high-end marketing company, attempts to gain professional and romantic-erotic power (cf. psychic vampire) over her up-and-coming subordinate, Isabelle. Christine's motivation is revenge because Isabelle is having an affair with her lover, Dirk Harriman (Paul Anderson). Christine is also motivated because Isabelle has spurned her sexual advances. Christine does everything to ruin Isabelle's reputation and relationships, trying to fire Isabelle's secretary, Dani (Karoline Herfurth), a lesbian in love with Isabelle. Because of these events, Isabelle seemingly becomes emotionally destitute developing an addiction to prescription drugs. After Christine is found dead, Isabelle is arrested, confessing to the murder

---

not make sense in the context of the film. Since the woman is gathering winter fuel, the term bread mother is apropos. This author stands by his interpretation in *Cinema Symbolism* but nevertheless wants to point out this potential discrepancy to his readers.

in a drug-induced trance. However, Isabelle quickly changes her story becoming desperate to prove her innocence; she informs the police that she has an alibi for the evening the murder took place. Dirk, drunk after being rejected by Christine, is arrested after a white scarf with Christine's blood turns up in his car. Isabelle is freed, and Dirk is charged with the murder despite his denials. It is also explained that Dirk's motivation for killing Christine is revenge because Christine threatened to expose Dirk's embezzlement from the advertising company.

At the climax, it is revealed that Isabelle is guilty of murdering Christine, and set everything up to convince everyone that she was having a nervous breakdown while framing Dirk for the crime. Dani reveals that she had captured Isabelle on video with her mobile device at various moments during the night of the murder. Dani then tries to blackmail Isabelle into becoming her lover. That evening, Isabelle has a bizarre dream wherein she strangles Dani to death after being seduced by her, but not before Dani sends the incriminating video of Isabelle to the investigating police detective, Inspector Bach (Rainer Bach). Suddenly, out of nowhere, Christine's deceased twin sister Clarissa miraculously appears, strangling Isabelle from behind with the bloodstained scarf. The next moment Isabelle wakes in her bedroom from the nightmare only to face a new one: Dani is dead at the foot of her bed. Nothing else is disclosed, and the movie abruptly ends.

Much of imagery of *Passion* indicates duality: a character that has a twin sibling and scenes that play out in front of mirrors and cameras. Dualism is a recurring theme of Brian De Palma's films *Sisters* (1973), *Obsession* (1976), *Body Double* (1984), *Raising Cain* (1992), and *Femme Fatal* (2002), and implies transition of the self. Alchemical change is present in *Passion*; however, De Palma paradoxically toys with the viewer since all is not symbolically as it seems. The film begins with Christine and Isabelle sitting on a sofa before an open Apple laptop computer. The symbolism is somewhat obvious: the Apple computer and its related emblem (an apple with a bite taken out) represent the forbidden fruit of the Garden of Eden; thus, the two women personify the two wives of the first man Adam: Lilith and Eve. But who is exactly who? Isabelle wears nothing but black throughout the film augmented by her raven locks, indicating she epitomizes alchemical blackness, death, *nigredo,* or the demon-trickster goddess, Lilith. Being a supreme con-artist, Isabelle is a feminized version of the Juggler or Magician card of the Tarot–the instigator of change–evidenced by her witty ad campaign. She is a master manipulator–or is she?

While the two women kibitz and flirt, the alchemical solar *citrinitas* enters the room in the form of Dirk, a minor, pathetic character drowned out by the raging estrogen of Christine, Isabelle, and Dani. He is not wanted having interrupted the two women's semi-erotic playtime. When Isabelle leaves, Christine gives her an elegant white scarf, a token of the lunar *albedo* and the sacred feminine (cf. Dorothy Gale's Silver Slippers from Baum's *The Wizard of Oz*), becoming an emblem of the women's unfettered sexuality, or *passion*, as the title of the film implies. The scarf turns up over and over again, eventually becoming a key piece of evidence. One thing is clear: *Passion* is all about the suppression of the masculine and the exaltation of the feminine. For example, Dirk wears a surreal white mask of Christine's face while he has sex with her, signifying she prefers sex with herself (cf. masturbation), or craves lesbianism over a heterosexual relationship; Christine becomes frustrated when she cannot achieve orgasm with him. Men are sexual outcasts in this movie, even Inspector Bach's apologetic advances are rejected; the divine masculine is persona non grata in *Passion*. The moon rules the day and night in this movie; the sacred feminine is out of control, the masculine is in a state of decay. The lunar-esque silver scarf, it is explained, belongs to Dirk, which is apropos since the scarf will be employed by Isabelle in implicating him in the murder of Christine, resulting in his incarceration. Subconsciously, the bloody scarf signifies the menstrual cycle, regulated by the moon.

Personifying Lilith, Isabelle is a mercurial loner, donning black clothing and lingerie, tokens of the alchemical *nigredo*, the Jungian archetypal shadow, during most of the movie. Isabelle is at first subservient to Christine, but Isabelle wishes to change alchemically into Christine *qua* Lilith: a ruthless executive, a sexually domineering bitch. Christine is callous and cavalier when she takes credit Isabelle's marketing idea, telling her that she did what she expects Isabelle to do if she was in her position (cf. dualism, role reversal). Christine also employs a variety of bondage devices, including a strap-on dildo, suggestive of Lilith's femme fatale deviant nature. Later, at a company party, she attempts to destroy Isabelle emotionally by showing a surveillance video of her wrecking her car in the parking garage. Thus, one has to ask: is Christine the personification of Lilith and not Isabelle? De Palma successfully implements this plot twist leaving the viewer in a state of confusion regarding the film's actual shadow persona. Christine adroitly hints at this by telling Isabelle, "You're more like me than you think." De Palma use of subliminal imagery to convey this message to the audience is, once again, superb and masterful. For example, Isabelle begins the movie wearing black, sitting crossed legged on Christine's sofa; later Christine sits in this *same posture* on the same sofa wearing black lingerie and stockings while waiting for Isabelle to come over to satisfy her lust.

Symbolizing Isabelle's metamorphosis into the wicked Christine, the color red, *rubedo*, is well-placed throughout the film, denoting alchemical finality. Christine's cigarette case is red; Christine wears sexy red lipstick; Christine employer, Koch Image International, logo and lettering is red; she wears a bright red turtleneck during a board meeting, and a red note left by Isabelle lures Christine with the promise of lesbian sex, only it turns out to be a calling card foreshadowing her demise. However, the starkest and abundant use of the color red is a pair of bondage-like red high heels that Christine presents to Isabelle, which she entices her to wear. This redness signifies Isabelle's desire to complete her Great Work by becoming Christine, which, in the end, she accomplishes. The shoes represent Christine's lesbian desires which she desperately wishes to refine with Isabelle. Christine's libido awakens when Isabelle puts on the red high heels in the back of a limousine, causing Christine to make homoerotic advances towards her. Christine is cutting loose her lesbian desires, while Isabelle secretly wants to become Christine. The red high heels are a metaphor for the secret longings these women seek to explore and embrace; what they want to *become* alchemically.

Eventually, Isabelle transforms into Christine only she is more ruthless and cunning. Isabelle, emulating Christine, acts unilaterally regarding a business decision, causing Christine to become envious of her; Christine now tries to destroy alchemically, or break down, Isabelle's sullen *nigredo* by turning it against her. Christine now becomes the trickster when she humiliates Isabelle by showing her a video of her having sex with Dirk, embarrassing her during a company party. However, not be outdone, Isabelle successfully one-ups Christine by cunningly masterminding her murder, pinning it on Dirk. Isabelle deceives Christine with a note promising lesbian sex, framing Dirk with the bloody scarf, echoing the trickster nature of the mercurial Juggler card. In jail, Isabelle's scornful, vengeful personality is symbolized by a drawing of Medusa that appears on the wall inside her cell. In the book, *Female Rage: Unlocking Its Secrets, Claiming Its Power*, Mary Valentis and Anne Devane note that, "When we asked women what female rage looks like to them, it was always Medusa, the snaky-haired monster of myth, who came to mind...In one interview after another we were told that Medusa is 'the most horrific woman in the world'...[though] none of the women we interviewed could remember the details of the myth."[537] Freed from jail, Isabelle emerges from her feigned psychosis and naiveté only to discover that she has been manipulated by Dani, her flaming redheaded assistant (cf. *rubedo*), having completed the Great Work. Dani has perfected a blackmail scheme which will chain Isabelle to her lesbian desires. Who is transforming into whom? Isabelle became the ruthless Christine, and Dani became Isabelle by becoming what Isabelle was to Christine, her subservient assistant, but now Dani *is* Christine, outwitting Isabelle. Embodying Christine, Dani is cruel, speaking down to Isabelle now returned to the role of the lowly servant. However, Isabelle is an archetype and Dani is a pretender; being darkness incarnate, Isabelle kills Dani at the film's finale. Before the movie ends, Christine's twin Clarissa manifests out of thin air wearing green high heels which are conspicuously shown to the audience. These same shoes appeared earlier when Christine and Isabelle preview a fashion show. How and why Clarissa comes to wear them is a mystery.

In her final moments, Dani's manages to send the incriminating video via a mobile device implicating Isabelle in Christine's death to Inspector Bach; then Clarissa strangles Isabelle with the white scarf, but this is only a nightmare. Or is it? Isabelle awakens from her nightmare only to be facing a new one: Dani is dead having been killed by her. Does this make Clarissa the mysterious and enigmatic Mercury? Is she the capricious Juggler after all? Who is the master of transition and who is the fledgling novice? Who, if anyone, sent the incriminating video to Inspector Bach? What was a dream and what was reality? What are merely figments of Isabelle's sinister imagination? The film concludes not answering these epistemological questions.

---

537 Cited in Stephen R. Wilk's *Medusa: Solving the Mystery of the Gorgon*, pp. 217-218.

Although it does not provide insight into the film's dubious ending, the number eight follows Isabelle like children followed the Pied Piper of Hamelin. For instance, there are eight letters in the name, Isabelle. Isabelle has been working with Christine for eight months, and while attending a soiree with Christine, the name *Octo* hangs on the wall behind them. *Octo*, the name of the company throwing the party, comes from the ancient Greek *okto* and Latin *octō* both meaning *eight*. Later, Isabelle is scheduled to meet an emotionally distraught Dirk at 8:00 pm. For Isabelle, the number eight is a veiled reference to the eighth card of the Tarot, Strength or Fortitude. On this card's archetypal negative qualities, occult author Richard Cavendish explains:

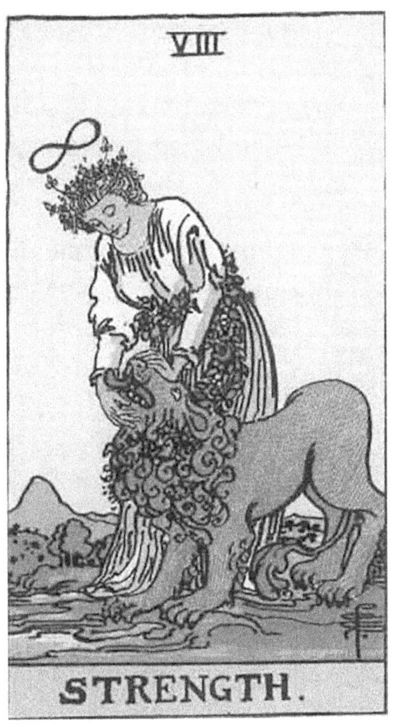

The eighth card of the Major Arcana is Strength, sometimes identified as Fortitude, from the Rider-Waite Tarot deck.

Strength of Force was originally a picture of Fortitude, … Abstract nouns in Greek and Latin are frequently feminine in gender, not neuter, which facilitated the personification of abstract ideas as goddess or demi-goddesses. …The lion can be identified with the Jungian concept of 'the shadow,' the dark and primitive, instinctive and dangerous part of each human being, which is feared and repressed. It is the Mr. Hyde who lives inside each Dr. Jekyll. …The Golden Dawn taught 'a dangerous secret,' not to be openly divulged, about the evil side of human personality: 'The evil persona can be rendered great and strong, yet trained, animal whereupon the man rideth…' In Crowley's version of the card, which he called Lust, the woman is riding of the Great Beast of Revelation, the apotheosis of evil, anarchy, and destruction. …The woman's unnatural dominance of the lion suggested to Crowley the discipline of submission to the abnormal and perverse.

…Waite (Arthur Edward Waite) had both alchemy and erotic symbolism in mind in designing his version of the card. The lion is red for the fiery, active, male principle of sulphur (which is red in its natural, unrefined state). The woman is closing the lion's mouth instead of opening it, which is another piece of sexual innuendo.[538]

Isabelle unleashes her inner Mr. Hyde by becoming a devious and vicious version of Christine. No longer repressed, Isabelle's evil personality, the Lilith within, alchemically awakens, murdering Christine. The solar *citrinitas* lion is degraded eventually destroyed by the feminine: Dirk is humiliated by Christine, framed for her death by Isabelle. Thus, like Crowley explained, the lion *qua* Dirk is submissive to Isabelle's disciplined dominance; the moon rules the sun which to Crowley was abnormal and perverse. Put another way, Isabelle manipulates the solar lion, becoming an apotheosis of evil, paralleling Crowley's interpretation of the card. Finally, Isabelle is forced into a lesbian relationship with Dani, which she finds repugnant, signifying, according to Waite, the card's sexual innuendo. The number eight is an adroitly concealed Tarot esoterica which identifies Isabelle's deviant and manipulative monkeyshines, making her a femme fatale archetype.

INDIA STOKER'S SADDLE SHOES: FETISHISM, MASTURBATION, SELF-LOATHING AND PSYCHOSIS

Park Chan-wook's *Stoker* is a symbolic epistemological conundrum. Like *The Wizard of Oz*, the film is multi-layered with allegories and metaphors, but in *Stoker* they intentionally contradict themselves. On one hand, we have a veiled transitional-alchemical storyline, but on the other, we are presented with sequences suggesting the transition was inevitable. In other words, *Stoker's* hidden alchemical colors and clues are nothing more than a red herring. On its surface, *Stoker* pays homage to Hitchcock's *A Shadow of a Doubt* (1943), a movie about a bored teenager named

---

538 Cavendish, *The Tarot*, pp. 97-98, "(Arthur Edward Waite)" added. cf. Crowley's *The Book of Thoth, passim.*

Charlotte "Charlie" Newton (Teresa Wright, 1918-2005) receiving wonderful news: her mother's younger brother (her namesake), Uncle Charlie Newton (Joseph Cotton, 1905-1994), is arriving for a visit. However, all is not what it seems. As the plot thickens, Charlotte discovers her uncle's murderous secrets but withholds them, allowing Charlie to be buried a hero. *Stoker* also references Kubrick's *The Shining*, pays homage to Hitchcock's *Psycho*, and even has a well-hidden *Black Swan* Easter egg. The Easter egg is not surprising since *Stoker's* production designer, Thérèse DePrez (1965-2017), was also the production designer of *Black Swan*.

Like all movies that feature alchemical change, a pilgrimage of transition, *Stoker* is a vast pallet of colors. The first color that jumps off the screen is green. It pervades the interior of Evelyn (Nicole Kidman) and India Stoker's mansion. Most of the movie is set inside the green walls and corridors of the Stoker manor, and although the home is lavish with well-manicured lawns and gardens, the house feels more like Kubrick's sinister Overlook Hotel than a home with a welcoming hearth. Instead, it's a restrictive, suffocating chastity belt that neither woman can shed. Over dinner Evelyn says she will "...stay locked up in this house for the rest of my life..." implying sexual abstinence. Within the confines of the nunnery-like estate the women are forced into an asexual reality; Evelyn has become a sarcastic, mean-spirited, frustrated taskmaster, while masturbation appease India's dark fantasies and yearnings. The house, with its labyrinth-like hallways, large rooms, and a foreboding dank basement is a giant, prohibitive maze that neither India nor Evelyn can escape from; it is an imposing castle forever holding a queen and princess prisoner from the rest of the world. The mansion is like *The Shining's* Overlook Hotel because both dwellings force their inhabitants to live in a repetitive cycle.

When India finally leaves the home's green walls at the end, the scene feels more like a prison break than an 18-year-old moving out. The color green, in the context of *Stoker*, symbolizes envy, green with envy, and the jealous game of one-upmanship that Evelyn and India engage to win the affections of Charlie Stoker (Matthew Goode). Charlie is the brother of the recently deceased Richard Stoker (Dermot Mulroney), Evelyn's husband and India's father. Charlie has moved into the household but has a dark secret the women are not aware of: Charlie is mentally ill, having been released from a mental institution by his brother. As the movie unfolds, it is

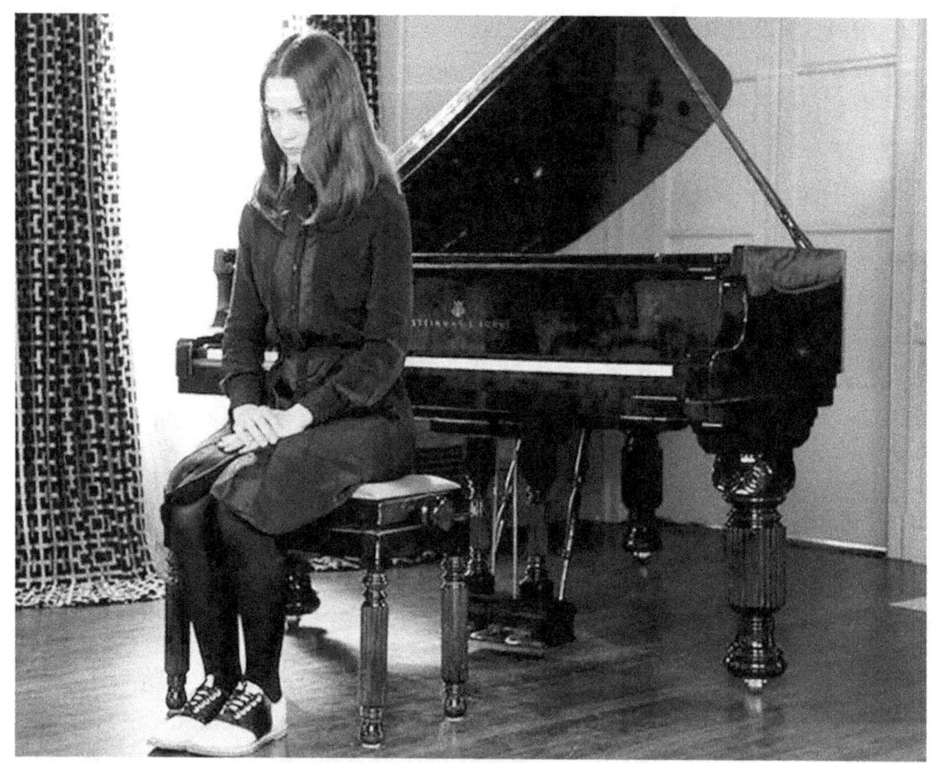

India Stoker, the eternal melancholic, dresses in black because of her father's death. Furthermore, India's black clothing identifies her with alchemy's *nigredo*–putrefaction and decay–characterizing her cruel, moribund personality.

explained that Richard's death was not accidental rather he was murdered by Charlie. The film is not a murder mystery, but a dark coming-of-age film esoterically invested with all the colors of Renaissance alchemy. But mirroring Kubrick's *The Shining*, Chan-wook turns against this occult color scheme by suggesting the alchemical change was inherent, predetermined, and incongruously predestined.

Exoterically, *Stoker* is the tale of the awkward transition from adolescence to adulthood, from innocence to experience; this is the journey that India Stoker, like all teenagers, must take. In other words, it is a coming-of-age film. Esoterically, *Stoker* is all about the alchemical metamorphosis of India from a melancholic teenager into a psychopathic adult; her order is chaos, her innocence is sexuality. India is a spoiled brat and a sociopath; she beautifully personifies the alchemical *nigredo*. Like all teenagers, she is bellicose and defiant, but her schizoid angst is more pronounced than most. She is obsessed with wearing black and white saddle shoes signifying dark against light, chaos and order, evil and good, which she receives every year on her birthday from an unknown benefactor. India fetishizes over her shoes by lying in bed with them like they were her lovers. She even changes the laces to reflect her emotions: they are black when she attends her father's funeral but become white after her mourning has passed. But she is outgrowing the shoes and losing her innocence; the shoes are now tight and uncomfortable producing blisters to form on her feet. On her 18th birthday, she finds the gift-wrapped box containing the shoes only this year the box contains a mysterious key. India also has a strange hobby for a teen-age girl: she is a huntress; her kills are taxidermy decorating the mansion.

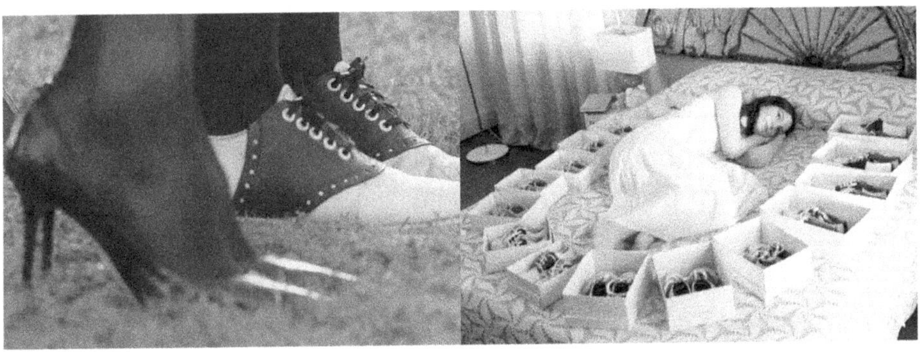

(Left) The Stoker Family shoe fetish. India's saddle shoes are not only an extension of her flesh but of her emotions as well. Attending her father's funeral, India has replaced the white laces with black ones representing her mourning. India's mother, seated next to her, wears black high heels anticipating India trading in her saddle shoes for sexier footwear. When India finally puts on the high heels, she welcomes the *nigredo*, becoming a murderess, achieving a bizarre form of adulthood. As India explains, "Only once you realize this do you become free, and to become adult is to become free." The "this" she refers to is her shadow self. (Right) The detestable India surrounds herself with her saddle shoes. She wears them, and only them, until she finally trades them in for sexy high heels at Charlie's behest; India's golden pyramid headboard is an emblem of the masculine heralding Charlie's (cf. *citrinitas*) dominance over her. India shoes play the role of alchemical trickster changing her from a teenager into a sophisticated yet murderous adult.

While grieving the death of her father, she reads *The Encyclopedia of Funerals and Mourning*, admonishing her mother for not lamenting the passing of her father enough. Misery loves company so India wants her mother to share her melancholy, even though Evelyn is trying to move on. India is not outgoing, caring little for what the outside world has to offer her. After the film's prologue, India appears dressed in mourning attire, complete with black stockings, symbolizing the sullen *nigredo*, exhibing the characteristics of the melancholic: she is miserable, antisocial, callous, aloof, has nothing but disdain for her peers, is friendless, devious, and is downright weird. For instance, during art class she does not draw the flowers; rather, she draws the inside of the vase holding the flowers. The vase's inside is red and yellow, the alchemical *citrinitas* and *rubedo*, signifying her alchemical change. India wallows in self-loathing, fostering a remorseless love-hate relationship with her mother, Evelyn. Evelyn embodies the alchemical *albedo*, the mature sophisticated feminine, seeking to unify with Charlie's *citrinitas*, thus perfecting the symbolic *Chymical Wedding of Christian Rosenkreutz*, the alchemical marriage of the sun and moon, Jung's syzygy The relationship seems natural because both Charlie and Evelyn are in their 40s, but this union never occurs because Charlie radiates the dark light of the *nigredo*; put another way, he is more akin to India than Evelyn. He is drawn to her and her to him so much so she will perfect alchemy by emotionally and psychologically becoming her uncle.

Charlie personifies the *citrinitas* stage, thus, India's forthcoming metamorphosis is symbolized by the color yellow (cf. the sun) which transcends India: yellow road lines, yellow birthday candles; a yellow spider crawls across the floor and up her black, stocking clad leg; deviled eggs; like a rising sun, a yellow plate hangs on the wall over her when she reads the funeral book; a yellow bird egg with blood on it (a metaphor for the bloodbath that will come); and a golden, pyramidal headboard stands over India's bed like an aesthetic tombstone. Later while sleeping, India dreams of the yellow spider crawling up her thigh (while still wearing black hosiery) making haste towards her erogenous zone, a reference to sexual awakening and adulthood. All this foreshadows the masculine, alchemical sun entering India's life, changing it forever.

The masculine sun arrives in the form of the mysterious, odd, pied piper- like Charlie, an enigma to both Evelyn and India. He immediately becomes the object of their affections, so they vie for his favor. Charlie plays his sister-in-law and niece against each other, eventually leading India down a pathway ending with her alchemically becoming his deviant personality. As the embodiment of the *citrinitas*, yellow surrounds Charlie: he gift-wraps India's saddle shoes with yellow ribbon and tissue; he wears a yellow sweater; the walls and curtains of his room in the psychiatric facility, the Crawford Institute, are yellow, and he carries a yellow umbrella. Like *Black Swan's* Thomas Leroy, Charlie emanates dark light, only his is much more deadly. He is Left-Hand Path Kabbalah, the ultimate saturnine black sun: Charlie Stoker is a suave murdering psychopath. But this sun has a powerful gravitational pull, drawing India to him like a moth to flame; Charlie's psyche is what India will ascend to: she will *become* Charlie by imitating his murderous ways while simultaneously trading youthful childhood innocence for mature adulthood.

To symbolize India's alchemical assumption of Charlie's twisted spirit, India is presented in a state ascendancy; she is maturing towards adulthood thus growing up. Her name implies this: *India* is a subtle reference to the mysterious land of India and the great Hindu trinity of Brahma, Vishnu, and Shiva who, despite being gods are subject to the sorcerers who, by means of their spells, exercise an ascendancy over theses mighty deities, making them bound to whatever commands their masters the magicians may please to issue.[539] Like a magical huntress, we see India ascend a small flight of steps (a hill) at school confronting and defeats a godlike bully named Chris Pitts (Lucas Till) by using a pencil as a defensive weapon. At night, she climbs the steps of a playground slide to become one with the bright full moon, the goddess Diana, the divine lunar huntress, symbolizing that India, already an expert in hunting and stalking prey, is about to take her game to a deadlier level. Twice India ascends a winding staircase in her mansion to become equal with Charlie, greeting her at the top. The first time to meet Charlie on his level, the second she ascends towards him, growing up, finally reaching adulthood when Charlie gives her a pair of high heels because she is now "of age," having reached her 18th birthday. When he puts them on her, India experiences rapture; the high heels are an aphrodisiac, she is no longer an adolescent but a sexy, mature adult. Gone are the childish saddle shoes, she has ripened, ready for the high-heeled sexual world of womanhood. But the esoteric symbolism of the shoes is veiled: from this moment on India *is* Charlie; she has reached him at the top of the steps (cf. ladder of ascension) welcoming his gift, but the high heels symbolically trick her by *changing her into him, change India from morose teenager to murdering adult*, the high heels are a demented, erotic version of the medieval philosopher's stone. From this point onward, she alchemically embodies his psychotic behavior and tendencies; Evelyn admonishes her, "India, who are you?" she asks her rebellious daughter. The question is

---

539 See Frazer's *The Golden Bough*, p. 51.

apropos because India herself no longer knows who she is, only that she is transitioning; her sense of identity confused. The mother-daughter love-hate relationship finally culminates with India's alchemical metamorphosis into Charlie's psyche, the *rubedo*, which occurs in Evelyn's red bedroom. Charlie tries to strangle Evelyn with his belt–the imagery parallels Charlie strangling Whip Taylor (Alden Ehrenreich)–but India shoots and kills him, finally transitioning from gloomy teenager to murderous adult; the conversion a triumph. Evelyn witnesses a *great becoming*: with Charlie dead, the melancholic teenage India also dies. India is reborn having successfully performed alchemy by changing herself into Charlie by assuming (or achieving) his adult yet insane mantle. India buries his body, fleeing the home wearing the high heels because she is now a woman; all her saddle shoes are left behind in a mess, symbolizing the chaotic, dysfunctional childish reality she thinks she is abandoning. Speeding away in Charlie's car, she is pulled over by Sheriff Howard whom she stabs with red-handled (cf. *rubedo*) gardening sheers, then shoots him for no reason other than sport. As Sheriff Howard tries to escape, his blood sprays white flowers turning them red recalling *Alice in Wonderland's* Rosicrucianism and gnosis; however, India is not Alice although Wasikowska portrays both in film; contrasting Alice, India does not receive wisdom rather she transforms into a high-heeled psychopath. Thus, she is now Charlie; the alchemical Great Work complete, she has become a deranged murderess. By killing Charlie and Sheriff Howard, she believes she has brought order out of chaos when, in fact, she has become chaos, a living embodiment of her deceased uncle and all his murderous, psychotic ways.

India's great alchemical becoming is symbolized by clues hidden in the celluloid, esoterically implying her coming-of-age, budding sexuality, and thus metamorphosis to a mature, ruthless killer. These clues reinforce the Renaissance alchemical color scheme but can be easily missed by the untrained eye. Charlie, clearly suffering Lolita Syndrome,[540] provides India with saddle shoes that she always wears, symbolizing her subconscious, erotic devotion to him. Charlie teases her with sexual innuendo, "But India ate everything, practically licked it clean," he tells her after she easts the meal that he prepared for her.

---

540 Lolita Syndrome is the sexual preference by an older person, usually understood to be an older man, for a girl in mid-to-late adolescence, the consummation of which is illegal in most jurisdictions.

India is humiliated yet aroused, repulsed yet excited. Charlie gives her wine from 1994, the year India was born, which she drinks, signifying the exchange of bodily fluids. He buys her ice cream, chocolate and vanilla (black and white, just like her shoes) and she makes an ice cream cone which she licks, conjuring fellatio. When India comes in from the pouring rain, seeing her mother and Charlie playing the piano, her drenched, dripping wet saddle shoes are shown, subtly suggesting vaginal secretion caused by sexual arousal. Her shoes symbolize pleasure and humiliation; not only are they are fetish but they're a bizarre form of bondage. Soaking wet, the shoes are a masturbatory talisman, akin to Elizabeth's black silk stockings, anticipating India's pitiful caresses when she takes a shower. It becomes apparent Evelyn is cruel and manipulative, trying to make her daughter envious of her relationship with Charlie. Later, India fantasizes about Charlie sitting beside her while she plays the piano. Soon he begins to tickle the ivories with her. As they perform their piano duet, India becomes seduced by the music they make; India becomes orgasmic by his imaginary presence. The symbolism of this scene is clear: India is trying to emulate the eroticism of her mature, voluptuous mother but she is trapped in a confused ontological limbo existing between youth and adulthood, innocence and experience, masturbation and sex. India even wears a green sweater (the same shade of the home's interior) symbolizing the overwhelming envy India feels towards her mother; India loves and hates Evelyn; so too does she love and hate herself. All of this is all part of the dark sexual game Charlie, Evelyn, and India are playing, but India is unaware that by engaging Charlie and Evelyn, she is morphing into a killer. Alternatively, Charlie and Evelyn think that by placating India they're ameliorating her distorted emotions when, in reality, their actions are making her more hostile. She is a pawn while he is king; it turns out the queenly Evelyn has no place in his (or India's) bizarre world. India is already huntress, but Charlie is a crazed murderer; he watches a program about birds of prey, about how they kill, and how sometimes they have to kill their siblings, foreshadowing India's discovery that Charlie is a monster murdering her father, Richard, killing their younger brother, Jonathan, as a child. Charlie wants India to know this: the mysterious key he substitutes for her saddle shoes unlocks a drawer in her father's desk circuitously revealing Charlie is a deranged psychopath. Most disturbingly, India is at ease when she discovers Charlie is a killer. Instead, she seems to embrace it, symbolizing her alchemy. She has no problem letting Charlie snap Whip's neck after he tries to sexually assault her (even though he has been incapacitated); is fine when she realizes Aunt Gwendolyn (a/k/a Auntie Gin, played by Jacki Weaver) has become one of his victims; does nothing when she discovers the body of the housekeeper Mrs. McGarrick (Phyllis Somerville) in the basement freezer, caring less that he has murdered her father. Most disturbingly, these killings do not repulse her, rather they sexually excite her. While taking a shower, India performs a mysterious baptism: she masturbates fantasizing about Charlie murdering Whip. Melancholically weeping, she climaxes when she recalls Charlie breaking Whip's neck, which

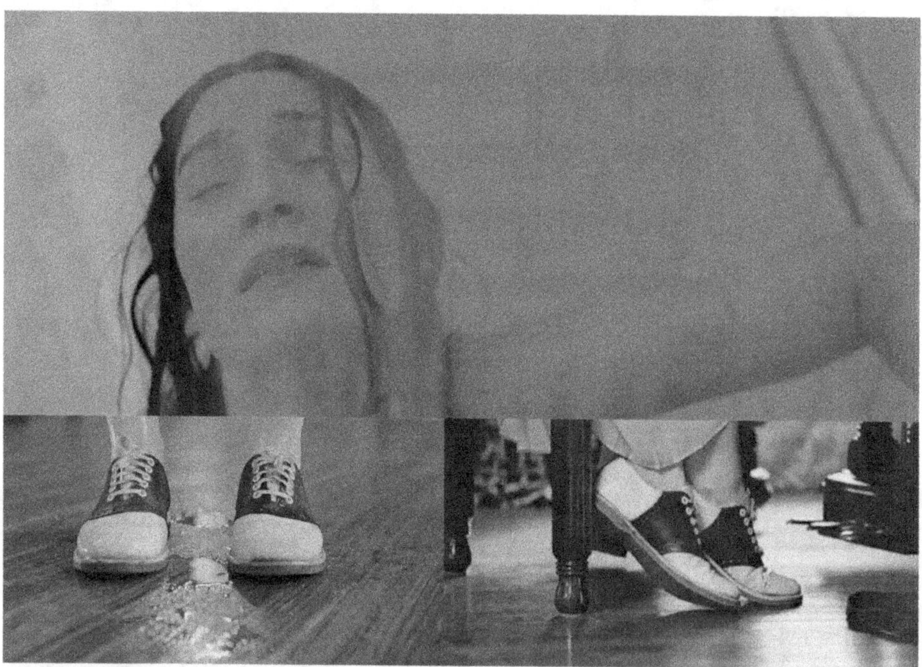

(Top) Like Elizabeth from *9 ½ Weeks* and Nina from *Black Swan* before her, India employs masturbation as part of her catharsis, her sable alchemical formula. Such a risqué theme is rare in mainstream cinema. (Bottom, Left and Right) Another common denominator between these three women is that they all have a fetish: Elizabeth takes pleasure by wearing black silk stockings, Nina's restrictive ballet slippers are a source of agony and ecstasy, India's black and white saddle shoes are pain and pleasure. India's perverse, unnatural fixation with her shoes reflects her toxic personality which eventually turns destructive. Furthermore, one could argue that India masturbates not only to orgasm, but to appease her bizarre shoe fetish.

puts a smile on her face. India gets off on Charlie's murderous ways; she admires him, wanting to become him psychologically. Here is wisdom: this metamorphosis is India Stoker's alchemy; her psychotic Magnum Opus perfected when she finally kills Charlie and Sheriff Howard.

However, Chan-wook betrays these alchemical allegories by bombarding the subconscious mind with repeating, duplicating images (and imagery) implying that India was destined to become a psychotic killer all along; there was no transition; instead, her murderous ways were predestined, almost a part of her DNA. Chan-wook imbues *Stoker* with Kubrick's *The Shining*, making the Stoker mansion feel like the Overlook Hotel, while transforming India into Jack Torrance-like character. At the beginning, India and Charlie are both introduced as silhouettes on the horizon, suggesting that India and Charlie are one and the same. To further convey this repetition, India is seen reading the book *A History of Pi* (1970) by Petr Beckmann. The number π (pi) is a mathematical constant, the ratio of a circle's circumference to its diameter, commonly approximated as 3.14159. Pi is an irrational number because it cannot be expressed in a fraction; its decimal representation never ends and never settles. Being an irrational and constant number, the book symbolizes that India's transformation into psychotic killer has always been part of her psyche, an unsettling inherent constant, her illogical and psychosis inevitable. Later, when India frolics with Whip in a playground at night, she symbolically becomes Pi by going 'round and 'round on a circular carousel, circumnavigating a circle's circumference.[541] The repetition continues: India sits across from a garden statue mirroring its posture. She is seen dripping wet in the rain anticipating her masturbatory shower scene, and later Evelyn is seen briefly taking a shower symbolizing her sexual frustration. Richard Stoker's sunglasses keep appearing, being worn by both India and Charlie. A bully takes a swing at India in art class, repeating this same motion later when India stands up to him, deflecting his oncoming punch with a pencil. When Whip

---

541 It's during this scene that India, subconsciously, hints that she will masturbate, which she does soon thereafter. While at the playground, the following dialog occurs between India and Whip: India: "Have you ever seen a photograph of yourself, taken when you didn't know you were being photographed, from an angle you don't get see when you look in a mirror, and you think, 'That's me… that's also me.' Do you, do you know what I'm talking about? Whip: Yeah, I think I do. India: Well, that's how I feel tonight. Whip: So you're surprised at yourself? You're not afraid of being touched anymore? India: Please don't spoil it."

is about to sexually assault India, he removes his belt while Charlie, sneaking up on him from behind him is also removing his belt, imitating each other, denoting repetition. Both India and Charlie kill while wearing other family members' clothes: Charlie wears and kills with his older brother's belt, and India wears her mother's blouse and father's belt when she kills Sheriff Howard. After having been killed by Charlie, Richard is set afire in his car, and later Evelyn makes a bonfire out of the taxidermy in the house; the former inferno purges Richard and the latter purges India. Both India and Charlie (as a child) handle the same water pistol. Charlie uses the same red-handled sheers India will later use to kill Sheriff Howard. However, the most unexpected use of repetition is when India makes a snow angel while lying on her mother's bed, which is seen later being made by Charlie as a child (in a flashback) after he buries his younger brother Jonathan. All this repetition indicates that psychologically India and Charlie are one and the same; they always have been and always will be. There is no alchemical transition. India is a huntress, so her metamorphosis into a deranged killer was not alchemical; rather, it had been a part of her the entire time, inherited. Chan-wook presents this conflicting symbolism leaving it to the viewer to decide what is alchemical, if anything, and what is predetermined. Such is the unusual nature of *Stoker* and all those inhabiting the Stoker mansion.

Concealed within this alchemy and repetition, Chan-wook also pays homage to Hitchcock's *Psycho*; the parallels between the two movies are uncanny. Both films feature a formidable home which is itself a character. There is taxidermy everywhere in Norman Bates' home and motel office, just like there is taxidermy throughout the Stoker mansion. Both Bates' home and the Stoker estate have creepy basements hiding preserved female corpses, and both basements have dangling light bulbs which end up swinging. Charlie bears a strong resemblance to Norman, and both men reflect each other psychologically and emotionally because they're both psychotic. Norman and Charlie like to murder while wearing their immediate family's clothing: Norman dresses as his dead mother while Charlie wears (and uses) his deceased older brother's belt. Both men have similar eerie catchphrases: Norman tells Marion Crane, "We all go a little mad sometimes," while Charlie tells India, "People disappear all the time." Marion sexually arouses Norman and India sexually arouses Charlie causing both men to kill, making their murders crimes of passion, not profit.

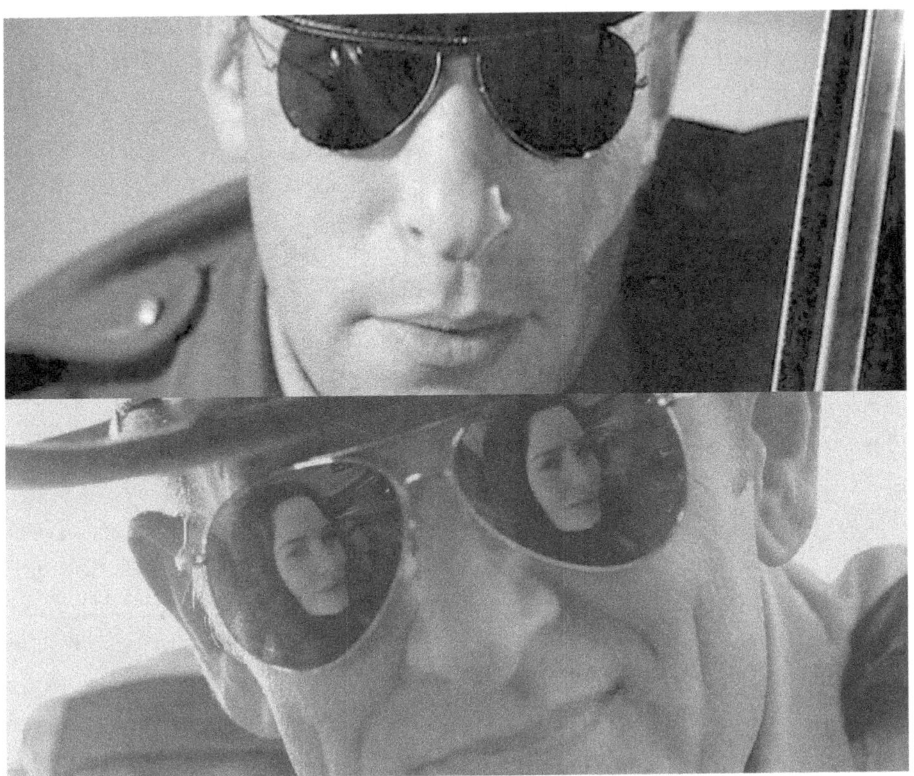

Comparative Cinema: (Top) Highway Patrol Officer (Mort Mills, 1919-1993) stops Marion Crane in Hitchcock's *Psycho*; (Bottom) Sheriff Howard stops India in *Stoker*. This cinematography is one of the similarities between the two movies.

Norman and Charlie prepare and serve meals to women, observing them dine, but neither man eats with them. Both men murder women at a motel no one stays at; Marion stays in Room 1 while Auntie Gin stays in Room 111 at their respective motels. The number one repeats: Marion, the love object of Norman, stays in Room 1 of the Bates Motel just as India, the love object of Charlie, lives at 101 Nicher Hill Road.[542] Both films feature the death of an investigator searching for a missing person: Sheriff Howard (Ralph Brown) is stabbed in *Stoker*, and a private detective Milton Arbogast (Martin Balsam, 1919-1996) is stabbed in *Psycho*. And both films feature a provocative shower scene: Marion Crane is violently stabbed to

---

542 The Stoker residence may be 101 Wicher Hill Road. The handwriting on the envelopes is difficult to read. Note that the number 1 repeats tying into the notion that India has been a psychopath the entire time.

death in *Psycho* and India masturbates while fantasizing about death in *Stoker*. By evoking these subtle analogies, *Stoker* feels uneasy, disturbed, unbalanced; like psychosis blossoms in its celluloid.

There is a well-hidden *Black Swan* Easter egg in *Stoker*. It appears in the flashback sequence when young Charlie murders his brother, Jonathan. Charlie is seen building a sandcastle complete with a winding staircase ascending towards a central Tourette, upon which he conspicuously places a small toy white swan like it was an object of veneration. Is this a lofty, anticipatory emblem foreshadowing his psychotic, virginal ideal which will later be personified by India? It seems that young Charlie envisions a virginal Odette-like female counterpart which Charlie, as an adult, has clearly projected upon his niece, obsessing over her. If the toy white swan is a symbol of India, and this author interprets it no other way, then the toy invests India with all the attributes of the White Swan herself, Nina Sayers. The similarities between Nina and India are remarkable: both are sexually frustrated young women living with their mothers; both their mothers are cruel and manipulative; both Nina and India are pessimistic and melancholy; both fall under the spell of a shadowy, enigmatic male figure seeking to control them; and both their fathers are absent. Both have celebratory cakes prepared for them; Nina's ballet slippers supply her with pain and pleasure as do India's saddle shoes; both the ballet slippers and saddle shoes are fetishes; both women masturbate to change themselves into something else, and both women turn to the dark side: Nina becomes a graceful Black Swan grotesque, and India becomes a murderess.[543] Lastly, both women associate with the moon: Nina is the archetypal personification of the Tarot's Moon card reversed (signifying lunacy among other things), while India is identified with Diana, the lunar goddess of the hunt.[544] India Stoker is Nina Sayers: a depressed masturbating virgin yearning to explore the black light of the Left-Hand Path and all the wickedness comes with it; to become a living, breathing Jungian shadow. The alchemical *nigredo* is India's *rubedo*; her intrinsic alchemical modus operandi is to absorb her uncle's sable *citrinitas*, to become a murderess. The transition was easier for India than *9 ½ Weeks'* Elizabeth and *Black Swan's* Nina because India's

---

543 Nina and India both masturbate in water: Nina while taking a bath and India while taking a shower. The water symbolizes baptism and rebirth which, for both women, is the generation of their Jungian shadow.

544 See Sullivan's *Cinema Symbolism*, Chapter XI.

ego is dormant; India has always been the *nigredo*. Her Uncle Charlie's unhealthy Luciferian-*citrinitas* light just magnified India's darkness, alchemically brought out the blackening murderous decay that was already within her. India perfects alchemy–the liberation of the shadow–allowing her to embrace her shadow, murdering without remorse. On the other end of the spectrum, this same alchemy–the release of the shadow self–destroys Elizabeth and Nina.

Discordia in Film: Basic Instinct, Fatal Attraction, and Repulsion

In *Cinema Symbolism*, this author discussed the importance of the goddess in film. The goddess, a personification of the sacred feminine, can assume many guises. She can be a cruel, manipulative mother; she can be loving or lustful; she can be a warrior, philosopher, or even the savior. In the guise of the evil mother (cf. the goddess Nemesis), we think of Pamela Voorhees (Betsy Palmer, 1926-2015) in *Friday the 13th* or the duplicitous computer, Mother, in *Alien* (1979). As the lustful (and loving) adventurer, one thinks of Barbarella (Jane Fonda) battling the evil Durand Durand (Milo O'Shea, 1926-2013) in 1968's psychotronic *Barbarella*. As the stalwart warrior, we think of Princess Leia in the *Star Wars* films and Katniss Everdeen (Jennifer Lawrence) in *The Hunger Games*;[545] as a Sophia-like philosopher one turns to Galadriel (Cate Blanchett) from *Lord of the Rings*, and as the savior, the Manichean heroine (a feminized sun, or lunar hero since she reflects the solar savior male archetype), Sarah Michelle Gellar's Buffy the Vampire Slayer or Ellen Ripley (Sigourney Weaver) come to mind. They are the dawn, the morning light that forces darkness to retreat.

These powerful women aside, one archetype that is popular in film and worth analyzing is the female oddball, an estrogen propelled Mercurius, the bane to all she encounters. She is erratic and hard to figure out; even she may not even know why she acts the way she does. This archetype comes straight from mythology; she is the goddess Discordia (Latin); in Greek

---

545 *The Hungers Games* released 2012; *The Hunger Games: Catching Fire* released 2014; *The Hunger Games: Mockingjay – Part 1* released 2014; and *The Hunger Games: Mockingjay – Part 2* released 2015.

Mythology, she is known as Eris. She is the goddess of chaos, strife, and discord. She is a problem and problematic; she is organized pandemonium. In her world there are no happy endings, only weird ones; her mood swings deadly, her actions erratic. Discordia shadows Marla Singer (Helena Bonham Carter) in *Fight Club*, frustrating and disrupting the Narrator, Tyler Durden, and the Space Monkeys in their quest for a nihilistic utopia. The archetype can also be comedic: Discordia thrives in the eccentric and overbearing Mrs. Lift (Anne Ramsay, 1929-1988) in 1987's *Throw Momma from the Train*, living to torment her timid son Owen (Danny DeVito). But to observe this archetype in action, we turn to three movies which present Discordia in all her chaotic splendor. The first is 1992's *Basic Instinct*, which sees Discordia come to life in the form of erotically charged Catherine Tramell (Sharon Stone), by sexually frustrating everyone she encounters, she gets away with murder. Discordia is personified by Alex Forrest (Glenn Close) in 1987's *Fatal Attraction* becoming a destructive force, terrorizing the ideal nuclear family of Reagan's America. Finally, the spirit of Discordia inhabits Carol Ledoux in 1965's *Repulsion* whose strife is internal; *Repulsion* documents Carol's lonely descent into madness and murder.

Catherine Tramell is a sexy, sly, beautiful female antagonist. She is an "evil genius" to quote Dr. Beth Garner (Jeanne Tripplehorn) in *Basic Instinct*; her Discordianism is the ability to get away with murder while seducing all those that enter her life, male and female. For Catherine, nothing is off limits: death, murder, drugs, passion, sadomasochism, and bisexuality are all part of her nebulous game. Only Catherine's game is murder, getting away with it by writing books about crimes that come to pass as she described them in her book, giving her the perfect alibi: who would commit a murder exactly the way one wrote about it in their book? Catherine would, but it has made her the prime suspect in the violent death of her boyfriend, Johnny Boz (Bill Cable, 1946-1998), a retired rock star viciously murdered with an ice pick during a kinky lovemaking session. Catherine is incriminated and, although she hangs out with a former murderess, Hazel Dobkins (Dorothy Malone), she is somehow able to remain at large. Catherine accomplishes this by projecting her guilt onto two people: her voyeuristic girlfriend, Roxanne Hardy (Leilani Sarelle) and Dr. Beth Garner, the latter she had a one-night stand with in college. Despite the fact that it was years ago, Beth still seems obsessed with Catherine. Although Roxanne and Beth are innocent, they fall victim to Discordia because neither of them survives the movie. Catherine seductively outwits the police during an interrogation, and has Detective Nick Curran (Michael Douglas) wrapped around her finger, despite the overwhelming evidence indicating she is the killer. The setting of her interrogation is symbolic: it takes place at the shooting range at police headquarters with Catherine as the target, while the police fire questions at her. But rather than be intimated, Discordia sows chaos instead: Catherine is not wearing panties, exposing herself to her inquisitors, diffusing the hostile situation.

She even projects her Discordianism onto Nick: shortly after they meet, he takes up his vices by smoking and drinking even though he vowed to quit. In turn, he projects her sexual aggressiveness onto Dr. Garner when, during a typical romantic interlude, he becomes violent, penetrating her anally against her wishes. It also comes to light Catherine may have murdered her parents as well as a former college counselor, but nothing can be definitively proven. Catherine even kills Detective Gus Moran (George Dzundza), managing to pin the murder on Beth, the good doctor is then killed by Nick in what appears to be self-defense. The movie concludes with Catherine and Nick in bed; she has seduced him, making him subject to her whims and desires. Instead of killing him with an ice pick she concealed beneath the bed, she embraces him; such is the anarchic nature of Discordia.

In *Fatal Instinct*, Discordia is a sensual seductress and would-be home wrecker. Alex Forrest has a one-night stand with Dan Gallagher (Michael Douglas) cajoling him into spending time with her. But Dan is married with a young daughter and breaks off the affair, arousing her Discordianism. At first, she harms herself by slashing her wrists but soon turns her hostilities toward her lover and his nuclear family. She begins stalking him, calling him both at work and at home repeatedly. She even tracks him to his new home in the country where she sees him play husband and father with his wife and child; Alex runs away, vomits, because normalcy's attributes make her sick. Next, she unleashes her chaos onto the Gallagher family construct: she destroys the family car with acid, kills their pet rabbit by boiling it to death, and abducts their daughter Ellen (Ellen Hamilton Latzen), terrifying the child by taking her on a roller coaster. Alex makes her final stand when she breaks into the Gallaghers' home, attempting to murder Dan's wife, Beth (Anne Archer), but is killed when Beth shoots her. The film ends by zeroing in on the object of Alex's Discordian derision: a family photo is shown depicting the Gallagher family happy and content. When watching this movie, pay attention to Alex's wardrobe: it is always black (cf. darkness, evil, shadow self), white (cf. light, positivity, ego), or black and white, symbolizing the love-hate passive-aggressive relationship she has with Dan and with herself. Her clothing is dualistic Hitchcockian cinema at its finest.

Finally, the spirit of Discordia resides in Carol Ledoux in Roman Polanski's *Repulsion*. This film is about the loss of self and the loss of sanity; it is a journey into the chaotic pit of madness. Carol, a beautiful Belgian manicurist obsessively biting her nails, lives in Kensington, London, with her older sister, Helen (Yvonne Furneaux). Carol practically sleepwalks through her days, interacting awkwardly with men because she is repulsed by sex. A would-be suitor, Colin (John Fraser), is flummoxed by her behavior as she rebuffs his advances, disgusted by them. She hides her head in her pillow against her sister's cries of sexual pleasure with her married boyfriend, Michael (Ian Hendry). When Helen leaves on a holiday to Italy with Michael, Carol appears even more distracted at work and gets sent home, remaining confined to the apartment. She leaves a raw skinned rabbit out to rot begins to hallucinate: first seeing the walls cracking, a man breaking in and molesting her, then hands reaching out of the walls to grab and attack her. Colin breaks open the door of her apartment when she refuses to acknowledge his adoration for her. He apologizes for his transgression telling her he wants to "be with [her] all the time," but Carol is not interested. She bludgeons him to death with a candlestick, dumps the body into the overflowing bathtub, nailing the broken door shut.

Later, the imperious landlord (Patrick Wymark, 1926-1970) breaks in looking for the late rent payment. Carol pays him, sitting on the sofa staring into space like a zombie. He remarks on the deteriorating state of the apartment, attempting to ingratiate himself by bringing her a glass of water as he leers at her in her nightgown. When he first propositions her, then sexually assaults her, she gets away. But he comes at her again, so she slashes him to death with a straight razor. When Helen and Michael return, they promptly discover the dead bodies. Michael goes for help. Helen, distraught, finds Carol hiding under a bed in a catatonic state. Neighbors soon arrive curious, concerned, and shocked. Michael returns, carrying Carol out, looking at her singular creepy wide-open eye,[546] face, and body. A family photograph depicts Carol as a girl, turned toward an adult male. The expression on young Carol's face is one of loathing and contempt. Although we are left to speculate, one can only assume Carol is taken to an insane asylum.

Carol's strife is psychological; Discordia is attacking all aspects of self-hood, destroying those around her. This film's symbolism is instinctive and unambiguous: the convent across the street indicates Carols' self-imposed celibacy; the violent cracks symbolize Carol's fractured psyche; the rotting rabbit and sprouting potatoes denote the tedious passage of time accompanied by her mental decay, and the intrusive hands signify her dislike of men and sex. It is implied that Carol's irrational-psychotic behavior is a result of child abuse evidenced by the photo in which she stares ominously at an adult male, the sexual predator. The movie's opening and ending are the same: a close-up of Carol's eye, because the eye is the window to the soul, a soul that is insane, lost. *Repulsion* is scary because Carol's reality is the precinct of nightmares, and from this terrible insanity the beautiful yet chaotic goddess is free to kill without remorse. Carol's empirical reality is gone, but it never existed in the first place; the dark maelstrom has always been her domain. Beneath whatever is left of her shattered ego, Carol is content with her destruction.

In Hollywood, there is always a dichotomy: the female can be pure, uplifting, and heroic but she can also be erotic, dark, melancholy, cruel and evil. Like the male, she is, after all, only human. In his book *The Occult: A History* Colin Wilson wrote, "I have mentioned already that in the occult tradition women are regarded as evil. In numerology, the female number 2, which represents gentleness, submissiveness, sweetness, is also the Devil's number. The Hindu goddess Kali, the Divine Mother, is also the goddess of violence and destruction. …A female assessment of a situation or a person is likely to accurate and delicate than a man's, but it lacks long-range vision. One might put it crudely by saying that women suffer from short-sightedness, and men from long-sightedness; woman cannot see what lies far away; man cannot see what is close. Thus, the two are ideal

---

546 Her other eye is concealed by shadow.

complements. The association of woman with evil arises from the situation in which the female assumes the male role, with short-term logic applied to long-term purposes. William Blake portrays the situation in his 'prophecy' *Europe*. Los is the male god of poetry, the sun and time; his consort, Enitharmon, the moon and space. But although they are the ideal 'man and wife' in eternity, they often fail to understand the other's nature in the realms of time."[547] In this paradigm, we find the female archetypes of this chapter: women trying to synthesize their dark sides to no avail; women undergoing painful alchemical transitions, women confusing and frustrating all those around them; women negating their egos to explore their shadows, women who kill and women who are insane. The erratic-sexual-diabolical female is just as powerful as the villainous male archenemy, and that's the way it should be. Since cinema is a reflection of us, the human condition, one thing is for sure: every moon has its dark side.

---

547 Colin Wilson, *The Occult: A History*, p. 417.

CHAPTER XII

THE ADVENTURES OF ROBIN HOOD: KABBALISTIC ARCHETYPES AND THE TAROT

"Come now, Sir Guy. You'd not kill a man for telling the truth?"
– Robin Hood, *The Adventures of Robin Hood*, 1938.

"In the year of Our Lord 1191 when Richard, the Lion-Heart,
set forth to drive the infidels from the Holy Land, he gave the
Regency of his Kingdom to his trusted friend, Longchamps,
instead of to his treacherous brother, Prince John. Bitterly resentful, John
hoped for some disaster to befall Richard so that he, with the
help of the Norman barons, might seize the throne for himself.
And then on a luckless day for the Saxons…"
– Title Cards, *The Adventures of Robin Hood*, 1938

"Bring Sir Robin food at once, do you hear?
Such impudence must support a mighty appetite."
– Prince John, *The Adventures of Robin Hood*, 1938.

"Is there nothing England's king can grant the outlaw
who showed him his duty to his country?"
– King Richard, *The Adventures of Robin Hood*, 1938.

During the opening credits of the 1938 Warner Brothers film, *The Adventures of Robin Hood*, one will read that the movie is, "Based Upon Ancient Robin Hood Legends." This statement is accurate; in my first book, *The Royal Arch of Enoch*, I explained that the Arthurian Legend is a solar and astrological metaphor best exemplified in the 1981 John Boorman film *Excalibur*.[548] Likewise, the lore of Robin Hood is equally steeped in mysticism, and this chapter will explain its archetypal

---

548 See Sullivan's *The Royal Arch of Enoch*, Chapter XV.

arcana. *Excalibur* is the best film to observe the veiled astrological-solar symbolism surrounding King Arthur and his Knights, although *Monty Python and the Holy Grail* (1975, see *Cinema Symbolism*, Chapter III) is a close second; the best movie to witness the occultism of Robin Hood is the Errol Flynn (1909-1959) classic, *The Adventures of Robin Hood*. Directed by Michael Curtiz (1886-1962) and William Keighley (1889-1984), the film features Flynn in the title role of Robin Hood; with Alan Hale (1892-1950) as John Little (a/k/a Little John); Patric Knowles (1911-1995) as Will Scarlet; Eugene Pallette (1889-1954) as Friar Tuck, with the villains: Claude Rains (1889-1967) as Prince John and Basil Rathbone (1892-1967) portraying Sir Guy of Gisbourne. Starring as the sacred feminine is Olivia de Havilland in the role of Lady Marian Fitzwalter, better known as Maid Marion. The "Ancient Robin Hood Legends" the film refers to are the mysteries of the Green Man, Tarot embodiment, and the kabalistic Tree of Life; these archaic archetypes live in the collective unconscious. They are forever embedded in the lore of Robin Hood and his Merry Men.

The movie opens informing the viewer that in 1191 (CE), Richard the Lionheart (Ian Hunter, 1900-1975), the King of England, has been captured by Leopold V, Duke of Austria, while returning from the Third Crusade. Richard's treacherous little brother, Prince John, seizes this opportunity to take power proceeding to oppress the Saxon commoners. John usurps the regency from his brother's trusted friend, Longchamps (who does not appear), raises their taxes supposedly to pay off Richard's ransom, but in reality, the money is to secure his position on the throne. The only nobleman opposing him is a Saxon knight, Sir Robin of Locksley. Robin acquires a loyal follower when he saves Much the Miller's Son (Herbert Mundin, 1898-1939) from being arrested by Sir Guy of Gisbourne for poaching in Sherwood Forest, having killed one of the king's deer to save himself from starvation. Next, Robin goes to see Prince John at Gisbourne's castle in Nottingham, announcing to John's assembled supporters and a contemptuous Lady Marian Fitzwalter that he will do all in his power to oppose John to restore Richard to his rightful place on the throne. John's nobles attempt to capture him but, in spite of their efforts, Robin escapes the castle.

With his lands and castle now forfeited with a price on his head, Robin flees with his friend Will à Gamwell, who, because of his red clothing, is known as Will Scarlet. They take refuge in Sherwood Forest recruiting

John Little–nicknamed Little John in jest–into their company after John trounces Robin in a bruising quarterstaff bout. Throughout the north of England, men join their growing band dubbed the Merry Men, in a revolt against John and his corrupt followers. Robin provokes the rotund Friar Tuck into a sword-fight. When the friar shows that he can give as good as he gets, Robin persuades him to join his band of outlaws to provide them with spiritual guidance. Soon after, Friar Tuck and Will have their first encounter when Will rides into camp with information that Gisbourne is transporting money and valuables through Sherwood. When Will gets off his horse, he notices the friar and draws his sword, whereupon Robin stays his hand telling Will that the friar is "one of us." Will quips, "One of us? He looks like three of us!"

Now known as the outlaw Robin Hood, he binds his men by an oath, to fight for a free England until King Richard triumphantly returns. They are to rob the rich only to give to the poor, to treat all women with courtesy, whether they be rich or poor, Norman or Saxon. In a short time, Prince John's Norman and Angevin cronies find themselves harassed beyond endurance, with many of their troops receiving swift and deadly retribution for their abuses, courtesy of the Merry Men's black arrows, the symbol of their rebellion. One day, Robin and his men capture a large party of Normans transporting monies through Sherwood. Among Robin's "guests" are Gisbourne, the cowardly Sheriff of Nottingham (Melville Cooper, 1896-1973), and Lady Marian. Robin and his men "liberate" the tax money, swearing to a man to contribute it towards King Richard's ransom. Marian is at first disdainful of Robin and his band of cut-throats but, seeing his beneficence in caring for hunted, maimed, and dispossessed Saxon families, she becomes convinced of his good intentions, beginning to see the reality of the Norman brutality. Observing that among the men being cared for is a Norman, she wonders why Robin has assisted him. Robin readily replies, "Norman or Saxon, what's that matter? It's injustice I hate, not the Normans." Marian now admires Robin for his goodness, honesty, and bravery. Robin allows the humiliated Gisbourne and Sheriff to depart Sherwood on foot, dressed in rags humbling them, informing them that Marian's presence spared their lives.

Incensed at the loss of 30,000 golden marks, with which he planned to pay off supporters, Prince John furiously accuses the Sheriff and Sir Guy of incompetence. Hoping to return to John's good graces, the Sheriff comes up with a cunning scheme to capture Robin by announcing an archery tournament. With the grand prize being a golden arrow to be presented by the Lady Marian to the victor, the Sheriff is sure Robin will be unable to resist the challenge. Everything goes as planned: Robin identifies himself by winning the competition, is taken prisoner, and is sentenced to be hanged for treason, turning Locksley into a hanged man (cf. traitor, Hanged Man Tarot card attributes. See Richard Cavendish's *The Tarot*, pp. 106-109). Marian, however, finds Robin's men in the village, helping them to plan an escape. Their plan works: the Merry Men rescue Robin on his way to the gallows. Later, under the cover of night, the outlaw sneaks back into the castle to thank Marion for her help. She and Robin pledge their love for each other, but Marian refuses Robin's offer to leave with him because she believes she can help the rebellion better by keeping an eye out for treachery in Gisbourne's castle. Robin agrees and departs.

King Richard, accompanied by a few of his loyal knights, secretly returns to England disguised as a band of merchants. While dining at an inn, the treacherous Bishop of the Black Canons (Montagu Love, 1880-1943) overhears one of Richard's men call him "Sire," hurrying to inform Prince John. Upon receiving the news, John and Gisbourne plot to dispose of Richard quietly before he can raise an army. Dickon Malbete (Harry Cording, 1891-1954), a disgraced former knight and Gisbourne's chief henchman, is sent to assassinate the King in return for the restoration of his rank and Robin's estate. Marian overhears them so she writes a note warning Robin, but Gisbourne discovers it and has her arrested for treason. Prince John assures her that, as soon as he is crowned King, he will be legally able to order the execution of a royal ward within two days. Marian's nurse, Bess (Una O'Connor, 1880-1959), has been romantically involved with Much since Gisbourne's party was intercepted in Sherwood, is dispatched to find him. Bess anxiously informs Much of Richard's reappearance, begging him to find Robin so he can save Marian. Much hastens off managing to intercept and kill Dickon after a desperate struggle.

Seeking Robin's help in reclaiming the throne, King Richard and his escort disguise themselves as wealthy monks journeying to Sherwood Forest. They are quickly accosted by Robin, requesting their money for the poor. When Richard assures him that he is traveling on the King's business, Robin happily invites him to dine in the forest. Soon after, Will comes across the injured Much, taking him back to Robin's camp. Much explains what Marian overheard telling Robin that, though he killed Dickon, he doesn't know where the King is now. Robin, anxious to protect Richard, begins to dispatch his men to locate him immediately. Convinced of Robin's loyalty, Richard and his men remove their monk's robes to receive the Merry Men's homage. Richard's knights all wear white tunics emblazoned with a large red cross (cf. Cross of St. George) identifying them as Knights Templar.

To stop John's coronation and save Marian, Robin devises a plan to sneak his forces into Nottingham Castle. He and the King visit the Bishop of the Black Canons, persuading him to include the outlaw band and Richard's knights (now disguised as monks) in his entourage. The plan succeeds, and during the coronation a melee breaks out. Robin and Gisbourne engage in a prolonged swordfight ending when Gisbourne is finally slain. Robin then fights his way down to the dungeon to rescues Marian from her cell; thereafter, Richard is restored to the English throne. John begs him for forgiveness but is rebuked by the Lionheart. Richard then exiles him and his followers, including the Sheriff and the Bishop, for the rest of their lives. He then pardons the outlaws, ennobles Robin as Baron of Locksley and Earl of Sherwood and Nottingham, ordering Robin to marry the Lady Marian who gladly accepts. Amidst the celebration, Robin and Marian sneak to the door of the great hall to depart, the former outlaw exclaiming, "May I obey all your commands with equal pleasure, sire!"

* * * *

European in origin, Tarot cards date from the 1370s and 1380s, and even then, it was not clear precisely where the cards originated. Brother John, a monk of Brefeld in Switzerland, wrote an essay on the cards stating, "…a certain game called the game of cards has come to us this year of our Lord 1377. In which game the state of the world as it is now is most excellently described and figured. But at what time it was invented, where, and by whom, I am entirely ignorant."[549] Shortly thereafter, the royal accounts of King Charles VI of France show that in 1392 a payment was made to "Jacquemin Gringonneur, a painter, for three packs of cards, gilded and colored, and ornamented with various devices, supplied to the

---

549 Quoted in Cavendish's *The Tarot*, p. 11.

King for his amusement."[550] The lore of Robin Hood also dates from the medieval period synchronizing with the Tarot's initial appearance. The Tarot and the Robin Hood archetypes are intertwined: Sir Guy of Gisbourne and Prince John are the first two Tarot archetypes introduced; Gisbourne is cruel, lusts after Marian, desiring to kill or enslave every Saxon, noble or surf. Gisbourne *qua* Robin Hood's chief antagonist is the Devil card of the Major Arcana. The card is a symbol of the application of brute force dominated by ignorance, wickedness, and intelligence used for evil ends, dovetailing with Sir Guy's vile persona.[551] Gisbourne's sole purpose is the destruction of the Saxons and, to them, Gisbourne is evil incarnate. For example, when Much the Miller's Son kills the king's deer, he is quickly apprehended by Sir Guy for poaching. After a brief verbal volley, Much emphatically states, "Sir Guy or the Devil!" implying the card's attributes. Later, assuming the role the wise and aloof Mephistopheles, Gisbourne's evil intelligence manifests when he concocts the plan to dispatch Dickon to assassinate King Richard under the cover of darkness.

Gisbourne is the chief disciple of a false ruler, Prince John, seeking to usurp the Throne of England by eliminating all those standing in his way. Being a *minor* and fraudulent monarch, John epitomizes a *lesser* card of the Tarot: the King of Swords reversed. John is, like Sir Guy of Gisbourne, a heartless and disloyal leader ruling by fear with an iron fist; taxing, enslaving, and killing all that oppose him. John thinks he can outwit his brother, Richard, having been kidnapped by King Leopold; the money he claims to be raising to pay Richard's ransom will instead be used to pave his way to the English Throne. The King of Swords reversed echoes Prince John's archetypal qualities: an evil man, selfish, obstinate, cold and calculating, cruel, sly, and perverse.[552] According to Crowley, the Sword-King is unable to progress in any direction except by accident.[553] Thus, Prince John's ascension to England's Throne is only made possible by the fortuitous abduction of King Richard.

---

550 Cavendish, *ibid*.

551 *ibid*, pp. 118-119.

552 *ibid*, p. 166.

553 *ibid*, see also page 160 of Crowley's *The Book of Thoth*: "Any action that he [King of Swords reversed or ill-dignified] takes is easily brushed aside by opposition. Inadequate violence spells futility."

When Gisbourne and Prince John scheme Richard's demise, John accidentally knocks over a goblet spilling wine. Prince John and Sir Guy have brought forth the Ace of Cups reversed (lesser arcana) indicating instability, unexpected and unwelcome change heralding the coming of Robin Hood, his Merry Men, and their fierce opposition to Norman rule.[554] The knocked over wine chalice foreshadows the trouble ahead for the pretender John, Gisbourne the Devil, and their allies; underlying discontent is alive in the paths and woods of Sherwood Forest.

This unrest within Sherwood Forest is fermented by the first two cards of the Major Arcana: the Fool and the Juggler-Magician. The Fool is Will Scarlet, and the Juggler is Robin Hood. Since the Fool is technically the first card followed by Juggler–the Juggler leads the Fool–hence Will is Robin's chief disciple. These two Tarot archetypes are introduced together riding to the rescue of Much the Miller's Son. The Fool archetype is, generally speaking, mad; however, his madness linked him not to humankind, but to God. There is an old Christian tradition of the fool being closer to God than other men.[555] The simpleton, removed from the

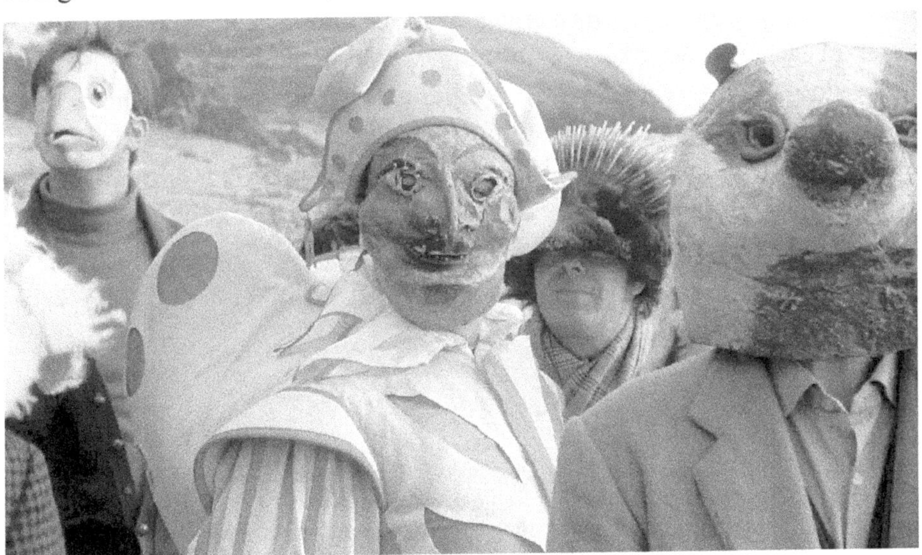

In *The Wicker Man*, Sergeant Neil Howie (Edward Woodward, 1930-2009) dons the costume of Punch becoming the Tarot's Fool, unknowingly offering himself up for sacrifice during Summerisle's May Day celebration. *Sumer Is Icumen In.*

554 *ibid*, p. 162.
555 *ibid*, p. 59.

complexities of everyday life with which he is helpless to cope, has a better set of values and a clearer perception of God than ordinary mortals, who are entangled in the complexities of life and are unable to see beyond them; the word *silly* originally meant *blessed*.[556] The bundle he carries contains his past experiences, which he values at nothing.[557] Thus, as a symbol of the perfected human spirit, the Fool is a child, "Truly, I say to you," Jesus told his disciples, "unless you turn and become like children, you will never enter the Kingdom of heaven."[558] The Fool has also been linked with Parsifal, the naïve knight of the Arthurian legends who, despite his innocence, overcomes all obstacles achieving the Holy Grail. Richard Wagner's (1813-1883) treatment of this theme in his 1882 opera *Parsifal* convinced Crowley and the O.T.O. that the great composer was also an adept of the occult and magic.[559] The Fool becomes *Back to the Future's* (1985) George McFly (Crispen Glover), mirroring the card, is simple, pure, and innocent. He is ignorant of the pitfalls that await him; McFly, like Parsifal, finds the Holy Grail which for him is his destiny: the love of Lorraine Baines (Lea Thompson) while overcoming his self-doubt by becoming a best-selling science fiction author. The Fool is about to enter an excellent adventure combining wisdom, madness, and folly[560] but make no mistake, when these ingredients are mixed in the right proportion, the results are miraculous, but when the mixture curdles, everything can end up in a sticky mess.[561] The Fool can be a madman or madwomen, a progenitor of disaster, someone wantonly opening Pandora's Box, not foreseeing the consequences of his or her actions.

* * * *

---

556 *ibid*, p. 59-64.

557 *ibid*. In *The Symbolism of the Tarot*, Ouspensky writes on pages 23-24 about the content of the Fool's sack, "'What has he in the bag?' I inquired, not why I asked. After a long silence the voice replied: 'The four magic symbols, the sceptre, the cup, the sword and the pentacle.' The fool always carries them, although he has long since forgotten what they mean. Nevertheless they belong to him, even though he does not know their use. The symbols have not lost their power, they retain it in themselves."

558 *ibid*, quoting Matthew 18:3.

559 *ibid*, p. 66.

560 See Hall's *The Secret Teachings of All Ages*, p. 414; see Nichol's *Jung and Tarot*, p. 24.

561 cf. Nichol's *Jung and Tarot*, p. 24.

Will Scarlet, Robin Hood's chief lieutenant, personifies the Fool Tarot card to kabalistic perfection. He is a silly, immature, buffoon-like amateur; Will is always ready with a witticism even when confronting a dangerous foe like Gisbourne. When Will and Robin rescue Much the Miller's Son, Will taunts Sir Guy that his actions are out of hand, a clever slight of Gisbourne's master, Prince John. After John signs a death warrant for Robin and all those that aid him, Will is not concerned about his dire predicament, complaining about irrelevant things; for him, ignorance is bliss. Instead of worrying about the death warrant and the gibbet, Will laments

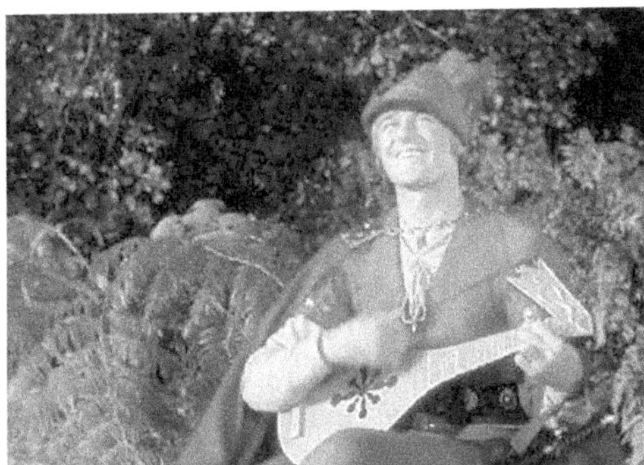
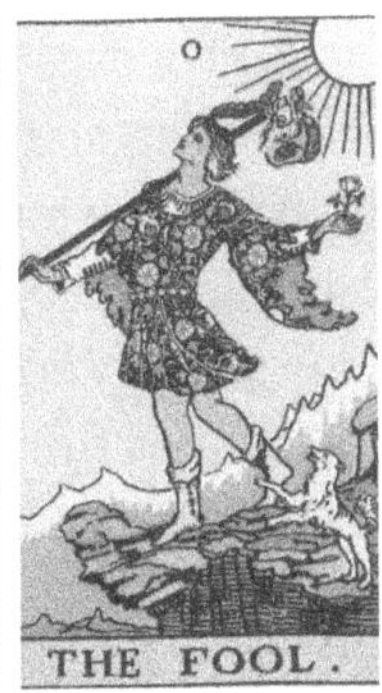

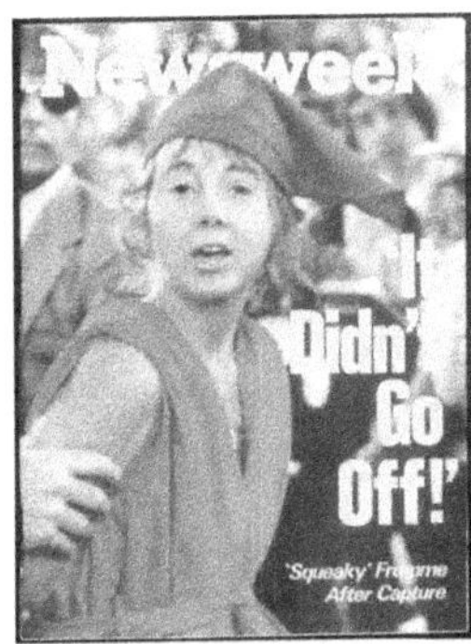

(Left) Like Nero fiddling while Rome burns, the foolish Will Scarlet passively strums his mandolin while watching Rob battle Little John, not caring about who wins or loses. (Center) The Fool Card of the Tarot, Rider-Waite deck, bears an eerie resemblance to *The Adventures of Robin Hood*'s Will Scarlet. (Right) 'It Didn't Go Off!' The Fool, ill dignified or reversed, incarnates as Lynette "Squeaky" Fromme on September 5th, 1975, when she unsuccessfully tried to assassinate President Gerald R. Ford (1913-2006) in Sacramento, California. Squeaky, a disciple of cult leader Charles Manson (1934-2017), choose not to play the jester's archetypal role of sarcastically mocking the establishment, instead she set out to eliminate the establishment altogether. Embodying the negative attributes of the Fool, Squeaky congruously wears the dunce cap of the misguided imbecile. Cover of *Newsweek*, September 15th, 1975.

that he had to sleep in the greenwood, pull seven acorns out of his ribs, that his teeth ache from chattering, and that an owl was hooting in his ear. When Robin battles John Little in a quarterstaff duel, Will decides to relax, watch on, and play his mandolin. In fact, Will obeys Little's command to play a livelier tune so that Robin can dance during their fight. Scarlet jests with Little John after the fight, later taunting the overweight Friar Tuck. However, Will is not a buffoon: echoing the positive attributes of the card, Will becomes the de facto leader of the Merry Men in Robin's absence, rescuing Much after his near-death fight with Dickon Malbete; he is the perfect mixture of folly and bravery enabling him to lead Sherwood's band of outlaws. Like the Merry Men, Will Scarlet can be playful yet can also be a Gnostic, enlightened warrior battling Norman brutality, serving justice at the same time by following Robin's mantra of *robbing from the rich and giving to poor.*[562]

The Juggler-Magician card is the next card after the Fool. Thus, the Fool *qua* Will Scarlet is led by the archetypal Juggler, Robin Hood. Concerning the Tarot, the Juggler card is in complete opposition to the Devil card; thus, Robin and Gisbourne oppose each other, they cannot coexist. Robin, reflecting the card's characteristics, is the clever trickster hiding in Sherwood Forest, becoming the bane to the Normans and their plans to topple King Richard. Like Mercury, Robin uses subterfuge, chicanery, and shenanigans to thwart John and his Norman sycophants. Robin brashly invites himself to a dinner of Norman nobles hosted by John, denouncing them as traitors, promising insurrection against them. Robin becomes a mercurial outlaw using every means necessary to combat the Normans while concealed in the woods. Make no mistake, this Juggler is bold appearing out of nowhere: he abducts Gisbourne, Maid Marian, and the Sheriff of Nottingham at sword-point, "inviting" them to a May Day-like feast hosted by himself and his Merry Men. As part of his deception, Robin wears the color Lincoln green to camouflage himself in Sherwood Forest, making him the personification of the legendary Green Man. The Green Man embodies the spirits of the trees, plants, and foliage which, for Robin, provides him with sanctuary and a base of operation.[563] The Green Man, a figure dressed in leaves and branches, led springtime processions in various parts of Europe, was sometimes connected with St. George, thus linking him to the Juggler or Magician of the Tarot. He is the principle of new life and new beginning, coming for the salvation of nature and humankind from darkness and dearth, the child of spring that alchemically transitions from the dead king of winter. Robin manipulates nature, using its greenery as a fortress to stop Gisbourne and John, to harness its energies and all that dwell within Sherwood to fight for righteousness. Robin's sidekick the Fool, or Will Scarlet, has no such plan; he only wants to enjoy his surroundings.

---

562 cf. Matthew 5.3: "Blessed are the poor in spirit: for theirs is the kingdom of heaven," and Luke 6:20: "And he lifted up his eyes on his disciples, and said, Blessed be ye poor: for yours is the kingdom of God."

563 See Guiley's *The Encyclopedia of Witches and Witchcraft*, p. 143.

Personifying Mercury, Robin is an agent of change: to restore King Richard while undermining John. Robin's mission is to holdout until Richard returns, bringing Saxon law and order back to England. Therefore, this is Robin's magical fairy tale mission and, in carrying it out, affects alchemy in the process. Although *The Adventures of Robin Hood* is not an alchemical film in the vein of *From Hell* or *Black Swan*, Robin does perform alchemy by transmuting Maid Marian from a cruel, unfeeling villainess to a compassionate, loving woman. She will revolt against her benefactors, John and Gisbourne, siding with Robin and his noble cause. Marion, as Robin's sacred feminine, the moon to his sun, his *anima*, is personified by the next card of the Major Arcana: the High Priestess (II) also known as the Female Pope. In terms of Kabbalah, the High Priestess card is the passive, female version of the active Juggler; she is the virgin Eve to the youthful Adam.[564] The unification of the two cards forms a perfected occult-alchemical wedding or Jung's syzygy. The Female Pope, when reversed, is Maid Marion when she is first introduced: a cold, spiteful, and malicious woman. When Marion is introduced, she is a mere lackey of Prince John and Sir Guy, she follows their whims without question, and like them, despises the Saxons. Marion is a spiteful siren likely based on Morgana le Fay, the great enchantress, and witch-queen of the Arthurian legends. Marion, playing the Female Pope reversed, embodies the legendary Morgana: a frosted spinster, acid, envious, frustrated, and deceptive. Similarly, the Greek Artemis and Roman Diana correspond to the Female Pope as a virgin goddess of the moon (positive), but there was another classical moon goddess of chilling and evil repute (negative-reversed). This goddess was Hecate, with whom the Egyptian Isis was identified as a lady of enchantments and a mistress of magic. Hecate was a goddess of witchcraft, ghosts, crossroads, nightmares, blood and terror, and her animal was the dog, the eater of corpses.[565] Although not an evil witch, Marion opens the film betrothed to Sir Guy the Devil; she is a detestable viper, spiting insults at Robin accusing him of treason when he crashes John's dinner party. However, through Robin's magic and alchemy, she symbolically transforms from the fearful Hecate to *gnosis* or *Sophia*: the intuitive

---

564 Cavendish, *The Tarot*, p. 71.
565 *ibid*, p. 75. See also Jeffrey Burton Russell's *A History of Witchcraft: Sorcerers, Heretics, and Pagans*, *passim*.

knowledge of God (cf. Minerva, Athena, Isis), the balance of the middle pillar, not brought by reason but from inspiration and insight, and intuition is by common consent a feminine gift.[566]

Robin Hood successfully performs alchemy by turning Maid Marion from an inverted personification of the High Priestess to her right-side-up version. The change takes place when Robin abducts Marion, Gisbourne, and Nottingham, making them the guests of honor at a woodland feast. Here, Robin proves to Marion that he is sincere: he and his Merry Men will not keep the 30,000 golden marks they stole from Gisbourne and Nottingham's caravan for themselves; instead, they will use it to pay off King Richard's ransom. Marion inquires what motivated Robin's turn from proud knight to renegade outlaw. He answers her by showing Marion the suffering and tortures that Gisbourne, John, and their tax gatherers have wrought to the ordinary people, both Saxon and Norman, men and women, young and old alike. Marion witnesses with her own eyes the injustice that Robin seeks to right. She now turns from the dark to light, her eyes opened, she "begins to see" to quote her; Marion is now alchemically changed forever. From here on out, Marion embodies the positive characteristics of the High Priestess card, primarily divine wisdom, the luminous light of Sophia, Isis, Artemis, and Diana, the kabalistic *Shekinah*.[567] In Jungian psychology, the Popess (the Moon as Marion) would represent for the man (the Sun, Robin Hood) a very high development of the *anima*.[568] It is she who would symbolize the archetypal figure which relates him to the collective unconscious.[569] For a woman, the Popess could be a highly differentiated form of Eros; she would symbolize womanliness, a spiritually developed self.[570] Marion, with the help of Robin, becomes archetypal female perfection: the two fall in love, and with the solar-lunar unification accomplished, Robin is now spiritually-equipped (cf. *ascensio*) to defeat Gisbourne and Prince

---

566 Cavendish, *ibid*.

567 cf. Hall's *The Secret Teachings of All Ages*, pp. 414-415; see *Crowley's The Book of Thoth*, pp. 72-73. See also J. Zohara Meyerhoff Hieronimus' *Kabbalstic Teachings of the Female Prophets*, pp. 15-16. Hieronimus writes on the feminine principle saying, "...the *Shechinah* is not a separate divine feminine presence in Judaism...rather *Shechinah* signifies the indwelling presence or Divine Immanence of the Creator Himself. ...Though some comparative writers might refer to the *Shechinah* as the divine feminine, the People of the Book regard God's being as one, not two."

568 Nichols, *Jung and Tarot*, p. 76.

569 *ibid*.

570 *ibid*.

John. Marion's wisdom shines she develops a plan to save Robin from the gallows pole. Marion also takes the initiative by dispatching Bess to locate Much so that he can intercept the Dickon the assassin. Fully devoted to Robin's cause, Marion anticipates *V for Vendetta's* Evey Hammond when Marion risks her life to warn Robin and Richard of the impending assassination attempt by Dickon. Standing before a kangaroo court, Marion is unrepentant; she is willing to suffer death for her beliefs; like Evey, she is ready to perish for what she knows to be right. The movie ends with Gisbourne dead, Prince John and his remaining followers deported, with Richard restored to the Throne of England. Robin and Marion are united together as one; the movie ends happily with villainy defeated. The moral of the Robin Hood legend is that for all of us, men and women alike, have available to us the powers of both the Juggler-Magician and Popess archetypes. Without these two polarities interacting inside ourselves there could be no life, no creativity.[571]

* * * *

Archetypal Tarot imagery surfaces in the characters' interactions. For instance, the quarterstaff bout between Little John and Robin Hood draws forth the Two of Rods Tarot (lesser arcana) from the collective unconscious. The two battle for superiority, epitomizing the Two of Rods: power, authority, influence over people, and good fortune.[572] Although John defeats Robin, he quickly joins his band of outlaws when he discovers the identity of his opponent; the conflict between the two combatants ends fortuitously with an alliance sown. Friar Tuck, a reclusive, austere monk, is the Hermit card of the Tarot, the wise, solitary sage. The Hermit archetype was thought to represent Diogenes of Sinope (ca. 412 BCE-323 BCE) in his quest to find an honest man. As a Christian, Friar Tuck is introduced fishing in a stream, an allegorical *fisher of men*, awakening from his slumber when Robin puts a fish in his lap–the astrological Piscean Age symbolism obvious (see Chapter I). At first, Robin jests with Tuck who rebukes him, engaging in a sword fight in water–Pisces is a water sign implying the watery, solar Age of Pisces–with the duel symbolizing the Two of Swords from the Tarot's lesser arcana. Prior to the duel, Little John explains to Much the Miller's

---

571 *ibid.*
572 See Cavendish's *The Tarot*, p. 159.

Son that Tuck is an expert swordfighter not to be underestimated; the card's attributes dovetail with Robin the outlaw and Tuck's piety. Although the two are briefly opposed, they unite when Tuck agrees to join the Merry Men, providing them with spiritual guidance and tranquility. The Two of Swords is harmony, concord, a balance of forces established, quarrels and differences reconciled, and faithful friendship,[573] all of which synchronize when Friar Tuck joins forces with Robin Hood. Like the Fool, the Hermit is a wanderer; his monk's cowl–the prototype for the Fool's cap–connect these two as brothers in spirit.[574] The first of the Merry Men that Friar Tuck interacts with is Will Scarlet, making fun of the overweight holy man; the Fool and the Hermit together again. The adverse aspects of the Hermit are secrecy, disguise, fear, timidity, and excessive caution which lurk in the Bishop of the Black Canons, Tuck's spiritual opposite.[575] The Bishop is a mere puppet of Prince John and Gisbourne, siding with them when it is opportunistic, but becomes gripped with anxiety upon learning of King Richard's return, and his confederates' plans to secretly assassinate him. The Bishop now wants out of his alliance with the Normans, but is immediately put in his place by Prince John scolding him, "How long will you retain your Abbey if Richard survives to find out what you've been up to these years he's been away?" Like a wounded animal, the Bishop cowers timidly in defeat; he is ordered to proclaim John the new king, which he obeys without question.

King Richard, the legitimate ruler of England, is the personification of the Emperor card (IV) of the Major Arcana. The Emperor represents divine right; he is the potential of the Juggler come to life.[576] It is the magical, revolutionary zeal of Robin which combats and thwarts the Normans, paving the way for John to return rightfully to the English Throne; the Juggler enables the Emperor to reclaim his divine right of kingship. The Emperor symbolizes patriarchal authority, government, the imposition of order on chaos, and conquest; all the archetypal earmarks of King Richard.

---

573 *ibid*, p. 165.

574 Nichols, *Jung and Tarot*, p. 165.

575 Cavendish, *The Tarot*, p. 171.

576 *ibid*, p. 80. On page 88 of *Criswell's Forbidden Predictions Based on Nostradamus and the Tarot*, Criswell describes Robin Hood's King Richard when he writes on the Emperor card saying , "Your [the Emperor] regal bearing, your keen judgment and leadership places you high in the control of others. Your mind is most active, but you will never become a plaything of passion due to your super intelligence."

He is the rightful king, bringing order out of the chaos that is, in the Robin Hood legend, the despotic Norman rule. Richard was also on a mission of conquest, being a Crusader in the Holy Land seeking to bring order out of chaos, returning Christian rule to Jerusalem. The Jungian interpretation harmonizes these attributes: The Emperor is a father, ruler and warrior, dominating and opinionated all of which King Richard embodies. Witches view the Emperor as one of the Tarot symbols of their horned god, the consort to their great goddess, supposed to have been worshipped with her since ancient times,[577] forging a nexus to Robin Hood as the pagan Green Man, the restorer of the Emperor *qua* witchcraft's horned god. The Emperor enthroned, Richard is fair and balanced: he does not order the death of his brother only his deportation, pardoning all the men of Sherwood. On the imagery of the Tarot card, it has been sug-

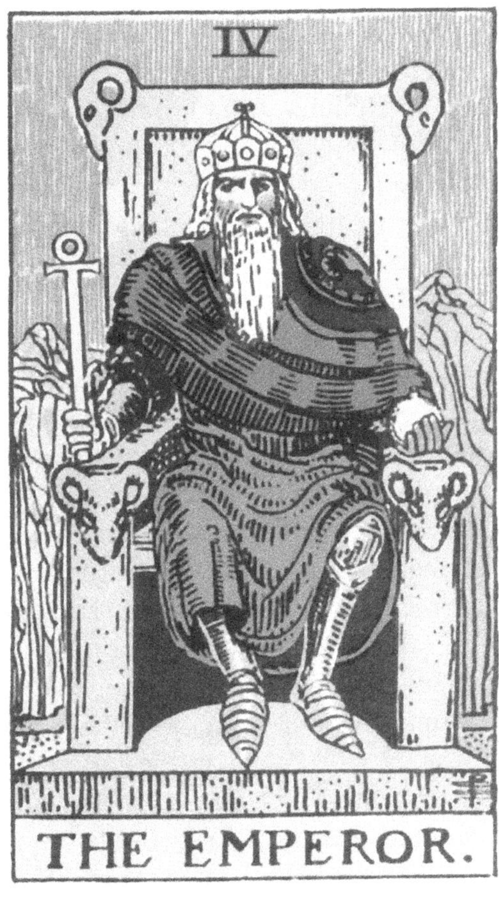

The Emperor Card (IV) from the Rider-Waite Tarot deck. The four ram skulls symbolize Aries the Ram and solar kingly rulership because the sign of Aries immediately follows the vernal equinox of March 20th-22nd. This is when the sun is resurrected from the three-month tomb of winter heralding its glorious reign in the northern hemisphere since the days are now longer and the nights shorter. The scepter signifies that, through his energy, a successful government has been established.

gested that the Emperor's robe, due to its tripartite folds, is a prototypical Masonic apron which, for Richard, is symbolically appropriate, since he is escorted back to England by a contingent of Knights Templar. According to Masonic philosopher Andrew Michael "the Chevalier" Ramsay, the Templars were godfathers of modern-day Freemasonry.

---

577 Cavendish, *ibid*, pp. 80-81.

* * * *

Not only are the dramatis personae of *The Adventures of Robin Hood* embodiments of the Tarot, or anthropomorphized Tarot cards, but they also synchronize to Kabbalah's twenty-two paths and ten *sefirot*. Sherwood Forest is an essential component within the Robin Hood legend, just like Gotham City is to the Batman-Dark Knight mythology, or Fangorn Forest is to J.R.R. Tolkien's *Lord of the Rings*; the Robin Hood tale could not be told without Sherwood Forest. Robin's home, with its dense woods and hidden paths, provides the perfect sanctuary for him and his outlaws to organize, providing them with shelter at the same time. If the heroes and villains of the Robin Hood tale personify Tarot archetypes, one wonders if there is any arcane symbolism surrounding Sherwood Forest? The answer to this question is yes: the trees of Sherwood conjure Kabbalah's Tree of Wisdom-Life– the emanation of God and the Tetragrammaton–which originates from the twenty-two letters of the Hebrew alphabet. In numerology, long before the Tarot was thought of, the number twenty-two had come to mean everything, totality, the whole world, all knowledge of God, all wisdom and truth, because of the Hebrew alphabet and its relationship to Kabbalah.[578] As such, the fact that there are twenty-two kabalistic paths, twenty-two Hebrew letters, and twenty-two Major Arcana cards is no coincidence; the number twenty-two, like the numbers three and seven, is numinous. This the why books by numerological and hermetically minded authors, intended to illuminate the mysteries of God and the world, are sometimes arranged in twenty-two parts. The Book of Revelation, as Christian Cabalists noticed, has twenty-two chapters and St. Augustine's *City of God* has twenty-two books. There are twenty-two chapters in each section of Levi's *Transcendental Magic, its Doctrine and Ritual* (a/k/a *Dogme et Rituel de la Haute Magie*, 1854-1856) and, again, in Crowley's *Magick in Theory and Practice* (the third part of his major work, *Magick or Book Four*).[579] When the Kabbalah and the symbolisms of its tree are applied to the ancient Robin Hood legends, appearing in *The Adventures of Robin Hood*, the Tarot card mysteries

---

578 *ibid*, pp. 55-56.

579 *ibid*. The first chapter, "The Magical Theory of the Universe," is Chapter 0 making the last chapter, "Of Black Magic," Chapter 22; i.e., zero equals one. See Contents of Crowley's *Magick*.

embodied by Sherwood Forest's inhabitants are both confirmed and revealed simultaneously. The varying personalities of the Robin Hood tale are but microcosms of a greater kabalistic macrocosm, connecting intuitively with the *unus mundus* or one world: a constant state of evolving and becoming.

In terms of the Kabbalah, the paths of the Juggler, the Fool, and the Female Pope emanate from the first *sefirah*, *Keter*, or Supreme Crown, which, in the Robin Hood legend, is personified by King Richard the Lionheart. The Fool card, or Will Scarlet, is path eleven, connecting *Keter* to the second *sefirah*, *Hokmah*, or Wisdom, and the Juggler, Robin Hood, is path twelve connecting *Keter* to the third *sefirah*, *Binah*, or Understanding. Maid Marian is path fourteen, the Female Pope, and her path emerges downward from *Keter*. Like the paths of Sherwood Forest, the paths of the

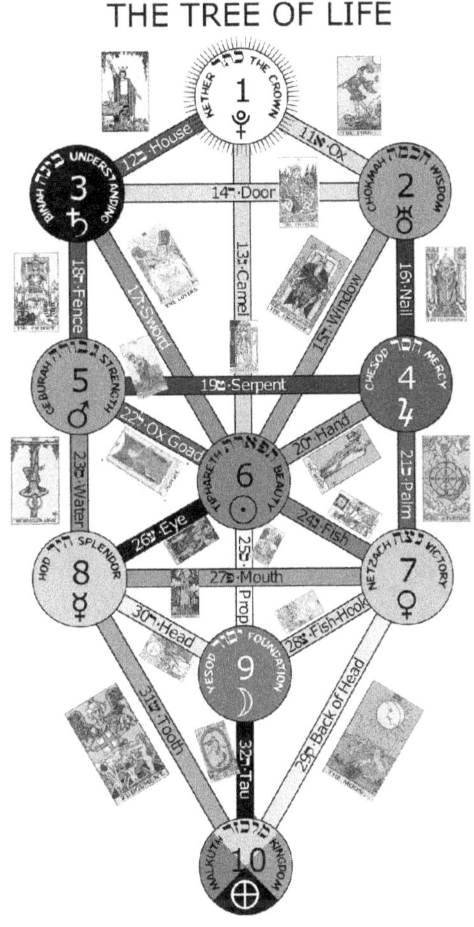

The twenty-two cards of the Major Arcana superimposed on Kabbalah's Tree of Life.

three primary protagonists of the Robin Hood tale form the uppermost part of the Tree of Life with first *sefirah*, *Keter*–the divine emanation from the hidden godhead–as its apex. The two great opposing principles, active and passive, male and female, are the *sefirot*, *Hokmah* (Male) and *Binah* (Female), personified by Robin (sun) and Marian (moon) unified: the finalization of the alchemical wedding. These three heroic archetypes, their corresponding paths, lead to Crown (*Keter*) which for Robin, Will, and Marian is the restoration of the proper English monarch, King Richard, ruling via the doctrine of the divine right of kings.[580] Richard is *Keter* incarnate: when he is finally restored and enthroned, the crown, potency, or divine will is properly returned to England. Once this is accomplished, the Juggler, the Female Pope, and the Fool have succeeded in their kabalistic and occult mission, because all three of their paths emanate from *Keter*: it is the microcosmic purpose of Robin, Marian, and Will to see King Richard seated back on the Throne of England with its macrocosmic *crown* worn by its legitimate monarch.[581]

Path twenty-six is Sir Guy of Gisbourne, the Devil card, connects the sixth *sefirah*, *Tifereth* (Beauty), and the eighth, *Hod* (Majesty). *Hod*, like Gisbourne, symbolizes the negative force behind flux and change, the sphere of mental faculties: intelligence, reason, considered reactions, the artificial and contrived.[582] *Tifereth* is Harmony and Balance, the equilibrium of opposite, and when both *sefirot* are symbolically combined, one gets Sir Guy of Gisbourne: the negative reactionary force within the Robin Hood legend, yet serves to complement and justify Robin Hood's sacred mission and purpose. Without Gisbourne, Robin Hood could not exist: in other words, Robin is action to Gisbourne's reaction. They represent light versus dark, the Devil and the Juggler harmonize each other, emphasizing the interdependence of good and evil. Finally, path twenty-six is the Hermit card, Friar Tuck, which connects *Tifereth* and the fourth *sefirah*, *Hesed*, which is Love and Mercy. The pious nature of Tuck is *Tifereth* bringing equilibrium to the renegade disposition of Robin Hood; in fact, Tuck jokes that he will join the Merry Men to turn the band from their outlawing ways. *Hesed*, echoing the devotions of Christianity and its adherents, is the impulse to do well, love others unconditionally, and to give charity–the tenets of Christian piety.

Legend is like religion: it is the passing down of wisdom from one generation to the next by teaching morality through archetypal characters, their interactions, their adventures, and their decision-making processes and related consequences; these stories are inherited, *they are the collective*

---

580 The divine right of kings, or divine-right theory of kingship, is a political and religious doctrine of royal and political legitimacy. It asserts that a monarch is subject to no earthly authority, deriving the right to rule directly from the will of God. See A.G. Dickens' *The English Reformation*, p. 399, *passim*.
581 cf. Pike's *Morals and Dogma*, p. 552 on the symbolism of the Kabbalah.
582 Cavendish, *The Tarot*, p. 52.

unconscious and part of the *unus mundus*. Such is the case regarding *The Adventures of Robin Hood* with its numinous Tarot embodiments and kabalistic iconography.

Cinema Symbolism 2 now shifts from the greenery of medieval Sherwood Forest to mid-nineteenth century industrialized New York City. This book concludes by revealing the lost history of the United States by analyzing the 2002 Martin Scorsese film, *Gangs of New York*.

CHAPTER XIII

LOST HISTORY AND
THE GANGS OF NEW YORK

"It's a funny feeling being took under the wing of a dragon,
it's warmer than you'd think."
– Amsterdam Vallon, *Gangs of New York*, 2002.

"I'm forty-seven. Forty-seven years old.
You know how I stayed alive this long? All these years?
Fear. The spectacle of fearsome acts. Somebody steals from me,
I cut off his hands. He offends me, I cut out his tongue.
He rises against me, I cut off his head, stick it on a pike, raise it high up
so all on the streets can see.
That's what preserves the order of things. Fear."
– Bill "the Butcher" Cutting, *Gangs of New York*, 2002.

"….We never knew how many New Yorkers died that week before
the city was finally delivered. My father told me we was all born of
blood and tribulation, and so then too was our great city…."
– Amsterdam Vallon, *Gangs of New York*, 2002.

"The appearance of law must be upheld,
especially while it's being broken."
– William "Boss" Tweed, *Gangs of New York*, 2002.

"When you kill a king, you don't stab him in the dark.
You kill him where the entire court can watch him die."
– Amsterdam Vallon, *Gangs of New York*, 2002.

At the end of 2002's Gangs of New York, the story's protagonist, Amsterdam Vallon (Leonardo DiCaprio), laments that no one will remember New York City's turbulent history during the run-up to, and during, the American Civil War (1861-1865) saying, "…And no matter what they did to build this city up again, for the rest of time, it will be like no-one even knew we was ever here." The purpose of this chapter is to resurrect some of the lost history of New York City and of the United States of America. This chapter will also provide the backstory behind the historical figures and gangs, depicted in *Gangs of New York*, which defined this lost history, forging modern-day America. Scorsese's film also projects arcane-Catholic thematic symbolism upon the viewer's subconscious mind. Scorsese's cinematography and plotline, when esoterically analyzed, reveals that *Gangs of New York* is an eternal religious struggle, going well beyond Catholic versus Protestant and immigrant against native. Released on December 20th, 2002–a little over a year after the September 11th, 2001 terrorist attack on the World Trade Center– the narrative parallels the post 9/11 world, depicting an epic battle between good and evil, God against the Devil, with Amsterdam Vallon emerging as New York City's deliverer by movie's end.

Gangs of New York begins on February 3rd, 1846, in Paradise Square in Lower Manhattan's Five Points. In the cruel and biting cold, a territorial skirmish of hand-to-hand combat takes place between Bill "the Butcher"[583] Cutting's (Daniel Day-Lewis) American-born Protestant Nativist gang and Priest Vallon's (Liam Neeson) Irish Catholic immigrant gang, the Dead Rabbits. Nativism is the political position of demanding a favored status for certain established inhabitants of a nation against the claims of newcomers or immigrants; in *Gangs of New York* the Natives–under Cutting's leadership–are hostile to Hibernian immigration. Cutting is introduced, staring down his Dead Rabbit opponents with his solitary evil eye, reminiscent of the dreaded basilisk's gaze, so terrible that it could kill with a single glance.[584] To combat the Natives, the Dead Rabbits ally with other New York gangs such as the Plug Uglies, the Chichesters, the Forty Thieves, and the Shirt Tails, as well as the mercenary, Walter "Monk" McGinn (Brendan

---

583 He is so nicknamed because he is an actual butcher, although Cutting has no problem applying his trade to his enemies.
584 Robert Masello, *Raising Hell*, pp. 43-44.

Gleeson), bludgeoning his opponents with a shillelagh. The battle concludes when Bill kills Priest, witnessed by Vallon's young son, Amsterdam (Cian McCormack). Bill declares the Dead Rabbits outlawed but orders that Vallon's body be buried with honor. Amsterdam seizes the knife used to kill his father, races off, burying it in a subterranean vault along with a medal depicting St. Michael casting out Satan which his father gave him before the battle. Young Vallon is raised in Hellgate orphanage.

In late 1862, an adult Amsterdam Vallon (now played by DiCaprio) returns to Five Points reuniting with an old friend, Johnny Sirocco (Henry Thomas). While playing cards in the bowels of Satan's Circus, Johnny introduces Amsterdam to Bill, not disclosing Amsterdam's true identity. Amsterdam finds that many of the former Dead Rabbits are now loyal to Bill, including "Happy Jack" Mulraney (John C. Reilly), now a corrupt police officer, as well as the bigot, Boyle McGloin (Gary Lewis). Amsterdam works his way into Bill's inner circle, learning that each year, Bill celebrates the anniversary of his victory over the Dead Rabbits. Amsterdam plans to avenge his father by killing Bill during the upcoming ceremony. Amsterdam also becomes more deeply involved with Tammany Hall, the double-dealing political empire of William "Boss" Tweed (Jim Broadbent), manipulating Bill while seemingly serving his interests concurrently. Politically, Bill the Butcher is a "Copperhead," the nickname given to northern Democrats that supported slavery, its expansion, and the Confederacy during the American Civil War.

Soon after Amsterdam and Johnny meet up, they run into Jenny Everdeane (Cameron Diaz), a discreet pickpocket and grifter. Later, Jenny pilfers the St. Michael medal that Amsterdam's father gave long ago. Amsterdam follows Jenny uptown, confronts her, retrieving his medal. Despite their hostilities, both have romantic feelings towards each other. However, his sexual interest in her is dampened once he learns she was Cutting's ward, still enjoying his affections.

During a theatrical performance of Harriet Beecher Stowe's (1811-1896) *Uncle Tom's Cabin*, Amsterdam thwarts an assassination attempt on Bill that leaves the latter wounded. Both retire to a brothel where Jenny nurses Bill, which causes Amsterdam and Jenny to argue, but they reconcile by making love. Later that night, Amsterdam is startled when he wakes to find Bill sitting near the bed, draped in a tattered American flag. Bill reminisces of how Priest Vallon was the last respectable enemy he fought; the Priest even once beat Bill soundly, allowing him live in shame rather than killing him. Bill now credits the incident with giving him the strength of will to come back strong, and that Amsterdam is like the son he never had. Soon thereafter, Johnny, jealous of Jenny and Amsterdam's relationship, exposes Amsterdam's true identity to Bill. On the night of the Bill's victory celebration at Sparrow's Chinese Theater, Bill consequently baits Amsterdam by mildly wounding Jenny during a knife-throwing act. During a toast, Amsterdam hurls a knife at Bill who deflects it, countering with a knife throw of his own, hitting Amsterdam square in the abdomen, then beats Amsterdam unconscious. Bill declares that he will let Amsterdam live as a freak, burning a hot knife blade into Amsterdam's cheek, marking him like Cain.

While in hiding, Jenny nurses Amsterdam back to health imploring him to leave New York for San Francisco with her. They are visited by McGinn, giving Amsterdam an old token of his father–a straight razor–inspiring Amsterdam to rise again. Amsterdam hangs a dead rabbit on a fence in Paradise Square as a warning to Bill, demanding that the corrupt Mulraney locate Amsterdam and dispose of him. Mulraney, however, is soon outmaneuvered by Amsterdam; he is strangled, and his dead body left hanging on a lamppost in the Square. In retaliation, Bill beats Johnny within an inch of his life, impaling him, mirroring Amsterdam's rabbit, on an iron fence in the Square; Amsterdam is forced to perform a mercy killing by shooting Johnny through the head.

Tweed, unhappy with Bill's violent methods, approaches Amsterdam with a plan to neutralize the Butcher: Tweed will back the candidacy of McGinn for local sheriff in return for the Irish vote. On Election Day, both Bill and Amsterdam's gangs use voter fraud and violent coercion to get citizens to vote, resulting in an impossible landslide victory for McGinn. Bill responds by publicly murdering McGinn in cold blood. During McGinn's funeral, Amsterdam challenges Bill to a traditional gang fight which the Butcher accepts. Jenny books passage to California believing Amsterdam will soon be dead.

On the day of the fight, the New York City Draft Riots (July 13th-16th, 1863) breakout, culminating in violence: many upper-class citizens and African-Americans are attacked by the rioters. The draft riots, known at the time as Draft Week, were bloodthirsty disturbances that were the culmination of working-class discontent with new laws passed by Congress that year to draft lower-class men to fight in the ongoing Civil War. The riots remain the largest civil and racial insurrection in American history, aside from the Civil War itself. During the film's finale, Union soldiers enter the city to suppress the riots. As the gangs meet, they are hit by cannon fire from naval ships in the harbor; most of the gang members are killed or dispersed. An enormous cloud of dust and debris covers the area, allowing Bill to strike Amsterdam with his knives, though the two are thrown to the ground by another shell blast. When the smoke clears, Bill discovers he has been hit by a piece of shrapnel, saying, "Thank God, I die a true American." Amsterdam then stabs Bill to death.

The Butcher is buried in Brooklyn next to Priest Vallon's grave, which Amsterdam and Jenny visit before they leave together. Amsterdam's disembodied voice declares that New York would be rebuilt, but they are no longer remembered, as if "we were never here." The scene then shifts, in a series of dissolves, to modern-day New York City being constructed, from the Brooklyn Bridge to the Empire State Building to the World Trade Center, while the graves of Cutting and Vallon gradually become overgrown and dilapidated symbolizing that they, and what they stood for, is lost to history.

* * * *

Scorsese, a Catholic, once planned to become a priest, clearly identifies Bill "the Butcher" Cutting with the Devil and Amsterdam Vallon as New York City's redeemer (a Christlike savior) when Priest Vallon invests his son with a medal of St. Michael defeating Satan. An esoteric nexus between the characters and their Biblical concomitants is established when Priest questions his young son regarding the religious symbolism of the medallion:

Priest Vallon: "Saint Michael the Archangel defend us in battle. Be ourprotector against the snares, and the wickedness of the Devil. Now son, who's that?" Young Amsterdam Vallon: "Saint Michael."

Priest Vallon: "Who is it?"

Young Amsterdam Vallon: "Saint Michael!"

Priest Vallon: "And what did he do?"

Young Amsterdam Vallon: "He cast Satan out of Paradise."

Priest Vallon: "Good boy."

The catechism complete, the battle between the Catholic Dead Rabbits and the Protestant Natives is for control of the Five Points, so named because it is the convergence of five streets.[585] During the 19th century, Five Points (near modern-day Chinatown) was one of the city's most notorious neighborhoods; the heart and soul of the Five Points was Paradise Square, central to the movie. The medal that Vallon gives his son of St. Michael casting out Satan implies that should the father fail, it will be Amsterdam's duty to cast Satan symbolically out of Paradise, or defeat the malignant Butcher and his gang of Natives, thereby *casting* them and their evil ways out of *Paradise* Square. Despite being a non-denominational Protestant, Bill the Butcher embodies archetypal qualities of Satan because is strong opposer of Priest Vallon's Catholic-Irish cause; the Hebrew term *Satan* is a noun from a verb meaning *to obstruct or oppose*.[586] The Butcher *qua* Mephistopheles rules his headquarters, Satan's Circus, the entrance guarded by a devil marionette. According to the Chinese, Bill drinks hellfire during the annual celebration of the Natives victory over the Dead Rabbits at Sparrow's Theater. Bill's one eye draws upon the mythology of Balor of the Evil Eye (sometimes spelled Balar or Bolar), a king of the Fomorians, a race of giants; note that the Butcher is introduced by zooming-in on his omnipresent, false evil eye. Balor, like Bill the Butcher, was a cyclops seeing all and everything with his single evil eye. According to mythologist and folklorist Alexander Hagerty Krappe (1894–1947), Balor was related to Kronos (the Roman Saturn) thus associating with death. Cutting, with his evil one eye, oversees everything in the Five Points, paralleling *Lord of the Rings*' Sauron (phonetically *Saturn*, see *Cinema Symbolism* Chapter X) watching over Mordor with his one all-seeing eye. The Eye of

---

585 "Mulberry Street... and Worth... Cross and Orange... and Little Water. Each of the Five Points is a finger. When I close my hand it becomes a fist. And, if I wish, I can turn it against you." - Bill "the Butcher" Cutting, *Gangs of New York*, 2002.
586 See Numbers 22:22, I Samuel 29:4, and Psalms 109:6.

Sauron, gazing endlessly atop the tower fortress Barad-dûr, one of Middle-earth's Two Towers, synchronizes Sauron and *The Two Towers* with Bill and *Gangs of New York* because both movies were released in the same year, 2002.

Bill the Butcher, his demonic attributes aside, was a historical person. *Gangs of New York's* Bill is based upon William Poole (1821-1855), also known by the *nom de guerre* "Bill the Butcher," was the leader of the New York City gang the Bowery Boys. Poole was a bare-knuckle boxer and a captain of the Know Nothing political movement. The Know Nothings, so named because their members answered that they "knew nothing" when questioned by authorities about their aggressive-violent activities,[587] operated on a national basis during the mid-1850s. The party promised to purify American socio-politics by limiting (or ending) the influence of Irish Catholics and other immigrants, thus reflecting Nativism and the violent Anti-Catholic sentiments of Scorsese's Bill the Butcher. Poole, like Bill Cutting, was a political gang leader and, although Bill was not a pugilist, he promotes the sport assisted by showman P.T. Barnum (1810-1891, portrayed by Roger Ashton-Griffiths). Poole never lived to see the American Civil War, having died eight years before the fictitious Bill the Butcher, but both utter similar last words. Poole's final words were, "Goodbye boys, I die a true American," and Bill's are "Thank God, I die a true American." Both were buried in a Brooklyn cemetery.

To ingratiate themselves with the Butcher and his circle, Johnny and Amsterdam agree to pull a job for him. The job involves looting a quarantined Portuguese ship in the harbor. However, upon boarding the ship it becomes clear that another gang, the Daybreak Boys, have beaten them to its cargo. Rather than leave empty handed, Amsterdam removes the corpse of the ship's captain, selling it to a nearby medical school. Amsterdam appears in an article in the Police Gazette under the headline: "Ghoul Gang Slaughters, Then Sells to Medical Science, A Fresh Outrage in the Five Points." A common purpose of body snatching, especially in the 19th century, was to sell the corpses for dissection during anatomy lectures in medical schools. Amsterdam, along with his cohorts, performs this gruesome task, making them ghouls. Bill admires their daring—not leaving the vessel empty-handed despite being under duress—and the morbid headline

---

587 Lauren R. Silberman, *Wicked Baltimore*, p. 62.

because, "Body snatching is a lost art. For many years the methods of the body-snatchers remained a mystery, …The body-snatchers jealously guarded the secrets of their craft, and fed only snippets of information to the inquisitive."[588] Body-snatchers, like Amsterdam and Johnny, were known as Resurrectionists or Resurrection Men, and their ghoulish nocturnal endeavor conjures the two most infamous murderers *qua* body-snatchers in history: William Burke (1792-1829) and William Hare (1792/1804–ca. 1858?) better known to history as Burke and

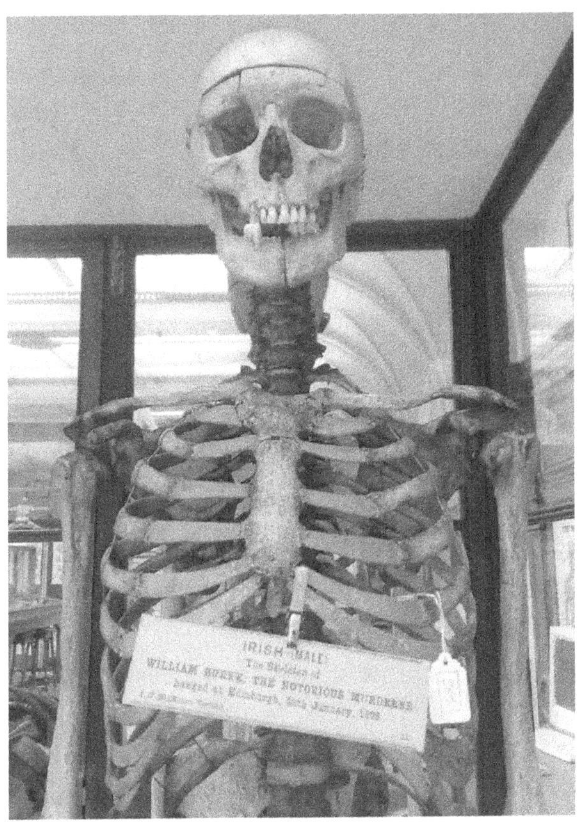

The skeleton of William Burke is on display in the Anatomy Museum of the Edinburgh Medical School, Scotland.

Hare. The Burke and Hare crimes, also known as the Edinburgh Body-Snatchers or the West Port Murders, were a series of killings committed in Edinburgh, Scotland, over a period of about ten months in 1828. The homicides were attributed to Irish immigrants William Burke and William Hare; the two men sold the corpses of their 16 victims to Dr. Robert Knox (1791-1862) as dissection material for his well-attended anatomy lectures. Burke and Hare's alleged accomplices were Burke's mistress, Helen McDougal, and Hare's wife, Margaret Laird. From their acts came the British word *burking*, originally meaning to smother a victim or to commit an anatomy murder, but which has since passed into general use as a word for any suppression or cover-up. Specifically, during trial Burke explained how burking was executed:

---

588 Norman Adams, *Dead and Buried?*, pp. 33, 37.

> We made the person drunk, and then suffocated them by holding the nostrils and mouth, and getting on the body. Sometimes I held the mouth and nose, while Hare went upon the body; and sometimes Hare held the mouth and nose, while I placed myself on the body.... We sometimes used a pillow...[589]

Burke and Hare hold a special place in the annals British criminal history, coming in a close second to the ghastly crimes of Jack the Ripper. In the end, Hare saved his neck by turning King's evidence. Their notoriety is pervasive: they have at least one Edinburgh public house named after them, and their ghoulish activities have thrilled cinemagoers over the years–more on this in a moment. Their wax effigies have an ever-lasting pitch in Madame Tussaud's Chamber of Horrors; the figure of Hare was modeled from life in Calton Jail, Edinburgh, before his release. Both waxworks are bearded; although in sketches at the time of the trial show the men to be clean shaven. It is possible Hare grew a beard in the weeks before his release so that he might not be easily recognized.[590] Like the corpses he delivered to Dr. Knox, William Burke's remains do not rest in peace: his skeleton has become a macabre relic on display in the Anatomy Museum of the Edinburgh Medical School.

Burke and Hare were not Resurrectionists in the truest sense of the word. As far as it is known they never robbed a grave, although Burke was supposed to have regularly watched funerals from the window of a house overlooking Greyfriars Kirkyard [churchyard]. Perhaps he wanted to substantiate a claim erroneously made by neighbors that he and his friend were body snatchers.[591] Likewise, Amsterdam Vallon and Johnny Sirocco never remove a corpse from its grave; however, the article in the Police Gazette clearly paints the duo as murderous grave-robbing ghouls. One of the Gazette's cartoonish illustrations depicts Amsterdam standing before a demonic, vampire-like creature watching him receive money from one of the medical school's doctors, signifying the wicked horrors of Burke and Hare. Burke and Hare, and body-snatching, have been the subject of several

---

589 Silberman, *Wicked Baltimore*, pp. 97-98 citing *West Port Murders: or, An Authentic Account of the Atrocious Murders Committed by Burke and his Associates*. London: Oxford University, 1829.
590 Adams, *Dead and Buried?*, p. 87.
591 *ibid*, "(churchyard)" added.

movies over the years, most notably the 1945 film, *The Body Snatcher*. Directed by Robert Wise (1814-2005) and produced by Val Lewton (1904-1951), the movie, set in 1831, features Boris Karloff as Cabman John Gray moonlighting as a body-snatcher. He raids Edinburgh kirkyards selling the corpses to Dr. Wolfe "Toddy" McFarland (Henry Daniell, 1893-1963) who uses them to teach anatomy at his medical school. Due to public outcry and increased security at cemeteries, Cabman Gray, like Burke and Hare, turns to murder to procure fresh bodies for McFarland, to be dissected during his lectures. At one point, Gray burkes Joseph (Bela Lugosi), the janitor at McFarland's academy when he attempts to blackmail Gray into giving him money to remain silent about Gray's nocturnal activities.

*　*　*　*

The Natives aside, some of the other street gangs featured in Scorsese's film have interesting histories themselves, such as the Dead Rabbits, the Chichesters, the Shirt Tails, the Forty Thieves, and arguably the most infamous of them all, the Plug Uglies. The Dead Rabbits were a crew of Irish-Catholic immigrants and the most feared gangs to emerge from the Five Points. Throughout the 1850s, the Dead Rabbits excelled at robbery, pick-pocketing and brawling particularly with their sworn enemies, William Poole's Bowery Boys, the muscle of the Know-Nothings. The gang was made up mostly of young men, but it was not unheard of for women to join the violence. According to legend, one of the most feared Dead Rabbits was Hell-Cat Maggie, a woman who reportedly filed her teeth to points and wore brass talons into battle; in *Gangs of New York*, she is portrayed by Cara Seymour. While the Dead Rabbits mostly dabbled in petty crime, they were also famous for the events of July 4th, 1857, when one of their street fights with the Bowery Boys turned into a bloody riot that killed a dozen people. The Dead Rabbits supposedly began as an offshoot of another gang called the Roach Guards, but some historians have suggested the two were one and the same. In fact, one popular theory argues that the term, *dead rabbit*, was a pejorative used by the Bowery Boys and the New York press about members of the Roach Guards as well as other Five Points gangs. Other historians suggest that the battle standard of the Dead Rabbits were rabbit pelts placed on a pike, hence the name, Dead Rabbits.

The Chichesters were an early Five Points street gang during the mid-19th century wearing their shirts on the outside of their pants as an insignia and sign of group affiliation. Members kept their weapons, as many as three or four at a time, concealed beneath their shirts; this discreet measure stands in contrast to competing gangs who flaunted their weapons to intimidate. The gang began stealing from stores and warehouses, selling the stolen goods to local fences in the 1820s, later becoming involved in illegal gambling and robbery. An ally of the Dead Rabbits against the Bowery Boys (cf. Nativism), the Chichesters maintained between 50 to 100 members lasting for more than 50 years before being absorbed by the Whyos.[592] much like many of the early gangs, following the Civil War in 1865. Never numbering more than a few hundred members, the Shirt Tails, like many other gangs, disappeared shortly before the American Civil War, although they did participate in a coalition of gangs under the Dead Rabbits, fighting against the Bowery Boys during the New York City Draft Riots, with its remaining members dissipating or joining one of the other various gangs.

The Forty Thieves, likely named after the folktale *Ali Baba and the Forty Thieves*,[593] was the first organized street gang in New York's history. Primarily consisting of Irish immigrants, they terrorized the Five Points for years. This violence, combined with the high crime rates, demonstrated that the Five Points desperately needed the aid of government support. The Forty Thieves saw this as an economic opportunity, establishing relations with Boss Tweed's Tammany Hall. This corrupt bureaucracy provided community services in exchange for money and support from its residents to fund their nefarious agendas. The juvenile delinquent Little Forty Thieves, the apprentice gang of the original Forty Thieves, would outlast their mentors, continuing to commit illegal activities throughout the 1850s, eventually joining other street gangs following the American Civil War.[594]

---

592 The Whyos, a collection of the various post-Civil War street gangs of New York City, was the city's dominant street gang during the late 19th century. The gang controlled most of Manhattan from the late 1860s until the early 1890s, when the Monk Eastman Gang defeated the last of the Whyos. The name came from the gang's cry, which sounded like a bird or owl calling, "Why-oh!" The Whyos do not appear in Gangs of New York.

593 The story is included in many versions of *One Thousand and One Nights*, added by Antoine Galland (1646-1715) in the 18th century. It is one of the most familiar of the *Arabian Nights* tales, and has been widely retold and performed in many media, especially for children, where the more violent aspects of the story are often suppressed.

594 Herbert Asbury, *The Gangs of New York*, passim.

Although New York City appears to be their thuggish abode, the street gang Plug Uglies were a heinous street gang operating on the west side of Baltimore in the 1850s. The Plug Uglies coalesced shortly after the creation of the Mount Vernon Hook-and-Ladder Company, a volunteer fire company on Biddle Street, between Pennsylvania Avenue and Ross Street (later Druid Hill). According to folklore, the name, Plug Ugly, refers to a single grotesque gang member but was nevertheless generous with his tobacco plugs; over time, the term would be linked to anyone considered rowdy.[595] Plug Ugly captains included lesser-known historical figures such as John English and James Morgan; other prominent members were Louis A. Carl, George Coulson, George "Howard" Davis, Henry Clay Gambrill, Alexander Levy, Erasmus "Ras" Levy, James Wardell, and Wesley Woodward. The gang associated with the Know Nothings, which was known as the American Party in Baltimore. Like similar associations in Baltimore and other United States cities during this period, the Plug Uglies' street influence made them useful to party politicians anxious to control the polls on Election Days. Some historians now contend that Edgar Allan Poe was shanghaied and beaten by the Plug Uglies on Election Day, October 1849, resulting in his death soon thereafter. The Plug Uglies were the central figures in the first election riot in Baltimore in October 1855. Together with the Rip Raps, they were also actively involved in deadly rioting during the October 1856 municipal election in Baltimore and in similar violence at the Know Nothing Riot in Washington in June 1857.[596] At the Washington riot, the National Guard was called out to quell the fighting, shooting and killing ten citizens. Accounts of the Washington riot appeared in newspapers nationally, gaining widespread notoriety for the Plug Uglies; the newspaper *Washington Star* described them, "…as pestilent and scrofulous a brood of scoundrels as hell itself could vomit from its vilest crater."[597] Besides Election Day fighting, the gang was involved in several assassinations, arsons, and shootings in Baltimore. Most notably, Plug Ugly Henry Clay Gambrill was implicated in the murder of a Baltimore police officer in September 1858. Gambrill's trial was presided

---

595 Silberman, *Wicked Baltimore*, p. 63 citing *The Sun*, October 17th, 1857.
596 Silberman, *ibid*, pp. 61-72, *passim*.
597 Silberman, *ibid*, p. 63 citing *Washington Star*, June 4th, 1857.

over by Judge Henry Stump (?-1865),[598] and the subsequent deadly violence relating to it, made the crime one of the most sensational of the era. The violence of the Plug Uglies and other political clubs had a substantial impact on Baltimore: they were primarily responsible for the creation of modern policing and a paid, professional fire department, as well as court and electoral reforms.[599] These reforms, together with the election of a Reform mayor and city council in October 1860 and then the Civil War, ultimately led to the disbandment of the Plug Uglies and the Know Nothings (American Party) in Baltimore.[600] On July 16th, 1863, during the New York City Draft Riots, the *New York Times* reported that Plug Uglies and Blood Tubs[601] gang members from Baltimore, as well as "Schuylkill Rangers and other rowdies of Philadelphia," had come to New York to participate in the riots alongside the Dead Rabbits and other New York gangs. The Times reported that "the scoundrels cannot afford to miss this golden opportunity of indulging their brutal natures, and at the same time serving their colleagues the Copperheads and secesh [secessionist] sympathizers."[602] Although the street gang has long since vanished, the Plug Uglies still haunt the shores of the Chesapeake Bay. Today, Plug Ugly's Publick House serves up food and booze, not mayhem, to the gentrified neighborhood of Canton in downtown Baltimore.[603]

The hidden hand manipulating Bill's Confederation of Natives,

Amsterdam Vallon's Dead Rabbits, and the other gangs is Tammany Hall, led by the mercurial and devious Boss Tweed. Tammany Hall, also known as the Society of St. Tammany, the Sons of St. Tammany, or the Columbian Order, was a New York City political organization founded in 1786, incorporated on May 12th, 1789, as the Tammany Society. It was named after Tamanend (ca. 1625-ca. 1701), a chief of one of the clans that

---

598 Stump served as Judge of the Criminal Court, 5th Judicial Circuit in Baltimore, Maryland, United States, from 1851 to 1860, one of the most lawless and politically violent decades in Baltimore history.

599 See Silberman's *Wicked Baltimore*, already cited.

600 Silberman, *ibid*, p. 70.

601 "The Blood Tubs, for example, drew their name because of their propensity to dunk their victims in buckets of pigs' [sic] blood and refuse." See Silberman, *ibid*, p. 66 citing John Thomas Scharf's *History of Baltimore City and County*.

602 "FACTS AND INCIDENTS OF THE RIOT.: THE MURDER OF COLORED PEOPLE IN THOMPSON AND SULLIVAN STREETS." *The New York Times*. July 16th, 1863, p. 1.

603 Visit http://www.pluguglyspub.com for more information.

made up the Lenni-Lenape Indian Nation in the Delaware Valley when the city of Philadelphia was established. Tamanend is best known as a lover of peace and friendship, playing a prominent role in developing amicable relations with the Lenape and the English settlers led by William Penn (1644-1718); a statue of Tamanend stands inside Tammany Hall's head-quarters. It was the Democratic Party's political machine that played a major role in controlling New York City and New York State politics and helping immigrants, most notably the Irish, rise to importance in American politics from the 1790s to the 1960s. It typically controlled Democratic Party nominations in Manhattan from the mayoral victory of Fernando Wood (1812-1881) in 1854, using its patronage resources to build a loyal, well-rewarded core of district and precinct leaders; after 1850 the vast ma-jority were Irish Catholics. Former governor and Masonic Grand Master of the State of New York DeWitt Clinton (1769-1828), was an early Brave (member) of Tammany Hall when it worked as a patriotic fraternal order mirroring Holland Lodge No. 8 and the Society of the Cincinnati; Clinton witnessed Tammany Hall's transformation into a morally defined middle class proto-Masonic fraternal order, at one level, to an opportunistic ersatz political party at another.[604]

The Tammany Society emerged as the center for Democratic-Republican Party politics in New York City in the early 19th century. After 1854, the Society expanded its political control even further by earning the loyal-ty of the city's rapidly growing immigrant community, which functioned as its base of political capital. The business community appreciated its readiness, at moderate cost, to cut through red tape and legislative maz-es to facilitate rapid economic growth. The Tammany Hall ward boss or ward heeler (wards were the city's smallest political units from 1786 to 1938) served as the local vote gatherer and provider of patronage. By 1872, Tammany had an Irish Catholic boss, and in 1928 a Tammany hero, New York Governor Al Smith (1873-1944) won the Democratic presi-dential nomination. However, Tammany Hall also served as an engine for graft and political corruption, perhaps most infamously under William M. "Boss" Tweed in the mid-19th century, depicted in *Gangs of New York*. By the 1880s, Tammany was building local clubs that appealed to social

---

604 See Sullivan's *The Royal Arch of Enoch*, Chapter VIII, *passim*.

activists from the ethnic middle-class.[605] In quiet times, the machine had the advantage of a core of solid supporters exercising control of politics and policymaking in Manhattan; it also played a significant role in the state legislature in Albany.

William Magear Tweed (1823-1878), known to history as Boss Tweed, was an American politician most notable for being the boss of Tammany Hall. At the height of his influence, Tweed was the third-largest landowner in New York City, a director of the Erie Railroad, the Tenth National Bank, and the New-York Printing Company, as well as proprietor of the Metropolitan Hotel. Tweed was elected to the United States House of Representatives in 1852 and the New York County Board of Supervisors in 1858, the year he became the head of the Tammany Hall political machine. He was also elected to the New York State Senate in 1867, but Tweed's greatest influence came from being an appointed member of numerous boards and commissions, his control over political patronage in New York City through Tammany, and his ability to ensure the loyalty of voters through jobs he could create and dispense on city-related projects. According to Tweed biographer Kenneth D. Ackerman:

> It's hard not to admire the skill behind Tweed's system ...The Tweed ring at its height was an engineering marvel, strong and solid, strategically deployed to control key power points: the courts, the legislature, the treasury and the ballot box. Its frauds had a grandeur of scale and an elegance of structure: money-laundering, profit sharing and organization.[606]

Tweed was convicted of stealing an amount estimated by an aldermen's committee in 1877 at between $25 and $45 million from New York City taxpayers through political corruption, although later estimates ranged as high as $200 million. Unable to make bail, he escaped from jail once, but was returned to custody, dying in the Ludlow Street Jail.

Tweed was a Freemason of Palestine Lodge as well as an Odd Fellow, and during the film, he is shown wearing Masonic and/or Odd Fellow

---

605 Roy V. Peel, *The Political Clubs of New York City, passim.*
606 Kenneth D. Ackerman, *Boss Tweed: The Rise and Fall of the Corrupt Pol Who Conceived the Soul of Modern New York,* quoted in Pete Hammill's "'Boss Tweed:' The Fellowship of the Ring" *The New York Times.* March 27th, 2005.

regalia. Within the world of conspiracy, the Masons are master manipulators, orchestrating political-socio-economical conflicts only to play both sides against the middle; hence, they are always assured a beneficial outcome no matter which side emerges victorious. This secret agenda plays out in *Gangs of New York* when Tweed first decides to ally with Bill, but upon discovering his violent anti-Irish sentiment, backs Amsterdam instead. The truth is that Tweed is only interested in getting votes, especially the Irish vote, and will obtain it by any means necessary, echoing a Masonic conspiracy by putting in motion a secret political agenda. After distancing himself from Bill, Tweed endorses an Irish Catholic, Walter "Monk" McGinn for Sheriff. Bill, in retaliation, kills the newly elected Irish Sheriff, causing Tweed to make threats against Bill, but the Butcher is too cunning. Cutting compares the lukewarm, duplicitous neutrality of Tammany Hall and Tweed to the spiritual lack of zeal of the indecisive Laodicean Church;[607] Bill cites Revelation 3:15-16: "I know thy works, that thou art neither cold nor hot: I would thou wert cold or hot. So then because thou art lukewarm, and neither cold nor hot, I will spue thee out of my mouth." Bill admonishes Tweed:

I know your works; you are neither cold nor hot. So, because you are lukewarm, I will spew you out of my mouth. You can build your filthy world without me. I took the father; now I'll take the son. You tell young Vallon I'm gonna paint Paradise Square with his blood, two coats. I'll festoon my bedchamber with his guts. As for you, Mr. Tammany-fucking-Hall, you come down to the Points again, and you'll be dispatched by my own hand. Get back to your celebration and let me eat in peace.

---

607 The Laodicean Church was a Christian community established in the ancient city of Laodicea on the river Lycus, in the Roman province of Asia, and one of the early centers of Christianity. The church was established in the Apostolic Age, the earliest period of Christianity, and is probably best known for being one of the Seven Churches of Asia (cf. Seventh Church Age) addressed by name in the Book of Revelation (Rev. 3.14-22). Katy Perry's song "Hot N Cold" (2008) is an esoteric parable about the noncommittal workings of Laodicean Church; Katy sings, "…I should know that you're no good for me. [Chorus:] 'Cause you're hot then you're cold, you're yes then you're no, you're in then you're out, you're up then you're down, you're wrong when it's right, it's black and it's white…." As such the "Hot N Cold" music video opens during a marriage ceremony in a church where the groom gets cold-feet and backs out of the ceremony.

For Bill, it is obvious that Tweed is only interested in obtaining votes by hook or by crook, and that Tweed's support of Nativism and the Know Nothings is self-serving. Bill parallels Tweed in that the latter is boss of Tammany Hall, while the former is the overseer of all that transpires in the Five Points; Bill's one eye never sleeps. During an exchange with Amsterdam, when Bill is seated draped in an American flag, the Butcher tells Amsterdam that he is 47 years old. Although Bill is not a Freemason, his rulership of the Five Points is esoterically symbolized by his age: the 47th Proposition of Euclid (a/k/a the Pythagorean Theorem) is the emblem of a Masonic Worshipful Master indicating rightful leadership.

*　*　*　*

Concealed within the celluloid of *Gangs of New York* is a battle for the future of the city. It is two versions of New York City which will collide: Bill the Butcher representing exclusion, pessimism, reaction, and repression; and Amsterdam, personifying a progressive, inclusive, and opportunistic New York City. Amsterdam Vallon is, literally, *New York City*: his forename, Amsterdam, esoterically references the original name of the village, New Amsterdam. Historically, New Amsterdam was a 17th-century Dutch settlement established at the southern tip of Manhattan Island, serving as the seat of the colonial government in New Netherland territory. It was renamed New York on September 8th, 1664, in honor of the then Duke of York–later James II (1633-1701) of England–after English forces seized control of Manhattan Island, along with the rest of the Dutch colony. Embodying *New* Amsterdam, DiCaprio's protagonist personifies New York City *moving forward* toward an egalitarian and democratic metropolis. Bill the Butcher is also a living version of New York City. He informs Vallon of this when they first meet in the bowels of Satan's Circus:

Bill Cutting: "You, whatever your name is, what is your name?"

Amsterdam Vallon: "Amsterdam, sir."

Bill Cutting: "Amsterdam? *I'm New York.* Don't you never come in here empty handed again, you gotta pay for the pleasure of my company."

Cutting embodies old New York: Nativist, antiquated, racist, steely, and stagnant. Their conflict is, therefore, more than a battle between the Natives and the Dead Rabbits, Catholic against Protestant, immigrant versus native; it is for the destiny of New York and America post-Civil War. In other words, the struggle between New York City's Natives and Dead Rabbits was but a microcosm of the macrocosm, the American Civil War. The war between the two New York gangs was a localized, condensed version of the two sides embattled in the Civil War–abolitionist against secessionist, north versus south–which engulfed the entire nation. Its outcome changed the destiny of the United States, forever. It is the old against the new.

However, Scorsese goes even further by imbuing the gang war with religious and eschatological overtones. He implies that the battle between the two microcosms, the Natives and the Dead Rabbits; and the macrocosm, the Civil War, run parallel, more than contrasting ideologies. Rather, the result will determine the destiny of the American Republic. Make no mistake; Amsterdam is thuggish like his counterpart Bill the Butcher. Despite being the son of a Catholic Priest, he is not a Christlike solar savior; rather, he should be thought of as a deliverer, midwifing Reconstructionist America. Amsterdam is heroic, but he is not a traditional hero: like a vengeful demon, he is unleashed from Hell, or Hellgate House of Reform, immediately disposing of his Bible by throwing it off a bridge. To kill his quarry, Bill the Butcher, Amsterdam befriends Johnny, joining his gang, doing the bidding of Bill's Natives. Like Christ and his Apostles, Amsterdam seeks to do battle with wickedness and villainy. However, before being born again, Amsterdam must first be betrayed by one of his helpers. Johnny, like Judas before him, betrays his master by revealing Amrsterdam's true identity and motives to the Butcher. The Butcher temporarily slays Amsterdam, but like all true deliverers, is resurrected like the sun at dawn. Like Christ, Amsterdam is kept in a subterranean tomb waiting to be reborn to do final battle with Bill and his band of cutthroats. Nursing Amsterdam back to life is the sacred feminine, Sophia, his Mary Magdalene, the Trinity to his Neo, Jenny Everdeane. Jenny is the keeper and protectress of Amrsterdam's body until he emerges from the tomb, resurrected, ready to battle Bill. Echoing the Gospel tales, Jenny resembles Mary Magdalene because Mary was the first to see Jesus rise from the dead, just like Jenny is with Amsterdam when he emerges from the crypt, his health restored. Jenny also mirrors Mary because Jenny is a prostitute, a moniker given to Mary albeit incorrectly. The concept of a female priestess (cf. sacred feminine, Jenny) nursing a savior or deliverer back to life can found in antiquity; Barbara Walker explains:

> The Gospels say no men attended Jesus' tomb, but only Mary Magdalene and her women. Only women announced Jesus' resurrection. This was because men were barred from the central mysteries of the Goddess.

> …Mary alone was the first to observe and report the alleged miracle. In just such a manner, pagan priestesses had been announcing the resurrection of savior gods like Orpheus, Dionysus, Attis, and Osiris every year for centuries… Mary Magdalene was described as a harlot; but in those times, harlots and priestesses were often one and the same. A sacred harlot in the Gilgamesh epic was connected with a victim-hero [cf. Amsterdam Vallon] in a similar way: 'The harlot who anointed you with fragrant ointment laments for you now.'…Under Christianity, priests soon took over all the rituals that had been conducted by women, declaring that women had no right to lead any religious ceremonies whatever.[608]

Symbolizing the spiritual nature of Amsterdam's struggle, is Jenny, the sacred feminine, throwing open the doors of the church at McGinn's funeral procession. During the funeral, Amsterdam challenges Bill to a final fight which the Butcher accepts, foreshadowing an End of Days scenario. This scene borrows from earlier cinematography; specifically, when McGinn kicks open the door of Priest Vallon headquarters, heralding the upcoming epic gang war between the Dead Rabbits and the Natives. These two scenes subtly suggest an overarching religious conflict (note that Priest Vallon's weapon of choice is a large crucifix) for the streets of New York going well beyond political-social-economic differences. McGinn, his nickname "Monk" smacks of Christian saintliness, combined with Jenny's forceful opening of the church's doors in the same fashion as McGinn implies, to the subconscious mind, battle, struggle, old against new, progressive against reactionary, life and death (cf. Priest Vallon's death and McGinn's

---

608 Acharya S, *The Christ Conspiracy*, p. 196 citing Barbara Walker's *The Woman's Dictionary of Symbols and Sacred Objects* and *The Woman's Encyclopedia of Myths and Secrets*.

funeral), and God against Devil. Their conflict is more than just a turf war between political ideologies; rather, it is for the heart and soul of the city and, by default, the nation as well.

After he is reborn and the Dead Rabbits with him (symbolized when Amsterdam hangs the rabbit pelt in Paradise Square), Christian iconography shadows Amsterdam throughout the remainder of the film. His base of operations is a Christian church; he kills Mulraney before Christ crucified then crucifies the body in Paradise Square. Amsterdam throws Boyle McGloin out of the church for blasphemy, scolding him, "You run with the Natives, you go pray with the Natives!" suggesting Jesus' rebellious nature towards secular and spiritual authorities. After the final battle (cf. Revelation), Amsterdam and Jenny stand before the graves of his father and the Butcher. Amsterdam informs the audience that their conflict forged a new city and in doing so a new nation, but that no one will remember them. Like Christ, a deliverer of spiritual newness, Amsterdam's earthly mission is now finished. Jenny and Amsterdam vanish forever from the history books, having transcended this world for a better one.

The *Gangs of New York* one-sheet poster features the phrase: "America was Born in the Streets." The film successfully documents that the street gangs of the nineteenth century were smaller representations of the country as a whole. The gangs

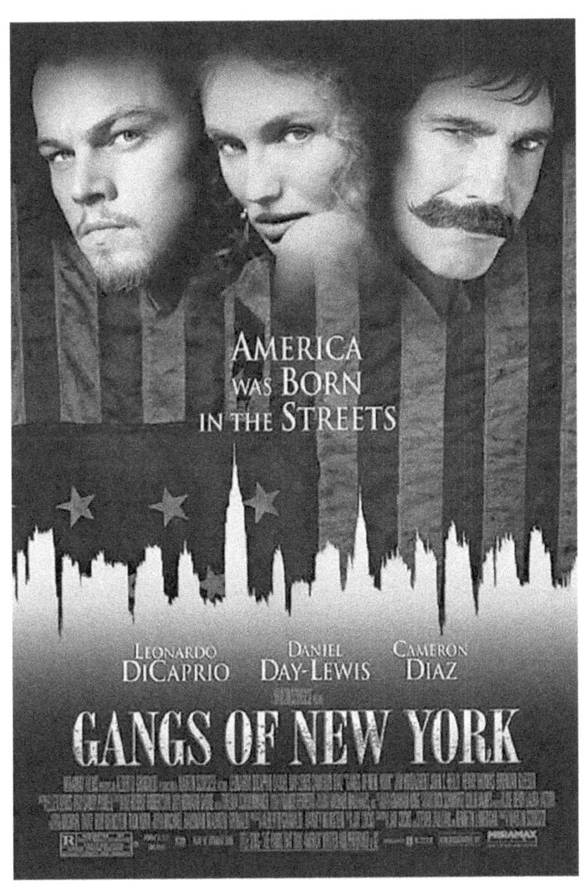

Gangs of New York one-sheet movie poster.

were microcosms of the divides and schisms of pre-Civil War America, and their differences were transformed during Reconstructionist America,

forging both a neo-New York City and United States. The street gangs were replaced with new gangs, or organizations that, again, mirrored post-Civil War America. Gone were the Abolitionists, Know Nothings, and the Natives, having been superseded by the Knights of Pythias, the Knights of Columbus, the Republican and Democratic Parties, and subversive organizations such as the Ku Klux Klan and the Knights of the Golden Circle; America's civil religious institutions, such as Freemasonry, Odd Fellowship, college fraternities and sororities, kept the Union intact. The Civil War and its related upheavals ultimately led to the Progressive Movement of the early 20th Century, unionized labor and women's suffrage, Prohibition and its repeal, the Great Depression, and the Civil Rights Movement of the 1960s. The movie poster is correct: modern-day America was born, or redeemed, out of the carnage produced by the urban street gangs of 1840s-1850s America. Their struggles and motivations, both material and spiritual, were not only a reflection of the social fabric of the country, but portents of its destiny as well.

CONCLUSION

"The world is changed. I feel it in the water, I feel it in the earth,
I smell it in the air. Much that once was is lost,
for none now live who remember it."
– Galadriel, *The Fellowship of the Ring*, 2001.

"It is like a finger pointing a way to the moon.
Don't concentrate on the finger or you will miss all that heavenly glory.
Do you understand?"
– Bruce Lee (credited as "Lee"), *Enter the Dragon*, 1973.

"Is that you John Wayne?
Is this me?"
– Private Joker, *Full Metal Jacket*, 1987.

"The droid stole a freighter?"
– Kylo Ren, *Star Wars: The Force Awakens*, 2015.

"I know now that my wife has become host to a Kandarian demon.
I fear that the only way to stop those possessed by the spirits
of the book is through the act of bodily dismemberment."
– Professor Raymond Knowby, *Evil Dead*, 1981

"It's been absolutely impossible to work through
these earth creatures. Their soul is too controlled."
– Eros, Plan 9 from Outer Space, 1959.

"Hate keeps a man alive. It gives him strength."
– Quintus Arrius, *Ben-Hur*, 1959.

"With the ship and the ray-gun gone they have no control."
– Col. Tom Edwards, *Plan 9 from Outer Space*, 1959.

Just like with *Cinema Symbolism*, this author originally intended to analyze more movies in this book, but to do so would have increased its length substantially. *Cinema Symbolism 2* would never end. Some of the films and television shows that were excised were David Lynch's television series *Twin Peaks* (1990-1991), and his films *Twin Peaks: Fire Walk with Me* (1992) and *Wild at Heart* (1990). This author also planned to analyze *The Hobbit: An Unexpected Journey* (2012), *The Hobbit: The Desolation of Smaug* (2013), and *The Hobbit: Battle of the Five Armies* (2014). As such, I have already begun outlining *Cinema Symbolism 3* which will include all these aforementioned movies. Tentatively, other films to be discussed in *Cinema Symbolism 3* include but not limited to *Snowpiercer* (2013), *Interstellar* (2014), *50 Shades of Grey* (2015), *Star Wars: The Force Awakens*, *Prometheus* (2012), *Donnie Darko* (2001), *The Neon Demon* (2016), *The Hunger Games* (2012, 2013, 2014, 2015), *The Adventures of Baron Munchausen* (1988), and *The Black Cauldron* (1985) among many others.

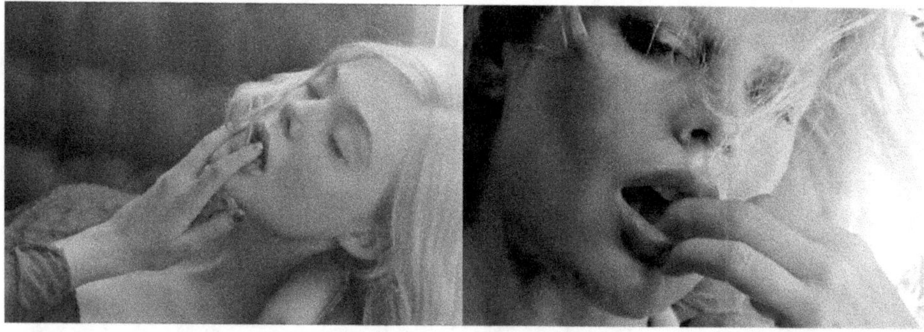

Comparative Cinema, Fingers and Lips: (Left) In *The Neon Demon*, Jesse (Elle Fanning) kindles Elizabeth's masturbatory rhapsody from *9 ½ Weeks* (right); their self-gratification is dark fantasy, destroying both women. *The Neon Demon* also conjures films like *Black Swan*, *The Shining*, *Suspiria*, *The Texas Chainsaw Massacre*, *The Matrix*, and *Mulholland Drive*, just to name a few. All this and more will be coming soon in *Cinema Symbolism 3*!

Once again, we ask: why are movies so crucial within popular culture? The answer: film is one of the most celebrated and influential mediums ever created; this is irrefutable. Cinema can alter our moods; affecting, shaping, and influencing our lives. Professor Eric Wilson, in his book *Secret Cinema*, commented:

He steps from the glare of the noonday sun into the cool and gloomy theater. In the lobby, an anteroom bathed in exotic lights, he already feels as is his personal history were a light reverie that he might slip on and off like a garment. As he makes his way into the auditorium proper, totally dark except for the trailer swimming on the screen, for a second he does not even know who he is. ...He is thirsty once more to undergo that exquisite forgetfulness that just washed over him as he crossed the threshold into the blackness.

The square goes white. The curtain closes and opens. The screen bursts into sound and brightness. It happens again. The burdened ego dissolves. The story, the actors, the director–these are immaterial. What matters is this: he is no longer *this* person in *that* job. He is unhindered by the schedules and the places that lock into one line of movement to the exclusion of others. He inhabits a dimension in which he can become whatever he wants. The film flickering before his witness has cleansed the grime holding him in a rut. The actual turns ghostly. He thrives in the possible.[609]

Movies not only entertain us, but can also inspire us; as such, hidden symbolism can impact us by projecting sublime mythology and esoteric icons onto our conscious and subconscious minds. Perhaps this is why occult cinema symbolism is such an interesting topic, a source of endless fascination.

I have stated in numerous radio and television interviews that I believe the placement and use of hidden symbolism are intentional. It invests the film with transcendental, occult meaning, transforming it into modern-day mythology. Decoding these movies is like playing a game of chess, discovering their arcane undercurrents, which only adds to the enjoyment and appreciation of the film.

But what about the idea that cinema is a predictive programming device? What of the phenomena of 9/11 appearing in movies prior the September 11th, 2001 attacks? This strange occurrence is often presented as the strongest evidence for predictive programming. Predictive programming theory holds that Hollywood, armed with the knowledge of pre-determined events, plants evidence of the upcoming catastrophes in films to prepare us, or subconsciously soften us, for the real incident when

---

609 Wilson, *Secret Cinema*, p. 33.

it inevitably occurs. So how does Hollywood know about these events before they happen? According to many, there is a vast and vicious conspiracy between Hollywood elites, filmmakers, secret government cabals, the Illuminati, the CIA, Skull and Bones and high degree Freemasons, staging global events designed to manipulate humankind, thereby leading it into a Luciferian, godless New World Order. Suffice to say, this theory does not hold up when subjected to critical and rational thinking. Numerous films have depicted invading space aliens, yet no invasion has occurred. It has been alleged that Princess Diana died (31 August 1997) as a result of an MI6 conspiracy, but no movies beforehand depict a famous princess, or member of a royal family, perishing in a car accident in Paris. If placing 9/11 in modern media was designed to soften us, it is safe to say they failed miserably. Nevertheless, this author believes the appearance of disguised and subtle 9/11 imagery in films and televisions shows before the terrorist attack is fascinating, and worthy of investigation. This author harkens back to what he said in the Preface, which is that this seems to be evidence that Jung's collective unconscious is not only be inherited but is also predictive, suggesting that notions of time, as we currently understand it, may not be linear. If this is so, and this author tends to believe it is, then 9/11 imagery would appear regardless of the filmmaker's conscious intent.

Finally, although this author does not want to reveal his methodology when it comes to analyzing cinema, I challenge the reader to pay attention to hidden themes next time while watching a movie. Ask yourself: is there an alchemical storyline present; is a character undergoing metamorphosis? Is the movie Gnostic; is a character or characters on a journey of self-discovery or enlightenment? Is there is a hero or heroine; if so, are elements of the monomyth present? If one can determine the movie's arcane context first, the next step is to start looking for and identifying hidden clues that reinforce it. Deducing the context is not easy to do, but if this can be done properly, this author believes the reader's appreciation of movies will be substantially increased. This author enjoys looking for esoteric imagery, connotations, and symbols in film and, even more so, writing about them. For me, I take comfort in knowing I have chosen seeking over stasis, investigation over apathy.

FILMOGRAPHY

The Abominable Dr. Phibes. Directed by Robert Fuest. Cast: Vincent Price, Joseph Cotten, Hugh Griffith. AIP, 1971.

The Adventures of Robin Hood. Directed by Michael Curtiz and William Keighley. Cast: Errol Flynn, Olivia de Havilland, Basil Rathbone. Warner Bros., 1938.

The African Queen. Directed by John Huston. Cast: Humphrey Bogart, Katharine Hepburn, Robert Morley. United Artists, 1951.

Alice in Wonderland. Directed by Clyde Geronimi and Wilfred Jackson. Cast: Kathryn Beaumont, Ed Wynn, Richard Haydn. Walt Disney Productions, 1951.

Alice in Wonderland. Directed by Tim Burton. Cast: Mia Wasikowska, Johnny Depp, Helena Bonham Carter. Walt Disney Pictures, 2010.

Alien. Directed by Ridley Scott. Cast: Sigourney Weaver, Tom Skerritt, John Hurt. Brandywine Productions, Twentieth Century-Fox Productions, 1979.

The Amityville Horror. Directed by Stuart Rosenberg. Cast: James Brolin, Margot Kidder, Rod Steiger. MGM, 1979.

Angel Heart. Directed by Alan Parker. Cast: Mickey Rourke, Lisa Bonnet, Robert De Niro, Charlotte Rampling. TriStar Pictures, 1987.

Angels and Demons. Directed by Ron Howard. Cast: Tom Hanks, Ewan McGregor, Ayelet Zurer. Columbia Pictures, 2009.

Animal House. Directed by John Landis. Cast: John Belushi, Karen Allen, Tom Hulce. Universal Pictures, 1978.

Back to the Future. Directed by Robert Zemeckis. Cast: Michael J. Fox, Christopher Lloyd, Lea Thompson. Universal Pictures, 1985.

Back to the Future II. Directed by Robert Zemeckis. Cast: Michael J. Fox, Christopher Lloyd, Lea Thompson. Universal Pictures, 1989.

Back to the Future III. Directed by Robert Zemeckis. Cast: Michael J. Fox, Christopher Lloyd, Lea Thompson. Universal Pictures, 1990.

Barbarella. Directed by Roger Vadim. Cast: Jane Fonda, John Phillip Law, Anita Pallenberg. Paramount Pictures, 1968.

Basic Instinct. Directed by Paul Verhoeven. Cast: Michael Douglas, Sharon Stone, George Dzundza. TriStar Pictures, 1992.

Bates Motel. Created by Anthony Cipriano, Carlton Cuse, Kerry Ehrin. Cast: Vera Farmiga, Freddie Highmore, Max Thieriot. A&E Television Networks, 2013-2017.

Batman. Directed by Tim Burton. Cast: Michael Keaton, Jack Nicholson, Kim Basinger. Warner Brothers, 1989.

Batman Returns. Directed by Tim Burton. Cast: Michael Keaton, Danny DeVito, Michelle Pfeiffer. Warner Bros., 1992.

Batman & Robin. Directed by Joel Schumacher. Cast: Arnold Schwarzenegger, George Clooney, Uma Thurman, Chris O'Donnell. Warner Bros., 1997.

Batman Begins. Directed by Christopher Nolan. Cast: Christian Bale, Michael Caine, Ken Watanabe. Warner Brothers, 2005.

Being There. Directed by Hal Ashby. Cast: Peter Sellers, Shirley MacLaine, Melvyn Douglas. BSB, CIP, Lorimar Film Entertainment, 1979.

Black Swan. Directed by Darren Aronofsky. Cast: Natalie Portman, Mila Kunis, Vincent Cassel. Twentieth Century Fox, 2010.

Blade Runner. Directed by Ridley Scott. Cast: Harrison Ford, Sean Young, Rutger Hauer, Darryl Hannah. Warner Bros., 1982.

Blue Velvet. Directed by David Lynch. Cast: Isabella Rossellini, Kyle MacLachlan, Dennis Hopper, Laura Dern. De Laurentiis Entertainment Group, 1986.

Body Double. Directed by Brian De Palma. Cast: Craig Wasson, Melanie Griffith, Gregg Henry. Columbia Pictures, 1984.

The Body Snatcher. Directed by Robert Wise. Cast: Boris Karloff, Bela Lugosi, Henry Daniell. RKO Radio Pictures, 1945.

Breakfast at Tiffany's. Directed by Blake Edwards. Cast: Audrey Hepburn, George Peppard, Patricia Neal. Paramount Pictures, 1961.

The Bride of Frankenstein. Directed by James Whale. Cast: Boris Karloff, Elsa Lanchester, Colin Clive. Universal Pictures, 1935.

Buffy the Vampire Slayer. Creator: Joss Whedon. Cast: Sarah Michelle Gellar, Nicholas Brendon, Alyson Hannigan. The WB and UPN, 1997-2003.

Cabin Fever. Directed by Eli Roth. Cast: Jordan Ladd, Rider Strong, James DeBello. Lions Gate Films, 2002.

The Cabinet of Dr. Caligari. Directed by Robert Wiene. Cast: Werner Krauss, Conrad Veidt, Friedrich Feher. Decla-Bioscop AG, 1920.

Caddyshack. Directed by Harold Ramis. Cast: Chevy Chase, Ted Knight, Rodney Dangerfield, Bill Murray. Warner Bros., 1980.

A Christmas Carol. Directed by Brian Desmond Hurst. Cast: Alastair Sim, Jack Warner, Kathleen Harrison. United Artists, 1951.

A Christmas Story. Directed by Bob Clark. Cast: Peter Billingsley, Melinda Dillon, Darren McGavin. MGM, 1983.

The Chronicles of Narnia: The Lion, the Witch and the Wardrobe. Directed by Andrew Adamson. Cast: Tilda Swinton, Georgie Henley, William Moseley. Walt Disney Pictures, 2005.

The Chronicles of Narnia: Prince Caspian. Directed by Andrew Adamson. Cast: Ben Barnes, Skandar Keynes, Georgie Henley. Walt Disney Pictures, 2008.

The Chronicles of Narnia: The Voyage of the Dawn Treader. Directed by Michael Apted. Cast: Ben Barnes, Skandar Keynes, Georgie Henley. Fox 2000 Pictures, 2010.

Cinderella. Directed by Clyde Geronimi and Wilfred Jackson. Cast: Ilene Woods, James MacDonald, Eleanor Audley. Walt Disney Productions, 1950.

Conan the Barbarian. Directed by John Milius. Cast: Arnold Schwarzenegger, James Earl Jones, Max von Sydow. Universal Pictures, 1982.

The Conjuring. Directed by James Wan. Cast: Patrick Wilson, Vera Farmiga, Ron Livingston. New Line Cinema, 2013.

Creepshow. Directed by George Romero. Cast: Hal Holbrook, Leslie Nielsen, Adrienne Barbeau. Warner Bros., 1982.

Crimson Peak. Directed by Guillermo del Toro. Cast: Mia Wasikowska, Jessica Chastain, Tom Hiddleston. Universal Pictures, 2015.

Dante's Inferno. Directed by Francesco Bertolini and Adolfo Padovan. Cast: Salvatore Papa, Arturo Pirovano, Giuseppe de Liguoro. Milano Film, 1911.

The Dark Knight. Directed by Christopher Nolan. Cast: Christian Bale, Heath Ledger, Aaron Eckhart. Warner Brothers, 2008.

The Dark Knight Rises. Directed by Christopher Nolan. Cast: Christian Bale, Tom Hardy, Anne Hathaway. Warner Brothers, 2012.

The Day the Earth Stood Still. Directed by Robert Wise. Cast: Michael Rennie, Patricia Neal, Hugh Marlowe. 20th Century Fox, 1951.

The Devil Rides Out. Directed by Terence Fisher. Cast: Christopher Lee, Charles Gray, Nike Arrighi. Hammer Films, 1968.

Dial M for Murder. Directed by Alfred Hitchcock. Cast: Ray Milland, Grace Kelly, Robert Cummings. Warner Bros., 1954.

District 9. Directed by Neill Blomkamp. Cast: Sharlto Copley, David James, Jason Cope. WingNut Films, 2009.

Dracula. Directed by Tod Browning and Karl Freund (un-credited). Cast: Béla Lugosi, Helen Chandler, David Manners. Universal Pictures, 1931.

Dracula. Directed by Francis Ford Coppola. Cast: Gary Oldman, Winona Ryder, Anthony Hopkins. American Zoetrope, Columbia Pictures Corporation, 1992.

Dracula's Daughter. Directed by Lambert Hillyer. Cast: Otto Kruger, Gloria Holden, Marguerite Churchill. Universal Pictures, 1936.

Dr. Jekyll and Mr. Hyde. Directed by John S. Robertson. Cast: John Barrymore, Martha Mansfield, Brandon Hurst. Famous Players-Lasky Corporation, 1920.

Dr. Jekyll and Mr. Hyde. Directed by Rouben Mamoulian. Cast: Fredric March, Miriam Hopkins, Rose Hobart. Paramount Pictures, 1932.

Dr. Jekyll and Mr. Hyde. Directed by Victor Fleming, Cast: Spencer Tracy, Ingrid Bergman, Lana Turner. MGM, 1941.

DuckTales. Cast: Alan Young, Russi Taylor, Terence McGovern. Disney Television Animation, 1987-1990.

Dune. Directed by David Lynch. Cast: Kyle MacLachlan, Virginia Madsen, Francesca Annis. Dino De Laurentiis Company, 1984.

Ed Wood. Directed by Tim Burton. Cast: Johnny Depp, Martin Landau, Sarah Jessica Parker. Buena Vista Pictures, 1994.

The Emperor's New Groove. Directed by Mark Dindal. Cast: David Spade, John Goodman, Eartha Kitt. Walt Disney Pictures, 2000.

Escape from New York. Directed by John Carpenter. Cast: Kurt Russell, Lee Van Cleef, Ernest Borgnine. Embassy Pictures, 1981.

Escape to Witch Mountain. Directed by John Hough. Cast: Eddie Albert, Ray Milland, Donald Pleasence. Buena Vista Distribution, 1975.

E.T. the Extra-Terrestrial. Directed by Steven Spielberg. Cast: Henry Thomas, Drew Barrymore, Peter Coyote. Universal Pictures, 1982.

Evilspeak. Directed by Eric Weston. Cast: Clint Howard, R.G. Armstrong, Joe Cortese. Warner Bros., 1981.

Excalibur. Directed by John Boorman. Cast: Nigel Terry, Helen Mirren, Nicolas Clay, Cheri Lunghi, Nicol Williamson. Warner Bros., 1981.

The Exorcist. Directed by William Friedkin. Cast: Linda Blair, Max von Sydow, Ellen Burstyn, Jason Miller, Kitty Winn. Warner Bros., 1973.

Express Yourself. Directed by David Fincher. Performed by Madonna. Propaganda Films, 1989.

Eyes Wide Shut. Directed by Stanley Kubrick. Cast: Tom Cruise, Nicole Kidman, Todd Field. Warner Bros., 1999.

Fantasia. Directed by James Algar and Samuel Armstrong. Cast: Leopold Stokowski, Deems Taylor, Corey Burton. Walt Disney Pictures, 1940.

Fast Times at Ridgemont High. Directed by Amy Heckerling. Cast: Sean Penn, Jennifer Jason Leigh, Judge Reinhold. Universal Pictures, Refugee Films, 1982.

Fatal Attraction. Directed by Adrian Lyne. Cast: Michael Douglas, Glenn Close, Anne Archer. Paramount Pictures, 1987.

Femme Fatale. Directed by Brian De Palma. Cast: Rebecca Romijn, Antonio Banderas, Peter Coyote. Quinta Communications, 2002.

Ferris Bueller's Day Off. Directed by John Hughes. Cast: Matthew Broderick, Alan Ruck, Mia Sara. Paramount Pictures, 1986.

Fifty Shades of Grey. Directed by Sam Taylor-Johnson. Cast: Dakota Johnson, Jamie Dornan, Jennifer Ehle. Universal Pictures, 2015.

Fight Club. Directed by David Fincher. Cast: Brad Pitt, Edward Norton, Helena Bonham Carter. Twentieth Century Fox, 1999.

A Fistful of Dollars. Directed by Sergio Leone. Cast: Clint Eastwood, Gian Maria Volontè, Marianne Koch. United Artists, 1964.

Flash Gordon. Directed by Mike Hodges. Cast: Sam J. Jones, Melody Anderson, Max von Sydow. Universal Pictures, 1980.

The Fly. Directed by David Cronenberg. Cast: Jeff Goldblum, Geena Davis, John Getz. SLM Production Group, 1986.

The Fog. Directed by John Carpenter. Cast: Adrienne Barbeau, Jamie Lee Curtis, Janet Leigh. Embassy Pictures, 1980.

For a Few Dollars More. Directed by Sergio Leone. Cast: Clint Eastwood, Lee Van Cleef, Gian Maria Volontè. United Artists, 1965.

47 Ronin. Directed by Carl Rinsch. Cast: Keanu Reeves, Hiroyuki Sanada, Ko Shibasaki. H2F Entertainment, 2013.

Frankenstein. Directed by James Whale. Cast: Colin Clive, Mae Clarke, Boris Karloff. Universal Pictures, 1931.

Friday the 13th. Directed by Sean S. Cunningham. Cast: Betsy Palmer, Adrienne King, Jeannine Taylor. Paramount Pictures, 1980.

The Frighteners. Directed by Peter Jackson. Cast: Michael J. Fox, Trini Alvarado, Peter Dobson. Universal Pictures, 1996.

From Hell. Directed by the Hughes Brothers. Cast: Johnny Depp, Heather Graham, Ian Holm. Twentieth Century Fox, 2001.

Fun and Fancy Free. Cast: Edgar Bergen, Dinah Shore, Charlie McCarthy. Walt Disney Productions, 1947.

Gangs of New York. Directed by Martin Scorsese. Cast: Leonardo DiCaprio, Cameron Diaz, Daniel Day-Lewis. Miramax, 2002.

Glen or Glenda. Directed by Edward D. Wood, Jr. Cast: Edward D. Wood, Jr. (as Daniel Davis), Béla Lugosi, Lyle Talbot, Delores Fuller, Conrad Brooks, Timothy Farrell. Screen Classics, 1953.

Goldfinger. Directed by Guy Hamilton. Cast: Sean Connery, Gert Fröbe, Honor Blackman. Eon Productions, 1964.

The Golem. Directed by Carl Boese and Paul Wegener. Cast: Paul Wegener, Albert Steinrück, Ernst Deutsch. Berliner Union-Film Studio, 1920.

The Good, the Bad and the Ugly. Directed by Sergio Leone. Cast: Clint Eastwood, Eli Wallach, Lee Van Cleef. United Artists, 1965.

The Greatest Story Ever Told. Directed by George Stevens, David Lean. Cast: Max von Sydow, Dorothy McGuire, Charlton Heston. United Artists, 1965.

The Green Hornet. Created by George W. Trendle. Cast: Van Williams, Bruce Lee, Wende Wagner. 20th Century Fox Television, 1966-1967.

The Green Mile. Directed by Frank Darabont. Cast: Tom Hanks, Michael Clarke Duncan, David Morse. Castle Rock Entertainment, 1999.

Halloween. Directed by John Carpenter. Cast: Jamie Lee Curtis, Donald Pleasence, Tony Moran. Compass International Pictures, 1978.

Halloween II. Directed by Rick Rosenthal. Cast: Jamie Lee Curtis, Donald Pleasence, Charles Cyphers. Dino De Laurentiis Company, Universal Pictures, 1981.

Halloween III: Season of the Witch. Directed by Tommy Lee Wallace. Cast: Tom Atkins, Stacey Nelkin, Dan O'Herlihy. Universal Pictures, 1982.

Hanky Panky. Directed by Sidney Poitier. Cast: Gene Wilder, Gilda Radner, Kathleen Quinlan. Columbia Pictures, 1982.

Harry Potter and the Sorcerer's Stone. Directed by Chris Columbus. Cast: Daniel Radcliffe, Emma Watson, Rupert Grint, Alan Rickman, Maggie Smith. Warner Bros., 2001.

Harry Potter and the Chamber of Secrets. Directed by Chris Columbus. Cast: Daniel Radcliffe, Emma Watson, Rupert Grint. Warner Bros., 2002.

Harry Potter and the Prisoner of Azkaban. Directed by Alfonso Cuarón. Cast: Daniel Radcliffe, Emma Watson, Rupert Grint. Warner Bros., 2004.

Harry Potter and the Goblet of Fire. Directed by Mike Newell. Cast: Daniel Radcliffe, Emma Watson, Rupert Grint. Warner Bros., 2005.

Harry Potter and the Order of the Phoenix. Directed by David Yates. Cast: Daniel Radcliffe, Emma Watson, Rupert Grint. Warner Bros., 2007.

Harry Potter and the Half-Blood Prince. Directed by David Yates. Cast: Daniel Radcliffe, Emma Watson, Rupert Grint. Warner Bros., 2009.

Harry Potter and the Deathly Hallows Part 1. Directed by David Yates. Cast: Daniel Radcliffe, Emma Watson, Rupert Grint, Evanna Lynch, Ralph Fiennes, Alan Rickman, Bonnie Wright. Warner Bros., 2010.

Harry Potter and the Deathly Hallows Part 2. Directed by David Yates. Cast: Daniel Radcliffe, Emma Watson, Rupert Grint, Evanna Lynch, Ralph Fiennes, Alan Rickman, Bonnie Wright. Warner Bros., 2011.

The Haunting. Directed by Robert Wise. Cast: Julie Harris, Claire Bloom, Richard Johnson. MGM, 1963.

The Haunting. Directed by Jan de Bont. Cast: Liam Neeson, Catherine Zeta- Jones, Owen Wilson. DreamWorks, 1999.

Head Office. Directed by Ken Finkleman. Cast: Judge Reinhold, Eddie Albert, Lori-Nan Engler. TriStar Pictures, 1986.

He-Man and the Masters of the Universe. Created by Roger Sweet, Mattel designer. Cast: John Erwin, Alan Oppenheimer, Linda Gary. Filmation Associates, 1983-1985.

Hitman. Directed by Xavier Gens. Cast: Timothy Olyphant, Dougray Scott, Olga Kurylenko. Twentieth Century Fox, 2007.

Hitman: Agent 47. Directed by Aleksander Bach. Cast: Rupert Friend, Hannah Ware, Zachary Quinto. Twentieth Century Fox, 2015.

Home Alone. Directed by Chris Columbus. Cast: Macaulay Culkin, Joe Pesci, Daniel Stern. Twentieth Century Fox, 1990.

Home Alone 2: Lost in New York. Directed by Chris Columbus. Cast: Macaulay Culkin, Joe Pesci, Daniel Stern. Twentieth Century Fox, 1992.

The Hound of the Baskervilles. Directed by Terence Fisher. Cast: Peter Cushing, André Morell, Christopher Lee. Hammer Film Productions, 1959.

The Hunger Games. Directed by Gary Ross. Cast: Jennifer Lawrence, Josh Hutcherson, Liam Hemsworth. Lionsgate, 2012.

Identity. Directed by James Mangold. Cast: John Cusack, Ray Liotta, Amanda Peet. Columbia Pictures, 2003.

Inauguration of the Pleasure Dome. Directed by Kenneth Anger (as Anger). Cast: Samson De Brier, Marjorie Cameron, Renate Druks, Joan Whitney. 1954.

Independence Day. Directed by Roland Emmerich. Cast: Will Smith, Bill Pullman, Jeff Goldblum. Twentieth Century Fox, 1996.

The Innocents. Directed by Jack Clayton. Cast: Deborah Kerr, Peter Wyngarde, Megs Jenkins. Twentieth Century Fox, 1961.

Invasion of the Body Snatchers. Directed by Don Siegel. Cast: Kevin McCarthy, Dana Wynter, Larry Gates. Allied Artists Pictures, 1956.

It's a Wonderful Life. Directed by Frank Capra. Cast: James Stewart, Donna Reed, Lionel Barrymore. RKO Radio Pictures, 1946.

Jacob's Ladder. Directed by Adrian Lyne. Cast: Tim Robbins, Elizabeth Peña, Danny Aiello. Carolco Pictures, 1990.

Jesus of Nazareth. Directed by Franco Zeffirelli. Cast: Robert Powell, Olivia Hussey, Laurence Olivier. ITC Films, 1977.

The King of Kings. Directed by Cecil B. DeMille. Cast: H.B. Warner, Dorothy Cumming, Ernest Torrence. DeMille Pictures Corporation, 1927.

King of Kings. Directed by Nicholas Ray. Cast: Jeffrey Hunter, Siobhan McKenna, Hurd Hatfield. MGM, 1961.

Knowing. Directed by Alex Proyas. Cast: Nicolas Cage, Chandler Canterbury, Rose Byrne. Summit Entertainment, 2009.

Krampus. Directed by Michael Dougherty. Cast: Adam Scott, Toni Collette, David Koechner. Universal Pictures, 2015.

Lara Croft: Tomb Raider. Directed by Simon West. Cast: Angelina Jolie, Jon Voight, Iain Glen. Paramount Pictures, 2001.

The Lion King. Directed by Roger Allers and Rob Minkoff. Cast: Matthew Broderick, Jeremy Irons, James Earl Jones. Walt Disney Pictures, 1994.

The Little Mermaid. Directed by Ron Clements, John Musker. Cast: Jodi Benson, Samuel E. Wright, Rene Auberjonois. Buena Vista Pictures, 1989.

Logan's Run. Directed by Michael Anderson. Cast: Michael York, Jenny Agutter, Richard Jordan. MGM, 1976.

The Lone Gunmen. Creators: Chris Carter, Vince Gilligan, John Shiban. Cast: Bruce Harwood, Tom Braidwood, Dean Haglund. 20th Century Fox Television, 2001.

The Lord of the Rings: The Fellowship of the Ring. Directed by Peter Jackson. Cast: Elijah Wood, Ian McKellen, Christopher Lee, Viggo Mortensen, Orlando Bloom. New Line Cinema, New Line Cinema, 2001.

The Lord of the Rings: The Two Towers. Directed by Peter Jackson. Cast: Elijah Wood, Ian McKellen, Christopher Lee, Viggo Mortensen, Orlando Bloom. New Line Cinema, New Line Cinema, 2002.

The Lord of the Rings: The Return of the King. Directed by Peter Jackson. Cast: Elijah Wood, Ian McKellen, Viggo Mortensen, Orlando Bloom. New Line Cinema, New Line Cinema, 2003.

Lost Highway. Directed by David Lynch. Cast: Bill Pullman, Patricia Arquette, Robert Blake. October Films, 1997.

The Lovely Bones. Directed by Peter Jackson. Cast: Rachel Weisz, Mark Wahlberg, Saoirse Ronan, Stanley Tucci. DreamWorks SKG, 2009.

Magic. Directed by Richard Attenborough. Cast: Anthony Hopkins, Ann-Margret, Burgess Meredith. Twentieth Century Fox, 1978.

The Magnificent Seven. Directed by John Sturges. Cast: Yul Brynner, Steve McQueen, Charles Bronson. United Artists, 1960.

Maleficent. Directed by Robert Stromberg. Cast: Angelina Jolie, Elle Fanning, Sharlto Copley. Walt Disney Studios, 2014.

Man of Steel. Directed by Zack Snyder. Cast: Henry Cavill, Amy Adams, Michael Shannon. Warner Bros., 2013.

The Manchurian Candidate. Directed by John Frankenheimer. Cast: Frank Sinatra, Laurence Harvey, Janet Leigh. United Artists, 1962.

Manhunter. Directed by Michael Mann. Cast: William Petersen, Kim Greist, Joan Allen. De Laurentiis Entertainment Group, 1986.

The Man Who Would Be King. Directed by John Huston. Cast: Sean Connery, Michael Caine, Christopher Plummer. Columbia Pictures, 1975.

Maria's Lovers. Directed by Andrey Konchalovskiy. Cast: Nastassja Kinski, John Savage, Keith Carradine. Cannon Films, 1984.

The Mask. Directed by Chuck Russell (as Charles Russell). Cast: Jim Carrey, Cameron Diaz, Peter Riegert. New Line Cinema, Dark Horse Entertainment, 1994.

The Masque of the Red Death. Directed by Roger Corman. Cast: Vincent Price, Hazel Court, Jane Asher. AIP, 1964.

Masters of the Universe. Directed by Gary Goddard. Cast: Dolph Lundgren, Frank Langella, Meg Foster. Golan-Globus Productions, 1987.

The Matrix. Directed by the Waschowski Brothers. Cast: Keanu Reeves, Laurence Fishburne, Hugo Weaving, Carrie-Anne Moss. Warner Bros., 1999.

The Matrix Reloaded. Directed by the Waschowski Brothers. Cast: Keanu Reeves, Laurence Fishburne, Hugo Weaving, Carrie-Anne Moss. Warner Bros., 2003.

The Matrix Revolutions. Directed by the Waschowski Brothers. Cast: Keanu Reeves, Laurence Fishburne, Hugo Weaving, Carrie-Anne Moss. Warner Bros., 2003.

Meatballs. Directed by Ivan Reitman. Cast: Bill Murray, Harvey Atkin, Kate Lynch. Paramount Pictures, 1979.

The Messiah (*Il Messia*). Directed by Roberto Rossellini. Cast: Pier Maria Rossi, Mita Ungaro, Carlos de Carvalho. Orizzonte 2000, 1975.

Metropolis. Directed by Fritz Lang. Cast: Brigitte Helm, Alfred Abel, Gustav Fröhlich. Parufamet, 1927.

Miracle on 34th Street. Directed by George Seaton. Cast: Edmund Gwenn, Maureen O'Hara, John Payne. Twentieth Century Fox Film Corporation, 1947.

Monty Python and the Holy Grail. Directed by Terry Gilliam and Terry Jones. Cast: Graham Chapman, John Cleese, Eric Idle, Michael Palin, Terry Gilliam, Terry Jones. Cinema 5, 1975.

Mulholland Drive. Directed by David Lynch. Cast: Naomi Watts, Laura Harring, Justin Theroux. Universal Pictures, 2001.

Murder by Decree. Directed by Bib Clark. Cast: Christopher Plummer, James Mason, David Hemmings. Embassy Pictures, 1979.

The Name of the Rose. Directed by Jean-Jacques Annaud. Cast: Sean Connery, Christian Slater, Helmut Qualtinger. Twentieth Century Fox, 1986.

National Lampoon's Vacation. Directed by Harold Ramis. Cast: Chevy Chase, Beverly D'Angelo, Imogene Coca. Warner Bros., 1983.

Nightbreed. Directed by Clive Barker. Cast: Craig Sheffer, David Cronenberg, Anne Bobby. 20th Century Fox, 1990.

The Neon Demon. Directed by Nicolas Winding Refn. Cast: Elle Fanning, Christina Hendricks, Keanu Reeves. Amazon Studios, 2016.

9 ½ Weeks. Directed by Adrian Lyne. Cast: Kim Basinger, Mickey Rourke, Margaret Whitton, Christine Baranski. MGM, 1986.

The Ninth Gate. Directed by Roman Polanski. Cast: Johnny Depp, Lena Olin, Frank Langella, Emmanuelle Seigner. Araba Films, 1999.

Now, Voyager. Directed by Irving Rapper. Cast: Bette Davis, Paul Henreid, Claude Rains. Warner Brothers, 1942.

Obsession. Directed by Brian De Palma. Cast: Cliff Robertson, Geneviève Bujold, John Lithgow. Columbia Pictures, 1976.

The Omega Man. Directed by Boris Sagal. Cast: Charlton Heston, Anthony Zerbe, Rosalind Cash. Walter Seltzer Productions, 1971.

Omen III: The Final Conflict. Directed by Graham Baker. Cast: Sam Neill, Lisa Harrow, Rossano Brazzi, Don Gordon. 20th Century Fox, 1981.

One Flew Over the Cuckoo's Nest. Directed by Milos Forman. Cast: Jack Nicholson, Louise Fletcher, Michael Berryman. United Artists, 1975.

101 Dalmatians. Directed by Clyde Geronimi, Hamilton Luske. Cast: Rod Taylor, Betty Lou Gerson, J. Pat O'Malley. Walt Disney Studios, 1961.

Passion. Directed by Brian De Palma. Cast: Rachel McAdams, Noomi Rapace, Karoline Herfurth. Entertainment One, 2012.

The Passion of the Christ. Directed by Mel Gibson. Cast: Jim Caviezel, Monica Bellucci, Maia Morgenstern. Newmarket Films, 2004.

The Patriot. Directed by Roland Emmerich. Cast: Mel Gibson, Heath Ledger, Joely Richardson. Columbia Pictures, 2000.

Pet Sematary. Directed by Mary Lambert. Cast: Dale Midkiff, Denise Crosby, Fred Gwynne. Paramount Pictures, 1989.

Phantasm. Directed by Don Coscarelli. Cast: A. Michael Baldwin, Bill Thornbury, Reggie Bannister, Angus Scrimm. AVCO Embassy Pictures, 1979.

The Pirates of the Caribbean: The Curse of the Black Pearl. Directed by Gore Verbinski. Cast: Johnny Depp, Geoffrey Rush, Orlando Bloom. Walt Disney Pictures, 2003.

Plan 9 from Outer Space. Directed by Edward D. Wood, Jr. Cast: Gregory Walcott, Vampira, Tom Keene, Conrad Brooks, Criswell, Tor Johnson, Paul Marco, Mona McKinnon. Reynolds Pictures, 1959.

Porky's. Directed by Bob Clark. Cast: Dan Monahan, Mark Herrier, Wyatt Knight. 20th Century Fox, 1981.

The Prisoner. Created by Patrick McGoohan. Cast: Patrick McGoohan, Angelo Muscat, Peter Swanwick. Everyman Films, 1967-1968.

Psycho. Directed by Alfred Hitchcock. Cast: Anthony Perkins, Janet Leigh, Vera Miles. Paramount Pictures, 1960.

Psycho II. Directed by Richard Franklin. Cast: Anthony Perkins, Vera Miles, Meg Tilly. Universal Pictures, 1983.

Pumpkinhead. Directed by Stan Winston. Cast: Lance Henriksen, Jeff East, John D'Aquino. De Laurentiis Entertainment Group (DEG), Lion Films, 1988.

Raiders of the Lost Ark. Directed by Steven Spielberg. Cast: Harrison Ford, Karen Allen, Paul Freeman. Paramount Pictures, 1981.

Raising Cain. Directed by Brian De Palma. Cast: John Lithgow, Lolita Davidovich, Steven Bauer. Universal Pictures, 1992.

Re-Animator. Directed by Stuart Gordon. Cast: Jeffrey Combs, Bruce Abbott, Barbara Crampton. Empire Pictures, 1985.

Rebecca. Directed by Alfred Hitchcock. Cast: Laurence Olivier, Joan Fontaine, George Sanders. United Artists, 1940.

Red Dragon. Directed by Brett Ratner. Cast: Anthony Hopkins, Edward Norton, Ralph Fiennes. Universal Pictures, 2002.

Red River. Directed by Howard Hawks and Arthur Rosson. Cast: John Wayne, Montgomery Clift, Joanne Dru. United Artists, 1948.

Repulsion. Directed by Roman Polanski. Cast: Catherine Deneuve, Ian Hendry, John Fraser. Compton Films, 1965.

The Rescuers. Directed by John Lounsbery, Wolfgang Reitherman. Cast: Bob Newhart, Eva Gabor, Geraldine Page. Walt Disney Productions, 1977.

Return from Witch Mountain. Directed by John Hough. Cast: Bette Davis, Christopher Lee, Kim Richards. Walt Disney Productions, 1978.

Rocky. Directed by John G. Avildsen. Cast: Sylvester Stallone, Talia Shire, Burt Young. United Artists, 1976.

Rosemary's Baby. Directed by Roman Polanski. Cast: Mia Farrow, John Cassavetes, Ruth Gordon. William Castle Productions, 1968.

Scarface. Directed by Brian De Palma. Cast: Al Pacino, Michelle Pfeiffer, Steven Bauer. Universal Pictures, 1983.

Scream Queens. Created by Ian Brennan, Brad Falchuk, Ryan Murphy. Cast: Emma Roberts, Lea Michele, Glen Powell. Fox, 2015-2016.

Secretary. Directed by Steven Shainberg. Cast: James Spader, Maggie Gyllenhaal, Jeremy Davies. Lions Gate Films, 2002.

Se7en. Directed by David Fincher. Cast: Morgan Freeman, Brad Pitt, Kevin Spacey, Gwyneth Paltrow. New Line Cinema, 1995.

Seven Samurai. Directed by Akira Kurosawa. Cast: Toshirô Mifune, Takashi Shimura, Keiko Tsushima. Toho Company, 1954.

Shadow of a Doubt. Directed by Alfred Hitchcock. Cast: Teresa Wright, Joseph Cotten, Macdonald Carey. Universal Pictures, 1943.

The Shawshank Redemption. Directed by Frank Darabont. Cast: Tim Robbins, Morgan Freeman, Bob Gunton. Columbia Pictures, 1994.

The Shining. Directed by Stanley Kubrick. Cast: Jack Nicholson, Shelley Duvall, Danny Lloyd. Warner Bros., 1980.

Sisters. Directed by Brian De Palma. Cast: Margot Kidder, Jennifer Salt, Charles Durning. AIP, 1973.

The Sixth Sense. Directed by M. Night Shyamalan. Cast: Bruce Willis, Haley Joel Osment, Toni Collette. Buena Vista Pictures, 1999.

Sleepy Hollow. Creators: Phillip Iscove, Alex Kurtzman, Roberto Orci. Cast: Tom Mison, Nicole Beharie, Lyndie Greenwood. Fox, 2013-2017.

Sleeping Beauty. Directed by Clyde Geronimi. Cast: Mary Costa, Bill Shirley, Eleanor Audley. Walt Disney Productions, 1959.

The Smurfs. Created by Peyo. Cast: Don Messick, Danny Goldman, Lucille Bliss. Hanna-Barbera Productions, 1981-1990.

The Smurfs. Directed by Raja Gosnell. Cast: Hank Azaria, Katy Perry, Jonathan Winters. Columbia Pictures, 2011.

The Smurfs 2. Directed by Raja Gosnell. Cast: Neil Patrick Harris, Jayma Mays, Katy Perry. Columbia Pictures, 2013.

Snow White and the Seven Dwarfs. Directed by William Cottrell and David Hand. Cast: Adriana Caselotti, Harry Stockwell, Lucille La Verne. Walt Disney Productions, 1937.

Soylent Green. Directed by Richard Fleischer. Cast: Charlton Heston, Edward G. Robinson, Leigh Taylor-Young. MGM, 1973.

The Spider Woman. Directed by Roy William Neill. Cast: Basil Rathbone, Nigel Bruce, Gale Sondergaard. Universal Pictures, 1944.

Stargate. Directed by Roland Emmerich. Cast: Kurt Russell, James Spader, Jaye Davidson. MGM, 1994.

Star Trek. Created by Gene Roddenberry. Cast: William Shatner, Leonard Nimoy, DeForest Kelley. Desilu Productions, 1966-1969.

Star Wars Episode I: The Phantom Menace. Directed by George Lucas. Cast: Ewan McGregor, Liam Neeson, Natalie Portman. Twentieth Century Fox, 1999.

Star Wars Episode II: Attack of the Clones. Directed by George Lucas. Cast: Hayden Christensen, Natalie Portman, Ewan McGregor. Twentieth Century Fox, 2002.

Star Wars Episode III: Revenge of the Sith. Directed by George Lucas. Cast: Hayden Christensen, Natalie Portman, Ewan McGregor. Twentieth Century Fox, 2005.

Star Wars Episode IV: A New Hope. Directed by George Lucas. Cast: Mark Hamill, Harrison Ford, Carrie Fisher. Twentieth Century Fox, 1977.

Star Wars Episode V: The Empire Strikes Back. Directed by Irvin Kershner. Cast: Mark Hamill, Harrison Ford, Carrie Fisher. Twentieth Century Fox, 1980.

Star Wars Episode VI: Return of the Jedi. Directed by Richard Marquand. Cast: Mark Hamill, Harrison Ford, Carrie Fisher. Twentieth Century Fox, 1983.

Star Wars Episode VII: The Force Awakens. Directed by J.J. Abrams. Cast: Daisy Ridley, John Boyega, Oscar Isaac. Walt Disney Studios, 2015.

The Stepford Wives. Directed by Bryan Forbes. Cast: Katharine Ross, Paula Prentiss, Peter Masterson. Columbia Pictures, 1975.

Stoker. Directed by Chan-wook Park. Cast: Mia Wasikowska, Nicole Kidman, Matthew Goode. Fox Searchlight Pictures, 2013.

Suicide Squad. Directed by David Ayer. Cast: Will Smith, Jared Leto, Margot Robbie. Warner Bros., 2016.

Sunset Blvd. Directed by Billy Wilder. Cast: William Holden, Gloria Swanson, Erich von Stroheim. Paramount Pictures, 1950.

Superman. Directed by Richard Donner. Cast: Christopher Reeve, Margot Kidder, Gene Hackman. Dovemead Films, 1978.

Suspiria. Directed by Dario Argento. Cast: Jessica Harper, Stefania Casini, Flavio Bucci. Produzioni Atlas Consorziate, 1977.

The Sword in the Stone. Directed by Wolfgang Reitherman. Cast: Rickie Sorensen, Sebastian Cabot, Karl Swenson. Walt Disney Productions, 1963.

The Ten Commandments. Directed by Cecil B. DeMille. Cast: Charlton Heston, Yul Brynner, Anne Baxter. Paramount, 1956.

The Terminator. Directed by James Cameron. Cast: Arnold Schwarzenegger, Linda Hamilton, Michael Biehn. Orion Pictures, 1984.

The Texas Chainsaw Massacre. Directed by Tobe Hooper. Cast: Marilyn Burns, Gunnar Hanson, Edwin Neal, Allen Danziger. Bryanston Distributing Company, 1974.

There Will Be Blood. Directed by Paul Thomas Anderson. Cast: Daniel Day-Lewis, Paul Dano, Ciarán Hinds. Miramax, 2007.

They Live. Directed by John Carpenter. Cast: Roddy Piper, Keith David, Meg Foster. Universal Pictures, 1988.

Throw Momma from the Train. Directed by Danny DeVito. Cast: Danny DeVito, Billy Crystal, Kim Greist. Orion Pictures, 1987.

Total Recall. Directed by Paul Verhoeven. Cast: Arnold Schwarzenegger, Sharon Stone, Michael Ironside. TriStar Pictures, 1990.

Transformers: Revenge of the Fallen. Directed by Michael Bay. Cast: Shia LaBeouf, Megan Fox, Josh Duhamel. DreamWorks, 2009.

Trick 'r Treat. Directed by Michael Dougherty. Cast: Anna Paquin, Brian Cox, Dylan Baker. Warner Bros., Warner Bros., 2007.

The Truman Show. Directed by Peter Weir. Cast: Jim Carrey, Laura Linney, Ed Harris. Paramount Pictures, 1998.

Twelve Monkeys. Directed by Terry Gilliam. Cast: Bruce Willis, Madeleine Stowe, Brad Pitt. Universal Pictures, 1995.

2001: A Space Odyssey. Directed by Stanley Kubrick. Cast: Keir Dullea, Gary Lockwood, William Sylvester. MGM, 1968.

V for Vendetta. Directed by James McTeigue. Cast: Hugo Weaving, Natalie Portman, Rupert Graves. Warner Bros., 2005.

Vertigo. Directed by Alfred Hitchcock. Cast: James Stewart, Kim Novak, Barbara Bel Geddes. Paramount Pictures, 1958.

The Warriors. Directed by Walter Hill. Cast: Michael Beck, James Remar, Dorsey Wright. Paramount Pictures, 1979.

Watchmen. Directed by Zack Snyder. Cast: Jackie Earle Haley, Patrick Wilson, Carla Gugino. Warner Bros., 2009.

The Wicker Man. Directed by Robin Hardy. Cast: Edward Woodward, Christopher Lee, Diane Cilento. British Lion Film Corp., 1973.

The Witch. Directed by Robert Eggers. Cast: Anya Taylor-Joy, Ralph Ineson, Kate Dickie. A24, 2015.

The Wizard of Oz. Directed by Victor Fleming and George Cukor (uncredited). Cast: Judy Garland, Frank Morgan, Ray Bolger, Billie Burke. MGM, 1939.

The Wolf Man. Directed by George Waggner. Cast: Claude Rains, Warren William, Ralph Bellamy, Lon Chaney, Jr., Evelyn Ankers. Universal Studios, 1941.

The Woman in Green. Directed by Roy William Neill. Cast: Basil Rathbone, Nigel Bruce, Hillary Brooke. Universal Pictures, 1945.

The X-Files. Created by Chris Carter. Cast: David Duchovny, Gillian Anderson, Mitch Pileggi. Fox, 1993-2018.

The X-Files: Fight the Future. Directed by Rob Bowman. Cast: David Duchovny, Gillian Anderson, John Neville. Twentieth Century Fox Film Corporation, 1998.

Yankee Doodle Dandy. Directed by Michael Curtiz. Cast: James Cagney, Joan Leslie, Walter Huston. Warner Bros., 1942.

BIBLIOGRAPHY

Abrams, M.H. *A Glossary of Literary Terms*. 7th ed. Boston: Heinle and Heinle, 1999.

Ackerman, Kenneth D.*BossTweed:TheRiseandFallofthe Corrupt Pol Who Conceived the Soul of Modern NewYork*. 2005. Reprint, Falls Church, Virginia: Viral History Press, 2011.

Adams, Norman, *Dead and Buried? The Horrible History of Bodysnatching*. New York: Bell Publishing Co., 1972.

Agrippa, Heinrich Cornelius. *Three Books of Occult Philosophy*. 1651. Reprint, translated by James Freake and edited and annotated by Donald Tyson, Woodbury, Minnesota: Llewellyn, 2009.

Alexander, Edward P. *Museum Masters: Their Museums and Their Influence*. London: AltaMira Press, 1995.

Alighieri, Dante. *The Divine Comedy*. 1555. Reprint, translation by C.H. Sisson, Oxford, England: Oxford University Press, 1993.

The American College of Heraldry, http://www. americancollegeofheraldry.org.

Anderson, Karl. *Astrology of the Old Testament or the Lost Word Regained*. 1892. Reprint, Pomeroy, Washington: Health Research, 1970.

Anson, Jay. *The Amityville Horror*. Upper Saddle River, New Jersey: Prentice Hall, 1977.

Apocalyptic Spirituality. Translated and introduction by Bernard McGinn. Mahwah, New Jersey: Paulist Press, 1979.

Ars Goetia: The Lesser Key of Solomon the King. Translated by Samuel Liddell MacGregor Mathers, Edited with Introduction by Aleister Crowley. 1904. Reprint, San Francisco: Weiser Books, 1997.

Asbury, Herbert. *The Gangs of New York: An Informal History of the Underworld*. 1927. Reprint, New York: Vintage Books, 2008.

Ascher, Rodney. (Director). (2012). *Room 237* [Documentary]. United States: Highland Park Classics.

Astoria, Dorothy. *The Name Book: Over 10,000 Names, Their Meanings, Origins, and Spiritual Significance*. Minneapolis, Minnesota: Bethany House Publishers, 1997.

Austerlitz, Saul. *Another Fine Mess: A History of American Film Comedy*. Chicago: Chicago Review Press, Inc., 2010.

Baigent, Michael, Richard Leigh and Henry Lincoln. *Holy Blood, Holy Grail*. New York: Dell Publishing Group, 1983.

Baigent, Michael and Richard Leigh. *The Temple and the Lodge*. London: Corgi Books, 1990.

Bakhtin, Mikhail. *Rabelais and His World*. Translated by Helene Iswolsky. Bloomington, Indiana: Indiana University Press, 2009.

Bangell08. (2015, October 23). *The Lion King and Hamlet: Similarities and Differences*. Retrieved February 25, 2016, from https://letterpile.com/ books/ Similarities-Between-The-Lion-King-and-Hamlet.

Barstow, Anne Llewellyn. *Witchcraze: A New History of the European Witch Hunts*. San Francisco: Pandora, 1994.

Baskin, Wade. *Dictionary of Satanism*. New York: Philosophical Library, 1972.

Baudrillard, Jean. *Simulacra and Simulation*. Translated by Shelia Faria Glaser. Ann Arbor, Michigan: University of Michigan Press, 1994.

Baum, L. Frank. *The Annotated Wizard of Oz Centennial Edition*. Edited by Michael Patrick Hearn and W.W. Denslow. New York: W. W. Norton & Company, 2000.

Beckmann, Petr. *A History of π*. New York: Golem Press, 1970.

Bergsen, Albert J., and Andrew M. Greely. *God in the Movies*. Piscataway, New Jersey: Transaction Publishers, 2000.

Besterman, Theodore. *Crystal-Gazing*. New York: Cosimo Classics, 2005.

Big Orange Landmarks: Exploring the Landmarks of Los Angeles, One Monument at a Time, http://bigorangelandmarks.blogspot.com.

Billington, James H. *Fire in the Minds of Men: Origins of theRevolutionary Faith.* New York: Basic Books, Inc., Publishers, 1980.

Bilstad, T. Allan. *The Lovecraft Necronomicon Primer: A Guide to the Cthulhu Mythos.* Woodbury, Minnesota: Llewellyn Worldwide, 2009.

Blake, William. *The Complete Poetry and Prose of William Blake.* Edited by David V. Erdman with commentary by Harold Bloom. Berkely and Los Angeles: University of California Press, 1982.

Blatty, William Peter. *The Exorcist.* New York: Harper & Row, Publishers, 1971.

Blavatsky, Helena P. *Isis Unveiled, Volumes I & II.* 1877. Reprint, Pasadena, California: Theosophical University Press, 1999.

Blavatsky, Helena P., *The Secret Doctrine.* 1888. Reprint, New York: Tarcher, 2009.

Bonwick, James. *Egyptian Belief and Modern Thought.* 1878. Reprint, Indian Hills, Colorado: Falcon's Wing Press, 1956.

Borst, Ronald V. *Graven Images: The Best of Horror, Fantasy, and Science-Fiction Film Art from the Collection of Ronald V. Borst.* New York: Grove Press, 1992.

Boucher, Geoff. (2009, May 11). "Leonard Nimoy: 'Star Trek' fans can be scary." *Hero Complex.* Los Angeles Times. Retrieved July 17, 2015, from http://herocomplex. latimes.com/uncategorized/leonard-nimoy-star-trek-fans-can-be-scary/.

Bowen, Catherine Drinker. *Francis Bacon: The Temper of a Man.* Boston: Little Brown and Company, 1963.

Box Office Mojo, www.boxofficemojo.com.

Boyle, Peter and Paul Rodhouse. *Cephalopods: Ecology and Fisheries.* Oxford, England: Wiley-Blackwell, 2005.

Brown, Robert Hewitt. *Stellar Theology and Masonic Astronomy or the Origin and Meaning of Ancient and Modern Mysteries Explained.* 1882. Reprint, Breinigsville, Pennsylvania: Merchant Books, 2009.

Buchan, John. *Oliver Cromwell.* Cambridge, Massachusetts: The Riverside Press, 1934.

Busenbark, Ernest. *Symbols, Sex, and the Stars in Popular Beliefs: An Outline of Moon and Sun Worship, Astrology, Sex Symbolism, Mystic Meaning of Numbers, the Cabala, and Many Popular Customs, Myths, Superstitions and Religious Beliefs.* 1949. Reprint, San Diego: The Book Tree, 2003.

Cabell, Craig. *Ian Fleming's Secret War.* Barnsley, South Yorkshire,England: Pen and Sword Books, 2008.

Campbell, Joseph. *The Hero with a Thousand Faces.* 1949. Reprint, Novato, California: New World Library, 2008.

Campbell, Joseph and Bill Moyers. *The Power of Myth.* New York: Anchor Books, 1991.

Caplen, Robert. *Shaken & Stirred: The Feminism of James Bond.* Bloomington, Indiana: Xlibris, 2010.

Carroll, Lewis. *The Complete Works of Lewis Carroll.* Introduction by Alexander Woollcott. Ware, Hertfordshire, England: Wordsworth Editions Ltd., 1991.

Carter, John. *Sex and Rockets: The Occult World of Jack Parsons.* Los Angeles: Feral House, 2004.

Case, Paul Foster. *The True and Invisible Rosicrucian Order.* York Beach, Maine: Samuel Weiser, Inc., 1985.

Cavendish, Richard. *The Tarot.* New York: Harper & Row, Publishers, 1975.

Churton, Tobias. *The Golden Builders: Alchemists, Rosicrucians, and the First Freemasons.* York Beach, Maine: Red Wheel/Weiser, LLC, 2005.

Churton, Tobias. *The Invisible History of the Rosicrucians: The World's Most Mysterious Secret Society.* Rochester, Vermont: Inner Traditions, 2009.

Churton, Tobias. *The Magus of Freemasonry: The Mysterious Life of Elias Ashmole – Scientist, Alchemist, and Founder of the Royal Society*. Rochester, Vermont: Inner Traditions, 2006.

Clauss, Manfred. *The Roman Cult of Mithras: The God and his Mysteries*. 1990. Reprint and translated by Richard Gordon, New York: Routledge, 2000.

Colbert, David. *The Magical Worlds of Harry Potter: The Magical Worlds of Harry Potter: A Treasury of Myths, Legends, and Fascinating Facts*. 2001. Reprint, New York: Berkley Books, 2008.

Colton, Ray C. *The Civil War in the Western Territories: Arizona, Colorado, New Mexico, and Utah*. Norman, Oklahoma: University of Oklahoma Press, 1959.

Conner, Miguel. *Voices of Gnosticism: Interviews with Elaine Pagels, Marvin Meyer, Bart Ehrman, Bruce Chilton and Other Leading Scholars*. Dublin, Ireland: Bardic Press, 2011.

Cooper, Milton William. *Behold a Pale Horse*. Flagstaff, Arizona: Light Technology Publishing, 1991.

Cooper, Tristan. (2015, June 15). "10 Harry Potter Easter Eggs That Will Take Over Your Life." *Dorkly.com*. Retrieved March 20, 2016, from http://www.dorkly. com/post/73435/harry-potter-easter-eggs.

Cornog, Evan. *The Birth of Empire: DeWitt Clinton and the American Experience, 1769-1828*. New York: Oxford University Press, 1998.

Cranston, Sylvia. *H.P.B.: The Extraordinary Life & Influence of Helena Blavatsky, Founder of the Modern Theosophical Movement*. New York: G.P. Putnam's Sons, 1993.

Criswell. *Criswell's Forbidden Predictions Based on Nostradamus and the Tarot*. Atlanta: Droke House/Hallux, Inc., 1972.

Criswell. *Criswell Predicts: From Now to the Year 2000*: Anderson, South Carolina: Droke House, 1968.

Criswell. *Criswell Predicts: Your Next Ten Years*. Anderson, South Carolina: Droke House, 1969.

Crowley, Aleister. *The Book of Thoth*. 1944. Reprint, San Francisco: Weiser Books, 2011.

Crowley, Aleister. *The Confessions of Aleister Crowley*. 1969. Reprint and edited by John Symonds and Kenneth Grant. London: Penguin/Arkana Books, 1989.

Crowley, Aleister. *Magick*. 1973. Reprint and edited by John Symonds and Kenneth Grant, London: Routledge & Kegan Paul, 1981.

Crowley, Aleister. *Magick Without Tears*. Edited and Introduction by Israel Regardie, Tempe, Arizona: New Falcon Publications, 1991.

Crowley, Aleister. *777 and other Qabalistic Writings of Aleister Crowley*. 1912. 1955. Reprint and edited by Israel Regardie, Boston: Red Wheel/ Weiser LLC, 1986.

Curl, James Stevens. *The Art and Architecture of Freemasonry*. London: B.T. Batsford, Ltd., 1991.

Daniels, Les. *Batman: The Complete History*. San Francisco: Chronicle Books, 2004.

Davidson, Gustav. *A Dictionary of Angels, Including The Fallen Angels*, 1967, Reprint, Florence, Massachusetts, 1994.

De Hoyos, Arturo and S. Brent Morris. *Is it True What they say About Freemasonry?* New York: M. Evans & Co., Inc, 2004.

Demos, John Putnam. *Entertaining Satan: Witchcraft and the Culture of Early New England*. Oxford, England: Oxford University Press, 1982.

Denisoff, R. Serge and William D. Romanowski. *Risky Business: Rock in Film*. New Brunswick, New Jersey: Transaction Publishers, 1991.

Devore, Nicholas. *Encyclopedia of Astrology*. New York: Bonanza Books, a Division of Crown Publishers, Inc., n.d.

Diamond, Stephen A., Ph.D. *Anger, Madness, and the Daimonic: The Psychological Genesis of Violence, Evil, and* Creativity. Albany, New York: SUNY Press, 1996.

Diamond, Stephen A., Ph.D. "Redeeming Our Devils and Demons," *Meeting the Shadow: The Hidden Power of the Dark Side of Human Nature*. New York: Tarcher/Putnam, 1991.

Dick, Philip K. *Do Androids Dream of Electric Sheep?* Introduction by Roger Zalazny. 1968. Reprint, New York: Del Rey, 1996.

Dickens, A.G. *The English Reformation*. London & Glasgow: Fontana/ Collins, 1978.

Doyle, Arthur Conan. *The Complete Sherlock Holmes: All Four Novels, All Fifty-Six Adventures*. Reprint, 1892-1927. New York: Bantam, n.d.

Doyle-White, Ethan. "Occultic World of Alan Moore." *Pentacle* (29), Summer 2009.

Duncan, Malcolm C. *Duncan's Masonic Ritual and Monitor; or, Guide to the Three Symbolic Degrees of the Ancient York Rite and to the Degrees of Mark Master, Past Master, Most Excellent Master, and the Royal Arch*. New York: Fitzgerald Publishing Corporation, n.d.

Duncan, Paul. *Stanley Kubrick*. Cologne, Germany: Taschen, 2011. Edinger, Edward. *Ego and Archetypes*. Boston: Shambhala Publications, 1992.

Edwards, Owen Dudley. *British Children's Fiction in the Second World War*. Edinburgh, Scotland: Edinburgh University Press, 2008

Egan, James Alan. *Elizabethan America*. Newport, Rhode Island: Cosmopolite Press, 2011.

Encyclopedia of Magic & Superstition: Alchemy, Charms, Dreams, Omens, Rituals, Talismans, Wishes. New York: Distributed by Crescent Books, a Division of Crown Publishers Inc., 1974.

Encyclopedia of World Mythology. New York: Galahad Books, 1975.

Eschenbach, Wolfram von. *Parzival*. Ca 1197- 1215. Translated with introduction by Helen M. Mustard and Charles E. Passage, New York: Vintage Books, 1966.

Estulin, Daniel. *The True Story of the Bilderberg Group*. Walterville, Oregon: Trine Day, 2009.

Evans, William Sloane, *A Grammar of British Heraldry consisting of Blazon and Marshalling*. London: J.R. Smith, 1854.

"FACTS AND INCIDENTS OF THE RIOT.: THE MURDER OF COLORED PEOPLE IN THOMPSON AND SULLIVAN STREETS." *The New York Times*. July 16, 1863. p. 1. Retrieved August 10, 2015, from http://www.nytimes.com/1863/07/16/news/facts-incidents-riot-murder-colored-people-thompson-sullivan-streets-sacking.html?pagewanted=all.

Flowers, Stephen E., *Fire & Ice: The History, Structure, and Rituals of Germany's Most Influential Modern Magical Order: The Brotherhood of Saturn*. St. Paul, Minnesota: Llewellyn Publications, 1994.

Foner, Eric. *Reconstruction: America's Unfinished Revolution, 1863- 1877*. New York: HarperCollins, 1988.

Ford, Kenneth W. and Diane Goldstein (Contributor). *The Quantum World: Quantum Physics for Everyone*. Cambridge, Massachusetts: Harvard University Press, 2005.

Ford, Luke. *A History of X: 100 Years of Sex in Film*. Amherst, New York: Prometheus Books, 1999.

Franklin, James. *The Science of Conjecture: Evidence and Probability Before Pascal*. Baltimore: Johns Hopkins University Press, 2001.

Fraser, Antonia. *Faith and Treason: The Story of the Gunpowder Plot*. New York: Anchor, 1997.

Frayling, Christopher. *Spaghetti Westerns: Cowboys and Europeans from Karl May to Sergio Leone*. 1981. Reprint, New York: Palgrave Macmillan, 2006.

Frazer, J.G. *The Golden Bough: A Study in Magic and Religion*. 1922.

Reprint, London: Papermac, 1994.

Freke, Timothy and Peter Gandy. *The Jesus Mysteries: Was the "Original Jesus" a Pagan God?* New York: Three Rivers Press, 2001.

French, Peter. *John Dee: The World of an Elizabethan Magus*. 1972. Reprint, London: Ark Paperbacks, 1987.

Frost, Gavin and Yvonne Frost. *The Magic Power of Witchcraft*. West Nyack, New York: Parker Publishing Company, Inc, 1976.

Freud, Sigmund. *Beyond the Pleasure Principle*. Edited and translated by James Strachey with an Introduction by Gregory Zilboorg and a Biographical Introduction by Peter Gay. New York: Norton, 1961.

Gabler, Neal. Walt Disney: *The Triumph of the American Imagination*. New York: Vintage Books, 2007.

Gardiner, Philip. *The Bond Code: The Dark World of Ian Fleming and James Bond*. Pompton Plains, New Jersey: New Page Books, 2008.

Gardiner, Philip. (Director). (2010). *The Initiation Of Alice In Wonderland: The Looking Glass Of Lewis Carroll* [Documentary]. United States: Reality Entertainment.

Gardner, Gerald B. *Witchcraft Today*. 1954. Reprint, London: Rider and Company, 1956.

Gibbs, Nancy and Michael Duffy. *The Presidents Club: Inside the World's Most Exclusive Fraternity*. New York: Simon & Schuster, 2013.

Gilbert, R.A. *The Golden Dawn Companion*. Boston: Red Wheel Weiser, 1986.

Ginzburg, Carlo. *The Night Battles: Witchcraft and Agrarian Cults in the Sixteenth and Seventeenth Centuries*. 1966-1983. Reprint, translated by John and Anne Tedeschi, Baltimore: The Johns Hopkins University Press, 1992.

Godwin, Joscelyn. *Athanasius Kircher's Theatre of the World: The Life and Work of the Last Man to Search for Universal Knowledge*. Rochester, Vermont: Inner Traditions, 2009.

Goldman, Jane. *X-Files Book of the Unexplained: Volumes 1 and 2*. New York: It Books (HaperCollins), 2008.

Grafton, Anthony. *Natural Particulars: Nature and the Disciplines in Renaissance Europe*. Cambridge, Massachusetts: MIT Press, 1999.

Greenwood, Earl and Kathleen Tracy. *Elvis: Top Secret – The Untold Story of Elvis Presley's Secret FBI Files*. New York: Signet Books, 1991.

Greer, John Michael. *The New Encyclopedia of the Occult*. St. Paul, Minnesota: Llewellyn Publications, 2004.

Grey, Rudolph. *Nightmare of Ecstasy: The Life and Art of Edward D.Wood, Jr.* Portland, Oregon: Feral House, 1992-1994.

Grimm, Jacob and Wilhelm Grimm, *The Original Folk and Fairy Tales of the Brothers Grimm: The Complete First Edition*. Translated by Jack Zipes. Princeton, New Jersey: Princeton University Press, 2014.

Griswold, John. *Ian Fleming's James Bond: Annotations and Chronologies for Ian Fleming's Bond Stories*. Bloomington, Indiana: AuthorHouse, 2006.

Guazzo, Francesco Maria. *Compendium Maleficarum: The Montague Summers Edition*. 1608. Reprint, Mineola, New York: Dover Publications, 1988.

Guiley, Rosemary Ellen. *The Encyclopedia of Witches and Witchcraft*. New York: Facts on File, Inc., 1989.

Hall, Manly Palmer. *Freemasonry of the Ancient Egyptians*. 1937. Reprint, Los Angeles: The Philosophical Research Society, Inc., 1965.

Hall, Manly Palmer. *Lectures on Ancient Philosophy*. 1984. Reprint, New York: TarcherPenguin, 2005.

Hall, Manly Palmer. *The Lost Keys of Freemasonry*. 1923. 1937. 1950. Reprint, New York: TarcherPenguin, 2006.

Hall, Manly Palmer. *The Secret Teachings of All Ages: An Encyclopedic Outline of Masonic, Hermetic, Qabbalistic and Rosicrucian Symbolic Philosophy*. 1928. Reprint, New York: TarcherPenguin, 2003.

Hall, Manly Palmer. *Twelve World Teachers*. Los Angeles: PhilosophicalResearch Society, Inc., 1965.

Hamill, Pete. (2005, March 27). "'Boss Tweed': The Fellowship of theRing.*" The New York Times*. March 27, 2005. http://www.nytimes.com/2005/03/27/books/ review/boss-tweed-the-fellowship-of-the-ring.html. Retrieved August 10, 2015.
Hamilton, Edith. *Mythology*. 1942. Reprint, New York: Back Bay Books, 2013.

Hancox, Joy. *The Byrom Collection and the Globe Theatre Mystery*. London: Jonathan Cape, 1992.

Haskins, Jim. *Voodoo and Hoodoo: The Craft as Revealed by Traditional Practitioners*. Portland, Oregon: Scarborough House, 1990.

Heathcote, Edwin. *Cinema Builders*. West Sussex, England: Wiley- Academy, 2001.

Heiddegger, Martin. *Being and Time*. Translated by John Macuarrie andEdward Robinson, New York: Harper, 1962.

Henry, John. *The Scientific Revolution and the Origins of Modern Science*. New York: Palgrave Macmillan, 2008.

Herbert, Frank. *Dune*. 1965. Reprint, New York: Ace Books, 1990. Herkin, Gregg. *Brotherhood of the Bomb: The Tangled Lives and*

Loyalties of Robert Oppenheimer, Ernest Lawrence, and Edward Teller. New York: Henry Holt and Company, LLC, 2002.

Higgins, Godfrey. *Anacalypsis: An Attempt to Draw Aside the Veil of the Saitic Isis or an Inquiry into the Origin of Languages, Nations and Religions, Volumes I & II*. 1833. Reprint, New York: A&B Book Distributors, Inc., 1992.

Higgins, Godfrey. *The Celtic Druids*. 1827-1829. Reprint, New York, Cosimo, Inc., 2007.

Higham, Charles. *The Adventures of Conan Doyle: The Life of the Creator of Sherlock Holmes*. New York: W. W. Norton & Company, 1976.

Hill Christopher. *Antichrist in Seventeenth-Century England*. 1971. Reprint, London: Verso, 1990.

Hill, Douglas and Pat Williams. *The Supernatural*. New York: Hawthorn Book Publishers, 1965.

Hieronimus, J. Zohara Meyerhoff. *Kabbalistic Teachings of the Female Prophets: The Seven Holy Women of Ancient Israel*. Rochester, Vermont: Inner Traditions, 2008.

Hoeller, Stephan A., *Gnosticism: New Light on the Ancient Tradition of Inner Knowing*. Wheaton, Illinois: Quest Books, 2002.

The Holy Bible containing all of the books of the Old and New Testament, King James version.

Hornung, Erik. *Conceptions of God in Ancient Egypt: The One and the Many*. Ithaca: Cornell University Press, 1996.

Hornung Erik, *The Secret Lore of Egypt: Its Impact on the West*. Ithaca: Cornell University Press, 2001.

Hothersall, David. *History of Psychology*. New York: McGraw-Hill, 2003. Hunter, M. Kelley. *Living Lilith: Four Dimensions of the Cosmic Feminine*. Bournemouth, England: The Wessex Astrologer Ltd, 2009.

Idel, Moeshe. *Golem: Jewish Magic and Mystical Traditions on the Artificial Anthropoid*. Albany, New York: State University of New York Press, 1990.

Internet Movie Database (IMDB), http://www.imdb.com.

Irwin, William. *The Matrix and Philosophy: Welcome to the Desert of the Real*. Chicago: Open Court, 2002.

"J.K. Rowling talks Harry Potter and the Deathly Hallows: Part 2 filming." *Snitchseeker.com*. July 6, 2011. http://www.snitchseeker.com/harry-potter-news/video-j-k-rowling-talks-deathly-hallows-part-2-film-production-lead-characters-82483/. Retrieved on March 21, 2016.

Jackson, Robert. *Witchcraft and the Occult*. Devizes, England: Quintet Publishing, 1995.

Jacobs, Joseph. *English Fairy Tales*. Edited by The Perfect Library. 1890. Reprint, CreateSpace Independent Publishing Platform, 2015.

Jonnys53. (2007, June 9). "What You May (or may not) Have Seen Hidden in *The Shining*." *Jonnys53.blogspot*. June 9, 2007. http://jonnys53.blogspot. com. Retrieved October 25, 2014.

Jung, C.G. *Collected Works, Alchemical Studies*. Princeton, N.J.: Princeton University Press, 1968.

Jung, Carl G.   *The Essential Jung*. Introduction by Anthony Storr. Princeton, New Jersey: Princeton University Press, 2013.

Jung, C.G. *Man and His Symbols*. New York: Dell, 1968.

Jung, Carl G. *Memories, Dreams, Reflections*. Reissue edited by Amelia Jaffe. Translated by Clara Winston and Richard Winston. New York: Vintage, 1989.

Jung, Carl G. *Mysterium Coniunctionis*. Vol. 14 of Collected Works of C.G. Jung. Edited by Sire Herbert Read et al. and translated by R.F.C. Hull. Princeton, New Jersey: Bollingen Press of Princeton University Press, 1967-.

Katz, Marcus. *Tarosophy*. Brisbane, Australia: Salamander and Sons, 2013.

Kern, Hermann. *Through the Labyrinth*. New York: Prestel, 2000. King, Stephen, *Pet Sematary*. New York: New American Library, 1984.

Knight, Richard P. *Symbolic Language of Ancient Art and Mythology*.

1892. Reprint, Whitefish, Montana: Kessinger Publishing LLC, 1993.

Knight, Stephen. *Jack the Ripper: The Final Solution*. New York: David McKay Company, Inc., 1976.

Kohler, Kaufmann, Ph.D. *Heaven and Hell in Comparative Religion with Special Reference to Dante's Divine Comedy*. New York: The MacMillan Company, 1923.

Kowalski, Dean. *The Philosophy of The X-Files*. Lexington, Kentucky: University of Kentucky Press, 2009.

Krappe, Alexander Hagerty. *Balor With The Evil Eye: Studies in Celtic and French Literature*. 1927. Reprint, Whitefish, Montana: Kessinger Publishing, LLC, 2006.

The Kubrick Corner, "Part 11: imperfect symmetries". Retrieved September 9, 2014, from http://kubrickfilms.tripod.com/id4.html.

Landis, John. *Monsters in the Movies: 100 Years of Cinematic Nightmares*. New York: DK, 2011.

Laqueur, Thomas A. *Solitary Sex: A Cultural History of Masturbation*. Brooklyn, New York: Zone Books, 2004.

LaVey, Anton Szandor. *The Compleat Witch or What to do When Virtue Fails.* New York: Dodd, Mead, & Company, 1971.

LaVey, Anton Szandor. *The Satanic Rituals.* New York: Avon Books, 1972.

Layton, Bentley. *The Gnostic Scriptures: Ancient Wisdom for the New Age.* 1987. Reprint, New York: Doubleday, 1995.

Levi, Eliphas. *The History of Magic.* 1860. Translated by Arthur Edward Waite, 1913. Reprint, London: Rider and Company, 1951.

Levi, Eliphas. *Transcendental Magic: Its Doctrine and Ritual.* 1854& 1856. Translated by Arthur Edward Waite, 1896. Reprint, Cambridge, Massachusetts: Cambridge University Press, 2013.

Levine, Ira. *Rosemary's Baby.* New York: Random House, 1967. Loncraine, Rebecca: *The Real Wizard of Oz: The Life and Times of L.*

Frank Baum. New York: Gotham Books, 2010.

Longair, Malcolm. *Quantum Concepts in Physics: An Alternative Approach to the Understanding of Quantum Mechanics.* Cambridge, Massachusetts: Cambridge University Press, 2013.

Lumpkin, Joseph B. *The Books of Enoch: A Complete Volume Containing 1 Enoch (The Ethiopic Book of Enoch), 2 Enoch (The Slavonic Secrets of Enoch), 3 Enoch (The Hebrew Book of Enoch).* Blountsville, Alabama: Fifth Estate, 2010.

Luton, Frith. *Bees, Honey and the Hive: Circumambulating the Centre; A Jungian Exploration of the Symbolism and Psychology.* Toronto: Inner City Books, 2011.

McGrath, Alister. *C. S. Lewis A Life: Eccentric Genius, Reluctant Prophet.* Carol Stream, Illinois: Tyndale House, 2013.

Mallory, Michael. *Universal Studios Monsters: A Legacy of Horror.* New York: Universal Publishing, 2009.

Macintyre, Ben. *For Your Eyes Only.* London: Bloomsbury Publishing, 2008.

Mackey, Albert Gallatin. *An Encyclopedia of Freemasonry and its Kindred Sciences,* Volumes I & II. New York and London: The Masonic History Company, 1921.

Macoy, Robert. *A Dictionary of Freemasonry*. 1869. Reprint, New York: Bell Publishing, 1989.

Maier, Bernard. *Dictionary of Celtic Religion and Culture*. Rochester, New York: Boydell Press, 1997.

Malory, Thomas. *Le Morte Darthur: The Winchester Manuscript*. 1470. Reprint and edited by Helen Cooper, New York: Oxford University Press, 2008.

Marshall, Peter. *The Magic Circle of Rudolf II: Alchemy and Astrology in Renaissance Prague*. New York: Walker & Company, 2006.

Marshall, Richard. *Witchcraft: The History and Mythology*. New York: Crescent Books, 1995.

Masello, Robert. *Raising Hell: A Concise History of the Black Arts – and Those Who Dared to Practice Them*. New York: Perigee Trade, 1996.

Mathers, Samuel Liddell MacGregor. *The Kabbalah Unveiled*. 1970. Reprint, York Beach, Maine: Samuel Weiser, 1997.

Maxwell, Jordan, Paul Tice and Gerald Snow. *That Old-Time Religion: The Story of Religious Foundations*. Escondido, California: The Book Tree, 2000.

May, Thomas. *Decoding Wagner: An Invitation to His World of Music Drama*. Milwaukee, Wisconson: Amadeus Press, 2004.

McCroy, Donald P. *No Ordinary Man: The Life and Times of Miguel de Cervantes*. Mineola, New York: Dover Publications, 2006.

McDonagh, Maitland. *Broken Mirrors/Broken Minds: The Dark Dreams of Dario Argento*. New York: Citadel, 1991.

McGilligan, Patrick. *Alfred Hitchcock: A Life in Darkness and Light*. New York: It Books, 2004.

McNally, Raymond T. and Radu Florescu. *In Search of Dracula: A True History of Dracula and Vampire Legends*. Greenwich, Connecticut: New York Graphic Society, 1972.

Melanson, Terry. *Perfectibilists: The 18th Century Bavarian Order of the Illuminati*. Walterville, Oregon: Trine Day, 2009.

Melville, Herman. *Moby Dick*. 1851. Reprint, New York: Pocket Books, 1999.

Miller, Jason. *Sex, Sorcery, and Spirit: The Secrets of Erotic Magic*. Pompton Plains, New Jersey: New Page Books, 2014

Miller, Scott. *The President and the Assassin: McKinley, Terror, and Empire at the Dawn of the American Century*. New York: Random House, 2011.

Morrison, Mark S. *Modern Alchemy: Occultism and the Emergence of Atomic Theory*. Oxford, England: Oxford University Press, 2007.

Murdock, D.M. *Did Moses Exist? The Myth of the Israelite Lawgiver*. Seattle: Stellar House Publishing, 2014.

Nahmad, Claire and Margaret Bailey, *The Secret Teachings of Mary Magdalene: Including the Lost Verses of The Gospel of Mary, Revealed and Published for the First Time*. London: Watkins Publishing, 2012.

Nelson, Victoria. *The Secret Life of Puppets*. Cambridge, Massachusetts:Harvard University Press, 2002.

Nichols, Sallie. *Jung and Tarot: An Archetypal Journey*. 1984. Reprint, San Francisco: Weiser Books, 2004.

Nietzsche, Friedrich. *Beyond Good and Evil*. 1886. Reprint, Mineola, New York: Dover Thrift Editions, 1997.

Nimoy, Leonard. *I Am Not Spock*. New York: Buccaneer Books, 1976.

Olcott, William Tyler. *Star Lore of All Ages*. 1911. Reprint, New York: G.P. Putnam's Sons, 1937.

Olcott, William Tyler. *Sun Lore of All Ages: A Collection of Myths and Legends*. 1914. Reprint, Mineola, New York: Dover Publications, Inc., 2005.

Opie, Iona and Peter Opie. *The Classic Fairy Tales*. Oxford, England: Oxford University Press, 1980.

Origen. *Contra Celsum*. 248 CE. Reprint, Boston: Cambridge University Press, 1980.

Osho. *Creativity: Unleashing the Forces Within*. New York: St. Martin's Griffin, 1999.

Osman, Ahmed. *Christianity: An Ancient Egyptian Religion*. Rochester, Vermont: Bear & Company, 2005.

Ouspensky, P.D., *The Symbolism of the Tarot: Philosophy of Occultism in Pictures and Numbers Pen-Pictures of the Twenty-Two Tarot Cards*. 1913. Translated by A.L. Pogossky. Reprint, Mansfield Centre, Connecticut: Martino Publishing, 2013.

The Overlook Hotel, www.theoverlookhotel.com.

Oxford English Dictionary, Second Edition. Oxford, England: Oxford University Press, 1989.

Parker, Derek and Julia Parker. *The Complete Astrologer*. New York: McGraw-Hill Book Company, 1971.

Parkin, Lance. *Magic Words: The Extraordinary Life of Alan Moore*. London: Aurum Press, 2013.

Pauwels, Louis, and Jacques Berger. *The Morning of the Magicians: Secret Societies, Conspiracies, and Vanished Civilizations*. 1960. Reprint, Rochester, Vermont: Destiny Books, 2009.

Pearson, Mike Parker. *Stonehenge – A New Understanding: Solving the Mysteries of the Greatest Stone Age Monument*. New York: The Experiment, LLC, 2013.

Peel, Roy V. *The Political Clubs of New York City*. New York: P. Putnam's Sons, 1935.

Perry, Mary Elizabeth, *Gender and Disorder in Early Modern Seville*, Princeton, New Jersey: Princeton University Press, 1990.

Pendle, George. *Strange Angel: The Otherworldly Life of Rocket Scientist John Whiteside Parsons*. Orlando, Florida: Harcourt, Inc., 2006.

Pietsch, Theodore W. *Trees of Life: A Visual History of Evolution*. Baltimore, Maryland: Johns Hopkins University Press, 2012.

Pike, Albert. *Morals and Dogma of the Ancient and Accepted Scottish Rite of Freemasonry*. 1871. Reprint, Richmond, Virginia: L.H. Jenkins, Inc., 1960.

Phillips, Gene D. *Stanley Kubrick: Interviews*. Oxford, Mississippi: University of Mississippi Press, 2001.

De Plancy, Collin. *Dictionary of Demonology*. 1818 published as *Dictionnaire Infernale*. Edited and Translated by Wade Baskin. Reprint, New York: Philosophical Library Inc., 1965.

Poe, Edgar Allan. *Edgar Allan Poe Complete Tales and Poems*. 2003. Reprint, New Jersey: Castle Books, 2009.

Potter, James V., Ph.D and Paula M. Potter, M.A. *Arrested Development and Personality Disorders: Understanding the Dr. Jekyll/Mr. Hyde Dual Personality*. Anderson, California: Advocare Publishing Co., 2011.

Price, Robert M. "Of Myth and Men: A Closer Look at the Originators of the Major Religions–What Did They Really Say and Do?" *Free Inquiry* (20/1). Amherst, New York, Winter 1999-2000.

Rarick, Ethan. *Desperate Passage: The Donner Party's Perilous Journey West*. New York: Oxford University Press, 2009.

Reiger, James. *Mutiny Within: The Heresies of Percy Bysshe Shelley*. New York: George Braziller, 1967.

Regardie, Israel. *The Complete Golden Dawn System of Magic*. Tempe, Arizona: New Falcon Publications, 1994.

Remes, Pauliina. *Neoplatonism: Ancient Philosophies*. Berkeley, California: University of California Press, 2008.

Renton, Jennie. (2001, 28 October) "The story behind the Potter legend: JK Rowling talks about how she created the Harry Potter books and the magic of Harry Potter's world." *Sydney Morning Herald*. Retrieved April 15, 2016, from http://www.accio-quote.org/articles/2001/1001-sydney-renton.htm.

Roark, David. (2010, February 18) "The Twisty Spirituality of Martin Scorsese." *Relevant Magazine*. Retrieved August 9, 2015, from http://www.relevantmagazine. com.

Robbins, Rossell Hope. *The Encyclopedia of Witchcraft and Demonology*. New York: Crown Publishers, Inc. 1959.

Rotten Tomatoes, www.rottentomatoes.com.

Rowling, J.K. *Harry Potter and Sorcerer's Stone*. New York: Scholastic, 1999.

Rudolph, Kurt. Gnosis: *The Nature and History of Gnosticism*. San Francisco: Harper SanFrancisco, 1987.

Russell, Jeffrey Burton. *The Devil: Perceptions of Evil from Antiquity to Primitive Christianity*. 1977. Reprint, Ithaca, New York: Cornell University Press, 1990.

Russell, Jeffrey Burton. *A History of Witchcraft: Sorcerers, Heretics, and Pagans*. 1980. Reprint, New York: Thames and Hudson Inc., 1991.

Russell, Jeffrey Burton. *Lucifer: The Devil in the Middle Ages*. Ithaca, New York: Cornell University Press, 1992.

Russell, Jeffrey Burton. *Mephistopheles: The Devil in the Modern World*. Ithaca, New York: Cornell University Press, 1992.

Russell, Jeffrey Burton. *The Prince of Darkness: Radical Evil and the Power of Good in History*. 1988. Reprint, Ithaca, New York: Cornell University Press, 1993.

Russell, Jeffrey Burton. *Satan: The Early Christian Tradition*. 1981. Reprint, Ithaca, New York: Cornell University Press, 1991.

Rumbelow, Donald. *The Complete Jack the Ripper*. 1975. Revised Edition, London: Penguin Books, 1988.

S, Acharya. *The Christ Conspiracy: The Greatest Story Ever Sold*. Kempton, Illinois: Adventures Unlimited Press, 1999.

S, Acharya. *Suns of God: Krishna, Buddha and Christ Unveiled*. Kempton, Illinois: Adventures Unlimited Press, 2004.

Sack, Ronald H. *Images of Nebuchadnezzar: The Emergence of a Legend*. Selinsgrove, Pennsylvania: Susquehanna University Press, 1991.

Saposnik, Irving S. *Robert Louis Stevenson*. New York: Twayne Publishers, 1975.

Schneider, Steven Jay. *101 Horror Movies You Must See Before You Die*. Hauppauge, New York: Barron's Educational Books, 2009.

Scholem, Gershom. *Kabbalah*. 1974. Reprint, New York: Meridian, 1978.

Scholem, Gershom. *On the Kabbalah and its Symbolism*. Translated by Ralph Manheim. New York: Schocken, 1996.

Schulzinger, Robert D. *The Wise Men of Foreign Affairs*. New York: Columbia University Press, 1984.

Scott, George Ryley. *The History of Torture Throughout the Ages*. London: Luxor Press, 1959.

Selby, Jenn. (2014, August 3) "Katy Perry says 'I want to join the Illuminati.'" *The Independent*. Retrieved December 1, 2014 from http:// www.independent.co.uk/ news/people/katy-perry-i-want-to-join-the- illuminati-9644920.html.

Shakespeare, William. *Cymbeline*. 1623. Reprint, New York: Simon & Schuster, 2003.

Shakespeare, William. *Hamlet*. 1603. Reprint, New York: Simon & Schuster, 2012.

Shakespeare, William. *Macbeth*. 1623. Reprint, New York: Washington Square Press, 1992.

Shakespeare, William. *Richard III*. 1623 (First Folio). Reprint, New York: Washington Square Press, 2004.

Sharp, Dennis. *The Picture Palace and Other Buildings for the Movies*. New york: Frederick A. Praeger, 1969.

Shelley, Mary. *Frankenstein*. 1818. Reprint, Mineola, New York: Dover Publications, 1984.

Shippy, Tom. *J.R.R. Tolkien: Author of the Century*. New York: Mariner Books, 2002.

Siegel, Carol. *Sex: Radical Cinema*. Bloomington, Indiana: Indiana University Press, 2015.

Silberman, Lauren R., *Wicked Baltimore: Charm City Sin and Scandal*. Charleston, South Carolina: The History Press, 2011.

Singer, June. *Blake, Jung, and the Collective Unconscious: The Conflict Between Reason and Imagination*. Lake Worth, Florida: Nicholas-Hayes, Inc., 2000.

Skal, David J. *The Monster Show: A Cultural History of Horror*. New York: W.W. Norton & Company, 1993.

Smith, Kevin. *Batman: The Widening Gyre*. Illustrated by Walter Flanagan. Burbank, California: D.C. Comics, 2011.

South, James B. *Buffy the Vampire Slayer and Philosophy: Fear and Trembling in Sunnydale*. Edited by William Irwin. Chicago: Open Court, 2011.

Snyder, Louis L. *Encyclopedia of the Third Reich*. 1976. Reprint, London: Robert Hale, 1998.

Sovatsky, Stuart. *Words from the Soul: Time, East/West Spirituality, and Psychotherapeutic Narrative*. Albany: State University of New York Press, 1998.

Spence, Lewis. *Ancient Egyptian Myths and Legends*. 1915. Reprint, New York: Dover Publications, 1990.

Spence, Richard B. *Secret Agent 666: Aleister Crowley, British Intelligence and the Occult*. Port Townsend, Washington: Feral House, 2008.

Spoto, Donald. *The Art of Alfred Hitchcock: Fifty Years of His Motion Pictures*. New York: Anchor Books, 1991.

St. Clair, Marisa. *Sun & Moon Signs: An Astrological Guide to Love, Career, & Destiny*. New York: Smithmark Publishers, 1999.

Stearn, Jess and Larry Geller. *Elvis' Search for God*. Austin, Texas: Greenleaf Publishers, 1998.

Steele, Valerie. *Fetish: Fashion, Sex & Power*. Oxford, England: Oxford University Press, 1996.

Stoker, Bram. *Dracula*. 1897. Reprint, New York: Random House, n.d. Stone, Bryan P. *Faith and Film: Theological Themes at the Cinema*. St. Louis: Chalice Press, 2000.

Sullivan, Gerald and Harvey Aronson. *High Hopes: The Amityville Murders.* New York: Coward McCann, 1981.

Sullivan, Robert W., IV. *The Royal Arch of Enoch: The Impact of Masonic Ritual, Philosophy, and Symbolism.* Burke, Virginia: Rocket Science Productions LLC, 2012.

Sullivan, Robert W., IV. *Cinema Symbolism: A Guide to Esoteric Imagery in Popular Music.* Burke, Virginia: Rocket Science Productions LLC, 2014.

Summers, Montague. *The Vampire: His Kith and Kin,* 1928. Reprinted as*The Vampire*, London: Senate, 1993.

Summers, Montague. *The History of Witchcraft and Demonology.* London: Kegan, Paul, Trench, Trubner & Co., Ltd., 1926.

Summers, Montague: *The Werewolf.* 1933. Reprint, New York: Bell Publishing, 1967.

Swartz, Mark Evan. *Oz Before the Rainbow: L. Frank Baum's The Wonderful Wizard of Oz on Stage and Screen to 1939.* Baltimore: The Johns Hopkins University Press, 2000.

Tsarion, Michael. *Astro-Theology and Sidereal Mythology.* Seattle: Taroscopes, 2008.

Tyson, Donald. *The Dream World of H. P. Lovecraft: His Life, His Demons, His Universe.* Woodbury, Minnesota: Llewellyn Worldwide, 2010.

Van der Zee, John. *The Greatest Men's Party on Earth: Inside the Bohemian Grove.* San Diego: Harcourt Brace Javonovich, 1974.

Versluis, Arthur. *Esoteric Origins of the American Renaissance.* Oxford, England: Oxford University Press, 2001.

Vitimus, Andrieh, *Hands-On Chaos Magic: Reality Manipulation through the Ovayki Current.* Woodbury, Minnesota: Llewellyn Publications, 2009

Voss, Roger. (2012, May 20) "*Blade Runner*–An Astro-Gnostic Fable (of the past – not the future)." *Vossnet.org.* Retrieved July 15, 2013, from http://www.vossnet.org.

Waite, Arthur Edward. *The Book of Black Magic.* 1972. Reprint, San Francisco: Weiser Books, 2008.

Walker, Barbara. *The Woman's Dictionary of Sacred Symbols and Objects.* San Francisco: Harper & Row, 1988.

Walker, Barbara. *The Woman's Encyclopedia of Myths and Secrets.* San Francisco: Harper & Row, 1983.

Warren, Bill and Bill Thomas (Contributor). *Keep Watching the Skies! American Science Fiction Movies of the Fifties: The 21st Century Edition.* Jefferson, North Carolina: McFarland & Company, Inc., Publishers, 2009.

Weaver, Tom, Michael Brunas and John Brunas. *Universal Horrors: The Studio's Classic Films, 1931-1946.* Jefferson, North Carolina: McFarland & Company, Inc., Publishers, 2007.

Webb, Thomas Smith. *Freemason's Monitor or Illustrations of Masonry.* 1797. 1802. Parts I and II in one volume, Salem, Massachusetts: Cushing and Appleton, 1808.

Weil, Simone. *Intimations of Christianity Among the Ancient Greeks.* London: Ark Paperbacks, 1987.

Wilk, Stephen R. *Medusa: Solving the Mystery of the Gorgon.* New York: Oxford University Press, 2000.

Wilson, Colin, *Aleister Crowley: The Nature of the Beast.* London: Aquarian Press, 1987.

Wilson, Colin. *The Occult: A History.* New York: Random House, 1971. Wilson, Eric G. *Secret Cinema: Gnostic Vision in Film.* New York: Continuum Publishing Group, 2006.

Wilson, Eric G. *The Strange World of David Lynch: Transcendental Irony from Eraserhead to Mulholland Dr.* New York: Continuum Publishing Group, 2007.

Woolf, Jenny. *The Mystery of Lewis Carroll: Discovering the Whimsical, Thoughtful, and Sometimes Lonely Man Who Created Alice in Wonderland.* New York: St. Martin's Press, 2011.

Worland, Rick. *The Horror Film: An Introduction*. Oxford, England: Wiley-Blackwell, 2006.

Yates, Frances. *Astraea: The Imperial Theme in the Sixteenth Century*, London: Routledge and Kegan Paul, 1975.

Yates, Frances. *Giordano Bruno and the Hermetic Tradition*. 1964, Reprint, London: University of Chicago Press, 1991

Yates, Frances. *The Occult Philosophy of the Elizabethan Age*. 1979, Reprint, New York: Routledge Classics, 2001-2015.

Yates, Frances. *The Rosicrucian Enlightenment*. 1972. Reprint, New York: Routledge Classics, 2002-2010.

Young, Julian. *Heidegger, Philosophy, Nazism*. Cambridge, Massachusetts: Cambridge University Press, 1997

INDEX

ABOUT THE AUTHOR

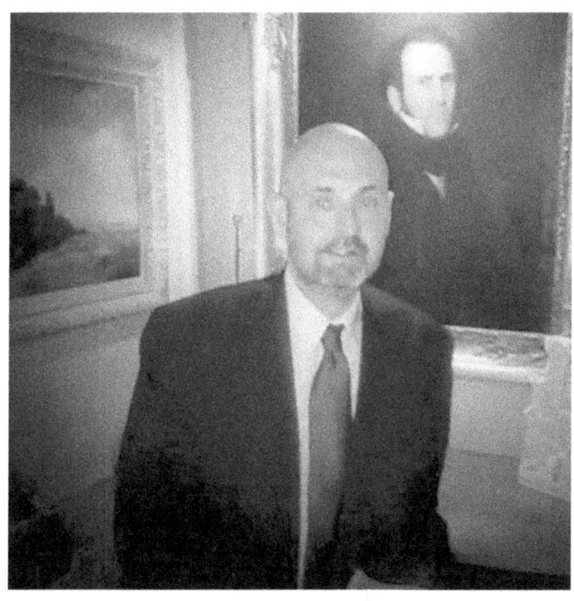

Robert W. Sullivan IV is a philosopher, historian, antiquarian, jurist, lay theologian, writer, and lawyer. He is the best-selling author of the books, *The Royal Arch of Enoch: The Impact of Masonic Ritual, Philosophy, and Symbolism* (2012, republished 2016) and *Cinema Symbolism: A Guide to Esoteric Imagery in Popular Movies* (2014, republished 2017). Mr. Sullivan received his B.A. (History) from Gettysburg College in 1995 having spent his entire junior year studying European history and philosophy at St. Catherine's College, Oxford University. He received his J.D. from Widener University (Delaware Campus) in 2000. Mr. Sullivan is a Freemason having joined Amicable-St. John's Lodge #25, Baltimore Maryland in 1997; in 1999 he became a 32nd degree Scottish Rite Mason, Valley of Baltimore, Orient of Maryland. A lifelong Marylander, he resides in Baltimore.

www.robertwsullivaniv.com
Follow: www.twitter.com/RobWSullivan4 or @RobWSullivan4
Subscribe: www.youtube.com/robertwsullivaniv